Los Angeles

timeout.com/los-angeles

Time Out Guides Ltd
Universal House
251 Tottenham Court Road
London W1T 7AB
United Kingdom
Tel: +44 (0)20 7813 3000
Fax: +44 (0)20 7813 6001
Email: guides@timeout.com
www.timeout.com

Published by Time Out Guides Ltd, a wholly owned subsidiary of Time Out Group Ltd.
Time Out and the Time Out logo are trademarks of Time Out Group Ltd.

© Time Out Group Ltd 2013
Previous editions 1997, 1999, 2001, 2004, 2006, 2008, 2011

10 9 8 7 6 5 4 3 2

This edition first published in Great Britain in 2013 by Ebury Publishing.
A Random House Group Company
20 Vauxhall Bridge Road, London SW1V 2SA

Random House Australia Pty Ltd 20 Alfred Street, Milsons Point, Sydney, New South Wales 2061, Australia

Random House New Zealand Ltd 18 Poland Road, Glenfield, Auckland 10, New Zealand

Random House South Africa (Pty) Ltd Isle of Houghton, Corner Boundary Road & Carse O'Gowrie, Houghton 2198, South Africa

Random House UK Limited Reg. No. 954009

Distributed in the US and Latin America by Publishers Group West (1-510-809-3700)
Distributed in Canada by Publishers Group Canada (1-800-747-8147)

For further distribution details, see www.timeout.com.

ISBN: 978-1-84670-395-9

A CIP catalogue record for this book is available from the British Library.

Printed and bound by Butler Tanner & Dennis, Frome, Somerset.

The Random House Group Limited supports the Forest Stewardship Council® (FSC®), the leading international forest-certification organisation. Our books carrying the FSC label are printed on FSC®-certified paper. FSC is the only forest-certification scheme supported by the leading environmental organisations, including Greenpeace. Our paper procurement policy can be found at www.randomhouse.co.uk/environment.

MIX
Paper from
responsible sources
FSC® C023561

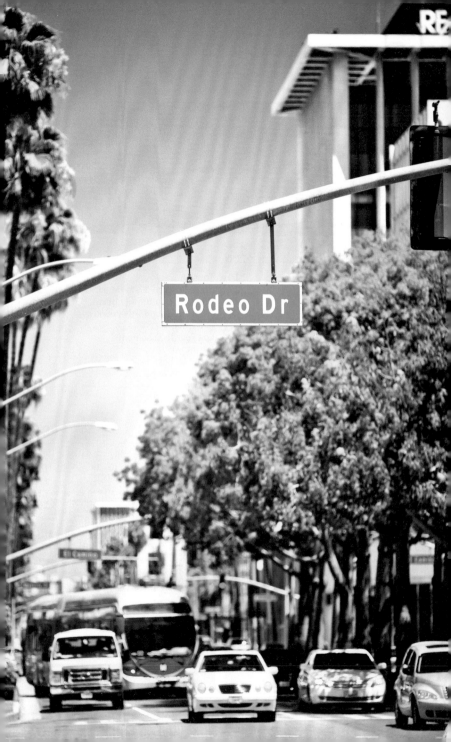

Contents

Arts & Entertainment 186

Escapes & Excursions 246

In Context 264

Essential Information 286

Maps 306

Introduction

Los Angeles is a city that many people think they know but few really do. Seen on screen over the decades, the plucky, built-from-nothing cow town has evolved into a 21st-century mix of glamour and grit, plastic boobs and deep tans. Right? Well, yes and no.

It's not that LA is misunderstood – because many of the clichés are true – it's more that most people don't get a chance to see it all, or even to scratch the surface. Beyond the permanent sunshine, dazzling teeth and the frozen foreheads is a real city – 89 cities, to be precise. And therein lies the issue: there really isn't such a thing as 'Los Angeles'. To get to grips with the whole of the sprawl, even on a surface level, takes weeks, months, arguably years. Gertrude Stein may have said 'There's no "there" there' of Oakland, but she could just as easily have been talking about Los Angeles.

Right now, though, just getting by is the priority of the average Angeleno (if there even is such a thing). This city was hit hard by the recession. The home foreclosure level and unemployment rate went through the roof and though there were early signs of improvement as this guide went to press, the sight of homeless people panhandling motorists in the shadow of the upscale Beverly Center is still a common one. For some, the American Dream has become the American Nightmare.

But what does this mean for the visitor? If it's your first time, you won't know any different. Those dazzling teeth are still there (the economy's tanking but you've still got to look the part). If you've been before, chances are you'll notice a few new things: first of all, higher prices (while it's possible to have a perfectly good time without a rock star's bank account, LA has never really been a 'budget' city).

You'll also see that Downtown is changing, with a new park, new museums and even the first inklings of a swanky new NFL stadium, provided a team can be lured here. There has also been a marked improvement in the area's food and drink options. Indeed, the restaurant scene in the whole of LA is evolving so quickly that it's hard to keep track. Yet, somehow, a city built on excess is learning to reign itself in, offering extended happy hours here and dining deals there.

LA may have – whisper it – toned itself down in the face of an economic meltdown, but the qualities that make it one of the most exciting, fascinating cities in the world will never go away. To use a cliché, it's business as usual in the City of Angels. *Lesley McCave, Editor*

About the Guide

GETTING AROUND

The back of the book contains street maps of Los Angeles, as well as overview maps of the city and its surroundings. The maps start on page 308; on them are marked the locations of hotels (❶), restaurants (❶), bars (❶) and coffeehouses (❶). Many businesses listed in this guide are located in the areas we've mapped; the grid-square references in the listings refer to these maps.

THE ESSENTIALS

For practical information, including visas, disabled access, emergency numbers, lost property, useful websites and local transport, please see the Essential Information. It begins on page 286.

THE LISTINGS

Addresses, phone numbers, websites, transport information, hours and prices are all included in our listings, as are selected other facilities. All were checked and correct at press time. However, business owners can alter their arrangements at any time, and fluctuating economic conditions can cause prices to change rapidly.

The very best venues in the city, the must-sees and must-dos in every category, have been marked with a red star (★). In the Sights chapters, we've also marked venues with free admission with a FREE symbol.

PHONE NUMBERS

Los Angeles has a number of different area codes, the most common ones being 310, 323 and 213. All local phone numbers in this guide are prefaced by a 1 and an area code. Always dial the 11-digit number as listed, including the 1, even if you're calling from a phone in the same area code.

From outside the US, dial your country's international access code (00 from the UK) or a '+' symbol, followed by the number as listed in this guide; here, the initial '1' serves as the US country code. So, to reach the Getty Center, dial +1-310 440 7300. For more on phones, see p296.

FEEDBACK

We welcome feedback on this guide, both on the venues we've included and on any other locations that you'd like to see featured in future editions. Please email us at guides@timeout.com.

Time Out Guides

Founded in 1968, Time Out has grown from humble beginnings into the leading resource for anyone wanting to know what's happening in the world's greatest cities. Alongside our influential weeklies in London, New York and Chicago, we publish more than 20 magazines in cities as varied as Beijing and Beirut; a range of travel books, with the City Guides now joined by the newer Shortlist series; and an information-packed website. The company remains proudly independent, still owned by Tony Elliott four decades after he launched *Time Out London*.

Written by local experts and illustrated with original photography, our books also retain their independence. No business has been featured because it has advertised, and all restaurants and bars are visited and reviewed anonymously.

ABOUT THE EDITOR

Having spent nine years at Time Out in London as editor and deputy series editor, Lesley McCave moved to Los Angeles in 2006. Since then she's written and edited articles for Time Out, Rough Guides, Lonely Planet, *Orange Coast* magazine, Vacationist.com, *The Independent*, *OC Weekly* and *LA Weekly*.

A full list of the book's contributors can be found on page 11.

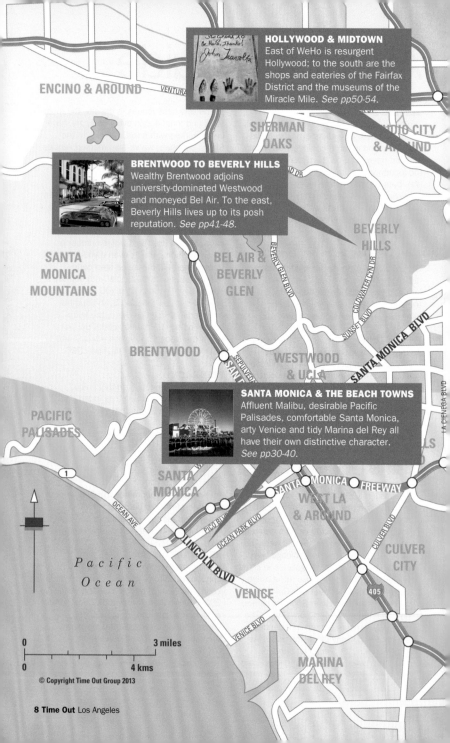

HOLLYWOOD & MIDTOWN
East of WeHo is resurgent Hollywood; to the south are the shops and eateries of the Fairfax District and the museums of the Miracle Mile. *See pp50-54.*

BRENTWOOD TO BEVERLY HILLS
Wealthy Brentwood adjoins university-dominated Westwood and moneyed Bel Air. To the east, Beverly Hills lives up to its posh reputation. *See pp41-48.*

SANTA MONICA & THE BEACH TOWNS
Affluent Malibu, desirable Pacific Palisades, comfortable Santa Monica, arty Venice and tidy Marina del Rey all have their own distinctive character. *See pp30-40.*

ENCINO & AROUND

SHERMAN OAKS

STUDIO CITY & AROUND

SANTA MONICA MOUNTAINS

BEL AIR & BEVERLY GLEN

BEVERLY HILLS

BRENTWOOD

WESTWOOD & UCLA

PACIFIC PALISADES

SANTA MONICA

WEST LA & AROUND

Pacific Ocean

VENICE

CULVER CITY

MARINA DEL REY

0 — 3 miles
0 — 4 kms

© Copyright Time Out Group 2013

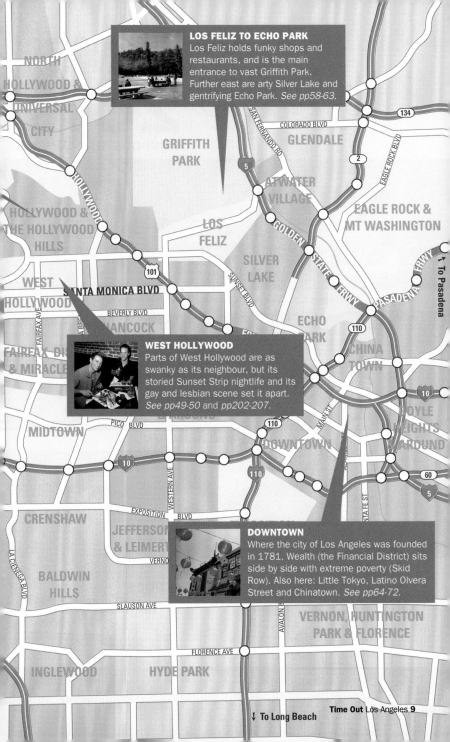

LOS FELIZ TO ECHO PARK
Los Feliz holds funky shops and restaurants, and is the main entrance to vast Griffith Park. Further east are arty Silver Lake and gentrifying Echo Park. *See pp58-63.*

WEST HOLLYWOOD
Parts of West Hollywood are as swanky as its neighbour, but its storied Sunset Strip nightlife and its gay and lesbian scene set it apart. *See pp49-50* and *pp202-207.*

DOWNTOWN
Where the city of Los Angeles was founded in 1781. Wealth (the Financial District) sits side by side with extreme poverty (Skid Row). Also here: Little Tokyo, Latino Olvera Street and Chinatown. *See pp64-72.*

NORTH HOLLYWOOD & UNIVERSAL CITY

GRIFFITH PARK

COLORADO BLVD

GLENDALE

134

2

HOLLYWOOD & THE HOLLYWOOD HILLS

ATWATER VILLAGE

5

LOS FELIZ

EAGLE ROCK & MT WASHINGTON

SILVER LAKE

GOLDEN STATE FRWY

WEST HOLLYWOOD

SANTA MONICA BLVD

101

SUNSET BLVD

PASADENA FRWY

To Pasadena

BEVERLY BLVD

HANCOCK

ECHO PARK

110

FAIRFAX DIS & MIRACLE

CHINA TOWN

10

PICO BLVD

MIDTOWN

110

MAIN ST

DOYLE HEIGHTS & AROUND

DOWNTOWN

10

110

60

5

WESTERN AVE

CRENSHAW

EXPOSITION BLVD

JEFFERSON & LEIMERT

VERNON

SANTA FE ST

BALDWIN HILLS

LA CIENEGA BLVD

SLAUSON AVE

AVALON

VERNON, HUNTINGTON PARK & FLORENCE

FLORENCE AVE

INGLEWOOD

HYDE PARK

↓ To Long Beach

Time Out Los Angeles

Editorial

Editor Lesley McCave
Deputy Editor Ros Sales
Listings Editors Ian Ritter, Tamar Love Grande
Proofreader Tamsin Shelton
Indexer Holly Pick

Editorial Director Sarah Guy
Management Accountant Margaret Wright

Design

Senior Designer Kei Ishimaru
Designer Darryl Bell, Thomas Havell
Group Commercial Senior Designer Jason Tansley

Picture Desk

Picture Editor Jael Marschner
Picture Researcher Ben Rowe
Freelance Picture Researcher Lizzie Owen

Advertising

Sales Director St John Betteridge
Advertising Sales Melissa Keller, Christine Legname, Christy Stewart

Marketing

Senior Publishing Brand Manager Luthfa Begum
Head of Circulation Dan Collins

Production

Production Controller Katie Mulhern-Bhudia

Time Out Group

Chairman & Founder Tony Elliott
Chief Executive Officer Aksel Van der Wal
Editor-in-Chief Tim Arthur
UK Chief Commercial Officer David Pepper
International Managing Director Cathy Runciman
Group IT Director Simon Chappell
Group Marketing Director Carolyn Sims

Contributors

Introduction Lesley McCave. **Los Angeles Today** Frances Anderton, Lesley McCave. **Eternal Fame** Lesley McCave. **Diary** Shana Nys Dambrot. **Sightseeing** Will Fulford-Jones, Lesley McCave, Miranda Morton, Kim Cooper (*Broadway Booming* Allison Milionis). **Hotels** Will Fulford-Jones, Lesley McCave, Allison Milionis. **Restaurants** Richard Foss, Lesley McCave (*Home made Heroes* Katherine Kims). **Coffeehouses** Lesley McCave, Katherine Spiers (*All Rise* Katherine Kims). **Bars** Julianne Gorman, Dennis Romero, Jonathan Cristaldi. **Shops & Services** Lesley McCave. **Children** Frances Anderton. **Film & TV** Jason Jude Chan (*Caught on Camera* Matthew Duersten; *Essential LA Films* Stephen Garrett, David Fear, Joshua Rothkopf, Keith Uhlich, David Fear). **Gay & Lesbian** Julian Hooper, Duane Wells. **Nightlife** Libby Molyneaux, Will Fulford-Jones, Natalie Nichols, Dennis Romero, Jeff Weiss (*Going Underground* Erika Stalder). **Performing Arts** Will Fulford-Jones, Don Shirley. **Sports & Fitness** Isaac Davis (*Wheel-life Adventures* Allison Milionis; *Catch a Break* Dennis Romero; *View from the Top* Zak Stone). **Escapes & Excursions** Will Fulford-Jones, Niamh McCormally, Ian Ritter (*Hollywood and Vines* Richard Foss). **History** Will Fulford-Jones, Lesley McCave. **Architecture** Frances Anderton. **Directory** Will Fulford-Jones, Niamh McCormally.

The Editor would like to thank Gayle Anderson at the MTA, James Mitchell, and contributors to the Time Out Los Angeles website and previous editions of this guide, whose work forms the basis for parts of it.

Maps john@jsgraphics.co.uk

Cover photograph Walt Disney Concert Hall by NiKreative/Alamy
Back cover photography Jakob N. Layman, Shutterstock.com, Barry J. Holmes

Photography Page 3 Andrey Bayda/Shutterstock.com; pages 6, 15, 260 Spirit of America/Shutterstock.com; pages 8 (top), 8 (bottom), 9 (top), 19, 38, 42, 45, 48, 50, 53, 59, 61, 62, 65 (bottom), 78, 79, 83, 86, 89, 139 (bottom), 161 (top), 173, 177, 188, 191, 198, 237, 239, 241, 244, 258, 277, 279, 281 Max Malandrino; page 8 (middle) Egd/Shutterstock.com; page 9 (bottom) Christian De Araujo/Shutterstock.com; page 12 Andrew Zarivny; page 16 John G. Mabanglo/epa/Corbis; page 17 Rodolfo Arpia/Shutterstock.com; page 18 Victor Decolongon; page 25 Courtesy Pasadena Chalk Festival; page 26 Mike Liu; pages 32, 92, 106, 121, 131, 136, 139 (top), 143, 146, 155, 161 (bottom), 165, 179, 186, 192, 208, 210, 211, 212, 220, 221, 222, 223 Sarah Hadley; pages 34, 36, 63, 65 (top), 70, 76, 229, 248 Shutterstock.com; pages 39, 94, 99, 122, 127, 133, 134, 149, 150, 152, 153, 157, 158 Jakob N. Layman; page 56 Alex Vertikoff; page 68 MMG1/Marlon Lopez; page 80 (top) Tim Street-Porter; page 80 (bottom left and right) Huntington Library and Botanical Gardens; page 85 Disney/Diego Uchitel; page 88 www.ThomasMcConville.com; page 90 Disney; page 95 Ed Rudolph; page 96 Alen Lin; pages 100, 111, 137, 140, 193, 194, 201, 206, 216, 235 Barry J. Holmes; page 102 Victor Leung; page 105 Skott Snider; pages 113, 129 Molly Cranna; page 114 Ming Tang-Evans; page 124 Courtesy Sassafras; page 171 Tim Griffith; page 182 Fred Licht; page 183 Ron Starr; page 199 Everett Collection/Rex Features; page 203 Ryan Forbes/Avablu; page 215 Mike Selsky; page 224 Jillian Sipkins; page 228 Joan Marcus; page 242 Benny Haddad; pages 246, 252, 255, 257 Heloise Bergman; page 251 David M. Schrader; page 262 David M. Albrecht; page 263 Courtesy San Diego CVB; page 264 Patricia Marroquin/Shutterstock.com; page 266 Paul Almasy/Corbis; page 269 Trekandshoot/Shutterstock.com; page 272 Pictorial Press Ltd/Alamy; page 274 iofoto/Shutterstock.com; page 276 John Gurzinski/EPA; page 286 Yusef El-Mansouri ; page 306 Bart Everett/Shutterstock.com

The following images were supplied by the featured establishments: pages 9 (middle), 21, 22, 31, 37, 51, 54, 118, 119, 132, 163, 168, 172, 174, 180, 184, 185, 204, 214, 226, 227, 230.

Los Angeles Today

Los Angeles may be down, but it will never be out.

TEXT: LESLEY MCCAVE & FRANCES ANDERTON

Spend even a short time in LA and you'll notice its residents have one thing on their mind: money. The same may be said for most of the rest of the world right now, admittedly, but for a metropolis built on big dreams and big houses, the recession hit hard. However, if Angelenos are paranoid about money, it's for good reason. LA was already an expensive place to live – polls frequently cite it as the second most expensive city in the US, after New York – but increasing unemployment and spiralling food costs in the wake of the world economic meltdown have made life harder for many. In the last few years, the state has teetered on the verge of bankruptcy, teachers have been laid off and museum and government office hours scaled back.

JUST ENOUGH FOR THE CITY?

LA has always been a city of extremes, it's just that the recession served to magnify them. Crime is at a low, yes, but then so is home ownership, with figures released in May 2012 showing that the proportion of households that are owner-occupied was on a par with 1997 levels. Homelessness, too, is officially down (for reasons that still aren't clear – it may well be that LA is simply too pricey even for homeless people), while animal shelters are bursting at the seams.

Angelenos may appear laid-back, but the reality is they don't take anything lying down. Even the city's charismatic former mayor Antonio Villaraigosa didn't escape criticism during his recent tenure, when he was lambasted for accepting tickets to sports and entertainment events at which he claimed (allegedly erroneously) to have ceremonial duties. LA still wants to have fun, it just doesn't want other people doing it at its expense.

GROWING PAINS

The space for constant reinvention once offered by Los Angeles is now harder than ever to find. The city has traditionally favoured houses over apartment blocks. However, as it struggles to cope with its ever-growing population, planners have been forced to consider building not outwards but upwards, gradually turning LA from a horizontal city to a vertical one. Downtown, in particular, has witnessed the birth of numerous high-rise apartment and/or retail complexes. Some plans, such as the Grand Avenue Project, have been scaled down, with Frank Gehry's proposed $3 billion hotel and mixed-use tower on hold, apparently indefinitely.

OIL BE DAMNED

Running hand in hand with these issues surrounding population density is the dreadful traffic that's now blighting a city once defined by its freewheeling, car-based culture. Built for the automobile, Los Angeles has also been ruined by it, as the ceaseless influx of people has made the lifestyle untenable. Day after day, citizens sit seething on clogged freeways and surface streets. The issue has been exacerbated by the lack of affordable housing: many Angelenos face lengthy commutes from outlying suburbs because they can't afford to live nearer to work.

The pro-growthers have justified their enthusiasm for new residential construction by promising new public transit systems to ease the burden on the roads. A number of new subway lines and rapid bus services have opened during the last decade, and more are on the way, but many longtime Angelenos don't even want an expanded public transport network because they don't want LA to change. Essentially, they want to turn back the clock to the good old days, to a time when you could sail 25 miles along an open freeway just to meet a friend for dinner. Just as pertinently, public transit plans have also become a locus for LA's racial tensions: some residents of the city's nicer neighbourhoods essentially prefer to keep the city segregated. And plans to extend the Purple Line subway under the streets of Beverly Hills have met with fierce opposition from members of the Beverly Hills Parent Teacher Association, who claim there is a serious risk of a methane explosion during drilling because the school sits above an oil field.

IT'S NOT EASY BEING GREEN

This sense that LA's car-based lifestyle is under assault has been intensified by rising gas prices and increasing awareness of global warming. The point of Los Angeles has always been consumption: large properties, oversized cars, ever-running air-conditioning, giant lawns drinking gallons of water channelled from outside the city. But the energy-inefficient lifestyle that locals have long taken for granted has not only become congested but expensive and, worse, guilt-inducing. Paradoxically, though, some of the more imaginative green design is being created here, and many leaders of the current American environmental movement are wealthy Angelenos. West Hollywood is the latest area to introduce a ban on plastic bags, following Los Angeles County, Malibu, Santa Monica and Long Beach. And many in the entertainment industry demonstrate

IN FOCUS

their greenness by driving biodiesel-fuelled cars or adding solar panels to their 6,000-square foot homes,

R 'N' R

Of course, LA is still huge fun. It remains the hub of the worldwide entertainment industry and likely always will be. Its obsession with celebrity continues, while real issues such as the legalisation of marijuana or gay marriage are given short shrift (either bill has yet to be passed, although ask anyone on the street and they're likely to be in favour of both).

NEIGHBOURHOOD WATCH

The city clearly still cares about its past – architecturally speaking, at least. Witness the emergence of Historic Preservation Overlay Zones. The first, covering the Victorian-era properties in Angelino Heights, was established in 1983. Today, the city of Los Angeles has 25 in total, with a dozen others under consideration. Because HPOZs outlaw the demolition of buildings within their boundaries and subject property owners to strict design reviews, they're the source of huge contention, pitting preservationists and house-proud home-owners against developers and other residents. It's a relief to know that after decades during which much of the city's heritage was

destroyed, the survival of some historic properties has been guaranteed. But it's also clear that Los Angeles will never be a static city. A constant flow of new residents has maintained an exciting and dynamic state of flux.

Unfortunately, some aspects of immigration have been destabilising. Perhaps most notable has been the arrival of huge numbers of Latin American immigrants (chiefly from Mexico) into neighbourhoods traditionally dominated by African Americans. As more Latinos have moved to LA, black Angelenos have found their communities transformed in ways they weren't anticipating, and their concerns haven't been helped by the anti-black prejudices held by some members of these new Latino communities. Black politicians have been left frustrated as they've lost ground to rising Latino political power; and on the streets, black gangs have found themselves outnumbered by Latino ones. This simmering anger hasn't been helped by deprivations that have affected many corners of LA: terrible public schools, for instance, and limited job opportunities. These long simmering tensions have led even the most idealistic activists to warn of an explosion on the streets as bad as the 1992 Rodney King riots.

California Governor **Jerry Brown**.

LOOK TO THE FUTURE NOW, IT'S ONLY JUST BEGUN

In early 2013, the first signs were good. Foreclosure rates were starting to dip, as was unemployment. House sales were on the rise – although, ironically, due to a shortage of decent homes for sale, bidding wars were driving up prices. Tourism was up: in 2012 LA welcomed a record 41.4 million visitors, a 2.5 per cent increase over the previous record high of the year before. And the public approval rating of California Governor Jerry Brown, elected in 2011, was at a two-year high of 57 per cent. A new Los Angeles mayor was about to be elected, replacing Villaraigosa (who was ineligible to run for a third term) as this guide went to press. Los Angeles has weathered the storm. Now it's time to have fun again.

IN FOCUS

Eternal Fame

Los Angeles is celebrity culture central.

TEXT: LESLEY MCCAVE

It's a typically hot afternoon on Robertson Boulevard in West Hollywood, as a black SUV with tinted windows drives up to the sidewalk. A figure emerges from the anonymity of the car and is immediately bundled into a nearby store by two burly bodyguards. A commotion ensues, quickly followed by the whirring of camera shutters. Shoppers stop to gawp at the scene. Within seconds, half of them have pulled out their cellphones and started to take their own photos. But of whom? Brangelina? J-Lo? LiLo? Could be. But it's just as likely to be a near-unknown whose face looks only vaguely familiar, whose name rings just a distant bell, and who, if it wasn't for the SUV and the bodyguards, would have slipped into the shop unnoticed. Welcome to 21st-century Los Angeles, where celebrity – or, at least, the impression of celebrity – remains the most valuable currency of all.

Seeing Stars

Our top five starry hangouts.

Where Brentwood Country Mart, Brentwood (*see p138*).
Who Jennifer Garner, Ben Affleck, Harrison Ford, Calista Flockhart, Anthony Bourdain, Helen Hunt, Cheryl Hines, Arnold Schwarzenegger, Reese Witherspoon, Larry David, Heidi Klum.
Insider tip Be like your favourite momshell and avoid the mart on weekends between noon and 2pm when it's jam-packed with local teens on lunch recess and parking is impossible. Want to really look like a local? Two words: riding boots.

Where Runyon Canyon, Hollywood (*see p53*).
Who Ryan Gosling, Justin Timberlake, Jessica Biel, Matthew McConaughey, Hayden Panettiere, Jake Gyllenhaal, Ben Stiller.
Insider tip If you've ever wanted to get within 15 feet of Ryan Gosling's abs, stake out the trail and be patient. Why not do some exercises while you wait?

Where Intelligentsia, Silver Lake (*see p136*).
Who Scott Speedman, Jesse Tyler Ferguson, Alia Shawkat, Jane Lynch, Tobey Maguire, Olivia Wilde, Zachary Quinto, Drew Barrymore.

Insider tip Arrive early, grab a seat at the coffee bar in the back, and set up your laptop so you can people-watch as everyone orders – even the most incognito stars won't escape your POV. The talent here tends to be more alternative – think: actors from quirky cult favourites such as *Arrested Development* or *The Dictator*.

Where Staples Center, Downtown (*see p238*).
Who Jack Nicholson, Dustin Hoffman, Andy Garcia, Anthony Kiedis, Flea, Kanye West, Kim Kardashian, Justin Timberlake, Jessica Biel, Jack Black, Nicky Hilton, Leonardo DiCaprio, Ciara, Rihanna, Tom Cruise, Antonio Banderas, Cameron Diaz, David Geffen, David Katzenberg.
Insider tip It's not that hard to see celebs in the 20,000-seat arena – just check the pricey front-row seats. Next to the Lakers' bench, you'll find A-listers borrowing David Geffen's two seats. Across from Jack Nicholson (who sits at half court) you'll see David Katzenberg with family and friends. A few rows behind Jack is funnyman Dustin Hoffman. Andy Garcia hangs out on the other side of the court in the third row.

Where Four Seasons Los Angeles at Beverly Hills (*see p175*).
Who Morgan Freeman, Katy Perry, John Mayer, Jessica Simpson, Enrique Iglesias, Jessica Alba, Jason Statham, Lauryn Hill, Kenny G.
Insider tip The restaurant, Culina, is popular with celebs (*Hustler* publisher Larry Flynt eats lunch here every day), but the spa is a mecca for Hollywood boldface names. Luxurious (and pricey) massages and facials are ever-popular. Just need a mani/pedi? Ask for Genia. She's prettied up the paws of Hollywood's poshest actresses.

IN FOCUS

PUBLIC IMAGE LTD

The entertainment industry is a global concern these days. However, as the city where it all began, and the city in which most of the major deals are still inked, Los Angeles remains its epicentre. In some ways, the business is much as it was in its early days: it still comes down to stars and studios with something to sell. But much has changed since the motion-picture studios were founded here, not least the ways in which celebrities interact with their public.

Once upon a time, the media had to rely on carefully edited publicity shots of Hollywood's latest and greatest. Any nascent scandals were swept under the carpet by the efficient studio-run publicity machine – major stars were not free agents, as they are today, but tied to individual studios. When stars did get caught with their trousers down, as happened most infamously with silent screen star Fatty Arbuckle in the early 1920s, it was huge news, but such misdemeanours hitting the headlines was the exception rather than the rule. Indeed, celebrities were rarely even seen out on the town; when they were spotted having dinner or at a première, it was a big deal.

This aura of untouchability has long since evaporated. In the 21st century, anyone – and we mean anyone – can become a celebrity in Los Angeles. Everyone from Lindsay Lohan's mum to Jerry Springer's bouncer has had their own reality shows. A flick through a typical week's TV schedule brings up such horrors as *Joan & Melissa: Joan Knows Best* ('Joan' being septuagenarian comedian Joan Rivers) and *Ice Loves Coco* ('Ice' being rapper-turned-actor Ice-T; even Wikipedia couldn't drum up more than 'The series follows the day-to-day life of Ice-T and his wife Coco Austin' as a description). And don't even get us started on *Snooki & JWoww* or *Here Comes Honey Boo Boo*. And if a 'real' celebrity is too busy (or too embarrassed) to show their face on camera, never fear, just focus on their spouses instead (how about *Mrs Eastwood & Company* for a prime example?). And that's before you get to the Real Housewives franchise, which currently has six separate shows, from New York City to Beverly Hills. Where *E! True Hollywood Story* used to profile the Kennedys, now it's the Kardashians. Naturally, the family also has its own show, *Keeping Up with the Kardashians*, which, at last count, had seven successful seasons and three spin-off series under its belt. Each week brings a new level of banality, a nadir being reached in August 2012 with the premiere of *Stars Earn Stripes*, in which celebrities competed in military training exercises, accompanied by members of the armed forces. Apparently, it wasn't until eight Nobel Peace Laureates including Desmond Tutu wrote an open letter to NBC complaining about the show that anyone thought it might be seen as glorifying war. Mercifully, only five episodes were aired.

THE PRESS GANG

At the forefront of Hollywood's star-making machine, as they have been for decades, are the American gossip magazines, which continue to track every move of more or less every celebrity in the US. And it's not just the ludicrous headlines: inane polls on the ensuing pages plumb new depths: 'Which Kardashian Are You?... Take the Test Now!'

However, it's now gone far beyond the point at which people are famous simply for being famous. Even people who blog about the famous are now stars in their own right. Case in point: Mario Armando Lavandeira Jr, aka Perez Hilton. Best known for his gossip website (www.perezhilton.com), Lavandeira at one point also had his own TV and radio shows, plus, incredibly, a clothing line (didn't anyone look at him before signing him up?).

IN FOCUS

Although Hilton's star has waned somewhat, the success of his often-vindictive blog has proved not just that the day-to-day lives of celebrities are of interest to the average Joe, but that those same celebrities are now considered fair game for a thorough kicking. Schadenfreude is alive and well in Los Angeles, presumably because it makes ordinary citizens feel better about their own problems. After all, if so-and-so isn't happy in the glamorous surroundings of Los Angeles, maybe our own dreary lives ain't so bad. The gossip magazines are now just the tip of the iceberg. Alongside Hilton's blog and the likes of TMZ (www.tmz.com), a website owned by a division of entertainment behemoth Time Warner that's famous for being the site that broke the news of Michael Jackson's death in 2009, every major news website from the BBC to CNN has a dedicated entertainment section. The *Daily Mail*'s website has proved popular Stateside, too, overtaking the *New York Times* in unique visitor numbers in early 2012. Indeed, the US appetite for all things British – celebrities included – is still as strong as ever. Now that David Beckham has left the Galaxy it remains to be seen how Angelenos will fill the void. As for gossipmonger and former *Mirror* editor Piers Morgan, who replaced Larry King as the host of CNN's flagship nightly talk show, the jury's still out. Some love him, some hate him, but after two years he's still fronting the New York-based programme.

This appetite for celebrity demands – what else? – more celebrities. Over and above the mothers, brothers and daughters, reality shows feature 'celebrities' that few people would have recognised at the height of their fame, let alone 15 years later. TMZ's site proudly shows off 'then' and 'now' photos on its 'Memba Him/Her?' pages, zeroing in with glee on every frown line, balding head and sagging gut.

At the heart of it all, of course, is money. The corporate world has been predictably quick to capitalise on the public's obsession with fame. Magazines pay millions of dollars for shots of stars or their offspring, knowing that sales will soar. Celebrity endorsements also bring in huge bucks, from those where the link between star and product is tangible (Michael Jordan and Nike, say) to those that it's difficult to believe even made it past the first meeting (Carlos Santana shoes, anyone?) And fashion lines send free clothing to celebrities in the hope that they'll wear it in public, preferably at the Oscars or the Golden Globes.

YOU CAN LOOK BUT YOU'D BETTER NOT TOUCH

Until just a few years ago, the closest any tourist got to spotting a celebrity in LA was on a guided tour of Beverly Hills, where, if they were very lucky, they'd catch a glimpse of their favourite star through the gate at the end of their driveway. More often than not, that hazy figure turned out to be a security guard or a housemaid, but at least it kept up the illusion of exclusivity. Nowadays, though, there's no unique allure. Many people can afford not only to visit Los Angeles but to stay in the hotels and restaurants frequented by the stars. Aside from the celebrities' own homes (and even that's debatable, thanks to reality TV), very few places are truly private.

The city's hotspots seem to change by the week, but spend just a short amount of time here and you're likely to run into someone famous. In addition to the locations we've singled out (*see p18* **Seeing Stars**), other places with good star-spotting opportunities include Joan's on Third, Urth Caffé, the Chateau Marmont and Equinox gym, all in West Hollywood. And if you like to shop while you stalk, forget Rodeo Drive and instead try the Grove. For fashion, Kitson on Robertson Boulevard and Fred Segal on Melrose Avenue are both good bets.

As a rule, mornings rather than afternoons are a better time to catch celebrities, but don't bother at weekends. And don't expect said celeb to pose for photos or sign autographs. Some will: if they're down the pecking order, they may be glad of the attention. But some won't. Above all, don't get too close without permission. The paparazzi may annoy celebs, but they haven't crossed the line into stalker territory. Yet.

Diary

Day or night, week in, week out – there's something going on in LA.

Besides Pilot Season, Première Season, Sweeps Season, Awards Season and Allergy Season, LA boasts an impressive year-round array of parades, sporting events and other spectacles, from the family-friendly to the far-out. Added to this is a wide range of cultural celebrations that reflect the city's status as a melting pot for communities from around the world, from Brazil to China to Mexico to Japan.

More happenings are listed throughout this guide: for film festivals, *see p195*; for gay and lesbian festivals, *see p201*; for musical festivals, *see p217*; for sporting events, *see pp237-240*. For event listings and reviews when you're in town, visit www.timeout.com/los-angeles. Note: be prepared for heavy traffic and road closures around popular street-based events such as Halloween and the Long Beach Grand Prix.

SPRING

Academy Awards
See p23 **And the Winner Is...**

Los Angeles Marathon
Starts at Dodger Stadium, Downtown; finishes at Ocean Avenue & California Street, Santa Monica (1-213 542 3000, www.lamarathon.com). **Date** mid Mar.
Every year, more than 23,000 runners and wheelchair racers take to the streets for this 26-mile slog through the city. But this is not a typical marathon: being LA, the route is dotted with some 1,000 cheerleaders, and neighbourhoods from Boyle Heights to Santa Monica celebrate the event with street performances.
▶ *LA also plays host to a variety of charity walks and other events, chief among them the annual AIDS walk (www.aidswalk.net/losangeles), held in October.*

Blessing of the Animals
El Pueblo de Los Angeles Historical Monument, Olvera Street, between US 101 & E César E Chávez Avenue, Downtown (1-213 485 8372, 1-213 485 6855, www.ci.la.ca.us/ELP). Metro Union Station/bus 33, 40, 42, 68, 70, 71, 78, 79/US 101, exit Alameda Street north. **Date** Sat before Easter. **Map** p315 D1.
Led by a cow festooned with flowers, this procession of farm animals and pets (with their owners) winds its way down LA's oldest street, where each animal is blessed with holy water.

Toyota Grand Prix of Long Beach
Downtown Long Beach (1-888 827 7333, 1-562 981 2600, www.gplb.com). Metro Transit Mall/bus 60, 232, 360/I-710, follow signs. **Date** mid Apr.
This high-speed extravaganza features the cars and stars of the IZOD IndyCar Series. The two-mile street circuit includes plenty of straights and curves; spectators should expect to spend the afternoon biting their nails.

★ LA Times Festival of Books
USC campus, Exposition Boulevard & South Figueroa Street, Downtown (1-213 237 2665, www.latimes.com/fob). Metro Expo Park/USC/ bus 38, 81, 102, 200, 204, 442, 550, 754/I-110, exit Exposition Boulevard. **Date** late Apr.
More than 140,000 people flock to the largest book festival in the country each spring to commune with authors giving readings and doing signings. Alongside the talks and discussions, booksellers set up stalls so that they can hawk their wares. During the event, sponsor Target runs free 'Bullseye' buses on a continuous loop between Union Station and USC.

Santa Clarita Cowboy Festival
Melody Ranch & Motion Picture Studio, just N of Hwy 14 (1-661 250 3735, www.cowboyfestival. org). Hwy 14, exit Santa Clarita. **Date** late Apr.

Pageant of the Masters.

Dig out your dude-ranch duds for this Western hoe-down. Attractions include the Melody Ranch Movie Night, Western art for sale, a cowboy couture fashion show, and plenty of cowboy music, poetry and chow. The festival is the only time that Gene Autry's ranch opens to the public.

▶ *For the Autry National Center: Museum of the American West, see p60.*

★ Fiesta Broadway/Cinco de Mayo
South Broadway and & W 1st Street, in & around City Hall, Downtown (1-310 914 0015, www.fiestabroadway.la). Various Metro stations & buses/I-110 or US 101, Downtown exits. **Map** p315 C1-C4. **Date** late Apr/early May.
Covering 12 square blocks and drawing crowds that top 500,000, this free fiesta does its best to live up to its reputation as the largest Cinco de Mayo celebration in the world – a festival marking the day in 1862 when Mexicans defeated French invaders. It's a blowout of feasting, *piñata*-breaking, music and general indulgence.

SUMMER

Pasadena Chalk Festival
Paseo Colorado, Pasadena (1-626 795 9100, www.pasadenachalkfestival.com). Metro Del Mar/bus 180, 181, 256, 780/I-110, exit Colorado Boulevard east. **Date** mid June.
Hundreds of artists create temporary masterpieces in chalk on the streets of Pasadena, while thousands

of onlookers watch where they walk. Eventually, awards are presented in a number of different categories, and then it's all washed away for good. *Photo p25.*

Independence Day
Across Los Angeles. **Date** 4 July.
The Hollywood Bowl (*see p228*) hosts LA's most famous fireworks display, synchronised to music by the LA Philharmonic. But celebrations aren't limited to the Bowl: Huntington Beach stages a parade during the day, capped by fireworks, and there's more patriotic razzle-dazzle at Venice Beach (*see p39*), the Rose Bowl and Disneyland (*see p90*). Note: many fireworks displays take place on the closest weekend to 4 July; check local listings for schedules.

Pageant of the Masters
650 Laguna Canyon Road, Laguna Beach, Orange County (1-949 494 1145, www. foapom.com). Pacific Coast Highway to Laguna Beach. **Date** early July-late Aug.
Art comes to life, literally: classic paintings, statues and murals take on a new dimension, as people dress and pose as *tableaux vivants* (living pictures) to recreate original masterpieces. A professional orchestra, a narrator, intricate sets and theatrical lighting help bring the works to life. Check the website for details of the Festival Art Show, held around the same time.

Lotus Festival
Echo Park Lake, between Glendale Avenue & Echo Park Boulevard, Echo Park (1-213 485 1310). Bus 2, 4, 92, 302, 603, 704/US 101, exit Glendale Boulevard north. **Date** wknd after 4 July. **Map** p314 D5.
Held among the lotus blooms in Echo Park, this low-key festival celebrates the cultures of Asia and the Pacific islands. Highlights include a market, live music and martial arts demonstrations.

US Open of Surfing
Huntington Beach Pier, at Main Street & Pacific Coast Highway, Huntington Beach, Orange County (www.usopenofsurfing.com). I-405, exit Beach Boulevard south. **Date** end July/start Aug.
America's largest pro surfing competition attracts the world's elite, who compete for big money while wowing 200,000 beach boys and girls with their skill, grace and innovative board designs. Heating up the festivities are live bands, a sports expo and after-parties with the friendly locals.
▶ *Surf-mad Huntington Beach is also home to the International Surfing Museum (see p89).*

Festival of the Chariots
Ocean Front Walk, Windward Circle, Venice Beach Boardwalk, Venice (1-310 836 2676, www.festivalofchariots.com). Santa Monica: Bus 2, 3, 4, 9, SM1, SM2/I-10, exit 4th-5th Street south.

IN FOCUS

And the Winner Is...

... Tinseltown. Hollywood loves to celebrate its own achievements.

There are now so many awards shows on the LA calendar that the already shaky concept of prize-giving has become devalued to the point of worthlessness. But from a star-spotting point of view, they're a red-carpet must. Some carry kudos: the **Screen Actors Guild (SAG) Awards** (www.sag.org), staged in late January at the Shrine Exposition Center; and the **Film Independent Spirit Awards** (www.spiritawards.com), a more casual event that's held in February or March in varying locations. Others, such as the **MTV Movie Awards** (www.mtv.com/ontv/movieawards; April, at the Gibson Amphitheatre in Universal City), are of no lasting importance. But for the industry mogul and star-spotter alike, there are three that stand well above the rest of the pack.

It's hard to exaggerate the importance of the **Academy Awards** (www.oscars.org) to LA. Oscar day is like LA's own Christmas.

The ceremony is held on a Sunday in late February or early March at the Dolby (formerly Kodak) Theatre on Hollywood Boulevard (*see p51*); fans queue for days to get places in the stands overlooking the red carpet.

The **Golden Globe Awards** (www.goldenglobes.org) are given out in January at the Beverly Hilton by the Hollywood Foreign Press Association. The Globes are often thought of as a precursor to the Oscars, but making predictions based on their results isn't always safe.

Essentially TV's Oscars, the **Emmys** (www.emmys.tv) are held in two stages: the **Daytime Emmys** are dished out in June (the 2012 event was held at the Beverly Hilton), with the **Primetime Emmys** handed out at the Nokia Theatre at L.A. LIVE (*see p218*), usually in September. You'll be treated to a full raft of stars from the small screen, as well as plenty of film stars acting as presenters for the evening.

IN FOCUS

Venice: Bus 1, 33, 733/I-10, exit 4th-5th Street south. **Date** 1st Sun in Aug. **Map** p310 A5-A6.
Hosted by the Hare Krishnas, this Indian tradition attracts 50,000 people, who chant and cheer for three honoured deities, representations of whom are paraded from the Santa Monica Civic Auditorium to Venice Beach on elaborately decorated chariots. A free Indian feast is held at the end of the route.

Nisei Week Japanese Festival
Little Tokyo, Downtown (1-213 687 7193, www.niseiweek.org). Metro Union Station/ bus 30, 40, 42/US 101, exit Alameda Street south. **Date** mid Aug. **Map** p315 D2-D3.
This nine-day festival celebrates Japanese culture with displays of martial arts, tea ceremonies, flower arranging and more, and starts with the coronation of the Nisei Week Queen. 'Nisei' refers to American-born children of Japanese who immigrated to the United States.

Watts Summer Festival
Ted Watkins Memorial Park, 1335 E 103rd Street, at S Central Avenue, Watts (1-213-361 4828, www.wattsfest.org). Harbor Fwy, exit Century Boulevard east. **Date** mid Aug.
Conceived in 1966, the year after the Watts Riots, this black pride event is the longest-running African American cultural festival in the US. Besides music, the event includes various other performances, a fashion show, a parade and a child-oriented area.

FYF Fest
Los Angeles State Historic Park, 1245 N Spring Street, Downtown (www.fyffest.com). CA-110, exit N Hill Street. **Date** early Sept.
The FYF Fest (Fuck Yeah Fest) rallies rowdy post-punkers, low-brow artists, anarchist skaters, caustic stand-ups and all manner of other virulently anti-establishment types for a weekend of indier-than-thou amp-busting fringe culture.

AUTUMN

Fiesta Hermosa Arts & Crafts Fair
Hermosa Beach, at Hermosa & Pier Avenues (1-310 376 0951, www.fiestahermosa.com). Bus 130/I-405, exit Rosecrans Boulevard west. **Date** Labor Day wknd (early Sept).
Wear a swimsuit under your clothes: after roaming the 250 stalls at this arts festival, sampling the fine foods and listening to the music, you may want to take a dip in the nearby ocean. There's another Fiesta over Memorial Day weekend (late May).

LA County Fair
Pomona County Fairplex, W McKinley & N White Avenues, Pomona (1-909 623 3111, www.lacountyfair.com). Metrolink shuttle from Union Staion/I-10, exit Fairplex Drive. **Date** early Sept-early Oct.
Los Angeles has changed immeasurably since 1921, when this event was first staged as an agricultural

---

**INSIDE TRACK
'TIS THE SEASON**

Towards Christmas, neighbourhood shopping events, where local independent stores provide discounts on merchandise and lay on festive food, drink and music, are held across town. Our favourites include the ones on Venice's Abbot Kinney Boulevard (www.abbotkinneyonline.com) and the Fairfax District's West Third Street (www.westthirdstreet.com). Check local listings for more information about what's on where.

---

fair. However, it still has farm-friendly appeal (livestock beauty contests, locally farmed produce) alongside the more modern acrobats, wine tastings, exhibitions and concerts.

West Hollywood Book Fair
West Hollywood Park, 647 N San Vicente Boulevard, between Santa Monica Boulevard & Melrose Avenue, West Hollywood (1-310 659 5550, www.westhollywoodbookfair.org). Bus 4, 105, 550, 704/I-10, exit La Cienega Boulevard north. **Date** late Sept. **Map** p312 A2.
Cruise the vendors at the nearby Pacific Design Center for the new bookshelves you'll probably need after a visit to the award-winning WeHo Book Fair. Readings, panel discussions and workshops are all among the IQ-elevating activities on the schedule.

Abbot Kinney Festival
Abbot Kinney Boulevard, between Main Street & Venice Boulevard, Venice (1-310 396 3772, www.abbotkinney.org). Bus 33, 733, SM1, SM2/I-10, exit 4th-5th Street south. **Date** late Sept/early Oct. **Map** p314 D5.
Take every artsy street fair you've ever attended, add all the stereotypes about the fun-loving Venice Beach locals you've ever heard, and you've got the general idea. Be sure to hit not only the guest vendors but also the locally owned galleries, shops and salons.

★ Halloween
Across Los Angeles. **Date** 31 Oct.
The main action is at the **West Hollywood Halloween Carnival**, held on Santa Monica Boulevard between La Cienega Boulevard and Doheny Drive (1-323 848 6503, www.weho.org, map p312 A/B2). Around 500,000 rowdy revellers are entertained by DJs, bands, costume contests, drag queen competitions and the crowning of the celebrity Honorary Mayor.

Día de los Muertos (Day of the Dead)
Across Los Angeles. **Date** early Nov.

Self Help Graphics & Art in Downtown LA (*see p66*) hosts music performances, arts and crafts vendors and a procession, which leaves Mariachi Plaza at 5pm, while the historic Downtown *paseo* of Olvera Street (*see p65*) offers a day of dancing and *piñata*-breaking, as well as nine nights of candlelit processions. Meanwhile, the haunting romance of the cinematic Golden Age is celebrated with the elaborate art-altar competition at the Hollywood Forever Cemetery (*see p53*). Most celebrations are held on 1 and 2 November, although some start in late October.

Mariachi Festival
Mariachi Plaza, at N Boyle Avenue & E 1st Street, Boyle Heights (1-951 224 4164, www.mariachi festival.info). Metro Mariachi Plaza/bus 30, 330/US 101, exit 1st Street east. **Date** mid Nov.
Decked out in ruffled, rainbow-coloured splendour, the itinerant musicians at this festival of Latino culture entertain visitors in mariachi styles. Tequila, tacos and other spicy specialities add further appeal.

WINTER

Hollywood Christmas Parade
Parade starts at TCL (formerly Grauman's) Chinese Theatre, travels east on Hollywood Boulevard, south on Vine Street, then west on Sunset Boulevard (1-866 727 2331, www.the hollywoodchristmasparade.com). **Date** Sun after Thanksgiving.
The event that inspired Gene Autry to write 'Here Comes Santa Claus' is a glitzy, star-studded presentation that attracts a million fans. First held in 1928, the parade features elaborate floats, pop stars, celebs riding in antique cars, equestrian shows and marching bands. Even with reserved bleacher seats, early arrival is a must, and parking is hideous.

Griffith Park Light Festival
Griffith Park, Crystal Springs Drive, between Los Feliz Boulevard & the Ventura Freeway, Los Feliz (1-323 913 4688, www.dwplightfestival.com). Bus 96/I-5, exit Crystal Springs Drive north. **Date** late Nov-1 Jan (closed 1 Dec). **Map** p314 C1.
Brighten up your holiday season with a drive along this mile-long stretch of lights. High points include flamboyant depictions of Hollywood landmarks composed of electric bulbs. Park your car at the LA Zoo and avoid the bumper-to-bumper traffic. The festival hasn't taken place for several years due to construction of a new water supply line on Crystal Springs Drive; check the website nearer the time to see if it's back on for 2013 and beyond.

Marina del Rey Holiday Boat Parade
Main channel, Marina del Rey (1-310 670 7130, www.mdrboatparade.org). Bus 108, C1, C7/I-405, exit Hwy 90 west. **Date** mid Dec.
It's anchors aweigh at this watery festival, as more than 70 ornamented boats compete for attention

and prizes. Watch proceedings from Fisherman's Village or Burton Chace Park.

Hanukkah Family Festival
Skirball Cultural Center, 2701 N Sepulveda Boulevard, at I-405, West LA (1-310 440 4500, www.skirball.org). Bus 761/I-405, exit Skirball Center/Mulholland Drive north. **Date** early Dec.
Enjoy the music, games, tastes and traditions that mark the Jewish festival of lights at the Skirball Center (*see p43*). Anyone can participate in a special Hanukkah event that changes yearly.

Las Posadas
Olvera Street, Downtown (1-213 625 7074, www.ci.la.ca.us/ELP). Metro Union Station/bus 33, 40, 42, 68, 70, 71, 78, 79/US 101, exit Alameda Street north. **Date** mid-late Dec. **Map** p315 C1.
This surprisingly cheerful re-enactment of Mary and Joseph's journey to Bethlehem features a candlelit procession, songs, dancing and *piñata*-breaking, with free candy for children and adults.

LA County Holiday Celebration
Dorothy Chandler Pavilion, Music Center Plaza, S Grand Avenue & W 1st Street, Downtown (www.lacountyarts.org/holiday.html). Metro Civic Center/Grand Park/Tom Bradley/bus 14, 37, 70, 71, 76, 78, 79, 96/I-110, exit 3rd Street east. **Date** 24 Dec. **Map** p315 B2.
This day-long festival of art, music and general merriment aims to represent the range of cultural and religious traditions that have put down roots in LA. It's an entertaining way to spend the last few hours before Christmas.

Tournament of Roses Parade
Parade starts in Pasadena at S Orange Grove Boulevard & Ellis Street, travels east on Colorado Boulevard & north on Sierra Madre Boulevard, ends at Paloma Street (1-626 449 4100, www.tournamentofroses.com). Various Metro stations & buses/I-110 to Pasadena (various exits). **Date** 1 Jan.
The first Rose Parade in 1890 was staged to show off California's sun-kissed climate. The tradition is still going strong, complete with elaborate floral floats, musical performances and equestrian troupes (not to mention the crowning of the fresh-faced Rose Queen and her Royal Court), but the celebration now draws more than 700,000 spectators, who line the streets of Pasadena. The Rose Bowl game (*see p238*) follows the parade. On May Day, the event is spoofed with a day of costumed mayhem at the **Doo Dah Parade** (1-626 590 1134, www.pasadenadoodah parade.info).

★ Chinese New Year
Parade starts on N Hill Street, then goes to Bernard Street, then N Broadway & ends at E César E Chávez Avenue, Downtown (1-213 617 0396, www.lagoldendragonparade.com). Metro Chinatown or Union Station/various buses/US 101, exit Alameda Street north. **Date** early-mid Feb.
The spectacular Golden Dragon Parade through Chinatown is the highlight of this annual two-day street fair, which also includes a carnival, lantern processions, arts and crafts, and plenty of food.

Brazilian Carnival
Club Nokia, 800 W Olympic Boulevard, at S Figueroa Street, Downtown (www.brazilian nites.com). Metro 7th Street/I-110, exit W Olympic Boulevard east. **Date** mid Feb.
If you can't make it all the way to Rio, you'll have to make do with this over-the-top explosion of feathers, sequins, production numbers and tan lines instead.

IN FOCUS

Pasadena Chalk Festival. See p22.

Explore

Tour LA

Get under the skin of this sprawling, fascinating city.

When sightseeing in LA, it doesn't necessarily pay to get up at the crack of dawn. Certainly, you should aim to arrive at the big theme parks (**Universal Studios**, **Disneyland** and **Six Flags**) as early as possible to beat the worst of the crowds. But otherwise, unless the museum or attraction you're hoping to visit is close to your hotel and can be easily reached without recourse to the freeway system, you may just end up stuck in horrendous rush-hour traffic.

JUST THE TICKET

If you're planning on seeing a number of attractions, it may be worth investing in a CityPASS. These small booklets grant decent discounts on admissions, and also allow pass-holders to jump most queues. The **Hollywood CityPASS** ($75, or $54 for 3-11s) includes admission to Madame Tussauds (*see p52*), a Hollywood Behind-the-Scenes tour, either a Starline tour of movie stars' homes or a narrated Hop-On, Hop-Off bus tour of 70 tourist spots around the city and either a guided tour of the Dolby Theater or entrance to the Hollywood Museum (*see p52*). The **Southern California CityPASS** ($306, or $269 for 3-9s) includes a three-day pass to both Disneyland parks (*see p90*), admission to Universal Studios (*see p80*) and, in San Diego, passes to SeaWorld (*see p261*). For an additional $33 ($25 for 3-9s), you can add either the San Diego Zoo or the zoo's separate Safari Park (*see p260*). You can buy a CityPASS from any participating attraction, or at www.citypass.com; special offers sometimes run.

GUIDED TOURS

In addition to the tours listed below, **Pasadena Heritage** (1-626 441 6333, www.pasadena heritage.org) runs tours of Old Town Pasadena on the first Saturday of the month; the **City of Beverly Hills** has year-round trolley tours and occasional walking tours (1-310 285 2500, www.beverlyhills.org); and the **Friends of the LA River** (1-323 223 0585, www.folar.org) offers regular walks along and around the river. For the **Sierra Club**, which organises hikes in Griffith Park and elsewhere in LA, *see p213*. For **Out and About** gay history tours, *see p205* **Tour of Booty**. Check www.time out.com/los-angeles for further ideas.

Children's Nature Institute

1-213 746 2966, www.childrensnaturei nstitute.org. **Tours** see website for details.
Rates $15; parents free.

Once a month on a Saturday, the CNI runs Tykes on Trails nature walks for families and under-eights in the Santa Monica Mountains and other areas, introducing families to the outdoors while instilling respect for nature. Most are stroller-accessible. Check the website for other activities.

★ Dearly Departed Tours

1-323 466 3696, www.dearlydepartedtours.com.
Tours see website for details. **Rates** $45-$55.

You don't have to have to be of a macabre mind to enjoy Scott Michaels' tours, but it helps, especially if you opt for the Tragical History Tour, which runs most days. Over the course of two and a half hours, participants are driven around in a minivan to nearly 100 celebrity murder and death sites (Janis Joplin, Michael Jackson, José and Kitty Menendez, to name but a few), plus other notorious spots such as the corner where Hugh Grant picked up Divine Brown. The drivers provide excellent commentary; Michaels himself is the host of the less-regular but fascinating Helter Skelter tours, which cover sites related to the Manson murders. Frequent Hollywood movie-site tours also offered. Insightful and highly recommended.

Esotouric

www.esotouric.com. **Tours** see website for details.
Rates $58.

The excellent Esotouric goes where most other tour companies fear to tread, operating a range of coach tours that take in an array of grittily fascinating sights and themes: the unsolved Black Dahlia murder, Raymond Chandler's Los Angeles and other similarly dark literary tours, the city's rock music heritage and so on. The majority of coach tours run for around three and a half hours, and early reservations are recommended. Über-ghouls should check the website for details of crime lab sessions.

★ Los Angeles Conservancy Walking Tours

Information 1-213 430 4219/reservations 1-213 623 2489, www.laconservancy.org.
Tours see website for details. **Rates** $10, $5 under-12s.

This praiseworthy organisation works to preserve and revitalise LA's urban architectural heritage, and then to educate the public about it. The Conservancy runs a wide variety of tours, covering everything from Downtown's historic theatres to tours of the Biltmore hotel. Reservations are required for many of the tours: they're understandably popular. Check the website for full details.

MONA Neon Cruises

1-213 489 9918, www.neonmona.org.
Tours *June-Sept* 7.30pm Sat. **Rates** $55.
For six months a year, the Museum of Neon Art (*see p84* **Inside Track**) runs nighttime tours (lasting three and a half hours) in an open-top double-decker bus, taking in neon signs both old and new along with movie-theatre marquees and other related landmarks. Book ahead.

Red Line Tours

1-323 402 1074, www.redlinetours.com. **Tours** *Hollywood: Behind the Scenes* 10am, noon, 2pm, 4pm daily. **Rates** $24.95; $15-$18 discounts; free under-9s with accompanying adult.
Red Line's popular Hollywood tour, which leaves from the Egyptian Theatre (6708 Hollywood Boulevard), visits many major local landmarks, taking in more than 100 years of Hollywood history. The 'live audio' system allows participants to hear the guide clearly via headphones while blotting out the omnipresent roar of traffic. Reservations are recommended but not required.

Starline Tours

1-800 959 3131, 1-323 402 1074 www. starlinetours.com. **Tours** see website for details. **Rates** $18-$82; discounts for multiple-day passes.
Starline runs a broad range of tours around Los Angeles, from one-hour trolley rides to day-long excursions. Its most popular tour is a two-hour loop around the homes of Hollywood stars; it leaves the TCL (formerly Grauman's) Chinese Theatre (*see p52*) every half-hour. Bonus: there's a free pick-up from most hotels in the LA area, as well as a new

'station' in Anaheim, from where passengers can take trips to San Diego, Legoland and Tijuana.

Undiscovered Chinatown Walking Tour

1-213 680 0243, www.chinatownla.com. **Tours** 1st Sat of mth. **Rates** $20; $10-$15 discounts.
Discover Chinatown's hidden spots, from a temple and herbal shop to an art gallery, antique stores and bargain shops on this monthly two-and-a-half-hour guided walking tour. Learn about the area's rich history while navigating through vibrant courtyards, alleyways and plazas.

STUDIO TOURS

The most famous studio tour is at **Universal Studios** (*see p80*), but a number of other major studios also offer the public a few brief glimpses behind the scenes. For some tours you need to bring ID – check in advance. Tours of NBC Studios in Burbank ended in 2012.

Paramount Studios

5555 Melrose Avenue, at N Gower Street, Hollywood (1-323 956 1777, www.paramount studiotour.com). **Tours** every 30mins, 9.30 am-2pm Mon-Fri. **Rates** $48; no under-12s allowed. **Map** p313 C3.
The only studio in Hollywood is once again welcoming visitors. The tours take roughly two hours, and reservations are required. For $150, you can opt for a four-and-and-a-half hour VIP tour that includes lunch and a few other not-really-worth-the-money amenities.

Sony Pictures Studios

10200 W Washington Boulevard, at Jasmine Avenue, Culver City (1-310 244 8687, www. sonypicturesstudios.com). **Tours** 9.30am, 10.30am, 1.30pm, 2.30pm Mon-Fri. **Rates** $35. **Parking** free.
Low-key walking tours, open only to over-12s, are offered during the week at this storied lot. Movies such as *The Wizard of Oz* were shot here in decades gone by; these days, it's used for both TV and film. Reservations are recommended.

Warner Brothers Studios

3400 Riverside Drive, at W Olive Avenue, Burbank (1-877 492 8687, http://vipstudiotour. warnerbros.com). **Tours** *VIP* regular intervals, 8.15am-11.45am Mon-Fri. *Deluxe* 10.20am Mon-Fri. **Rates** *VIP* $49. *Deluxe* $250. **Parking** $7.
The two-and-a-half hour VIP tour of Warners' Burbank studios takes in a goodly portion of the facility before ending at a small museum. The Deluxe tours last five hours and go even further behind the scenes; reservations are recommended. Leave under-eights at home.

EXPLORE

Santa Monica & the Beach Towns

Going coastal.

With the Santa Monica Mountains to the north and the shimmering Pacific to the west, the palm tree-lined cliffs and year-round sun tempered by ocean breezes, Santa Monica's natural surroundings couldn't be bettered. The roads, buildings and gardens that have grown up around it are immaculate: clean, tidy and easy on the eye.

To the north lies Malibu. Although it was incorporated as a city in 1990, Malibu is not a place so much as a 27-mile stretch of the Pacific Coast Highway that winds through some of Southern California's most magnificent coastal terrain. Parts of it are lined, on the ocean side, by beach houses of varying sizes and styles, with largely mediocre commercial buildings on the inland side nestling against the mountains.

To the south of Santa Monica is Venice, still a popular tourist haunt but a gritty shadow of its former self, trendy Abbot Kinney Boulevard aside.

Map p310	**Coffeehouses** p131
Restaurants p94	**Hotels** p164
Bars p118	

Map p310   **Coffeehouses** p131
Restaurants p94   **Hotels** p164
Bars p118

MALIBU

Malibu is such a desirable spot that its wildly wealthy locals, including privacy-hungry stars and publicity-shy industry moguls, are willing to live with the threat of fires and floods, and have formed a group dedicated to preventing new development from marring their lifestyle. Home-owners with properties backing on to Broad Beach and Carbon Beach have long tried to prevent plebs from playing on the sandbar, but public protests have resulted in increased access.

Leaving aside **Adamson House** (*see right*) and the reservation-only garden tours at the 22-acre **Ramirez Canyon Park** (5750 Ramirez Canyon Road, 1-310 589 2850), donated to the Santa Monica Mountains Conservancy by Barbra Streisand, Malibu has virtually no tourist attractions, unless you count the outdoor Malibu Country Mart and neighbouring Malibu

Lumber Yard, which are nice for a stroll in the sun. Elsewhere, treats lie in its beaches and canyons: within yards of the entrance to one of the many trails, you can be out of view of the city and communing with coyotes and red-tailed hawks. Also worthy of a look is the historic **Malibu Pier** (www.malibupiersport fishing.com) – originally built in 1905 – which reopened a few years ago after a $10 million refurb. It's still very low-key, but includes a café and a small surf museum, as well as whale-watching tours, and fishing and watersports equipment rental.

Adamson House

23200 Pacific Coast Highway (1-310 456 8432, www.adamsonhouse.org). Bus 534/I-10, exit PCH north. **Open** *House tours* 11am-2pm *Wed-Sat. Garden tours* 10am Fri. **Admission** *All tours* $7; $2 discounts; free under-6s. **No credit cards.**

This striking 1929 Spanish-style building sits, along with the Malibu Lagoon Museum, inside the confines of Malibu Lagoon State Park. The major attraction at Adamson House is the array of decorative tiles manufactured at the once-celebrated but now-closed Malibu Tile Works. The guided tours (be sure to arrive 15 minutes in advance) allow visitors access to much of the property. Tours of the 1930s-style gardens are followed by a tour of the house, at no extra cost. If it's raining, the house tours don't run.

Malibu Chamber of Commerce
23805 Stuart Ranch Road, Suite 105, at Civic Center Way (1-310 456 9025, www.malibu.org). I-10, exit PCH north. **Open** 9am-5pm Mon-Fri.

PACIFIC PALISADES

Between Malibu and Santa Monica lies Pacific Palisades, a small, rich community with a lower profile than its neighbours. The immaculate green lawns and large bungalows are straight out of *Leave It to Beaver*, but contained within its Santa Monica Mountains location are some wonderful, rugged places; among them are **Rustic Canyon Park** (1-310 454 5734), **Temescal Gateway Park** (1-310 454 1395) and **Will Rogers State Historic Park** (*see p33*). Nearby are the **Self-Realization Fellowship Lake Shrine** (*see p33*); and **Will Rogers State Beach**, a gay-friendly spot (*see p209* **Gay Beaches**). However, the highlight for visitors is the **Getty Villa**, open to visitors who book ahead.

Eames House
203 Chautauqua Boulevard, off PCH (1-310 459 9663, www.eamesfoundation.org). Bus SM9/I-10, exit PCH north. **Open** *Exterior tours, by arrangement only* 10am-4pm Mon, Tue, Thur-Sat. **Admission** $10. **Credit** MC, V.
Charles and Ray Eames' landmark experiment in home design, built in 1949, is now a National Historic Landmark. Interested visitors are welcome to take a self-guided tour of the exterior on an appointment-only basis by booking at least 48 hours in advance. Note that there's (free) parking on Corona del Mar, but none at the house itself.

★ FREE Getty Villa
17985 Pacific Coast Highway (1-310 440 7300, www.getty.edu). Bus 534/I-10, exit PCH north. **Open** 10am-5pm Mon, Wed-Sun; reservations required. **Admission** free. *Parking* $15. **Credit** AmEx, DC, Disc, MC, V.
In 1974, oil magnate J Paul Getty opened a museum of his holdings in a faux villa in Malibu, based on the remains of the Villa dei Papiri in Herculaneum. Derision from critics and ridicule from art experts followed, but the Getty grew into a beloved local attraction. In 1997, the decorative arts and paintings were moved to the Getty Center (*see p41*), and the villa was closed for conversion into a museum for Getty's collection of Mediterranean antiquities. When it reopened in 2006, part-restored and part-transformed by architects Jorge Silvetti and Rodolfo Machado, the press were rather kinder.

There are roughly 1,200 artefacts on display at any one time, dating from 6500 BC to AD 400, and

EXPLORE

Malibu Country Mart.

Green and Serene

These tranquil spots are the perfect places to escape to.

One great surprise that LA holds for first-time visitors is its greenness. Some of the city's many iconic palm trees produce dates, the favourite food of the wild green parrots that can be heard screeching above Hollywood and points east. And those parrots know that LA is dotted with dozens of gardens, many of them the treasured retreats of locals.

Although it's run by UCLA, the **Hannah Carter Japanese Garden** is not in Westwood but on a quiet street in nearby Bel Air. Once through the heavy gate, you'll enter a quiet world of exquisite, traditional Japanese landscaping. Paths meander over bridges and by waterfalls, with views of wooden tea houses, ancient statues and fat koi in cool ponds. Unfortunately, as this guide went to press, the garden was closed to the public as UCLA tries to sell it, claiming the limited parking in the area had kept visitor numbers too low for it to be properly maintained. There's an online petition to have the garden reopened at http://hannahcarterjapanesegarden.com.

Just inland from the Pacific Coast Highway and easy to miss when you're rushing to catch the sunset, the mystical, mysterious **Self-Realization Fellowship Lake Shrine** (*see p33*) is run by a non-denominational order that welcomes visitors but doesn't proselytise to them. Set on a ten-acre site that was used as a film set during the silent era, the lovely gardens evoke old Hollywood: look out for the Dutch windmill chapel, the Mississippi houseboat and a number of gliding swans. The East, meanwhile, is represented by a gilded lotus gate enclosing a shrine that contains some of Gandhi's ashes.

Further along the coast in Malibu, the 23-acre **Serra Retreat** (3401 Serra Road, 1-310 456 6631, www.serraretreat.com) is run by Franciscan friars. The gardens and walkways, dotted with statues, offer a peaceful respite amid a backdrop of stunning ocean and mountain views. Advance notice is required at weekends.

Few visitors to Frank Gehry's crumpled **Walt Disney Concert Hall** (*see p229*) realise that atop the structure stands a charming roof garden that affords views over the city. Designed by Melinda Taylor as a tribute to flower-loving patroness Lillian Disney, Walt's wife, it's stocked with flowering trees and

Self-Realization Fellowship Lake Shrine.

colourful shrubbery, its meandering paths leading to a lotus-shaped Delftware mosaic fountain. Also keep an eye (and nose) out for the culinary garden, which onsite restaurant Patina (www.patinarestaurant.com) makes good use of; its website has a detailed map of the herbs and plants.

Not all of LA's secret gardens are open to just anyone. To tour Beachwood Canyon's unusual **Garden of Oz** (on Ledgewood Drive, not far from the Hollywood sign), you'll need to make friends with one of the select group of neighbours who hold a key, or be lucky enough to drop by when someone is already inside. Created by Gail Cottman with the help of a number of artists, the hilly site is so comprehensively covered with mosaic paths, sculptures, doll parts and loving messages that even peeking over the wall is a delightful sight.

EXPLORE

organised under such themes as Gods and Goddesses and Stories of the Trojan War. If you're a novice, start in the TimeScape room (room 113), where a wall-mounted frieze maps the different civilisations along with the art and statuary they created.

You could easily spend a few hours idly wandering through the galleries, but some exhibits really stand out. In room 101C, look for an amazing Greek perfume container that dates back to around 400 BC: it's incredibly elegant and, despite its age, entirely intact. Room 101 holds a collection of disparate items relating to Greek gods and some delicate painted oil jars. The outlandish, stag-spouted drinking horn in room 105 is gloriously absurd. And in room 108 stands a 1,900-year-old statue of Herakles, an alpha-male figure who reputedly inspired Getty to build the museum in the design of a Roman villa.

Upstairs, room 217 holds an eerie limestone statue of a Cypriot fertility goddess from around 3000 BC, her six toes implying superhuman qualities. But the highlight is room 212, where you'll find some intricate Roman gems and coins alongside an unnerving miniature skeleton cast in bronze.

The site also holds conservation laboratories, seminar rooms and a research library (not open to the public), plus temporary exhibitions. Note that you'll need to book a timed ticket (free) in order to visit the museum (if you're coming by bus, make sure you get your ticket hole-punched by the driver before arriving). At peak times, be sure to book well in advance; and try and get your ticket for early in the morning in order to beat the crowds.

▶ *Check the website for details of tours, talks, lectures, performances, films and family activities at both the Getty Villa and Getty Center in Brentwood (see p41).*

FREE Self-Realization Fellowship Lake Shrine
17190 Sunset Boulevard, at Pacific Coast Highway (1-310 454 4114, www.lakeshrine.org). Bus 2, 302/I-10, exit PCH north. **Open** *Gardens 9am-4.30pm Tue-Sat; noon-4.30pm Sun. Visitors' centre 9am-4pm Tue-Sat; noon-4pm Sun.* **Admission** free.
See p32 **Green and Serene**.

FREE Will Rogers State Historic Park
1501 Will Rogers State Park Road, at Sunset Boulevard (1-310 454 8212, www.parks.ca.gov). Bus 2, 302, 476/I-405, exit Sunset Boulevard west. **Open** *Park 8am-sunset daily. House tours hourly 11am-3pm Thur, Fri; hourly 10am-4pm Sat, Sun.* **Admission** free. *Parking* $12.
The former home of writer, cowboy philosopher, trick-roper and the first honorary mayor of Beverly Hills has been maintained as it was in the 1930s. The 186-acre grounds give access to some good hikes; one path takes you to Inspiration Point, from where you get a breathtaking view of mountains and sea. You can also take horse-riding lessons (call or check

online for details). Polo matches are held at the park on weekends between April and September or October (www.willrogerspolo.org).

SANTA MONICA
Map p310
The area around Santa Monica was inhabited for centuries by the Gabrielino Native Americans, then by Spanish settlers who named the city and many of its major streets. Acquired by Anglo pioneers in the late 19th century, it soon snowballed from a small holiday resort into today's city, with a population of 84,000. Nowadays sunseekers mix with Iranians, health fiends, beach bums, families, young-free-and-singles, retirees, entertainment industry titans and entertainment industry wannabes. Apart from the frequent fogs, the living is easy in Santa Monica, especially if you've money in your pocket.

At the other end of the scale, you'll also find plenty of homeless Angelenos ambling along its streets and beaches. The city's government has long taken a humanitarian approach to the issue of homelessness, part of a famously benevolent attitude to social problems. Indeed, the self-satisfied middle-class Santa Monica liberal has become a familiar political trope across both the region and the country, oft cited both by supporters and enemies.

As well as the tourist-oriented beaches and the strings of shops, Santa Monica also boasts some excellent, daring modern architecture. Much of Frank Gehry's work is here, including his own house, but Santa Monica also contains art deco landmarks such as the **Shangri-La** hotel (*see p168*) and some fine 1950s buildings. The **Strick House** at 1911 La Mesa Drive, which falls into the latter category, is the only home in the country designed by Oscar Niemeyer, albeit from a distance: the architect never set foot in the US.

What you won't find in Santa Monica is a cutting edge. The nightlife here is all white bread and mayo; outside of the galleries at Bergamot Station, the cultural scene is deeply indifferent; and while there are good places to eat here, too many of the restaurants promise more than they deliver. Still, such trifling issues don't seem to worry the locals, who seem convinced that they've found a suburban paradise by the Pacific. And you know what? They might be right.

Montana Avenue

Four blocks north of Wilshire Boulevard, Santa Monica's main east–west artery, **Montana Avenue**, is situated towards the northern end of Santa Monica, bordering

EXPLORE

Beachy Keen

Towel? Check. Sunscreen? Check. Now head for these unmissable spots of sand.

Ever since Vasco Núñez de Balboa laid eyes on the Pacific Ocean in 1513, the world has gazed upon the Southern California coastline with wonder. With its gorgeous interface of sea and sky against a chiselled mountain backdrop, the 30-mile stretch of beaches along LA County's coastline – from Malibu in the north, through Santa Monica and Venice, and on to the South Bay – is incomparable.

Despite LA's surf city reputation, the Pacific is chillingly cold for nine months of the year. But in July and August, when oceanside temperatures hover around 90°F (32°C), the water can reach 70°F (21°C). The further you are from Santa Monica Bay, where waste is pumped into the ocean, the cleaner the water. That said, even the water in Santa Monica has improved under the auspices of **Heal the Bay** (1-310 451 1500, www.healthebay.org), an environmental outfit devoted to monitoring pollution. Swimming is permitted on all beaches in LA County, but strong currents and pounding waves make it difficult.

Beaches officially open at 7am and close at 10pm. Many have space and rental gear for in-line skating, roller-hockey, cycling, surfing and volleyball, as well as refreshment stands, showers and toilets. Alcohol, pets and nudity are prohibited; bonfires are permitted only at Dockweiler State Beach in Vista del Mar, and then only in designated fire rings. Lifeguards may not be on duty at all beaches. Occasionally, due to rough rip tides, shark sightings and pollution, beaches may be closed. In summer, check the *LA Times* for ratings of all the local beaches.

Though there is limited free parking on the Pacific Coast Highway, parking can be difficult and expensive. Still, it's better to pay for a space than have your vehicle towed. For more information on beaches in LA, check the Department of Beaches & Harbors website at http://beaches.co.la.ca.us. The following are the pick of LA's beaches, from north to south.

El Matador State Beach

Around 32350 Pacific Coast Highway.
Small, beautiful and dominated by rocky outcrops, El Matador looks not unlike a European beach. Six miles north of Malibu and 25 miles from Santa Monica, it's just

past Zuma Beach (*see below*), accessible via a steep gravelly path. Wear shoes and don't bring too much heavy gear. There are no lifeguards or other facilities, so you should be able to find some privacy on the beach; spread your towel in the cupped hands of the rocks. Arriving early or staying late should reward you with a memorable dawn or sunset. El Matador and nearby **El Pescador** and **La Piedra** beaches collectively form the **Robert H Meyer Memorial Beaches**. All three are worth a visit.

Zuma Beach

Around 30000 Pacific Coast Highway.
The four-mile sprawl of immaculate sand that makes up family-friendly Zuma Beach is ideal for surfing, swimming, volleyball, sunbathing and long walks; the water is clean and the sand soft beneath your feet. Zuma can get crowded, and getting there along the traffic-congested PCH can be a challenge at weekends. There are lifeguards, toilets and showers. You can buy food from stands, but packing a picnic basket is a better idea.

Malibu

Surfrider Beach: around 23050 Pacific Coast Highway. For Malibu, see p30.
The public are legally allowed access to all beaches in Malibu, but finding the routes to them can be difficult: many of the houses that back on to them are owned by privacy-hungry celebrities. The public beaches are nothing out of the ordinary but are popular for swimming, sunning and watching the surfers at Surfrider Beach. There are also tidepools, a marine preserve, and volleyball and picnic areas. Drive out towards Point

Venice Beach.

Dume to see the opulent houses of the rich and famous, some sitting precariously on the edge of rocky bluffs.

Santa Monica State Beach

For Santa Monica, see p33.
This big beach, which effectively runs the length of Santa Monica itself, is usually crowded and has a festive feel to it. The big attraction is Santa Monica Pier (on a level with Colorado Avenue), roughly three city blocks in length and packed with typical and endearingly low-tech distractions: pier fishing, video arcades, free twilight dance concerts in summer, fortune tellers, fairground games, rides and a Ferris wheel.

Venice Beach

For Venice, see p38.
People-watching is the raison d'être at Venice Beach, which effectively continues from the southern end of Santa Monica Beach without a break. Jump into the flow of the winding Venice Boardwalk, where you can skate or cycle, watch or play volleyball or basketball, and check out the gym bunnies who work out at Muscle Beach. Street parking is usually jammed, but there are several beachside lots.

Manhattan Beach

For Manhattan Beach, see p85.
South of LAX, Manhattan Beach is right out of a Southern California postcard, offering clean water, sand that stretches out of sight, small piers and all kinds of activities: volleyball (there's an annual Volleyball Open each August), sailing and walking, cycling and in-line skating on the ocean front paths. The charm is the local flavour; visitors can swim, picnic and bask in the sun alongside residents and local fishermen. The surf isn't bad either.

Huntington State Beach

For Huntington Beach, see p88.
Essentially, more of the above, just further south (Huntington Beach is about 15 miles south of Long Beach). Its chief attraction is its surfing: Huntington Beach picks up swells from a variety of directions, which makes for good waves, and the water is often less crowded than at Malibu's Surfrider Beach.

on the Santa Monica Canyons. A drab commercial strip during the 1970s, the street has since morphed into the Rodeo Drive of the coast, although conspicuous consumption here comes with a little more subtlety and a lot less flash. Designer stores sit alongside small boutiques (including upscale jewellery store Roseark, at No.1111), cut-above cake shops (Sweet Lady Jane, at No.1631) and trendy coffee shops (Primo Passo, at No.702).

North of Montana, the streets get wider, the houses get broader and the gardens get more manicured. The four lanes of **San Vicente Boulevard** are separated by a grass verge lined with coral trees, which all but eliminates the impression that this is just another four-lane rat-run. The locale looks less like Santa Monica than Brentwood; which is, to the east at 26th Street, what it eventually becomes (*see p41*).

Third Street Promenade

Drifting south from Montana Avenue, Santa Monica gets steadily more commercial until you reach traffic-soaked Wilshire Boulevard and, eventually, the **Third Street Promenade**. A four-block pedestrianised stretch that runs down 3rd Street from Wilshire to Colorado Avenue, it's a pleasant but bland parade of mostly familiar names (Gap, Starbucks et al). The restaurants are ordinary, but the Wednesday morning farmers' market makes up for it. At the Promenade's southern end is **Santa Monica Place** shopping centre (*see p140*).

Santa Monica History Museum

1350 7th Street, between Arizona Avenue & Santa Monica Boulevard (1-310 395 2290, www.santamonicahistory.org). Bus 4, 20, 33, 704, 720, 733, SM1, SM2, SM3, SM7, SM8, SM9, SM10/I-10, exit Lincoln Boulevard north.
Open noon-8pm Tue, Thur; 10am-5pm Wed, Fri, Sat. **Admission** $5; $3 discounts; free under-12s. **Credit** AmEx, Disc, MC, V. **Map** p310 B3.
Founded in the 1970s, the SMHM houses a variety of material relating to the art, history and culture of the town. Housed in the same building as the Santa Monica Public Library, the 5,000sq ft museum has displays featuring historical artefacts and documents, plus interactive exhibits and a gallery with both permanent and temporary art shows.

Santa Monica Beach

For a different perspective, head a block north and a block west from the Third Street Promenade to the Penthouse bar and restaurant at the **Huntley Hotel** (1111 2nd Street; *see p165*). On a clear day, you can see to Santa Catalina Island and the endless lizard's back of the jagged San Bernardino Mountain peaks.

EXPLORE

Continuing a couple of blocks west will bring you to hotel-lined Ocean Avenue and, across the road, **Santa Monica Beach**. The focal point is **Santa Monica Pier** (at Colorado Avenue); on it is **Pacific Park** (free; www.pacpark.com), a traditional set-up stocked with a shiny Ferris wheel, fairground games and cotton-candy stands. On warm weekends, the stretch is busy with families, beach bums and gym bunnies, who work out in public at the original **Muscle Beach** just south of the pier. Those who'd rather not get sand between their toes hole up at the posh terrace bar at **Shutters on the Beach** (*see p167*) before adjourning to the **Viceroy** (*see p167*) to sup cosmopolitans with the beautiful people.

★ Santa Monica Pier Aquarium

1600 Ocean Front Walk, at Colorado Avenue (1-310 393 6149, www.healthebay.org/santa-monica-pier-aquarium). Bus 33, 733, SM1, SM4, SM7, SM8, SM10/I-10, exit 4th/5th Street north. **Open** *Summer* 2-6pm Tue-Fri; 12.30-6pm Sat, Sun. *Winter* 2-5pm Tue-Fri; 12.30-5pm Sat, Sun. **Admission** $3-$5; free under-13s. **Credit** MC, V. **Map** p310 A3.

Run by environmental charity Heal the Bay and located underneath the pier, the Santa Monica Pier Aquarium takes an educational tack; indeed, it's closed during the morning to allow for school field trips. It's a low-key place, a galaxy away from the likes of SeaWorld, but there's fun here for young-sters in the form of touch tanks full of crabs, snails and the like – more than 100 species of animals and plants in total, each of which can be found living within Santa Monica Bay itself. Shark Sundays (3.30pm every Sunday), featuring informative talks

on the much-maligned creatures, are justifiably pop-ular; check the website for other events and themed weekends. A good option for parents who can't bear the raucous atmosphere on the pier.

Ocean Park & Main Street

Beginning at the bottom of the Third Street Promenade, **Main Street** leads drivers past the conflicting designs of the 1930s-era **Santa Monica City Hall** (No.1685) and the '50s-era **Santa Monica Civic Auditorium** before ending in the heart of Venice. However, its most interesting stretch runs between Pico Boulevard and Rose Avenue. This is the hilly locale of **Ocean Park**, immortalised often in paintings by local artist Richard Diebenkorn.

The third of Santa Monica's three main commercial drags (after Montana Avenue and the Third Street Promenade), Main Street is an upmarket strip, and the stretch between Ocean Park Avenue and Marine Street is the most charming part of Ocean Park. Dating from the early 20th century, its buildings are populated by a range of largely independent coffeehouses, restaurants and gift shops. Also here is the **California Heritage Museum** (*see below*) and the **Edgemar Center for the Arts** (No.2437, 1-310 399 3666, www.edgemarcenter. org), a Frank Gehry-designed cultural mall that hosts theatrical performances and classes.

California Heritage Museum

2612 Main Street, at Ocean Park Boulevard (1-310 392 8537, www.californiaheritagemuseum. org). Bus 33, 733, SM1, SM2, SM8, SM10/I-10, exit 4th/5th Street south. **Open** 11am-4pm Wed-

EXPLORE

Santa Monica Pier.

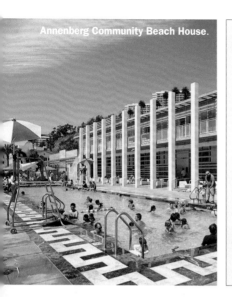

Annenberg Community Beach House.

**INSIDE TRACK
COMMUNITY SPIRIT**

What started as an opulent beachfront estate built by William Randolph Hearst for Hollywood star Marion Davies in the 1920s is now a modern, community beach club open to the public, thanks to Wallis Annenberg of the Annenberg Foundation, who provided $27.5 million for the transformation. The five-acre **Annenberg Community Beach House** (1-310-458-4904, http://beachhouse.smgov.net) is located at 415 Pacific Coast Highway in Santa Monica. It accommodates a main house with a rec room for board games, ping pong and classes and events, a swimming pool, a splash pad, beach volleyball and tennis courts, soccer fields, canopies, a café and rentals for paddle boards. Most amenities are free, while pool access is $4-$10/day and parking is $3/hour or $6/day.

Sun. **Admission** $8; $5 discounts; free under-12s. *Parking* free. **Credit** DC, MC, V. **Map** p310 A3.
This is an engaging, enthusiastically run operation, housed in an 1894 house and largely devoted to the decorative arts. The exhibits take the shape of rooms decorated in period style, among them a Victorian-era dining room and a 1930s kitchen. This permanent collection is supplemented by temporary displays; past shows have been devoted to everything from surfboards to old fruit-box labels. It's at its busiest on Sundays, though only outside: it hosts a popular farmers' market every Sunday morning (*see p151*).

Santa Monica Convention & Visitors Bureau

1920 Main Street, between Pico Boulevard & Bay Street (1-310 393 7593, www.santamonica.com). Bus 33, 733, SM1, SM4, SM7, SM8, SM10/I-10, exit 4th/5th Street south. **Open** 9am-5.30pm daily. **Map** p310 A3.
Other locations Palisades Park, 1400 Ocean Avenue, Santa Monica (1-310 393 0410); 322 Santa Monica Pier (no phone); cart at 1300 block of Third Street Promenade (1-310 309 9139).

Inland Santa Monica

Although inland Santa Monica is chiefly residential, it does hold pockets of interest for the visitor. Chief among them is **Bergamot Station**, a complex of art galleries created at a former Red Trolley terminus (2525 Michigan Avenue, at Cloverfield Boulevard; *see p154*). Its most famous tenant is the **Santa Monica Museum of Art** (*see right*), but many of its

other, commercial, galleries merit attention; *see p154*. The other major museum is the **Museum of Flying** (*see below*) at the **Santa Monica Airport**, itself home to an antiques market (*see p160*).

Museum of Flying

3100 Airport Avenue, between Walgrove & S Centinela Avenues (1-310 398 2500, www. museumofflying.com). Bus SM8/I-10, exit Bundy Drive south. **Open** 10am-5pm daily. **Admission** $10; $6-$8 discounts; free under-5s. **Credit** AmEx, MC, V. **Map** p310 D5.
Dedicated to the history of aviation, this small museum has around 15 aircraft, including a replica of the Wright Flyer, plus artefacts, personal effects and displays emphasising the history of the Santa Monica Airport and the Douglas Aircraft Company (don't miss the mural by Mike Machat).

Santa Monica Museum of Art

Building G1, Bergamot Station, 2525 Michigan Avenue, at Cloverfield Boulevard (1-310 586 6488, www.smmoa.org). Bus SM1, SM4, SM5, SM7/I-10, exit Cloverfield Boulevard north. **Open** 11am-6pm Tue-Sat. **Admission** *Suggested donation* $5; $3 discounts. **Credit** AmEx, MC, V. **Map** p310 D3.
The West Side's art scene continues to offer interesting shows, with new galleries cropping up at regular intervals. However, this contemporary art gallery is the most prestigious of the lot. Housed in the former trolley stop on the LA–Santa Monica Red Line that has become home to a complex of art galleries (Bergamot Station, *see p154*), the Santa Monica

EXPLORE

Muscle Beach. *See p40*.

EXPLORE

Museum of Art attracts sizeable crowds to its openings, which herald lively temporary exhibitions of work by a variety of local, national and international artists. Keep an eye out for the special events (lectures, workshops for adults and children and the like).

VENICE

Map p310

Despite gentrification in and around the area, its continued popularity with tourists, and the fact that its name long ago passed into cliché as a byword for hippiedom, Venice retains its edge. However, things are changing, and fast. The artists and dropouts who've long defined the area remain, but they're being usurped by young creatives in search of a countercultural edge, and by families driven down from their ideal-world home of Santa Monica by spiralling property prices. The uneasy mix is completed by low-income black and Latino communities in the troubled but improving Oakwood area, bounded by Lincoln and Venice Boulevards and Sunset and Electric Avenues.

Venice owes its existence to entrepreneur Abbot Kinney, who founded the city at the start of the 20th century in the hope that it would become the hub of an American cultural renaissance. The lagoon, the mock-Italian buildings and the canals were all his doing, as were the two dozen gondoliers imported from Italy. The cultural rebirth never quite

happened, but Kinney's creation did grow into a lively and successful resort that was known, in its heyday, as the 'Playland of the Pacific'.

It wasn't until later, after many of its canals were tarmacked, that Venice became a cultural hotbed. Artists and writers have been attracted to the area for decades, drawn by the sense of community and cheap rents. If you're here in May, look out for the annual **Venice Artwalk** (www.veniceartwalk.org), a fundraiser for the Venice Family Clinic that offers visitors the opportunity to tour more than 60 artists' studios. Year-round, though, keep your eyes peeled for the public art. Jonathan Borofsky's *Ballerina Clown*, on the corner of Main Street and Rose Avenue, is the most striking, but Ocean Front Walk and its surrounding streets are home to more examples, including many murals.

In the 1980s, Venice became a hive of architectural activity. The locale punches well above its weight with regard to the design of its buildings, and an enjoyable few hours can be spent touring its more notable spots. Frank Gehry's **Norton** and **Spiller Houses** (2509 Ocean Front Walk and 39 Horizon Avenue) are overshadowed only by his **Chiat/Day Building** (340 Main Street), its entrance marked by a gigantic pair of Claes Oldenburg-designed binoculars. Among other striking buildings are Brian Murphy's **Hopper House** (326 Indiana Avenue); and several new apartment buildings by such notable local architects as Steven Ehrlich (the **Venice Beach Lofts**, 25 Brooks Avenue), Koning Eizenberg (the **Electric ArtBlock**, 499 Santa Clara Avenue) and Mark Mack (the **Abbot Kinney Lofts**, 1200 Abbot Kinney Boulevard).

Abbot Kinney Boulevard

Venice's founder is commemorated in the name of its main thoroughfare, the increasingly chi-chi **Abbot Kinney Boulevard**. Not long ago, this was a ragged stretch of road that struggled to leave much of a lasting impression on locals or visitors. How times change. These days, at least between Broadway and California Avenues, where it's lined with small stores, bars and restaurants, it's a nice place to stroll and shop.

Abbot Kinney has mostly resisted the chains that crop up elsewhere in LA. However, the big brands are circling. When frozen yoghurt chain Pinkberry opened a store on Abbot Kinney in 2007, local grass-roots organisation Venice Unchained encouraged shoppers to boycott it. Three years later it closed. And talk that Starbucks might worm its way in has had locals concerned that the area may become too homogeneous. For now, though, the businesses, stocking everything from designer duds to handmade toys, are proud of their independence.

Among our favourites are **Strange Invisible Perfumes** (No.1138; *see p159*) and the flagship store of Venice-founded charity shoe brand **TOMS** (No.1344; 1-310 314 9700, www.toms.com).

On the first Friday of every month, Abbot Kinney's galleries, bars, restaurants and shops participate in the imaginatively named 'First Fridays' event. It's a good time to explore the street, although it can get extremely crowded and clogged with food trucks, so arrive early (around 5 or 6pm) to grab a parking space.

Venice Beach

While affluent new Venice can be seen in all its glory along Abbot Kinney Boulevard, shambolic old Venice remains in evidence along **Venice Beach** (*see p34* **Beachy Keen**). It's long been known as a mecca for kooky California culture and, up to a point, it remains so; repeated efforts by the authorities to rein in the vendors and entertainers have so far come to nothing. However, in the 21st century, it's as much of a tourist attraction as the Hollywood Walk

Juice is the Word

This new crop is cleansing Angelenos from the inside out.

It makes sense that the neighbourhood most associated with hippies and health food would be home to a store devoted to all things juice. Although it wasn't the first juicery to open in LA – that accolade goes to the still-popular **Beverly Hills Juice** (8382 Beverly Boulevard, 1-323 655 8300, www.beverlyhillsjuice.com), which opened way back in 1975 – **Moon Juice** (507 Rose Avenue, Venice, 1-310 399 2929, www.moonjuiceshop.com) has helped boost the recent growth spurt. In addition to cold-pressed juices and smoothies in such combos as fennel, frond and herb, the tiny shop sells dried fruit and nuts and supplements including bee pollen and probiotics.

Pressed Juicery (www.pressedjuicery. com), meanwhile, began with home-delivery juice kits, but now has storefronts all over LA, including Downtown and West Hollywood, plus a truck. Flavours include coconut cinnamon, watermelon mint and the rather scary-sounding Green Alkalizer

(cucumber, apple, lemon, ginger, cayenne). In Pacific Palisades and Brentwood (with more locations and a roving truck planned), **Juice Crafters** (www.juicecrafters.com) creates both cold-pressed juices and 'powerhouse smoothies' – regular ones just don't do it any more – topped off with a scoop of superfood such as chia seed or royal jelly. Near the Miracle Mile, **Clover** (342 S La Brea Avenue, 1-323 609 3903, www.cloverjuice.com) stocks bottled, cold-pressed juices – try the eponymous Clover, with pear, lime, coriander, mint and kale or a concoction such as the cold-weather comfort of the Seasonal, made with yam, carrot, apple, cinnamon and ginger.

By the time you read this, more spaces will have sprouted (plans for a second Moon Juice in Silver Lake were announced at press time, as well as Juice Served Here on trendy West 3rd Street). Just remember, if someone suggests a liquid lunch, check first whether they mean Beaujolais or beetroot.

Clover.

of Fame – the henna tattooists, abysmal performers and chips-cheap stalls recall nothing so much as Camden Market under the sun.

But for all its tackiness and attempts at eccentricity, the Boardwalk continues to entertain. From sightseers on Segways to radical pamphleteers, from romancing couples to steroid-stuffed bodybuilders at **Muscle Beach** (just north of Venice Boulevard), the people-watching is tremendous. And while the goods and services on offer are largely junk (cheap sunglasses, cheaper T-shirts, inedible snacks), there are a few beacons of civility along here. Snag some lunch at **Figtree's Café** (429 Ocean Front Walk, 1-310 392 4937, www.figtreescafe.com) before scanning the shelves at the excellent **Small World Books** (1407 Ocean Front Walk; *see p141*). Parallel with the bookstore, right on the beach, is the new 16,000-square-foot **Venice Beach Skate Park** (*see p242*).

It's worth diving off the beach and exploring the so-called 'walk-streets' that join the main road to the beach. These skinny little alleys are lined on either side with houses and apartments, an implausibly cosy arrangement that depends on community spirit for its success. Luckily, Venice has such spirit in spades, and houses along here remain highly sought-after properties. There's a more extensive network of walk-streets further inland, just west of Lincoln Boulevard.

The canals

Many of Venice's original canals were filled in during the 1920s by authorities unwilling to maintain them. However, a handful remain intact, offering a charming window into the way this neighbourhood must once have looked. Located south-east of the intersection of Venice Boulevard and Pacific Avenue, this small network of waterways is almost idyllic, a world away from the brashness of the beach.

It's worth spending a while idling along these waterways, sneaking a peek into the homes of the lucky locals. You won't for one second believe that you're in Italy, but that doesn't matter – this area has a character all its own.

MARINA DEL REY & AROUND

Considering that Los Angeles is located next to the largest area of open water on the planet, it's slightly strange that more attention isn't paid to its community of sailors. However, while the city's surfers get all the fame, many other Angelenos keep boats at **Marina del Rey Harbor**, a resort and residential complex just south of Venice. Conceived a century ago but only completed in 1965, the marina consists of an artificial harbour with eight basins named to evoke the South Seas (Tahiti Way, Bora Bora

Way) and filled with bobbing yachts, motor boats and flashy cruisers.

Like many similar resorts around the world, it's not a handsome place on land. Indeed, with the possible exception of Fisherman's Village, a cheesy re-creation of a New England fishing town, it's actually pretty ugly. The marina is surrounded by apartment blocks and bland hotels. Still, you'd no more visit Marina del Rey for the architecture than you'd visit Downtown LA for the surfing – it's really missing the point.

The Marina's attractions are all recreational. Picnic, jog and cycle (the Marina is a link in the 21-mile coastal bike path) in **Burton W Chace Park** and **Admiralty Park** at the northern end; fish from a dock at the west end of Chace Park or rent a boat to go ocean-fishing at **Fisherman's Village**; or join whale-watching excursions run during winter by any number of charter companies. But otherwise, save your money: the shopping is touristy, and most eateries are to be recommended more for their waterside charm than their food.

Playa del Rey & Playa Vista

Playa del Rey is separated from Marina del Rey only by the skinny little Ballona Creek, but it feels like a very different place. Small and unfancy, it's more down to earth than its neighbour – although there's a small hotel (the **Inn at Playa del Rey**; *see p170*), Playa del Rey as a whole seems unenthusiastic about attracting tourists. There's a curious variety of buildings on the stretch of **Vista del Mar** that sits just north of Culver Boulevard: look out, in particular, for the unexpectedly wonky green property at No.6672, designed by Eric Owen Moss in 1977. And there's a sweet little beach too. But otherwise, there's not that much to see in the heart of what's basically a seaside village.

Hugging Ballona Creek are the **Ballona Wetlands**. This nature reserve once stretched to 2,000 acres, but years of over-construction (including Marina del Rey) have reduced it to just a tenth of that size. Despite the intrusion, more than 200 species of birds can still be seen here. See www.ballonafriends.org for details of tours and other events.

Developers have been trying to get their hands on the remaining stretch of the Ballona Wetlands for years, so far without success. And if the rather sterile new residential neighbourhood of **Playa Vista** on the other side of Lincoln Boulevard is any indication of the kind of construction that might take its place, it's a good job that the area remains untamed. This huge development has been dogged by controversy since its inception, and there may well still be courtroom battles to be fought about proposed additions to the site in future years.

Brentwood to Beverly Hills

Money, money, money.

There is wealth in many corners of LA. However, nowhere is it displayed with quite such panache as in Beverly Hills. Its commercial thoroughfares are lined with high-end shops and eateries, its residential streets are immaculately manicured, and both foot and motor traffic are pristine.

Heading west, tourist attractions are few and far between in **Century City**, although in neighbouring **Westwood** it's pleasant to stroll around the UCLA campus. Further west lies **Brentwood**; today the area feels like a small town but it consisted of farms and fields until 1915, when a real estate agent named Bundy saw its potential. Landscape architects were asked to create 'flora, arbor and artistic park attractions'; everything that suggested a formal city was to be avoided. To the south, formerly film-focused **Culver City** is enoying a resurgence, aided by the recent arrival of the Metro train system in the area.

Map p311	Coffeehouses p132
Restaurants p98	Hotels p170
Bars p120	

BRENTWOOD

Today, as ever, Brentwood is a leafy, largely residential neighbourhood; cruise up **Kenter Avenue** and **Bonhill Road** for a peek through the keyhole. There are numerous notable buildings: designed by Frank Lloyd Wright, the **Sturges House** (449 Skyewiay Road) is wedged dramatically on to a hill; and Eric Owen Moss's work in Culver City (*see p44*) finds a small but scintillating echo in the building he designed at **167 S Westgate Avenue**. However, there's also plenty of grandiose architectural mediocrity and an awful lot of tall, paparazzi-proof hedges.

Brentwood has always drawn the wealthy and the famous: Raymond Chandler wrote *High Window* while living at 12216 Shetland Place, and Marilyn Monroe died a lonely death at 12305 5th Helena Drive. However, it was another star who really put the area on the global map, although the exact parts he put on it are no longer there. The condo of murdered Nicole Brown Simpson (formerly 875 S Bundy Drive) has been relandscaped to deter sightseers, while OJ Simpson's house (formerly 360 N Rockingham Avenue) was bulldozed in 1998.

San Vicente Boulevard, the area's main road, has running down its centre a line of coral trees, the official tree of the city. At the corner of San Vicente and 26th Street is the **Brentwood Country Mart** (www.brentwood countrymart.com), a small outdoor mall that's home to upmarket shops and eateries, among them James Perse, Diesel bookstore, **Caffe Luxxe** (*see p131*), **Sweet Rose Creamery** (*see p134* **Cold Comfort**) and **Farmshop** (*see p99*).

★ FREE Getty Center

1200 Getty Center Drive, at I-405 (1-310 440 7300, www.getty.edu). Bus 761/I-405, exit Getty Center Drive. **Open** 10am-5.30pm Tue-Fri, Sun;

EXPLORE

10am-9pm Sat. **Admission** free. *Parking* $15; $10 after 5pm Mon-Fri for events & after 5pm Sat.

Los Angeles's hilltop acropolis was conceived as a home for the hitherto disparate entities of the J Paul Getty Trust, but that's the only straightforward thing about it. Architect Richard Meier was hired to build the museum in 1984, but it took 13 years, several additional designers (to work on the interior and the landscaping) and $1 billion to complete. The end result is a remarkable complex of travertine and white metal-clad pavilions that resembles a kind of monastic retreat designed for James Bond. Its relative inaccessibility is more than compensated for by the panoramic views, from the hills and the ocean in the west all the way around to Downtown in the east.

Once you've parked at the bottom and taken the electric tram ride up the hill, one thing becomes apparent: it's a big place. To the west of the plaza is a café, a restaurant (*see p99*) and the circular Research Institute, which houses one of the world's largest art and architecture libraries, and a roster of public exhibits. Beyond it is the Central Garden, designed by Robert Irwin. North are the Getty Conservation Institute and the Getty Foundation (not open to the public) and the Harold M Williams Auditorium, where talks and symposia alternate with concerts and film screenings. To the south, up a grand Spanish Steps-style stairway, is the museum lobby, an airy, luminous rotunda that opens to a fountain-filled courtyard surrounded by six pavilions housing the permanent collection and often-excellent temporary shows, spanning everything from fashion in the Middle Ages to Cuba in art.

Collections

The Getty's budget is the envy of museums the world over, but it was a Johnny-come-lately to European art; and while its collections may not match the major museums of the Old World, certain aspects – post-Renaissance decorative arts, the photography selection – are magnificent, and others are fast improving.

The collections are spread over four two-level pavilions, all linked on both levels by walkways. The art is displayed more or less chronologically: the North Pavilion contains pieces from prior to 1700; the East and South Pavilions feature works from the 17th and 18th centuries; and the West Pavilion runs from 1800 to the present day. The plaza level of each pavilion contains sculpture and decorative arts,

Getty Center.

along with temporary exhibits in other disciplines; the second floors are given over to paintings.

On the ground floor of the North Pavilion, room N104 contains an intriguing array of glass objects dating from the 1400s to the 1600s, while N105 is home to a rotating series of small-scale displays drawn from the Getty's collection of illuminated manuscripts. Upstairs is dominated by Italian religious painting from the 15th and 16th centuries; highlights include a vast altarpiece by Bartolomeo Vivarini (N202) and a scintillating *Venus & Adonis* by Titian (N205).

The East Pavilion is heavy on the Dutch and Flemish masters. Notable pieces include Gerrit van Honthorst's *Christ Crowned with Thorns* (E201); several works by Rubens, among them *The Entombment* (E202); and Gerrit Dou's intensely detailed *Astronomer by Candlelight* (E205).

One of the museum's strengths is its collection of 17th- and 18th-century decorative arts, most of it French, that monopolises the ground-floor galleries in the South Pavilion. Some rooms contain individual exhibits (seek out the bed in S109); others are virtual reconstructions of French drawing rooms, complete with original panelling. Next to this opulent array, the galleries upstairs can't compete, but they do house two Gainsboroughs (S202) and Odilon Redon's *Baronne de Domecy*, a dream-like piece that overshadows the rest of the pastels and watercolours in S206.

INSIDE TRACK ROAD RAGE

As part of a plan to widen the I-405 through the **Sepulveda Pass**, drivers can expect roadworks and congestion on and around the freeway until the project's completion in late 2013. Check the dedicated page on Metro's website (www.metro.net/projects/I-405) for details and updates.

The ground-floor galleries in the West Pavilion are given over to European sculpture and decorative arts from the late 18th and 19th centuries plus, in W104-W106, changing exhibits from the Getty's drawings collection. Upstairs is a strong-ish selection of paintings, mostly from the 19th century. Room W202 contains the luminous *Modern Rome – Campo Vaccino* by Turner, and in neighbouring gallery W201, a seascape by Turner entitled *Van Tromp, Going about to Please his Masters, Ships a Sea, Getting a Good Wetting*. However, the key works are in W204: several Monet pieces, a Cézanne still life, a delightfully raffish Renoir portrait of composer Albert Cahen d'Anvers, and Van Gogh's *Irises*. Recent acquisitions include *Portrait of Madame Brunet* by Manet (Room W203) and *The Italian Comedians* by Watteau (Room S202).

Elsewhere, look out for the rotating displays culled from the museum's world-class photography holdings. And don't miss the fine sculpture gardens at the museum's entrance and by the West Pavilion, home to works by (among others) Miró and Moore.

★ Skirball Cultural Center

2701 N Sepulveda Boulevard, at I-405 (1-310 440 4500, www.skirball.org). Bus 761/I-405, exit Skirball Center/Mulholland Drive north.
Open noon-5pm Tue-Fri; 10am-5pm Sat, Sun.
Admission $10; $5-$7 discounts; free under-2s.
Free to all Thur. *Parking* free. **Credit** DC, MC, V.
Something of a local powerhouse, the Skirball is a cultural centre as distinct from a museum, and aims to look at connections between 4,000 years of Jewish heritage and the American democratic life. Those with an interest in Jewish history will get the most from some of the exhibits (the 30,000-object collection is one of the largest holdings of Judaica in the US), but this is an egalitarian enterprise that should interest most visitors with a sense of cultural adventure.

Visions and Values: Jewish Life from Antiquity to America, the central exhibit, offers a lengthy but interesting trawl through Jewish history and culture, taking in everything from Jewish holidays to the American Jewish experience. It is joined by Noah's Ark, a wonderful kid-oriented exhibit that explores cultural differences through a retelling of the old animals-two-by-two tale (entrance with free timed tickets only; advance reservations recommended). Folk art-esque animals hang from the ceilings and peer out from a mock-ark; hands-on interaction is encouraged as part of what's the most enjoyable family-friendly exhibit in the LA region.

These two headline-grabbing permanent exhibits are supplemented by a decent café and a pleasing garden; a lively programme of temporary exhibitions on everything from America's founding documents to the art of Maira Kalman; talks and discussions, many related to ongoing displays; and an unexpectedly rich schedule of concerts and other performances. The Skirball might be off the beaten tourist track, but it's well worth the diversion.

CULVER CITY

Forget Hollywood: Culver City was once the cradle of the American movie industry. Many major motion-picture studios conducted their business from these streets, among them MGM and RKO; films of the calibre of *Citizen Kane* and *The Wizard of Oz* were shot here, at a time when the town produced more than half of all the movies shot in America. The entertainment industry retains a presence in the area: **Sony Pictures** is squeezed in on part of the old MGM lot between W Washington and Culver Boulevards, just east of Overland Avenue (for tours, *see p29*). But there's more to the area than mere nostalgia for some long-lost cinematic golden age. Culver City, possibly for the first time in its existence, is hip.

After years as little more than a suburban adjunct to the more engaging neighbourhoods to the west and north, Culver City has spent the last decade or so turning itself around. The town's focal point is the downtown intersection of **Main Street** and **Culver Boulevard**, around which sit a low-key but lively collection of galleries, shops and restaurants. New venues are constantly springing up, and the number looks set to grow further now, thanks to the opening of the new Metro train station – part of the Expo line – at Washington and National Boulevards.

For all its cultural appeal, the area doesn't really offer much for the sightseer. At the junction of Culver Boulevard and Irving Place, **Town Plaza** is surely the only block in the city with two fountain sculptures: Eric Orr's untitled triangular granite pole, and Douglas Olmsted Freeman's more eye-catching *Lion's Fountain*. A few yards to the west are a couple of historic structures: the **Culver Hotel**, built in the '20s, and the **Kirk Douglas Theatre** (*see p233*), an old '40s cinema topped by an iconic neon-lit tower. And north of here, across Culver Boulevard, is the fabulous **Museum of Jurassic Technology** (*see p44*).

However, Culver City's renaissance is best symbolised by an 11-acre complex of buildings located at the corner of Venice Boulevard and Helms Avenue. Local baker Helms baked its last loaf here in 1969, but its old premises have been spared the wrecking ball by forward-thinking local preservationists. Its glorious neon sign now fully restored, the **Helms Bakery** (www.helmsbakerydistrict.com) today houses an array of galleries, furniture shops and eateries such as Father's Office (*see p119*).

Not far from here, on the 3500 block of Hayden Avenue near the junction with National Boulevard, is perhaps the most eye-catching architectural project in LA. In the 1940s and '50s, the **Hayden Tract** was a thriving

EXPLORE

INSIDE TRACK LOTS OF LOTS

Not everything in Beverly Hills costs a fortune: handily for visitors, there are numerous parking structures in the Golden Triangle, some of which offer free parking for one or two hours. Try the ones on Crescent, Camden, Canon, Bedford, Beverly or Rexford Drives, or Dayton or Brighton Ways. Visit www.beverlyhills.org for a map of the locations.

industrial area, but by the '80s the businesses had largely moved out. Enter Frederick Smith, an entrepreneur with a vision of how to regenerate the area, and Eric Owen Moss, the experimental architect he chose to give it life. Some of the old factories remain, but others have been replaced by Moss's odd yet dazzling office buildings. Park outside the daunting black hulk of the **Samitaur Stealth Building** (3528 Hayden Avenue); walk under it and into the parking lot to see Moss's singular style in full effect. In one corner stands the **Umbrella** (No.3542), its crazed exterior staircase leading nowhere; across the way is another building with a frontage that leans precariously forward, echoing the angles of the Stealth building. Back on the main road sits the demented façade of **3535 Hayden Avenue**, all spiky wood and awkward concrete. (For a brief overview of Moss's new and planned constructions, *see p282.*)

The area south of Culver City holds little of interest to visitors, save for the small but fascinating **Wende Museum**, an earnest exhibition compiled by Justinian Jampol, a Cold War-obsessed academic. There are Stasi artefacts here, along with propaganda posters, remnants of the East German counterculture, segments of the Berlin Wall and East German ruler Erich Honecker's personal papers (5741 Buckingham Parkway, 1-310 216 1600, www.wendemuseum.org; closed Sat, Sun; by appt only Mon-Thur). Nearby is the Catholic **Holy Cross Cemetery** (5835 W Slauson Avenue, 1-310 836 5500, www.holycross mortuary.com), the final resting place of numerous stars, including Sharon Tate, Bing Crosby, John Candy and *Wizard of Oz* actors Ray Bolger and Jack Haley.

★ Museum of Jurassic Technology

9341 Venice Boulevard, at Bagley Avenue (1-310 836 6131, www.mjt.org). Metro Culver City/ bus 33, 220, 733, SM12/I-10, exit Robertson Boulevard south. **Open** 2-8pm Thur; noon-6pm Fri-Sun. **Admission** *Suggested donation* $8; $5 discounts; free under-12s. **Credit** AmEx, MC, V.

Don't be fooled by the name: this is not some kind of Spielbergian dinosaurland. It's far more interesting than that. Hidden behind an unassuming, window-less storefront, David Wilson's Museum of Jurassic Technology presents itself as a repository of curiosi-ties (opera singer Madelena Delani, who suffered from terrible memory failings), scientific wonders (a bat that can fly through walls) and artistic miracles (the 'microminiatures' of Soviet-Armenian refugee Hagop Sandaldjian, who painted impossibly tiny sculptures that fit within the eye of a needle).

Fact is mixed with the fantastical, through the elaborate and beautiful treatment (dramatically lit vitrines, audio-visual displays) accorded to every-thing from the history of trailer parks to 17th-cen-tury Renaissance man Athanasius Kircher. Which exhibits, if any, are bona fide? Which, if any, are satirical? And, most crucially of all, does it matter? A subversive, witty and brilliant enterprise, the Museum of Jurassic Technology challenges the very nature of what a museum is or should be, while also taking its place as one of the most fascinating attrac-tions in the entire city. The Borzoi Kabinet Theater (a 14-seat cinema) and Tula Tea Room screen short films and serve Georgian tea for part of the day. Unique and unreservedly recommended.

Star Eco Station

10101 W Jefferson Boulevard, between Overland & Duquesne Avenues, Culver City (1-310 842 8060, www.ecostation.org). Bus C3, C4/I-10, exit Overland Avenue south. **Open** *July, Aug* 1-5pm Mon-Fri; 10am-4pm Sat, Sun. *Sept-June* 1-5pm Fri; 10am-4pm Sat, Sun. **Admission** $8; $6-$7 discounts; free infants. *Parking* free. **Credit** DC, Disc, MC, V.

Part wildlife rescue centre, part educational facility, this very family-friendly enterprise practises what it preaches in terms of environmental awareness – it was even built from recycled materials. Staff pro-vide care for unwanted exotic animals, many of which have either been donated by the public or con-fiscated by government agencies. Guided tours are compulsory (the last one leaves an hour before the building closes) and offer visitors the chance to pet the animals while learning about endangered species, environmental concerns and how kids can make a change. A number of other exhibits add further con-text; call or check online for details of special events.

WESTWOOD & AROUND

The Westwood neighbourhood is dominated by the University of California, Los Angeles, better known as **UCLA**. The handsome and suitably cultured 400-acre campus makes for an agreeable diversion. To reach it, drive up Westwood Boulevard and follow the right-hand fork into Westwood Plaza.

South of UCLA, centred around Westwood Boulevard and Broxton Avenue, Westwood's commercial district is walkable but not hugely inspiring. There's less to buy but more to see at the **Hammer Museum** (*see below*) and **Westwood Memorial Park** (1218 Glendon Avenue, at Wilshire Boulevard, 1-310 474 1579), the final resting place of Marilyn Monroe, Natalie Wood, Burt Lancaster, Billy Wilder and, in an unmarked grave next to actor Lew Ayres, Frank Zappa.

South of here, the area rather peters out. Wilshire Boulevard is dominated by drab skyscrapers; below it, Westwood Boulevard contains a few ethnic restaurants but not much else. The most powerful presence in the area is the **Mormon Temple** (10777 Santa Monica Boulevard, at Overland Avenue), topped by a 257-foot tower that's crowned with a gold-leaf statue of the angel Moroni. The temple, the largest Mormon place of worship outside Salt Lake City, is open only to church members, but the manicured lawn and white stone building are an awe-inspiring sight even if you're not Mormonically inclined. Similarly expansive but less impressive is the **Westside Pavilion**, a classic 1980s mall that was spruced up some years ago and is now home to the **Landmark** cineplex (*see p194*).

Hammer Museum

10899 Wilshire Boulevard, at Westwood Boulevard (1-310 443 7000, www.hammer. ucla.edu). Bus 20, 720/I-405, exit Wilshire Boulevard east. **Open** 11am-8pm Tue-Fri; 11am-5pm Sat, Sun. **Admission** $10; $5 discounts; free under-17s. Free to all Thur. *Parking* $3 1st 3hrs with validation. **Credit** AmEx, DC, MC, V. **Map** p311 A4.

Industrialist Armand Hammer founded this museum, primarily to house his own collection. Now, under the ownership of UCLA, the Hammer stages fascinating themed shows of modern art, photography and design. The former have included everything from video installations to American comic art; the last are often drawn from UCLA's Grunwald collection of graphic arts. The shows are supplemented by the Hammer Projects series, focused on emerging artists; works from Hammer's permanent collections (from Rembrandt to Ruscha); and an excellent, largely free events programme that takes in music, films, symposia and so on. The bookstore is terrific too.

BEL AIR

After it was developed by Alphonzo E Bell in the early 1920s, this sleepy hillside community north of Westwood became a favoured location among stars who wanted to have privacy as well as fantastic views. Celebrities still abound, but there's not a great deal for the outsider to see along the winding roads. The **Hotel Bel-Air** (*see p172*) on Stone Canyon Road, which opened in 2011 after a major renovation, mirrors the tranquil, dripping-with-money locale, with its beautifully manicured gardens and luxuriant lake.

EXPLORE

UCLA campus.

CENTURY CITY

Century City was once a movie backlot, where Tom Mix filmed his Westerns. It's still home to Fox Studios, but it's also now characterised by a skyline-dominating overabundance of high-rise buildings. Most are nondescript, but there are a couple of exceptions, both by Minoru Yamasaki: the triangular **Century Plaza Towers** and the **Century Plaza Hotel** (now the **Hyatt Regency Century Plaza**; *see p173*), a huge, high-rise ellipse. Several other cloudbusters were recently added to the mix, including two apartment complexes: the 24-storey Carlyle (10776 Wilshire Boulevard) and the 42-storey Century (next to the Hyatt Regency). However, business dominates, and the main attraction is the **Westfield Century City** mall (*see p141*). There is a little culture here too, in the form of the **Annenberg Space for Photography** (*see p154*), which stages small yet thoughtful exhibitions. And if the Westside Subway Extension ends up wending its way through Century City, as at least one plan proposes, more change is bound to come.

BEVERLY HILLS

Map p311

Beverly Hills has been a star magnet for decades. Douglas Fairbanks and Mary Pickford were the first to move here in 1920, to a Wallace Neff-designed mansion at 1143 Summit Drive they called Pickfair (later demolished by Pia Zadora), and the celeb power remains strong. You'll occasionally see streetside vendors selling 'star maps', purporting to pinpoint celebrities' homes. It probably goes without saying that they're about as reliable as, say, Lindsay Lohan.

North of Santa Monica Boulevard

The best way to introduce yourself to Beverly Hills is to drive the residential streets in the area bounded by **Sunset Boulevard**, **Doheny Drive**, **Santa Monica Boulevard** and **Walden Drive**. There's an eerie quiet throughout: traffic is sparse, and the only people on foot are gardeners. If you get the feeling you're being watched, you probably are: as tiny signs on almost every fencepost or lawn detail, security firms patrol these streets.

The area is anything but homogeneous. When you have as much money as the folks around here, you don't just buy a house: you build your own. And, of course, you build it exactly as you please, which might not be in anything like the same way as your neighbours. As a result, the architecture is a wild blend of styles: everything from squat modernist boxes

to palatial mansions and Spanish villas, often all on the same street. Still, nothing is quite as wild as the fairytale folly of the 1921 **Spadena House**, also known as the Witch's House (516 N Walden Drive, at Carmelita Avenue). Built in Culver City to house a movie studio's offices, the fantastical structure was moved here in 1934. It's now privately owned, and snooping is discouraged, but you can get a proper look at the façade from the street.

At the north-eastern junction of Santa Monica and Wilshire Boulevards sits another slice of old Beverly Hills. Harnessing **Beverly Gardens**, a pleasant but unremarkable stretch of greenery, stands the **Electric Fountain**, built by architect Ralph Flewelling and sculptor Merrell Gage. Upon completion in 1931, the dramatic water displays and neon lighting stopped traffic. The fountain is still a fine sight. Its focal point is a Native American praying for rain.

Two landmarks sit north on Sunset Boulevard, by the junction with Beverly Drive. Known as the 'Pink Palace', the **Beverly Hills Hotel & Bungalows** (No.9641; *see p173*) was one of the first buildings to be constructed in the city. Close by is **Will Rogers Memorial Park**; it was here, in the park's public toilets, that George Michael was arrested in 1998.

The houses north of here, around **Benedict** and **Coldwater Canyons**, are grander than those south of Sunset, none more so than the **Greystone Mansion** (905 Loma Vista Drive, 1-310 550 4796, www.greystonemansion.org). Built in 1927 by oil millionaire Edward L Doheny for his son, who was shot dead within weeks of moving in, this 55-room Tudor-style home has featured in films such as *The Witches of Eastwick* and *Indecent Proposal*. The house is closed to the public (apart from occasional special events), but its 18 acres of landscaped gardens are usually open 10am-5pm daily (check first before making a special trip).

South of Santa Monica Boulevard

If the streets north of Santa Monica Boulevard are where the locals live, the roads south of it are where they spend their money. The pocket bounded by Wilshire Boulevard, Canon Drive and Little (or South) Santa Monica Boulevard, which includes **Rodeo Drive**, Dayton Way and Brighton Way, is known as the **Golden Triangle**. A few more prosaic chains have arrived in recent years, but the pedestrian-friendly area is still famous for the array of high-end fashion designers with shops here. **Two Rodeo**, a $200 million ersatz-European cobbled walkway, is always busy with window-shopping tourists and serious spenders.

Signs of wealth abound along **Little Santa Monica Boulevard**. The **Peninsula Beverly**

Hills (No.9882, at Charleville Boulevard; *see p175*) is a good place for celebrity-spotting. And next door (9830 Wilshire Boulevard) stands a stunning building designed by IM Pei for über-agent Michael Ovitz's Creative Artists Agency, all white marble and cantilevered glass. (CAA moved to Century City in 2007, but the building remains.) **Beverly Hills Rent-A-Car** (9732 Little Santa Monica Boulevard, at S Linden Drive) deals not in Fords and Chevys but Porsches and Ferraris, while **Sprinkles** (*see p133* **All Rise**) sells delicious $3.25

cupcakes to Hillbillies who are watching their figure only *so* closely. Other women sit in shop windows getting their hair coiffed. And at Little Santa Monica Boulevard and Rexford Drive sits the Spanish baroque-style **Civic Center**, as carefully maintained as any film set. Nearby, construction work is under way on the site of the old Beverly Hills Post Office – the historic building will become part of the new Wallis Annenberg Center for the Performing Arts, which is expected to open in autumn 2013.

Ghouls' Paradise

In LA, you may end up more famous dead than alive.

When it comes to violent celebrity deaths, Los Angeles is in a league of its own. Murder happens on a grand scale here: you live big, you die big. And, in many cases, you die young.

Probably the most famous murders in LA history occurred on the night of 8 August 1969, when five people – including actress **Sharon Tate**, wife of film director Roman Polanski – were slain by hippie followers of self-styled guru Charles Manson. The house where the murders took place, at 10050 Cielo Drive (off Benedict Canyon Drive, north of Beverly Hills), was demolished in 1994; the property that now stands on the site is numbered 10066. The following night, Leno and Rosemary LaBianca were murdered by members of Manson's 'Family' at their home at 3301 Waverly Drive, Los Feliz (later renumbered 3311). Their connection to Manson? Simply that, a year earlier, he'd attended a party at the house next door.

A quarter of a century later, another brutal murder made headlines. On the night of 12 June 1994, Nicole Brown Simpson and her friend Ronald Goldman were stabbed to death at Simpson's house at 875 (now 879) S Bundy Drive in Brentwood. Five days later, following a notorious police chase along the LA freeways, football star, actor and Nicole's ex-husband **OJ Simpson** was arrested and then charged with their murders. Simpson was found not guilty in 1995, but was later deemed liable in a civil trial. He's currently in jail in Nevada, having been found guilty of kidnapping and armed robbery in a Las Vegas hotel room in 2007.

As well as the famous, there are the forgotten. *Rebel Without A Cause* star **Sal Mineo** was knifed to death during a botched robbery in his garage at 8569

Holloway Drive, just off the Sunset Strip, on 12 February 1976. Two decades later, actor **Haing S Ngor** – who survived life under the Khmer Rouge in Cambodia, and later won an Oscar for his performance in 1995's *The Killing Fields* – was murdered in an apparent robbery-gone-wrong outside his home at 945 N Beaudry Avenue, Chinatown, on 25 February 1996.

Some of LA's most notorious murders remain unsolved, among them that of mobster **Bugsy Siegel**, who was shot dead at 810 N Linden Drive in Beverly Hills on 20 June 1947; it's just a few streets away from Lana Turner's former house, at 730 N Linden Drive, where her daughter, Cheryl Crane, stabbed and killed Turner's lover, **Johnny Stompanato**, on 4 April 1958, allegedly in self-defence. Also unsolved is the slaying of rapper **Biggie Smalls**, aka the Notorious BIG, gunned down outside the Petersen Automotive Museum (*see p56*) on 9 March 1997. In 2007, Smalls' relatives filed a wrongful death suit against the City of LA, claiming it deliberately concealed the identity of – and failed to pursue – the killers. And then, of course, there's legendary record producer **Phil Spector**, accused of murdering waitress and B-movie actress Lana Clarkson at his 'Pyrenees Castle' in Alhambra (1700 Grand View Drive) on 3 February 2003. After a mis-trial, Spector was retried and convicted of second-degree murder in 2009.

Such deaths continue to generate both intrigue and revenue. Guided tours of famous death sites have become major tourist attractions (try the excellent **Dearly Departed Tours**; *see p28*). There's even the **Museum of Death** (6031 Hollywood Boulevard, 1-323 466 8011, www.museumofdeath.net) in Hollywood.

EXPLORE

But for all the glamour, numerous remnants of old Beverly Hills have survived intact. **Nate 'n Al** (414 N Beverly Drive, at Brighton Way; *see p102*) is a too-Jewish-to-be-true deli that draws a mixed crowd of young bucks and ancient ladies who lunch; south, the stretch of Beverly Drive between Wilshire and Pico Boulevards is a great example of classic LA 1950s architecture. Close by Civic Center, the **Union 76** gas station on the corner of Little Santa Monica Boulevard and Crescent Drive boasts a 1950s cantilevered concrete canopy.

Beverly Hills Visitor Center

9400 S Santa Monica Boulevard, at N Canon Drive (1-310 248 1000, www.lovebeverlyhills.com). Bus 4, 14, 16, 316, 704/I-10, exit Robertson Boulevard north. **Open** 9am-5pm Mon-Fri; 10am-5pm Sat, Sun. **Map** p311 C2.

★ Museum of Tolerance

Simon Wiesenthal Plaza, 9786 W Pico Boulevard, at Roxbury Drive (1-310 553 8403, www.museum oftolerance.com). Bus SM7, SM13/I-10, exit Overland Avenue north. **Open** *Apr-Oct* 10am-5pm Mon-Fri; 11am-5pm Sun. *Nov-Mar* 10am-5pm Mon-Thur; 10am-3pm Fri; 11am-5pm Sun. **Admission** $15; $11-$12 discounts; free under-5s. *Parking* free. **Credit** AmEx, DC, MC, V. **Map** p311 C4.

Greystone Mansion. *See p46.*

Founded in 1993 by the Simon Wiesenthal Center, a Jewish organisation named after the famous Nazi-hunter and devoted to combating anti-semitism and other forms of prejudice, the Museum of Tolerance was seen as a daring enterprise: a museum devoted to an abstract concept rather than a specific type of artefact. However, while it's adventurous in concept, it's also extremely enlightening, not least because the museum's set-up is careful to leave it to the visitor to come up with their own definition of the word.

The main exhibit is an involving hour-long walk-through on the Holocaust, which blends taped narration with photos, film footage, personal testimonies, dioramas and World War II artefacts. At the start of the exhibit, you're given a 'passport' with a child's photograph; their fate is revealed to you at the end of the tour. You can explore the subject further on the computers in the Multimedia Center (the material is online at http://motlc.wiesenthal.com), via displays of other Holocaust documents, and in conversation with a number of survivors, who regularly visit the museum to give talks and host discussions. Their stories are moving and endlessly fascinating. A newer acquisition, and the centrepiece of a new interactive exhibit, is the Hitler Letter, a signed document from 1919 that reveals the beginnings of Hitler's goal to destroy the Jewish people.

Elsewhere, the Tolerancenter is an interactive exhibit that aims to spur visitors into thinking about their own prejudices. It's used as an educational aid by local schools, and for LAPD officer training. One of the three major exhibits is Finding Our Families, Finding Ourselves, in which the likes of Carlos Santana, Maya Angelou and Billy Crystal tell of their heritage as immigrants and children of immigrants.

Call or check online for details of special exhibits, talks and discussions. Advance booking is advised (call 1-310 772 2505); the museum is closed on Saturdays, Jewish holidays and most other holidays.

Paley Center for Media

465 N Beverly Drive, at S Santa Monica Boulevard (1-310 786 1000, www.paleycenter.org). Bus 4, 20, 704, 720/I-10, exit Robertson Boulevard north. **Open** noon-5pm Wed-Sun. **Admission** *Suggested donation* $10; $5-$8 discounts. *Parking* free 1st 2hrs, then $1 every additional 30mins. **No credit cards**. **Map** p311 C3.

Formerly the Museum of Television & Radio but now renamed after its co-founder, former CBS president William S Paley, the Paley Center has a collection of more than 150,000 TV, radio and new media programmes. The collection is accessible to the public for on-site viewing (search the database and request a programme); the centre, designed by Getty Villa architect Richard Meier, also organises regular screenings, public seminars and discussions in its theatre. The annual PaleyFest, held in March at the Saban Theatre on Wilshire Boulevard, features panel discussions from the casts of current TV shows such as *New Girl* and *The Big Bang Theory*.

West Hollywood, Hollywood & Midtown

Mainstream sights and gay delights.

An independent city since 1984, tiny West Hollywood – a little under two square miles – is the epicentre of gay and lesbian life in LA, with Santa Monica Boulevard as its main thoroughfare. It's also home to the straight nightclubs of the fabled Sunset Strip, and, in the east, a community of immigrant Russians. Further east, Hollywood is reclaiming some of the glamour long associated with its name. And talking of names, to the south, the Miracle Mile might be an exaggeration these days, but it does hold some interesting sights, including a museum devoted to the Holocaust.

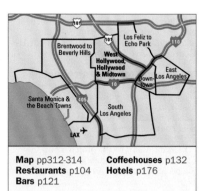

Map pp312-314	Coffeehouses p132
Restaurants p104	Hotels p176
Bars p121	

WEST HOLLYWOOD

Map p312

As well as its vibrant gay and lesbian community, West Hollywood is synonymous with the **Sunset Strip**, the stretch of W Sunset Boulevard running from Doheny Drive to Laurel Canyon, which was developed in 1924. By the 1930s, it was Hollywood's playground: at the Trocadero and Ciro's, singers such as Lena Horne belted out sets for stars, businessmen and mobsters. However, it was a very different type of nightlife that gave the Sunset Strip something approaching iconic status. Located at 8901 W Sunset, the **Whisky a Go-Go** (*see p222*) became the first discothèque on the West Coast when it opened in 1964, and was a hit almost from the moment it opened. Other clubs followed, and the area became the centre of LA youth culture during the 1960s, with everyone from the Byrds to the Doors playing regularly.

The area still has its nightlife, though nowadays it's largely the haunt of tourists. The **Comedy Store**, on the site where Ciro's once stood (No.8433; *see p225*), helped to break stars such as Robin Williams. The venerable **Roxy** (No.9009; *see p222*) and the younger **House of Blues** (No.8430; *see p217*) continue to host fine

acts, but the Whisky long ago lost its spark. The Strip is kept alive by hotels such as the **Chateau Marmont** (No.8221; *see p176*) and **Mondrian** (No.8440; *see p177*), trendy **Equinox** gym (No.8590; *see p206*) and a stretch of restaurants and shops between Holloway Drive and Alta Loma Road, known as the Sunset Plaza mall.

West Hollywood's main points of interest during daylight hours are the massive advertising billboards, some as big as the buildings to which they're attached. However, some structures, such as the immense **Beverly Center** mall (8500 Beverly Boulevard; *see p138*), dominate the horizon but don't particularly impress with anything except their scale. Similarly vast is César Pelli's **Pacific Design Center** (8687 Melrose Avenue, at San Vicente Boulevard, 1-310 657 0800, www.pacificdesign center.com), a huge glass shed that's been generously nicknamed 'the Blue Whale'. A third red building is scheduled to join the existing blue and green behemoths by late 2013, adding offices, a conference hall and two restaurants. Built to house outlets for the interior design trade, the PDC is underused for its size, although MoCA (*see p71*) stages exhibitions here and it's also home to the local tourist information centre, **Visit West Hollywood** (*see p50*).

Away from the area's main roads, the residential streets of West Hollywood are cosy, densely packed and pleasingly free of pretence. A detour on wheels or on foot is an agreeable way to while away an afternoon, stopping off for a latte on Melrose Avenue at **Urth Caffé** (No.8565; *see p134*) or **Le Pain Quotidien** (No.8607), or browsing the mix of upscale and affordable shops on Robertson Boulevard, part of which is pleasingly in Beverly Hills.

Several small buildings are notable. The angular **Lloyd Wright Home & Studio** (858 N Doheny Drive) was designed by Frank's son, but the real gem is at 835 N Kings Road: built as a live-work space by Rudolf Schindler, the extraordinary structure now houses the **MAK Center for Art & Architecture**.

MAK Center for Art & Architecture

Schindler House, 835 N Kings Road, between Waring & Willoughby Avenues (1-323 651 1510, www.makcenter.org). Bus 10, 105/I-10, exit La Cienega Boulevard north. **Open** 11am-6pm Wed-Sun. **Tours** Sat, Sun (call for details). **Admission** $7; $6 discounts; free under-12s. Free to all 4-6pm Fri. **Credit** AmEx, MC, V. **Map** p312 B2.
Constructed in 1922 by radical Austrian architect Rudolf Schindler, this LA landmark is a dazzling

combination of concrete walls, redwood partitions, rooftop 'sleeping baskets' and outdoor living rooms. Docent-led tours of the modest house are offered at weekends, and the building also hosts a variety of exhibitions, discussions, screenings and concerts, based on decidedly non-mainstream themes.

Visit West Hollywood

Pacific Design Center, 8687 Melrose Avenue, at N San Vicente Boulevard (1-800 368 6020, 1-310 289 2525, www.visitwesthollywood.com). **Open** 8.30am-5.30pm Mon-Fri. **Map** p312 A2.

HOLLYWOOD

Map p313

For years, tourists arrived in Hollywood expecting to walk on to a movie set: camera crews on every corner, paparazzi crowding the sidewalks. What they found was a shabby, glamour-free shambles. Granted, the floodlit paradise of filmic immortality conjured up by the name was the creation of imaginative press officers: movies haven't been filmed here for decades, and the continued use of its name as shorthand for the movie industry is misleading. Still, few visitors were prepared for what they found. Word spread; people stopped coming.

EXPLORE

Streets of Glory

Try to spot your favourite celebrity as you pound the pavement.

From Bud 'Who's on first?' Abbott to bearded Texan bluesmen ZZ Top, more than 2,000 figures from the world of entertainment have been immortalised on the **Hollywood Walk of Fame** since actress Joanne Woodward first received the honour in 1960. Made of pink terrazzo inset with gold lettering and one of five symbols that denote the recipient's profession (film, TV, radio, music or stage), the stars line Hollywood Boulevard, between La Brea Avenue and Gower Street, and a stretch of Vine Street.

Stars are awarded by a mysterious committee convened through the Hollywood Chamber of Commerce; if your nomination is successful, you (or, more likely, your movie producers, TV network or record label) must stump up $25,000. Alongside huge names such as Paul Newman and Vivien Leigh sits a parade of forgotten actors, a wrestling promoter (Vince MacMahon), three dogs (Lassie,

MICHAEL JACKSON

Rin Tin Tin and Strongheart, the latter solely remembered for stumbling into a hot studio light and dying in 1929) and a murderer (western swing musician Spade Cooley, who beat his wife to death in 1961). Meanwhile, bona fide celebs such as Richard Burton aren't honoured until decades after their death: the Welsh actor finally received a star on 1 March 2013 – appropriately, St David's Day – right next to former wife Liz Taylor at 6336 Hollywood Boulevard.

The Hollywood Walk of Fame is one of LA's great glories, and precisely the landmark that Hollywood deserves: dazzling and bewildering, laughable and sentimental. But it is also the most blatant illustration of a truth that's dominated Hollywood for a century. If you're lucky, talent will take you to the top of your profession. But a big pile of cash, a bulging contacts book and a great agent will get you there quicker.

Things have changed. Since the late 1990s, the city has made an effort to restore a little glitter to the area, and both tourists and locals have returned in droves. The regeneration hasn't been without its critics – essentially, LA has done to parts of Hollywood what New York did to Times Square in the '90s. But the gripers have been outnumbered by moneyed night owls, savvy entrepreneurs, tourists and, tellingly, construction workers. Condo towers are springing up all over the area, as sure a sign as you'll find that Hollywood's resurgence is more than just a flash in the pan.

Hollywood Boulevard

The stretch of Hollywood Boulevard between La Brea Avenue and Vine Street was one of the city's seamier thoroughfares by the mid '90s, a decaying parade of adult theatres, souvenir stores and ne'er-do-wells. But now, re-dubbed the Hollywood Entertainment District after a makeover, it's once more a family-friendly tourist attraction with plenty of appeal.

The centrepiece of the regeneration is the four-storey **Hollywood & Highland** centre (*see p140*), an awkwardly designed but popular complex that's home to 75 shops and restaurants, from Sephora to the Hard Rock Café, plus an upscale bowling alley (**Lucky Strike Lanes**; *see p241*), the **Dolby** (formerly Kodak) **Theatre** (*see below*) and, connected at the rear, a Loews hotel (*see p179*). However, perhaps the mall's greatest asset is its multi-level (and reasonably priced) parking garage; the entrance to it is on Highland Avenue.

Hollywood & Highland is slick and modern, but for glamour, you'll need to head next door to **Grauman's Chinese Theatre**, recently renamed **TCL Chinese Theatre** after the company that bought the naming rights to the world-famous sight (*see p52*). Indeed, the Hollywood buildings that exude the most star quality are the old cinemas: **El Capitan**, opposite Grauman's (No.6838), and the historic **Egyptian Theatre** (No.6712; *see p198*), home to the American Cinematheque. The **Hollywood Museum** (*see p52*) adds context, with glitz coming courtesy of the **Hollywood Roosevelt** (No.7000; *see p179*), built in 1927.

There's less glamour on Hollywood Boulevard to the east of Highland Avenue, where touristy attractions (the **Hollywood Wax Museum**, *see p52*, and **Ripley's Believe it or Not!**, *see p52*) jostle for attention with souvenir shops, an adult theatre and a vast Scientology centre. On **Cahuenga Boulevard** between Hollywood and Sunset Boulevards, you'll find pricey and, in some cases, exclusive bars, restaurants and clubs.

The area's resurgence as a residential quarter is most apparent around the famous

TCL Chinese Theatre. *See p52.*

Hollywood and Vine intersection. A huge **W** hotel and condominium complex (*see p178*) opened at 6250 Hollywood Boulevard in early 2010, followed a few months later by another hotel, the small but perfectly packaged **Redbury** (1717 Vine Street; *see p178*), across the road from the 13-storey **Capitol Records Building** (No.1750). Thankfully, all these new and newly converted buildings haven't quite overshadowed the tower, a genuine Hollywood icon since it was completed in 1956. Instantly recognisable, it's shaped like a stack of records and topped with a stylus, reputedly the idea of songwriter Johnny Mercer and singer Nat 'King' Cole. Proposals for a controversial $664-million Millennium Project – which would include two massive skyscrapers – were being put forward by the owners of Capitol Records as this guide went to press. Not surprisingly, the idea has been met with opposition from those who claim that, among other things, the new buildings would block views of the iconic Hollywood sign and, ironically, the Capitol Records tower itself.

Dolby Theatre

Hollywood & Highland, 6801 Hollywood Boulevard, at N Highland Avenue (1-323 308 6300, www.dolbytheatre.com). Metro Hollywood-Highland/bus 210, 212, 217, 310/US 101, exit Highland Avenue south. **Open** *Tours* every 30mins 10.30am-4pm Mon-Fri; 8.30-11.30am Sat, Sun. **Admission** $15; $10 discounts; free under-3s. **Credit** AmEx, DC, MC, V. **Map** p313 A1. The 3,300-seat home of the Academy Awards is a slick building that's underused the rest of the year. Half-hour guided tours are offered daily, but call or check online before making the trip: on performance days, the theatre may not run its normal schedule.

EXPLORE

★ Hollywood Museum

1660 N Highland Avenue, between Hawthorn Avenue & Hollywood Boulevard (1-323 464 7776, www.thehollywoodmuseum.com). Metro Hollywood-Highland/bus 210, 212, 217, 310/US 101, exit Highland Avenue south. **Open** 10am-5pm Wed-Sun. **Admission** $15; $5-$12 discounts. **Credit** AmEx, DC, MC, V. **Map** p313 A2.

Designed as the Hollywood Fire & Safe Building in 1914, this building was converted in 1928 into a beauty salon by Max Factor. A refurbishment seven years later turned it into an art deco classic; it's now a museum dedicated to the movies, with more than 10,000 pieces of memorabilia covering 100 years. The ground floor has been decorated to resemble the original Factor shop, its walls lined with memorabilia related to stars of the 1930s, '40s and '50s. Out the back sits Cary Grant's gleaming 1965 Rolls-Royce. The top two floors bring things closer to the present day (Stallone's boxing gloves from *Rocky*, plus items from *Star Trek*, *Transformers* and *Glee*), while the basement holds a mock-up of Hannibal Lecter's cell from *The Silence of the Lambs*, plus costumes from Jason, Freddie and Chucky. Other items include props from *Gone with the Wind*, a collection of Marilyn Monroe documents and artefacts, plus Elvis's bathrobe and, hilariously, Roddy McDowall's bathroom. An understated gem.

Hollywood Wax Museum

6767 Hollywood Boulevard, at N Highland Avenue (1-323 462 5991, www.hollywoodwax.com). Metro Hollywood-Highland/bus 210, 212, 217, 310/US 101, exit Highland Avenue south. **Admission** 10am-midnight daily. **Admission** $16.99; $8.99-$14.99 discounts; free under-5s. **Credit** AmEx, DC, Disc, MC, V. **Map** p313 A1.

Hollywood is pushing itself into the 21st century with vigour, but some attractions remain stuck in the past. The Hollywood Wax Museum harks back to days long gone, when a poorly proportioned wax model of someone famous was liable to draw gasps of astonishment from fun-starved crowds. There's fun to be had trying to recognise the stars, but perhaps not 17 bucks' worth. Combined tickets are available with the Guinness World of Records Museum (No.6764) across the street and Ripley's Believe it or Not! (*see right*).

Madame Tussauds

6933 Hollywood Boulevard, at N Orange Drive (1-323 798 1670, www.madametussauds.com). Metro Hollywood-Highland/bus 210, 212, 217, 310/US 101, exit Highland Avenue south. **Open** 10am-6pm Mon-Thur; 10am-8pm Fri-Sun. **Admission** $25.95; $18.95-$20.95 discounts; free under-4s. **Credit** AmEx, MC, Disc, V. **Map** p313 A1.

No prizes for guessing what's at this museum, part of the worldwide franchise, which opened in 2009. From old-school icons (James Dean, Clark Gable) to modern-day movie stars (Johnny Depp, Salma Hayek), via singers (Beyoncé, Lady Gaga), sporting heroes (David Beckham), movie directors (Tarantino) and TV stars (Jane Lynch, Robert Pattinson), they're all here. Even Madame T herself is immortalised. C'mon, if you're going to visit Madame Tussauds anywhere, why not here? At least you might get the chance to compare the figures with the real thing outside.

Ripley's Believe it or Not!

6780 Hollywood Boulevard, at N Highland Avenue (1-323 466 6335, http://hollywood.ripleys.com). Metro Hollywood-Highland/bus 210, 212, 217, 310/US 101, exit Highland Avenue south. **Open** 10am-midnight daily. **Admission** $16.99; $8.99 discounts; free under-4s. **Credit** AmEx, Disc, MC, V. **Map** p313 A1.

This is one of many Ripley's museums around the US, and if you've been to any of the others, you can skip this, a gurning parade of bizarre 'facts' that stretches the definition of the word 'museum' to breaking point. Not surprisingly, kids love it.

TCL Chinese Theatre

6925 Hollywood Boulevard, between N Orange Drive & N McCadden Place (1-323 464 8111, www.manntheatres.com). Metro Hollywood-Highland/bus 210, 212, 217, 310/US 101, exit Highland Avenue south. **Open** *Tours* every 30mins 10am-8.30pm daily. **Admission** *Tours* $13.75; $6.50-$11.50 discounts. **Credit** AmEx, DC, MC, V. **Map** p313 A1.

It's a great place to catch a movie, but most people come to the Chinese Theatre for the hand and/or foot imprints of around 200 Hollywood stars. As legend has it, Norma Talmadge accidentally stepped into the wet cement outside the new building during construction; theatre owner Sid Grauman then fetched Mary Pickford and Douglas Fairbanks to repeat the 'mistake' with their feet and hands, beginning the tradition. The courtyard is usually choked with tourists; it's just a pity that its appeal is tempered by the tour hawkers and the ticket agents in the forecourt. For a half-hour tour, book in advance (1-323 463 9576 or go online) or just turn up; tours don't take place if there's a special event on. *Photo p51.*

South of Hollywood Boulevard

Few visitors leave Hollywood Boulevard during their visit to Hollywood; few locals blame them. Still, though there's less obvious tourist appeal away from the main drag, it's a relief to escape the throngs and get into a neighbourhood with a little more dirt under its fingernails.

Walking two blocks south on Vine Street will take you to **Sunset Boulevard**, a formerly sleazy road (Hugh Grant met Divine Brown on the north-east corner of Sunset and Courtney Avenue) that's a little nicer these days. The

Hollywood Forever Cemetery.

main attraction isn't even on Sunset: rather, it's the view from the intersection with Bronson Avenue, one of the best vantage points from which to see the **Hollywood sign** (*see p269* **Times of the Sign**). South is the **Hollywood Forever Cemetery** (*see below*); nearby is **Paramount Studios** (*see p29*), the only working studio in Hollywood.

Back on Sunset, and heading west, the attractions are largely commercial. While the tourists wander Hollywood & Highland hoping to see a star, the in-the-know celeb-hunters are at the **ArcLight** cinemas (No.6360; *see p194*). A few blocks west sits the **Crossroads of the World** (No.6671), a formerly charming outdoor shopping plaza (now offices) built in 1936 that pre-dates LA's strip mall explosion by 50 years.

★ FREE **Hollywood Forever Cemetery**
6000 Santa Monica Boulevard, between N Gower Street & N Van Ness Avenue (1-323 469 1181, www.hollywoodforever.com). Bus 4, 704/US 101, exit Santa Monica Boulevard west. **Open** *Summer* 8am-7pm daily. *Winter* 8am-6pm daily. **Admission** free. **Parking** free. **Map** p313 C2.
Despite being located off busy Santa Monica Boulevard, Hollywood Forever is a serene final resting place for such celluloid luminaries as Cecil B DeMille, Jayne Mansfield and Rudolph Valentino (legend has it that a mysterious 'Woman in Black' still stalks the cemetery, mourning the demise of Hollywood's original lover man). Mel Blanc's headstone says 'That's All, Folks!', while Douglas Fairbanks Sr and Jr are in a huge tomb in front of a lake guarded by a fountain and three black swans. William Andrews Clark Jr, founder of the LA Philharmonic, has an even bigger mausoleum in the

middle of a lake. Note that the cemetery's closing time varies according to sunset, so call ahead if making a special trip.
▶ *Aside from late celebs, Hollywood Forever is also home to summer outdoor movie screenings; Cinespia-hosted sleepovers with projected films (see p200), live music and games; as well as a number of unique concert events (past performers include Bon Iver, the XX and Sigúr Ros).*

The Hollywood Hills

For perspective on the **Hollywood Hills**, the tail end of the Santa Monica Mountains that divide LA from the San Fernando Valley, take a ride along soaring, precarious **Mulholland Drive**. A mix of Hollywood-style spectacle and wild rural bramble that offers views in every direction, the road springs to life above the Hollywood Bowl (there's an amazing overlook at this eastern end), follows the crest of the hills and the mountains, and ends in Malibu, with a seven-mile stretch in the middle that's closed to traffic (Dirt Mulholland). Along its length, buildings are wedged into hillsides or perched on slopes, all the better to enjoy the amazing sunrises and sunsets. Scenic overlooks dot the roadside, offering fresh perspectives on the city and its suburbs. But Mulholland Drive is at its most mysterious after dark, with no street lights to guide the way and the city shimmering below like the treasure at the bottom of the ocean. It's LA's most spectacular road.

North of the West Hollywood strip, **Runyon Canyon Park** is a strip of canyon wilderness running from Mulholland Drive to Franklin Avenue (entrances on Fuller Avenue and Vista Street; www.laparks.org). Trails of varying lengths and difficulty lead to breathtaking 360-degree viewpoints. Finding a parking spot close to the entrance can be a chore, however, especially at weekends.

Between Runyon Canyon and US 101 is the architecturally affecting **Hollywood Bowl** (*see p228*). Across US 101, the **Hollywood Reservoir** (*see p54*) provides a chance to muse on LA's debt to William Mulholland. To the east are the hills of **Griffith Park** (*see p59*); one way to access them is to hire a horse from **Sunset Ranch** (*see p242*).

EXPLORE

INSIDE TRACK
CLOSING (FOR) CEREMONY

Note that some sights along Hollywood Boulevard close or operate to reduced hours on and around the day of the Oscars, in February/March. Call or go to their websites to check.

EXPLORE

INSIDE TRACK
GOING TO THE DOGS

Perennially packed **Pink's**, a hot dog joint at the corner of Melrose Avenue and N La Brea Avenue, has been at this site since 1946 (there are now locations at LAX, Universal CityWalk and Knott's Berry Farm, among others). Among its bestselling combos are Mulholland Drive Dog, named after the 2001 movie in which it featured, and the bacon burrito dog, stuffed with two hot dogs, cheese, bacon, chili and onions. Finish with some coconut or marble cake if you dare.

FREE Hollywood Bowl Museum
2301 N Highland Avenue, at US 101 (1-323 850 2058, www.hollywoodbowl.com). Bus 156/US 101, exit Highland Avenue north. **Open** *Mid June-mid Sept* 10am-showtime Tue-Sat; 4pm-showtime Sun. *Mid Sept-mid June* 10am-5pm Tue-Fri; by appointment Sat. **Admission** free. *Parking* free. This fine little museum presents a lively account of the Hollywood Bowl's history, through archival film footage, audio clips, photography and all manner of other memorabilia. A new exhibit, LIVE at the Bowl!, showcasing broadcasts and recordings from the Bowl via vintage phonographs, radios and TVs, runs from July 2013 to May 2014.

Hollywood Reservoir & Dog Park
Lake Hollywood Drive, Hollywood Hills. Bus 156/US 101, exit Barham Boulevard north. Formed in 1924 when the Mulholland Dam was built, the Hollywood Reservoir was a landmark piece of engineering. Holding 2.5 billion US gallons, it provided the drinking water to facilitate the city's spread, piped in from 300 miles away through the Owens River Aqueduct system. Now most of its water storage is underground, but the pretty lake attracts runners, walkers and the occasional cyclist to its waterside trails, which offer a fantastic view of the Hollywood sign. Tucked behind the reservoir up Beachwood Canyon is the Hollywood Dog Park.

FAIRFAX DISTRICT

Map p312
Although LA's first major Jewish community settled in Boyle Heights, the stretch of **Fairfax Avenue** between Beverly Boulevard and Melrose Avenue has been the city's main Jewish drag since the 1940s. Grocers, butcher's shops, restaurants and bakeries line the street, nicknamed the 'Kosher Canyon'; all are excellent, and, naturally, almost all are closed on Saturdays. Open 24-7, however, is the legendary **Canter's Deli** (No.419; *see p107*).

Just south of the Beverly–Fairfax intersection lies **CBS Television City**, a studio complex built in 1952 and still in use today. Looking at it, you'd never guess the site once held a major sporting stadium: built in 1939, Gilmore Field was home to the minor-league Hollywood Stars baseball team until their demise in 1957, when CBS bought the lot and razed the ballpark. Next door, at the junction of W 3rd Street and Fairfax Avenue, is the tag-team retail experience of the **Grove** (*see p140*) and the **Farmers Market**. Next door, in the north-west corner of Pan Pacific Park, is the riveting **Los Angeles Museum of the Holocaust** (*see p55*).

One of LA's most popular malls, the Grove is dominated by the usual chains, along with some new Brit imports such as Topshop and Gordon Ramsay's disappointing Fat Cow restaurant. However, its spacey, open-air layout helps make it one of the most pleasant shopping centres in the city. The Farmers Market, meanwhile, pre-dates the Grove by more than 60 years. Although the farmers who set up here in 1934 have long since moved on, food still dominates this wonderfully old-fashioned commercial corner. Some of the stalls sell fruit, fudge and sundry temptations; others are full-service food counters.

There's plenty of excellent shopping nearby. To the north, the stretch of **Melrose Avenue** around Fairfax Avenue is lined with independent stores, with fashion dominating the landscape. And to the south, the stretch of W 3rd Street between Fairfax and the Beverly Center holds several dozen small retailers, from shops selling everything from travel books to cupcakes to excellent sushi restaurant Izakaya by Katsuya.

Los Angeles Museum of the Holocaust.

★ FREE Los Angeles Museum of the Holocaust

100 S The Grove Drive, at Beverly Boulevard (1-323 651 3704, www.lamoth.org). Bus 14, 20, 217, 714/I-10, exit Fairfax Avenue north. **Open** 10am-5pm Mon-Thur, Sat, Sun; 10am-2pm Fri. **Admission** free; donations welcome. **Credit** AmEx, MC, V. **Map** p312 C3.

While Beverly Hills has the Museum of Tolerance (*see p48*), the Fairfax District is home to the Museum of the Holocaust, which opened in 2010. The subject matter is, naturally, dark, but the museum treats it in a sensitive manner, providing audio guides that lead visitors through a succession of rooms detailing the rise of Nazism through the concentration camps, the Holocaust, and its aftermath. It's easy to spend hours here, immersed in the history and the horror. Guided tours and talks from survivors are also given on a regular basis, while temporary exhibitions round things out.

MIRACLE MILE & MIDTOWN

Map p312

Stretching along Wilshire Boulevard between Fairfax and La Brea Avenues, the **Miracle Mile** got its nickname from its astonishing commercial growth during the 1920s. Although many of the old buildings remain, including some real art deco glories, the street doesn't live up to its old moniker any more. The department stores that made its nickname have long since closed, as have smaller landmarks such as iconic Googie diner **Johnie's** (No.6101).

Still, the Miracle Mile is far from deserted, and is even making something of a comeback. The main attraction is the **Los Angeles County Museum of Art** (*see right*). It's been joined in recent years by a number of small commercial galleries, including several in the building at 6150 Wilshire Boulevard. Also here are four other very different museums: the **Petersen Automotive Museum** (*see p56*), the **Craft & Folk Art Museum** (*see right*), the **A+D Museum** (*see below*) and, best of all, the **Page Museum at the La Brea Tar Pits** (*see p56*), which explores the area's unexpected natural quirks.

A+D Museum

6032 Wilshire Boulevard, at S Orange Grove Avenue (1-323 932 9393, www.aplusd.org). Bus 20, 217, 218, 720/I-10, exit Fairfax Avenue north. **Open** 11am-5pm Tue-Fri; noon-6pm Sat, Sun. **Admission** $10; $5 discounts; free under-12s. **Credit** AmEx, Disc, MC, V. **Map** p312 C4.

The A+D Museum – 'A' for architecture, 'D' for design – offers an interesting roster of exhibitions on the likes of Richard Neutra and Eero Saarinen, supplemented by a programme of urban hikes, discussions and workshops.

Craft & Folk Art Museum

5814 Wilshire Boulevard, at S Curson Avenue (1-323 937 4230, www.cafam.org). Bus 20, 217, 218, 720/I-10, exit Fairfax Avenue north. **Open** 11am-5pm Tue-Fri; noon-6pm Sat, Sun. **Admission** $7; $5 discounts; free under-10s. Free 1st Wed of mth. **Credit** A§mEx, DC, MC, V. **Map** p312 C4.

LA's only public showcase devoted to contemporary craft and community-based folk art continues to broaden its programming, and with the help of its sister community outreach programme, Folk Art Everywhere (www.folkarteverywhere.com), it bridges the gap between global and local cultures.

★ Los Angeles County Museum of Art (LACMA)

5905 Wilshire Boulevard, at S Fairfax Avenue (1-323 857 6000, www.lacma.org). Bus 20, 217, 218, 720, 761/I-10, exit Fairfax Avenue north. **Open** noon-8pm Mon, Tue, Thur; noon-9pm Fri; 11am-8pm Sat, Sun. **Admission** *General admission* $15; $10 discounts; free under-17s. Pay what you wish after 5pm daily. Free to all 2nd Tue of mth. *Special exhibitions* prices vary. **Parking** $7. **Credit** AmEx, DC, MC, V. **Map** p312 C4.

While LACMA's collections have long been the most impressive in the city, the 20-acre complex of buildings in which they've been housed has been quite the reverse. A bewildering jumble of architectural styles blighted still further by abysmally poor signage, they never really did the artworks justice.

At last, though, things have improved. Funding difficulties and public outrage forced the museum to abandon Rem Koolhaas's original plans to rebuild almost the entire complex from scratch in 2002. However, Renzo Piano's subsequent blueprint for a less dramatic and less expensive redevelopment of the museum did get the go-ahead. With two new buildings for art, an outdoor bar and restaurant and monumental outdoor artworks, the museum has become a lot more visitor-friendly.

It all starts with the new **BP Grand Entrance Pavilion**, which at last gives the museum a proper focal point. On either side of the entrance are Chris Burden's *Urban Light*, a piece made up of 202 cast-iron street lamps gathered from around LA, restored to working order, and Michael Heizer's *Levitated Mass*, a 340-tonne boulder suspended over a 456-foot-long slot through which visitors pass.

In addition to the 45,000sq ft **Lynda and Stewart Resnick Exhibition Pavilion**, which opened in 2010 to house temporary exhibitions, the most exciting development is the Piano-designed **Broad Contemporary Art Museum (BCAM)**, funded by LA philanthropists Eli and Edythe Broad, and now home to a dazzling selection of contemporary works. Spread over three floors, the selection of pieces on display is strong on American artists – there's a very impressive Richard Serra piece on the first floor, a Nam June Paik video installation and Chris Burden's *Metropolis II*, a room-sized tangle of miniature free-

EXPLORE

ways and train tracks. The **Ahmanson Building** has also been spruced up as part of the renovation work, and the collections reorganised. The modern collection on the second floor holds a gallery of 20 Picassos, plus works by the likes of Mondrian, Klee and Kandinsky; upstairs, the Greek and Roman art collections are now housed in a space that benefits from huge windows and lots of natural light.

The American art collection has been reinstalled on the second floor of the **Art of the Americas** building, where you'll also find the Latin American collection. Despite all this activity, the work is far from complete. The Academy of Motion Picture Arts and Sciences has plans to move into the old May Co department store building at the corner of Wilshire and Fairfax to create, by 2016, a new Academy Museum of Motion Pictures, designed by Renzo Piano and Zoltan Pali. Future plans for LACMA provisionally call for the renovation of the galleries untouched by Piano, which at present contain European art (including Impressionist and post-Impressionist pieces by the likes of Cézanne, Gauguin and Degas), Egyptian art, and world-renowned collections of art from Korea, Japan, South and South-east Asia and the Middle East. The precise plans for the next phase of building have yet to be finalised and may require the temporary closure of some galleries – call ahead if your interest is limited to a particular area.

The permanent collections are supplemented by some excellent temporary shows and a very strong programme of events, among them family days, film screenings and plenty of free music. Full details of all events, including the frequent tours, are available on the museum's website.

▶ *Even if you're not lingering at LACMA for hours, it's worth exploring the museum's recent eating and drinking additions, including Ray's (farm-to-table fare), Stark Bar (craft cocktails) and, for hot drinks and pastries, C+M (Coffee and Milk).*

Page Museum at the La Brea Tar Pits

5801 Wilshire Boulevard, between S Stanley & S Curson Avenues (1-323 934 7243, www. tarpits.org). Bus 20, 217, 218, 720/I-10, exit Fairfax Avenue north. **Open** 9.30am-5pm daily. **Admission** $12; $2-$4.50 discounts; free under-2s. Free 1st Tue of mth. **Parking** $7 with validation. **Credit** AmEx, DC, Disc, MC, V. **Map** p312 C4.
In 1875, a group of amateur palaeontologists discovered animal remains in the pits at Rancho La Brea, which bubbled with asphalt from a petroleum lake under what is now Hancock Park. Nearly 140 years later, the pros are still at work here, having dragged more than 3.5 million fossils from the mire in the intervening years. Some are up to 40,000 years old; the museum estimates that about 10,000 animals have been found. Small mammals inadvertently came into contact with the sticky asphalt and were immobilised. A single, mired large herbivore might attract the attention of a dozen predatory birds and mammals, some of which would in turn become

LACMA.

trapped and provide more food for other carnivores. This cycle was repeated over time.

Many of these specimens are now on display in this delightfully old-fashioned museum, which can't have changed much since it opened in 1977. Interactivity is limited to windows on to the Fishbowl Lab, where scientists work on bone preservation; the bulk of the museum is made up of simple displays of items found in the pits. Most are bones – of jackrabbits, gophers, a 160lb bison, skunks and a 15,000lb Columbian mammoth, plus an extraordinary wall of 400 wolf skulls – though there are also early cave drawings and human accoutrements such as bowls and hairpins. Outside, the pits still bubble with black goo; in summer, you can watch palaeontologists at work.

In 2009, during construction of an underground car park for LACMA next door, 16 fossil deposits – containing the remains of up to 700 specimens, including a near-intact mammoth dubbed Zed – were uncovered and removed, filling 23 crates. The resulting Project 23 can be followed online via the museum's website.

Petersen Automotive Museum

6060 Wilshire Boulevard, at N Fairfax Avenue (1-323 964 6315/930 2277, www.petersen.org). Bus 20, 217, 218, 720/I-10, exit Fairfax Avenue north. **Open** 10am-6pm Tue-Sun. **Admission** $12; $3-$8 discounts; free under-5s. **Credit** AmEx, DC, MC, V. **Map** p312 C4.
The Miracle Mile was the first commercial development in LA designed expressly for the benefit of drivers, and so this former department store makes an apt home for this museum of automobile culture. The story of how LA – and much of the West Coast – was built around the needs of drivers is a fascinating tale. Unfortunately, the Petersen doesn't tell it in any great detail, preferring instead to dazzle visitors with an admittedly impressive collection of autos from the last century. Some of the vehicles wear their history with pride: a delivery truck from Culver City's iconic Helms

Bakery and an old Vincent motorcycle, for instance. Others look ahead, such as the Batmobile from the Tim Burton movies. While the life-size dioramas of garages and diners evoke the early days of the US car obsession, the museum misses its chance to tell a story that warrants telling. But the cars are lovely, and the themed temporary exhibitions are often a treat.

HANCOCK PARK

Map p313

A handsome residential neighbourhood dating back to 1910, **Hancock Park** is home to some of LA's most palatial mansions, at least outside Beverly Hills and Bel Air. Historically an Anglo enclave, Hancock Park excluded blacks and Jews until 1948, when Nat 'King' Cole became the first African American to move to the neighbourhood. He wasn't to be the last, but Hancock Park remains a bastion of wealthy middle-class Anglo values. Bounded by Wilshire Boulevard and Van Ness, Highland and Melrose Avenues, the area is at its best at Christmas, when homeowners try to outdo each other with decorative displays of festive jollity.

The area's main commercial drag is **Larchmont Boulevard**, between Beverly Boulevard and W 1st Street and informally known as **Larchmont Village**. A little snatch of Main Street Middle America in the heart of Los Angeles, the two-block stretch is lined with bijou restaurants, antiques shops and the like. Some are chains but most are independently owned, and many are housed in handsome buildings that date back to the 1920s. Our favourites include **Larchmont Beauty Center** (No.208; *see p159*), **Babycakes** for vegan and gluten-free cupcakes (No.236), the West Coast outpost of minimalist toiletries brand **Malin + Goetz** (No.238) and family-centric **Chevalier's Books** (No.126). Also don't miss the farmers' market, held every Sunday from 10am to 2pm south of Beverly Boulevard.

KOREATOWN & AROUND

Map p313 & p314

Roughly bordered by Wilshire and Pico Boulevards, and Western and Vermont Avenues, **Koreatown** has made a comeback since being torched in the riots of 1992. Tensions between the Korean and African American communities (and, to a lesser extent, the Central American population) haven't entirely abated. But an accord of sorts seems to have been reached.

Korean businesses are still visible: some pre-dating the riots, others established only in the last decade. Banks, men's clubs and shop-front grocers abound along Pico and Olympic Boulevards, and the area is dotted with Korean restaurants such as **Soot Bull**

Jeep (3136 W 8th Street; *see p109*). However, despite its name, the district's character comes more from the Latin Americans who now outnumber the Koreans by around four to one. Among Anglos, **El Cholo** (1121 S Western Avenue) is the most popular Mexican restaurant (*see p108*).

Wilshire Boulevard and N Western Avenue, Koreatown's north-western corner, is dominated by the **Wiltern Center**. A green art deco pile built in 1931, it lingered in a state of advanced decay during much of the 1970s and '80s before being rescued and turned into a performing arts and commercial centre. The **Wiltern** (*see p218*) hosts rock shows and club nights.

Across the street from the Bounty bar (*see p124*) sits the site of the old Ambassador Hotel (No.3400), a once-glamorous resort built in the 1920s but known to most as the site of Robert F Kennedy's assassination. Despite numerous protests, the hotel was demolished in 2006 to make way for a new high school.

WESTLAKE

Map p314

Two parks anchor the down-at-heel area of Westlake, just west of Downtown: **Lafayette Park** (on Wilshire Boulevard, by the junction of S Hoover Street), and its larger neighbour, **MacArthur Park** (also on Wilshire, between S Alvarado and S Park View Streets). For years populated chiefly by gang members, drug dealers and the homeless, MacArthur Park is safer now than it's been for a while. Its former grandeur is only fleetingly apparent, even after the restoration of its lake and 500-foot (152-metre) water spout, but it's still not difficult to see how the park could have inspired Jimmy Webb to pen his epic song in its honour.

If you'd like to leave a cake out in the rain here, your best bet is to head to **Langer's Delicatessen** (704 S Alvarado Street, 1-213 483 8050, www.langersdeli.com), which is considered by many to have the best pastrami sandwich in town.

Grier Musser Museum

403 S Bonnie Brae Street, between W 4th & W 5th Streets (1-213 413 1814, www.griermusser museum.org). Metro Westlake-MacArthur/bus 18, 200/US 101, exit Alvarado Street south. **Open** noon-4pm Wed-Sat; reservations required. **Admission** $10; $5-$7 discounts. *Parking* free. **No credit cards. Map** p314 C6.
This Victorian house, located on a residential street just north-east of MacArthur Park, has been maintained to reflect its origins, and is thus stuffed almost to bursting with antique fixtures, fittings and general ephemera. Special events include annual presentations at Halloween and Christmas.

EXPLORE

Los Feliz to Echo Park

Incredible architecture and one of the country's best parks.

Desirable but never flashy, understated rather than fashionable, Los Feliz is a fluid melding of yuppie demand, hipster distinction and immigrant influence. Drive around the blocks leading to Griffith Park (the area's main attraction) and you'll find huge mansions, luscious flora and fauna and signs from the local fire department directing you not to indulge in cigarettes while 'in the hills'.

Neighbouring Silver Lake is trendy, and still edgy in parts – as are Echo Park, to the south-east, and Highland Park, to the north-east – but essentially these are residential areas with a mellower pace of life than elsewhere in Los Angeles.

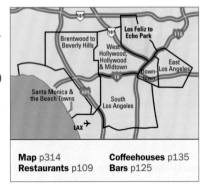

Map p314	**Coffeehouses** p135
Restaurants p109	**Bars** p125

EXPLORE

LOS FELIZ

Map p314

Los Feliz is named in honour of José Feliz, a soldier who claimed the area in the 19th century and whose family held on to the district until they lost it 50 years later in a legal snafu. The area housed a number of film studios in the silent era: a set for DW Griffith's *Intolerance* stood at the Sunset Boulevard and Hillhurst Avenue site now occupied by the single-screen, Egyptian-flavoured **Vista** cinema. Walking north-west from here up Hollywood Boulevard will lead you past a scattering of shops towards **Barnsdall Art Park** (*see p59*).

The stretch of **Vermont Avenue** that runs north of here, between bustling Hollywood Boulevard and bucolic Franklin Avenue, is one of Los Feliz's two main streets. It's a very pedestrian-friendly area, its hipster boutiques and eateries best approached on foot. Shops include fashion favourites **SquaresVille** (No.1800; *see p148*) and **Y-Que** (No.1770), and bookstore **Skylight** (No.1818; *see p141*); the pick of the eating options is **Fred 62** (No.1850; *see p109*); and there's entertainment of sorts at the **Dresden Room** (No.1760; *see p125*), where you'll find ultra-campy lounge duo Marty & Elayne. The arty vibe is completed by the **Los Feliz 3 Cinemas** (No.1822, 1-323 664 2169).

Parallel to Vermont Avenue lies **Hillhurst Avenue**, a similarly wanderable stretch of road dotted with pleasing shops and approachable eateries, such as Carol Young's organic **Undesigned** clothing boutique (No.19532, 1-323 663 0088, www.undesigned.com), the **Alcove Café & Bakery** (No.1929, 1-323 644 0100, www.alcovecafe.com), housed in two bungalows, and the smart **Vinoteca Farfalla** (No.1968, 1-323 661 8070, www.vinotecafarfalla.com).

The residential streets in Los Feliz are almost all handsome, but a few properties stand out. One is Frank Lloyd Wright's **Ennis-Brown House** (2655 Glendower Avenue, north-east of Vermont Avenue, www.ennishouse.com), a boxily exotic concrete construction from 1924 that suffered horrible damage in the 1994 earthquake. In 2009, the house was placed on the market for a cool $15 million, eventually selling for less than a third of the asking price (one condition of the sale is that the new owner allow it to be open to the public for a minimum of 12 days a year). Not far away, Richard Neutra's International Modern **Lovell House** (4616 Dundee Drive) was built in 1929, but it's most famous for its starring role 70 years later in *L.A. Confidential*. Slightly further east, at **4053 Woking Way**, the fairytale structure just visible behind high walls and greenery was the home of Walt Disney from 1932 until 1949.

Barnsdall Art Park & Hollyhock House

4800 Hollywood Boulevard, between Edgemont Street & Vermont Avenue (Barnsdall Art Park www.barnsdall.org, Hollyhock House 1-323 644 6269, www.hollyhockhouse.net). Metro Sunset-Vermont/bus 204, 754, LDH/US 101, exit Sunset Boulevard east. **Open** *Hollyhock House tours* phone for details. **Admission** *Hollyhock House tours* phone for details. **No credit cards. Map** p314 A2.

After oil heiress and philanthropist Aline Barnsdall bought this cute little hill following World War I, she engaged Frank Lloyd Wright to build her a group of buildings at its summit. The complex was designed to include a cinema, a theatre and an array of artists' studios alongside Hollyhock House (1919-21), Barnsdall's proposed home, but it was never completed and she never moved in.

Barnsdall went on to donate the house, guest house and 11 acres of the land to the city on the premise that they be used as a public art park. More than eight decades later, the site still fulfils that role, with exhibitions in a variety of different gallery spaces. Tours of the restored buildings – a Historic National Monument that is under renovation until mid 2013 – are offered Wednesday to Sunday; call for details of times and admission prices.

Griffith Park

In 1896, mining tycoon Griffith J Griffith donated five square miles of land to the city for use as a public park. Expanded down the decades with other land donations and purchases, **Griffith Park** is now the largest city-run park in the US (five times the size of New York's Central Park), its vastness separating Los Feliz and the Hollywood Hills from Glendale and Burbank.

It's an immense, dramatic place. Some patches are flat, packed on warm weekends with picnickers, football-tossers, drumming circles and Frisbee-throwers. Other sections have been civilised by golf courses, tennis courts, soccer pitches and even the occasional museum. However, despite much-criticised plans to develop parts of Griffith Park with aerial tramways, multi-level parking garages and an array of commercial activity, supported by controversial local city councilman Tom

Griffith Park.

LaBonge, it remains wild, rugged and untamed. The downside? It's prone to occasional but potentially destructive wildfires: in 2007, a major blaze devastated roughly one-quarter of the park. But such incidents are mercifully rare.

The 53 miles of hiking trails offer far more variety than you'd expect from an urban park. One of the most popular trails is the half-hour schlep from Griffith Observatory to the 1,625-foot (495-metre) peak of Mount Hollywood, and not without good reason: the views from the top are awesome, the city spreadeagled around you in all its hazy majesty. Details of the park's trails can be obtained from the **Ranger Station** in the park's south-east corner (4730 Crystal Springs Drive), but be warned: the current hiking maps are poor. You might be better off joining one of the **Sierra Club**'s evening walks around the park (*see p242*), which run year-round and are especially wonderful under moonlit skies. In the south-west of the park is Bronson Canyon, where everything from *Gunsmoke* to *The Monkees* to the *Batman* series has been filmed (look out for the entrance to the 'Bat Cave'). You need to hike to the site; the nearest car park can be reached by taking Canyon Drive from Franklin Avenue, but as the location is so remote and tricky to find, we recommend asking at the Ranger Station. Hiking the park is highly recommended – *see p242 and p243* **View From the Top** – but be sure to take extra precautions, including plenty of water and sunscreen, in very hot weather.

Away from the trails, the park's man-made attractions include the **Los Angeles Zoo**, the **Griffith Observatory**, the **Autry National Center of the American West** and the open-air **Greek Theatre** (*see p217*). The gorgeous 1926 **Merry-Go-Round**, between the Los Feliz entrance and the zoo, is open daily in summer and weekends and public holidays in winter (1-323 665 3051). The opening hours of the other attractions mentioned above vary; see

---

**INSIDE TRACK
WHEEL MEET AGAIN**

With a gradient of 33 per cent, Fargo Street in Echo Park is said to be the steepest road in California. For 30 years, the **LA Wheelmen cycling club** (www.lawheelmen.org) has organised a ride up it, usually in March; barely half the riders make the top.

We're Jammin'

How to make your sightseeing more fruitful.

When, during the 19th century, the railways promoted California tourism in an attempt to boost winter ticket sales, they used images of pretty Spanish señoritas holding fat, juicy oranges and grapes hanging from the vine. The orange groves and vineyards have long gone, replaced by suburbs and shopping centres, but LA's gentle climate fosters fruit without the help of farmers. Wild edibles grow all over the city: on steep hillsides and in people's yards, alongside freeways, even between cracks in the sidewalks. Legally, anything found growing on public property is ripe for the taking, including fruit on branches hanging over garden fences on to the street.

Created by artist-activists Dave Burns and Austin Young and writer Matias Viegener, **www.fallenfruit.org** maps the locations and growing seasons of urban edibles in LA. Printable maps, including ones of Echo Park, Silver Lake and Sunset Junction, reveal where you can find seasonal guavas, figs, prickly pears, bananas, passionfruit, avocados, nectarines, apples, grapes, elderberries, loquats, persimmons, olives, walnuts, pomegranates and – yes – fat, juicy oranges. It's a tasty excuse to take a leisurely stroll around some neighbourhoods you might not otherwise have visited, so grab a sack and get picking.

Burns, Young and Viegener's hard work has borne fruit elsewhere, too: if you're hungry and happen to find yourself in Hawthorne (south-east of LAX), stop by the **Del Aire Public Fruit Park** – the first of its kind in California – which opened in January 2013. Nearly 30 trees, from apricot to pluot, have been planted in the orchard, along with dwarf lemon and rosemary plants. Just give them a little time to grow first…

the reviews below for individual details. However, regardless of the season, Griffith Park itself is open from 5.30am to 10pm every day. For more information, call 1-323 913 4688 or see www.laparks.org.

Note that ongoing road and pipeline repairs in the park until late 2013 means there may be traffic diversions: if you have a particular sight in mind, call first to check.

★ Autry National Center of the American West

4700 Western Heritage Way, opposite LA Zoo (1-323 667 2000, www.theautry.org). Bus 96/I-5, exit Zoo Drive west. **Open** 10am-4pm Tue-Fri; 11am-5pm Sat, Sun. **Admission** $10; $4-$5 discounts; free under-3s. *Parking* free. **Credit** AmEx, DC, MC, V.

You might expect this Griffith Park museum to be a kitschy exhibition about the life and works of the famous singing cowboy. However, although there's an annual Gene Autry Founder's Day installation in the lobby around the time of Autry's birth (29 September), it's actually a very engaging exploration of the western US, outlining its history and detailing the myths that came to surround it.

The museum is bigger than it looks, spread over two floors with temporary exhibitions in two galleries and periodically rotating permanent exhibits in the rest of the space. Ground-floor galleries offer iconographic cowboy art and Western art in all its variety, plus ephemera from the golden age of the Western. Downstairs galleries tell the story of western migration by different communities, with illuminating exhibits on how they lived, what they hunted, where they settled and so on. Due homage is paid to the Mexican *vaqueros*, the original pioneering cowboys of the Old West whom Hollywood largely wrote out of the history books. However, fans of Western myth and legend will enjoy catching sight of Doc Holliday's revolver from the shootout at the OK Corral, the only gun positively attributed to Billy the Kid, the 200-strong Colt Firearms Collection and movie memorabilia such as the Lone Ranger's original costume. Kids will find fun around every corner, dressing up in cowboy clothes and 'riding' a life-size replica horse, panning for gold and more.

The Autry is currently in the midst of redesigning its permanent galleries. In addition to strengthening its collections, programmes and infrastructure, the Griffith Park facility is scheduled to open its new Art of the West exhibition in June 2013, as well as several galleries devoted to the environment and the history of native peoples in California in the coming years. Meanwhile, a new Autry Resource Center in Burbank is under construction to house the vast collection, the Autry's two research libraries and the Institute for the Study of the American West.

★ FREE Griffith Observatory

2800 E Observatory Road (1-213 473 0800, www. griffithobservatory.org). Bus 180, 181, 380, then long, steep uphill walk/I-5, exit Los Feliz Boulevard west. **Open** *Observatory* noon-10pm Wed-Fri;

10am-10pm Sat, Sun. *Planetarium* 8 shows, 12.45-8.45pm Wed-Fri; 10 shows, 10.45am-8.45pm Sat, Sun. **Admission** *Observatory* free. *Planetarium* $7; $3-$5 discounts; free under-5s (only admitted to 1st show daily). *Parking* free. **Map** p314 A1.

'If every person could look through that telescope,' declared Griffith J Griffith, 'it would revolutionize the world.' Nearly 80 years after this iconic building opened, the world remains unrevolutionised, and the city smog means that the views are not as clear as they were in Griffith's day. However, in 2006, after a five-year renovation programme, the 12in Zeiss refracting telescope and the restored, expanded building reopened to the public, providing the crowning glory for this wonderful old art deco landmark. Free public telescope viewing is available each evening the observatory is open and the skies are clear.

You could comfortably spend a few hours here. The ground floor holds the Hall of the Sky and Hall of the Eye, where complementary exhibit galleries focus on humans' relationship to the stars; a Foucault pendulum, directly under Hugo Ballin's famed mural on the central rotunda; and the live shows in the handsome, high-tech Samuel Oschin Planetarium. Downstairs, accessible via the campy displays of space-themed jewellery in the Cosmic Connection Corridor, you'll find two large exhibit galleries. At the Leonard Nimoy Event Horizon theatre, you can see a short film about the history and resurgence of the observatory. Pieces of the Sky documents, brightly and informatively, the impact made on earth by meteorites and other falling space debris. The Gunther Depths of Space exhibit contains crisp and colourful descriptions of the planets, a bronze of Albert Einstein and a vast, 150ft by 20ft, 2.46-gigapixel image of the night sky – the largest in the world – taken from the Palomar Observatory in San Diego County.

Autry National Center of the American West.

However, the star attraction remains the building itself, both inside and out. Famous for its appearances in movies both acclaimed (*Rebel Without a Cause*) and disdained (*Lawnmower Man 2: Beyond Cyberspace*), this LA icon is one of the city's must-see attractions.

Los Angeles Zoo

5333 Zoo Drive (1-323 644 4200, www.lazoo.org). Bus 96/I-5, exit Zoo Drive west. **Open** 10am-5pm daily. Last entry 1hr before closing. **Admission** $17; $12 discounts; free under-2s. *Parking* free. **Credit** AmEx, DC, Disc, MC, V.

The LA Zoo's greatest asset is its location, in the isolated hills of Griffith Park. It's a pretty popular place, but the zoo's size – 80 acres, plus a huge parking lot – means that it rarely feels busy. Highlights include the Campo Gorilla Reserve, which serves as a home for six great apes, and the LAIR ('Living Amphibians, Invertebrates and Reptiles'), housing Komodo dragons, alligators and tortoises. Elsewhere, a flock of flamingos flutter in a pond close to the entrance, while a nearby meerkat stands guard over proceedings. Sea lions slither and swim and a jaguar takes another nap. As a visitor attraction, it's a success; however, certain enclosures feel slightly despondent, and the zoo continues to draw criticism (in 2012, for instance, an LA judge passed down a scathing judgement about the treatment of the inhabitants of the Elephants of Asia exhibit). A new exhibit, Rain Forest of the Americas, showcasing species native to Central and South America, is scheduled for completion in late 2013. Check the website for details of tours and tickets.

Bear in mind that some bigger animals may seek shady refuge from the extreme heat on warm summer days, and that some animals are led inside from 4pm.

FREE Travel Town Museum

5200 Zoo Drive (1-323 662 5874, http://travel town.org). Bus 96/Hwy 134, exit Forest Lawn Drive. **Open** *Summer* 10am-5pm Mon-Fri; 10am-6pm Sat, Sun. *Winter* 10am-4pm Mon-Fri; 10am-5pm Sat, Sun. **Admission** *Museum* free; donations appreciated. *Travel Town rides* $2.50; $2 discounts. *Parking* free. **No credit cards**.

This endearing outdoor museum in Griffith Park's north-west corner is made up of restored railroad cars from the Union Pacific, Atchison and Santa Fe lines, an early 20th-century milk delivery truck, and more than a dozen steam and diesel locomotives.
► *Adjacent to Travel Town is Los Angeles Live Steamers (1-323 662 8030, www.lals.org), a club of rail enthusiasts that constructs and runs scale replicas of diesel, steam and electric engines. Free rides are offered every Sunday from 11am to 3pm.*

SILVER LAKE

Map p314

Gang activity still nibbles at its edges, and the clothes on sale in its boutiques won't confuse anyone into thinking they're on Rodeo Drive,

EXPLORE

but not even *Vanity Fair* tagging Silver Lake as the 'coolest neighbourhood in LA' several years ago has stopped its rise. Its blend of art school types, left-of-centre industry folk and immigrant communities has managed to stave off the chain stores. Instead, Silver Lake is dominated by bijou shops, restaurants and bars.

The convergence of W Sunset Boulevard and Santa Monica Boulevard – known as **Sunset Junction** – is the axis of Silver Lake. Between here and the junction of Silver Lake Boulevard, Sunset Boulevard is dotted with shops trading in everything from quirky gifts (**Serifos**, No.3814, 1-323 660 7467) to trendy leather bags (**Clare Vivier**, No.3339, 1-323 665 2476) to spices, salts, sugars and teas (**Spice Station**, No.3819, 1-323 660 2565, http://spicestation silverlake.com). To see the locale in all its glory, visit the **Sunset Junction Street Fair** in August.

The neighbourhood's namesake boulevard is worth driving, if only for the curves around Silver Lake itself, glittery at night and enveloped by some of the area's nicest homes. This residential neighbourhood is a bastion of old LA glamour: some of the city's finest architects worked here in the 1920s and 1930s. The many RM Schindler properties include the **Droste** and **Walker Houses** at 2025 and 2100 Kenilworth Avenue, and the daunting **Olive House** at 2236 Micheltorena Street. Also on Micheltorena are two buildings by John Lautner: **Silvertop** (No.2138) and **Lautner's own residence** (No.2007). Austrian-born architect Richard Neutra is represented by a cluster of buildings on Silver Lake Boulevard and on Neutra Place.

ECHO PARK

Map p314

In the early 1900s, a suburb called Edendale became a film industry hotbed, attracting movie-makers with its bright sun and clear days. Now known as **Echo Park**, the area is still a draw, albeit for different reasons: it's the gateway neighbourhood to LA's predominantly Latino east side, but is also home to a Major League baseball stadium, two parks and some delightfully preserved century-old buildings.

The neighbourhood of Echo Park is often defined as the area to the north of US 101 and east of Alvarado Street, but many locals mark the border with the 'Foot Clinic' sign at Benton Way and W Sunset Boulevard. This area, with Alvarado and Sunset as its nucleus, supports many of Echo Park's best cafés and shops, plus the **Echo Park Film Center** (No.1200; *see p200*). Beyond here, most of the area is residential.

To the south-east of the junction of Sunset and Alvarado sits the green space from which the neighbourhood takes its name. **Echo Park** looks to be more water than land, the park's

green space ringing a long, thin lake centred on a large fountain. The park was laid out in the 1890s by architect Joseph Henry Taylor to resemble an English garden. Take a paddleboat ride through the blossoming lotuses in the lake, celebrated at July's **Lotus Festival** (*see p22*).

Emerging on the west side of Echo Park will lead you into **Angelino Heights**, a residential enclave famous for its Victorian mansions. There's scarcely an ugly building within its confines (it's loosely bordered by W Sunset Boulevard, Boylston Street, US 101 and Echo Park), but the 1300 block of Carroll Avenue is especially attractive. North-east is **Dodger Stadium**, home of the Los Angeles Dodgers baseball team (*see p237*).

Beyond the outfield lies the vast **Elysian Park**, a jumble of nature and development, less scenic than Griffith Park, but not without decent trails and picnic spots. **Bishops Canyon** hosts Little League baseball games; slightly further along the same road, **Angels Point** affords views of Dodger Stadium and the Downtown skyline from Peter Shire's eye-catching Glass-Simons Memorial. Unexpectedly, it also features the **Los Angeles Police Academy** (1880 N Academy Drive), established in the 1920s as a shooting club for LAPD officers.

North-east of Elysian Park, the Echo Park neighbourhood is at its cosiest. The roads are skinny and the houses are packed together, exaggerated by the dramatic hills. The likes of **Ewing Street** and **Avon Street** are almost San Franciscan in their peaks and troughs: pray that your brakes don't fail on the way down.

Scattered throughout the neighbourhood are a number of quaint stairways – some from the 19th century, others reconstructed – that provide access from the streets. A couple are especially notable: at 232 steps, the **Baxter Steps** (at

Silver Lake.

Los Angeles River.

Baxter and Avon Streets) are believed to be the city's tallest, while at **923-927 N Vendome Street** are the steps up which Laurel and Hardy drag a piano in their 1932 film *The Music Box*.

MT WASHINGTON TO EAGLE ROCK

North-east of Echo Park, on the other side of I-5 and the **Los Angeles River**, sit a handful of interesting residential neighbourhoods. Just past the slightly sketchy neighbourhood of **Cypress Park** is **Mt Washington**, formerly an artists' colony of sorts and still an independent-minded community. You can get a glimpse of the area's character by heading north up winding Mt Washington Drive to San Rafael Avenue; however, the only real attraction is, or was, the **Southwest Museum of the American Indian** (234 Museum Drive, at Marmion Way). Founded in 1907 by Charles Fletcher Lummis, the museum and its collection of 250,000 Native American artefacts were bought in 2003 by the Autry National Center and later moved to the Autry National Center in Griffith Park (*see p60*). The old gallery space is currently being used for conservation and preservation work; highlights of the collection are on view from 10am to 4pm on Saturdays; in future, the building may also be used as an education or cultural centre.

Highland Park

Just north-east of here, more or less between Mt Washington and the area of **Eagle Rock**, is the historic neighbourhood of **Highland Park**. Popular with LA's artistic community in the late 19th and early 20th centuries, it's not been without its problems, and Latino gang violence remains a concern. But what trouble there is here is easily avoided. Roughly halfway between Downtown Los Angeles and Pasadena, Highland Park is often described as LA's first suburb. Certainly, it's more attractive than the 'burbs that followed: its streets are dotted with grand

old residences. Notable buildings include **Judson Studios** (200 S Avenue 66, at York Boulevard, 1-323 255 0131, www.judsonstudios. com), originally the home of the Los Angeles College of Fine Arts and now a stained-glass studio and gallery; and the residences on S Avenue 59 south of Figueroa Street. Highland Park is also hot: a recent influx of artists and entrepreneurs has helped transform the area into a lively multicultural hub with eclectic shopping (smoke shops and second-hand threads share kerb space with art galleries and bookstores) and dining choices (from *taquerias* and *panaderias* to gastropubs and urban coffee klatches). And, thanks to a recent $100,000 grant, York Boulevard and environs is getting a facelift, with expanded sidewalks and benches to support the area's booming café culture and foot traffic.

FREE El Alisal (Lummis Home)

200 E Avenue 43, at Carlota Boulevard (1-323 222 0546, www.socalhistory.org). Metro Southwest Museum/bus 81, 83/Hwy 110, exit Avenue 43 west. **Open** *Tours* noon-4pm Fri-Sun. **Admission** free. *Parking* free.
Built at the turn of the 19th century by adventurous jack-of-all-trades Charles Fletcher Lummis, this strange but admirable building is open for low-key tours at weekends. Reservations aren't required.

Heritage Square

3800 Homer Street, at E Avenue 43 (1-323 225 2700, www.heritagesquare.org). Metro Heritage Square or Southwest Museum/bus 81, 83/Hwy 110, exit Avenue 43 west. **Open** *Apr-Oct* noon-5pm Fri-Sun. *Nov-Mar* 11.30am-4.30pm Fri-Sun. **Admission** $10; $5-$8 discounts; free under-6s. *Parking* free. **Credit** MC, Disc, V.
Preservation, LA-style. The buildings that together make up this open-air museum were all moved here from other locations: a railroad station from Century City, a church from Pasadena, a colonial drug store and a variety of formerly private residences from across the city. Tours run on the hour between noon and 3pm; there's no entry after the last one leaves.

Downtown

A change is gonna come.

By day, Downtown LA is a crisp political district, a bustling centre of finance and commerce, a Mexican shopping mall, a convention hub, a multi-million-dollar fashion market and more. But by night, at least until recently, it wasn't much at all. However, the last few years have seen the locale transformed in a dramatic manner. L.A. LIVE and Disney Hall have helped lure outsiders back to the area; a number of excellent restaurants and smart new bars have superseded the once-divey nightlife scene; and the low-key emergence of a small local arts district has added a little grassroots culture. The residential population, too, has grown dramatically, as young, educated dwellers move into swanky new loft apartments all over the district, from Chinatown to Broadway. Right now, Downtown might just be the most fascinating neighbourhood in Los Angeles.

Map p314	**Coffeehouses** p136
Restaurants p110	**Hotels** p181
Bars p127	

CHINATOWN

LA's original Chinatown sprang up in the 1850s around Alameda Street. A thriving area at the turn of the 19th century, it began to fade soon after, and the land that held it was redeveloped as Union Station in the 1930s. (One remaining building from the original Chinatown holds the **Chinese American Museum**; *see p66*.)

However, although the Chinese community leaders had failed to secure a future for their neighbourhood, their children soon managed to establish a second Chinatown in an area just north-west of Union Station in what was once Little Italy. These pioneers set about building a neighbourhood that would serve the local Chinese American community while also appealing to tourists. In June 1938, Chinatown's Central Plaza, an inauthentic yet strangely exotic confection, opened to the public.

Some 75 years later, Central Plaza is still the focal point of Chinatown, but Chinatown is no longer the focal point of LA's Chinese American communities: that role falls to Monterey Park, north-east of here. The small district feels a little forlorn these days, the streets often quiet outside of **Chinese New Year** (*see p25*).

However, it has undergone a small revival of late, a cluster of galleries and bars making an interesting juxtaposition with the dusty old Chinese-owned bric-a-brac stores. For additional context, follow the excellent self-guided walking tour detailed on panels throughout the area; it starts at Chinatown station but you can pick it up at any point.

N Broadway and, to a lesser extent, **N Spring Street** are the main roads, home to banks, grocers, bakeries (try the Phoenix, at 969 N Broadway) and a Metro station. Further north on Broadway is **Central Plaza** (947 N Broadway), one of the nation's first pedestrian malls. These days, its businesses are a mix of old-fashioned restaurants and bars, tacky souvenir shops on Gin Ling Way, and new(er)comers such as hipster-friendly Asian eaterie **Via Café** (451 Gin Ling Way, 1-213 617 1481). A statue of Republic of China founder Dr Sun Yat-Sen sternly oversees proceedings.

North of Central Plaza, the volunteer-run **Chinese Historical Society** (411 Bernard Street, 1-323 222 0856, www.chssc.org, closed Sat) contains information on Chinatown's past. A block further north stand **St Peter's Church** and the **Casa Italiana** (1051 N

EXPLORE

Broadway, www.casaitaliana.org), two extant reminders of the Italian community that lived here before the Chinese arrived.

To the west of Broadway, **Hill Street** holds more Chinese businesses. On Thursdays from 4pm to 8pm, a farmers' market is held in the parking lot adjacent to No.727. But perhaps the area's most interesting street is skinny **Chung King Road**, just behind it. Some of its old Chinese shops remain, but others have been taken over by Anglos and converted into tiny galleries. Among them are the Happy Lion (No.963) and Black Dragon Society (No.961).

OLVERA STREET & THE PLAZA

Just across César E Chávez Avenue from Chinatown is **El Pueblo de Los Angeles Historical Monument**, a restored 44-acre historic park that purports to be on the site of the original settlement of LA. In fact, the first settlement was half a mile from here, but no trace of it remains; LA's official birthday is 4 September 1781, the day that the first Spanish settlers began farming and building ranches.

It's a curious jumble of buildings, most built in the late 19th and early 20th centuries and used today for all manner of purposes. To get a feel for the area, it's worth joining one of the family-friendly free tours run by Las Angelitas del Pueblo (www.lasangelitas. org), which depart from the Las Angelitas office on the south side of the Plaza at 10am, 11am and noon from Tuesday to Saturday. Booking isn't required unless you're travelling with a large group.

Running east of Main Street, is **Olvera Street**, a narrow, pedestrianised thoroughfare. Renovated in 1930 as a Mexican marketplace, it's now a tourist trap, albeit a generally enjoyable one. In between the odiferous taco stands and the stalls hawking colourful hats and shirts, keep an eye out for the **Avila Adobe**, the oldest existing house in LA. Built in 1818, this small ranch-style home has been restored, and now operates as a museum; there's also a visitors' centre in the courtyard. The nearby **Sepulveda House** contains the **América Tropical Interpretive Center** (www.americatropical.org), a new museum and observation deck explaining the social and political influences behind the *América Tropical* mural painted here by David Alfaro Siqueiros. The mural caused such controversy when it was unveiled in 1932 it was subsequently whitewashed over.

At the southern end of Olvera Street sits the circular **Plaza**, the bustling focal point of El Pueblo. South of the Plaza is a cluster of old and not-so-old buildings; one, a 19th-century fire station, houses a diverting collection of

Chinatown.

INSIDE TRACK
CAUGHT ON CAMERA

Some of Downtown's most striking buildings have been immortalised in film over the decades. In *Blade Runner* (1982), Rutger Hauer tracks Harrison Ford through the Bradbury Building (*see p72*), and in *War of the Worlds* (1953) City Hall (*see p68*) is blown up by Martians. More recently, in *2012* (2009), the US Bank Tower collapses following an earthquake.

old firefighting equipment. And just across Main Street from the Plaza are more historic buildings, including the oldest Catholic church in LA: Our Lady, Queen of the Angels, commonly known as **La Placita**.

Visible from the Plaza is **Union Station** (800 N Alameda Street). Opened in 1939 on the site of the original Chinatown, it was the last of the great American rail stations to be built, at a cost at the time of $11 million. By 1971, just seven passenger trains a day were running here; however, it's a bit busier today, and its Mission-style exterior, marble floors, high ceilings and decorative tiles make it a handsome place. Try not to confuse it with the Spanish colonial post office that stands next to it.

To the south-west of La Plaza, the new **LA Plaza de Cultura y Artes** (501 North Main Street, 1-888 488 8083, http://lapca.org, closed Tue) celebrates Mexican American culture and arts via interactive exhibits and a re-creation of a 1920s-era Main Street. The project caused controversy even before it opened in 2011, when construction work unearthed a large number of human bones from an abandoned Catholic cemetery next door. The bones were later reinterred. Nearby, the **Italian American Museum of Los Angeles** (644 Main Street, 1-213 485 8432, www.italianhall.org), which aims to explore the history of Italian Americans in the US via exhibitions and educational programmes, is due to open in early 2014.

Chinese American Museum

425 N Los Angeles Street, at Arcadia Street (1-213 485 8567, www.camla.org). Metro Union Station/bus 76/US 101, exit Los Angeles Street south. **Open** 10am-3pm Tue-Sun. **Admission** *Suggested donation* $3; $2 discounts. **Credit** MC, V. **Map** p315 C1.

While CAM's location in El Pueblo might seem a little incongruous, its location is actually very appropriate. This was LA's original Chinatown, and the Garnier building, in which part of the museum sits, is the most historic Chinese structure in the area: built in 1890, when Chinese immigrants dominated

this part of town, it has been home to a number of community organisations. Exhibits spotlight the history of LA's Chinatown and examine the more general experience of Chinese Americans in the US.

LITTLE TOKYO TO SKID ROW

Head south down Alameda Street, past Temple Street to Central Avenue, and you'll reach the **Geffen Contemporary** wing of the **Museum of Contemporary Art** (*see p71*), housed in a former warehouse converted by Frank Gehry. Right by the museum, Roger Yanagita's *Go for Broke* monument commemorates the Japanese American soldiers who fought in World War II, experiences dramatised in the 1951 movie *Go for Broke*. Further down Central Avenue is the **Japanese American National Museum** (*see p67*). Opposite, partly housed in the 1925 Nishi Hongwanji Buddhist Temple, is the JANM's **National Center for the Preservation of Democracy**.

It's at this corner that Little Tokyo really begins. Just across the road, running between 1st and 2nd Streets just west of Central Avenue, is the **Japanese Village Plaza**, a mini-mall with restaurants, shops and karaoke bars. Across from the Japanese Village Plaza is the **James Irvine Garden**, a lovely, romantic example of a traditional Japanese garden. The gardens are accessible by taking an elevator to the basement of the **Japanese American Cultural & Community Center** (244 S San Pedro Street, 1-213 628 2725, www.jaccc.org).

To the east, relocated from Boyle Heights, is one of LA's best-known arts institutions. Founded in the early 1970s, the **Self Help Graphics & Art** cultural centre (1300 E 1st Street, 1-323 881 6444, www.selfhelp graphics.com) runs community art workshops, stages sporadic sales and exhibits work by established and up-and-coming Latino artists. However, it's most famous for its annual **Dia de Los Muertos** (Day of the Dead) celebrations each autumn (*see p24*).

There's more to see to the west of Japanese Village Plaza. Pedestrianised **Astronaut Ellison S Onizuka Street**, which runs diagonally south between 1st Street and the corner of 2nd and San Pedro Streets, is named for one of the astronauts who died in the *Challenger* crash in 1986; a model of the shuttle commemorates his life. A little further west is the 19th-century St Vibiana's Cathedral (210 S Main Street), now a private-hire party and events venue. To the south-east stands the **Higashi Honganji Buddhist Temple** (505 E 3rd Street), which blends neatly and sweetly into its otherwise Western locale.

Walking further south of Little Tokyo will bring you to LA's infamous **Skid Row**, centred

EXPLORE

on 5th Street between Main and Alameda Streets. The homeless have long congregated here, but the area has also become both a magnet for lowlifes and troubled souls of every stripe. Creeping gentrification at the area's western extremity has lifted the area, but these changes have had their critics – some observers have claimed that a number of transients have been unlawfully forced from residential hotels by developers anxious to convert the buildings to posh apartments. The battle looks set to continue for a while.

★ Japanese American National Museum

100 N Central Avenue, at E 1st Street (1-213 625 0414, www.janm.org). Metro Little Tokyo/Arts District/bus 30, 40, 42/US 101, exit Alameda Street south. **Open** 11am-5pm Tue, Wed, Fri-Sun; noon-8pm Thur. **Admission** $9; $5 discounts; free under-5s. Free to all 3rd Thur of mth & 5-8pm all other Thurs. **Credit** AmEx, DC, MC, V. **Map** p315 D2.

The story of Japanese immigration to the US really begins in 1882, when bosses were barred from importing cheap Chinese labour by the Chinese Exclusion Act. Thousands of Japanese arrived to take their place; many settled in the San Joaquin Valley and became farmers. But the Japanese were then excluded from American life in much the same way as the Chinese had suffered before them: they were prevented from owning land in 1913, banned from immigrating in 1924 and sent to internment camps during World War II. Only in 1952 were people born in Japan allowed to become American citizens. This museum, one of the city's best, tells the story of Japanese immigration to the US in lucid, engaging fashion. Even if you've no prior interest in the subject, you'll be drawn in to it by the perfectly pitched displays. Aside from the permanent exhibition, the museum has an engaging roster of documentary and art exhibitions, including a wrenching yet beautiful display of images and artefacts from the aforementioned internment camps. To cap it all off, there's a lovely gift shop and a Chado tea room.

CIVIC CENTER & AROUND

Civic Center

Just north-east of Little Tokyo, there's a neat intersection of immigrant communities: **Judge John Aiso Street**, named after the highest-ranking *nisei* to serve for the Allies during World War II, connects to Temple Street at the **Edward R Roybal Federal Building** (255 E Temple Street), named after California's first Mexican American congressman. Outside the latter is Jonathan Borofsky's sculpture *Molecule Man*, a quartet of huge metal figures.

The majority of LA's administrative and political institutions are based in this area,

Public Art

Striking structures as you stroll.

The one characteristic that links every part of Downtown LA is the preponderance of public art: outside skyscrapers, on the walls of public buildings, even in the form of bicycle racks. Ruth Wallach's Public Art in LA website (www.publicartinla.com) is an unbeatable resource to the hundreds of works; here are five of the best.

Hammering Man

Jonathan Borofsky (1988)
California Market Center, 110 E 9th Street, at S Main Street
This hulking, hammering silhouette is one of three Borofsky works in Downtown. The others are *Molecule Man*, outside the Federal Building (*see left*); and *I Dreamed I Could Fly*, six figures suspended above the platform at Civic Center station.

Mind, Body and Spirit

Gidon Graetz (1986)
SW corner of 4th & Hope Streets
This twisty horn, made from stainless steel and bronze, forms part of a sculpture garden outside the YMCA. Other works here include two sports-themed pieces by Milton Hebald and a gymnast cast in bronze by Michael Zapponi.

Source Figure

Robert Graham (1991)
Hope Place, between 4th & 5th Streets
This three-foot bronze nude stands proudly atop a column in a fountain halfway up the Bunker Hill Steps.

Friendship Knot

Shinkichi Tajiri (1972)
2nd & San Pedro Streets
Tajiri has long favoured knots in his works, which include sculptures such as this towering fibreglass object in Little Tokyo.

Bicycle Rack

Randall Wilson (1998)
corner of College & Yale Streets
Wilson's pair of inverted hearts are one of ten bike racks designed by students at the Southern California Institute of Architecture; others stand in Pershing Square, outside the Geffen Contemporary and by the LA Times Building.

EXPLORE

known as Civic Center. Just north of the Federal Building, at Aliso and Los Angeles Streets, is the **Metropolitan Detention Center**. Designed to blend in with the office blocks around it, the building looks nothing like a conventional jail; legend has it that a group of Japanese tourists once tried to check in, thinking it was a hotel.

To the west is the art deco-styled **City Hall** (200 N Spring Street), built in 1928 and LA's tallest building until 1957. Free tours of the handsome old building are offered at 10am and 11am from Monday to Friday; you'll need to book in advance by calling 1-213 978 1995. However, you don't need to join a tour in order to visit the little-used observation deck, one of the best-kept secrets in Downtown. Simply ask for a free pass at the reception desk (9am-5pm daily) and then head up to the 27th floor, where you'll get some fabulous views of the city.

Back across 1st Street stands the 1930s **LA Times Building** (202 W 1st Street), still home to the *Los Angeles Times*. It's overshadowed by its neighbours, but the interior holds some treasures. A series of displays traces the history of the paper; in the centre, a rotating globe is set into a marbled plinth and ringed by a Hugo Ballin mural. Two quotations take pride of place: one by 19th-century religious reformer Henry Ward Beecher. 'The newspaper,' wrote Beecher, rather piously, 'is a greater treasure to the people than uncounted millions of gold.' To gain access, you need to book a tour – they're free but must be reserved at least a month in advance by calling 1-213 237 3178.

Two other buildings stand just east of here along Main Street, both of them new. Hemmed in by Spring, Main, 1st and 2nd Streets, the DMJM-designed **LAPD Headquarters** provides a suitably dramatic neighbour for Thom Mayne's **Caltrans District 7 Headquarters**, which occupies the whole of the next block to the east at Main and 1st Streets. In its vast, flat dimensions and enormous scale, it resembles a huge, shiny ocean liner.

Disney Hall & around

Though Downtown contains a surprising number of historic buildings, it's best known for two of its newest. The **Cathedral of Our Lady of the Angels** (555 W Temple Street) has had a number of nicknames pinned to it since its dedication in 2002: perhaps the most memorable is 'Our Lady of the 101', after the freeway from which it can clearly be seen.

It's a fine structure, but it's overshadowed by its neighbour. The **Walt Disney Concert Hall** (111 S Grand Avenue; *see p229*) opened in 2003 after an odyssey of promises, delays, starts, stops, shutdowns, ego battles, funding problems and structural concerns. But it was

Richard J Riordan Central Library. *See p71.*

all worth it: bold, brash yet also sensual in its reflective glory, Frank Gehry's building sits like a reclining steel butterfly, its wings fanning languidly atop Bunker Hill. It's just as wonderful inside: the acoustic of the hall is said to be the best in the US.

Facing each other across 1st Street, Disney Hall and the buildings that comprise the **Music Center** (home to the **Dorothy Chandler Pavilion**, the **Ahmanson Theatre** and the **Mark Taper Forum**; *see p231*) are wildly different structures borne of different eras and of very different approaches to the same task. They don't gel as a unit at all, but it's daft to hold Gehry responsible for the architectural failings of earlier generations.

This area looks set to change dramatically in the next few years, thanks to the government-backed $3 billion **Grand Avenue Project** (www.grandavenuecommittee.org). Although plans for condo buildings, a hotel (designed by Gehry), various entertainment venues and a shopping mall are currently on hold – probably indefinitely – due to money worries, the 16-acre **Grand Park** between the DWP Building and

City Hall opened in 2012, with entrances at Grand Avenue, Hill Street, Broadway and Spring Street. The park is so far proving popular, with a Tuesday farmers' market and free yoga and music events; check the website (http://grandparkla.org) for full details. And while not officially part of the project, the long-awaited **Broad** contemporary art museum, named after its benefactors, Eli and Edythe Broad, will be a major boon to the area. The 120,000-square-foot, three-storey museum, designed by Diller Scofidio + Renfro, is due to be completed in 2014.

THE FINANCIAL DISTRICT & BUNKER HILL

South of Disney Hall, art meets commerce. At Grand Avenue and 3rd Street is the **Museum of Contemporary Art** (MOCA; *see p71*), part of the billion-dollar California Plaza. While the museum is undeniably the highlight of the area, the plaza is by no means unmemorable, whether for the computer-operated fountain spraying 40-foot (12-metre) geysers or the daily concerts in summer. Across the road, meanwhile, sits the **Wells Fargo Center** (333 S Grand Avenue); as well as being a banking powerhouse, it's home to the **Wells Fargo History Museum** (1-213 253 7166), which tells the story of the bank founded in the heyday of the Gold Rush.

Known as **Bunker Hill**, this was where LA's wealthiest citizens built their houses a century ago: grand Victorian mansions, powerful illustrations of their owners' riches. However, after the once-exclusive area began to decay in the 1940s and '50s, the mansions were razed. Eventually, a slew of shiny but architecturally unremarkable skyscrapers were built in their place, and Bunker Hill began to enjoy a second life as LA's financial district.

The only surviving remnant of the old Bunker Hill is **Angels Flight** (Hill Street, between 3rd & 4th Streets, 50¢ one way, or 25¢ with a valid Metro ticket or TAP card), the world's shortest railway. Built in 1901 to ferry citizens to their hilltop homes, closed in 1969, reopened 27 years later and then shut down again after a fatal accident in 2001, it finally reopened in March 2010.

A couple of blocks south sits **Pershing Square**. A public meeting place since 1866, it was renamed in 1918 after the commander of the US Army in World War I. Nowadays it hosts concerts in summer and an ice rink in winter but is a pretty drab, depressing place. In February 2013, it was announced that Anschutz Entertainment Group (AEG), the company behind the proposed new Downtown NFL stadium, would donate $700,000 in seed money to help 're-envision' the park. No time frame

has been set, but a revamp couldn't come soon enough. Dominating the edge of the square is the grand **Millennium Biltmore** (*see p181*), built in 1923.

Continue directly south from Pershing Square down Olive or Hill Streets and you'll immediately find yourself in the Jewelry District, six square blocks bounded by 6th Street, Broadway, 8th Street and Olive Street. There are some 5,000 businesses here, set up in individual stores or in sprawling indoor marketplaces, and the area is a polyglot's delight: expect to hear anything from Hebrew to Armenian as the stallholders and repairers go about their exotic business.

A little west of Pershing Square is the **Richard J Riordan Central Library** (*see p71*), a striking Beaux Arts building from 1926. After a fire in the 1980s, it was refurbished with money stumped up by the developers of **US Bank Tower** (formerly Library Tower, 633 W 5th Street); built by IM Pei in 1990 and towering 1,018 feet (310 metres) into the Downtown sky, it's the tallest building in LA. In front of the library is the oasis of the **Robert F Maguire Gardens**; the wide, graceful sweep of the 103 Bunker Hill Steps, linking 5th and Hope Streets.

Heading west from here along 5th Street will bring you within range of two major hotels. The hip **Standard** (550 S Flower Street; *see p181*) is housed in Claude Beelman's sturdy old Standard Oil Building, but it's overshadowed by the five-tower, business-oriented **Westin Bonaventure** (404 S Figueroa Street); built by John Portman in the 1970s, it still looks futuristic from the outside. These streets have also been resettled in recent years by moneyed twenty- and hirtysomethings hungry for an urban lifestyle: the **Pegasus Lofts** (Flower

EXPLORE

INSIDE TRACK
EAST OF ALAMEDA

Previously known as the Warehouse District, the area to the east of Alameda Street, roughly between 1st and 7th Streets, recently began redefining itself as the 'Arts District'. And while some streets can feel desolate, there are increasing signs that the area is up and coming, with decent restaurants and bars continuing to crop up. Our favourites so far include German-style sausage hall **Wurstküche** (*see p115*), **Daily Dose** café (*see p136*), authentic French bistro **Church & State** (1850 Industrial Street, 1-213 405 1434), **Pourhaus** (*see p128*) and burger and beer den **Villains Tavern** (www.villainstavern.com).

Broadway Booming

Bringing back the halcyon days.

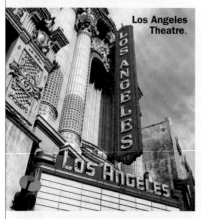

Los Angeles Theatre.

As lively as Broadway is in the 21st century, it was livelier in the 1920s, when it was home to the largest theatre district west of the Mississippi. The grand theatres on the street, some a century old, have lain dormant for years. However, a group of locals is helping to return Broadway to its former glory.

Broadway went through several identities before becoming LA's theatrical centre in the early 20th century, its venues offering both live performances (Harry Houdini, WC Fields) and silent movies. Among the popular theatres and nickelodeons were the **Cameo** at No.528, completed in 1910 as Clunes Broadway, and the **Palace** at No.630, which opened in the following year as the Orpheum.

For all its popularity, Broadway remained a pretty low-rent part of town until one man arrived with a vision and the cash to make it happen. Built by Sid Grauman in 1918 for a then-outrageous seven-figure sum, the extravagant **Million Dollar Theater** (No.307) was the first truly grand theatre to open in Downtown. Staging a spread of shows and movies, it single-handedly elevated Broadway above its low-rent vaudeville origins.

Inspired by Grauman, other promoters followed suit. The Rialto was joined on Broadway's 800 block by the **Orpheum** (No.842), which opened in 1926 as a vaudeville palace, and the **Tower** (No.802), a movie theatre completed in 1927, which

is currently being turned into a concert venue. The same year saw the arrival of the **United Artists Theatre** (No.933), built by the UA studio to screen its own movies. And in 1931, the plush **Los Angeles Theatre** (No.615) was built in just 90 days at a cost of $1 million.

The party didn't last. As Downtown gave way to the suburbs in the years following World War II, its theatres fell on hard times. A resurgence during the 1960s was brief, and the remaining venues fell into decrepitude or closed their doors for good.

Happily, most miraculously survived. Not all are in decent shape: the lobbies of several, including the Cameo and the **Rialto** (No.820), are home to a sad agglomeration of stalls, and the UA Theatre is now a church. However, a 20-plus-year effort by the LA Conservancy has helped bring about change.

In 2008, councilman José Huizar, with support from the mayor and local property owners, announced Bringing Back Broadway (www.bringingbackbroadway. com), a public-private initiative designed to return vitality and splendour to the street over the course of the next decade. The ambitious group wants to complete the renovation of the theatres, while also introducing other forms of entertainment, attracting big retail names and even reviving the old streetcar network; in December 2012, voters approved $62.5 million in funding for the latter.

The rehabilitation of the theatres is already under way. After restoration, the Orpheum (*see p218*) is once again staging concerts; the Palace and the Los Angeles Theatre are both used for filming (www.losangelestheatre.com); and the Million Dollar Theater reopened in 2008 after renovations that ran to, yes, a million dollars (www.milliondollartheater.com).

Access to most of the theatres is limited to tours run by the LA Conservancy every Saturday at 10am. But visitors to LA in May and June have the chance to watch a classic film in one of the old palaces as part of the Conservancy's **Last Remaining Seats** event, which offers a glimpse of the glamour of yesteryear. Booking ahead is essential; for more on the tours and Last Remaining Seats, see www.lac onservancy.org.

Street, between 6th Street and Wilshire Boulevard) is one such typical conversion.

Heading south down Figueroa Street will bring you to one of LA's best-known sculptures: Terry Allen's *Corporate Head*, a lifesize effigy of a corporate executive with its head disappearing into the side of the Citicorp office building (725 S Figueroa Street). It's the highlight of **Poet's Walk**, an assortment of verse inscriptions and public art.

This stretch of 7th Street, heading east, has added some decent new bars and restaurants of late; standouts currently include Bottega Louie (1-213 802 1470, www.bottegalouie.com), a gourmet market-cum-restaurant at the corner of Grand Avenue and 7th Street, while the new FIGat7th mall (www.figat7th.com) at, you guessed it, 7th and Figueroa, continues to attract decent stores and restaurants.

★ Museum of Contemporary Art, Los Angeles

MOCA Grand Avenue *250 S Grand Avenue, at 3rd Street. Metro Civic Center/Grand Park/ Tom Bradley/bus 16, 18, 55, 62/I-110, exit 4th Street east.* **Map** p315 B2.
Geffen Contemporary at MOCA *152 N Central Avenue, at 1st Street. Metro Little Tokyo/Arts District/bus 30, 40, 42/US 101, exit Alameda Street south.* **Map** p315 D2.
Both *1-213 626 6222, www.moca.org.* **Open** 11am-5pm Mon, Fri; 11am-8pm Thur; 11am-6pm Sat, Sun. **Admission** *Combined ticket* $12; $7 discounts; free under-12s. Free to all 5-8pm Thur. **Credit** AmEx, DC, MC, V.
The city's premier showcase for post-war contemporary art, MOCA started life in a police warehouse on the edge of Little Tokyo. It's now the Geffen Contemporary, its spacious, raw interior designed by Frank Gehry in the 1980s; it's considered by some to be one of his gutsiest spaces. When MOCA's main building, designed by Japan's Arata Isozaki, was completed a few blocks from the Civic Center, the museum was able simultaneously to mount ambitious survey exhibitions and to showcase items from its fine permanent collection, which includes pieces by Rauschenberg, Rothko, Twombly, Mondrian and Pollock. Up to half a dozen shows can be viewed at any one time between the two galleries and its West Hollywood outpost at the Pacific Design Center (*see p49*). A programme of talks and performance events rounds out the scene.
▶ *MOCA's dedicated YouTube channel, www. youtube.com/mocatv, features short videos on art and culture, including dance and music.*

FREE Richard J Riordan Central Library

630 W 5th Street, between S Grand Avenue & S Flower Street (1-213 228 7000, www.lapl.org/ branches/central-library). Metro Pershing Square or 7th Street-Metro Center/bus 16, 18, 55, 62/

I-110, exit 6th Street east. **Open** 10am-8pm Mon-Thur; 10am-5.30pm Fri, Sat. **Admission** free. **Map** p315 B3.
Designed by Bertram Goodhue, completed in 1926 and renamed after the city's former mayor in 2001, LA's main library is worth a look even if you've no interest in borrowing books. The exterior is a Beaux Arts beauty, crowned with a dramatic, tiled pyramid tower and decorated with bas-reliefs by Lee Lawrie, but there's also plenty to see inside. The main lobby is topped with an unexpectedly colourful ceiling mural by Venice artist Renée Petropoulos; other highlights include a frieze that retells Walter Scott's Ivanhoe and a series of murals dedicated to California history. The Annenberg Gallery shows rare LA-related pieces from the library's collection; the Getty Gallery stages temporary exhibitions; and there's a fine programme of lectures and discussions in the Mark Taper Auditorium (for details, see www.lfla.org/aloud). *Photo p68.*

BROADWAY

Between 1st Street and Olympic Boulevard (effectively 10th Street), Downtown's liveliest road is an intoxicating blend of LA history, Latino culture, old-world trade and modern-day wealth. Classic '20s theatres stand shoulder to shoulder with Hispanic markets and street traders; jewellers look out from shop windows at Downtown's wandering homeless. Even the scruffier buildings carry with them a grandeur bestowed by simple survival; the street life is the stuff of photographers' dreams.

Start at 1st and Broadway and wander south. After a quick detour east down 3rd Street to see Eloy Torrez's mammoth mural of Mexican American actor Anthony Quinn, arms spread

EXPLORE

wide as he looks down over a parking lot on the north side of 3rd between Broadway and Spring Street, you'll reach the magnificent **Bradbury Building** (304 S Broadway). Designed by otherwise unknown architect George Wyman in 1893, it's an extraordinary building, defined by its ornate cast-iron fittings and the natural light that floods it. It's used as offices, but visitors are welcome to take a look around the lobby and wander up the stairwell to the first landing.

Across the street from the Bradbury Building sits the enclosed **Grand Central Market**, a perpetually busy Mexican-style market with stalls selling everything from fresh meat to fruit smoothies. A proposed makeover, which could see trendy food entrepreneurs move in among the old-school family-run businesses, has some locals worried about gentrification and price rises. Nearby is the **Million Dollar Theatre** (No.307), where Sid Grauman launched his West Coast operations. For more on the theatre and on the others that once constituted LA's Little White Way, *see p70* **Broadway Booming**.

After several blocks dominated by Latino retailers, ancient theatres and, between 6th and 8th Streets, jewellers (this is the edge of the Jewelry District), you'll reach a key link between old and new Downtown. Designed by Claude Beelman and completed in 1929, the 13-storey **Eastern Columbia Building** (at the north-west corner of Broadway and 9th Street) is a gorgeous, turquoise art deco pile that has been converted into loft apartments.

THE FASHION DISTRICT & THE FLOWER DISTRICT

East of the Jewelry District are two other commercial hubs. Centred on 8th and Wall Streets, the **Flower District** (www.laflower district.com) and the **Los Angeles Flower Market** (closed Sunday) are at their liveliest at the start of the day. Get here pre-dawn for a colourful riot of activity, as wholesalers unload truckloads of lilies, roses, orchids and tulips.

Close by, the roads around Los Angeles Street south of 7th Street received a rebranding in the 1980s when real estate owners attempted to modernise the area. It seems to have worked: formerly the Garment District, a workaday name for a workaday area, the rechristened **Fashion District** (www.fashiondistrict.org), which spans the street south of here down to the I10 freeway, now pulses with activity. Clothes are still made here in decades-old warehouses, but many more are brought in from elsewhere and sold.

The four main market centres are all grouped together; spread over three 13-storey buildings housing 1,000 showrooms, the **California Market Center** (110 E 9th Street, www. californiamarketcenter.com) is the biggest.

However, apart from the ground-floor fashion bookstore and Jonathan Borofsky's sculpture *Hammering Man*, or unless you're here for one of the sample sales (held on the last Friday of most months), there's not much to see.

SOUTH PARK & L.A. LIVE

Edging out cautiously from around the intersection of the Harbor Freeway and the Santa Monica Freeway (I-110 and I-10), South Park isn't actually a park at all but a rather drab locale that's been slowly resuscitated by a number of big-money developments. First to arrive was the **Los Angeles Convention Center**, open since 1971 and expanded 22 years later. In 1999, it was joined by the 20,000-capacity, $400 million **Staples Center** (*see p218*), which was built next door, providing Downtown with a major venue for shows and sporting events. However, both venues have recently been overshadowed by a newer arrival, just a stone's throw away.

Hemmed in by Olympic Boulevard, Figueroa Street, 11th Street and the Harbor Freeway, the $2.5 billion **L.A. LIVE** development, built in three phases and completed in 2010, was billed by those behind it as 'Times Square West', an adult playground aimed at attracting moneyed suburbanites back to LA's urban core. There's no doubt it has a lot to offer – not least two major hotels (the Ritz-Carlton and adjoining JW Marriott; *see p181*), plenty of bars, restaurants and clubs (highlights include the Conga Room and WP24; *see p115*), plus enough entertainment to keep visitors busy all year round (the 7,000-capacity Nokia Theatre (*see p218*), the GRAMMY Museum, Lucky Strike Lanes (*see p241*) – and Staples Center itself, which is officially considered part of L.A. LIVE), but it's anyone's guess what it will mean in the long term for the area.

★ GRAMMY Museum

800 W Olympic Boulevard, Suite A245, at S Figueroa Street (1-213 765 6800, www. grammymuseum.org). Metro Pico/bus 81, 381, 442, 460/I-110, exit Olympic Boulevard east. **Open** 11.30am-7.30pm Mon-Fri; 10am-7.30pm Sat, Sun. **Admission** $12.95, $10.95-$11.95 discounts. *Parking* from $5. **Credit** AmEx, MC, V. **Map** p315 B4.

This 30,000sq ft museum in the L.A. LIVE district celebrates music, exploring everything from the creative process to the technology of the recording studio to the Grammy awards themselves. It's set over four floors, with interactive, permanent and temporary exhibits (past shows have included John Lennon, Songwriter and Hip Hop: A Cultural Odyssey). Check the website for details of programmes, including discussions, films and performances.

East Los Angeles

This gritty, historic area warrants exploration.

Officially, the unincorporated area of East LA takes Indiana Street as its western boundary. However, in modern-day shorthand, it also includes hilly Boyle Heights (part of the City of LA), which separates Downtown and East LA and takes the Los Angeles River and Indiana Street as its western and eastern borders. And some have argued that East LA's true spiritual starting point is Olvera Street, just across the river in Downtown.

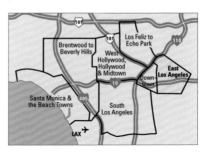

Commercial activity in East LA is centred on César E Chávez Avenue, 1st Street and Whittier Boulevard, three parallel east–west streets. Still, for all its points of cultural interest, the area is visually and architecturally undistinguished. Aside from a few handsome Victorian homes and a number of newer murals, the charisma of East LA comes from the people rather than the buildings, which are mostly bland and unremarkable.

AREA HISTORY

Many non-Anglo immigrant groups settled in East Los Angeles when they first arrived in the city. In the early 20th century, there was a sizeable Jewish community here; the Jews were then followed by Asians, blacks, Italians and, eventually, Mexicans, who have dominated the area for more than four years.

Back in the 1960s, East LA's political clout was so negligible that the area was torn asunder by freeway construction. However, it remains a lively area with a strong sense of Latino identity. And with Latinos now wielding more political power than at any point in LA's history (in 2005, Boyle Heights native Antonio Villaraigosa became the city's first Hispanic mayor in more than 130 years), the future is as bright here as it's been for some time. And the arrival of the Metro's Gold Line, which now connects this downtrodden part of the city to its newly thriving Downtown core, will no doubt help the area's long-term prospects.

BOYLE HEIGHTS

Named after the founder and former president of the United Farm Workers union, **César E Chávez Avenue** is actually a continuation of Sunset Boulevard, running from north of

Downtown through Boyle Heights into East LA. The commercial activity begins just east of I-10, and is at its liveliest along Chávez Avenue between N Cummings and N Fickett Street. This stretch of road, the heart of Boyle Heights, is lined with earthy restaurants, basic-looking shops stocked with cheap clothing and other inessentials, street vendors hawking everything from papayas to bargain jewellery, and even strolling musicians, who will play a romantic bolero or two on their well-worn guitars for a reasonable fee as you dine at **La Parrilla** (2126 E César E Chávez Avenue, 1-323 262 3434, www.laparrillarestaurant.com). At the intersection of Chávez and Soto Street, look out for several murals by local artists.

Compared to Chávez Avenue, 1st Street (two blocks to the south) is pretty mellow. The main point of interest is at 1st Street and Boyle Avenue, just east of the 101 freeway: **Mariachi Plaza**, one of the largest congregations of freelance mariachi musicians outside Mexico City's Garibaldi Square. Sporting traditional black ranchero outfits, the musicians gather here and wait for passing drivers to hire them to play at social and family events. The square is charmingly scruffy, although the historic (1889) and formerly dilapidated **Boyle Hotel** was recently given a $24 million

EXPLORE

makeover, spearheaded by the non-profit East Los Angeles Community Corporation, which added affordable housing units, a community room and a mariachi centre.

Most of the other attractions along 1st Street are culinary; chief among them is **La Serenata de Garibaldi** (No.1842, 1-323 265 2887, www.laserenataonline.com), which offers Mexican haute cuisine (the fresh fish is the star of the show). Further east is **El Mercado** (No.3425, at Cheesebroughs Lane), a multi-level market reminiscent of those in Mexican cities. Upstairs, you'll find restaurants with duelling mariachi bands, each seeking to lure clientele from the others; downstairs teems with stalls selling all manner of clothes, food and consumer goods. It's tremendous fun.

Elsewhere, Boyle Heights and its surrounding streets boast three very pleasant parks, the largest of them just north of the I-10 on the cusp of Lincoln Heights. Among the attractions in **Lincoln Park** are some statues of Mexican revolutionary heroes and the **Plaza**

de la Raza (www.plazadelaraza.org), a popular arts centre in a converted boathouse by the lake that offers art classes to children after school. The area's other parks include **Hollenbeck Park** (at 4th and Cummings Streets), built to an English model, and the heart-shaped **Prospect Park** (off Chávez Avenue at Echandia Street), a legacy of the local Jewish community.

EAST LOS ANGELES

Indiana Street serves as the eastern boundary of both Boyle Heights and the City of Los Angeles. Beyond it lies an unincorporated area officially known as East Los Angeles, which itself borders Monterey Park to the north (*see p84*), Montebello to the east and City of Commerce to the south. For the most part, this area is similar in character and appearance to Boyle Heights: both neighbourhoods are dominated by Latin Americans, both are slightly deprived and yet both retain a tangible pride in their local identities.

South of Highway 60 and **Calvary Cemetery** (one of two big local graveyards) is **Whittier Boulevard**, which is to East LA what Chávez Avenue is to Boyle Heights. Between Eastern Avenue and Atlantic Boulevard, Whittier is just as busy as Chávez, if not more so: the road is lined with clothes shops, restaurants, *botánicas* (selling herbs and incense), bakeries, nightclubs and bars, and traffic can be tough.

Whittier Boulevard was once the main drag for locals who wanted to display their low-rider hot rods, until the local police eventually put a stop to the tradition. However, East LA remains the LA capital of hot rod design. If you're lucky, you'll see a spectacular example cruising the street while you wait in the traffic. Look out, too, for customised low-rider motorbikes.

The culture of East Los Angeles spills over into its north-eastern neighbour, the city of **Monterey Park**. **Luminarias** (3500 Ramona Boulevard, 1-323 268 4177, www.luminariasrestaurant.com), one of several Latino restaurants, offers an array of Mexican favourites. Nearby is the **Vincent Price Art Museum** at East Los Angeles College (1301 Avenida César Chávez, 1-323 265 8841, http://vincentpriceartmuseum.org; closed mid Dec-late Jan), which reopened in 2011 in a swanky new 40,000-square-foot building designed by Arquitectonica. The museum is named after the horror film icon and art enthusiast who donated more than 2,000 works of art from his personal collection (including many Latino pieces); because, as he put it, 'this is where it's needed'.

In the Line of Duty

The Ruben Salazar story.

On 29 August 1970, Whittier Boulevard was the scene of a 'police riot' when a Chicano anti-war demonstration was attacked by police. During the disturbances, 42-year-old Chicano journalist Ruben Salazar was killed in the Silver Dollar café-bar (No.4945, at S La Verne Avenue, but long since closed) by a police tear-gas pellet to the head. The death of Salazar, a reporter for the *Los Angeles Times*, was thought by some to be retribution for his criticism of the sheriff's department's abusive behaviour towards people of colour. Recently released files, however, point more towards a tragic, preventable accident, the policeman in question having fired into a packed bar on the basis of an eyewitness mistakenly reporting armed gunmen inside. The Ruben Salazar Project, a PBS documentary aiming to offer more insight into the event, was in production as this guide went to press; follow http://cityprojects.net/projects/ruben-salazar for updates. Back west along Whittier, a couple of blocks from the border with Indiana Street, a small green space has been renamed Salazar Park in his honour, and stands as a symbol of the 1970s Chicano Movement.

South Los Angeles

These deprived neighbourhoods hold some fascinating sights.

South Los Angeles owes its black identity to the era of restrictive covenants. Instituted in the early 20th century and finally repealed in 1948, these segregationalist laws confined African Americans to a tight area around Central Avenue. In the past two decades, however, growing numbers of African Americans have headed to the suburbs and in their place have moved Latino families, who've made their mark in the form of a vibrant sidewalk culture.

Between the mid 1970s and the LA Riots of 1992, South Central developed a reputation as one of the most deprived, gang-ridden and violent areas in the US. It developed such a bad name that, in 2003, the city council passed an ordinance that officially changed it to South Los Angeles in a bid to help the area shed its appalling image. However, many still refer to the area by its more infamous moniker. Whichever name you use, the area is not necessarily dangerous, but it can be bleak: unrelieved by hills or sea, South LA appears as nothing but relentless flatlands of concrete and asphalt.

EXPOSITION PARK & AROUND

In the 19th century farmers sold food and plants in an open-air market at Agricultural Park to the south of Downtown LA. By 1910, the park had crumbled into a shadow of its former self, attracting not farmers but deadbeats, gamblers and prostitutes. Local attorney William C Bowers began a campaign to reclaim the land and build on it a public park and educational centre. In 1913, his vision became reality with the opening of the renovated and renamed Exposition Park.

If you approach Exposition Park from Downtown along Figueroa Avenue, you may be alarmed by the sight of a large plane directly in front of you, seemingly in the middle of the road. Don't worry: the decommissioned DC-8 is merely the frontage of the **California Science Center**'s air and space exhibits gallery (*see right*). Close by is the **Californian African American Museum** (*see right*);

the park's northern frontier, meanwhile, is home to the seven-acre **Rose Garden** (closed Jan-mid Mar). The park's main attraction, though, is also its oldest: the **Natural History Museum of Los Angeles County** (*see p77*).

The south side of the park is dominated by the hulking **Los Angeles Memorial Coliseum**, built in 1923 and the main stadium for the Olympics of both 1932 and 1984. These days, it's used in autumn by the University of Southern California's Trojans football team (*see p238*).

FREE California African American Museum

Exposition Park, 600 State Drive, between S Figueroa Street & S Vermont Avenue (1-213 744 7432, www.caamuseum.org). Metro Expo/Vermont or Expo Park/USC/bus 40, 42, 81, 102, 550/I-110, exit Exposition Boulevard west. **Open** 10am-5pm Tue-Sat; 11am-5pm Sun. **Admission** free. *Parking* $10.

This handsome museum, conference centre and research library focuses on the artistic and historical achievements of African Americans. The permanent exhibit loosely tells the story of African Americans' journey from Africa, through emancipation and into the 21st century, using an assortment of paintings, textiles, photographs, ceremonial objects, personal testimonies and other memorabilia. In addition, curated and travelling exhibitions are held throughout the year, as well as screenings and workshops.

FREE California Science Center

Exposition Park, 700 State Drive, between S Figueroa Street & S Vermont Avenue (1-323 724 3623, www.californiasciencecenter.org). Metro

Towers of Strength

How a bunch of junk became a famous landmark.

When Italian-born tilesetter Sabato (aka Simon) Rodia moved to Watts, the neighbourhood was ethnically mixed. Three decades later, when he left, it was predominantly black and Latino, widely seen as the heart of LA's African American community. In the intervening years, though, Rodia had constructed its single iconic structure, an extraordinary piece of folk art that's one of only a handful of National Historic Landmarks in Los Angeles.

Rodia started work on constructing what have become known as the **Watts Towers** (1765 E 107th Street) shortly after purchasing a triangular lot in the area and moving on to the site in 1921. Using nothing but found objects (salvaged metal rods, cast-off pipe structures, broken bed frames), Rodia sent his towers inching gradually skywards, reinforcing them with steel and cement to prevent interference from both neighbours and the authorities.

Scaling the towers on a window-washer's belt and bucket, Rodia gradually decorated his towers with a patchwork of yet more found materials that inadvertently act as a reliquary of early and mid 20th-century consumer objects. The glass is mostly green and comes from bottles of 7-Up or Canada Dry; the tiles came from Malibu Pottery, where Rodia was employed in the late 1920s. Other objects clearly visible on the towers' coarse, gaudy 'skin' include jewellery, marble and an estimated 25,000 seashells.

The towers' construction, by a single pair of hands over a 33-year span, are part of their legend. But so is their wan, spectral beauty. Like skeletal echoes of Antoni Gaudí's voluptuous Barcelona church steeples, the towers reach for the sky in an elaborate network of spindly, curved tendrils, connected with equally playful, decorous webs. There are 17 of them in all, the tallest stretching 99 feet (30 metres) high.

The locals, though, were never especially supportive of his endeavours. Miscreant kids regularly smashed the towers' glass and tiling; during the war, a rumour even started that Rodia was sending classified information to the Japanese through the towers, which didn't endear him to his neighbours. In 1954, after years of abuse and vandalism, the 75-year-old Rodia abruptly gave the land to a neighbour and moved away.

After Rodia's departure, the towers changed hands several times, but were issued with a demolition order in 1957 on the basis that they were structurally unsound.

A public outcry ensued, and two years later the city agreed to test the towers' stability. A stress load of 10,000 pounds was applied, but they didn't budge an inch… Unlike the crane applying the stress, which buckled under the strain.

It's not all been plain sailing, however. The towers have gradually deteriorated over the years, and were damaged in the 1994 earthquake. For details of tours of the towers, which run from Thursday to Sunday, call 1-213 847 4646.

Expo/Vermont or Expo Park/USC/bus 40, 42, 81, 102, 550/I-110, exit Exposition Boulevard west. **Open** 10am-5pm daily. **Admission** *Museum* free. *IMAX* $5-$8.25. *Temporary exhibits* prices vary. *Parking* $10. **Credit** *IMAX* DC, MC, V.

The California Science Center opened in 1998 in an airy building directly in front of the Rose Garden in Exposition Park. Permanent exhibit galleries include World of Life and Creative World, along with the SKETCH Foundation Gallery air and space exhibits. Ecosystems, the permanent exhibition wing, presents 11 different environments using a combination of hands-on exhibits and live habitats. Adjoining each gallery is a Discovery Room with activities that allow kids and parents to take a closer look at the science.

Exhibit highlights include the Kelp Tank, populated with 1,500 fish, kelp and other marine life; the ever-popular High-Wire Bicycle, which allows the brave to ride a bike along a 1in wire some 43ft (13m) above the ground in order to demonstrate the power of gravity; Tess, the 50ft (15m) body simulator and star of the BodyWorks show; and space capsules from the Mercury, Gemini and Apollo-Soyuz missions. The biggest news in recent years, however, was the arrival of the Space Shuttle Endeavour, in October 2012. It's housed in the Samuel Oschin Space Shuttle Endeavour Display Pavilion for the next few years while the new Samuel Oschin Air and Space Center is built. A timed ticket for the Endeavour Exhibition can be purchased on the Science Center website for a service fee of $2 (or $3 if booked by phone).

There's more to see and do in the Special Exhibits Gallery, which changes exhibits regularly, and in the IMAX cinema, which has a seven-storey-high screen and shows films that complement the exhibits.

FREE Natural History Museum of Los Angeles County

Exposition Park, 900 Exposition Boulevard, between S Figueroa Street & S Vermont Avenue (1-213 763 3466, www.nhm.org). Metro Expo/ Vermont or Expo Park/USC/bus 40, 42, 81, 102, 550/I-110, exit Exposition Boulevard west. **Open** 9.30am-5pm daily. **Admission** $12; $2-$6.50 discounts; free under-2s. *Parking* $10. **Credit** AmEx, DC, Disc, MC, V.

The NHM's original Beaux Arts structure was LA's first museum building, opening with Exposition Park itself back in 1913. Its massive collection spans more than 35 million objects and specimens, making it second in size only to the Smithsonian's. It's an immense place, so it's worth planning your visit. Those with only a little time to spare should head directly to the dazzling collections in the Gem & Mineral Hall, where the exhibits include a 4,644-carat topaz, a 2,200-carat opal sphere and a quartz crystal ball which, with a diameter of 10.9in and a weight of 65lb, is one of the biggest on earth. Other highlights include three old-school diorama halls; the creepy-crawly Insect Zoo; and the Visible Vault, easily the most interesting of the anthropological exhibits.

Some of the exhibits here were showing their age, but things are brighter now that a seven-year, $135 million programme of renovations is finishing; completion is due for summer 2013, to mark the museum's centenary. The skylight that crowns the museum's rotunda has already been restored to beautiful effect, and the Age of Mammals exhibit opened in 2010, followed, in 2011, by the Dinosaur Hall, showcasing more than 300 fossils. An outdoor wilderness exhibit was set to open in summer 2013 too. The website has details of special events; among them is the First Friday programme held on the first Friday night of the month, which features tours, lectures and music.

University of Southern California (USC) & around

The **University of Southern California** is just north of Exposition Park, bounded by Figueroa Street, Exposition Boulevard, Vermont Avenue and Jefferson Boulevard. Established in 1880, the campus has several areas worth exploring, whether alone (maps are available from www.usc.edu or at the campus entrances) or as part of the free 90-minute tours that run on weekdays (call 1-213 740 6605 for details).

Directly north of USC sits the 6,300-capacity **Shrine Auditorium** (665 W Jefferson Boulevard, at Royal Street). Built in 1926, this huge, Moorish structure hosts the annual Screen Actors Guild (SAG) awards in January.

CENTRAL AVENUE

Between the 1920s and the '50s, the stretch of **Central Avenue** between Washington Boulevard and Vernon Avenue was a hub of LA's African community, home to some of the first financial enterprises, theatres, churches and social institutions established exclusively to serve blacks. The road found a measure of nationwide fame for the music that boomed out of its bars and nightclubs: jazz at first, then R&B. This musical heritage is celebrated every summer with the **Central Avenue Jazz Festival** (www.centralavejazz.org), but modern-day Central Avenue is a rather sad place. Many of its buildings and businesses have seen better days, and the African American influence has been partly usurped by Latino culture.

WATTS

After the jazz era, blacks continued migrating south along Central Avenue towards Watts. The area is notorious for the riots of 1965 and 1992, but it is also home to an LA landmark, the **Watts Towers** (*see p74* **Towers of Strength**). The **Watts Towers Arts Center** (1727 E 107th Street, 1-213 847 4646) hosts exhibitions, festivals and concerts; guided tours are also available.

EXPLORE

The Valleys

Over the hills but not far away.

Located directly north of the Hollywood Hills, the
San Fernando Valley is most famous for its girls –
namely, the gum-popping, air-headed Valley Girl,
immortalised by the Frank Zappa song and the
Martha Coolidge movie of the same name. While
The Brady Bunch was being filmed in a split-level
1960s ranch house, other San Fernando backyards
found girls in curls and guys in tight trousers
doing a lot more than playing ball. Paul Thomas
Anderson fictionalised this sordid past (and
present) in *Boogie Nights*.

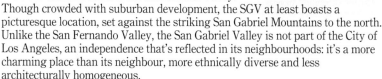

To the east and south is the San Gabriel Valley.
Though crowded with suburban development, the SGV at least boasts a
picturesque location, set against the striking San Gabriel Mountains to the north.
Unlike the San Fernando Valley, the San Gabriel Valley is not part of the City of
Los Angeles, an independence that's reflected in its neighbourhoods: it's a more
charming place than its neighbour, more ethnically diverse and less
architecturally homogeneous.

SAN FERNANDO VALLEY

Just over the hill from West Hollywood via
Laurel Canyon Boulevard is pricey **Studio
City**. It's named after the studio developed in the
area by actor/director Mack Sennett in the 1920s,
although today it's home to a different studio –
CBS – along with industry types and other
wealthy professionals. The area's main drag,
Ventura Boulevard, is increasingly welcoming
interesting, often independent, stores, bars
and restaurants into the fold, which sit nicely
alongside veterans such as Art's Deli (*see p115*).

To the west sit **Sherman Oaks**, once Valley
Girl Central, but now considerably more diverse;
Tarzana, where you'll find fabulously scruffy
rock club **Paladino's** (6101 Reseda Boulevard,
1-818 342 1563); and **Northridge**, most notable
for the Googie-style **First Lutheran Church
of Northridge**, better known as **Life House**
(18355 Roscoe Boulevard, 1-818 885 6861, www.
lifehouse.la), aka the 'First Church of Elroy
Jetson', and for being the site of a powerful
earthquake in 1994. To the north is **Sylmar**,
which boasts the two **Nethercutt Collection**
museums (*see p79*); and **Mission Hills** and
the **Mission San Fernando Rey de España**
(15151 San Fernando Mission Boulevard, 1-818
361 0186), founded in 1797 and rebuilt after the

1971 earthquake; Lenny Bruce and Groucho
Marx are buried at nearby **Eden Memorial
Park** (11500 Sepulveda Boulevard, (1-818 361
7161, www.eden-memorialpark.com).

Further north is **Santa Clarita**, home to
the ever-popular **Six Flags Magic Mountain**
park (*see p79*), while to the west is **Simi
Valley**, home of the **Ronald W Reagan
Presidential Library & Museum** (*see p79*).

The Valley's two main cities, however,
are Glendale and Burbank, which sit more
or less side by side, north of Griffith Park.
Crisply pressed **Glendale** is larger and more
charismatic than tidy **Burbank**. Still, both
are ultimately pretty bland places that bring to
mind Mark Twain's quote that 'Los Angeles is
a great place to live, but I wouldn't want to visit'.
Indeed, Glendale's main attraction is a cemetery:
the **Forest Lawn Memorial Park** (1712 S
Glendale Avenue, 1-800 204-3131, www.forest
lawn.com), the final resting place of celebrities
such as Walt Disney, Errol Flynn, Spencer
Tracy, Nat 'King' Cole, Clark Gable and Michael
Jackson. Glendale is also home to the third-
largest Armenian community outside Armenia,
plus two back-to-back malls (Americana
at Brand and Glendale Galleria; *see p138*).

The film industry's influence runs so deep
in Burbank that it was used as the last name

Santa Monica Mountains.

for Jim Carrey's character in *The Truman Show*. **Warner Brothers** (*see p29*), NBC and Disney have studios here. However, aside from iconic drive-in **Bob's Big Boy** (4211 Riverside Drive) and a few decent bars in the up-and-coming North Hollywood ('NoHo') area to the west, there's not much to see. Better, perhaps, to drive to **Universal Studios** (*see p80*).

Suburbia aside, the San Fernando Valley is the gateway to the wonderful **Santa Monica Mountains**, one of the country's most beautiful and environmentally fragile urban mountain ranges. Separating the valley from the city basin and the ocean, the mountains are dotted with hiking and biking trails, and contain many ranches that once belonged to movie stars and the studios that employed them: there's the **Paramount Ranch** (2903 Cornell Road, off Kanan Road, Agoura, 1-818 597 9192, www.theparamountranch.com), which has stood in for Tombstone and Dodge City and was used for the TV series *Dr Quinn, Medicine Woman*. For more on the area, contact the **Santa Monica Mountains National Recreation Area** (1-805 370 2301, www.nps.gov/samo).

For more information on the area, contact the **Valley Visitors Bureau** (5121 Van Nuys Boulevard, Sherman Oaks, 1-818 379 7000, www.thevalley.net).

FREE Nethercutt Collection

Nethercutt Museum *15151 Bledsoe Street, at San Fernando Road, Sylmar.* **Open** 9am-4.30pm Tue-Sat.
San Sylmar *15200 Bledsoe Street, at San Fernando Road, Sylmar.* **Open** *Tours* 10am, 1.30pm Thur-Sat. Booking essential.

Both *1-818 364 6464, www.nethercuttcollection. org. Bus 94, 794/I-5, exit Roxford Street east.*
Admission free. **Parking** free.
The collection of eccentric cosmetics heirs and philanthropists Dorothy and JB Nethercutt makes for a striking pair of museums. The San Sylmar site holds a collection of old, fancy but functional objects, all in working order: everything from gorgeous old cars and Steuben Glass hood ornaments to French furniture and automated musical instruments. Among the sporadic events are recitals on the Mighty Wurlitzer theatre organ. Nethercutt Museum, meanwhile, provides a handsome home for 100 of the Nethercutts' 230-plus classic cars: Daimlers, Lincolns, Packards and Duesenbergs, all kept in immaculate order.

Ronald W Reagan Presidential Library & Museum

40 Presidential Drive, at Madera Road, Simi Valley (1-800 410 8354, www.reaganlibrary.com). Hwy 118, exit Madera Road south. **Open** 10am-5pm daily. **Admission** $21; $15-$18 discounts; free under-3s. *Parking* free. **Credit** AmEx, DC, Disc, MC, V.
This place is great for fans of the Gipper, but liberals will probably see red. The museum contains an array of exhibits detailing Reagan's childhood and his years in office and supplemented by more general displays covering American history. He is also buried here.

Six Flags Magic Mountain

Magic Mountain Parkway, off I-5, Valencia (Magic Mountain 1-661 255 4100, Hurricane Harbor 1-661 255 452, www.sixflags.com). I-5, exit Magic Mountain Parkway for both parks. **Open** Hours vary by day & by season: call or

---

INSIDE TRACK THEME PARK TIPS

Theme parks in the LA area are popular for a reason, but their sheer scale can be overwhelming. It's virtually impossible to cover any park in its entirety in one day. It's worth going online in advance, therefore, to figure out which rides and attractions you really want to see (bearing in mind, if you're coming with kids, that some have height restrictions). Costs can add up quickly, too, so spend some time investigating the various packages and deals on offer. Also check opening and closing times – many vary on an almost daily basis, and some parks are closed out of season. Two other top tips: bring lots of sunscreen and, unless you really love crowds, avoid peak times, which, as well as most of the summer, include Thanksgiving, Christmas and New Year.

EXPLORE

Huntington Library, Art Collections & Botanical Gardens. *See p82*

check online for full details. *Magic Mountain: Summer* usually from 10.30am daily. *Winter* usually from 10.30am only weekends & school hols. *Hurricane Harbor: Summer* usually from 10.30am daily, only during summer. **Admission** *Magic Mountain* $64.99; free under-2s. *Hurricane Harbor* $38.99; $24.99 discounts; free under-2s. *Parking* $17. **Credit** AmEx, DC, Disc, MC, V. Comprising Magic Mountain and Hurricane Harbor, Six Flags delivers thrills for all but the most joyless and crowd-phobic holidaymakers. The park offers rollercoasters and water rides for every level of screamer: while there are some gentle rides here, the park is most famous for the ones that'll push your heart into your mouth and your lunch on to the person in front of you. It's a raucous place, both on the rides and off them: for very young kids, Disneyland and Universal Studios are better bets.

Perhaps the most terrifying of all the park's rides is the Riddler's Revenge, the world's tallest, longest and fastest stand-up rollercoaster. However, it's got stiff competition, not least from the Green Lantern, the first vertical track spinning coaster in the US. Other highlights include the Colossus, billed as 'the tallest and fastest wooden coaster in the West'; the ludicrous Viper, which soars 188ft (56m) in the air; and X2, a 'fifth-dimensional rollercoaster'. New for 2013 are Full Throttle, with a mind-blowing 160ft

(49m) loop, and LEX LUTHOR: Drop of Doom, the world's tallest drop tower ride. Happily, there are a number of activities suitable for riders of a nervous disposition, among them the gentler-than-it-sounds Canyon Blaster.

Hurricane Harbor, generally open only in summer, is Magic Mountain's smaller, watery cousin. As you might expect, the rides here are a little milder, but there are still thrills to be had: try Tornado, billed as a 'six-storey funnel of fear'.

▶ *Note that many rides have height restrictions, starting at around 48in (1.22m).*

Universal Studios & CityWalk

100 Universal City Plaza, Universal City (1-818 622 4455, www.universalstudioshollywood.com, www.citywalkhollywood.com). Metro Universal City/Studio City/bus 96, 156, 166/US 101, exit Universal Center Drive.
Universal Studios Open Hours vary; call or check online for details. *Summer* usually from 9am daily. *Winter* usually from 10am daily. **Admission** $80; $72 for under 48in; free under-3s. *Parking* $15.
Citywalk Open Hours vary; call or check online for details. Usually from 8am daily. **Admission** free. *Parking* $15.
Both Credit AmEx, DC, Disc, MC, V.

EXPLORE

More than any of its Southern California competitors, Universal Studios is a theme park with a capital 'T'. The theme here, of course, is the movies. The park offers a necessarily selective ramble through the studio's hits and even one or two of its misses; it's difficult to know whether the park is here to promote the movies or vice versa. Either way, it's hard to shake the feeling that you've bought tickets to a colossal marketing exercise.

The rides aren't as exciting as you might expect: certainly, they lack both Disneyland's charm and the sheer terror inspired by Six Flags Magic Mountain. You're here for the illusion of glamour, the silver-screen memories brought back by the rides rather than the rides themselves. Adults and teens will enjoy the Jurassic Park river adventure, while kids of all ages should be tickled by the ride based on *The Simpsons*. Other films brought to something approaching life include *The Mummy* and, bizarrely, *Waterworld*. However, the pick of the themed attractions, for both grown-ups and kids, is the cheeky *Shrek 4-D* movie and the truly terrifying Transformers: The Ride-3D.

Similarly, the studio tour itself is more about association than excitement. Despite all the hype boasting of how you're being let behind the scenes, the closest you'll likely get to seeing some actual action is spying the occasional spark's car parked behind an otherwise faceless sound stage. Still, once you've resigned yourself (and your kids) to a star-free afternoon, there's a great deal to enjoy, from old movie sets seemingly left lying around by careless stagehands, to the cheesily compiled set pieces and a dazzling chase sequence inspired by the Vin Diesel movie *The Fast and the Furious*, as well as King Kong 360 3-D, created by Peter Jackson himself.

Most attractions have the decency to save their souvenir shops until the end. Not here. You can't reach Universal Studios without strolling down CityWalk, a loud, colourful and oppressive pedestrian street crammed with souvenir hawkers and junk-food retailers. If you've got children, don't be too surprised to find your finances severely depleted before you've even reached the gates of the studios.

Note that the prices detailed above are for basic admission only. A large variety of queue-jumping tickets are also available, with prices ranging from $129 for an off-season 'Front of Line' pass to $289 for a VIP ticket.

SAN GABRIEL VALLEY
Pasadena & around

Pasadena is one of the most attractive towns in the region, and one of the few parts of Southern California where the term 'old money' still means something. It was developed in the 1870s and became popular with Midwesterners over the subsequent two decades; indeed, the famous **Tournament of Roses Parade**

(*see p25*) was founded in 1890 as a marketing exercise, an attempt by the city fathers to show off Pasadena's immaculate climate to outsiders. More than a century later, the locals remain immensely proud of their city. And key to the area's continued appeal is its sense of history, and the locals' enthusiasm for preserving it.

The focal point is **Old Town Pasadena** (http://oldpasadena.org), centred on Colorado Boulevard and bounded by N Marengo Avenue, West Del Mar Avenue, South Pasadena Avenue and Green Street. This area is a perfect example of the way in which Pasadena fuses tradition with the 21st century. As recently as the mid 1980s, it was a sorry, run-down picture of boarded-up dereliction. Today, however, packs of teenagers mingle with families and couples in a tidy mix of restored old buildings and new construction. Despite the obvious presence of chains, a number of independent stores and eateries do thrive here, and the district's approachable streetscape is a world away from the Valley mall culture.

This keen preservationist instinct carries over into other parts of Pasadena, both in civic structures such as the grand old **Pasadena City Hall** (100 N Garfield Avenue) and in the handsome houses that line the city's residential corners. Charles and Henry Greene's **Gamble House** (*see p82*) is deservedly the most famous; however, the streets around it, especially **Arroyo Terrace** (designed by the Greenes) and **Grand Avenue**, are lined with similarly delightful century-old homes. A self-guided tour of the area is available from the Gamble House's shop. Other notable residential districts include **Oak Knoll**, especially Hillcrest and Wentworth Avenues, and the **Bungalow Heaven** district, hemmed in by Washington Boulevard, Hill Avenue, Orange Grove Boulevard and Lake Street.

Pasadena also distinguishes itself with its array of visitor attractions, more interesting and varied than any other town in the valley. Among its museums are the **Norton Simon Museum** (*see p83*), the **Pacific Asia Museum** (*see p83*), the **Pasadena Museum of California Art** (*see p84*) and **Kidspace** (*see p83*) – all are worth a peek. The **Tournament House** (*see p84*) offers another window into the area's past; elsewhere, NASA's **Jet Propulsion Laboratory** (*see p82*) and the **Mount Wilson Observatory** (466 Foothill Boulevard, 1-626 440 9016, www.mtwilson.edu) can provide unexpected glimpses of things very far beyond the San Gabriel Valley.

Two pleasant communities adjoin Pasadena. North-west is the picturesque hillside town of **La Cañada Flintridge**, home of the peaceful **Descanso Gardens** (*see p82*). And to the

EXPLORE

south is the wealthy suburb of **San Marino**, developed by land and railroad baron Henry Huntington at the start of the 20th century. Huntington's former estate (*see right*) is open to the public.

Descanso Gardens

1418 Descanso Drive, at Oakwood Avenue & Knight Way, La Cañada Flintridge (1-818 949 4200, www.descansogardens.org). I-210, exit Angeles Crest Hwy. **Open** *9am-4.30pm daily.* **Admission** $8; $3-$6 discounts; free under-4s. *Parking* free. **Credit** DC, MC, V.

This delightful tribute to the horticultural magic of Southern California includes more than 600 varieties of camellia (these are best seen between the middle of February and early May, when there are around 34,000 of the plants in bloom) and some five acres of roses. There are also lilac, orchid, fern and California native plant areas, as well as an oriental tea house donated by the Japanese-American community. Yoga classes are held amid the greenery from 8.30am to 10am, and tram tours run throughout the day.

Gamble House

4 Westmoreland Place, at Walnut Street, Pasadena (1-626 793 3334, www.gamblehouse. org). Bus 267/Hwy 110 to Pasadena (hwy ends at Glenarm Street). **Open** *Tours approx every 20mins, noon-3pm Thur-Sun.* **Admission** $12.50-$13.75; $7-$11 discounts; free under-12s. *Parking* free. **Credit** AmEx, DC, MC, V.

When brothers Charles and Henry Greene moved to Pasadena from Cincinnati in 1893, the Arts and Crafts movement had yet to take hold in California. By the time they built this house in 1908 for the Gamble family (as in Procter & Gamble), their influence had travelled far and wide. This handsome house, on a leafy Pasadena street, is perhaps the leading example of Southern California's 'Craftsman' bungalow style, influenced – in typical fashion – by both Japanese and Swiss architecture. The house was almost sold by Gamble's daughter-in-law in 1962, but when she overheard the prospective buyers discussing their plans to paint everything white, she immediately pulled the home off the market. It's now in the hands of the University of Southern California. More recently, it featured as the home of 'Doc' Brown in the *Back to the Future* trilogy.

Highlights of the informative tours include the nature-themed frieze made from California redwood; Emil Lange's stunning glass doors; and the unexpected presence in the kitchen of the same tiling that was then used on the New York subway. Add in Tiffany lamps and Greene-designed furniture, and it's easy to see how the cost of the home escalated to $60,000 at a time when the average house in the area cost a mere $1,200. The bookshop is strong on architecture, and also offers a sheet detailing many other notable houses in the neighbourhood. Reservations

are highly recommended; buy tickets online for a small discount. Look out for the thought-provoking lectures from November through to May too.

★ Huntington Library, Art Collections & Botanical Gardens

1151 Oxford Road, off Huntington Drive, San Marino (1-626 405 2100, www.huntington.org). Bus 79/Hwy 110 to Pasadena (hwy ends at Glenarm Street). **Open** *Memorial Day-Labor Day* 10.30am-4.30pm Mon, Wed-Fri; 10.30am-4.30pm Sat, Sun. **Admission** $20-$23; $8-$18 discounts; free under-5s. Free to all 1st Thur of mth (tickets required; call 1-800 838 3006). *Parking* free. **Credit** AmEx, DC, Disc, MC, V.

The bequest of entrepreneur Henry E Huntington is now one of the most enjoyable attractions in the Los Angeles region. It's also not a destination that you should attempt to explore in full during a single day: between the art, the library holdings and the spread-eagled outdoor spaces, there's plenty to see, and most of it is best enjoyed at lingering leisure rather than as part of a mad dash.

Once you've paid your admission, you'll be close to the main library, which holds more than six million items and is open only to researchers (apply for credentials in advance of your visit). However, some of its most notable holdings, among them a Gutenberg Bible and the earliest known edition of Chaucer's *The Canterbury Tales*, are always on display in the adjoining exhibition hall, alongside regular themed temporary shows. The art collection is almost as notable as the library's collection. Built in 1910, the main house is home to a very impressive collection of British painting, which includes Gainsborough's *The Blue Boy* alongside works by Blake, Reynolds and Turner. And over in the newer Scott and Erburu Galleries, you'll find a selection of American paintings.

However, despite all these cultural glories, the Huntington's highlights are outdoors in its vast jigsaw of botanical gardens, which are arguably the most glorious in the entire Los Angeles region. The 207 acres of gardens, 120 acres of which are open to the public, are divided into a variety of themes: the Desert Garden, now a century old, is packed with cacti and other succulents; the Shakespeare Garden evokes a kind of Englishness rarely seen in England these days; the Children's Garden is a delightful mix of educational features and entertaining diversions; and the Chinese-themed Garden of Flowing Fragrance is a delicate environment built in part by Chinese artisans. After a $6.8 million upgrade, the quietly, unassumingly magical Japanese Garden reopened in 2012; renovations include the installation of a ceremonial teahouse, donated to the Huntington by the Pasadena Buddhist Temple. *Photos p80.*

FREE Jet Propulsion Laboratory

4800 Oak Grove Drive, north of Foothill Boulevard (1-818 354 4321, www.jpl.nasa.gov). Bus 268/

Hwy 110 to Pasadena (hwy ends at Glenarm Street). **Open** *Tours* call for details. **Admission** free. *Parking* free.

Employing 5,000 people, and equipped with an annual budget of $1.4 billion, the JPL designed, built and now operates NASA's Deep Space Network; it was also responsible for the *Mars Pathfinder* and the *Spirit Rover*'s mission to Mars. Once a week on alternating Mondays/Wednesdays, the lab opens its doors to the public; the two- to two-and-a-half-hour tour begins with a multimedia overview of the setup, after which the public is shown around the Space Flight Operations Facility and the Spacecraft Assembly Facility. Demand is high and security measures mean you must book three weeks in advance. US citizens will need to present a driver's licence, while citizens of other countries must declare their nationality prior to booking and bring a passport and/or green card on the day. For full security and booking details, check the website.

Kidspace Children's Museum

Brookside Park, 480 N Arroyo Boulevard, at W Holly Street, Pasadena (1-626 449 9144, www. kidspacemuseum.org). Bus 267/Hwy 110 to Pasadena (hwy ends at Glenarm Street). **Open** *Sept-May* 9.30am-5pm Tue-Fri; 10am-5pm Sat, Sun. *June-Aug* 9.30am-5pm Mon-Fri; 10am-5pm Sat, Sun. **Admission** $10; free under-1s. *Parking* free. **Credit** AmEx, DC, Disc, MC, V.

Norton Simon Museum.

This popular interactive children's museum features a wide variety of exhibits and entertainment, from the Kaleidoscope entrance to the educational gardens and the Splash Dance water feature in the central courtyard, the perfect way to cool down on a baking Valley afternoon. In summer 2012, the museum unveiled its Galvin Physics Forest, with new hands-on exhibits. Free Family Night is the first Tuesday of every month (except September), from 4pm to 8pm.

FREE Norton Simon Museum

411 W Colorado Boulevard, between N Orange Grove Boulevard & N St John Avenue, Pasadena (1-626 449 6840, www.nortonsimon.org). Bus 180, 181, 256, 380/Hwy 110 to Pasadena (hwy ends at Glenarm Street). **Open** noon-6pm Mon, Wed-Sun. **Admission** $10; $7 discounts; free under-18s. Free to all 6-9pm 1st Thur of mth. *Parking* free. **Credit** AmEx, DC, Disc, MC, V.

The Norton Simon's Gehry-helmed makeover in the late 1990s raised the museum's profile, but it also helped it expand the range of its collection, giving it more space and creating a calm, simple environment in which to display it. And this is a beautifully designed museum, its collection sympathetically mounted and immaculately captioned.

The museum is still best known for its impressive collection of Old Masters, notably pieces by 17th-century Dutch painters such as Rembrandt (a particularly rakish self-portrait), Brueghel and Frans Hals. The French Impressionists are represented by, among others, Monet, Manet and Renoir. Other valuable holdings include a generous array of Degas' underappreciated ballerina bronzes, some excellent modern works – including a haunting Modigliani portrait of his wife, some Diego Rivera paintings, and plenty of works by the so-called Blue Four (Feininger, Jawlensky, Klee and Kandinsky) – and large collections of European prints, Far Eastern art and Buddhist artefacts. After you've checked out the temporary shows, head into the excellent sculpture garden. All told, a terrific museum.

Pacific Asia Museum

46 N Los Robles Avenue, at E Colorado Boulevard West, Pasadena (1-626 449 2742, www.pacific asiamuseum.org). Metro Memorial Park/bus 180, 181, 267, 687/Hwy 110 to Pasadena (hwy ends at Glenarm Street). **Open** 10am-6pm Wed-Sun. **Admission** $9; $7 discounts; free under-11s. Free to all 4th Fri of mth. Half-price if you've visited the Pasadena Museum of California Art *(see p84)* on same day. *Parking* free. **Credit** AmEx, DC, Disc, MC, V.

Art and artefacts from Asia and the Pacific Rim are displayed in the historic Grace Nicholson Building, a re-creation of a northern Chinese palace with a charming Chinese Garden Court to match. Taken from the museum's collection of 14,000 items, the permanent displays include both contemporary and

EXPLORE

traditional Asian arts; they're supplemented by temporary shows, which tend to run for roughly four months at a time. Look out for special events.

Pasadena Convention & Visitors Bureau

300 E Green Street, at S Euclid Avenue, Pasadena (1-626 795 9311, 1-800 307 7977, www.pasadenacal.com). Metro Del Mar/bus 180, 181, 267, 687/Hwy 110 to Pasadena (hwy ends at Glenarm Street). **Open** 8am-5pm Mon-Fri.

Pasadena Museum of California Art

490 East Union Street, between N Los Robles & N Oakland Avenues, Pasadena (1-626 568 3665, www.pmcaonline.org). Metro Memorial Park/bus 180, 181, 267, 687/Hwy 110 to Pasadena (hwy ends at Glenarm Street). **Open** noon-5pm Wed-Sun. **Admission** $7; $5 discounts. Free to all 1st Fri of mth & 3rd Thur 5-8pm. Half-price if you've visited the Pacific Asia Museum on same day. **Parking** free. **Credit** AmEx, DC, MC, V.

An open-air staircase beautified by moody lightplay from an oculus above it creates a striking entrance into this three-storey facility. The museum is dedicated to California art and design from the last 150 years, and often runs several temporary exhibitions simultaneously in its gallery spaces: you might find a collection of paintings by Pasadena Impressionist Benjamin Chambers Brown alongside a show devoted to toy culture. One admission price covers all shows.

FREE Tournament House & the Wrigley Gardens

391 S Orange Grove Boulevard, between W Del Mar & W California Boulevards, Pasadena (1-626 449 4100, www.tournamentofroses.com). Metro Memorial Park/bus 180, 181, 267, 687/Hwy 110 to Pasadena (hwy ends at Glenarm Street). **Open** *Tours* Feb-Aug 2pm, 3pm Thur. **Admission** free. *Parking* free.

Formerly owned by chewing-gum magnate William Wrigley Jr, this grand old mansion is now the official headquarters of the Tournament of Roses Association, which organises the annual Rose Parade and Rose Bowl Game. It's open for tours for six months of the year, and is worth a look as much for its stately gardens as for its handsome and occasionally stunning interior.

Heading east

As you head inland from Pasadena, points of interest become fewer and further between. In Arcadia sits an elegant 1930s racetrack, **Santa Anita Park** (*see p239*), and the **Los Angeles County Arboretum & Botanic Garden** (*see below*). Beyond are acres of suburbia, enlivened only by a handful of older foothill communities along the Foothill Freeway. Both **Sierra Madre** and **Monrovia**, which lie in the shadow of the San Gabriel Mountains, have charming early 20th-century downtown areas.

Continuing east on I-210, you'll eventually reach **Claremont** and the Claremont Colleges, a collection of six educational institutions near East Foothill Boulevard. The town's 'Village' (east of Indian Hill Boulevard, between 1st and 4th Streets) is another delightful downtown area, featuring buildings from the 1920s. South-east of Claremont is **Pomona**, home to California State Polytechnic University and, each autumn, the month-long **LA County Fair** (*see p23*). The area remains an important agricultural centre; you'll see the same giant vegetables and prize-winning pigs as you would in the Midwest.

The area south of Pasadena holds greater variety. The bustling suburbs of **Monterey Park**, **Alhambra** and **San Gabriel** have largely Chinese and Chinese American populations, many of them immigrants from Taiwan and Hong Kong. Forget Chinatown, just north of Downtown LA: this is one of the largest Chinese settlements in the US. The strips of Atlantic Boulevard and Garfield Avenue contain Chinese restaurants of every sort, as well as groceries, bakeries and chemists.

Los Angeles County Arboretum & Botanic Garden

301 N Baldwin Avenue, between W Colorado Boulevard & Campus Drive, Arcadia (1-626 821 3222, www.arboretum.org). Bus 79, 264, 268/ I-210, exit Baldwin Avenue south. **Open** 9am-4.30pm daily. **Admission** $8; $3-$6 discounts; free under-5s. Free to all 3rd Tue of mth. *Parking* free. **No credit cards.**

These gorgeous grounds in Arcadia, very close to the Santa Anita racetrack, have been designed as an educational facility (tours are available), but many people simply come here for a little peace and quiet. You could wander these gardens for hours; many do, taking in tropical forests and waterfalls, trees and fish. There's also a café on site.

EXPLORE

Heading South

A lotus land of glorious beaches and the Happiest Place on Earth.

Orange County feels a million miles away from LA – and it likes it that way. Here, clifftop mansions still cost several million dollars, despite the recession, and retirees both young and old really do spend their time shopping, eating and going to the beach. (Their main problem is deciding which stretch of immaculate sand to park their plastic bodies on.) Elsewhere, there's urban grit in the form of San Pedro and Long Beach, both of which have spruced up of late and both of which offer genuine points of cultural interest, including a Latin art museum, an aquarium and a ship that may or may not be haunted.

The South Bay & Long Beach

THE SOUTH BAY

El Segundo to Redondo Beach

Getting to the South Bay is half the fun. The beachside Vista del Mar road starts about a mile south of **Marina del Rey**, off Culver Avenue at Dockweiler State Beach. Zip past LAX and you're in the district of **El Segundo**. The best non-aquatic attraction here is an old-fashioned cinema: the fabulous **Old Town Music Hall** (140 Richmond Street, 1-310 322 2592), which features pre-1960s movies and organ concerts on Fridays through Sundays.

Continue south on Vista del Mar (which becomes Highland Avenue) until you reach Manhattan Beach Boulevard and then make a right towards the ocean. This is the heart of **Manhattan Beach**, formerly a low-key, quasi-bohemian town that's been transformed over the last half-decade into an affluent, casually fashionable pocket of LA. The pedestrianised shopping streets hold more than their share of independent stores, but no business better epitomises modernised Manhattan Beach than the **Shade Hotel** (1221 N Valley Drive; *see p183*), an unexpectedly sleek boutique. The beach itself is less eccentric than Venice but also less people-crazed than Santa Monica; its fame is drawn from its status as the spiritual home of beach volleyball.

The surfside flavour continues south into nearby **Hermosa Beach** and **Redondo Beach**, the latter with one of the area's most developed piers in the shape of King Harbor (at the end of Portofino Way). Purists might find its shops, restaurants, fish markets and marina rather cheesy, but Redondo is the most family-oriented of the South Bay's beaches.

Palos Verdes & San Pedro

One of the best drives in Southern California is the loop around the scenic Palos Verdes Peninsula. Take the Pacific Coast Highway (Highway 1, aka the PCH) south to Palos Verdes Boulevard, go south again to Palos Verdes Drive West, along Paseo del Mar and then to Palos Verdes Drive South. On the way, stop at the lovely glass-and-stone **Wayfarers Chapel** (5755 Palos Verdes Drive South, 1-310 377 1650, www.wayfarers chapel.org), the most visited building by architect Lloyd Wright (Frank's son), and the **South Coast Botanic Garden** (26300 Crenshaw Boulevard, 1-310 544 1948, www. southcoastbotanicgarden.org); both are open until 5pm every day.

And ritzy Palos Verdes shares the peninsula with one of LA's most colourful working-class communities: **San Pedro**, traditionally the home of fishermen, dockers, Navy staff, immigrants and the massive Port of Los Angeles. It's a surprisingly charismatic little place, proudly awash with reminders of its history but also possessed of a quietly tangible

EXPLORE

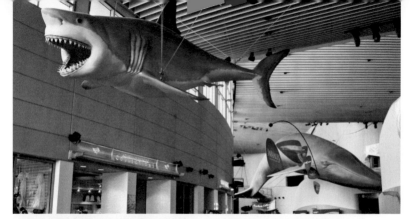

Aquarium of the Pacific.

ambition to smarten itself up a little: witness
the handsome mock-vintage tram cars that
run along the waterfront (Fri, Sat, Sun, and
the rest of the week when cruise ships are in
port). Also here is World War II battleship
USS Iowa, (1-877 446 9261, http://pacificbattle
ship.com), which opened to the public as a
museum in July 2012.

Downtown San Pedro is centred on 6th
Street between Pacific Avenue and Harbor
Boulevard, dotted with cute independent
shops and restaurants, but the highlight is
the **Warner Grand Theatre** (478 W 6th
Street, 1-310 548 7672, www.warnergrand.org),
a restored 1931 movie palace that screens
classic films and stages occasional concerts.
Close at hand, just on the waterfront, is the
Los Angeles Maritime Museum (*see p87*).

Head south from Downtown along S Gaffey
Street and you'll eventually reach **Angels
Gate Park**. The views from the top are
fantastic, arching out eastwards over industrial
San Pedro, the harbour, the broad sweep of
Cabrillo Beach, the Frank Gehry-designed
Cabrillo Marine Aquarium (*see right*) and
the isolated **Angels Gate Lighthouse**. Some
of the best views to the south, meanwhile, are
accessed from the **Friendship Bell**: presented
by South Korea to the United States on the
occasion of the latter's bicentennial in 1976,
it's housed in a traditional Korean pavilion.

Across the park is **Fort McArthur**, a
slightly bedraggled and dissociated collection
of buildings that are mostly closed to the
public. Further south is one of the area's
most charming buildings: the **Point Fermin
Lighthouse** (807 W Paseo del Mar, 1-310
241 0684, www.pointferminlighthouse.org,
closed Mon), a gentle wooden house from 1874
that's unexpectedly topped with a lighthouse
tower. Look out, too, for the mysterious,
haunting 'Sunken City', a formerly wealthy
neighbourhood that effectively slid into the
ocean during the 1920s and '30s.

FREE **Cabrillo Marine Aquarium**
*3720 Stephen M. White Drive, at Pacific Avenue,
San Pedro (1-310 548 7562, www.cabrillomarine
aquarium.org). I-110, exit Harbor Boulevard west.*
Open noon-5pm Tue-Fri; 10am-5pm Sat, Sun.
Admission free; donations requested. *Parking
free-$1/hr.* **No credit cards**.
Dedicated to Southern Californian marine life,
Cabrillo Marine Aquarium is friendly, low-key and
home to an Aquatic Nursery, Exploration Center,
Marine Research Library, a hands-on tidal pool
exhibit and 30 ocean-life tanks. Special seasonal
events include two-hour whale-watching trips,
occasional guided walks to the tidal pools at Point
Fermin Marine Life Refuge and grunion runs (held
during the migrating season of this small, pencil-
sized fish).

Los Angeles Maritime Museum
Berth 84, end of W 6th Street, San Pedro (1-310 548 7618, www.lamaritimemuseum.org). I-110, exit Harbor Boulevard west. **Open** 10am-5pm Tue-Sun. **Admission** $3; $1 discounts. *Parking* free. **No credit cards.**
The largest maritime museum in the state contains a potted history of fishing in California, the story of San Pedro's canning industry, and an array of model boats and ships. Check online for details of temporary shows, which cover related topics. The handsome 1940s streamline moderne building that houses the museum once acted as a ferry terminal.

Long Beach

The Long Beach of popular imagination is one of dockers, deadbeats and cops debating what they should do with all the drunken sailors. But since the factories closed and Navy work dwindled in the 1980s, it's changed beyond recognition. The area is smarter than it's ever been, and more cultured. However, those in search of its old edge can still find it: turf wars between rival black, Latino and Cambodian gangs keep up tensions.

Long Beach's metamorphosis from blue-collar grittiness to white-collar tidiness is most tangible along **Ocean Boulevard**. However, the broad, near-waterside sweep of street deserves better than the collection of flat-pack modern skyscrapers that line it. Familiar hotels and financial institutions sit in familiar-looking buildings; were it not for the aroma of salty sea air, you could be in any Middle American city. By far the most charismatic building is the unexpected, French Gothic-styled **Villa Riviera** apartment building (800 E Ocean Boulevard), completed just before the Depression and spruced up by developers a few years ago.

Long Beach's two primary tourist attractions sit to the south of Ocean Boulevard, alongside or on the water. The excellent **Aquarium of the Pacific** (*see right*) is at Rainbow Harbor, along with the **Pike at Rainbow Harbor**, a newish retail development (aside from lacklustre chains, there's a decent AVIA hotel); while the **Queen Mary** (*see p88*) ocean liner is moored across the Queensway Bay Bridge. North of Ocean Boulevard, commerce is centred on Pine Avenue, though the shops are generally less interesting than the historic buildings that house them: look out, in particular, for the handsome **Farmers & Merchants Bank** at the north-east corner of Pine and 3rd Streets, and the old **Press-Telegram Building** at Pine and 6th, expected to be converted into apartments. East of here, at the corner of Alamitos Avenue and 7th Street, sits the **Museum of Latin American Art** (*see p88*).

Just east of Downtown Long Beach is the **Long Beach Museum of Art** (2300 E Ocean Boulevard, 1-562 439 2119, www.lbma.org), whose attractions include some notable Californian works of art as well as a cultured roster of temporary exhibits. Further east, Ocean Boulevard turns into E Livingston Drive and then leads into the neighbourhood of **Belmont Shore**. The stretch of E 2nd Street east of Livingston is worth a look for its interesting shops and restaurants, such as independent record store **Fingerprints** (No.4612; *see p161*). North of Downtown, the Bixby Knolls neighbourhood is home to such cultural draws as the 1844 **Rancho Los Cerritos** (4600 Virginia Road, 1-562 570 1755, www.rancholoscerritos.org, closed Mon, Tue), one of the last surviving two-storey adobe houses in Southern California, and the **Long Beach Shakespeare Company** (4250 Atlantic Avenue, 1-562 997 1494, www.lbshakespeare.org).

★ Aquarium of the Pacific
100 Aquarium Way, at Shoreline Drive (1-562 590 3100, www.aquariumofpacific.org). Metro 1st Street/I-710, exit Shoreline Drive east. **Open** 9am-6pm daily. **Admission** $25.95; $14.95-$22.95 discounts. *Parking* $8. **Credit** AmEx, DC, MC, V.
Dedicated as much to education as entertainment, this spectacular aquarium more than justifies the drive down to Long Beach, especially if the alternative is the razzle-dazzle of San Diego's considerably pricier SeaWorld. Inevitably, the Shark Lagoon is the most popular exhibit; other highlights include feeding the birds in the colourful Lorikeet Forest aviary. The theme for 2013 is Ocean Exploration, with new shows and an exhibit entitled Wonders of the Deep set to debut as this guide went to press. Much of the rest of the aquarium is divided geographically: loveable sea lions in the Southern California/Baja section, exotic fish in the Tropical Pacific area, and sea otters, jellies and other cold-water critters in the Northern Pacific. If the real thing isn't enough for the kids, they may enjoy an animated and exaggerated version of the same in the shape of *Turtle Vision 4-D* ($4). Visitors can also embark on daily boat cruises and behind-the-scenes tours through combo tickets.

EXPLORE

INSIDE TRACK ON THE BUSES
Buses in Long Beach include a free 'Passport' shuttle service, which connects some of the city's major sights, including the Aquarium of the Pacific and the *Queen Mary*. For full details, see www.lbtransit.com. For up-to-date information on buses elsewhere in Orange County, visit www.octa.net.

Long Beach Area Convention & Visitors Bureau
301 E Ocean Boulevard, Suite 1900, at Long Beach Boulevard (1-562 436 3645, www.visitlongbeach.com). Metro Transit Mall/I-710, exit Shoreline Drive east. **Open** 8am-5pm Mon-Fri.

★ Museum of Latin American Art
628 Alamitos Avenue, at E 6th Street (1-562 437 1689, www.molaa.com). Metro 5th Street/I-710, exit Alamitos Avenue north. **Open** 11am-5pm Wed, Fri-Sun; 11am-9pm Thur. **Admission** $9; $6 discounts; free under-12s. Free to all Sun. *Parking* free. **Credit** AmEx, DC, MC, V.

MoLAA is located on land that once housed the Balboa Amusement Producing Company, the most productive silent film studio of its day. Founded in 1996, MoLAA is the only museum in the US exclusively dedicated to modern and contemporary Latin American art. An expansion in 2007, designed by architect Manuel Rosen, resulted in eye-catching additions to the museum that more than doubled its total exhibition space and added a large sculpture garden.

The core of the museum is its permanent collection, now numbering over 1,300 works of art from Mexico, Central and South America and the Spanish-speaking Caribbean. The Project Room gallery features installations and exhibitions of cutting-edge Latin American artists. A range of temporary shows and a programme of special events provide added interest, as does Café Viva, serving Latin American dishes. A lovely day out.

Queen Mary
1126 Queens Highway (1-562 435 3511, www.queenmary.com). Metro Transit Mall, then bus or taxi, I-405, then I-710 south. **Open** 10am-6pm Mon-Thur; 10am-7pm Fri-Sun.. **Admission** $24.95-$75; $14.95-$24.95 reductions. *Parking* free 0-30mins; $3 31mins-1hr; $12 more than 1hr. **Credit** AmEx, DC, Disc, MC, V.

This grand old ocean liner disproves F Scott Fitzgerald's contention that there are no second acts in American lives. Constructed by Clydeside shipbuilders John Brown & Company in the 1930s, the *Queen Mary* sailed the Atlantic for three decades before easing into a second existence as a tourist attraction. Most of its appeal comes courtesy of the self-guided tours, which afford porthole views of the ways in which moneyed guests might have spent their leisurely weeks crossing the ocean alongside similar glimpses of the life enjoyed by the boat's crew. Look out for the displays of archive photographs, and be sure to have a drink in the gorgeous, recently restored Observation Bar, an art deco gem. In addition to self-guided audio tours, there are several other tours, some of which run in the evening (check the website for details), as well as popular exhibits such as Diana: Legacy of a Princess, which debuted in 2012. And if you really like the place, you can spend the night in one of the cabins: the ship doubles as a hotel *(see p184)*.

Orange County
THE SOUTH COAST

Just south of the LA County border, **Seal Beach** and **Sunset Beach** begin the 50-mile stretch of beach bliss that is coastal Orange County, flanked in its entirety by the Pacific Coast Highway (aka PCH, or Highway 1). Alongside its almost immaculate sandbar, major sights are few and far between: Seal Beach is notable only for the presence of a 9,000-resident retirement community called Leisure World, while Sunset Beach's sole claim to fame is the epoch-definingly abysmal soap opera of the same name that it inspired in the 1990s. It's really all about location, location, location: time your visit right, and you'll see why Sunset Beach got its name.

The real OC action starts south of here in **Huntington Beach**, an altogether livelier pocket of beach-bum culture. Hang out at the pier or on the sand and you'll see how the city got its nickname of 'Surf City'. From dawn to dark, surfers head here in search of the perfect wave, before retreating to a regenerated and slightly anodyne Main Street that's lined with surf-gear stores and buzzing bars and restaurants with names like the Longboard and Baja Sharkeez. There's even a surfing museum here *(see p89)*.

South of here, **Newport Beach** is a more intriguing proposition. Southern California's moneyed leisure classes cluster in the lavish

Museum of Latin American Art.

homes that overlook **Newport Harbor**, popping over to the upscale **Fashion Island** open-air mall (*see p140*) to pick up some treats. However, things are considerably earthier on the stretches of Balboa and Newport Boulevards between 21st and 30th Streets, a mix of smart-ass stores, biker-friendly bars and old-school restaurants such as the **Crab Cooker** (2200 Newport Boulevard). This is the sunny, mellow and pedestrian-friendly **Balboa Peninsula**, home to an iconic Ferris wheel and the **ExplorOcean/Newport Harbor Nautical Museum** (600 East Bay Avenue, 1-949 675 8915, www.nhnm.org, open most days, but call first to check), which is set to expand over the next few years. It's linked to the man-made **Balboa Island** by a regular ferry service. Grab a Balboa Bar ice-cream as you wander the island's lovely streets.

Inland of Newport, **Costa Mesa** is known chiefly for the mammoth **South Coast Plaza** mall (*see p141*) and nearby **Segerstrom Center for the Arts** (*see p232*). Further down the coast, **Laguna Beach** began as an artists' colony and is now the home of the admired **Laguna Art Museum** (307 Cliff Drive, 1-949 494 8971, www.lagunaartmuseum. org). With its pick-up basketball and volleyball games, Main Beach offers excellent people-watching. A little further south, **San Juan Capistrano** is famous for the swallows that return to **Mission San Juan Capistrano** (1-949 234 1300, www.missionsjc.com) each spring, although the beautifully maintained structure is worth visiting on its own account. And at the county's end, **San Clemente** has all the sun and waves but few of the crowds of its neighbours.

International Surfing Museum

411 Olive Avenue, between Main & 5th Streets, Huntington Beach (1-714 960 3483, www.surfing-museum.org). Metro 5th Street/I-405, exit Beach Boulevard south. **Open** noon-5pm Mon, Wed-Fri; noon-9pm Tue; 11am-6pm Sat, Sun. **Admission** $2; free under-12s. **Credit** (over $10) MC, V. *Parking* free.

This small museum honours Duke Kahanamoku, the godfather of surfing, and celebrates surf music, surf life-saving and – of course – surf babes. Temporary exhibits come and go like the waves, but there's usually something here to see. The museum is staffed with volunteers who are full of surfing stories, some of which may actually be true.

Anaheim & inland

An archetype of both the sunny Southern Californian lifestyle and the suburban American dream, the populous city of **Anaheim** is dominated by one landmark:

Queen Mary.

Disneyland (*see p90*), open since 1955 and still the engine that drives the area's economy. Away from the Happiest Place on Earth, the town holds little of interest, although the two local sports teams – baseball's **Angels** (*see p237*) and the hockey-playing **Ducks** (*see p240*) – draw impressively loyal crowds.

The towns around Anaheim are similarly short on charisma, although there are some notable sights amid the miles of featureless residential and commercial sprawl. North-west of Anaheim is **Buena Park**, home to the old-fashioned theme-park attractions of **Knott's Berry Farm** (*see p91*). To the north is **Fullerton**, enlivened by the presence of California State University. And further east is Yorba Linda, where you'll find the **Richard Nixon Library & Birthplace** (*see p91*).

South-west of Anaheim, the town of **Westminster** is notable for the presence of what's reputed to be the largest Vietnamese community outside Vietnam. The Little Saigon neighbourhood has a number of Vietnamese food shops and restaurants; **S Vietnamese Fine Dining** (545 Westminster Mall Drive, 1-714 898 5092) is the smartest and probably the best.

Conversely, nearby **Santa Ana** is a distinctly Latino city. Strolling along busy 4th Street between French and Ross Streets, with its colourful storefronts and hum of Spanish, you could almost believe you were walking through a small city in Mexico (or, at least, in East LA). The excellent **Bowers Museum of Cultural Art** (2002 N Main Street, 1-714 567 3600, www.bowers.org) has a strong Native American collection. Further north, at 2500 Main Street, you can't miss the Arquitectonica-designed black cube that

EXPLORE

is the kid-friendly **Discovery Science Center** (1-714 542 2823, www.discovery cube.org), which contains more than 120 interactive exhibits.

Anaheim/Orange County Visitor & Convention Bureau

800 W Katella Avenue, at Harbor Boulevard (1-714 765 8888, www.anaheimoc.org). **Open** 8am-5pm Mon-Fri.

★ Disneyland

1313 S Harbor Boulevard, between Katella Avenue & Ball Road, Anaheim (1-714 781 4565, www.disneyland.com). I-5, exit Disneyland Drive.
Disneyland Open hours vary: call or check website for details. *Summer* usually 8am-midnight daily. *Winter* usually 9am-8pm Mon-Thur; 8am-midnight Fri, Sat; 9am-9pm Sun.
California Adventure Open hours vary: call or check website for details. *Summer* usually 10am-10pm daily. *Winter* usually 10am-8pm Mon-Thur; 10am-10pm Fri-Sun.
Both Admission *1 park for 1 day* $87; $81 discounts; free under-3s. *Both parks for 1 day* $125; $119 discounts; free under-3s. Call or check online for details of multi-day tickets. *Parking* $15.
Credit AmEx, DC, Disc, MC, V.
The longstanding Disneyland resort isn't just a set of theme parks: it's a spectacular piece of pop art that's as bright or as dark as you'd like it to be. Incorporating two parks – the nearly 60-year-old, near-mythic Disneyland, plus the younger and less celebrated Disney's California Adventure – the resort calls itself 'The Happiest Place on Earth'.

Certainly, Disney does all it can to get you in the right mood. Disneyland isn't so much a park as its own separate world; there are even three Disney-operated hotels (*see p184*) in the resort, so you need not have the illusion shattered at the end of the day. The hotels, though, do bring to attention the main drawback to spending time here: the sheer expense. You can save hundreds of dollars staying at one of the non-Disney hotels just outside the property, and you may need to do so in order to afford the steep prices of food, drink and admission. It's worth noting, though, that ticket prices drop if you visit for multiple days, recommended if you want to get a real feel for the place and enjoy all the rides.

Both parks have dozens of dining spots, with cuisine ranging from burgers and pizza to pastas and seafood. Still, you may want to dine at Downtown Disney, a pedestrian-only avenue of nightclubs (including a House of Blues) and restaurants between the two parks. It's not that the food is that much better, but if you're going to be paying Disney's high prices, you might need a drink or two in order to soften the blow: liquor sales were banned from Disneyland by Walt himself, citing the undesirable 'carnie atmosphere' booze might have created, and alcohol remains banned from the park itself.

Disneyland.

The other main demerit against Disneyland is the crowds: they can be overwhelming, particularly in summer and, unexpectedly, on Christmas Day. (Top tip: few visit on Super Bowl Sunday.) But the crowds can't be helped, and they're very unlikely to improve: Disneyland is popular for a reason.

Disneyland

Disneyland is packed with must-do attractions spread over seven 'lands', all immaculately themed in every detail. **Main Street USA** embodies turn-of-the-19th-century America, while **Frontierland** takes on Westward expansion (the John Wayne version) and **New Orleans Square** is exactly like its namesake – only without the poverty. **Adventureland** offers thrills of the jungle variety; **Tomorrowland** is a kitschily charming look into the future; **Critter Country** is the wooded home of Winnie the Pooh and Br'er Rabbit; and **Fantasyland** is where Disney's animated films come to life. As for the iconic mouse, you're most likely to find him scurrying about with his pals in **Mickey's Toontown**.

The secret of Disneyland's charm lies in its special history. Unlike the company's other parks, it was largely designed by Walt himself, and it's the only one in which he ever set foot. As a result, Disneyland is practically a biography of its creator's life, if you know where to look. Try reading the names in Main Street's upper-level windows; you'll find many of Disney's collaborators and artists listed. And in Frontierland, you'll find the petrified tree Walt once gave his wife as an anniversary present.

But most people, of course, are here for the rides. Among the best are **Space Mountain** (located in Tomorrowland), a legitimately thrilling indoor roller-coaster ride through 'deep space'; the epic **Indiana**

Jones Adventure (in Adventureland), based on the Spielberg adventure movies; **Pirates of the Caribbean** (in New Orleans Square), the basis for the hit Johnny Depp film franchise and one of the most detail-packed and atmospheric rides in the park; and the **Matterhorn** (in Fantasyland), a breakneck bobsled ride around and through a scaled-down replica of the Swiss peak. The popular **Star Tours** thrill ride/galactic excursion added all-new 'destinations', viewed through 3D glasses, in 2011.

Beyond that, there are dozens of carnival-style 'dark' rides, boat trips, rollercoasters, flume rides and Audio-Animatronics shows, many of them wonderfully charismatic and touchingly old-fashioned. If anything defines Disneyland, it's the human touch that's so obviously been lavished on many of its featured rides and attractions. Certainly, it's difficult to imagine Universal Studios retaining anything as charming as the **It's a Small World** boat ride or the fabulous **Enchanted Tiki Room**.

Disney's California Adventure

Located in a former car park, this decent little enterprise is no match for Disneyland in terms of size or attention to detail, but it does a decent job of celebrating the geography, culture and history of its namesake state. Also, unlike Disneyland, it serves alcohol, and has done so since opening day. A $1.1 billion renovation of the park was completed in 2013 with the introduction of a new Buena Vista Street entryway and the spectacular **Cars Land**, inspired by the movie *Cars* and featuring three new attractions including **Radiator Springs Racers**. Other new attractions, which opened earlier in the renovation timeline, are **Toy Story Midway Mania**, an interactive ride/video game, **World of Color**, an after-dark water and special effects show, and **The Little Mermaid: Ariel's Undersea Adventure**, a next generation 'dark ride' in the Disneyland Fantasyland tradition.

While DCA doesn't have anything as engrossing as Pirates of the Caribbean, it does feature some decent rides. The **Twilight Zone Tower of Terror**, a special effects-packed 'drop'-ride based on the classic TV show and housed in the **Hollywood Land** section of the park, is worth a look, as is **Soarin' over California**, a beautiful flight simulator. Soarin' over California is located in the **Condor Flats** section, itself split up into separate areas that pay homage to (among other places) San Francisco and the Wine Country. The highlight of the **Paradise Pier** section, meanwhile, is the **California Screamin'** rollercoaster, the tallest and fastest coaster ever built in a Disney park. Not every ride is suitable for kids of all ages, but very young children are welcome in **A Bug's Land**.

★ Knott's Berry Farm

8039 Beach Boulevard, at La Palma Avenue, Buena Park (1-714 220 5200, www.knotts.com). I-5, exit Beach Boulevard south.

Knott's Berry Farm Open hours vary; call or check website for details. **Admission** $59.99; $30.99 discounts; free under-3s. Call or check online for details of multi-day tickets. **Soak City Open** Late May-mid Sept; call or check website for details. **Admission** $34.99; $24.99 discounts; free under-3s. Call or check website for details of multi-day tickets. **Both Parking** $15. **Credit** AmEx, DC, Disc, MC, V.

Knott's Berry Farm started as a farm selling the home-made preserves of one Mrs Cordelia Knott. Although Ma Knott is long gone, her jams are still on sale. But on the whole, Knott's Berry Farm seems to have realized that it can't get by on nostalgia alone: there seems to have been a concerted effort to bring this once old-fashioned enterprise up to date.

Some charming remnants of the park's early years remain: most notably in the **Ghost Town** section, which contains a number of buildings that have been transplanted from old mining towns. The continued presence of Snoopy as the park's mascot is another gentle nod to tradition (younger visitors in particular love the Charlie Brown Speedway, part of Camp Snoopy). Ultimately, though, the thrill-seekers win out over the sentimentalists thanks to a number of water rides, the stomach-churning **Xcelerator**, and rollercoasters such as the **Sierra Sidewinder** and the **Pony Express** and, new for summer 2013, the 52ft-high **Coast Rider**.

Next door to the Berry Farm sits **Soak City**, a mammoth water park that's open in summer. Combination tickets are available for the two attractions; check online for more information, and for details of the exact opening times of both parks.

Richard Nixon Library & Birthplace

18001 Yorba Linda Boulevard, at Imperial Highway, Yorba Linda (1-714 993 5075, www. nixonfoundation.org). Hwy 90, exit Yorba Linda Boulevard west. **Open** 10am-5pm Mon-Sat; 11am-5pm Sun. **Admission** $11.95; $4.75-$8.50 discounts; free under-6s. *Parking* free. **Credit** AmEx, DC, Disc, MC, V.

Tricky Dickie is remembered chiefly for two ignominious events: his defeat at the hands of John F Kennedy in 1960, and the Watergate scandal that led to him becoming the only American president to resign his post. Both events are discussed in this museum, housed on the site where Nixon was born in January 1913; other highlights include a rare 1823 facsimile of the Declaration of Independence and a gallery devoted to America's space programme. Nixon and wife Pat are enjoying their afterlives in the gardens. A new exhibit celebrating the centenary of his birth – Patriot. President. Peacemaker. (http://nixon100.org) – runs throughout 2013, and possibly beyond.

▶ *Nixon's western White House, the Spanish-inspired Casa Pacifica, can be seen from the beach at San Clemente (see p89).*

EXPLORE

Consume

Restaurants

Food, glorious food.

When it comes to restaurants in Los Angeles, nobody knows it all. Indeed, nobody even knows most of it. The city's dining scene is constantly evolving, with restaurants seeming to spring up from nowhere overnight and others shutting up shop forever, victims of the economy or a bad location. The good news is that LA now offers some of the best cuisine in the country, from the high end of the price scale (hotel restaurants, in particular, have impressed recently) to the low end (the city's fabled ethnic eateries remain consistently reliable). The downside, however, is that as soon as a restaurant gets a white-hot reputation, the chef is besieged with offers from investors, and often leaves to open a new place. Most of the following should keep going strong into the foreseeable future, but it's worth checking in advance if you have your heart set on a particular chef or dish. Also visit www.timeout.com/los-angeles for reviews and roundups of the latest and best restaurants and bars.

INSIDE INFORMATION

Always book in advance if possible, and be sure to phone ahead if you're running late. Many restaurants take reservations via online services such as www.opentable.com, but no restaurant books all its tables in this way: if you call, you might get into a place that the internet claims is full. Even with a reservation, there's often a wait: if you have theatre tickets or other time constraints, let the host know when you arrive and advise your server as you order.

Some restaurants that double as nightspots increase the volume of the music and dim the lights at a certain point in the evening. If you suspect this might happen, ask to be seated in a quiet area. And although the term 'California casual' was invented here, don't push your luck: some of the finer eateries draw the line at shorts and, in rare instances, jeans. Smoking is banned in all restaurants, including outdoor patios.

Many restaurants and cafés provide valet parking. It's often worth the expense

as it beats driving around fruitlessly trying to find a parking spot on the street.

If you're happy with the service, tip at least 15 per cent; anything less is taken as severe criticism. A few restaurants add a service charge, but most are decent enough to inform diners before they total the bill.

Please note that prices given throughout this chapter are for an average main course. We've used the $ symbol to indicate operations offering particularly good value: restaurants with main courses or tapas for around $10 or less (exclusive of tax).

SANTA MONICA & THE BEACH TOWNS

Malibu

Inn of the Seventh Ray

128 Old Topanga Canyon Road, at Riding Lane, Topanga (1-310 455 1311, www.innoftheseventh ray.com). I-10, exit PCH north. **Open** 11.30am-3pm, 5.30-10pm Mon-Fri; 10.30am-3pm, 5.30-10pm Sat; 9.30am-3pm, 5.30-10pm Sun. **Main courses** *Lunch* $15. *Dinner* $30. **Credit** AmEx, DC, MC, V.
Californian
This famous hippie haven has gone haute cuisine, but it hasn't lost touch with its roots: stylish vegan

❶ Blue numbers given in this chapter correspond to the location of restaurants on the street maps. *See pp310-315.*

CONSUME

dishes sit with the likes of hoisin-glazed lamb belly with tamari barley and apple cider vinaigrette. Sunday brunch is great, especially the wholegrain Belgian waffles, and the romantic garden setting has to be seen to be believed. Allow extra time: the inn is accessible only by a two-lane road that can be slow going. Closed Mondays in winter.

Moonshadows

20356 Pacific Coast Highway, west of Big Rock Drive (1-310 456 3010, www.moonshadows malibu.com). Bus 534/I-10, exit PCH north. **Open** 11.30am-3.30pm, 4.30-10.30pm Mon-Thur; 11.30am-3.30pm, 4.30pm-midnight Fri, Sat; 11am-3.30pm, 4.30-10.30pm Sun. *Dinner* $28. **Credit** AmEx, DC, MC, V. **Seafood**
A few years back, Moonshadows made changes to both its menu and its decor in an attempt to attract a younger crowd, but people head here for the same reason they always have: to dine on seafood while enjoying unparalleled views of the ocean. The simple dishes are still the best.

★ Nobu

22706 Pacific Coast Highway, east of Sweetwater Canyon Drive (1-310 317 9140, www.nobu restaurants.com). Bus 534/I-10, exit PCH north. **Open** 5.45-10pm Mon-Thur, Sun; 5.45-11pm Fri, Sat. **Main courses** $29. **Credit** AmEx, DC, MC, V. **Japanese**
Formerly housed in the Malibu Country Mart, chef Nobu Matsuhisa's relocated restaurant, overlooking Surfrider Beach and the Malibu Pier, is so close to the beach you can see the footprints in the sand. Nobu's minimalist aesthetic – wood panelling, no tablecloths – creates an understated feel that complements its environment; the menu is as stellar as its surroundings. The WeHo location is, if anything, more glam, attracting a celeb crowd on a nightly basis.
Other locations 903 N La Cienega Boulevard, West Hollywood (1-310 657 5711).

Santa Monica

Galley

2442 Main Street, between Ocean Park Boulevard & Hollister Avenue (1-310 452 1934, www.the galleyrestaurant.net). Bus SM1, SM2, SM8, SM10/I-10, exit 4th/5th Street south. **Open** 5-10pm Mon-Sat; 1-10pm Sun. **Main courses** $28. **Credit** AmEx, DC, Disc, MC, V. **Map** p310 A4 ❶ **American**
During the 75-plus years it's been in business, the oldest restaurant in Santa Monica has accumulated an amiable clutter of nautical junk lit by garish fairy lights, not to mention a cluster of jocular local characters at the bar. Steaks and seafood are decent, and the house special salad dressing is legendary.

★ Huckleberry

1014 Wilshire Boulevard, at 10th Street (1-310 451 2311, www.huckleberrycafe.com). Bus 2, 20/ I-10, exit Lincoln Boulevard south. **Open** 8am-8pm Mon-Fri; 8am-5pm Sat, Sun. **Main courses** $12. **Credit** AmEx, MC, V. **Map** p310 B2 ❷ **American**

CONSUME

Tar & Roses. *See p97.*

CONSUME

Superba Snack Bar. *See p98.*

Huckleberry is a local institution. And for one good reason, namely husband-and-wife team Josh Loeb and Zoe Nathan's menu of seasonal, farmers' market produce. From the Verve Coffee Roasters coffee to the baked goods to the sandwiches to the salads, everything is outstanding. It's always packed, so expect to share a table. Loeb and Nathan also run nearby Rustic Canyon (1119 Wilshire Boulevard, 1-310 393 7050, www.rusticcanyonwinebar.com), Milo & Olive (see p97) and Sweet Rose Creamery at the Brentwood Country Mart (see p134 **Cold Comfort**).

Josie

2424 Pico Boulevard, at 25th Street (1-310 581 9888, www.josierestaurant.com). Bus SM7, SM10, 44/I-10, exit Cloverfield Boulevard south/20th Street south. **Open** 6-9pm Mon-Thur; 6-10pm Fri, Sat; 5.30-9pm Sun. **Main courses** $32. **Credit** AmEx, Disc, MC, V. **Map** p310 D4 ❸ **American**
Josie LeBalch and two other female chefs work in the kitchen while LeBalch's husband Frank manages front of house at this greatly admired Santa Monica favourite. Progressive American, French and Italian influences abound, producing combinations such as buffalo burger with truffle fries.

Mélisse

1104 Wilshire Boulevard, between 11th Street & 12th Street (1-310 395 0881, www.melisse.com). Bus 20, 41, 720, SM2/I-10, exit Lincoln Boulevard north. **Open** 6-9.30pm Tue-Thur; 6-9.45pm Fri; 5.45-9.45pm Sat. **Tasting menus** $125-$250. **Credit** AmEx, DC, Disc, MC, V. **Map** p310 B2 ❹ **French**
Josiah Citrin is one of the best chefs in Los Angeles, and the long, expensive meals he serves at this white-tablecloth operation are the stuff of both legend and controversy. Tasting menus of Provence-meets-Pacific cooking with fine wines can easily run to $400 and take three hours.

Milo & Olive

2723 Wilshire Boulevard, at Harvard Street (1-310 453 6776, www.miloandolive.com). Bus 20, 720, SM2/I-10, exit Cloverfield Boulevard north/20th Street north. **Open** 8am-11pm daily. **Main courses** $16. **Credit** AmEx, DC, Disc, MC, V. **Map** p310 D2 ❺ **Italian**
The newest outpost of Huckleberry (see p95) owners Josh Loeb and Zoe Nathan is a smallish space serving everything wood-baked, from the must-have garlic knots to pizzas, pastas and salads. And that's before you get to the amazing sweet treats, including doughnuts that change daily and a brioche that's filled with a tangy and creamy crème fraîche centre. *See also p133* **All Rise**.

★ Tar & Roses

602 Santa Monica Boulevard, at 6th Street (1-310 587 0700, http://tarandroses.com). Bus 1, 4, 7, 8, 10/I-10, exit 5th Street.

Open 5.30-10.30pm Mon-Sat; 5.30-9.30pm Sun. **Main courses** $25. **Credit** AmEx, DC, Disc, MC, V. **Map** p310 B3 ❻ **American**
At Tar & Roses, everything that can be is cooked using either the wood-burning oven or grill. The menu doesn't really propose to reinvent anything: rather, chef/owner Andrew Kirschner simply focuses on doing it better, with a little extra finesse. The perfect duck leg confit mingles with wood-roasted grapes and hazelnuts, and you won't find a better roast chicken than the one here. Happily, the use of the wood-fired oven doesn't exclude desserts: the strawberry tart is sublime. The most coveted seats are the ones at the back, on the quaint, enclosed patio. *Photo p95.*

Warszawa

1414 Lincoln Boulevard, at Santa Monica Boulevard (1-310 393 8831, www.warszawarestaurant.com). Bus 4, 10, 704, SM1, SM5, SM7, SM8, SM10/I-10, exit Lincoln Boulevard north. **Open** 6-11pm Tue-Sat; 5-10pm Sun. **Main courses** $19. **Credit** AmEx, DC, Disc, MC, V. **Map** p310 B3 ❼ **Polish**
There are few Polish restaurants in LA, but this one has become popular far outside its own community. Although Polish isn't exactly the hip cuisine of the moment, stylish young diners join Polish expats in this genteel converted cottage to create a lively ambience. Specialities include crisp-skinned fried duck, the stew called *bigos*, and the addictive ravioli, *pierogis*.

CONSUME

Venice

Baby Blues

444 Lincoln Boulevard, at Sunset Avenue (1-310 396 7675, www.babybluesvenice.com). Bus SM1, SM4, 7, 8, 10/I-10, exit Lincoln Boulevard south. **Open** 11.30am-10pm daily. **Main courses** $20. **Credit** AmEx, DC, Disc, MC, V. **Map** p310 B5 ❽ **American**

Though Baby Blues is best known for its succulent barbecued meats, there's a lot more to love on its menu: catfish and shrimp, both corn-topped with Mexican *cotija* cheese, and very good sautéed collard greens. Vegetarians can dine here happily, soaking up the artsy atmosphere and making a meal of sides, while others tuck into massive plates of pork and beef. **Other locations** 7953 Santa Monica Boulevard, West Hollywood (1-323 656 1277).

Gjelina

1429 Abbot Kinney Boulevard, at Milwood Avenue (1-310 450 1429, www.gjelina.com). Bus SM1, 33, 733/CA-90, exit Lincoln Boulevard west. **Open** 11.30am-midnight Mon-Fri; 9am-midnight Sat, Sun. **Main courses** $15. **Credit** AmEx, DC, Disc, MC, V. **Map** p310 A6 ❾ **American**

Pack in with the beautiful people at this Abbot Kinney hotspot. There's always a wait, but the scene is buzzing and the food good. Order plates to share – you can't go wrong with any of the seasonal vegetables and pizzas baked in the wood-burning oven. Snag a seat on the patio for brunch or a place at a communal table for dinner. A takeout offshoot is next door.

Joe's

1023 Abbot Kinney Boulevard, between Broadway & Westminster Avenues (1-310 399 5811, www.joesrestaurant.com). Bus 33, SM1/I-10, exit 4th/5th Street south. **Open** noon-2.30pm, 6-10pm Tue-Thur; noon-2.30pm, 6-11pm Fri; 11am-2.30pm, 6-11pm Sat; 11am-2.30pm, 6-10pm Sun. **Main courses** *Lunch* $15. *Dinner* $28. **Credit** AmEx, DC, Disc, MC, V. **Map** p310 A5 ❿ **Californian**

When chef Joseph Miller opened this restaurant in 1991, Abbot Kinney was a rough area. However, the gangs have now been replaced by valet parking, and Joe's is now one of the top dining destinations on what's become a very hip street. Brunch and lunch are a bargain, especially the prix fixe; the excellent Cal-French dinners are also fairly priced. Get recommendations from your server or from Miller himself, who's often found out front chatting with diners.

★ Superba Snack Bar

533 Rose Avenue, at Dimmick Avenue (1-310 399 6400, www.superbasnackbar.com). Bus SM1/PCH, exit Rose Avenue. **Open** 6-10.30pm Mon-Thur; 11am-3pm, 5-11.30pm Fri; 10am-3pm, 5-11.30pm Sat; 10am-3pm, 5-10pm Sun. **Main courses** $18. **Credit** AmEx, DC, Disc, MC, V. **Map** p310 B5 ⓫ **Italian**

Superba Snack Bar is a self-defined 'modern pastaria'. The root of the menu is in chef Jason Neroni's handmade pasta dishes, like the beautiful plate of smoked bucatini carbonara made with noodles as thick as bootlaces and swirled with salty pancetta and a neatly poached egg. On warm nights, the patio is a perfect spot to dine. On cold ones, grab a seat at the bar to marvel over the action in the open kitchen. All in all, a welcome, rare Venice restaurant where scene doesn't trump substance. Note: reservations are only taken for parties of six or more. *Photo p96.*

Marina del Rey to LAX

Café del Rey

4451 Admiralty Way, between Bali & Promenade Ways (1-310 823 6395, www.cafedelreymarina. com). Bus 108, 358/Hwy 90, exit Mindanao Way. **Open** 11.30am-2.30pm, 5.30-10pm Mon-Sat; 10.30am-2.30pm, 5-9.30pm Sun. **Main courses** *Lunch* $18. *Dinner* $34. **Credit** AmEx, DC, Disc, MC, V. **Californian**

By day, the view of the marina from Café del Rey is lovely; by night, the whole interior seems to glow. The signature is executive chef Daniel Roberts' creative use of fresh, locally sourced vegetables and seafood, cooked using French, Asian and Californian ideas.

Truxton's

8611 Truxton Avenue, at W Manchester Avenue, Westchester (1-310 417 8789, www.truxtons americanbistro.com). Bus 3, 6, 102, 115/I-10, exit La Tijera Boulevard south. **Open** 11am-10pm Mon-Fri; 9am-10pm Sat, Sun. **Main courses** $13. **Credit** AmEx, DC, Disc, MC, V. **American**

Specialising in comforting American cuisine, this hopping sidestreet spot uses market produce and smokes brisket overnight; not wildly unusual in LA, but unique in this particular culinary desert. The food is comfortably the best in the area.

BRENTWOOD TO BEVERLY HILLS

Brentwood

★ Farmshop

Brentwood Country Mart, 225 26th Street, at San Vicente Boulevard (1-310 566 2400, www.farm shopla.com). Bus 4, 14/I-10, exit Cloverfield Boulevard. **Open** *Restaurant* 7.30-11am, 11.15am-2.30pm, 5.30-9.30pm Mon-Fri; 8am-2pm, 5.30-9.30pm Sat; 8am-2pm, 5-9pm Sun. *Bakery* 7am-6pm daily. *Market* 7am-7pm daily. **Main courses** $20. **Credit** AmEx, DC, Disc, MC, V. **American**

Restaurant, bakery and market, Brentwood Country Mart's Farmshop is the one-stop shop for Angelenos with an expense account. Brunch, lunch and dinner – at the helm of Thomas Keller's ex-right hand man Jeffrey Cerciello, who never fires a misstep – focuses on seasonal, local ingredients. Brunch is standup –

Lukshon. *See p100.*

try the French toast of thick brioche slices topped with seasonal fruit or house-made pastrami and eggs – while to-go items like Sunday fried chicken and pre-made sandwiches are perfect for a gourmet picnic.

★ Restaurant at the Getty Center

1200 Getty Center Drive, at I-405 (1-310 440 6810, www.getty.edu). Bus 761/I-405, exit Getty Center Drive. **Open** 11.30am-2.30pm Tue-Fri; 11.30am-2.30pm, 5-9pm Sat; 11am-3pm Sun. **Main courses** *Lunch* $17. *Dinner* $34. **Credit** AmEx, DC, MC, V. **American**

The Getty's restaurant operates limited hours; still, no matter how much you need to tweak your schedule, it's worth the effort. Enjoy spectacular views of the city and the coastline, including the vineyard of a private winery, while dining on excellent modern American cuisine. Dishes such as sea scallops with pork belly and sunchokes, and Dungeness crab cakes with smoked paprika aioli are both marvellous. For a quicker bite, try the café or garden terrace café.

▶ *The Getty Villa in Malibu (see p31) now offers 'Tea by the Sea' ($36) on Thursday afternoons, with a menu inspired by the villa's recreated first-century Roman gardens.*

Takao

11656 San Vicente Boulevard, at Darlington Avenue (1-310 207 8636, www.takaobrentwood. com). Bus 14, SM3, SM4/I-10, exit Bundy Drive north. **Open** 11.30am-2.30pm, 5.30-10.30pm

Mon-Sat; 5-10pm Sun. **Main courses** $35. **Credit** AmEx, DC, MC, V. **Japanese**

Takao Izumida is famous in Los Angeles as an alumnus of celebrity chef Nobu's kitchen. However, at his own restaurant, he serves sushi without the Peruvian embellishments. The quality here is very high, and the $70-$120 *omakase* menu is a real highlight: tell the chef your likes and dislikes and then fasten your seatbelt, because things are sure to get interesting.

Culver City

La Dijonaise

8703 Washington Boulevard, at Helms Avenue (1-310 287 2770, www.ladijonaise.com). Metro Culver City/bus 33, C1/I-10, exit Robertson Boulevard south. **Open** 7am-9pm Mon-Fri; 8am-9pm Sat; 8am-5pm Sun. **Main courses** $15. **Credit** AmEx, DC, MC, V. **French**

INSIDE TRACK EATING AT LAX

As part of its continuing renovation, LAX's Tom Bradley terminal is welcoming some good new eateries over the coming years, including branches of **Umami Burger**, **Petrossian** (*see p153*), **Short Cake** (*see p133* **All Rise**), **ink.sack** (a spinoff of Michael Voltaggio's Ink; *see p104*) and Suzanne Goin's **Larder at Tavern**.

The French country cooking at this appealing bistro-bakery is very good and the prices are fair. Don't expect innovation or a high-class atmosphere, but if you want steak Bordelaise, bouillabaisse or (of course) chicken Dijon for under $20 with a glass of wine, this is the place. At breakfast, there are excellent omelettes and pastries.

Lukshon
3239 Helms Avenue, between Washington & Venice Boulevards (1-310 202 6808, www. lukshon.com). Metro Culver City/bus 33, C1/ I-10, exit Venice Boulevard south. **Open** noon-3pm, 5.30-10.30pm Tue-Thur; noon-3pm, 5.30-10.30pm Fri; 5.30-10.30pm Sat. **Main courses** $15. **Credit** AmEx, DC, MC, V. **Thai**
Sang Yoon's Lukshon, in the Helms Bakery complex, is just steps away from his other eaterie, Father's Office (*see p119*). But the similarities end there. Where Father's Office is one of the city's first gastropubs with a decidedly American menu, Lukshon is the first of its own kind – an upscale and polished restaurant that reinterprets South-east Asian flavours. While dishes such as *dan dan* noodles and Chinese black mushrooms may seem ordinary, they're reinvented just enough so you don't mind paying the upscale prices. To end, the nightly changing dessert is complimentary and, invariably, fantastic. *Photo p99.*

$ Tender Greens
9523 Culver Boulevard, at Cardiff Avenue (1-310 842 8300, www.tendergreensfood.com). Bus 6, 12, 33, 733, C1/I-10, exit Robertson Boulevard south. **Open** 11.30am-9pm daily. **Main courses** $10. **Open** DC, MC, V. **American**
This casual spot has become a locals' favourite, and with good reason: the mainly organic food is decent and, just as importantly, it's dished up in next to no time from a poshed-up canteen-style counter. Choose from something meaty and/or something salady, made from local ingredients, then repair to a nearby table with the food and a glass of wine. Best for lunch. **Other locations** 8759 Santa Monica Boulevard, West Hollywood (1-310 358 1919); 6290 Sunset Boulevard, Hollywood (1-323 382 0380); 210 Arizona Avenue, Santa Monica (1-310 587 2777).

West LA

$ Apple Pan
10801 W Pico Boulevard, at Glendon Avenue (1-310 475 3585). Bus SM1, C3, SM7, SM8, SM12, SM13/I-10, exit Overland Avenue north. **Open** 11am-midnight Tue-Thur, Sun; 11am-1am Fri, Sat. **Main courses** $7. **No credit cards**. **Map** p311 A5 ⑫ **Cafés & diners**
See p106 **Vintage Vittles**.

Tlapazola Grill
11676 West Gateway Boulevard, at S Barrington Avenue (1-310 477 1577, www.tlapazola.com).

Bus SM2, SM8/I-10, exit Bundy Drive south. **Open** 11am-3pm, 5-10pm Tue-Thur; 11.30am-3pm, 5-10pm Fri; 4-10pm Sat, Sun. **Main courses** $14. **Credit** DC, Disc, MC, V. **Mexican**
This is one of the few eateries in LA that offers innovative versions of Oaxacan food, a cuisine that's subtler and more interesting than run-of-the-mill Mexican fare. The menu includes the likes of salmon in a pumpkin seed *mole*, trout with salsa fresca and barbacoa braised lamb.

Upstairs2
2311 Cotner Avenue, between W Pico & W Olympic Boulevards (1-310 231 0316, www. upstairs2.com). Bus 6, SM4, SM5, SM7/I-405, exit Santa Monica Boulevard east. **Open** 5.30-10pm Wed, Thur; 5.30-11pm Fri, Sat. **Tapas** $12. **Credit** AmEx, DC, MC, V. **Mediterranean**
When LA's largest wine store decided to open a restaurant upstairs, it did what you might expect: created a stellar wine list and paired it with the food. The prices are surprisingly reasonable, but you can end up spending serious money if you start exploring the upper reaches of the wine list. Still, if you really like one of the wines, you can go downstairs and buy a few bottles to take home.

Westwood

Nanbankan
11330 Santa Monica Boulevard, at Corinth Avenue (1-310 478 1591). Bus 1, 4, 11/ I-405, exit Santa Monica Boulevard west.

Bazaar by José Andrés.

CONSUME

INSIDE TRACK DINE LA

DineLA's restaurant week, a 12-day event that comes around twice a year (usually late January/early February and October), allows diners to eat at otherwise unaffordable top spots for a song. The three-course prix-fixe menus cost $15/$20/$25 for lunch (depending on the restaurant) and $25/$35/$45 for dinner. Around 300 eateries participate and some even throw in extras, such as a glass of wine. Visit http://discover losangeles.com to search by cuisine, price and location. Advance booking recommended.

Open 5.30-10.30pm daily. **Main courses** $22. **Credit** DC, MC, V. **Japanese**
LA's original *robatayaki* restaurant is still one of the best, in terms of both selection and execution. Diners line up for a wide variety of meats and vegetables, grilled with subtle Japanese seasonings and served with beer, saké or wine. Large parties should steer clear on the busier nights: the seating policy means that you may never get a table while smaller groups are seated ahead of you.

$ Native Foods
1114 Gayley Avenue, at Kinross Avenue (1-310 209 1055, www.nativefoods.com). Bus 1, 2, 3, 6, 8, 11, 12, 233, 761/I-405, exit Wilshire Boulevard east. **Open** 11am-10pm daily. **Main courses** $10. **Credit** AmEx, DC, Disc, MC, V. **Eclectic**
This vegan café has become popular with students thanks to the healthy food, the fast service and prices that won't break a budget. The dishes are good: even non-vegetarians may be seduced by Moroccan, Greek or Indian-style rice and veggie bowls.
Other locations 9343 Culver Boulevard, Culver City (1-310 559 3601); 2901 Ocean Park Boulevard, Santa Monica (1-310 314 4333).

Century City

Clementine
1751 Ensley Avenue, at Santa Monica Boulevard (1-310 552 1080, www.clementineonline.com). Bus 4, 16, 28, 316, 728/I-405, exit Santa Monica Boulevard east. **Open** 7am-7.30pm Mon-Fri; 8am-5pm Sat. **Main courses** *Breakfast* $8. *Lunch* $15. **Credit** AmEx, DC, Disc, MC, V. **Map** p311 B3 🅭
American
Annie Miller's lovely, low-key café-bakery offers delicious fuel to the neighbourhood's shoppers and office workers. The food ranges from the deeply healthy (home-made granola) to the even more profoundly naughty (look out for a BBQ menu during

the summer); don't leave without trying one of the appetising and ever-changing array of sweet things.
Other locations 9346 Civic Center Drive, Beverly Hills (1-310 461 0600).

Beverly Hills

★ Bazaar by José Andrés
SLS Hotel at Beverly Hills, 465 S La Cienega Boulevard, at Clifton Way (1-310 246 5555, www.thebazaar.com). Bus 3, 105, 330/I-10, exit La Cienega Boulevard north. **Open** 6-10pm Mon-Wed; 6-11pm Thur-Sun. **Tapas** $14. **Credit** AmEx, DC, MC, V. **Map** p312 B3 🅮 **Spanish**
Inside the sexy and playful SLS (*see p175*), the Bazaar by José Andrés is a carnival of food and drink offerings that are as whimsical and sleek as the Philippe Starck-designed space. Grab a drink – expect martinis with olive foam and 'salt air' margaritas – at the swanky Bar Centro or at the al fresco Bar Centro Terrace. Of course, the real star is the Spanish chef's modern cooking. Indulge in an intimate tasting menu inside the hidden dining room Saam or share tapas like 'Philly cheesesteak' made with seared Wagyu beef atop 'air bread' and uni and avocado buns.

★ BierBeisl
9669 S Santa Monica Boulevard, between N Roxbury & N Bedford Drives (1-310 271 7274, www.bierbeisl-la.com). Bus 4, 14, 16, 704/I-10, exit Robertson Boulevard north. **Open** noon-midnight Mon, Tue, Thur-Sat. **Main courses** $28. **Credit** AmEx, DC, MC, V. **Map** p311 C3 🅯
Austrian
'Unassuming' and 'Beverly Hills' are not words you often see in the same sentence, but that's exactly what BierBeisl is. Here, Patina-alum Bernhard Mairinger – all six feet seven inches of him – serves Austrian fare that anticipates, then exceeds, your expectations. There is, of course, schnitzel, which pairs well with a savoury mustard fingerling potato salad. Sausages get their own menu and they're similarly elevated well beyond the norm. For dessert, you'll likely be drawn to the flaky apfelstrudel, but also consider the *kaiserschmarrn*, a light, fluffy pancake served alongside home-made plum compôte.

CUT
Beverly Wilshire Hotel, 9500 Wilshire Boulevard, at S Rodeo Drive (1-310 276 8500, www.wolfgang puck.com). Bus 14, 20, 37/I-405, exit Wilshire Boulevard east. **Open** 6-10pm Mon-Thur; 6-11pm Fri; 5.30-11pm Sat. **Main courses** $50. **Credit** AmEx, DC, Disc, MC, V. **Map** p311 D3 🅰
American
Set within the confines of a Four Seasons hotel, Wolfgang Puck's steakhouse is designed to impress. Unsurprisingly, meat, from sirloin to Wagyu, is a forte; add sauces and sides and prepare to get stuck in. Whatever your main course, do save room for dessert (we recommend the baked Alaska).

Picca.

chopping and drizzling before presenting you with your finished salad. Your lunch will cost you more than at Subway next door, but the ingredients are well above average and portions are huge. The Century City location also serves breakfast.
Other locations 1888 Century Park East, Century City (1-424 239 8700).

Grill on the Alley
9560 Dayton Way, at Wilshire Boulevard (1-310 276 0615, www.thegrill.com). Bus 14, 20, 37/I-405, exit Wilshire Boulevard east. **Open** 11.30am-9pm Mon, Tue-Thur; 11.30am-10.30pm Fri, Sat; 5-9pm Sun. **Main courses** *Lunch* $28. *Dinner* $35. **Credit** AmEx, DC, Disc, MC, V. **Map** p311 C3 ⓳ **American**
The food is good, but that's not actually the reason why most people come here: along with Mastro's Steakhouse (246 N Canon Drive, 1-310 888 8782, www.mastrosrestaurants.com) and the fabled Polo Lounge at the Beverly Hills Hotel (*see p173*), this is Hollywood power-lunch central. Even though the restaurant has only been here since the 1980s, it already feels like an old-money hangout. Order a steak or Crab Louie, gawk at the stars, and enjoy being pampered by consummate professionals who treat everybody like they're somebody.
Other locations Grill on Hollywood, 6801 Hollywood Boulevard, Hollywood (1-323 856 5530).

Matsuhisa
129 N La Cienega Boulevard, between Wilshire Boulevard & Clifton Way (1-310 659 9639, www.nobumatsuhisa.com). Bus 30, 105, 330/I-10, exit La Cienega Boulevard north. **Open** 11.45am-2.15pm, 5.45-10.15pm Mon-Fri; 5.45-10.15pm Sat, Sun. **Main courses** *Lunch* $25. *Dinner* $25. **Credit** AmEx, DC, MC, V. **Map** p312 B4 ⓴ **Japanese**
Celebrity chef Nobuyuki Matsuhisa's empire began at this Beverly Hills operation, which continues to thrive. Matsuhisa's masterful merging of Japanese and Peruvian cuisines is best experienced at the *omakase* dinners of seven courses or more (starting at $90). Tell the chef your likes and dislikes and then let him loose on your tastebuds.

Nate 'n Al
414 N Beverly Drive, between Santa Monica Boulevard & Brighton Way (1-310 274 0101, www.natenal.com). Bus 4, 14, 16, 37, 316/I-405, exit Wilshire Boulevard east. **Open** 7am-9pm daily. **Main courses** $15. **Credit** AmEx, DC, MC, V. **Map** p311 C3 ㉑ **Jewish**
Nate 'n Al's isn't the best Jewish deli in greater LA, but 70 years of service have certainly made it an institution. The food is heavy but good, and the servers are seasoned veterans who've seen everything and treat punks, millionaires, families and elderly Jewish matrons exactly the same.

Fogo de Chao
133 N La Cienega Boulevard, between Wilshire Boulevard & Clifton Way (1-310 289 7755, www.fogodechao.com). Bus 30, 105, 330/I-10, exit La Cienega Boulevard north. **Open** 11.30am-2pm, 5-10pm Mon-Fri; 4.30-10.30pm Sun. **Main courses** *Lunch* $35. *Dinner* $58. **Credit** AmEx, DC, Disc, MC, V. **Map** p312 B4 ⓱ **Brazilian**
Most Brazilian barbecues supplement good meat with carelessly prepared side dishes that are an obvious afterthought. Fogo de Chao is different: the beautiful salad bar and the buffet are both full of fine cold dishes made with premium ingredients. This is the priciest *churrascaria* in LA but by far the best, aided by its exceptional South American wine list.

★ $ Greenleaf Gourmet Chop Shop
9671 Wilshire Boulevard, at N Bedford Drive (1-310 246 0756, www.greenleafchopshop.com). Bus 20/I-405, exit Wilshire Boulevard east. **Open** 11am-6pm Mon-Fri; 11am-4pm Sat. **Main courses** $10. **Credit** AmEx, Disc, MC, V. **Map** p311 C3 ⓲ **American**
In an area otherwise dominated by high-end hotel eateries and mediocre coffeeshops, this place is a find. Choose your ingredients from the lengthy chalkboard menu and the chefs will get to work

Around the World

... with LA's best ethnic cuisines.

Most big cities have a few neighbourhoods that feel as if they've been dropped in from another corner of the planet. LA celebrates its own ethnic enclaves with enthusiasm: everyone from expats to chefs head to them in search of authentic foods that are unavailable elsewhere. Here are five areas in which to explore LA's culinary diversity:

CHINESE: MONTEREY PARK

LA's Chinatown has several good restaurants, but the best and most authentic Chinese food is to the east near Monterey Park and Alhambra. Try the Shandong beef rolls at **101 Noodle Express** (1408 E Valley Boulevard, Alhambra, 1-626 300 8654), or dim sum at any of a hundred places: we recommend **Empress Harbor** (*see p116*).

INDIAN: LITTLE BOMBAY, ARTESIA

The best Indian food in LA is served in Artesia along a stretch of Pioneer Boulevard. Try **Jay Bharat** (No.18701, 1-562 924 3310) or **Udupi Palace** (No.18635, 1-562 860 1950) for hearty South Indian vegetarian food.

MEXICAN: PLAZA MEXICO, LYNWOOD

Mexican restaurants are everywhere in LA, but Lynwood's Plaza Mexico mall stands out for its diversity. There are eateries specialising in goat stew, seafood from Yucatán and other regional delicacies, but we really like **Guelaguetza** (*see p109*), a branch of the Koreatown favourite (although now under different ownership).

THAI: THAI TOWN, HOLLYWOOD

Most Thai restaurants in LA serve a mild, Americanised version of the cuisine. The exceptions are in Hollywood's Thai Town, home to America's largest Thai community. Try northern Thai cuisine at **Ocha Classic** (various locations) or southern Thai at **Jitlada** (5233 W Sunset Boulevard, 1-323 663 3104, www.jitladala.wordpress.com). Tell your server you want your food Thai hot, not *farang* hot.

VIETNAMESE: LITTLE SAIGON, WESTMINSTER

The largest Vietnamese community outside Vietnam is in Westminster, Orange County. One of the area's best restaurants is **Pho Thang Long** (15579 Brookhurst Street, 1-714 839 4955), famous for spicy noodle soup and the wok-fried steak called shaking beef. Just want a sandwich? Go to **Lee's Sandwiches** or **Mr Baguette** (various locations): both specialise in *banh mi*, French-style sandwiches filled with Vietnamese meat and vegetables.

CONSUME

Picca

9575 West Pico Boulevard, between Smithwood & Edris Drives (1-310 277 0133, www.picca peru.com). Bus 7, 13/I-10, exit Robertson Boulevard north. **Open** 6-11pm Mon-Thur, Sun; 6pm-midnight Fri, Sat. **Main courses** $15. **Credit** AmEx, DC, MC, V. **Map** p311 D4 ㉒ **Peruvian**

Peruvian food is the new black, and nobody wears it better than Ricardo Zarate, who serves a sophisticated interpretation of the cuisine of his motherland. The menu offers a rather exhaustive list of small plates: chicken skin *chicharrones*, pig trotter stew, sea bass ceviche, duck confit with black beer sauce, rare skirt steak topped with a fried egg and plantains. There's also an entire menu devoted to Peruvian-style sushi, which is served on potatoes instead of rice. Service can be harried.
▶ *Downstairs, Sotto (1-310 277 0210) serves excellent Neapolitan-style pizzas, pastas and Italian-style small plates by chefs Steve Samson and Zach Pollack, formerly of Pizzeria Ortica (see p117; closed Mon.*

Scarpetta

Montage Beverly Hills, 225 N Canon Drive, at Clifton Way (1-310 860 7970, www.montage beverlyhills.com). Bus 14, 20, 37/I-405, exit Wilshire Boulevard east. **Open** 6-10pm Mon-Thur; 6-10.30pm Fri, Sat; 11am-3pm, 5.30-9pm Sun. **Main courses** $28. **Credit** AmEx, Disc, MC, V. **Map** p311 D3 ㉓ **Italian**

Scott Conant's upscale Italian cuisine more than matches the Montage's posh surroundings. Granted, not all diners will be prepared to spend $24 on a simple plate of spaghetti with tomato and basil, but one bite will change anyone's mind. The rest of the menu roams pastas, meats and fish dishes, and the desserts are divine. Attentive service, too. Sommelier Mark Hefter's wine list amounts to a staggering 800 bottles.

Spago

176 N Canon Drive, between Clifton Way & Wilshire Boulevard (1-310 385 0880, www. wolfgangpuck.com). Bus 14, 20, 37/I-10, exit Robertson Boulevard north. **Open** 5.30-10.30pm Mon; noon-2.15pm, 5.30-10.30pm Tue-Thur;

11.30am-2.15pm, 5.30-10.30pm Fri; noon-2.15pm, 5.30-10.30pm Sat; 6-10pm Sun. **Main courses** $35. **Credit** AmEx, DC, Disc, MC, V. **Map** p311 D3 ㉔ **Californian**

Even before Spago reopened in October 2012 after a three-month makeunder, everyone was buzzing about Wolfgang Puck's rebooted fine-dining staple. With the restaurant's success over 30 years, a built-in audience arrives, eager to coo over executive chef Lee Hefter's reworked, cross-cultural bill of fare. In addition to California – over whose cuisine Puck still reigns – Asia, Italy and France influence the menu. Service isn't always perfect, and at these prices it should be. Still, on any given night you're bound to spot a celeb or two, including Puck himself.

Urasawa

218 N Rodeo Drive, at Wilshire Boulevard (1-310 247 8939). Bus 14, 20, 37/I-10, exit Robertson Boulevard north. **Open** 6-8.30pm Tue-Sat. **Main courses** *Set menu* $395. **Credit** AmEx, DC, MC, V. **Map** p311 C3 ㉕ **Japanese**

LA is awash with sushi bars, but Urasawa is at the top of the heap. Flown in daily, the fish is prepared by chef Hiroyuki Urasawa and one assistant. Meals stretch to 25 artfully prepared courses; the experience will be amazing and expensive. Booking is imperative (there are no walk-ins) and an early-evening slot is best: if you come at 8pm, each course will arrive as soon as you've finished the previous tidbit.

WEST HOLLYWOOD, HOLLYWOOD & MIDTOWN

West Hollywood

★ AOC

8700 W 3rd Street, at S Hamel Road (1-310 859 9859, www.aocwinebar.com). Bus 16, 220, 316/I-10, exit Fairfax Avenue north. **Open** 6-10pm Mon-Thur; 6-11pm Fri; 5.30-11pm Sat; 5.30-10pm Sun. **Main courses** $15. **Credit** AmEx, DC, MC, V. **Map** p312 A3 ㉖ **French**

The acronym stands for Appellation d'Origine Contrôlée, the system for certifying the region of origin of food and wine in France and ensuring its quality. AOC might be a long way from France, but the

---

THE BEST
OLD-FANGLED INSTITUTIONS

The classic dishes can't be beat.
Apple Pan. *See p100.*

Vintage Hollywood.
Musso & Frank Grill. *See p105.*

Cramped, authentic and fun.
Dan Tana's. *See above.*

---

food is Gallic in its perfection. As this guide went to press, AOC had just moved from its old digs up the street into this location near the Beverly Center, a gorgeous space with a lovely patio area. Small plates plus platters to share will continue to feature on the dinner menu, while lunchtime offerings will cater to the business and shopping crowds. The newly bolstered cocktail and wine lists are impressive, too.

BLT Steak

8720 W Sunset Boulevard, between Palm Avenue & Alta Loma Road, West Hollywood (1-310 360 1950, www.bltsteak.com). Bus 2, 30, 105, 302, 330/I-10, exit La Cienega Boulevard north. **Open** 6-10.30pm Tue-Thur; 6-11.30pm Fri, Sat. **Main courses** $40. **Credit** AmEx, DC, Disc, MC, V. **Map** p312 B2 ㉗ **American/French**

BLT is short for Bistro Laurent Tourondel, and while the famed French chef split from the restaurant in 2010, it continues to deliver high-quality steaks (including Kobe beef) and seafood. However, it's the sides, especially the featherlight popovers, and the desserts, such as the passionfruit crêpe soufflé, that steal the show.

Dan Tana's

9071 Santa Monica Boulevard, between N Doheny Drive & Nemo Street (1-310 275 9444, www.dantanasrestaurant.com). Bus 4/I-10, exit Robertson Boulevard north. **Open** 5pm-1.30am daily. **Main courses** $25. **Credit** AmEx, DC, Disc, MC, V. **Map** p312 A2 ㉘ **Italian**

No one comes here for the food. It's not that the simple, old-fashioned Italian fare is bad (it's expensive, but portions are huge): it's more that the old Hollywood atmosphere is wonderfully thick. The older servers can tell you what LA was like back when this food was cutting edge, a time when they were much younger but Dan Tana's looked the same. It's favoured by celebs with respect to olde Hollywood (George Clooney, for instance, after whom one of the dishes is named).

$ Griddle Café

7916 W Sunset Boulevard, at N Fairfax Avenue (1-323 874 0377, www.thegriddlecafe.com). Bus 2, 302/I-10, exit Fairfax Avenue north. **Open** 7am-4pm Mon-Fri; 8am-4pm Sat, Sun. **Main courses** $10. **Credit** AmEx, DC, MC, V. **Map** p312 C1 ㉙ **Cafés & diners**

A useful standby in this part of town, this is a greasy spoon as only West Hollywood knows how, which is to say that it's not in the least bit greasy. Buff young hunks and hunkettes chow down on immense pancakes and lunchtime sandwiches; they're watching your figure, even if you aren't.

Ink

8360 Melrose Avenue, at N Kings Road (1-323 651 5866, www.mvink.com). Bus 10, 48, 105/I-10, exit La Cienega Boulevard north.

CONSUME

Open 6-11pm Mon-Thur, Sun; 6pm-midnight Fri, Sat. **Main courses** $20. **Credit** AmEx, DC, MC, V. **Map** p312 B2 ③⓪ **American**
Former Top Chef winner Michael Voltaggio is LA's most avant-garde chef, and when it comes to 'cooking' with liquid nitrogen, nobody in California does it better. Nothing is ever quite what it seems: pork belly might seem at first as if it's been slow-smoked over charcoal, but then you realise the smoky flavour is actually coming not from the meat but from the accompanying drizzle of oil. It's a riot of fun, and it's almost always stunningly delicious. The wine list is just as challenging and thought-provoking as the kitchen menu. Note: the interior is very sexy but the noise levels can be extremely high.

Lucques

8474 Melrose Avenue, at Clinton Street (1-323 655 6277, www.lucques.com). Bus 10, 48, 105/I-10, exit La Cienega Boulevard north. **Open** 6-10pm Mon; noon-2.30pm, 6-10pm Tue-Thur; noon-2.30pm, 6-10.30pm Fri, Sat; 5-10pm Sun. **Main courses** *Lunch* $20. *Dinner* $33. **Credit** AmEx, DC, MC, V. **Map** p312 B2 ③① **French**
To get in the right frame of mind for this modern French-Mediterranean restaurant, decide that you're willing to try absolutely anything. Chef Suzanne Goin is fantastically inventive, using obscure ingredients in exuberant and unlikely combinations. Fill the centre of your table with appetizers and then order a main or two. The lunch and Sunday-night prix fixe menus are among the best deals in town. Along with business partner Caroline Styne, Goin also runs AOC (*see p104*) and upscale Tavern in Brentwood (11648 San Vicente Boulevard, 1-310 806 6464).

Red O.

Red O

8155 Melrose Avenue, at N Kilkea Drive (1-323 655 5009, www.redorestaurant.com). Bus 10, 48, 217, 218/I-405 exit La Cienega Boulevard south. **Open** 6-10pm Mon; 6-11pm Tue-Thur; 6pm-midnight Fri; 10.30am-3pm, 6pm-midnight Sat; 10.30am-3pm, 6-10pm Sun. **Main courses** $22. **Credit** AmEx, DC, Disc, MC, V. **Map** p312 B2 ③② **Mexican**
Led by celeb chef Rick Bayless, Red O opened to great fanfare in 2010, making it almost impossible to get a table. In the course of its first three years, reviews have been mixed, and at least one chef has left. Still, there's no denying the room is beautiful, and we've enjoyed meals of duck *taquitos*, chicken *mole poblano* and *buñuelos* with salted caramel ice-cream here. Just lose the heavy security mob at the door, please.

Hollywood

Cleo

Redbury Hotel, 1717 Vine Street, at Hollywood Boulevard (1-323 962 1711, www.cleo restaurant.com). Metro Hollywood-Vine/bus 180, 181, 210, 212, 217, 222, 312, 780, LDH/US 101, exit Vine Street south. **Open** 6-11pm daily. **Tapas** $13. **Credit** AmEx, DC, MC, V. **Map** p313 B1 ③③ **Middle Eastern**
Standouts are numerous on Danny Elmaleh's menu of rustic-style Middle Eastern dishes, but include roast Sonoma lamb with lebaneh and couscous, and the addictive Brussels sprouts with capers, parsley, almonds and red wine vinaigrette. Prices are reasonable if you don't over-order – despite the small plates-style set-up, portions aren't tiny. The room itself, on the ground floor of the funky Redbury, is lovely, if loud, but the food will soon distract you.

Mario's Peruvian & Seafood

5786 Melrose Avenue, at N Vine Street (1-323 466 4181). Bus 10, 48, 210/I-10, exit La Brea Avenue north. **Open** 11.30am-8pm Mon-Thur, Sun; 11.30am-9.30pm Fri, Sat. **Main courses** $13. **Credit** AmEx, DC, Disc, MC, V. **Map** p313 B3 ③④ **Peruvian**
Mario's was one of the first restaurants to bring Peruvian cuisine into the LA mainstream. The place has the ambience of an old lunch counter and there's often a queue, but the food keeps people coming back: seafood fried rice, beef sautéed with potato and onion, citrusy fish ceviches and so on. The green sauce on your table is spicier than it looks, but it's so flavourful that you'll use too much of it anyway.

Musso & Frank Grill

6667 Hollywood Boulevard, at N Cherokee Avenue (1-323 467 7788, www.mussoand frank.com). Metro Hollywood-Highland/bus 156, 212, 217, 222, 312, LDH/US 101, exit Highland Avenue north. **Open** 11am-11pm

CONSUME

Tue-Sat. **Main courses** $35. **Credit** AmEx, DC, Disc, MC, V. **Map** p313 A1 ③⑤ **Russian** *See below* **Vintage Vittles**.

★ **Pizzeria Mozza**
641 N Highland Avenue, at Melrose Avenue (1-323 297 0101, www.pizzeriamozza.com). Bus 10, 48/I-10, exit La Brea Avenue north. **Open** noon-midnight daily. **Main courses** $17. **Credit** AmEx, DC, MC, V. **Map** p313 A3 ③⑥ Italian

Serving what may be the best pies in LA, Pizzeria Mozza is led by chef Mario Batali, La Brea Bakery founder Nancy Silverton and wine expert Joe Bastianich. The menu covers meats, salads, *bruschette* and pizzas; there's also a daily dish such as lasagne or crispy duck leg with lentils. The butterscotch *budino* is a must-have for dessert. Next door is Osteria Mozza (1-323 297 0100), run by the same team, serving upscale Italian food, and with a dedicated mozzarella bar. **Other locations**: 800 W Coast Highway, Newport Beach (1-949 945 1126).

Vintage Vittles

Top marks for old-school eateries.

Although LA tends to look forwards rather than backwards, it's home to a smattering of historic restaurants that have gallantly resisted the urge to modernise. Squint through their windows and it's easy to imagine yourself in the city of red-car trains and starlets on soda-fountain stools. And then look down at the plate: are you sure your 21st-century palate wants to sample *that*? Happily, a few of these evocatively old-fashioned dining destinations serve food you might actually want to eat.

Open since 1919, the **Musso & Frank Grill** (*see p105*) is Hollywood's oldest restaurant, a steak-and-cocktails joint formerly favoured by Charlie Chaplin and Raymond Chandler. With its obscure dishes and individually priced sides (and salad dressings!), the menu can be daunting. However, some items are fail-safes. At breakfast, grab an order of crêpe-thin flannel cakes; later in the day, the grilled meats are excellent. And every table gets a half-loaf of house-made sourdough bread, the perfect accompaniment to a dry martini.

In business since 1908, **Philippe the Original** (*see p113*) is one of two local spots that claims to have invented the French dip sandwich. Savvy customers select the traditional lamb or lighter turkey filling, then ask the server to double-dip the bread in the meaty juice; a French-dip sandwich is also incomplete without some of the sinus-clearing house mustard. The wines by the glass aren't bad, a concession to the lunch trade from nearby City Hall.

The **Pacific Dining Car** (*see p112*) is an elegant throwback to the early 20th century, when robber barons met over thick steaks and thicker cigar smoke. The bargain-hunter's secret is the breakfast menu (available 24 hours): among the spins on eggy standards is a great Creole benedict.

Musso & Frank Grill.

The Scottish-themed **Tam O'Shanter** (*see p110*) was Walt Disney's favourite restaurant, and remains resolutely old-fashioned. Prime rib with horseradish is a classic; for a more casual option, eat in the bar from the sandwich carving station. For dessert, it's got to be CC Brown's Hot Fudge Sundae, a perfect replica of the late, lamented Hollywood Boulevard original.

Over at West LA's **Apple Pan** (*see p100*), diners ring a U-shaped counter to inhale burgers slathered with hickory sauce. However, the burgers aren't anything to write home about. For a more satisfying experience, stick with the classic tuna or egg salad sandwich, crispy fries and a slice of luscious banana cream pie.

CONSUME

★ Providence

5955 Melrose Avenue, at Cole Avenue (1-323 460 4170, www.providencela.com). Bus 10, 48/ US 101, exit Melrose Avenue west. **Open** 6-10pm Mon-Thur; noon-2pm, 6-10pm Fri; 5.30-10pm Sat; 5.30-9pm Sun. **Main courses** *Lunch* $35; set menu $75. *Dinner* set menus $85-$175. **Credit** AmEx, DC, MC, V. **Map** p313 B3 ☞ **Seafood**

One of the most talked-about restaurants in Los Angeles in recent times is, in fact, a modern but nonetheless cosy place on a rather dull stretch of Melrose Avenue. Chef Michael Cimarusti is most famous for his wizardry with seafood, but the kitchen team works wonders with everything. The tasting menus are pricey but excellent and the presentation is second to none.

$ Roscoe's House of Chicken & Waffles

1514 N Gower Street, at W Sunset Boulevard (1-323 466 7453, www.roscoeschickenandwaffles. com). Metro Hollywood-Vine/bus 2, 302, LDHWI/US 101, exit Sunset Boulevard west. **Open** 8.30am-midnight Mon-Thur, Sun; 8.30am-4am Fri, Sat. **Main courses** $10. **Credit** AmEx, DC, Disc, MC, V. **Map** p313 B2 ☞ **American**

You can find better chicken in LA, and better waffles – but for both under one roof, Roscoe's is king. The Hollywood branch is the fanciest.

Other locations throughout LA.

Yamashiro

1999 N Sycamore Avenue, north of Franklin Avenue (1-323 466 5125, www.yamashiro hollywood.com). Metro Hollywood-Highland/bus 156, 180, 181, 212, 217, 222, 312, 780, LDH/US 101, exit Highland Avenue south. **Open** 5.30-9.30pm Mon-Thur, Sun; 5.30-10.30pm Fri, Sat. **Main courses** $32. **Credit** AmEx, DC, Disc, MC, V. **Map** p313 A1 ☞ **Pan-Asian**

Yamashiro, meaning 'mountain palace', was built in 1914 as a private art museum made to look like a palace near Kyoto. For years, it was a beautiful building in which to eat bad food, but the kitchen team has made a major difference in recent years: the restaurant is now worth a visit even if you don't snag a table with a view. With executive chef Brock Kleweno at the helm, Japanese, Korean and Chinese traditional items are presented alongside sensible and occasionally daring fusion ideas.

Fairfax District

Canter's Deli

419 N Fairfax Avenue, at Oakwood Avenue (1-323 651 2030, www.cantersdeli.com). Bus 217, 218/I-10, exit Fairfax Avenue north. **Open** 24hrs daily. **Main courses** $14. **Credit** DC, Disc, MC, V. **Map** p312 C3 ☞ **Jewish**

This reliable piece of local history, still owned by the Canter family after more than 80 years, is both a fine old-school Jewish deli and one of LA's favourite after-hours places. Come here at 2am, and you're bound to see musicians from all over town who've just got off stage and want to tuck into some blintzes or a stacked pastrami sandwich. The mural by the car park chronicles Jewish history in LA.

Farmers Market

6333 W 3rd Street, at Fairfax Avenue (1-323 933 9211, www.farmersmarketla.com). Bus 16, 217, 218, 316, 780/I-10, exit Fairfax Avenue north. **Open** 9am-9pm Mon-Fri; 9am-8pm Sat; 10am-7pm Sun. **Main courses** vary. **Credit** varies. **Map** p312 C3 ☞ **Various**

Back in 1934, local farmers began selling produce at the corner of 3rd and Fairfax. A handful of stalls still proffer groceries, but they're outnumbered by 30-plus catering stands offering a culinary round-the-world trip. Alongside the American comfort food served at the historic, 24-hour Du-Par's restaurant, you can get everything from Texas barbecue (Bryan's Pit BBQ) to Parisian crêpes (French Crepe Company), N'awleens po'boys (Gumbo Pot) to sunny Mexican fare (¡Loteria!). For dessert, you can't beat Bennett's Old-Fashioned Ice-Cream. More recent top-notch additions include Short Order, serving burgers, fries and custard shakes, and its spinoff Short Cake, specialising in baked goods and coffee. Hot dog addicts, meanwhile, should swing by Fritzi Dog for superior franks and tater tots.

► *For more on Bennett's Old-Fashioned Ice-Cream, see p134 Cold Comfort. For more on Short Cake, see p133 All Rise.*

★ $ Joan's on Third

8350 W 3rd Street, between S Kings Road & S Flores Street (1-323 655 2285, www.joanson third.com). Bus 16, 218, 316/I-10, exit Fairfax Avenue north. **Open** 8am-8pm Mon-Sat; 8am-6pm Sun. **Main courses** $10. **Credit** AmEx, DC, MC, V. **Map** p312 B3 ☞ **Cafés & diners**

This über-trendy yet friendly café-deli is a great place at which to stock up on supplies for a picnic, but it's also a lovely spot for a sit-down breakfast or lunch. Prices are on the high side, but the food is beautifully prepared. Don't leave without a cupcake – or two. A second branch, in Studio City, was in the works at the time of writing.

M Café de Chaya

7119 Melrose Avenue, at N La Brea Avenue (1-323 525 0588, www.mcafedechaya.com). Bus 10, 48, 212, 312/US 101, exit Highland Avenue south. **Open** 9am-10pm Mon-Sat; 9am-9pm Sun. **Main courses** $11. **Credit** AmEx, DC, MC, V. **Map** p312 D2 ☞ **Eclectic**

Macrobiotic food can have rather muted flavours; it's to the kitchen's immense credit that M Café de Chaya has managed to popularise it. The stylish room is, of course, filled with vegetarians and vegans, but it also serves exceptional sushi and a mild but tasty version of Korean *bibimbap*. It's not unusual to see diners taking pictures of the beautifully prepared food. **Other locations** 9433 Brighton Way, Beverly Hills (1-310 858 8459).

$ Mendocino Farms
175 S Fairfax Avenue, at W 3rd Street (1-323 934 4261, http://mendocinofarms.com). Bus 14/I-10, exit Fairfax Avenue north. **Open** 11am-9pm daily. **Main courses** $9. **Credit** AmEx, MC, V. **Map** p312 C3 **㊾ Sandwiches**
Big, hearty sandwiches with superior ingredients on a variety of breads (including gluten free) are the order of the day at this growing mini chain. Classics include BBQ pulled pork and turkey avocado and *kurobuta* pork belly *banh mi*, and there are also vegan options and salads. Be prepared to wait during busy times. **Other locations** throughout LA.

Son of a Gun
8370 W 3rd Street, between S Orlando Avenue & S Kings Road (1-323 782 9033, www.sonofagun restaurant.com). Bus 16, 218, 316, LDF/I-10, exit Fairfax Avenue north. **Open** 11.30am-2.30pm, 6-11pm Mon-Thur; 11.30am-2.30pm, 6pm-midnight Fri; 6pm-midnight Sat; 6-11pm Sun. **Main courses** $16. **Credit** AmEx, DC, MC, V. **Map** p312 B3 **㊸ Seafood**
Vinny Dotolo and Jon Shook's second restaurant – the first being the meat-intensive Animal (435 N Fairfax Avenue, Fairfax District, 1-323 782 9225) – focuses on fish. Nautical-themed knick-knacks frame the walls, but a dive Son of a Gun is not. Its version of lobster roll, for instance, takes beautiful chunks of lobster draped in lemon aioli and plops them on a plump, albeit tiny, brioche bun. Other hits: shrimp toast with Sriracha mayo and the fried chicken sandwich. Get there early to nab a seat at the communal table or the bar; otherwise, limited reservations are available.

★ Sycamore Kitchen
143 S La Brea Avenue, between W 1st & W 2nd Street (1-323 939 0151, http://thesycamore kitchen.com). Bus 212, 312/101, exit Silver Lake Boulevard west. **Open** 8am-5pm daily. **Main courses** $11. **Credit** AmEx, DC, MC, V. **Map** p312 D3 **㊻ Sandwiches**

**THE BEST
NEW-FANGLED MUST-VISITS**

Worth the hype? Yes.
Bazaar by José Andrés. *See p101.*

Italian comfort food at its best.
Pizzeria Mozza. *See p106.*

Big Meaty flavours.
Animal. *See above* **Son of a Gun.**

Karen Hatfield follows up her fine dining Hatfield's (6703 Melrose Avenue, 1-323 935 2977) with a casual bakery and café that serves the breakfast and lunch crowd with morning pastries and sandwiches all on house-made bread. Order at the register and take a seat at the lofty outdoor patio. Late-afternoon sweet seekers – the sticky bun is a must – are rewarded with pastries that are half price from 4.30pm.

Miracle Mile & Midtown

Luna Park
672 S La Brea Avenue, between Wilshire Boulevard & W 6th Street (1-323 934 2110, www.lunaparkla.com). Bus 20, 212, 312, 720/I-10, exit La Brea Avenue north. **Open** 11.30am-10.30pm Mon-Thur; 11.30am-11.30pm Fri; 10am-11.30pm Sat; 10am-10pm Sun. **Main courses** *Lunch* $15. *Dinner* $23. **Credit** AmEx, DC, MC, V. **Map** p312 D4 **㊼ Italian**
This loud but friendly diner-restaurant is relatively affordable and fairly speedy, making it a good option if you're heading on to a concert at the nearby Wiltern. The cooking is simple and exuberant: rock shrimp pizza with mozzarella, arugula and aioli is recommended, as are the red wine braised boneless short ribs. Your enjoyment of the evening may be aided by the lethal cocktails served at the bar.

$ Versailles
1415 S La Cienega Boulevard, between W Pico Boulevard & Alcott Street (1-310 289 0392, www.versaillescuban.com). Bus 7, 13, 105, 705/I-10, exit La Cienega Boulevard north. **Open** 11am-10pm Mon-Thur, Sun; 11am-11pm Fri, Sat. **Main courses** $10. **Credit** AmEx, DC, MC, V. **Map** p312 B5 **㊾ Cuban**
Although this bustling Cuban joint boasts a large menu, you should go straight for the garlic chicken served with sweet onion, fried plantains and white rice with black beans. Service is brisk but not rude. **Other locations** throughout LA.

Koreatown & around

El Cholo
1121 S Western Avenue, between W 11th Street & Country Club Drive (1-323 734 2773, www. elcholo.com). Bus 28, 207, 728, 757/I-10, exit Western Avenue north. **Open** 11am-10pm Mon-Thur; 11am-11pm Fri, Sat; 11am-9pm Sun. **Main courses** $13. **Credit** AmEx, DC, Disc, MC, V. **Map** p313 D6 **㊾ Mexican**
Having opened in 1923, El Cholo is Los Angeles' oldest continuously operated Mexican restaurant, and it probably hasn't been at the cutting edge of cuisine for more than 80 years. Still, the Mexican comfort food is decent and the atmosphere is historic in a way very few other LA eateries can manage. Must-have options include guacamole (made tableside), green corn tamales and the margaritas.

Other locations 1025 Wilshire Boulevard, Santa Monica (1-310 899 1106); 1037 S Flower Street, Downtown (1-213 746 7750).

Chosun Galbee
3330 W Olympic Boulevard, at S Manhattan Place (1-323 734 3330, www.chosungalbee.com). Bus 28, 207, 728, 757/I-10, exit Western Avenue north. **Open** 11am-11pm daily. **Main courses** $32. **Credit** AmEx, DC, Disc, MC, V. **Map** p313 C6 🔟 **Korean**

If you're new to Korean food but fancy learning a little more about it, this upscale Koreatown spot is a good choice. The grub is tasty, authentic and popular with Koreans, but it isn't the spiciest in town, and the servers speak fluent English. The menu includes noodles, rice dishes and casseroles; however, you should try *gal bi*, marinated short ribs grilled at your table and served with a delicate tang.

Guelaguetza
3014 W Olympic Boulevard, at Irolo Street (1-213 427 0608, www.guelaguetzarestaurante. com). Metro Wilshire-Normandie/bus 28, 206, 728/I-10, exit Vermont Avenue north. **Open** 9am-10pm Mon-Thur, Sun; 9am-11pm Fri, Sat. **Main courses** $11. **Credit** AmEx, DC, Disc, MC, V. **Map** p313 D6 🔟 **Mexican**

The *guelaguetza* is a Oaxacan dance; its use as the name of this restaurant is a reminder that the food served here differs from classic Mexican. The speciality is meat (chicken, beef or pork) served with richly fragrant and spicy sauces called *moles*, which use fresh-ground herbs and chocolate to create a depth of flavour. Try the oxtail stew or a *tlayuda*, a strange pizza-like corn cake, with a fresh juice.

Papa Cristo's
2771 W Pico Boulevard, at S Normandie Avenue (1-323 737 2970, www.papacristos.com). Bus 30, 206, 330/I-10, exit Normandie Avenue north. **Open** 9.30am-8pm Tue-Sat; 9am-4pm Sun. **Main courses** $12. **Credit** AmEx, DC, Disc, MC, V. **Map** p313 D6 🔟 **Greek**

Papa Cristo's sits in the shadow of the Greek Orthodox cathedral in LA's Byzantine-Latino District, one of the more interesting cultural fusions in this very mixed city. The simple grilled meats and seafood are always good, but the best day to visit is on a Thursday, when the restaurant offers complete family-style dinners with wine tastings and entertainment for $24 per person. Good fun.

Soot Bull Jeep
3136 W 8th Street, between S Kenmore & S Catalina Streets (1-213 387 3865). Metro Wilshire-Western/bus 66, 204, 206/I-10, exit Vermont Avenue north. **Open** 11am-11pm daily. **Main courses** $20. **Credit** AmEx, DC, Disc, MC, V. **Map** p314 A6 🔟 **Korean**

Soot Bull Jeep is one of the few Koreatown restaurants that hasn't switched to gas or electric grills, and the smoke from the charcoal fires permeates everything. The side items are good but basic; the real attraction is the excellent meat, which comes with a predictably but pleasingly smoky flavour and spicy sauce.

Taylor's Steak House
3361 W 8th Street, at S Ardmore Avenue (1-213 382 8449, www.taylorssteakhouse.com). Metro Wilshire-Normandie/bus 66, 206/I-10, exit Western Avenue north. **Open** 11.30am-9.30pm Mon-Thur; 11.30am-10.30pm Fri; 4-10.30pm Sat; 4-9.30pm Sun. **Main courses** *Lunch* $16. *Dinner* $25. **Credit** AmEx, DC, Disc, MC, V. **Map** p313 D5 🔟 **American**

In this city of illusions, it should come as no surprise to stumble upon a steakhouse that looks and feels decades older than it actually is. Founded in 1953 but on this site only since 1970, Taylor's cultivates a 1930s feel. The old-fashioned atmosphere and hearty food have kept the restaurant in business, even as the neighbourhood has changed around it.

LOS FELIZ TO ECHO PARK
Los Feliz

Fred 62
1850 N Vermont Avenue, at Franklin Avenue (1-323 667 0062, www.fred62.com). Bus 180, 181/US 101, exit Vermont Avenue north. **Open** 24hrs daily. **Main courses** $11. **Credit** AmEx, DC, Disc, MC, V. **Map** p314 A2 🔟 **Cafés & diners**

Chef Fred Eric was born in 1962, which explains the name of this 24-7 diner on Vermont. The food can be a bit erratic, though the breakfasts and the meatloaf are among the best in the city. Still, even if the cooking doesn't knock you out, the funky decor and the good service should be enough to raise your spirits.

Little Dom's
2128 Hillhurst Avenue, at Avocado Street (1-323 661 0055, www.littledoms.com). Bus 180, 181/ I-5, exit Los Feliz Boulevard west. **Open** 8am-3pm, 5.30-11pm Mon-Thur, Sun; 8am-midnight Fri, Sat. **Main courses** $16. **Credit** AmEx, DC, MC, V. **Map** p314 B1 🔟 **Italian**

Since opening in 2008, this popular neighbourhood joint, younger brother of 60-year-old Dominick's in West Hollywood (8715 Beverly Boulevard, 1-310 652 2335), has stayed crammed with hipsters, young families and celebs alike. The ricotta and blueberry pancakes are absurdly good, while the three-course Monday-night dinner for $15 is a steal.

SanSui
2040 Hillhurst Avenue, between Ambrose & Finley Avenues (1-323 660 3868, www.san-sui.com). Bus 180, 181/I-5, exit Los Feliz Boulevard west. **Open**

CONSUME

11.30am-2pm, 5.30-9.45pm Mon-Fri; 5.30-9.45pm Sat, Sun. **Main courses** *Lunch* $11. *Dinner* $20. *Sushi* $8. **Credit** AmEx, DC, Disc, MC, V. **Map** p314 B2 ⑰ **Japanese**

Unlike most Japanese restaurants in LA, this tranquil eaterie specialises in what it calls 'mountain cuisine'. Bowls of hearty udon soup are available, as is sushi, but why not try one of the rice bowls with burdock or lotus root and mushrooms? A peaceful venue in the middle of a hectic nightlife district.

Tropicalia

1966 Hillhurst Avenue, at Clarissa Avenue (1-323 644 1798, www.tropicaliabraziliangrill.com). Bus 180, 181/I-5, exit Los Feliz Boulevard west. **Open** 11am-10.30pm Mon-Thur, Sun; 11am-11.30pm Fri, Sat. **Main courses** $13. **Credit** AmEx, DC, Disc, MC, V. **Map** p314 B2 ⑱ **Brazilian**

Most Brazilian restaurants in LA focus on *churrascaria*, essentially a special occasion barbecue feast. Tropicalia, though, is more interesting, offering a range of rainforest and coastal recipes. The restaurant's owners are also wine merchants, which helps explain the well-chosen and interesting list.

Silver Lake

Alegria on Sunset

3510 W Sunset Boulevard, at Maltman Avenue (1-323 913 1422, www.alegriaonsunset.com). Bus 2, 175, 302/US 101, exit Silver Lake Boulevard north. **Open** 11am-10pm Mon-Thur; 11am-11pm Fri; 10am-11pm Sat. **Main courses** *Breakfast & lunch* $10. *Dinner* $15. **Credit** AmEx, DC, MC, V. **Map** p314 C3 ⑲ **Mexican**

Located in a seen-better-days strip mall, Alegria transcends its unbecoming location with some lively and agreeably messy Mexican food. The dinners are good, but you may have to wait for a table (it doesn't take reservations); breakfast and lunch are perfectly acceptable alternatives.

Café Stella

3932 W Sunset Boulevard, between Sanborn & Hyperion Avenues (1-323 666 0265, www.cafestella.com). Bus 2, 175, 302/US 101, exit Silver Lake Boulevard north. **Open** 6-11pm Mon-Sat; 6-10pm Sun. **Main courses** $25. **Credit** AmEx, DC, MC, V. **Map** p314 B3 ⑳ **French**

Located just near Sunset Junction, Café Stella can get pretty cramped, and the service is sometimes poor when the restaurant is busy. However, on mellower nights, the atmosphere is charming, and the French bistro food is usually very good: order steak frites, mussels or the famous beet salad.

Edendale

2838 Rowena Avenue, between Hyperion Avenue & Glendale Boulevard (1-323 666 2000, www.theedendale.com). Bus 92, 96, 201/I-5, exit Hyperion Avenue west. **Open** 5-10pm Mon-Wed; 5-11pm Thur-Sat; 11am-3pm, 5-10pm Sun. **Main courses** $20. **Credit** AmEx, DC, MC, V. **Map** p314 D2 ㉑ **American**

The building that houses the Edendale spent most of its life as a fire station, but the land on which it sits has long-established ties to the movie industry: cinema buffs will enjoy looking at the old prints on the weathered brick walls. Deals are done in the restaurant over seared New Zealand salmon or the legendarily good bacon-wrapped lamb meatballs.

$ Millie's

3524 W Sunset Boulevard, at Maltman Avenue (1-323 664 0404, www.milliescafe.net). Bus 2, 4, 302/US 101, exit Silver Lake Boulevard north. **Open** 7.30am-4pm daily. **Main courses** $10. **Credit** DC, Disc, MC, V. **Map** p314 C3 ㉒ **Cafés & diners**

This cheerful little breakfast and lunch joint is tiny and often packed, but the inexpensive but generous food is worth the wait and the servers rise to the challenge of delivering it quickly to the hungry hordes of diners. Try the home-made granola or the weird but alluring hangover cure called the Devil's Mess.

Atwater Village

Tam O'Shanter

2980 Los Feliz Boulevard, between Revere & Boyce Avenues (1-323 664 0228, www.lawrysonline.com/tam-oshanter). Bus 180, 181, 201/I-5, exit Los Feliz Boulevard east. **Open** *Restaurant* 11am-2pm, 5-9pm Mon-Thur; 11am-2pm, 5-10pm Fri; 11am-4pm, 4-10pm Sat; 10.30am-2.30pm, 4-9pm Sun. *Sandwich & ale bar* 11am-11pm daily. **Main courses** *Lunch* $25. *Dinner* $34. **Credit** AmEx, DC, Disc, MC, V. **American**

See p106 **Vintage Vittles**.

DOWNTOWN

★ Bäco Mercat

408 S Main Street, between W 4th & Winston Streets (1-213 673 1480, www.bacomercat.com). Bus 1, 33/I-110, exit Bristol Street. **Open** 11.30am-2.30pm, 5.30-11pm Mon-Thur; 11.30am-3pm, 5.30pm-midnight Fri, Sat; 11.30am-3pm, 5-10pm Sun. **Main courses** $15. **Map** p315 C3 ㉓ **Mediterranean**

Chef Josef Centeno's first solo venture captures not only the zeitgeist of Downtown's white-hot dining but also the incredible multiculti spirit of Los Angeles at large. The centrepiece is the *bäco*, an unlikely hybrid that is equal parts Mediterranean flatbread, Mexican taco and sheer, mad genius. It's available in seven or eight iterations, including the original: a soft, pillowy flatbread stuffed with Centeno's unique take on *carnitas* (normally just pork, his includes beef) along with fresh herbs, baby greens and a tomato spread. Also excellent: the vegetable dishes and the cocktails. *Photo p113.*

CONSUME

Meals on Wheels

LA's mobile food vans keep on truckin'.

Life in Los Angeles revolves around two things: cars and food. So it makes sense that the two would eventually come together in a big way. While *loncheras* – food trucks serving Mexican food to Latino workers – have been roaming the streets of LA for decades, the last few years have seen a huge growth in the number of other culinary carts doing the rounds.

The pattern is simple and familiar: a truck Tweets its location, and hungry followers turn up and wait in line. Sometimes for hours.

The vehicle widely credited with kicking off the recent trend is the **Kogi** Korean barbecue truck (http://kogibbq.com). From one lowly truck dishing out orders of 'blackjack' quesadillas and short rib tacos in 2008, owner Roy Choi has now grown his business into a fleet of four vans, upwards of 100,000 Twitter followers and a bricks-and-mortar restaurant, Alibi Room (12236 Washington Boulevard, Culver City, 1-310 390 9300, www.alibiroomla.com). As Choi told us, 'I just threw the ball on the field… the other (truck)s can kick it around.'

And kick it around they have. Through the internet, excitement about Kogi spread, and other budding wheeler-dealers started spotting the potential. These days, there are dozens of trucks in LA and OC, several Twitter stream aggregators (such as www.findlafoodtrucks.com) and websites such as http://roaminghunger.com, which shows the current location of food trucks on a map. There are even food truck festivals – the summertime **LA Street Food Fest** at the Pasadena Rose Bowl (http://www.lastreetfoodfest.com) and a regular **Truckit** fest (www.truckitfest.com), which runs in conjunction with Downtown LA's monthly art walk (second Thursday of the month), to name but two. (And talking of names, we wonder if there's a secret contest going on for the worst pun: Crepe'n Around, Shrimp Pimp or… wait for it… Truck Norris – groan – serving Hawaiian Filipino fusion.)

Just as the city is a melting pot of people and cuisines, all types of ethnic food are served up from LA's food trucks, from the **Mighty Boba**'s tapioca tea and Taiwanese sausage (http://mightyboba.com) to **India Jones**'s butter chicken curry and the like

(https://twitter.com/IndiaJonesCT). And it's not just savoury fare: ice-cream sandwiches from **Coolhaus** (www.eatcoolhaus.com; *see also p134* **Cold Comfort**) and cupcakes and other naughty treats from B Sweet (www.mybsweet.com) are up for grabs, too.

And let's not forget staples. Busting for a burger? Napalm Death (with Pepper Jack cheese, jalapeños and *habanero aioli*) with a side of über-popular tater tots from **Grill 'Em All** (www.grillemalltruck.com) will see you right, as will the chilli cheese fries from **Frysmith** (www.eatfrysmith.com). Too lazy to put together a grilled cheese sandwich? Ta-da! Someone's done it for you (www.thegrilledcheesetruck.com). Overdid it on the booze last night? There's nothing like the **Buttermilk** truck's (http://buttermilktruck.com) biscuit breakfast sandwich, with cheese, fried egg, bacon and a side order of rosemary garlic hash browns, to soothe those sore guts. Or try brekkie-slinging **Egg Slut** (http://eggslut.com), frequently found outside Handsome Coffee Roasters in Downtown LA and the Palihotel in the Fairfax District. Not fancy enough? How about a lobster roll from the **Lobsta** truck (www.lobstatruck.com). We've even heard rumours of a devilled eggs truck. (What next? A caviar and champagne truck?)

Of course, it's not all been plain sailing (or driving). Critics complain that when trucks pitch up en masse at events such as Venice's First Fridays (*see p39*), they clog the already packed streets, creating major congestion. Indeed, that's the one obvious drawback to the food truck phenomenon: you've driven to the truck – now where's the valet?

CONSUME

THE BEST FOR LUNCH

Sausage and fries and beer, oh my!
Wurstküche. *See p115.*

Superbly fresh ingredients that shine.
Huckleberry Café. *See p95.*

Cafeteria-style grub on the go.
Lemonade. *See right.*

▶ *Josef Centeno also runs nearby Bar Amá (118 West 4th Street, Downtown, 1-213 673 1480), serving Tex-Mex grub inspired by family recipes and a drinks list that's heavy on tequila, mezcal and Mexican beer.*

Drago Centro

525 S Flower Street, between W 5th & W 6th Streets (1-213 228 8998, www.celestinodrago. com). Metro 7th Street-Metro Center/bus 14, 37, 70, 71, 76, 78, 79, 96, 378, 487, 498, 707/ I-110, exit 6th Street east. **Open** 11.30am-2.30pm, 5-10pm Mon-Fri; 5-10pm Sat; 5-9pm Sun. **Main courses** *Lunch* $20. *Dinner* $29. **Credit** AmEx, DC, Disc, MC, V. **Map** p315 B3 ⓺4 **Italian**
The Drago family's Los Angeles restaurant empire started out in 1991 in Santa Monica, and it was a celebrity-friendly hangout that was worth the often rather substantial expense required to dine there. But that location closed in 2012, and now Drago Centro is the family of restaurants' flagship location and it continues to serve stylishly arranged but mostly traditional renditions of Italian regional cuisine.
Other locations Enoteca Drago, 410 N Canon Drive, Beverly Hills (1-310 786 8236); Il Pastiao Ristorante, 400 N Canon Drive, Beverly Hills (1-310 205 544); Osteria Drago, 8741 W Sunset Boulevard (1-310 657 1182).

Lazy Ox Canteen

241 S San Pedro Street, between E 2nd & E 3rd Streets (1-213 626 5299, www.lazyoxcanteen. com). Metro Little Tokyo/Arts District/bus 30, 40, 42, 330, 442/I-101, exit 4th Street. **Open** 11.30am-2.30pm, 5-11pm Mon-Wed; 11.30am-2.30pm, 5pm-midnight Thur-Fri; 10am-3pm, 5pm-midnight Sat; 10am-3pm, 5-11pm Sun. **Main courses** $20. **Credit** AmEx, Disc, MC, V. **Map** p315 D3 ⓺5 **Gastropub**
Michael Cardenas' casual eaterie is thriving, despite changes in personnel (original chef Josef Centeno went to open Bäco Mercat (*see p110*), and his replacement, Perfecto Rocher, left not long after). As a nod to its Little Tokyo location, Asian influences are dotted throughout the menu, but you'll also find classic gastropub fare such as burgers. Dinner can get pricey; come for lunch instead, when the pulled

pork sandwich with tomato confit and pickled red onions on a house-made brioche bun reigns supreme.

★ $ Lemonade

515 S Flower Street, at 5th Street (1-213 488 0299, www.lemonadela.com). Metro 7th Street-Metro Center/bus 14, 37, 70, 71, 76, 78, 79, 96, 378, 487, 498, 707/I-110, exit 6th Street east. **Open** 11am-3pm Mon-Fri. **Main courses** $8. **Credit** AmEx, Disc, MC, V. **Map** p314 B3 ⓺6 **American**
LA needs more of this type of mini-chain. The lengthy menu covers cafeteria-style dishes (braises such as red miso beef short rib), rices, noodles, pastas and side dishes, plus toothsome sandwiches (beef and horseradish aioli, for instance). To drink, there are basic coffees, plus soft drinks including a variety of lemonades. OK, the $1 cupcakes won't grab any awards, and at busy times the ordering system can get a bit chaotic, but overall Lemonade is a winner. Some branches are open at weekends.
Other locations throughout LA.

Ocean Seafood

750 N Hill Street, between Ord & Alpine Streets (1-213 687 3088, www.oceansf.com). Metro Union Station/bus 45, 68, 81, 84, 90, 91, 96, 796/US 101, exit Alameda Street north. **Open** 9am-10pm Mon-Fri; 8am-10pm Sat, Sun. **Main courses** $14. **Credit** AmEx, DC, Disc, MC, V. **Map** p315 C1 ⓺7 **Chinese**
The culinary capital of Chinese food in LA is now Monterey Park, but the restaurants in Chinatown still have a devoted following. Ocean Seafood is the best bet in the area for Hong Kong-style dim sum, and also offers fresh fish from the tanks. The big upstairs room is packed every weekend; however, if you go during the week, you're unlikely to wait.

Original Pantry

877 S Figueroa Street, at 9th Street (1-213 972 9279, www.pantrycafe.com). Metro 7th Street-Metro Center/bus 28, 442, 493, 497, 498, 499, 701, 721/I-110, exit 9th Street east. **Open** 24hrs daily. **Main courses** $13. **No credit cards**. **Map** p315 B4 ⓺8 **Cafés & diners**
There's no lock on the door, nor does there need to be: now owned by former mayor Richard Riordan, this greasy spoon has been open 24-7 since 1934, with only the briefest of breaks to rework the kitchen into modern health standards. Expect American diner favourites in gargantuan portions; nothing is exceptional, but everything is good.

Pacific Dining Car

1310 W 6th Street, at Columbia Avenue (1-213 483 6000, www.pacificdiningcar.com). Bus 18, 20, 720/I-110, exit 6th Street west. **Open** 24hrs daily. **Main courses** $40. **Credit** AmEx, DC, Disc, MC, V. **American**
See p106 **Vintage Vittles**.

Bäco Mercat. See p110.

Parish

840 S Spring Street, at S Main Street (1-213 225 2400, www.theparishla.com). Bus 10, 33, 48, 55, 66, 92, 355, 721/I-10, exit Maple Avenue. **Open** 8am-midnight Mon-Wed; 8am-2am Thur, Fri; 9am-2am Sat; 9am-midnight Sun. **Main courses** $17. **Credit** AmEx, DC, MC, V. **Map** p315 C4 ⑥⑨ Gastropub

Rising star chef Casey Lane's laid-back, two-storey English-inspired gastropub is perfectly calibrated for its still-gentrifying 'hood. To get a good feel for the place, sit on the upstairs patio beneath a lovely shady tree, order a couple of rounds of devilled eggs and fried olives and sit back with a strong cocktail. Is it a bar? Is it a pub? Is it a restaurant? The lines are seamlessly blurred. Standout dishes include the poutine (fries covered in a topping such as pig trotter ragu), the buttermilk fried chicken and the marrowbone.

▶ *The Parish is the perfect pre- or post- hangout for the gorgeous Orpheum theatre (see p218), where there's always something interesting going on.*

Patina

Walt Disney Concert Hall, 141 S Grand Avenue, between W 2nd & W 3rd Streets (1-213 972 3331, www.patinarestaurant.com). Metro Civic Center/Grand Park/Tom Bradley/bus 10, 14, 37, 70, 71, 76, 78, 79, 96, 378, 442/I-110, exit 3rd Street east. **Open** 5-9.30pm Tue-Sat; 4-9pm Sun. **Closed** from 9.30pm on nights when there is no performance. **Main courses** $42. **Credit** AmEx, DC, Disc, MC, V. **Map** p315 B2 ⑦⓪ Italian

For a while, the Patina Group opened new restaurants at a fearsome pace. The quality suffered, and it took time for it to regain its previous consistency. This Disney Hall restaurant seems to be the group's current flagship, and is as adventurous as the Patina of old: Charles Olalia took over as chef de cuisine in mid 2012: here's hoping he keeps standards high. Expensive, but worth it.

$ Philippe the Original

1001 N Alameda Street, at Ord Street (1-213 628 3781, www.philippes.com). Metro Union Station/bus 10, 45, 68, 83, 84, 96/US 101, exit Alameda Street north. **Open** 6am-10pm daily. **Main courses** $8. **No credit cards.** **Map** p315 D1 ⑦① Cafés & diners

See p106 **Vintage Vittles.**

Rivera

1050 S Flower Street, at W 11th Street (1-213 749 1460, www.riverarestaurant.com). Bus 81, 442, 460/I-110, exit 6th Street/9th Street. **Open** 11.30am-2pm, 5.30-10.30pm Mon-Wed; 11.30am-2pm, 5.30pm-midnight Thur, Fri; 5.30-10.30pm Sat; 5.30-10pm Sun. **Main courses** $25. **Credit** AmEx, MC, V. **Map** p315 B5 ⑦② Latin

If one single thing were needed to illustrate Downtown's revival in the last few years, it would be Rivera. Newcomers may have stolen the spotlight somewhat, but this restaurant is still a contender. From the cocktails through to the desserts, chef John Sedlar's inventive pan-Latin cuisine merits multiple explorations, not least because there are three menus, one for each separate room within the restaurant.

Spring Street Smokehouse

640 N Spring Street, at E César E Chávez Avenue (1-213 626 0535, www.sssmokehouse.com). Metro Union Station/bus 10, 45, 68, 76, 83, 84, 96/US 101, exit Alameda Street north. **Open** 10.30am-9pm Mon-Thur; 10.30am-10pm Fri; noon-10pm Sat; noon-9pm Sun. **Main courses** $14. **Credit** AmEx, DC, Disc, MC, V. **Map** p315 C1 ⑦③ American

Located on the edge of Chinatown, the Spring Street Smokehouse is a barbecue joint that was formerly owned by the catering service for the nearby county jail. However, never fear, you'll eat better than the prisoners. Served with very spicy sauce, the pork ribs and beef brisket are the standouts, but the kitchen also turns out good sandwiches and, if you

CONSUME

Pancake Perfection

A handful of the city's better batters.

Angelenos often get a bum rap for being overly carb-conscious, but that's not quite true. Come brunch time, you'll see that for every egg white omelette and seasonal fruit bowl on the table, there are also stacks of pancakes drowning in thick, melting pats of butter and maple syrup. Diet be damned.

On Sundays, Koreatown craft beer bar **Beer Belly** (532 S Western Avenue, 1-213 387 2337, http://beerbellyla.com) serves up a boozy bevy of brunch dishes to help you sop up that wicked morning hangover. Snickers pancakes are perfect for morning munchies: bits of Snickers bar are embedded like gold nuggets in a huge, dinner-plate-sized pancake that's worth every carb. Whatever risk it runs of being too sweet is balanced by the savoury maple syrup served alongside. And to drink? Beer, natch. If it's on tap, the Firestone Velvet Merlin, an oatmeal stout, makes a particularly good pairing. Beer and pancakes: the breakfast of champions.

At weekends, the sidewalk outside Hollywood's **Square One Dining** (4854 Fountain Avenue, 1-323 661 1109, www.squareonedining.com) is packed with neighbourhood locals waiting for a table – and taking in the view of the blue Scientology building across the street. The buttermilk pancakes have purists rejoicing, but they're just the starting point for pancake deviants, who like to add bacon-enriched caramel sauce.

Pity the blueberry ricotta pancake on any menu other than the one at **BLD** in the Fairfax District (7450 Beverly Boulevard, 1-323 930 9744, www.bldrestaurant.com). Indeed, the restaurant's blueberry ricotta pancakes are so good they're the standard to which all others are compared. BLD's version has a richness courtesy of the ricotta, and there are enough blueberries dotting the pancake landscape to guarantee a burst of sweetness in every bite. On the side, Berkshire maple syrup is served in a log cabin-shaped tin. At weekends, be prepared for a wait.

The seasonal fare at **Cooks County** (8009 Beverly Boulevard, 1-323 653 8009, www.cookscountyrestaurant.com), also in the Fairfax District, makes the restaurant a popular dinner destination for neighbourhood locals, so it's no surprise that the same crowd shows up on weekend mornings for brunch. And a good number of those folks order the lovely – and enormous – buttermilk pancake. With crisp, chewy edges and a sweet, toothsome interior, the cast iron skillet-baked creation is finished with a dusting of powdered sugar; it's somehow improved with the accompanying huckleberry compôte and bourbon-barrel maple syrup.

Located in the beachside Fairmont Miramar hotel in Santa Monica, **Fig** (101 Wilshire Boulevard, 1-310 319 3111, www.figsantamonica.com) gives you the choice of brunching in its gorgeous dining room or outside next to a bluer-than-blue pool. Thankfully, it doesn't rely only on its ambience to convince you that it's one of the best brunch spots on the Westside; instead, it offers luxurious lemon ricotta pancakes that strike just the right, subtle balance between sweet and tangy (and at $15, they should). And that thick pat of almond-blueberry butter? The icing on the pancake.

If you have a longstanding grudge against wholegrain pancakes – they usually taste like cardboard or are too dense to eat more than a forkful – get yourself to Venice's **Axe** (1009 Abbot Kinney Boulevard, 1-310 664 9787, www.axerestaurant.com). There, the nine-grain pancake forces you to rethink your preconceptions. Made with the brown oats, flax, millet and other grains that wouldn't be out of place in a proper wholegrain loaf or a satisfying bowl of granola, the pancake here is everything you thought it wouldn't be. Light. Flavourful. Sweet. Delicious. It's also huge, so order one to share.

CONSUME

call ahead, smoked turkey. You can also expect a good selection of beers and a weekday happy hour that begins at 3pm.

Traxx

Union Station, 800 N Alameda Street, between US 101 & E César E Chávez Avenue (1-213 625 1999, www.traxxrestaurant.com). Metro Union Station/bus 4, 10, 40, 68, 84, 442/US 101, exit Alameda Street north. **Open** *Restaurant* 11.30am-2.30pm, 5.30-9pm Mon-Fri; 5-9pm Sat. *Bar* 11.30am-10pm Mon-Sat. **Main courses** *Lunch* $20. *Dinner* $23. **Credit** AmEx, DC, MC, V. **Map** p315 D1 ⑰ **American**

People with no plans to take a train often come to dine at Traxx in Union Station: the food really is that good. It's surprisingly adventurous: crispy parsnip pancakes with smoked salmon, crème fraîche and chives, striped bass with caramelized fennel and coriander vinaigrette, house-cured pork chops with fig polenta. The art deco appearance and the excellent people-watching from the terrace add visual appeal.

★ WP24

Ritz-Carlton Hotel, 900 W Olympic Boulevard, at Georgia Street (1-213 743 8824, www.wolfgangpuck.com). Bus 28, 81, 442, 460/I-110, exit 6th Street/9th Street. **Open** 5.30-10pm Mon-Sat; 5.30-9pm Sun. **Main courses** *Set menus* $80-$110. **Credit** AmEx, DC, Disc, MC, V. **Map** p315 A4 ⑮ **Asian**

As if the setting itself – the 24th floor of the Ritz-Carlton – wasn't exciting enough (check out those views of Downtown LA), Wolfgang Puck's Asian menu is also a knockout. Diners choose from one of the set menus, but if they seem too pricey, head for the equally gorgeous adjacent bar, which offers a similar menu. Whichever you opt for, don't miss the pork belly dumplings, spicy chicken *dan dan* dumplings or the pumpkin pie cake.

$ Wurstküche

800 E 3rd Street, at Traction Avenue (1-213 687 4444, www.wurstkucherestaurant.com). Bus 30, 40, 330/I-10, exit 4th Street. **Open** 11am-midnight daily. **Main courses** $7. **Credit** AmEx, MC, V. **Gastropub**

If you've a hankering for hearty comfort food, this is the place for you. Order at the front counter then head to the cavernous German beer hall-style back room and wait for your grub to arrive. Sausages range from the basic (bratwurst, bockwurst) to the exotic (rattlesnake and rabbit, anyone?) and the fries come with dipping sauces. There are interesting Belgian and German beers on draft and tap, too. **Other locations** 625 Lincoln Boulevard, Venice (1-213 687 4444).

▶ *Other sausage-centric eateries in LA include Berlin Currywurst (www.berlincurrywurst.com), with locations in Silver Lake (3827 W Sunset*

Boulevard, 1-323 663 1989) and Hollywood (1620 N Cahuenga Boulevard, 1-323 467 7593), and Wirsthaus (345 N La Brea Avenue, Fairfax District, 1-323 931 9291, www.wirsthausla.com).

THE VALLEYS
San Fernando Valley

Alcazar

17239 Ventura Boulevard, between Louise & Amestoy Avenues, Encino (1-818 789 0991, www.al-cazar.com). Bus 150, 240/I-405, exit Ventura Boulevard west. **Open** 5-10pm Tue-Thur; 5pm-midnight Fri; noon-2am Sat; noon-9pm Sun. **Main courses** $15. **Credit** AmEx, DC, Disc, MC, V. **Lebanese**

Los Angeles has few high-style, high-end Lebanese restaurants, but Alcazar stands out among the not particularly vigorous competition. The oriental opulence of the dining room is a perfect setting for the high-quality Arabic food on the menu: order one of the combination plates or pile the table with appetisers from the list of mezedes.

Art's Deli

12224 Ventura Boulevard, between Laurel Canyon Boulevard & Whitsett Avenue, Studio City (1-818 762 1221, www.artsdeli.com). Bus 150, 240/US 101, exit Laurel Canyon Boulevard south. **Open** 7am-9pm daily. **Main courses** *Breakfast* $13. *Lunch/Dinner* $15. **Credit** AmEx, DC, Disc, MC, V. **Jewish**

Opened in 1957, Art Ginsburg's deli has built a great reputation and a very loyal following with its menu of hefty sandwiches and excellent chicken noodle and cabbage soups. If you stick to the traditional dishes, you're assured of a good meal.

Dr Hogly-Wogly's Tyler Texas BBQ

8136 Sepulveda Boulevard, between Roscoe Boulevard & Lanark Street, Panorama City (1-818 780 6701, www.hoglywogly.com). Bus 152, 234, 734/I-405, exit Roscoe Boulevard east. **Open** 11.30am-10pm daily. **Main courses** $13. **Credit** AmEx, DC, Disc, MC, V. **American**

Many people swear that this by-the-roadside shack is the only authentic Texas barbecue joint in Los Angeles; whether that's true or not, it's without doubt one of the best. Supplement your slabs of smoky meat and dollops of spicy sauce with potato salad and coleslaw, and try to save room for a slice of pecan pie.

Saddle Peak Lodge

419 Cold Canyon Road, at Piuma Road, Calabasas (1-818 222 3888, www.saddlepeaklodge.com). No bus/PCH, exit Malibu Canyon Road. **Open** 6-9pm Wed, Thur; 6-10pm Fri; 5-10pm Sat; 10.30am-2pm, 5-9pm Sun. **Main courses** $40. **Credit** AmEx, DC, Disc, MC, V. **American**

CONSUME

This upscale lodge at the end of a country road was a Hollywood star retreat in the 1920s, and retains an Old West feel. The speciality is game: partridge, elk and venison are favourites, though the specials can include even more exotic fare. The weekend brunch is popular with people out for a day in the country; alternatively, come to view sunset from the upper dining rooms.

$ Sushi Yotsuya

18760 Ventura Boulevard, between Burbank Boulevard & Yolanda Avenue, Tarzana (1-818 708 9675). Bus 150, 154, 240, 741/US 101, exit Reseda Boulevard south. **Open** noon-2pm, 6-10pm Tue-Fri; 5.30-10pm Sat; 5.30-8.30pm Sun. **Sushi** $4-$10. **Credit** AmEx, DC, MC, V. **Japanese**
Ventura Boulevard is known as Sushi Row because of the number and quality of Japanese restaurants along its length; Yotsuya is among the most celebrated of them. Chef Masa Matsumoto is a traditionalist: there are no novelties here, just lovely fresh fish on warm rice with delicate Japanese seasonings.

San Gabriel Valley

Empress Harbor

111 N Atlantic Boulevard, at W Garvey Avenue, Monterey Park (1-626 300 8833, www.empress harbor.net). Bus 70, 260, 762, 770/I-10, exit Atlantic Boulevard south. **Open** 9am-10pm daily. **Main courses** $15. **Credit** AmEx, DC, MC, V. **Chinese**
The city of Monterey Park fills to capacity every weekend with Chinese families shopping and eating dim sum. If you're after the latter, Empress Harbor is a great bet: it's a huge place, but service is brisk and the food is very decent. The English-language skills of the servers are only moderate, but that's nonetheless a step above many other restaurants in the area.

Japon Bistro

927 E Colorado Boulevard, between N Lake & N Mentor Avenues, Pasadena (1-626 744 1751, www.japonbistro-pasadena.com). Metro Lake/bus 20, 180, 181, 187, 256, 485, 780/I-210, exit Lake Avenue south. **Open** 11.30am-2.30pm Mon; 11.30am-2.30pm, 5-9.30pm Tue-Thur; 11.30am-2.30pm, 5-10.30pm Fri; 5-10.30pm Sat; 5-9.30pm Sun. **Main courses** *Lunch* $12. *Dinner* $23. **Credit** AmEx, DC, MC, V. **Japanese**
Japanese ideas are modernised with references to other cuisines at Japon Bistro. Try the different sushis, but pay close attention to the specials. The saké bar has some limited-release Japanese varieties that can be expensive but might stretch your definition of perfection.

La Luna Negra

44 W Green Street, between S Fair Oaks & S De Lacey Avenues, Pasadena (1-626 844 4331, www.lalunanegrarestaurant.com). Metro Del Mar/bus 10, 260, 686, 687/Hwy 134, exit Orange Grove Boulevard south. **Open** 11am-2pm, 5-10pm Tue-Thur; 11am-11pm Fri, Sat; 11am-10pm Sun. **Main courses** $25. **Tapas** $11. **Credit** AmEx, DC, MC, V. **Spanish**
La Luna Negra attracts a young, party-hearty crowd every night. The tables are tightly packed and the room is boisterous; on nights when there's a band playing, you can forget conversation. However, the food is worth attention, with standard tapas, paellas and roasts joined by more modern oddities.

Wahib's Middle East Restaurant

910 E Main Street, at S Granada Avenue, Alhambra (1-626 281 1006, www.wahib middleeast.com). Bus 78, 79, 176, 378/I-10, exit Garfield Avenue north. **Open** 9am-10pm daily. **Main courses** *Breakfast* $6. *Lunch/ dinner* $14. **Credit** AmEx, DC, Disc, MC, V. **Middle Eastern**
A lunch spot and casual family restaurant during the week, Wahib's morphs into a nightclub at the weekends. The kitchen bakes its own breads and pastries; the lamb dishes are superb. On Sundays, there's an amazing all-in buffet for only $14.95.

$ Yazmin

27 E Main Street, between Garfield Avenue & N Stoneman Avenue, Alhambra (1-626 308 2036, http://yazminmalaysian.tumblr.com). Bus 78, 176, 258, 378/I-10, exit Garfield Avenue north. **Open** 11am-3pm, 5-9.30pm Mon, Wed, Thur; 11am-3pm, 5-10pm Fri; 11am-10pm Sat; 11am-9.30pm Sun. **Main courses** $9. **Credit** DC, MC, V. **Malaysian**
LA has few Malaysian and Singaporean restaurants, but the community near the imposing mosque has supported all manner of nearby eateries, among them Yazmin. It's a bright, cheerful and inexpensive place; menu highlights include laksa soup.

HEADING SOUTH
The South Bay

Darren's

1141 Manhattan Avenue, at 12th Street, Manhattan Beach (1-310 802 1973, www. darrensrestaurant.com). Bus 126, 232/I-405, exit Hawthorne Boulevard north. **Open** 5-10.30pm Mon-Sat. **Main courses** $28. **Credit** AmEx, DC, MC, V. **Californian**
Chef Darren Weiss has built a reputation on full-flavoured dishes such as beet and haricot vert salad, rock shrimp ravioli and Thai peanut-crusted salmon. At this elegant salon-like room, he serves all his old favourites and daily specials inspired by the market.

★ Manhattan Beach Post

1142 Manhattan Avenue, at Center Place, Manhattan Beach (1-310 545 5405,

*www.eatmbpost.com). Bus 102, 109, 438/I-405,
exit Rosecrans Avenue west.* **Open** 5-10pm Mon-
Thur; 11.30am-10.30pm Fri; 10am-10.30pm Sat;
10am-10pm Sun. **Main courses** $15. **Credit**
AmEx, Disc, MC, V. **American**
You've probably never dreamed of eating brunch in a
post office, but that's the experience at chef David
LeFevre's hip, rustic restaurant. MB Post – the restaurant takes its name from its former resident, the
Manhattan Beach Post Office – delivers a daily changing menu that echoes the farm-to-table California
mantra. Steak is grilled over white oak and layered
with a poached egg, broccolini and red chimichurri
sauce. A slew of communal tables make for a social
brunch, with a batch of seasonal cocktails at the ready.

Restaurant Christine
*24530 Hawthorne Boulevard, at Newton Street,
Torrance (1-310 373 1952, www.restaurant
christine.com). Bus 344/I-110, exit Hwy 1 west.*
Open 11.30am-2pm, 5-9pm Mon-Fri; 5-10pm Sat.
Main courses *Lunch* $15. *Dinner* $25. **Credit**
AmEx, DC, Disc, MC, V. **American**
At her eponymous restaurant, Christine Brown has
invented an original fusion of Asian, French and
Southwestern dishes. She even sometimes discusses
her philosophy of cooking while working at the
stove in the centre of her restaurant. The menu
changes, but the value and service do not: this is top-
class cooking at suburban prices.

Orange County

Jagerhaus
*2525 E Ball Road, at S Sunkist Street, Anaheim
(1-714 520 9500, www.jagerhaus.net). I-5, exit
Ball Road east.* **Open** 7am-9pm Mon-Fri; 8am-9pm
Sat, Sun. **Main courses** $15. **Credit** AmEx, DC,
MC, V. **German**
Anaheim was established by German immigrants
in the 1800s, so it makes sense that some of them are
still here running restaurants. Jagerhaus is open for
breakfast to dinner, and the Austrian raisin
pancakes will give you the strength to trek through
Disneyland. Come back for a dinner of home-made
sausage, braised wild boar or *sauerbraten* (beef marinated and roasted) with great brown bread. Note:
the car park entry is from Sunkist Street.

El Misti Picanteria Arequipeña
*3070 W Lincoln Avenue, at Beach Boulevard,
Anaheim (1-714 995 5944). I-405, exit Beach
Boulevard north.* **Open** 11am-8pm Tue-Fri;
10am-9pm Sat; 10am-8pm Sun. **Main courses**
$12. **Credit** DC, MC, V. **Peruvian**
El Misti is the best Peruvian restaurant in the region,
an unpretentious spot decorated with colourful
murals. Come here for inexpensive and tasty seafood
dishes, grilled lamb ribs and stir-fry with potatoes,
all of them Peruvian mainstays. The *lucuma*-
flavoured ice-cream is a tropical delight.

★ Napa Rose
*Disney's Grand Californian Hotel & Spa, 1600
S Disneyland Drive, at Katella Avenue, Anaheim
(1-714 300 7170). I-5, exit Harbor Boulevard
south.* **Open** 5.30-10pm daily. **Main courses** $42.
Credit AmEx, DC, Disc, MC, V. **Californian**
Believe it or not, Napa Rose actually would do well
in Napa, or in any other food- and wine-crazed town.
Strawberry sage barbecue duck breast is not what
you might expect at a Disney hotel, but it's served
here and is wonderful. The wine list is amazing and
fairly priced, and service is top-notch.

★ Pizzeria Ortica
*650 Anton Boulevard, at Avenue of the Arts,
Costa Mesa (1-714 445 4900, www.pizzeria
ortica.com). Bus 55, 57, 216, 464/I-405, exit
Bristol Street.* **Open** 11.30am-2pm, 5-10pm
Mon-Fri; 5-10pm Sat, Sun. **Main courses** $17.
Credit AmEx, DC, Disc, MC, V. **Italian**
David Myers' Italian restaurant couldn't look more
out of place, located on a bland but busy street near
the South Coast Plaza mall. But it's the quality of the
authentic Italian cooking that counts. Don't miss the
pizza with home-made sausage and fennel, the
squash tortelli or, for dessert, the *budino di ciocco-
lato*. Myers is also responsible for French bistro
Comme Ça (8479 Melrose Avenue, West Hollywood,
1-323 782 1104, www.commecarestaurant.com) and
Hinoki & the Bird (10 West Century Drive, Century
City, 1-310 552 1200, www.hinokiandthebird.com).
▶ *Restaurants worth seeking out within
South Coast Plaza include Charlie Palmer at
Bloomingdale's (www.charliepalmer.com) and
Marché Moderne (www.marchemoderne.net).*

Sapphire
*1200 South Coast Highway, at Brooks Street,
Laguna Beach (1-949 715 9888, www.sapphire
llc.com). I-405, exit Hwy 133 south.* **Open** 11am-
10.30pm Mon-Thur; 11am-11pm Fri, Sat; 10am-
10.30pm Sun. **Main courses** $30. **Credit** AmEx,
DC, MC, V. **American**
Chef Azmin Ghahreman claims to cook a truly
global cuisine, and he has a better case than most.
The food at Sapphire is an incomparable modern
blend: everything from baked kurobuta pork shank
with spaetzle to Hawaiian-style steamed mahi mahi,
all of it excellent. The location is lovely, too.

★ Stonehill Tavern
*St Regis Monarch Beach Resort, 1 Monarch Beach
Resort, Dana Point (1-949 234 3318, www.stregis
mb.com/stonehill-tavern). I-5, exit Crown Valley
south.* **Open** 5.30-11pm Wed-Sun. **Main courses**
$40. **Credit** AmEx, DC, Disc, MC, V. **American**
Celebrated chef Michael Mina offers up his twist on
modern tavern fare (the term is used in its lightest
sense). Seasonal tasting menus and wine pairings
are always worth a try and the deluxe resort setting
is hard to beat.

CONSUME

Bars

Liquid assets.

LA's bars have seen a renaissance in the last few years. It's almost as if the American recession has forced owners to finally face the market's desires and move away from basic five-beer menus, velvet ropes and plush banquettes. Sure, there's still plenty of cheese around, but the new wave of molecular cocktail artists, craft beer sommeliers and vintage-bar revivalists has injected LA's bar life with a foodie-like sense of value and adventure.

With the new cocktail and craft beer culture has come a new sense of occasion, and it's now common to see men wearing jackets and women in hats and heels. Some people still dress like slobs here, however. One's power is inversely proportional to the quality of one's threads, and often the richest guy at the table is wearing flip-flops – because he can.

The Time Out LA website (www.timeout.com/los-angeles) also keeps track of the latest openings. For our favourite hotel bars, *see p185* **Raising the Bar**.

SMOKING
Los Angeles, Beverly Hills and Santa Monica forbid smoking in outdoor patios at cafés. Sorry folks, but if your choice of venue is a restaurant with a bar or lounge, it might be hard to find a place nearby to light up. The good news is that outdoor smoking areas at bars are still usually exempt from the snuff-'em-out rules.

BOOZE & THE LAW
Los Angeles can be a frustrating place. A city on the edge of a tech-savvy, Pacific-leaning new world order has the alcohol hours of old, Protestant America. It's true, you'll have a hard time finding a drink after 2am, and most places clear the glasses by 1.45am.

Still, if you make the right friends in town, there are places that serve sauce after-hours, including some Asian restaurants that offer 'cold tea'. And if you're a weekend warrior you can always imbibe at 6am, when bars are allowed to serve anew. But with the exception of a few clubs and bars, the sunrise scenery

> ❶ Green numbers given in this chapter correspond to the location of each bar on the street maps. *See pp310-315.*

isn't as picturesque as a lounge at 11pm – unless your idea of beauty is something out of a Charles Bukowski story.

It goes without saying that you shouldn't drink and drive. Parts of Hollywood and Downtown – and, now, Culver City – are well connected by the Metro train system; otherwise, take the bus or a cab.

SANTA MONICA & THE BEACH TOWNS
Santa Monica

Bar Copa
2810 Main Street, at Ashland Avenue (1-310 452 2445, www.barcopa-la.com). Bus 33, 733, SM1, SM2, SM8, SM10/I-10, exit 4th/5th Street south. **Open** 9pm-2am Wed-Sat. **Credit** AmEx, DC, MC, V. **Map** p310 A4 ❶
The sexy, scarlet and black minimalist vibe and the soul-funk grooves have both proved hits with cool West Side kids. With tracks from the golden age of hip hop, some soul, funk and a bit of '80s thrown in alongside the strong speciality drinks, the dance-floor stays good and loose. If it looks too full, then just a little down the street is the Circle Bar (2926 Main Street, 1-310 450 0508, www.thecirclebar.com), which is another staple for pretty young twenty- and thirtysomethings.

Chez Jay

1657 Ocean Avenue, between Colorado Avenue & Pico Boulevard (1-310 395 1741, www.chez jays.com). Bus 33, 733, SM1, SM7, SM8, SM10/I-10, exit 4th/5th Street south. **Open** 2pm-2am Mon; 11.30am-2am Tue-Fri; 9am-2am Sat, Sun. **Credit** AmEx, DC, MC, V. **Map** p310 A3 **②**

This divey but loveable spot close to Santa Monica Pier was a regular haunt for Brian Wilson back in the day. The traces of sawdust on the floor and the coterie of leathery beach locals hanging around the small bar probably haven't changed much since he last swung by. The full dinner menu helps grant the place a constantly ticking trade.

★ Father's Office

1018 Montana Avenue, at 10th Street (1-310 393 2337, www.fathersoffice.com). Bus SM3/I-10, exit Lincoln Boulevard north. **Open** 5pm-1am Mon-Thur; 4pm-2am Fri; noon-2am Sat; noon-midnight Sun. **Credit** AmEx, DC, Disc, MC, V. **Map** p310 B2 **③**

A convivial buzz fills this airy place even when there's just a handful of people inside it. Blame, or credit, the 30-plus beers, many from Californian microbreweries; there's also a nice range of wines. Food-wise, forgo the tapas in favour of the fabled Office burger, and be sure to eat it in the way the menu suggests: no additions and no substitutions. The Culver City branch is sleeker and more minimalist, but it still draws a standing room-only crowd.

Other locations Helms Bakery, 3229 Helms Avenue, Culver City (1-310 736 2224).

Renée's Courtyard Café & Bar

522 Wilshire Boulevard, between 5th & 6th Streets (1-310 451 9341, www.reneescourtyardcafe.com). Bus 4, 20, 33, 704, 720, 733, SM1, SM5, SM7,

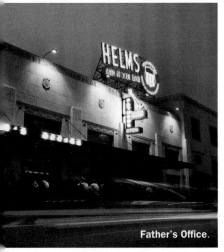

Father's Office.

INSIDE TRACK
SHOW YOUR AGE

Don't forget to carry photo ID, such as a driver's licence or passport, at all times. Even those who look well over the legal drinking age of 21 may get 'carded' while trying to order drinks at the bar.

SM8, SM10/I-10, exit 4th/5th Street north. **Open** 5.30pm-2am daily. **Credit** AmEx, DC, Disc, MC, V. **Map** p310 B2 **④**

It's likely that you've walked past this lesser-known Santa Monica dive. Inside, it's a kitschy, knick-knack-filled café and bar that's a cluttered cross between an old enchanted forest and your crazy aunt's home. On offer is pub-like fare of burgers and buffalo wings, a basic beer and wine selection, and a not-so-special speciality drinks list (think lemon drops and mai tais).

Shorebar

112 W Channel Road, at PCH (1-210 429 1851, www.shorebarsm.com). Bus, 534, SM9/I-10, exit PCH north. **Open** 7pm-1am Tue-Sun. **Credit** AmEx, DC, MC, V. **Map** p310 A1 **⑤**

Shorebar is a beach-club inspired cosy space that features white wood panelling, blue and white striped walls, comfy below-deck-style booth seating and submarine-theme lighting fixtures illuminating vintage photos of local lifeguards (no *Baywatch* paraphernalia here). Once on board, get ready to drown yourself in a sea of sophisticated cocktails.

Venice

Brig

1515 Abbot Kinney Boulevard, at Palms Boulevard (1-310 399 7537, www.thebrig.com). Bus 33, 733/I-10, exit Lincoln Boulevard south. **Open** 6pm-2am Mon-Thur; 5pm-2am Fri; noon-2am Sat, Sun. **Credit** AmEx, DC, MC, V. **Map** p310 A6 **⑥**

Once a dive bar, the Brig underwent a facelift a few years back. The pool table and the solid jukebox remain as reminders of its seedier past, and the stainless steel fittings are a little less lustrous these days. Still, it remains sleek, although it's more a neighbourhood hangout than a destination spot.

Otheroom

1201 Abbot Kinney Boulevard, at San Juan Avenue & Aragon Court (1-310 396 6230, www.theotheroom.com). Bus 33, 733, SM2/I-10, exit Lincoln Boulevard south; or I-405, exit Marina Freeway. **Open** 5pm-2am daily. **Credit** AmEx, DC, Disc, MC, V. **Map** p310 A5 **⑦**

Wide-open windows welcome patrons into this dark, sexy wine bar, which epitomises the best aspects of the newer, slicker Venice. Get there early during the

CONSUME

week if you're hoping to enjoy a mellow conversation over one of the numerous wines by the glass, or show up after 8pm for some serious mingling.

Venice Beach Wines

529 Rose Avenue, at Rennie Avenue (1-310 606 2529, www.venicebeachwines.com). Bus C1/ I-10, exit Lincoln Boulevard south. **Open** 4-11pm Mon-Thur; 4pm-midnight Fri; 9am-midnight Sat; 9am-11pm Sun. **Credit** AmEx, DC, MC, V. **Map** p310 B6 ❽

The smoky scent of grilled paninis and pizzas fills the interior and tented patio spaces that comprise this wine bar and retail store owned by Norma Alvarado and Oscar Hermosillo. There's also an array of wines by the glass, beers and a small plates menu designed by *Next Iron Chef* Jill Davie. Venice's eclectic, artsy posh crowd convenes here, but it's casual nonetheless.

BRENTWOOD TO BEVERLY HILLS

Culver City

Blind Barber

10797 Washington Boulevard, between Midway & Overland Avenues (1-310 841 6679, www. blindbarber.com). Bus 1/I-10, exit National Boulevard west. **Open** noon-9pm Mon-Sat; noon-6pm Sun. **Credit** AmEx, DC, Disc, MC, V.

Joshua Boyd, Adam Kirsch and Jeff Laub have brought their NYC barbershop/cocktail show to Culver City. The front room is stark white with four barber stations (call ahead for availability). If a shave or trim aren't on the cards, you'll be steered through a nondescript door revealing a speakeasy, decked out with dim lighting, old wood panelling and yellow fading wallpaper. In between dancing there's plenty of great cocktails and delectable grilled cheese options.

Bottle Rock

3847 Main Street, between Venice & Culver Boulevards (1-310 836 9463, www.bottlerock culvercity.com). Bus 33, 733, C1/I-10, exit

THE BEST HAPPY HOUR SPOTS

3-7pm & 10pm-1.30am daily
Weiland Brewery. *See p129.*

4-7pm Mon-Fri
Corkbar. *See p127.*

5-7pm Wed-Fri
Edison. *See p128.*

3-7pm daily
Public House 1739. *See p125.*

Robertson Boulevard south. **Open** 4-11pm Mon-Thur, Sun; noon-1am Fri, Sat. **Credit** AmEx, DC, Disc, MC, V.

Bottle Rock performs double-duty as a sophisticated wine bar and an upscale wine store: trying before you buy is encouraged. Small plates of meats, cheeses and salads complement the liquid refreshment, which also stretches to one of the city's best selections of beers.

Other locations 1050 Flower Street, Downtown (1-213 747 1100).

Buggy Whip

7420 La Tijera Boulevard, at I-405 (1-310 645 7131, www.buggywhipsteakhouse.com). Bus 102/I-405, exit La Tijera Boulevard west. **Open** 4-11pm daily. **Credit** AmEx, DC, MC, V.

Veteran piano man Peter Wagner holds court in the dining lounge of the Buggy Whip every night from Wednesday to Saturday. Dinner reservations for the bar area are strongly recommended if you want to secure a front-row seat while Wagner sings the familiar likes of 'You Belong to Me'. Resolutely retro, and all the better for it.

Corner Door

12477 W Washington Boulevard, at Wasatch Avenue (1-310 313 5810, www.thecornerdoor la.com). Bus 102/I-405, exit Culver Boulevard/ Washington Boulevard. **Open** 5.30pm-midnight Mon, Tue, Sun; 5.30pm-2am Wed-Sat. **Credit** AmEx, DC, Disc, MC, V.

The Corner Door feels like a neighbourhood place where everybody knows your name. The drinks menu features craft cocktail specials as well as a set list of classics, eight beers on tap (along with bottled brews) from California and Colorado breweries and a decent selection of Italian, French, New Zealand and domestic wines. Food-wise, there's an excellent choice of hearty, traditional American fare to match.

Mandrake Bar

2692 S La Cienega Boulevard, between Venice & Washington Boulevards (1-310 837 3297, www.mandrakebar.com). Bus 33, 105, 534, 705, 733/I-10, exit La Cienega Boulevard south. **Open** 6pm-midnight Mon, Sun; 5pm-midnight Tue-Thur; 5pm-1am Fri, Sat. **Credit** AmEx, DC, Disc, MC, V.

Tucked away from its competitors, the Mandrake is convenient for the local arts district, and even has its own gallery space. The bar itself is a mellow locals' hangout, with unpretentious service and reasonably priced drinks. The fake-tree-stump patio seating provides a fine setting for smoking and conversation.

Oldfield's Liquor Room

10899 Venice Boulevard, at Kelton & Girard Avenue (1-310 842 8066, www.oldfields liquorroom.com). Bus 33, 733/I-405, exit

Bar Lubitsch.

Venice Boulevard west. **Open** 5pm-2am daily. **Credit** AmEx, DC, Disc, MC, V.

This cocktail bar takes its name from former racing driver and actor Barney Oldfield. For all the excitement in Barney's life, Oldfield's offers a subdued, neighbourhood-bar experience. Locals congregate comfortably around a smartly designed bar with pockets for small groups to mingle over the pared-down cocktail list, representative of 1933 Group's dedication to post-Prohibition drinks.

Beverly Hills

Bar Nineteen 12

Beverly Hills Hotel & Bungalows, 9641 W Sunset Boulevard, at N Crescent Drive (1-310 273 1912, www.beverlyhillshotel.com/bar-nineteen12). Bus 2, 302/I-405, exit Sunset Boulevard east. **Open** 6pm-2am daily. **Credit** AmEx, DC, Disc, MC, V. **Map** p311 B2

This historic hotel *(see p173)* boasts a stylish indoor-outdoor lounge. It's worth calling ahead to get on the guest list; however, if that doesn't work, simply turn up and stake your claim before the doorman arrives for the 8pm shift – they won't kick you out if you're already in. Also within the hotel is the famous Polo Lounge, which attracts a glam, moneyed crowd.

Livello at L'Ermitage Beverly Hills

L'Ermitage Hotel, 9291 Burton Way, between N Foothill Road & N Elm Drive (1-310 278 3344, www.lermitagebh.com). Bus 16, 4/ I-405, exit Wilshire Boulevard east. **Open** 9.30am-midnight Mon-Wed, Sun; 10.30am-2am Thur-Sat. **Credit** AmEx, DC, Disc, MC, V. **Map** p311 D2

The hotel setting and upscale decor help make this bar into the kind of place in which you can have a conversation without the need to raise your voice. And if that conversation just so happens to be about swinging the financing of your new film, then so much the better: you'll be in good company as this has been an industry haunt for years.

WEST HOLLYWOOD, HOLLYWOOD & MIDTOWN

West Hollywood

For the area's gay bars, *see pp203-204.*

Bar Lubitsch

7702 Santa Monica Boulevard, between N Spaulding & N Stanley Avenues (1-323 654 1234). Bus 4, 217, 218, 704/I-10, exit Fairfax Avenue north. **Open** 7pm-2am Mon-Fri; 8pm-2am Sat, Sun. **Credit** AmEx, DC, Disc, MC, V. **Map** p312 C2

Although there's a pronounced Russian theme at Bar Lubitsch, West Hollywood's small and pensionable Russian community have yet to show their faces. This is a modern WeHo archetype: the decor is more kitsch than authentic, and the drinks (inevitably, heavy on the vodka) are strong and expensive. Still, it's a likeable spot, more relaxed and less pretentious than you might expect, with the option to grind away on a moderately sized dancefloor.

Bar Marmont

8171 W Sunset Boulevard, between N Harper Avenue & Havenhurst Drive (1-323 650 0575, www.chateaumarmont.com/barmarmont.php). Bus 2, 302/I-10, exit La Cienega Boulevard north. **Open** 6pm-2am daily. **Credit** AmEx, DC, Disc, MC, V. **Map** p312 B1

Although it's not actually within the Chateau Marmont hotel *(see p176)* – it's a very short walk away – this is its affiliated bar. And just like the hotel, Bar Marmont is both fabulously elegant and gently exclusive. The decor is beautiful (the butterflies pinned to the ceiling are a lovely touch) and the gastropubby food comes courtesy of Carolynn Spence, formerly of New York's fabled Spotted Pig. A gem.

Formosa Café

7156 Santa Monica Boulevard, at Formosa Avenue (1-323 850 9050). Bus 4, 212, 312,

CONSUME

704/I-10, exit La Brea Avenue north. **Open** 4pm-2am Mon-Fri; 6pm-2am Sat, Sun. **Credit** AmEx, DC, Disc, MC, V. **Map** p312 D2 ⑬

There's a full Asian-influenced menu, but the food comes a poor third to the history and the strong drinks here. In business for nearly 75 years, the Formosa was a hangout of the Hollywood aristocracy during the '40s and '50s. The clientele these days is younger and less famous, but the walls remain lined with images of the stars that once graced the still-atmospheric bar and the dark booths. *L.A. Confidential* fans will recognise it from the film.

Surly Goat

7929 Santa Monica Boulevard, at N Fairfax Avenue (1-323 650 4628, www.surlygoat.com). Bus 4, 217, 218, 704/I-10, exit Fairfax Avenue north. **Open** 6pm-2am Mon-Fri; 1pm-2am Sat, Sun. **Credit** AmEx, Disc, MC, V. **Map** p312 C2 ⑭

With brewmaster Ryan Sweeney at the helm, this craft beer bar more than meets expectations – the other co-owner is nightlife and dining vet Adolfo Suaya. Inside the moody, candlelit space, choose from two dozen beers on tap and over 40 rare and international bottles.

Hollywood

Boardner's

1652 N Cherokee Avenue, at Hollywood Boulevard (1-323 462 9621, www.boardners.com). Metro Hollywood-Highland/bus 156, 163, 212, 217, 363, 656, 780, LDH/US 101, exit Sunset Boulevard west. **Open** 5pm-2am Mon-Fri; 4pm-2am Sat, Sun. **Credit** AmEx, DC, Disc, MC, V. **Map** p313 A2 ⑮

A locals' bar is a rarity amid the tourist bustle of the boulevard. But here it is, Boardner's, long and elegant in its 1920s provenance, but somehow also punk in its come-as-you-are attitude. There's also a nice patio and the B52 club, featuring 20-ft ceilings and giant dancefloor. Apparently, the Black Dahlia had her last drink here.

Cat & Fiddle

6530 W Sunset Boulevard, between Seward Street & N Hudson Avenue (1-323 468 3800, www.thecatandfiddle.com). Bus 2, 302/US 101, exit Sunset Boulevard west. **Open** 11.30am-2am Mon-Fri; 10am-2am Sat, Sun. **Credit** AmEx, MC, V. **Map** p313 B2 ⑯

We can't claim that the English pub interior is especially authentic, but it does have one of the best patios in Hollywood. The food, on the whole, is pretty ordinary. Still, happy hour here is great and the locals are a chummy bunch.

Drai's

W Hotel, 6250 Hollywood Boulevard, between Vine Street & Argyle Avenue (1-323 962 1111, www.drais.net). Metro Hollywood-Vine/bus 163, 180, 181, 210, 212, 217, 312, 363, 780/US 101, exit Hollywood Boulevard west. **Open** 5.30pm-2am Thur-Sun. **Credit** AmEx, DC, MC, V. **Map** p313 B2 ⑰

This bar, restaurant and lounge on the rooftop of the swanky W hotel is known more for its celeb sightings than for its cocktails and continental cuisine. If you must get an eyeful of the fabulous life in LA, this is the place to find pretty people getting pretty drunk next to a picturesque pool. We suggest going early, soaking up the Hollywood view, and leaving before the amateurs arrive. Call or check the website for opening days and times, which vary by season.

★ Frolic Room

6245 Hollywood Boulevard, at N Argyle Avenue (1-323 462 5890). Metro Hollywood-Vine/bus 163, 180, 181, 210, 212, 217, 312, 363, 780, LDH/US 101, exit Vine Street south. **Open** 11am-2am Mon-Fri; 10am-2am Sat, Sun. **Credit** AmEx, DC, Disc, MC, V. **Map** p313 B1 ⑲

In business since the '30s and with one of the finest neon signs in the entire Los Angeles region, the Frolic Room remains what it's always been: a straightforward, friendly little room in which to get

Pour Vous.

loaded with others of a similar mindset, a neighbourhood hangout in a neighbourhood without many of them. Look out for the beautiful Al Hirschfeld cartoon mural on the back wall. Movie buffs will recognise this place from *L.A. Confidential* – Kevin Spacey's character stops by here for a drink.

Piano Bar

6429 Selma Avenue, at N Cahuenga Boulevard (1-323 466 2750, www.pianobarhollywood.com). Metro Hollywood-Vine/bus 163, 180, 181, 210, 212, 217, 312, 780, LDH/US 101, exit Hollywood Boulevard west. **Open** 4pm-2am daily. **Credit** AmEx, DC, Disc, MC, V. **Map** p313 B2 ⑲

This is a rare find in the heart of Hollywood: a low-key and friendly dive. On any given night, the house piano man generally keeps things lively in this endearingly contrived Brit-themed hangout. Refreshingly, just as management claims, there's no cover charge, guest list or dress code.

★ Pour Vous

5574 Melrose Avenue, at N Gower Street (1-323 871 8699, www.pourvousla.com). Bus 10, 48, 210/I-10, exit La Brea Avenue north. **Open** 8pm-2am Mon-Sat. **Credit** AmEx, DC, MC, V. **Map** p313 B3 ⑳

This jazz-age Parisian salon has brought a touch of class to Melrose. Inside, blue and amber theatrical lighting illuminates various corners of a parlour-style room. The central fixture is a cosy fireplace that gives way to circular, café seating under a dome. The cocktail list is simplified to feature tried-and-true staples, plus some ingenious concoctions, and sultry burlesque performances bring a temporary mesmerising hush over the room. Reservations are encouraged but not necessary for a small group dressed in proper 'cocktail attire' (which is the only way you're getting in anyway).

Sassafras

1233 N Vine Street, at Fountain Avenue (1-323 467 2800, www.sassafrassaloon.com). Bus 210, LDH/I-10, exit La Brea Avenue north. **Open** 5pm-2am daily. **Credit** AmEx, Disc, MC, V. **Map** p313 B2 ㉑

The barrel-aged cocktail is front and centre at Sassafras, a throwback to the Old South. Walk past what looks like a patio on the Bayou to the long bar framed by odd family heirlooms and dangling bottles of barrel-aged cocktails in constant rotation (literally, on an ancient dry-cleaning rack). Behind the bar sits an actual Savannah townhouse. If the scenery is too much, focus on the menu – house-brewed ginger-beer concoctions alongside the oak barrel-aged cocktails, and Southern grub such as jambalaya and sweet potato pie. *Photo p124.*

Room at the Roosevelt Hotel

Hollywood Roosevelt Hotel, 7000 Hollywood Boulevard, at N Orange Drive (1-323 769 7296, *www.spareroomhollywood.com). Metro Hollywood-Highland/bus 163, 180, 181, 210, 212, 217, 312, 780, LDH/US 101, exit Hollywood Boulevard west.* **Open** 8pm-2am Mon, Wed-Sat. **Credit** AmEx, DC, Disc, MC, V. **Map** p313 A1 ㉒

Entering the Spare Room is like stepping into another era, where classic cocktails – served by waitresses in Gatsby-era dresses – pour freely and people make merry all night long. The big draw is Monday game night, when an exclusive bowling league competes – get on the waiting list and be prepared to pay $100 an hour to reserve one of two lanes for six people. Or just chill in the lounge and cosy up to your neighbours with a friendly game of Monopoly or Connect Four. On Wednesdays from 8pm to 10pm there's half-price bowling and happy hour-priced food and drinks.
▶ *Also within the Roosevelt is the poolside Tropicana Bar, featuring stiff and expensive drinks, acres of attitude, a few famous actors and models, and the richly furnished Library Bar.*

La Velvet Margarita Cantina

1612 Cahuenga Boulevard, between Selma Avenue & Hollywood Boulevard (1-323 469 2000, www.velvetmargarita.com). Metro Hollywood-Vine/bus 163, 180, 181, 210, 212, 217, 312, 780, LDH/US 101, exit Hollywood Boulevard west. **Open** 11.30am-2am Mon-Fri; 6pm-2am Sat, Sun. **Credit** AmEx, DC, Disc, MC, V. **Map** p313 B2 ㉓

The Mexi-Goth styling may seem a little on the heavy-handed side, but after your first drink, all that black velvet will start to feel about right. If you like your Día de los Muertos on the kitschy side, you're more than ready to order a flaming margarita, and maybe something from the dinner menu: the drinks are not designed to be enjoyed on an empty stomach.

Woods

1533 N La Brea Avenue, between W Sunset Boulevard & Hawthorn Avenue (1-323 876 6612, www.vintagebargroup.com/the-woods.php). Metro Hollywood-Highland/bus 156, 163, 212, 217, 656, 780, LDH/US 101, exit Sunset Boulevard west. **Open** 6pm-2am Mon-Fri; 8pm-2am Sat, Sun. **Credit** AmEx, DC, MC, V. **Map** p313 A2 ㉔

This hangout is just far enough from the thick of the Hollywood action to deter the worst of the bar-hopping crowds; as such, it's popular but, happily for its fans, not too popular. The forestry theme could have ended up looking terribly kitsch, but it's actually pretty good fun. It's expensive, but then so's everywhere around here.

Fairfax District

Canter's Kibitz Room

419 N Fairfax Avenue, at Oakwood Avenue (1-323 651 2030, www.cantersdeli.com). Bus 14, 217, 218/I-10, exit Fairfax Avenue north. **Open** 10.30am-1.40am daily. **Credit** AmEx, DC, Disc, MC, V. **Map** p312 C3 ㉕

CONSUME

This agreeably worse-for-wear little taproom is tucked off to the side of Canter's Deli. The mood is matey and the drinking tends to be pretty focused. It's sometimes quiet, but alt-rocking bands drop in most evenings and liven things a little. Drinks are predictably strong. Across the road is the Dime (442 N Fairfax Avenue), a swanky attempt at mimicking this kind of dive-bar culture.

El Carmen

8138 W 3rd Street, between S La Jolla Avenue & S Crescent Heights Boulevard (1-323 852 1552). Bus 16, 217, 218, 316/I-10, exit La Cienega Boulevard north. **Open** 5pm-2am Mon-Fri; 7pm-2am Sat, Sun. **Credit** AmEx, DC, Disc, MC, V. **Map** p312 C3 ㉖

The *lucha libre* theme at this lively spot goes well beyond mere motif: the Mexican-inspired decor is several thousand feet over the top. The healthy selection of tequilas and mescals together combine to create innumerable excuses for the inevitable morning-after hangover. The lauded El Perfecto margarita is a highlight.

Miracle Mile

Tom Bergin's Tavern

840 S Fairfax Avenue, between Wilshire & San Vicente Boulevards (1-323 936 7151, www.tom bergins.com). Bus 20, 217, 720, LDF/I-10, exit Fairfax Avenue north. **Open** 11.30am-2am Mon-Fri; 10.30am-2am Sat, Sun. **Credit** AmEx, DC, Disc, MC, V. **Map** p312 C4 ㉗

When Tom Bergin's temporarily closed for renovations in 2011, everyone was concerned about the shamrocks bearing the names of regulars of past and present tacked to the ceiling. Thankfully, they survived, as did the lovely U-shaped bar and dark wood panels. New owners Warner Ebbink and chef Brandon Boudet have focused on retaining the tavern's history while modernising: the beer taps are new, the green leather booths have a shiny sheen and the menu now features slightly upscale Irish fare.

▶ *For a swankier sip in the area, visit the Patina group's Ray's and Stark Bar at LACMA (see p55).*

Koreatown

Brass Monkey

3440 Wilshire Boulevard, at S Mariposa Avenue (1-213 381 7047, www.cafebrassmonkey.com). Metro Wilshire-Normandie/bus 20, 720/I-10, exit Normandie Avenue north. **Open** 11am-2am Mon-Fri; 4pm-2am Sat, Sun. **Credit** AmEx, DC, Disc, MC, V. **Map** p313 D5 ㉘

On the ground floor of a nondescript office building (park and enter at the back), this ski lodge-styled room has one of the most comprehensive karaoke songbooks in the city. Waiting times on weekends routinely hit 45 minutes, so you'll have time to down plenty of liquid courage before you get your shot at the stage.

Sassafras. *See p123.*

HMS Bounty

3357 Wilshire Boulevard, at S Kenmore Avenue (1-213 385 7275, www.thehmsbounty.com). Metro Wilshire-Normandie/bus 20, 204, 720/I-10, exit Western Avenue north. **Open** 11am-midnight Mon, Sun; 11am-1am Tue-Sat. **Credit** AmEx, DC, Disc, MC, V. **Map** p313 D5 ㉙

Naturally enough, one of LA's best nautical-themed bars sits fully 15 miles from the water. This agreeably egalitarian place is famed for the warmth of its welcome and the cheapness of its drinks, characteristics that are embraced by everyone from visiting rockers to residents of the apartment hotel directly above the taproom. Well-seasoned waitresses handle the table service, distributing dishes from a traditional American menu.

Prince

3198½ W 7th Street, at S Catalina Street (1-213 389 2007, www.theprincela.com). Metro Wilshire-Vermont/bus 20, 720, LDWCK/I-10, exit Vermont Avenue north. **Open** 4pm-2am daily. **Credit** AmEx, DC, Disc, MC, V. **Map** p314 A6 ㉚

The management is Korean, as is the music, but the rest of the place resembles a bizarre cross between a bordello and an English gentlemen's club. Drinks aren't cheap, so stick to something simple (bottled Hite, perhaps) and then order the unusual yet delicious fruit platter.

R Bar

3331 W 8th Street, at Irolo Street (1-213 387 7227). Metro Wilshire-Vermont/bus 20, 720, LDWCK/I-10, exit Vermont Avenue north. **Open** 7pm-2am daily. **Credit** AmEx, DC, Disc, MC, V. **Map** p313 D5 ㉛

A speakeasy-style bar in a rough, historic neighbourhood behind the remnants of the Ambassador

Hotel (where Robert Kennedy was murdered), R Bar relies on a secret-password system (via its Facebook page, www.facebook.com/rbarktown). Once inside it's a down-to-earth, local-hipster spot with bottom-shelf spirits, karaoke on Wednesdays and occasional comedy nights. There's food (burgers) and more than a little intrigue. And sometimes the doorman will let you in without the magic words anyway.

LOS FELIZ TO ECHO PARK
Los Feliz

★ Bar Covell
4628 Hollywood Boulevard, between N Vermont & Hillhurst Avenues (1-323 660 4400, www.bar covell.com). Bus 4, 156, 204, 754/US 101, exit Hollywood Boulevard east. **Open** 5pm-midnight Mon-Fri; 5pm-2am Sat, Sun. **Credit** AmEx, DC, Disc, MC, V. **Map** p314 A3 ㉜

The focus here is on small production, off-the-beaten-path old world and new world beer and wine selections from around the globe. There's also a selection of light-fare snacks: try the Carnivore's Special Flatbread with a glass of something leathery and French. Candles and dim bulbs illuminate a well-dressed neighbourhood crowd of food and wine buffs. There's no printed menu, so let someone behind the bar expertly guide you.

Dresden Room
1760 N Vermont Avenue, between Kingswell & Melbourne Avenues (1-323 665 4294, www.the dresden.com). Metro Vermont-Sunset/bus 4, 156, 204, 754/US 101, exit Vermont Avenue north. **Open** 4.30pm-2am Mon-Sat; 5pm-midnight Sun. **Credit** AmEx, Disc, MC, V. **Map** p314 A2 ㉝

Retrace key scenes from *Swingers* and you'll end up at the Dresden Room, settled in for an evening with inimitable musical duo Marty & Elayne. A beacon of genuine, unironic kitsch, nothing has changed here in umpteen years, from the corkboard walls to the wrought-iron lighting fixtures.

**THE BEST
FOOD-SERVING BARS**

For 'upscale' hardier dishes
Corner Door. *See p120.*

For burgers
Mohawk Bend. *See p126.*

For grilled cheese
Blind Barber. *See p120.*

For guilty deep-fried pleasures
One-Eyed Gypsy. *See p128.*

Good Luck Bar
1514 N Hillhurst Avenue, at Hollywood Boulevard (1-323 666 3524). Bus 4, 156, 204, 754/US 101, exit Hollywood Boulevard east. **Open** 7pm-2am Mon-Fri; 8pm-2am Sat, Sun. **Credit** AmEx, DC, MC, V. **Map** p314 B3 ㉞

Aside from the party-pleasing favourites on its jukebox, Good Luck Bar is Mandarin-themed to the max: red-soaked, black-lacquered and windowless in a way that makes you feel as if you're on a movie set moments before the aerodynamic kung fu scene kicks off. Cocktails come with borderline-iconic dragon stirrers, but beer and shots are still the bestsellers.

Public House 1739
1739 N Vermont Avenue, at Kingswell Avenue (1-323 663 1739). Metro Vermont-Sunset/bus 4, 156, 204, 754/US 101, exit Vermont Avenue north. **Open** 11am-2am daily. **Credit** AmEx, DC, MC, V. **Map** p314 A2 ㉟

This gastropub has renovated and reopened in a space directly adjacent to its former home. But it's still the place to go when you want to gather with fellow Lakers or Dodgers fans and catch the game on the multiple screens throughout the premises, while an array of new bar games – dartboards, pool, shuffle board – will keep you busy if sport isn't your thing. Were it not for the straightforward menu of burgers, mac and cheese and the like, along with an extensive beer list, 1739 would be the quintessential local dive. The outdoor seating is great for people watching. Note that a wine bar, steakhouse and Indian restaurant are slated to open on the site in 2013.

Atwater Village

Bigfoot Lodge
3172 Los Feliz Boulevard, between Edenhurst Avenue & Glenfeliz Boulevard (1-323 662 9227, www.bigfootlodge.com). Bus 180, 181/I-5, exit Los Feliz Boulevard east. **Open** 5pm-2am daily. **Credit** AmEx, DC, Disc, MC, V.

Every log cabin experience you've ever endured will come flooding back when you step through the doors of this engaging spot. From the fireplace to the signage, rendered in that quaint '50s National Park font, management hasn't missed a beat in its bid to rebuild the wilderness in Atwater Village.

Griffin
3000 Los Feliz Boulevard, at Boyce Avenue (1-323 644 0444). Bus 180, 181/I-5, exit Los Feliz Boulevard east. **Open** 5pm-2am daily. **Credit** AmEx, Disc, MC, V.

The stylish Griffin is the kind of low-key, hipster-happy lounge you'd like to have in your neighbourhood. The music is perfectly pitched and the drinks are decent, but the ambience is key here: friendly without being over-friendly, stylish yet unpretentious. A nice local spot.

CONSUME

Silver Lake

Bar Stella

*3932 W Sunset Boulevard, between Sanborn
& Hyperion Avenues (1-323 666 0265, www.cafe
stella.com). Bus 2, 4, 175, 302, 704/US 101, exit
Silver Lake Boulevard north.* **Open** 6pm-late daily.
Credit AmEx, DC, Disc, MC, V. **Map** p314 B3 ⑯

The folks at Café Stella (*see p110*) have taken up the
craft cocktail craze with Bar Stella – in the same location – a den of exposed brick that feels like a Baja-
Californian guesthouse furnished with Caribbean-
style furniture. You might pass right by (the door is
somewhat concealed), but double-back and grab a
seat along the back wall where you can sip away at
well-mixed drinks, imagining what inspired the art
behind the bar.

Cha Cha Lounge

*2375 Glendale Boulevard, at Silver Lake Boulevard
(1-323 660 7595, www.chachalounge.com). Bus
92/I-5, exit Glendale Boulevard south.* **Open** 5pm-
2am daily. **Credit** AmEx, DC, Disc, MC, V. **Map**
p314 D2 ⑰

Hipsters pack this Tijuana-themed, Silver Lake
party bar illuminated by a lone 'Lounge' sign out
front. Stop in the thatched roof bar for a Pacifico by
the bottle or PBR on tap. Take in the colourful
Mexican paraphernalia, and the portraits of drag
queens and blacklight paintings on the walls. It's a
confusing conundrum of decor that gives the bar its
particular appeal. Photo booth, table football and
shiny black booths – all present and correct.

Good Microbrew & Grill

*3725 W Sunset Boulevard, at Lucille Avenue (1-
323 660 3645, www.goodmicrobrew.com). Bus 2,
175, 302/US 101, exit Vermont Avenue north.*
Open 11am-10pm Mon, Tue; 11am-11pm Wed;
11am-midnight Thur-Sat; 9am-10pm Sun. **Credit**
AmEx, DC, Disc, MC, V. **Map** p314 B3 ⑱

On weekend nights this place is packed with beer
aficionados, and for good reason. It has a list of ales,
pilsners, bocks, lagers and stouts to rival anywhere
in town. The food – sweet potato fries, quesadillas,
chicken wings – might be predictable, but the amazing inventory of brew will satisfy even the most
jaded international beer hound.

Smog Cutter

*864 N Virgil Avenue, between Normal & Burns
Avenues (1-323 660 4626). Bus 10, 26/US 101,
exit Vermont Avenue north.* **Open** 2pm-2am
daily. **No credit cards. Map** p314 B4 ⑲

As the sign says, 'Hangovers installed and serviced'.
Your hosts are no-nonsense Korean bartenders who
keep the funny business – excesses of alcoholic
bravado, arguments with the staff – to a minimum.
Your soundtrack is the karaoke stylings of assorted
drunken hipsters: when it gets going, this place is
even rowdier than the Brass Monkey (*see p124*).

Thirsty Crow

*2939 W Sunset Boulevard, between Westerly
Terrace & Silver Lake Boulevard (1-323 661
6007, www.thirstycrowbar.com). Bus 2, 4, 302,
704/US 101, exit Silver Lake Boulevard north.*
Open 5pm-2am Mon-Sat; 2pm-2am Sun. **Credit**
AmEx, DC, Disc, MC, V. **Map** p314 C4 ⑳

Another winner from 1933 Group (responsible for
Oldfield's, *see p120*, and Sassafras, *see p123*, among
others). Once you're past the doorman, you might
notice a stuffed dusty crow mascot perched in the
rafters, but what should catch your eye is the whisky
display behind the horseshoe-shaped bar, covering
100-plus whiskies and 60-plus small-batch bourbons.
The only other view is brick walls through paned
glass windows, while dim lights under sconces round
out the room to give the bar a sinister glow – but you'll
likely be bothered for a smoke rather than a duel.

Tiki-Ti

*4427 W Sunset Boulevard, between Hillhurst &
Fountain Avenues (1-323 669 9381, www.tiki-
ti.com). Bus 2, 175, 302/US 101, exit Vermont
Avenue north.* **Open** 4pm-2am Wed-Sat. **No
credit cards. Map** p314 B3 ㉑

Jam-packed with blowfish, tribal masks and faux
tropical foliage, entering Sunset's tiki bar is like taking a tropical holiday without the cost of a plane
ticket. As you'd expect, it serves brightly coloured
tropical drinks – a mai tai or blue hawaiian usually
does the trick. Surprisingly, this place generally
packs a long line, not because there's a red velvet
rope out front, but because of its minuscule size.

Echo Park

Gold Room

*1558 W Sunset Boulevard, at Echo Park Avenue
(1-213 482 5259). Bus 2, 4, 302, 704/US 101,
exit Glendale Boulevard.* **Open** noon-2am daily.
Credit AmEx, DC, MC, V. **Map** p314 D5 ㉒

While the neighbourhood around it gentrifies, this
mostly locals dive keeps things honest with top-shelf
tequilas and Mexican League *fútbol*. The crowd is
mainly made up of thirtysomething males taking a
break over cheap drinks in an atmosphere teeming
with casino-waitress hospitality. Not the place to
flaunt a weird haircut or bust out a lofty attitude:
locals and staff have zero tolerance for poseurs.

Mohawk Bend

*2141 W Sunset Boulevard, between N Alvarado
& Mohawk Streets (1-213 483 2337, www.
mohawk.la). Bus 2, 4, 302, 704/US 101, exit
Glendale Boulevard.* **Open** noon-2am Mon-Fri;
9.30am-2am Sat; 9.30am-1am Sun. **Credit** AmEx,
DC, Disc, MC, V. **Map** p314 D4 ㉓

This vegan-friendly bar-restaurant has taken over
what was once an old vaudeville theatre, redesigned
to feature lofty, vaulted ceilings and light fixtures that
might have come from a dressing room. There's an

CONSUME

Mohawk Bend.

impressive fleet of 72 beers on tap – all from California brewers (save for one monthly featured out of state brewery) – is at your beck and call.

▶ *Owner Tony Yanow also runs Tony's Darts Away (1710 W Magnolia Boulevard, Burbank, 1-818 253 1710, www. http://tonysda.com).*

Highland Park & Eagle Rock

Johnny's Bar
5006 York Boulevard, at N Avenue 50 (1-323 982 0775). Metro Highland Park/bus 83/I-110, exit Avenue 52 north. **Open** 2pm-2am Mon, Wed-Sun; 5pm-2am Tue. **Credit** AmEx, DC, Disc, MC, V.
This old boozer, divey without really being a dive, has been discovered by artsy indie kids, who mix freely with locals and refugees from the nearby York (*see below*). Entertainment from the excellent jukebox is supplemented by projections of classic movies like *The Godfather*; a pool table provides additional diversion.

York
5018 York Boulevard, between N Avenues 50 & 51 (1-323 255 9675, www.theyorkonyork.com). Metro Highland Park/bus 83/I-110, exit Avenue 52 north. **Open** 10.30am-2am daily. **Credit** AmEx, DC, Disc, MC, V.
The grown-up epicentre of Highland Park's social scene, this gastropub offers a carefully edited selection of microbrews and a shortish food menu that's a cut above usual bar fare. The banquettes and exposed brick walls lend a warm boho personality; and you can hear your own conversation even when it's full.

DOWNTOWN

In addition to the following, the bar at **WP24** within the Ritz-Carlton (*see p181*) is lovely.

Bar 107
107 W 4th Street, at S Main Street (1-213 625 7382). Metro Pershing Square/bus 33, 55, 83, *92/US 101, exit Main Street south.* **Open** 4pm-2am Mon-Fri; 3pm-2am Sat, Sun. **Credit** AmEx, MC, V. **Map** p315 C3 ④
The local hangout of choice for the converted loft community, Bar 107 is painted red and gold all the way up to its 20ft ceilings. The architectural bones may be fancy but the vibe is that of a mellow dive. Bar 107 prides itself on its no-dance-music policy, instead preferring to soundtrack its evenings with hipster-friendly rock and country.

★ Caña Rum Bar
714 W Olympic Boulevard, at Flower Street (1-213 745 7090, www.canarumbar.com). Metro Pershing Square/bus 2, 4, 30, 40, 42, 48/I-110, exit 9th Street east. **Open** 6pm-2am Wed-Fri; 8pm-2am Mon, Tue, Sat, Sun. **Credit** AmEx, DC, Disc, MC, V. **Map** p315 B4 ④
Downtown nightlife entrepreneur Cedd Moses' experiment with a private bar charging $2,200 in annual dues didn't exactly come at the right time, and so the precious cocktail museum that was the Doheny soon morphed into something more Latin and vibrant. Caña Rum Bar features 140 gourmet rums for cocktails that include mojitos, Tiki drinks and margaritas. The sense of exclusivity isn't gone, but the $2,200 membership is. It's now only $20.

★ Corkbar
403 W 12th Street, at S Grand Avenue (1-213 746 0050, www.corkbar.com). Metro Pico/bus 81, 246, 344, 381, 442, 460/I-110, exit Adams Boulevard. **Open** 11.30am-10pm Mon-Fri; 3pm-11pm Sat, Sun. **Credit** AmEx, Disc, MC, V. **Map** p315 B5 ④
Locavore wine enthusiasts will find refuge at this hip wine bistro where the focus is almost exclusively on California wine – there are roughly 70 by the glass, stored in temperature controlled fridges. Collectors and winos alike marvel at Corkbar's impressive two-storey backdrop of shelves of carefully placed empty bottles in varying and alternating

CONSUME

facings. Thankfully, the knowledgeable and passionate wine staff help navigate the list.

Edison

108 W 2nd Street, at S Main Street (1-213 613 0000, www.edisondowntown.com). Metro Pershing Square/bus 33, 55, 83, 92/US 101, exit Main Street south. **Open** 5pm-2am Wed-Fri; 7pm-2am Sat. **Credit** AmEx, DC, Disc, MC, V. **Map** p315 C2 ㊼
Don't let the dress code (no T-shirts, sportswear, sneakers or baggy jeans) scare you off: you'll be thankful you made the effort when you set foot inside this power plant-turned-Downtown hotspot. The names of the party lounges (Tesla, Generator) pay homage to the building's past, and there's a live band on Thursdays, plus DJs on Fridays and Saturdays.

Golden Gopher

417 W 8th Street, between Hill & Olive Streets (1-213 614 8001, http://213nightlife.com/golden gopher). Metro 7th Street-Metro Center/bus 14, 37, 70, 71, 76, 78, 79, 81, 96/I-110, exit 9th Street east. **Open** 8pm-2am Mon, Sat, Sun; 5pm-2am Tue-Fri. **Credit** AmEx, DC, Disc, MC, V. **Map** p315 B4 ㊽
Cedd Moses, aka Mr Downtown, is behind this haunt, which is a perfect mix of high and low, where you can come for a quick PBR – or a fancy, well-made cocktail. Prices are reasonable, the jukebox is stocked with oldies-meets-Coachella, and a retro arcade (think Pac-Man) allows for friendly drinking games. Do note, however, that dress code is enforced.

Hank's Bar

Stillwell Hotel, 840 S Grand Avenue, between W 8th & W 9th Streets (1-213 623 7718). Metro 7th Street-Metro Center/bus 14, 37, 70, 71, 76, 78, 79, 96/I-110, exit 9th Street east. **Open** noon-1.30am daily. **Credit** MC, V. **Map** p315 B4 ㊾
The streets around it are constantly being rebuilt, but this old residential hotel remains unchanged. The same can be said for its ground-floor bar: divey yet approachable, unpredictable and charismatic, it's a little piece of the past in a neighbourhood that's mostly anxious to press on towards the future.

One-Eyed Gypsy

901 E 1st Street, at N Vignes Street (1-626 340 3529, http://one-eyedgypsy.com). Metro Little Tokyo/ Arts District/US 101, exit Mission Road. **Open** 7pm-2am Wed-Sat. **Credit** AmEx, Disc, MC, V.
If the LA County Fair set up tent Downtown, the One-Eyed Gypsy – a sweet and spicy cocktails and canned beer, heart-attack snacks-inspired dive – would be its main attraction. It's a mix of Mardi Gras meets East India Trading Company-inspired decor – with hanging beads, ornate walls and large mirrors behind the bar, where cherub-like statues preside over a team of busy goth and hipster bartenders. You can pile into the photo booth then hit the Skee Ball machines or ask the gypsy tarot card quarter machine to tell you your fortune. Later, snag a table near the stage for a decent view of the band or occasional burlesque act.

Pourhaus

1820 Industrial Street, at Mill Street (1-213 327 0304, www.pourhauswinebar.com). Bus 60, 62, 760/I-10, exit Mateo Street. **Open** noon-10pm Mon-Thur, Sun; noon-midnight Fri; 3pm-midnight Sat. **Credit** AmEx, Disc, MC, V.
The revitalisation of Downtown LA is alive and well at this wine bar/retail store. Owner (and wine pro) Lorena Porras offers global wines she's passionate about, from small-production, family-owned producers. The atmosphere is derived from the friendly, easygoing staff, Porras included, who'll help you decide on a wine by the glass or a monthly rotating flight. If you really liked a wine you tasted, grab it off the shelf and take it home for more imbibing.

Rooftop Bar at the Standard

Standard Hotel, 550 S Flower Street, between W 5th & W 6th Streets (1-213 892 8080, www.standardhotels.com). Metro 7th Street-Metro Center/bus 16, 18, 55, 62/I-110, exit 6th Street east. **Open** noon-1.30am daily. **Credit** AmEx, DC, Disc, MC, V. **Map** p315 B3 ㊿
Although this hotel rooftop bar isn't as happening as it once was, the clientele of models, wannabes and admirers hanging out around the pool continue to look, and act, like they've sprung from the pages of *Vice*. It's best on weekend afternoons, with DJs spinning, liquor flowing and terrific views of Downtown.

★ Seven Grand

515 W 7th Street, at S Olive Street (1-213 614 0737, www.sevengrand.la). Metro 7th Street-Metro Center/bus 14, 37, 70, 71, 76, 78, 79, 81, 96/I-10, exit 3rd/4th Street. **Open** 5pm-2am Mon-Wed; 4pm-2am Thur, Fri; 7pm-2am Sat, Sun. **Credit** AmEx, DC, MC, V. **Map** p315 B4 (51)
From the neon stag on the sign outside to the impressive selection of whiskies inside (and the impressive staff who pour them), Seven Grand's theme is manliness. Pool tables, plaid wallpaper and mounted game help create an atmosphere influenced by tradition but with a very modern sense of humour. A dress code is enforced: no baggy clothes or flip-flops.

★ Varnish

118 E 6th Street, at S Main Street (1-213 622 9999, http://213nightlife.com/thevarnish). Metro Pershing Square/bus 33, 55, 83, 92/US 101, exit Main Street south. **Open** 7pm-2am daily. **Credit** AmEx, DC, Disc, MC, V. **Map** p315 C3 (52)
Classic craft cocktail aficionado Sasha Petraske is a big deal in New York, so when he teamed up with the ubiquitous Cedd Moses and barman Eric Alperin in 2009 to launch a bar in Los Angeles, it quickly became the godfather of the local craft cocktail

The New Brew Crew

LA is polishing its taps and sowing its suds with microbreweries and brewpubs.

Like many other cities, LA is seeing a surge in craft breweries and brewpubs, putting the stalwart brands of decades past in serious competition for tap space with small-batch beers, from stouts and IPAs to Belgian-style brews. According to the Brewers Association, in 2011 alone there were 250 brewery openings (174 microbreweries and 76 brewpubs) across the US, bringing the total number of breweries in America to 2,126.

The craze is catching on in retail stores and bars in Tinseltown, aided by the annual LA Beer Week in September, which in 2012 saw 11 straight days of celebrating beer with tastings and events, putting St Patrick's Day to shame and possibly taking the record for the longest booze-fuelled festival in recent history (what wine festivals go on that long?).

When did it all start? Perhaps when Jeremy Raub's **Eagle Rock Brewing Company** (3056 Roswell Street, Atwater Village, 1-323 257 7866, http://eaglerock brewery.com) was officially the first brewery to open within city limits in 2009, or when Ryan Sweeney (of the **Surly Goat**, *see p122*, in WeHo and the **Blind Donkey**, *see p130*, in Pasadena) introduced Pliny the Younger, a Triple IPA from Russian River Brewing Co, at the now-defunct BoHo gastropub. Then came Tony Yanow (**Tony's Darts Away** and **Mohawk Bend**, *see p126*), who in 2011 co-founded **Golden Road Brewing** (5410 West San Fernando Road, 1-213 373 4677, http://goldenroad.la), a pub and brewery in Atwater Village. Here, the order of the day was canned – not bottled – craft beer (also available on tap). His business partner is Meg Gill who, at 28, was the youngest female brewery owner in the world at the time of writing. In less than a year, Golden Road was on draft in over 400 locations in LA and 1,500 shops around the country – helping further the case that canned beer is better suited to preserve freshness and taste than bottled beer, as Gill had convinced Yanow. Indeed, that seems to be the beer connoisseur's new adage.

Downtown LA's continued renaissance is improved by the addition of the **Buzz Wine Beer Shop** (460 S Spring Street, 1-213 622 2222, www.buzzwinebeershop.com), a superb hub boasting 200-plus beer facings and Friday beer flights. **Weiland Brewing Company** (www.weilandbrewery.net), has two spots: 400 E 1st Street (1-213 680 2881)

Glendale Tap.

and an 'Underground' location (505 S Flower Street, 1-213 622 1125). Also look out for **Bonaventure Brewing Co**'s fourth-floor restaurant on the pool deck level of the Westin Bonaventure hotel (404 S Figueroa Street, 1-213 236 0802, www.bonaventurebrewing.com) and the newly revamped **Angel City Brewery** (216 S Alameda Street, 1-213 622 1261, http://angelcitybrewery.com).

Several brewpubs are focusing their menus solely on California beers, with a sprinkling from other domestic and international craft producers. Check out Mohawk Bend, the Surly Goat, the **Glendale Tap** (*see p130*) and **Venice Ale House** (2 Rose Avenue, 1-310 314 8253, www.venicealehouse.com). Meanwhile, **Culver City Home Brewing** (4358½ Sepulveda Boulevard, Culver City, www.brewsupply.com) offers classes in home brewing. Venturing to Pasadena you'll discover tasting rooms at **Stone Brewing Co** (220 S Raymond Avenue, 1-626 440 7243, www.stonebrew.com) and, south of LA, in Torrance, a group of breweries including the **Monkish Brewing Co** (20311 S Western Avenue, 1-310 295 2157, www.monkish brewing.com) and **Strand Brewing** (23520 Telo Avenue, 1-310 517 0900, www.strandbrewing.com); **Smog City Brewing Co** (www.smogcitybrewing.com) was due to join the party as this guide went to press.

Unlike the cocktail craze, where $15-$20 was the norm per drink, the majority of these brews will cost you between $5 and $10 on tap. And if you spring for a can, know that the craft beer industry has got your back.

movement. The Downtown speakeasy sits inside Cole's restaurant, past a discreet rear door, marked only by a drawing of a coupé glass. Standing at the bar is not permitted, so snag a vintage booth and take in the live piano music; but, of course, the main draw here is the drinks. You can't go wrong with a classic old-fashioned or aviation.

THE VALLEYS
San Fernando Valley

Bow & Truss
11122 Magnolia Boulevard, between Lankershim Boulevard & Vineland Avenue, North Hollywood (1-818 985 8787, www.bowandtruss.com). Metro North Hollywood/CA 170, exit Magnolia Boulevard. **Open** 11.30am-late Mon-Sat; 10am-late Sun. **Credit** AmEx, Disc, MC, V.
Bow & Truss aims to elevate the craft cocktail scene of this once-sleepy neighbourhood. The self-described 'Latin' theme runs from bull-and-matador artwork on the walls to a menu featuring paellas, cheeses, charcuterie and tacos (don't miss the chicken confit version), while drinks from LA's finest ministers of cocktailing, Aidan Demarest and Marcos Tello, include some intriguing sherry-based quaffs.

Federal Bar
5303 Lankershim Boulevard, at Chandler Boulevard, North Hollywood (1-818 980 2555, www.thefederalbar.com). Metro North Hollywood/CA 170-North, exit Magnolia Boulevard. **Open** 11.30am-2am daily. **Credit** AmEx, DC, Disc, MC, V.
This burgers and beer joint features a great selection of micro beers, bourbons and scotches, an eclectic wine

---

INSIDE TRACK WE'RE ONLY HERE FOR THE BEER

Desperate for a proper pint? In addition to the Cat & Fiddle, LA has a few other English pubs worth stopping by. Ye Olde King's Head (116 Santa Monica Boulevard, Santa Monica, 1-310 451 1402; and 12969 Ventura Boulevard, Studio City, 1-818 990 9055; www.yeoldekingshead.com) offers pub grub and Premier League football games, as does the more upmarket Village Idiot (7383 Melrose Avenue, 1-323 655 3331, Fairfax District, www.village idiotla.com). Even posher – despite the name – is the Pikey (7617 W Sunset Boulevard, Hollywood, 1-323 850 5400, www.thepikeyla.com); the restaurant is decent – definitely order the fish and chips – but the attached dimly lit bar is the real draw.

---

list featuring California and some new world wines, and a menu of comfort food. Decor-wise, it's modern leather-industrial design meets deco copper ceilings and eccentrically fashionable furniture. Sometimes there's a $10 cover for live music or comedy upstairs.

San Gabriel Valley

Blind Donkey
53 E Union Street, between N Raymond & N Fair Oaks Avenues, Pasadena (1-626 792 1833, www.theblinddonkey.com). Metro Memorial Park/bus 20, 40, 51, 52, 177, 187/I-110, exit Arroyo Parkway north. **Open** 4pm-2am Mon-Fri; 1pm-2am Sat, Sun. **Credit** AmEx, Disc, MC, V.
The name of this bar – brought to you by Ryan Sweeney from the Surly Goat (*see p122*), Verdugo Bar and the Little Bear – pays homage to the blindfolded donkeys of old who walked round and round pulling a millstone to grind corn. Here, whisky lovers get to indulge in a list boasting 100-plus whiskies from America, Scotland, Ireland and Canada. The decor features those popular Edison bulbs dangling from a tall ceiling, exposed brick and random pics of donkeys; communal tables provide space for groups and two televisions offer some sports intake. Stick to whisky or beer as cocktails are pretty run-of-the mill.

★ Glendale Tap
4227 San Fernando Road, at W Cypress Street, Glendale (1-818 241 4227). Bus 94, 603/I-5, exit Los Feliz Boulevard. **Open** 5pm-2am Mon-Fri; noon-2am Sat, Sun. **Credit** MC, V.
Feeding LA's craft beer mania, the Glendale Tap is a faux-dive bar replete with a seasonal rotating list of 50-plus beers on tap/cask that won't break the bank. Two free pool tables commandeer the centre of the room, and even though the joint has the markings of a dive – beer, beards, bar games, humidity and a fairly unmarked façade – this is the place for serious beer connoisseurs to sample mostly California, Colorado and Belgian craft beers from pristine taps served by bartenders who have tasted every beer and can talk you through the list.

Tap Room
Langham Huntington Hotel, 1401 S Oak Knoll Avenue, at Wentworth Avenue, Pasadena (1-626 585 6457, http://langhamtaproom.com). Bus 485/I-110, exit Glenarm Street east. **Open** 2pm-1am Mon-Thur; noon-2am Fri, Sat; noon-midnight Sun. **Credit** AmEx, DC, Disc, MC, V.
A nod to the original hotel bar that opened just after Prohibition ended, the Tap Room is a high-class joint with an elegant bar and pretty patio in one of the most beautiful hotels in the Pasadena area. On Thursday nights, chef Jesse Flores serves small plates and the bar gets busy with spirits tastings, drink specials and live jazz. The Stephen Boyd Band's residency on Friday and Saturday nights keeps this cosy spot swinging.

Coffeehouses

The bean scene.

Many Angelenos like to try and make their hard-earned wealth seem accidental, and there's no better way to cultivate an aura of leisure than to while away a few workday hours in a coffeehouse. The variety of venues gets broader by the year, although the most recent trend is for upscale coffeehouses: decadent lunches and pastries on the menu, outrageously expensive equipment churning behind the bar. Still, plenty of relaxed hangouts remain – as, of course, do the major chains. Starbucks is as unavoidable here as in any other city. However, it's given plenty of competition by the equally lacklustre Coffee Bean & Tea Leaf (www.coffeebean.com), a California-based chain. A better alternative is Peet's (www.peets.com), which originally opened in Berkeley in 1966 (its aficionados are dubbed 'Peetnicks') and now has around 200 branches, mainly in California.

SANTA MONICA & THE BEACH TOWNS

Santa Monica

★ Caffe Luxxe

925 Montana Avenue, between 9th & 10th Streets (1-310 394 2222, www.caffeluxxe.com). Bus SM3/I-10, exit Lincoln Boulevard north. **Open** 6am-7pm Mon-Fri; 6.30am-7pm Sat, Sun. **Credit** AmEx, MC, V. **Map** p310 B2 ❶

Gary Chau and Mark Wain's café has brought a touch of European-style elegance to this stretch of Montana Avenue. The drinks are all handmade, and the beans and leaves are sourced from small family-owned businesses around the world; the coffee is roasted in Luxxe's own roastery. Pastries and savoury goods are baked locally and there's a small selection of gift items. In fact, the only thing Luxxe doesn't have is internet – deliberately so. You'll find cheaper coffee elsewhere, but you won't find better. More branches are planned; note that this one stays open later than the others.

Other locations Brentwood Country Mart, 225 26th Street, Santa Monica (1-310 394 2222); 11975 San Vicente Boulevard, Brentwood (1-310 394 2222).

18th Street Coffee House

1725 Broadway, at 18th Street (1-310 264 0662). Bus 4, SM1, SM10/I-10, exit Cloverfield Boulevard north. **Open** 7am-7pm Mon-Thur; 7am-6.30pm Fri; 8am-6pm Sat. **Credit** DC, Disc, MC, V. **Map** p310 C3 ❷

Serving decent coffee alongside a range of sweets and savouries, the moody-broody 18th Street Coffee House draws a loyal crowd of locals who also happen to be successful screenwriters and/or red-carpet celebrities. There's a no-cellphone policy inside and a patio outside.

Funnel Mill

930 Broadway, at 10th Street (1-310 393 1617, www.funnelmill.com). Bus 4, 20, 33, 704, 720, 733, SM1, SM5, SM7, SM8, SM10 /I-10, exit Lincoln Boulevard north. **Open** 9am-7pm Mon-Fri; 10am-7pm Sat. **Credit** MC, V. **Map** p310 B3 ❸

At this low-key, independent shop, an array of rare coffees is elegantly served on silver trays with milk and sugar on the side. The most notable item on the menu is a $90 cup of coffee, made from beans that have already passed through the digestive system of a creature called the Sumatran Paradoxurus (tasting by appointment only!). All the more delicious on your lips.

> ❶ Yellow numbers given in this chapter correspond to the location of coffeehouses on the street maps. *See pp310-315.*

CONSUME

Urth Caffé. See p134.

Venice

Abbot's Habit
1401 Abbot Kinney Boulevard, at California Avenue (1-310 399 1171). Bus 33, 733, SM1, SM2/I-10, exit 4th/5th Street south. **Open** *Summer* 6am-10pm daily. *Winter* 6am-9pm daily. **Credit** DC, MC, V. **Map** p310 A6 ④
Venice attracts a mixed crowd; and this café, which arrived on Abbot Kinney long before most of its neighbours, is no exception. Affluent home-owners mix with starving artists; while the coffee's not outstanding, the scene makes this a Venice classic.

★ Jin Patisserie
1202 Abbot Kinney Boulevard, at San Juan Avenue (1-310 399 8801, www.jinpatisserie.com). Bus 33, 733, SM1, SM2/I-10, exit 4th/5th Street south. **Open** 11am-6pm Tue-Sun. **Credit** AmEx, Disc, MC, V. **Map** p310 A5 ⑤
At Jin Patisserie, liquid refreshment comes second to desserts: there's something for every self-indulgent fancy, from green tea-flavoured treats to chocolate concoctions. Don't miss the delectable *macarons*. The tiny garden is a civilised spot in which to take a break from the low-grade insanity on Abbot Kinney.

Marina del Rey to LAX

Tanner's Coffee Co
200 Culver Boulevard, at Vista del Mar (1-310 574 2739). Bus 115/I-405, exit Manchester

Boulevard west. **Open** 6am-7pm Mon-Fri; 6.30am-7pm Sat; 6.45am-7pm Sun. **Credit** DC, MC, V.
The coffee served here is pretty good, the range of pastries is laudable, and there's free Wi-Fi too. Still, since it's adjacent to a park and one block from the beach, you'll probably want your caffeine fix to go.

BRENTWOOD TO BEVERLY HILLS
Culver City

Cognoscenti Coffee
6114 Washington Boulevard, at Roberts Avenue (1-213 986 6624, http://popupcoffee.com). Metro Culver City/bus 33, 733, C1/I-10, exit Washington Boulevard south. **Open** 8am-5pm Mon-Sat. **Credit** AmEx, DC, MC, V.
Yeekai Lim's Cognoscenti Coffee now has a second location, in Culver City's Arts District (the other is within Atwater Village's excellent Proof Bakery, 1-323 664 8633). The minimalist storefront feels like someone's home, with a large, wood-countered island and round communal tables with limited seating that spills out on to the outdoor patio. Expect meticulous precision in espresso-based drinks and pour-over coffee from roasters such as Phil & Sebastian, Counter Culture, Wrecking Ball and Ritual.

Beverly Hills

Caffe Dell'arte
428 N Bedford Drive, at Brighton Way (1-310 271 6842). Bus 20, 720/I-405, exit Wilshire Boulevard east. **Open** 6.30am-6pm Mon-Fri; 7.30am-4pm Sat. **Credit** MC, V. **Map** p311 C3 ⑥
This unpretentious little café can get lost amid the flash and glitz of the luxury emporiums around it. However, if you're looking for a cheap pick-me-up after a marathon shopping session, this is the place.

WEST HOLLYWOOD, HOLLYWOOD & MIDTOWN
West Hollywood

Alfred Coffee & Kitchen
8428 Melrose Place, at N Croft Avenue (1-323 944 0811, www.alfredcoffee.com). Bus 4, 105, 305, 550, 704/I-10, exit La Cienega Boulevard north. **Open** 8am-6pm Mon-Sat; 9am-3pm Sun. **Credit** AmEx, DC, MC, V. **Map** p312 B2 ⑦
A welcome newcomer to the area, Alfred blends in to its trendy locale with hardwood floors, communal tables and a lovely tiled (working) fireplace. Coffee is from Stumptown, while a short menu of salads and sandwiches complements the pastries, muffins and scones. It's right on the doorstep of the Sunday farmers' market, but a perfect spot for

All Rise

LA's bakeries are popping up faster than you can say, 'What Dukan Diet?'

Surprisingly, for a place whose citizens seem to be on a permanent diet, Los Angeles is home to a huge number of bakeries. Indeed, while every café worth its sugar offers a range of cakes and pastries, the region has recently seen an explosion in specialist bakeshops and nostalgic throwbacks.

One of the city's best is inside mid-city art museum LACMA (*see p55*). **C+M** (1-323 857 6180, www.patina group.com) stands for Coffee and Milk, which it serves, alongside nostalgic riffs on pop tarts and Oreo cookies, plus hand-held pies – buttery, refined and irresistible – and delicate Meyer lemon curd and lavender-sprinkled pop tarts that showcase chef Josh Graves's sophisticated knack for pastry.

On the heels of the highly anticipated burger destination Short Order came the opening of its sweet counterpart **Short Cake** (1-323 761 7976, www.shortcake la.com), both located in the Fairfax District's Farmers Market. It offers its own take on classics such as fruit pies, peanut butter bars and classic yellow cake. Baker Hourie Sahakian offers her goodies with heart (not sass) that's completely infectious.

At nearby **Sycamore Kitchen** (*see p108*), Karen Hatfield has taken a detour from her fine dining restaurant, Hatfield's, with a casual bakery/café that serves morning pastries and sandwiches on house-made bread. The addictive salted caramel pecan bobka roll is quickly becoming a signature item. Bonus: late afternoon sweet-seekers are rewarded with half-price pastries from 4.30pm.

The Westside's flour queen Zoe Nathan has opened **Milo & Olive** (*see p97*), an ode to all things wood-baked. Mini-cupcakes, éclairs and lemon bars are replaced with (vegan) chocolate-banana and pistachio cakes, wholewheat croissants – they'll convert any traditionalist – and killer skillet bread.

Downtown, meanwhile, boasts **Semi Sweet Bakery** (105 E 6th Street, 1-213 228 9975, http://semisweetbakery.com), whose owner and chef Sharlena Fong has years of pastry cred under her belt. Fong amped up the baked goods selection at nearby Nickel Diner and made maple-bacon doughnuts a city-wide craving. Semi Sweet does a riff on the famed creation with a maple-bacon sticky bun made with light brioche. Doughnuts include a fab strawberry shortcake variety.

Over in Pacific Palisades, the bakery at Alain Giraud's restaurant, **Maison Giraud** (1032 Swarthmore Avenue, 1-310 459 7561, www. maison-giraud.com), turns out some of the best viennoiseries this side of the Seine. Take away a freshly baked baguette or try that ubiquitous pâtisserie staple, a croissant – buttery, flaky and one of the best in the city.

But if all you crave is a cupcake, have no fear: LA's obsession with the diminutive treat shows no sign of slowing down. On the contrary: 2012 saw the opening of DC import **Georgetown Cupcake** on trendy South Robertson Boulevard (No.143, 1-310 893 2866, www.georgetowncupcake.com), while long-time favourite **Sprinkles** installed an ATM-style cake-dispensing machine outside its flagship (9635 Little Santa Monica Boulevard, 1-310 274 8765, www.sprinkles.com) for salivating fans who couldn't face the long lines – as well as an ice-cream shop next door. It also has a new – already thriving – outpost at the **Grove** (*see p140*). Equally good are the concoctions at **Frosted Cupcakery** (1200 North Highland Avenue, Hollywood, 1-323 467 1080, www.frostedcupcakery.com) and **Joan's on Third** on W 3rd Street (*see p107*). By comparison, the cupcakes at **Magnolia Bakery** (8389 West 3rd Street, 1-323 951 0636, www.magnoliabakery.com), just across the street from Joan's, fall short, but the moist coconut cake and the retro banana pudding more than compensate.

For more throwback treats, visit Susan Sarich's **SusieCakes** in Brentwood (11708 San Vicente Boulevard, 1-310 442 2253, www.susiecakesla.com), a self-styled 'all-American home-style bake shop' selling whoopee pies and other retro treats.

CONSUME

people-watching any day of the week. Plans for live acoustic music on Friday afternoons were in the works as this guide went to press.

Kings Road Café

8361 Beverly Boulevard, at N Kings Road (1-323 655 9044, www.kingsroadcafe.com). Bus 16/I-10, exit La Cienega Boulevard north. **Open** 7am-6pm daily. **Credit** AmEx, MC, V. **Map** p312 B3 ⑧
This sceney but down-to-earth joint gets packed at weekends, when there's a wait for outdoor tables. The baked goods can be a let-down but stick with

salads and sandwiches – not to mention the addictive vanilla blended latte – and you can't go wrong. The occasional celeb spot is a bonus.
Other locations 12401 Ventura Boulevard, Studio City (1-818 985 3600).

★ Urth Caffé

8565 Melrose Avenue, at Westmount Drive (1-310 659 0628, www.urthcaffe.com). Bus 4, 105, 550, 704/I-10, exit La Cienega Boulevard north. **Open** 6.30am-11.30pm daily. **Credit** AmEx, DC, Disc, MC, V. **Map** p312 B2 ⑨

Cold Comfort

The hottest coolest places in town.

In 2006, not long after Pinkberry opened its first branch on a quiet West Hollywood sidestreet, the *LA Times* dubbed it 'the taste that launched 1,000 parking tickets'. Fast-forward seven years and while frozen yoghurt is still popular (particularly among more weight-conscious denizens), the bubble has definitely burst. Pinkberry's original location has gone, as have several of its other stores, but you can still get your froyo fix at remaining branches (including the one in the Beverly Center; *see p138*), plus other chains such as **Yogurtland** (at the neighbouring Beverly Connection mall) and independent one-offs such as WeHo favourite **Yogurt Stop** (8803 Santa Monica Boulevard, 1-310 652 6830, www.yogurtstop.net).

Mother Moo.

Today, however, the city's former froyo junkies have found a new obsession: ice-cream. LA has recently witnessed a surge in ice-creameries, from the retro to the revolutionary. For the former, take the vintage-style **Sweet Rose Creamery** at the Brentwood Country Mart (1-310 260 2663, www.sweetrose creamery.com). The concoctions served here are made using ingredients such as Valrhona chocolate. The salted caramel flavour is addictive.

Over in the Malibu Village mall, **Grom** (3886 Cross Creek Road, 1-310 456 9797, www.grom.it) is the first West Coast branch of a small chain of artisan gelaterias founded in Italy. Here, the premium is on superior ingredients such as Syrian pistachios and Piedmont nougat. Rich, authentic gelato in flavours such as

English toffee is also served at the **Gelato Bar**, a popular family-run joint in Los Feliz (1936 Hillhurst Avenue, 1-323 668 0606, www.gelatobarla.com).

True ice-cream aficionados, however, swear by **Scoops**. Six years after its launch, Tai Kim's ice-cream shop in Hollywood (712 N Heliotrope Drive, 1-323 906 2649), next to **Cafecito Orgánico** (*see right*), still has fans lining up for signature flavours such as brown bread and the weird-sounding-but-subtle-tasting Guinness and chocolate. Flavours change daily, but catch the luscious honey and salt combo if you can. The store drew such a following that a second location opened in 2010 in Palms (3400 Overland Avenue, 1-323 405 7055, www.scoopswestside.com), followed by a third in 2012 (5105 York Boulevard, Highland Park).

Another unconventional choice is **Mashti Malone's** (1525 N La Brea Avenue,

Urth has four locations in Los Angeles, but this one is the starlets' hangout of choice. The focus is on the organic coffees, teas and food, all of which are good (the pumpkin pie is unmissable) – but the real point of interest is the collection of minor, medium and occasionally major celebrities who come here… and the paparazzi parked outside to document their caffeine habits and companions. *Photo p132.*
Other locations 2327 Main Street, Santa Monica (1-310 314 7040); 267 S Beverly Drive, Beverly Hills (1-310 205 9311); 451 S Hewitt Street, Downtown (1-213 797 4534).

Hollywood, 1-323 874 0144, www.mash timalone.com), where you can cool down with delicately perfumed Persian ice-cream in flavours such as rosewater saffron. Like all the best places to eat in LA, it's located in a strip mall.

Those hankering after a truly old-school experience, meanwhile, should head to the Farmers Market in the Fairfax District, where two ice-cream stands – **Gill's Old-Fashioned Ice Cream** and **Bennett's** – are still churning out the cold stuff, decades on. And if you're overheating in the San Gabriel Valley, be sure to stop by long-time fave **Buster's** (*see p136*) in South Pasadena, newbie **Mother Moo** in Sierra Madre (17 Kersting Court, 1-626 355 9650, www.mothermoo.com) to the east and, to the south, legendary, nigh-on 100-year-old **Fosselman's** in Alhambra (1824 W Main Street, 1-626 282 6533, www.fosselmans.com).

Or you could do what any other self-respecting local does and wait for the ice-cream to come to you. Forget cardboard cones for the ice-cream van: how about a potato chip and butterscotch ice-cream cookie from the **Coolhaus** truck? Launched in 2008, the brand has proved so popular it now has a presence in four other cities, plus a bricks-and-mortar outlet in Culver City (8588 Washington Boulevard, 1-310 424 5559, www.eatcoolhaus.com).

In a similar vein, there's **Beachy Cream**, whose truck pitches up at special events and food markets, serving organic ice-cream with SoCal-themed names such as Strawberry Surfer Girl and Ginger Wipe Out. Likewise, it now has a store (1209 Wilshire Boulevard, Santa Monica, 1-310 656 4999, www.beachycream.com).

Hollywood

Bourgeois Pig
5931 Franklin Avenue, between Tamarind & N Bronson Avenues (1-323 464 6008). Bus 180, 181, 207, 217, LDH/US 101, exit Gower Street north. **Open** 8am-2am Mon-Thur, Sun; 8am-2.30pm Fri, Sat. **Credit** MC, V. **Map** p313 C1 ⑩
The dimly lit Bourgeois Pig sits on a strip of Franklin Avenue in Hollywood that's hip right now, thanks in no small part to the presence nearby of the Upright Citizens Brigade Theatre (*see p227*). Pop in for tea or an espresso before the show, but not if you're in a hurry – service is notoriously slow.

Fairfax District

Susina
7122 Beverly Boulevard, at N Detroit Street (1-323 934 7900, www.susinabakery.com). Bus 14, 212/I-10, exit La Brea Avenue north. **Open** 7am-11pm Mon-Fri; 8am-11pm Sat, Sun. **Credit** AmEx, MC, V. **Map** p312 D3 ⑪
Susina is one of the most popular bakeries in town, and with good reason. The café itself is charming, with a Vienna-at-the-turn-of-the-century vibe, and both coffees and cakes are excellent: in particular, the summer berries cake is the stuff of legend. Staff are happy for you to linger with your cuppa for as long as you wish.

LOS FELIZ TO ECHO PARK
Los Feliz

Café Los Feliz
2118 Hillhurst Avenue, at Avocado Street (1-323 664 7111). Bus 180, 181/I-5, exit Los Feliz Boulevard west. **Open** 7am-6pm Mon-Sat; 7am-3pm Sun. **Credit** AmEx, MC, V. **Map** p314 B1 ⑫
Kick back at this quaint, family-run café that serves salads, sandwiches and more (although it's best known most for its delicious pastries and French coffee). Savoury or sweet, the croissants are a must-try.

Silver Lake

Cafecito Orgánico
534 N Hoover Street, at Bellevue Avenue (1-213 537 8367, www.cafecitoorganico.com). Bus 10/US 101, exit Silver Lake Boulevard north. **Open** 6am-7pm Mon-Fri; 7am-7pm Sat, Sun. **Credit** AmEx, DC, Disc, MC, V. **Map** p314 B4 ⑬
Tourists may wait in 20-minute lines at Intelligentsia (*see p136*) up the street, but locals prefer Cafecito, the quieter shop on Hoover. Here you'll find less pretension and more privacy – as well as pastries and the addictive Espresso Clandestino and free Wi-Fi.
Other locations 710 N Heliotrope Drive, Hollywood (1-213 537 8367); 29169 Heathercliff Road, Malibu (1-213 537 8367).

CONSUME

Café Tropical

2900 W Sunset Boulevard, at Silver Lake Boulevard (1-323 661 8391, www.cafe tropicalla.com). Bus 92, 201/I-5, exit Hyperion Avenue west. **Open** 6am-10pm daily. **Credit** MC, V. **Map** p314 C4 ⓔ

This much-cherished Cuban café offers a nice selection of coffee, extra-sweet pastries and lovely *empanadas*. With its cosy and earnest Cuban American vibe, it's a wonderful change from the chain-store establishments. Coffee is both strong and excellent.

★ Intelligentsia

3922 W Sunset Boulevard, at Sanborn Avenue (1-323 663 6173, www.intelligentsiacoffee.com). Bus 2, 4, 175, 302, 704/US 101, exit Silver Lake Boulevard north. **Open** 6am-8pm Mon-Wed, Sun; 6am-11pm Thur-Sat. **Credit** AmEx, Disc, MC, V. **Map** p314 B3 ⓕ

Intelligentsia's gorgeous tiled patio is always chock-full with beautiful people having very important discussions. Coffee is expensive, but it's also better than at nearly every other café in LA (the Black Cat Espresso is always a winner). Parking can be a pain, though.

Other locations 1331 Abbot Kinney Boulevard, Venice (1-310 399 1233); 55 E Colorado Boulevard, Pasadena (1-626 578 1270).

DOWNTOWN

Daily Dose

1820 Industrial Street, at Mill Street (1-213 281 9300, www.dailydoseinc.com). Bus 60, 62, 760/I-10, exit Mateo Street. **Open** 7am-6pm Mon-Fri; 9am-6pm Sat; 10am-3pm Sun. **Credit** AmEx, DC, MC, V.

A coffee shop and café serving up artisanal coffee and soul-satisfying food, made with natural ingredients sourced from local farmers, ranchers and fisheries. The food is fresh and seasonal, while the drinks menu has fun options, like Disco lemonade (Meyer lemonade with agave-marinated cherries).

Groundwork

108 W 2nd Street, at S Main Street (1-213 620 9668, www.lacoffee.com). Metro Little Tokyo/Arts District or Pershing Square/bus 33, 55, 83, 92/US 101, exit Main Street south. **Open** 6am-5pm Mon-Fri; 8am-2pm Sat. **Credit** DC, Disc, MC, V. **Map** p315 C2 ⓖ

This mini-chain is the venue of choice among many of the city's coffee snobs, and this location is popular with the denizens of the arts district in Downtown. The decor's not much to look at, but the quality of the drinks and sweet and savoury grub speaks for itself. **Other locations** throughout LA.

THE VALLEYS

San Gabriel Valley

Buster's Ice Cream & Coffee Shop

1006 Mission Street, at Meridian Avenue, South Pasadena (1-626 441 0744). Metro South Pasadena/bus 176/Hwy 110, exit Fair Oaks Avenue south or Orange Grove Avenue south. **Open** 6.30am-7pm Mon-Wed; 6.30am-8pm Thur; 6.30am-9pm Fri; 7am-9pm Sat; 7am-8pm Sun. **No credit cards**.

Buster's only adds to the quaint aura of charming South Pasadena. The menu includes everything from simple drip coffees to elaborate sundaes (made with Fosselman's ice-cream), and the coffeehouse is a perfect place in which to rest after a day spent ogling Craftsman homes. Note that it closes an hour earlier on Fridays and Saturdays in winter.

Zona Rosa Caffe

15 S El Molino Avenue, at E Colorado Boulevard, Pasadena (1-626 793 2334, www.zonarosacaffe.com). Metro Memorial Park/bus 180, 181, 267, 687/Hwy 110 to Pasadena (hwy ends at Glenarm Street). **Open** 7.30am-9pm Mon; 7.30am-11pm Tue-Thur; 7.30am-midnight Fri, Sat; 9am-10pm Sun. **No credit cards**.

Carrying with it a funky Latin feel, this café injects a little tang into Pasadena. The second floor houses a gallery, while the ground floor is full of goods imported from Latin America. Check out the Mexican hot chocolate.

Susina. See p135.

CONSUME

Shops & Services

Shop! In the name of love.

Popular cliché equates shopping in LA with the high-priced, star-studded glamour of Rodeo Drive. The fabled Beverly Hills street lives up to its reputation, but there's more to the city's shopping scene than its super-pricey designer stores. From the independent boutiques of Venice to the chain-packed malls that dot every corner of the region, LA doesn't lack variety; your main concern will be beating the traffic. And while the faltering exchange rate means that, for European visitors, the US in general isn't the bargain it once was, there's still plenty of retail therapy to be had.

THE LA SHOPPING SCENE

Shop hours are generally 10am to 6pm, though some stores open at 9am or remain open until 7pm, and most malls are open until at least 9pm. Return policies in the big chains are nearly always in the buyer's favour, but some smaller boutiques will go to the end of the world to avoid giving you a refund. A sales tax of 9 per cent will be added to the marked price of all merchandise and services in most of LA County; in Orange County, the sales tax is currently eight per cent.

The following selection is just a snapshot of what the city has to offer; keep abreast of new openings at www.timeout.com/los-angeles.

General

DEPARTMENT STORES

Barneys New York

9570 Wilshire Boulevard, at S Camden Drive, Beverly Hills (1-310 276 4400, www.barneys.com). Bus 4, 16, 20, 720/I-10, exit Robertson Boulevard north. **Open** 10am-7pm Mon-Wed, Fri, Sat; 10am-8pm Thur; noon-6pm Sun. **Credit** AmEx, DC, Disc, MC, V. **Map** p311 C3.

Every fashionista's best friend, the Los Angeles outpost of the legendary New York department store offers five floors of cosmetics, jewellery, shoes, designer clothes (for both sexes), lingerie and home accessories; the high-end likes of Prada, Fendi and Marc Jacobs are typical of the fare for sale. Above sits more elegance: Barney Greengrass, a classy rooftop restaurant.

Bloomingdale's

Westfield Century City (see p141), Century City (1-310 772 2100, www.bloomingdales.com). Bus 4, 16, 28, 316, 704, 728/I-405, exit Santa Monica Boulevard east. **Open** 10am-9pm Mon-Sat; 11am-7pm Sun. **Credit** AmEx, Disc, MC, V. **Map** p311 B4.

Presenting a range of stock that falls somewhere between middlebrow Macy's and upmarket Neiman Marcus in the pricing stakes, Bloomie's specialises in just-about-affordable designer clothing (Calvin Klein, DKNY, Alice + Olivia and others), jewellery, shoes and accessories: it's strong on handbags and there's an excellent selection of sunglasses.

Other locations throughout LA.

Macy's

Beverly Center (see p138), West Hollywood (1-310 854 6655, www.macys.com). Bus 14, 16, 105, 316, LDF/I-10, exit La Cienega Boulevard north. **Open** 10am-9.30pm Mon-Sat; 11am-8pm Sun. **Credit** AmEx, DC, Disc, MC, V. **Map** p312 B3.

Middle-market Macy's has spent the past decade or so expanding from its original New York home right across the nation. Its wares include costly garments from American designers, but also more affordable and casual clothing lines (from the likes of Rachel Roy and Tommy Hilfiger), accessories and cosmetics. The separate menswear store at the Beverly Center is especially well stocked.

Other locations throughout LA.

Neiman Marcus

9700 Wilshire Boulevard, at S Roxbury Drive, Beverly Hills (1-310 550 5900, www.neiman marcus.com). Bus 4, 16, 20, 720/I-10, exit

Robertson Boulevard north. **Open** 10am-7pm
Mon-Wed, Sat; 10am-8pm Thur; noon-6pm Sun.
Credit AmEx. **Map** p311 C3.

Residing at or near the top of the department store
tree, Neiman Marcus is widely nicknamed 'Needless
Mark-ups'. But nothing is really overpriced here: the
goods are simply top-of-the-line, and you're paying
for the quality (and the label: expect to find clothes
from the likes of Diane von Furstenberg, Jean Paul
Gaultier and Chloé). Good shoe department.
Other locations Fashion Island (*see p140*;
1-949 759 1900).

Nordstrom

*Westside Pavilion, 10800 W Pico Boulevar, at
Overland Avenue, West LA (1-310 470 6155,
www.nordstrom.com). Bus C3, SM7, SM8, SM12,
SM13/I-10, exit Overland Boulevard north.* **Open**
10am-9pm Mon-Fri; 10am-8pm Sat; 11am-7pm Sun.
Credit AmEx, DC, Disc, MC, V. **Map** p311 A5.

In the hierarchy of department stores, Nordstrom
falls neatly into the middle: not as swish as Neiman
Marcus, but smarter than Macy's. Designers in stock
range from Diesel to DKNY; the shoe and cosmetics
departments are uniformly excellent.
Other locations throughout LA.

Saks Fifth Avenue

*9634 Wilshire Boulevard, at S Peck Drive, Beverly
Hills (1-310 275 4211, www.saksfifthavenue.com).
Bus 4, 16, 20, 720/I-10, exit Robertson Boulevard
north.* **Open** 10am-7pm Mon-Wed, Fri, Sat; 10am-
8pm Thur; noon-6pm Sun. **Credit** AmEx, DC, MC,
V. **Map** p311 C3.

Saks opened its Beverly Hills branch in 1938 and
draws the city's biggest spenders with a carefully
glamorous selection of fashion. There's a menswear
store at 9634 Wilshire Boulevard (1-310 275 4211).
Other locations South Coast Plaza (*see p141*;
1-714 540 3233).

Target

*7100 Santa Monica Boulevard, at N La Brea
Avenue, West Hollywood (1-323 603 0004,
www.target.com). Bus 4, 212, 312, 704/I-10, exit
La Brea Avenue north.* **Open** 8am-11pm Mon-Sat;
8am-10pm Sun. **Credit** AmEx, DC, Disc, MC, V.
Map p312 D2.

Formerly dowdy and prosaic, this hugely successful
countrywide chain has reinvented itself over the last
decade with the help of well-known fashion names
such as Isaac Mizrahi and, during the holidays, a line
of Neiman Marcus merchandise more affordably
priced than at the mother store. But for all its aspirations, it's basically still a reliable supplier of low-
cost clothes, along with cheap appliances and
housewares. Some branches, including this one,
have a pharmacy, photo-development centre and
grocery section; also look for Starbucks outposts at
most stores.
Other locations throughout LA.

MALLS

For the following we've included general
opening hours; some stores open or close
later. Check the malls' websites for details.

Americana at Brand

*889 Americana Way, between Central Avenue
& Grand Boulevard, Glendale (1-877 897 2097,
www.americanaatbrand.com). Bus 92, 180, 181,
183, 201/I-5, exit Colorado Street east.* **Open**
10am-9pm Mon-Thur; 10am-10pm Fri, Sat;
11am-8pm Sun.

This immaculate, open-air mall mimics the Grove,
its sister operation, with Vegas-esque architecture
and a slew of upscale shops. Among the highlights
are Cole Haan, Anthropologie, Kate Spade, Kiehl's
and Tiffany & Co; there's also a range of restaurants
(including a branch of trendy Japanese joint
Katsuya) and an 18-screen cineplex.

The nearby **Glendale Galleria** (100 West
Broadway, 1-818 246 6737, www.glendalegalleria.com)
has more than 200 separate operations, among them
several department stores (Macy's, Nordstrom, JC
Penney and a huge Target) and mid-market fashion
faves (Abercrombie & Fitch, Gap, Victoria's Secret).

Beverly Center

*8500 Beverly Boulevard, at S La Cienega
Boulevard, West Hollywood (1-310 854 0071,
www.beverlycenter.com). Bus 14, 16, 105, 316,
LDF/I-10, exit La Cienega Boulevard north.*
Open 10am-9pm Mon-Fri; 10am-8pm Sat;
11am-6pm Sun. **Map** p312 B3.

It won't win any architectural awards, but this hulking, ugly mall is a good one-stop all-rounder. It's
anchored by two department stores, Henri Bendel,
Bloomingdale's and Macy's, and a list of fashion
retailers that includes Diesel, Coach, Tiffany, Dolce
& Gabbana and Burberry. Other shops include
Aveda, Sephora and Bed, Bath & Beyond; there's
also a decent food court and a cineplex. For cheaper
brands Old Navy, Nordstrom Rack and Ross Dress
for Less, as well as CVS, Target and restaurant
chains such as Johnny Rockets, Souplantation and
Corner Bakery Café, cross La Cienega Boulevard to
the Beverly Connection mall (www.thebeverly
connection.com).

Brentwood Country Mart

*225 26th Street, at San Vicente Boulevard,
Brentwood (1-310 451 9877, www.brentwood
countrymart.com).* **Open** 10am-7pm Mon-Sat;
11am-6pm Sun.

This small barn-themed retail village features luxe
shopping (Space NK, James Perse, Sugar Paper), sipping (Caffe Luxxe; *see p131*) and dining (Farmshop;
see p98) amid such quirky touches as old-fashioned
kids' mechanical rides, a rotisserie chicken joint
(Reddi Chick fries are legendary), author appearances
at the Diesel bookstore and al fresco summer movies.

Where to Shop

LA's best shopping neighbourhoods in brief.

SANTA MONICA & VENICE

Santa Monica's pedestrianised, chain-packed **Third Street Promenade** is popular, as is the new **Santa Monica Place** mall, but there's more interesting shopping to be found north on **Montana Avenue**, tidily lined with upscale boutiques. South of Santa Monica, **Main Street** in Ocean Park has a variety of stores selling clothes and gifts. And in Venice, head first to the proudly independent gift, clothing and art stores on **Abbot Kinney Boulevard** before you think of heading to the **Boardwalk** for $2 shades and African masks.

BEVERLY HILLS

A few familiar chains have moved into the **Golden Triangle**, bounded by Santa Monica Boulevard, Wilshire Boulevard and Rexford Drive, but this is still swank central. Chi-chi boutiques are also in abundance on the stretch of **Robertson Boulevard** south of Beverly Boulevard, where paparazzi regularly snap starlets shopping.

WEST HOLLYWOOD & HOLLYWOOD

The highlight of West Hollywood's shopping – if you're into designer brands – is the area on and around **Melrose Place**, just east of La Cienega.. Shopping in Hollywood itself is mixed, but the **Hollywood & Highland** complex does hold some worthwhile stores.

Hollywood & Highland.

FAIRFAX & MELROSE DISTRICTS

There's plenty of stylish shopping on **Melrose Avenue** between Fairfax Avenue and San Vicente Boulevard. South and east of here, the stretch of **W 3rd Street** between La Cienega and Crescent Heights Boulevards is also awash with great independent shops and cafés.

LOS FELIZ & SILVER LAKE

Both these East Side neighbourhoods offer a cultured, alt-slanted selection of stores. In Los Feliz, head to **Vermont Avenue** and **Hillhurst Avenue**; Silver Lake's shopping is concentrated around **Sunset Junction** and along **Sunset Boulevard**.

DOWNTOWN

Central **Downtown** doesn't offer much (although a few chains are moving into the area), but its edges contain treasures. Both **Chinatown** and **Little Tokyo** have worthwhile multicultural shopping; further south, the **Fashion District** offers bargains galore, not all of them legit.

THE VALLEYS

Shopping in the Valleys is focused around malls, but Old Town in **Pasadena** breaks the mould. Centred around Colorado Boulevard, its old buildings have been modernised to form a handsome, strollable street.

Fashion District.

Grove.

Fashion Island

401 Newport Center Drive, at San Miguel Drive, Newport Beach (1-949 721 2000, www.shopfashionisland.com). I-5 to Hwy 55 south to Hwy 73 south. **Open** 10am-9pm Mon-Fri; 10am-7pm Sat; 11am-6pm Sun; check with individual stores and restaurants for extended hours.

This gorgeous outdoor oceanside mall is a good one-stop shop if you're in the area. There are four department stores (Macy's, Bloomingdale's, Nordstrom and Neiman Marcus), along with an Apple Store, a Barnes & Noble and a selection of fashion stores that are a cut above the usual mall fare (Anthropologie, Elie Tahari, Trina Turk). It can get hellishly busy on weekends.

★ Grove

189 The Grove Drive, at W 3rd Street, Fairfax District (1-323 900 8080, www.thegrovela.com). Bus 16, 217, 218, 316, LDF/I-10, exit Fairfax Avenue north. **Open** 10am-9pm Mon-Thur; 10am-10pm Fri, Sat; 11am-8pm Sun. **Map** p312 C3.

In a town where most malls are housed inside bland, air-conditioned structures, this upscale open-air centre has been a hit. There are only around 50 retailers, but the selection is strong (an Apple Store, Barneys New York Co-Op, Crate & Barrel, and flagships of Abercrombie & Fitch and Topshop/Topman). There's also a Nordstrom and a decent movie theatre.

Hollywood & Highland

6801 Hollywood Boulevard, at N Highland Avenue, Hollywood (1-323 817 0220, www. hollywoodandhighland.com). Metro Hollywood-Highland/bus 156, 163, 212, 217, 363, 656, 780, LDH/US 101, exit Hollywood Boulevard west. **Open** 10am-10pm Mon-Sat; 10am-7pm Sun. **Map** p313 A1.

It's difficult to say whether Hollywood & Highland has helped drive Hollywood's recent commercial renaissance, or whether it's ridden to success on its coat-tails. Either way, this ambitious mall has become a popular destination after a shaky start. The stores are a jumble of familiar favourites (Gap, American Eagle, Sephora) and smaller chains (Bebe, Hot Topic, Fossil); it's designed to appeal to a younger crowd. For grub, there's a California Pizza Kitchen and Hard Rock Café, among others. The parking entrance is on Highland Avenue; parking is just $2 for two hours (with validation).

Santa Monica Place

315 Colorado Avenue, at 4th Street, Santa Monica (1-310 394 5451, www.santamonicaplace.com). Bus 4, 20, 704, 720, SM1, SM2, SM3, SM4, SM5, SM7, SM8, SM9, SM10/I-10, exit 4th/5th Street north. **Open** 10am-9pm Mon-Sat; 10am-8pm Sun. **Map** p310 A3.

This former down-at-heel mall reopened in 2010 after a two-and-a-half-year transformation. While the new open-air centre looks the part, with a sweeping rooftop dining deck with views of the ocean (although a better choice is Dr Andrew Weil's eaterie, True Food Kitchen, on the ground level. The shops themselves are a strange mix of obscure and well known (the latter includes two department stores, Bloomingdale's and Nordstrom, plus 7 For All Mankind, Michael Kors and Louis Vuitton); Kate Spade, Camper and the Art of Shaving were due to open later in 2013. Worth a wander if you're in the area.

South Coast Plaza

3333 Bristol Street, at I-405, Costa Mesa (1-800 782 8888, www.southcoastplaza.com). I-405, exit Bristol Street north. **Open** 10am-9pm Mon-Fri; 10am-8pm Sat; 11am-6.30pm Sun.

This monster is the third largest shopping centre in the US, with around 250 stores. Chains and luxury boutiques dominate, but whatever you want, you can probably find it here, whether in one of the five department stores (from Sears to Saks Fifth Avenue), the vast array of fashion retailers, or in one of the many specialist stores that sell everything from jewellery to sneakers. And if not, then you're very close to the Lab 'antimall' (2930 Bristol Street, 1-714 966 6660, www.thelab.com), which has a more youth-oriented range of retailers (Urban Outfitters, Buffalo Exchange and the like). With such high-end shopping comes high-end dining: Charlie Palmer at Bloomingdale's and Marché Moderne make SCP a destination in its own right.

Westfield Century City

10250 Santa Monica Boulevard, between Century Park W & Avenue of the Stars, Century City (1-310 277 3898, www.westfield.com/centurycity). Bus 4, 16, 28, 316, 704, 728/I-405, exit Santa Monica Boulevard. **Open** 10am-9pm Mon-Sat; noon-7pm Sun. **Map** p311 B4.

This immense mall has moved slightly upmarket in recent years, adding some smarter shops to its roster of main-street perennials. The likes of Gap and Sunglass Hut now rub shoulders with Brooks

---

INSIDE TRACK 'BU'S WHO

Worth a look if you're driving to the beach are two upscale outdoor malls in Malibu. The **Malibu Country Mart** (3835 Cross Creek Road, Malibu, www.malibucountrymart.com) has branches of Chrome Hearts, Oliver Peoples (*see p158*) and Planet Blue, among others. Next door, standouts at the **Malibu Lumber Yard** (3939 Cross Creek Road, Malibu, www.the malibulumberyard.com) include J Crew (*see p145*), James Perse (*see p144*) and designer boutique Intermix (www.intermixonline.com).

Brothers, Kate Spade, Thomas Pink and even Swarovski; however, the mall's two department stores remain Bloomingdale's and Macy's. There's also a 15-screen movie theatre (*see p194*). The car park is a horror during peak times.

MARKETS

For food markets, *see p151*. For antiques markets and flea markets, *see p160*.

Specialist

BOOKS & MAGAZINES
General

Although the number of **Barnes & Noble** bookstores has diminished in recent years, you can still visit the best ones at the Grove (1-323 525 0270, www.bn.com), which hosts celebrity book signings, and on Santa Monica's Third Street Promenade (1-310 260 9110).

★ Book Soup

8818 Sunset Boulevard, between Larabee Street & Horn Avenue, West Hollywood (1-310 659 3110, www.booksoup.com). Bus 2, 105, 302/I-10, exit La Cienega Boulevard north. **Open** 9am-10pm Mon-Sat; 9am-7pm Sun. **Credit** AmEx, DC, Disc, MC, V. **Map** p312 A2.

The variety of stock at Book Soup is huge and diverse, even if the space itself is a little squeezed, and the newsstand outside is well stocked with domestic and international papers and magazines. Celebrity authors tend to give readings here, so if you strike out elsewhere, you may be able to catch sight of a few famous people here.

Skylight Books

1818 N Vermont Avenue, at Melbourne Avenue, Los Feliz (1-323 660 1175, www. skylightbooks.com). Metro Vermont-Sunset/ bus 4, 156, 180, 181, 204, 754/US 101, exit Vermont Avenue north. **Open** 10am-10pm daily. **Credit** AmEx, DC, Disc, MC, V. **Map** p314 A2.

This much-cherished bookstore strikes a neat balance between intellectual crowd-pleasers and more unusual fare. Open since the mid 1990s, it bucked book-industry trends by expanding into the premises at the adjoining 1814 N Vermont Avenue a few years ago.

Small World Books

1407 Ocean Front Walk, at Horizon Avenue, Venice (1-310 399 2360, www.smallworld books.com). Bus 33, 733, SM1, SM2/I-10, exit 4th/5th Street south. **Open** 10am-8pm daily. **Credit** AmEx, DC, MC, V. **Map** p310 A5.

Tucked away amid the T-shirt hawkers and jewellery makers on the Venice Boardwalk is this great indie bookseller. The stock carried is an all-round mix, everything from pop fiction to scientific tomes, but store cat Conan is one of the main draws.

★ Vroman's

695 E Colorado Boulevard, between N El Molino & N Oak Knoll Avenues, Pasadena (1-626 449 5320, www.vromansbookstore.com). Metro Lake/bus 180, 181, 485/Hwy 110 to Pasadena (hwy ends at Glenarm Street). **Open** 9am-9pm Mon-Thur; 9am-10pm Fri, Sat; 10am-8pm Sun. **Credit** AmEx, DC, Disc, MC, V.

The largest independent bookshop in Southern California was founded over a century ago and is still going strong. The stock is excellent and the staff very helpful. Keep an eye out for the regular readings and the book signings. There's also a gift and stationery store up the road at No.667.

Specialist

Aside from the speciality shops below, LA has bookstores devoted to film (**Larry Edmunds Bookshop**, 6644 Hollywood Boulevard, Hollywood, 1-323 463 3273, www.larryedmunds.com), comics (**Meltdown**, 7522 W Sunset Boulevard, Hollywood, 1-323 851 7223, www.meltcomics.com) and African American literature (**Eso Won**, 4327 Degnan Boulevard, Leimert Park, 1-323 290 1048, www.esowonbookstore.com), among other subjects. Many have frequent book signings, some by big-name authors; call or check the websites for details. Sadly, much-loved spirituality bookstore **Bodhi Tree** closed its doors on Melrose Avenue at the end of 2011, but it's worth checking its website – www.bodhitree.com – as there are rumours it may come back to life.

Children's Book World

10580½ W Pico Boulevard, between Prosser & Manning Avenues, West LA (1-310 559 2665, www.childrensbookworld.com). Bus C3, SM7, SM8, SM12, SM13/I-10, exit Overland Boulevard north. **Open** 10am-5.30pm Mon-Fri; 10am-5pm Sat. **Credit** DC, MC, V. **Map** p311 B5.

This huge children's bookshop offers 80,000 titles and super-knowledgeable staff. Storytelling sessions are held most Saturdays at 10.30am.

Samuel French

7623 W Sunset Boulevard, between N Stanley & N Curson Avenues, West Hollywood (1-866 598 8449, www.samuelfrench.com). Bus 2, 302/ I-10, exit Fairfax Avenue north. **Open** 10am-6pm Mon-Fri; 10am-5pm Sat; noon-5pm Sun. **Credit** AmEx, DC, Disc, MC, V. **Map** p312 C1.

From silver screen to printed page: Samuel French sells just about every film script in print, plus myriad theatre scripts and books about drama and film.

★ Traveler's Bookcase

8375 W 3rd Street, at S King's Road, Fairfax District (1-323 655 0575, www.travelbooks.com). Bus 16, 105, 218, 316/I-10, exit La Cienega Boulevard north. **Open** 11am-7pm Mon; 10am-7pm Tue-Sat; noon-6pm Sun. **Credit** AmEx, DC, MC, V. **Map** p312 B3.

The best travel bookshop in Southern California offers a broad range of guidebooks and maps, along with an impeccably chosen selection of travel literature. The staff are friendly and helpful.

Used & antiquarian

Other fine used bookshops include the funky **Counterpoint Records & Books** in Hollywood (5911 Franklin Avenue, 1-323 957 7965, www.counterpointrecordsandbooks.com) and the musty **Cliff's Books** in Pasadena (630 E Colorado Boulevard, 1-626 449 9541).

Brand Bookshop

231 N Brand Boulevard, between W California & W Wilson Avenues, Glendale (1-818 507 4390, www.abebooks.com). Bus 92, 180, 181, 183, 201/I-5, exit Colorado Street east. **Open** 11am-8pm Mon-Thur; 10am-10pm Fri, Sat; 11am-6pm Sun. **Credit** AmEx, DC, Disc, MC, V.

Arguably the best reason to visit Glendale, Brand offers upwards of 100,000 used books on more or less every subject imaginable. You're bound to find something you like, and can also bring in your own tomes to trade.

CHILDREN
Fashion

There are branches of **Gap Kids** everywhere, including one on the Third Street Promenade in Santa Monica (No.1355, 1-310 393 0719, www.gap.com). Upmarket chains with a presence in LA include **Janie & Jack** and **Pottery Barn Kids**, both at the Grove; *see p140*.

Entertaining Elephants

12053½ Ventura Place, at Ventura Boulevard, Studio City (1-818 766 9177, www.entertaining elephants.com). Bus 150, 240, 750/US 101, exit Laurel Canyon Boulevard south. **Open** 10am-6pm Mon-Sat; 8am-2pm Sun. **Credit** AmEx, DC, MC, V.

Entertaining Elephants offers sophisticated, modern clothes and accessories, plus furniture and toys, from around the globe. There's an emphasis on natural, fair-trade materials, and the own-brand organic line is made locally.

CONSUME

Traveler's Bookcase.

Kitson Kids

*116 N Robertson Boulevard, at Alden Drive,
Beverly Hills (1-310 657 0450, www.shop
kitson.com). Bus 14, 16/I-10, exit Robertson
Boulevard north.* **Open** 9.30am-7pm Mon-Fri;
8.30am-7pm Sat; 11am-6pm Sun. **Credit** AmEx,
DC, MC, V. **Map** p312 A3.

Hipsters with families love the goods on offer here,
from the likes of Trunk, Diesel, True Religion and
Great China Wall. This stretch of Robertson is home
to the whole Kitson empire: womenswear is at
No.115; menswear is at No.146; and Kitson Studio,
stocking accessories, is at No.142.
Other locations throughout LA.

Toys

★ Dinosaur Farm

*1510 Mission Street, between Fair Oaks &
Fremont Avenues, South Pasadena (1-626 441
2767, www.dinosaurfarm.com). Metro South
Pasadena/bus 176/Hwy 110, exit Fair Oaks
Avenue south.* **Open** 10am-6pm Mon-Sat; 11am-
5pm Sun. **Credit** AmEx, DC, MC, V.

Adored by families throughout the LA area, this
award-winning toy shop is a must-visit if you have
kids in tow. Not surprisingly, the stock is heavy on
dinos (toys, books and costumes), but there are also
mainstream names such as Thomas the Tank
Engine, plus a room full of girly gear.

Puzzle Zoo

*1411 Third Street Promenade, at Santa Monica
Boulevard, Santa Monica (1-310 393 9201,
www.puzzlezoo.com). Bus 4, 20, 704, 720/I-10,*
exit 4th/5th Street north. **Open** 10am-10pm
Mon-Thur, Sun; 10am-11pm Fri, Sat. **Credit**
AmEx, DC, Disc, MC, V. **Map** p310 A3.

Jigsaws remain a speciality at this friendly favourite,
but there are also tons of board games, action figures, dolls and whizz-bang modern goodies.

ELECTRONICS & PHOTOGRAPHY

General

There are several branches of **Best Buy**, the
biggest general electronics chain in the country,
in LA; the most central is at 1015 N La Brea
Avenue in West Hollywood (1-323 883 0219,
www.bestbuy.com). Gadget geeks should seek
out **Fry's**, which has branches in Anaheim,
Manhattan Beach, Woodland Hills and Burbank
(2311 N Hollywood Way, 1-818 526 8100,
www.frys.com).

Specialist

Mac stalwarts should head for the **Apple
Store** at the Grove (*see p140*; 1-323 965 8400,
www.apple.com). For photographic supplies,
try **Samy's Camera** chain (branches include
one at 431 S Fairfax Avenue, Fairfax District,
1-323 938 2420, www.samys.com). And
if you're looking to rent a cellphone, try
TripTel (www.triptel.com), which has a
branch at LAX (1-310 645 3500) but also
delivers to addresses within a 15-mile
radius of the airport.

FASHION

Designer

You'll find every designer label under the sun in Los Angeles: the array of shops rivals those in better-known fashion cities such as New York, London and Paris. Alongside the well-known names, LA also boasts a growing stable of home-grown designers, who mix Hollywood glitz, hippie chic and beachy sportswear.

The swankiest shopping area is the so-called Golden Triangle in **Beverly Hills**, with **Rodeo Drive** housing many of fashion's big names. In **Two Rodeo**, a complex at the corner of Rodeo Drive and Wilshire Boulevard, you'll find **Versace** (No.248, 1-310 205 3921, www.versace.com); on Rodeo itself, designers include **Christian Dior** (No.309, 1-310 859 4700, www.dior.com), **Dolce & Gabbana** (women's at No.312 & men's at No.314, 1-310 888 8701, www.dolcegabbana.com/), **Hermès** (No.428, 1-310 278 6440, www.hermes.com), **Ralph Lauren** (No.444, 1-310 281 7200, www.polo.com), **Miu Miu** (No.317, 1-310 247 2227, www.miumiu.com) and **Prada** (No.343, 1-310 278 8661, www.prada.com). **Chanel**, a former Rodeo resident, is now located at 125 N Robertson Boulevard, 1-310 278 5500, Beverly Hills (www.chanel.com).

The British invasion of Los Angeles continues. Among the imports are **Ted Baker** (131 N Robertson Boulevard, Beverly Hills, 1-310 550 7855, www.tedbaker.com), **Burberry**'s flagship store (9560 Wilshire Boulevard, Beverly Hills, 1-310 550 4500, www.burberry.com), **Paul Smith** (8221 Melrose Avenue, West Hollywood, 1-323 951 4800, www.paulsmith.co.uk), **Stella McCartney** (8823 Beverly Boulevard, West Hollywood, 1-310 273 7051, www.stella mccartney.com) and **Alexander McQueen** (8379 Melrose Avenue, West Hollywood, 1-323 782 4983, www.alexandermcqueen.com). **Vivienne Westwood** (8320 Melrose Avenue, West Hollywood, 1-323 951 0021, www.vivienne westwood.co.uk) and **Joseph** (156 S Robertson Boulevard, Beverly Hills, 1-318 385 7187) round out the pack.

For charts comparing British, French and US clothes and shoe sizes, *see p297*.

Diane von Furstenberg

8407 Melrose Avenue, at N Orlando Avenue, West Hollywood (1-323 951 1947, www.dvf.com). Bus 10, 105/I-10, exit La Cienega Boulevard north. **Open** 11am-7pm Mon-Sat; noon-6pm Sun. **Credit** AmEx, DC, Disc, MC, V. **Map** p312 C2.
Diane von Furstenberg invented the wrap dress, but her LA boutique shows there's much more to her designs. From evening gowns to sports gear, everything is chic yet practical.

★ James Perse

8914 Melrose Avenue, between N Almont & N La Peer Drives, West Hollywood (1-310 276 7277, www.jamesperse.com). Bus 4, 105, 550, 704/I-10, exit La Cienega Boulevard north. **Open** 10am-6pm Mon-Sat; noon-5pm Sun. **Credit** AmEx, DC, Disc, MC, V. **Map** p312 A2.
Perse offers casually classic clothes for men, women and children, made from refined fabrics and featuring appropriately seasonal colours.
Other locations throughout LA.

Marc Jacobs

8400 Melrose Place, between N Orlando & N Croft Avenues, West Hollywood (1-323 653 5100, www.marcjacobs.com). Bus 10, 105/I-10, exit La Cienega Boulevard north. **Open** 11am-7pm Mon-Sat; noon-6pm Sun. **Credit** AmEx, DC, Disc, MC, V. **Map** p312 B2.
More than any other collection, Jacobs' designs epitomise the style of young Hollywood. This store is dedicated to the womenswear collection (menswear is at No.8409): from clothing to accessories, everything is gorgeous, but be prepared to spend high – or aim for the more affordable Marc by Marc Jacobs around the corner (8410 Melrose Avenue, both men- and womenswear). Rounding out the empire is Bookmarc, selling coffee-table books on fashion and culture, at 8407 Melrose Place.

Trina Turk

8008 W 3rd Street, between S Crescent Heights Boulevard & S Edinburgh Avenue, Fairfax District (1-323 651 1382, www.trinaturk.com). Bus 16, 217, 218, 316/I-10, exit Fairfax Avenue north. **Open** 11am-6pm Mon-Sat; noon-6pm Sun. **Credit** AmEx, DC, MC, V. **Map** p312 C3.
Turk's striking collections come with a retro Palm Springs feel. Funky shades and bags complete the look, and the friendly staff are happy to help.

★ Vanessa Bruno

8448 Melrose Avenue, between N Croft Avenue & N Alfred Street, West Hollywood (1-323 655 5300, www.vanessabruno.com). Bus 10, 105/I-10, exit La Cienega Boulevard north. **Open** 11am-7pm Mon-Sat; noon-6pm Sun. **Credit** AmEx, DC, Disc, MC, V. **Map** p312 B2.
Paris-born Bruno has a loyal following of LA-based celebrity fans, and it's easy to see why. This US flagship store carries her full range, from her main collection and Athé diffusion line to beautiful footwear and accessories such as her signature Grand Cabas tote bag.

Discount

The nearest outlet malls are **Citadel Outlets** south-east of Downtown (100 Citadel Drive, Commerce, 1-323 888 1724, www.citadel outlets.com), where you'll find the likes of Calvin

Klein, Kenneth Cole and Reebok, and **Premium Outlets**, 45 minutes north of LA (740 E Ventura Boulevard, Camarillo, 1-805 445 8520, www. premiumoutlets.com), where Barneys, DKNY and Nike are among the 160 stores. For **Desert Hills Premium Outlets** near Palm Springs, *see p254*.

In Downtown's **Fashion District** (*see p72*), vendors hawk clothing, accessories and fabrics for low prices from 10am to 5pm daily. Still, it's not exactly guilt-free shopping: LA has become an international manufacturing centre for fake designer accessories.

General

All the major mid-market chains have stores in LA, and some have several. In particular, branches of **Old Navy** (Beverly Connection; *see p138*), **Gap** (1355 Third Street Promenade, Santa Monica, 1-310 393 0719, www.gap.com) and **Banana Republic** (357 N Beverly Drive, Beverly Hills, 1-310 858 7900, www.banana republic.com) abound throughout the city. Based in LA, **American Apparel** also has stores around town, including one in Venice Beach (701 Ocean Front Walk, 1-310 396 3332, www.americanapparel.net).

Abercrombie & Fitch's West Coast flagship is at the Grove (*see p140*; 1-323 954 1500, www.abercrombie.com). Also at the Grove are branches of **Forever 21** (1-323 934 0018, www.forever21.com), which is great for cheap, Topshop-style clothes and bags, as well as **Topshop** itself (along with **Topman**, together in a 30,000-square-foot flagship; 1-323 938 1085). For preppy-but-wearable gear, try **J Crew** (1-323 939 1070, www.jcrew.com); and, for well-priced basics, **Zara** (No.6333, 1-323 935 5041, www.zara.com). One of **Diesel**'s LA stores is at the Third Street Promenade in Santa Monica (No.1340, 1-310 899 3055, www.diesel.com), where you'll also find funky **Urban Outfitters** (No.1440, 1-310 394 1404, www.urbanoutfitters.com) and the reliable clothes of **American Eagle** (301 Arizona Avenue, 1-310 255 0223, www.ae.com).

British chains that have found a home in and around LA include upmarket **Reiss** (145 N Robertson Boulevard, Beverly Hills, 1-310 276 0060, www.reissonline.com) and mid-market **Jigsaw** (Paseo Colorado, 340 E Colorado Boulevard, Pasadena, 1-626 577 7300, www.jigsaw-london.com). Swedish brand **H&M** is at the Beverly Center (*see p138*) and 8580 Sunset Boulevard, West Hollywood (1-310 855 9683, www.hm.com), among other locations.

American Rag
150 S La Brea Avenue, between W 1st & W 2nd Streets, Fairfax District (1-323 935 3154, www.amrag.com). Bus 14, 16, 212/I-10, exit La Brea Avenue north. **Open** 10am-9pm Mon-Sat; noon-7pm Sun. **Credit** AmEx, DC, MC, V. **Map** p312 D3.
One of the city's largest collections of designer wear in a relaxed, warehouse setting. New clothing covers a huge array of brands for both men and women, along with accessories, shoes and the 'World Denim Bar', but the vintage section is equally browsable.
Other locations Fashion Island (*see p140*; 1-949 760 1510).

Anthropologie
211 S Beverly Drive, at Charleville Boulevard, Beverly Hills (1-310 385 7390, www. anthropologie.com). Bus 14, 20, 37/I-405, exit Wilshire Boulevard east. **Open** 10am-8pm Mon-Sat; 11am-6pm Sun. **Credit** AmEx, DC, Disc, MC, V. **Map** p311 D3.
Girly gear designed to get you noticed, including pretty dresses, designer jeans, brightly printed hand-bags, A-line skirts and must-have shoes.
Other locations throughout LA.

Blues Jean Bar
1409 Montana Avenue, at 14th Street, Santa Monica (1-310 393 4100, www.bluesjeanbar.com). Bus SM3/I-10, exit Lincoln Boulevard north. **Open** 10am-6pm Mon-Sat; 11am-5pm Sun. **Credit** AmEx, DC, MC, V. **Map** p310 B2.
Struggling to decide on jeans that fit properly? Fret no more. The Blues Jean Bar offers 'denim on tap', whereby customers browse the jeans at the wooden bar and then enlist the services of the 'bartender' to help choose. The 30-strong collection of brands rotates regularly but usually includes Joe's, Paige, James and 7 For All Mankind.

Fred Segal
8118 Melrose Avenue, between N Crescent Heights Boulevard & N Kilkea Drive, West Hollywood (1-323 651 1935, www.fredsegal.com). Bus 10/I-10, exit Fairfax Avenue north. **Open** 10am-7pm Mon-Sat; noon-6pm Sun. **Credit** AmEx, DC, MC, V. **Map** p328 C2.

**THE BEST
FASHIONISTA DESTINATIONS**

For big brands at big prices
Golden Triangle and Rodeo Drive.
See p139.

For vintage gems
Decades. *See p147.*

For the journey alone
South Coast Plaza. *See p141.*

CONSUME

Insider's Guide to Melrose Avenue

A stroll along this popular shopping street.

In a city with so much sprawl, shopping in Los Angeles can be tricky. But Melrose Avenue is one of those rare destinations with some of the best shops for every need. Here's the best way to browse this eclectic strip.

Decades (No.8214; *see p147*) is a mainstay for vintage fans, but they also flock to **Resurrection** (No.8006, 1-323 651 5516, www.resurrectionvintage.com), which is practically a religious experience for those with a penchant for pieces that are a little bit gypsy, a little bit avant-garde. The shop's sweet spot is its collection of pieces from the swinging 1960s and '70s: mini shift dresses from Pierre Cardin and Courrèges, hanging alongside floaty boho frocks by Ossie Clark and Thea Porter. Be sure to check out owner Katy Rodriguez's own fashion and jewellery lines, too.

Fred Segal (No.8118; *see p145*) is perhaps the most recognisable name in LA retail, thanks to a series of high-profile shout-outs in *Clueless* and *Legally Blonde*. If it's a souvenir tote you're after, we recommend the Melrose outpost, but if you're just visiting to kill time before lunch, all signs point to the SaMo location (500 Broadway, 1-310 451 7178), where LA burger chain Umami has a space.

Kelly Wearstler (No.8440, 1-323 895 7880, www.kellywearstler.com) got her start as one of LA's most buzzed-about interior designers, then forayed into fashion with a womenswear line. Now she has added retailer to her résumé, opening a Melrose flagship store that brings all of her creative pursuits together in one place. Get the designer's swoon-worthy look with painterly print blouses, pants and biker jackets; sculptural brass jewellery; and objects for the home, from vintage club chairs to tableware to quirky *objets d'art*.

No self-respecting Angeleno (or visitor) can possibly do without a pair of statement sunglasses, and the **Guise Archives** (No.7928, 1-323 782 1093, www.guise shop.com) is a great place to stock up, carrying an array of hard-to-find frames both vintage (Carrera, Ray-Ban) and modern (Benjamin Eyewear, Wildfox). They also have regular eyeglasses by brands like Salt Optics and Tavat.

Jade Lai's **Creatures of Comfort** (No.7971, 1-323 655 7855, www.creatures ofcomfort.us) is a rare refuge of peace on Melrose. Inside, you'll find unobtrusively cool brands from both near (Clare Vivier handbags, All For the Mountain jewellery) and far (Isabel Marant and Rachel Comey). Our favourite pieces, however, have to be from CoC's in-house clothing line, filled with the kind of perfect basics you'll wear over and over – slouchy tees, cropped trousers and pretty patterned blouses, to name just a few.

Around the back of Melrose Place, pastel-painted boutique **TenOverSix** (No.8425, 1-323 330 9355, www.tenover6.com) is often referred to as one of the city's best spots for gift shopping, but we prefer to stop by when we're looking for something for ourselves. Accessories are the name of the game, with a roster of so-hot-right-now names – Clare Vivier bags, Pamela Love jewellery – and lesser-known designers, many of them local. We usually head straight for the women's shoe section, with its neatly edited collection of Dieppa Restrepo's cheerfully coloured loafers.

Decades.

CONSUME

A number of shops under one roof, Fred Segal sells hip casual clothes and expensive designer gear, plus gifts, furniture and beauty goods. It's a great platform for local designers. There's a spa and salon at the Santa Monica branch (No.420).
Other locations 420 & 500 Broadway, Santa Monica (1-310 394 1271).

Jill Roberts

363 N Beverly Drive, at Brighton Way, Beverly Hills (1-310 860 1617, www.jillroberts.com). Bus 4, 16, 20, 720/I-10, exit Robertson Boulevard north. **Open** 10am-6pm Mon-Sat; noon-5pm Sun. **Credit** AmEx, DC, MC, V. **Map** p311 D3.
A who's who of top designers is offered at this Beverly Hills boutique, from Claudie Pierlot to Gryphon, plus Seaton (Roberts' own line of casual luxury). Clutches, footwear by Golden Goose and beachwear by Melissa Odabash are further reasons to visit.
Other locations 920 Montana Avenue, Santa Monica (1-310 260 1966).

Lululemon Athletica

334 N Beverly Drive, between Dayton & Brighton Ways, Beverly Hills (1-310 858 8339, www.lululemon.com). Bus 4, 16, 20, 720/I-10, exit Robertson Boulevard north. **Open** 10am-7pm Mon-Sat; 11am-6pm Sun. **Credit** AmEx, Disc, MC, V. **Map** p311 D3.
That logo you've seen on all those hot bodies around town? It's Lululemon's. What began as a retail space next to a yoga studio in Vancouver in 1998 has since burgeoned into a worldwide brand of chic workout gear, from tank tops to jackets to trousers to accessories such as bags and yoga mats.
Other locations throughout LA.

Madison

8115 Melrose Avenue, between N Crescent Heights Boulevard & N Kilkea Drive, West Hollywood (1-323 651 3662, www.madisonlos angeles.com). Bus 10/I-10, exit Fairfax Avenue north. **Open** 11am-7pm Mon-Sat; noon-5pm Sun. **Credit** AmEx, DC, MC, V. **Map** p312 C2.
Beloved by the city's style mavens, this store is a treasure trove of designer wear, shoes and bags, featuring obscure names alongside the well-known likes of Chloé, Marc Jacobs and Paul & Joe. Start browsing here and you may never leave.
Other locations throughout LA.

★ Polkadots & Moonbeams

8367 & 8381 W 3rd Street, between S Kings Road & S Orlando Avenue, Fairfax District (modern 1-323 655 3880, vintage 1-323 651 1746, www.polkadotsandmoonbeams.com). Bus 16, 105, 218, 316/I-10, exit La Cienega Boulevard north. **Open** 11am-7pm Mon-Sat; 11am-6pm Sun. **Credit** AmEx, DC, MC, V. **Map** p312 B3.

Two stores close to each other: No.8381 sells new designer pieces (Ella Moss, Corey Lynn Calter) and jewellery by Sheila Fajl, while No.8367 has a mix of vintage clothing and new but vintage-inspired items (Trashy Diva dresses, for example).

Rag & Bone

8533 Melrose Avenue, at W Knoll Drive, West Hollywood (1-424 245 4816, www.rag-bone.com). Bus 4, 105, 550, 704/I-10, exit La Cienega Boulevard north. **Open** 11am-8pm Mon-Sat; noon-7pm Sun. **Credit** AmEx, DC, MC, V. **Map** p312 B2.
With no formal fashion training, it's with sheer talent that the British design team behind Rag & Bone, David Neville and Marcus Wainwright, have created a wildly successful and coveted fashion brand based around well-tailored, edgy basics. The LA flagship is a one-stop shop for the brand's extensive collection of menswear, womenswear, bags, shoes, accessories and their popular Rag & Bone Jean line of denim and basic T-shirts.

Used & vintage

At **Buffalo Exchange** (131 N La Brea Avenue, Fairfax District, 1-323 938 8604, www.buffaloexchange.com) and **Crossroads Trading Co** (7409 Melrose Avenue, Fairfax District, 1-323 782 8100, www.crossroads trading.com), gently used clothes are sold at low prices. Each chain has several LA locations.
See also p145 **American Rag** *and left* **Polkadots & Moonbeams**.

★ Decades/Decadestwo

8214 Melrose Avenue, at N Harper Avenue, West Hollywood (1-323 655 1960, www.decadesinc. com). Bus 10/I-10, exit La Cienega Boulevard north. **Open** 11am-6pm Mon-Sat; noon-5pm Sun. **Credit** AmEx, DC, MC, V. **Map** p312 B2.
Head up the stairs to America's most glamorous vintage shop, which boasts couture classics from the 1960s and '70s, chic outfits by the likes of Hermès, Thierry Mugler and Ossie Clark hand-picked by owner Cameron Silver. Also here is Decadestwo, the contemporary consignment store.

It's a Wrap!

3315 W Magnolia Boulevard, between N Lima & N California Streets, Burbank (1-818 567 7366, www.itsawraphollywood.com). Bus 163, 183/I-5, exit Olive Avenue west. **Open** 11am-8pm Mon-Fri; 11am-6pm Sat, Sun. **Credit** DC, Disc, MC, V.
Dress like a star, literally: this massive shop sells clothes worn by actors and actresses in films and TV shows, from sleek designer clothes to absurd *Star Trek* costumes. Prices are decent.
Other locations 1164 S Robertson Boulevard, Beverly Hills (1-310 246 9727).

CONSUME

Squaresville

1800 N Vermont Avenue, at Melbourne Avenue, Los Feliz (1-323 669 8464). Metro Vermont-Sunset/bus 4, 156, 204, 754/US 101, exit Vermont Avenue north. **Open** *noon-7pm Mon; 11am-8pm Tue, Wed; 11am-9pm Thur; 11am-10pm Fri, Sat; noon-9pm Sun.* **Credit** AmEx, DC, Disc, MC, V. **Map** p314 A2.

A funky selection of old threads is offered at this local favourite: some smart, but most casual and agreeably hipster-friendly. Prices are keen.

FASHION ACCESSORIES & SERVICES

Clothing hire

Men's Wearhouse

Beverly Connection, 100 N La Cienega Boulevard, between W 3rd Street & Beverly Boulevard, West Hollywood (1-310 358 0748, www.menswear house.com). Bus 14, 16, 105, 316, LDF/I-10, exit La Cienega Boulevard north. **Open** *10am-9pm Mon-Fri; 9.30am-9pm Sat; 11am-6pm Sun.* **Credit** AmEx, DC, Disc, MC, V. **Map** p312 B3.

Nominated for an Oscar and forgotten your jacket? Tuxedos are available here for purchase or rental. **Other locations** throughout LA.

One Night Affair

1726 S Sepulveda Boulevard, at Santa Monica Boulevard, West LA (1-310 474 7808, www.one nightaffair.com). Bus 4, 704, C6, SM1/I-405, exit Santa Monica Boulevard east. **Open** *by appt only (11am-7pm Tue-Fri; 9am-6pm Sat).* **Credit** AmEx, DC, Disc, MC, V.

The place to rent everything from cocktail dresses to wedding gowns, some by Versace, Vera Wang and Badgley Mischka.

Cleaning & repairs

Many strip malls in LA have a dry-cleaner: you're never far from one.

Brown's Cleaners

1223 Montana Avenue, between 12th & Euclid Streets, Santa Monica (1-310 451 8531). Bus SM3/I-10, exit Lincoln Boulevard north. **Open** *7am-6pm Mon-Fri; 7am-noon Sat.* **Credit** DC, MC, V. **Map** p310 B2.

It's not exactly cheap, but Brown's is a classic of its kind, and the service is excellent. As well as dry-cleaning, there's a tailor available to carry out repairs.

Handbags

★ Clare Vivier

3339 West Sunset Boulevard, at Micheltorena Street, Silver Lake (1-213 483 2247, www. clarevivier.com). Bus 2, 4, 175, 302/US 101,

exit Silver Lake Boulevard north. **Open** *11am-6pm Mon-Sat.* **Credit** AmEx, Disc, MC, V. **Map** p314 C4.

If you don't live in Silver Lake, there are few places that warrant making the drive there. This is one of them. The flagship namesake store of the French-born, Los Angeles-dwelling designer features her wide array of leather totes, duffels, clutches and pouches in a rainbow of hues. Other finds like scented candles, jewellery and seasonal accessories from other brands.

Hats

Goorin Brothers

7627 Melrose Avenue, between N Stanley & N Curson Avenues, Fairfax District (1-323 951 0393, www.goorin.com). Bus 10, 217, 218, LDF/I-10, exit Fairfax Avenue north. **Open** *11am-7pm Mon-Thur; 11am-8pm Fri, Sat; 11am-6pm Sun.* **Credit** AmEx, DC, MC, V. **Map** p312 C2.

The hats at this longstanding San Francisco firm run from the subtly stylish to the overwhelmingly garish. But with everything from baseball caps to fedoras, there should be something to suit almost every taste.

Jewellery

There's a huge branch of **Tiffany** at 210 N Rodeo Drive (1-310 273 8880, www.tiffany.com), and one at the **Beverly Center** (*see p138*).

★ Alexis Bittar

8383 W 3rd Street, at S Orlando Avenue, West Hollywood (1-323 951 9803, www.alexis bittar.com). Bus 16, 105, 218, 316/I-10, exit La Cienega Boulevard north. **Open** *10am-6pm Mon-Sat; noon-5pm Sun.* **Credit** AmEx, DC, Disc, MC, V. **Map** p312 B3.

This sweet boutique stocks Brooklyn-born, New York-based jeweller Bittar's signature sculpted metal pieces, including bracelets, rings, earrings and necklaces. It's virtually impossible to leave without buying something.

Other locations 1612 Abbot Kinney Boulevard, Venice (1-310 452 6901).

Arp

8311½ W 3rd Street, between S Sweetzer & S Flores Avenues, Fairfax District (1-323 653 7764, http://arplosangeles.com). Bus 16, 105, 218, 316/I-10, exit La Cienega Boulevard north. **Open** *noon-6pm Mon-Sat; by appointment Sun.* **Credit** AmEx, DC, MC, V. **Map** p312 B3.

Arp stocks beautiful pieces of fine jewellery made by Ted Muehling and his protégés; names to look out for here include Gabriella Kiss, Nicole Landaw and Lola Brooks.

CONSUME

Lingerie & underwear

Nationwide chain **Victoria's Secret** has shops throughout the LA conurbation, including the Third Street Promenade (*see p35*; 1-310 395 3182, www.victoriassecret.com).

Agent Provocateur
7961 Melrose Avenue, between N Hayworth & N Edinburgh Avenues, West Hollywood (1-323 653 0229, www.agentprovocateur.com). Bus 10, LDF/ I-10, exit Fairfax Avenue north. **Open** 11am-7pm Mon-Sat; noon-6pm Sun. **Credit** AmEx, DC, MC, V. **Map** p312 C2.

Thanks to its saucy window displays and huge star following, Brit chain Agent Provocateur has become the most talked-about lingerie retailer in the world. Signature items include half- and quarter-cup bras, sexy corsets, suspenders and slips.
Other locations 242 N Rodeo Drive, Beverly Hills (1-310 888 0050).

Faire Frou Frou
13017 Ventura Boulevard, at Coldwater Canyon, Studio City (1-818 783 4970, www.fairefrou frou.com). Bus 150, 240/US 101, exit Coldwater Canyon Avenue. **Open** 10am-6pm Mon-Sat; noon-4.30pm Sun. **Credit** AmEx, DC, MC, V.

The Valley may seem like an unlikely place for one of the city's best collections of avant-garde lingerie, but the brand list at Faire Frou Frou is like a roll call of today's most directional lingerie designers. While a lot of what's here isn't suited for everyday wear, there's plenty for those who like sporting something special under their work clothes.

Shoes

London Sole
1331 Montana Avenue, at 14th Street, Santa Monica (1-310 255 0937, www.londonsole.com). Bus SM3/I-10, exit Lincoln Boulevard north. **Open** 10am-6.30pm Mon-Sat; 11am-6pm Sun. **Credit** AmEx, DC, MC, V. **Map** p310 B2.

Classic ballet flats in all colours and designs. There are solid shades, glittery and leopard print pairs, and they're all comfy. *Photo p150.*

Re-Mix Shoe Company
7605½ Beverly Boulevard, at N Curson Avenue, Fairfax District (1-323 936 6210, www.remix vintageshoes.com). Bus 14, 217, 218/I-10, exit Fairfax Avenue north. **Open** noon-7pm Mon-Sat; noon-6pm Sun. **Credit** AmEx, DC, Disc, MC, V. **Map** p312 C3.

Despite its URL, not everything at Re-Mix is old: besides the rows of vintage shoes is its own brand of retro creations, from wingtips to slingbacks.

Undefeated
2654 Main Street, between Ocean Park Boulevard & Hill Street, Santa Monica (1-310 399 4195, www.undftd.com). Bus 33, 733, SM1, SM2, SM8, SM10/I-10, exit 4th/5th Street south. **Open** 11am-7pm Mon-Sat; 11am-5pm Sun. **Credit** AmEx, MC, V. **Map** p310 A4.

CONSUME

Squaresville.

London Sole. *See p149.*

CONSUME

An über-cool hangout for sneaker geeks, Undefeated stocks limited editions from the likes of Vans and Nike, along with its own clothing. Fans should also try Waraku down in Venice (1225 Abbot Kinney Boulevard, 1-310 452 5300, www.warakuusa.com). **Other locations** 112 S La Brea Avenue, Fairfax District (1-323 937 6077); 3827 W Sunset Boulevard, Silver Lake (1-323 668 1315).

FOOD & DRINK
Bakeries

See also pp131-136 **Coffeehouses**.

★ La Brea Bakery
460 S La Brea Avenue, between W 4th & 6th Streets, Miracle Mile (1-323 939 6813, www.labreabakery.com). Bus 20, 212/I-10, exit La Brea Avenue north. **Open** 7.30am-6pm Mon-Fri; 8am-6pm Sat; 8am-4pm Sun. **Credit** AmEx, DC, MC, V. **Map** p312 D4.
Nancy Silverton is credited with single-handedly introducing Angelenos to the joys of the fresh, flavoursome loaf. In the 25 years since her store opened, she's become a household name and her store has grown into an international operation, supplying restaurants such as Campanile (sadly now defunct) and Mozza. At the original store, dough reigns supreme – along with tarts, pastries and sandwiches.

La Maison du Pain
5373 W Pico Boulevard, between S Ridgeley Drive & S Burnside Avenue, Midtown (1-323 934 5858, www.lamaisondupainla.com). Bus SM5, SM7, SM13/I-10, exit Fairfax Avenue north. **Open** 8am-6pm Tue-Sat. **Credit** AmEx, DC, Disc, MC, V. **Map** p313 A6.
It's hard to believe that two Filipina sisters with no baking experience opened this lovely café nearly ten years ago. They set their sights high, remortgaging their properties in order to fly in kitchen equipment and a young chef from France. The result? The best croissants and cinnamon rolls in the city, to this day.

Chocolates

★ Compartés Chocolatier
912 S Barrington Avenue, between San Vicente Boulevard & Darlington Avenue, Brentwood (1-310 826 3380, www.compartes.com). SM3, SM4, SM14/I-405, exit Wilshire Boulevard. **Open** 10am-6pm Mon-Sat. **Credit** AmEx, MC, V.
A Brentwood fixture for more than six decades, Compartés has been newly remodelled to include a spiffier showroom and a patio out front where chocoholics can savour their purchases in peace. These are more like works of art than mere chocolates, with over 200 alternating organic and all-natural flavour combos and designs. Don't miss the special-occasion treats around holidays and Valentine's Day. Of note: Compartés is the only chocolatier ever to earn a perfect score from *Bon Appétit*.

Valerie Confections
3360 W 1st Street, between S Virgil & S Commonwealth Avenues, Silver Lake (1-213 739 8149, www.valerieconfections.com). Bus 14, 37, 201/Metro Vermont-Beverly/US-101, exit Silver

Lake Boulevard. **Open** 11am-6pm Mon-Sat.
Credit AmEx, MC, V. **Map** p314 B5.
At this small store, Valerie Gordon offers beautifully packaged, gourmet confectionery (caramels, truffles, toffee) along with cakes, pastries and jams that are also for sale at the Santa Monica and Hollywood farmers markets. The petits fours, in flavours such as rose petal and early grey, are justly renowned.

Drinks

Du Vin

540 N San Vicente Boulevard, at Melrose Avenue, West Hollywood (1-310 855 1161, www.du-vin.net). Bus 4, 105, 550, 704/I-10, exit La Cienega Boulevard north. **Open** 10am-7pm Mon-Sat.
Credit AmEx, DC, Disc, MC, V. **Map** p312 A2.
The cobblestone courtyard entrance to Du Vin is more Europe than LA; inside, it's more wine cellar than shop. Californian, Italian and, especially, French wines are supplemented by spirits, beers and accessories. Excellent customer service, too.

★ Galco's Soda Pop Stop

5702 York Boulevard, at N Avenue 57, Highland Park (1-323 255 7115, www.sodapopstop.com). Metro Highland Park/bus 83/I-110, exit Avenue 52 north. **Open** 9am-6.30pm Mon-Sat; 9am-4pm Sun. **Credit** DC, MC, V.
This extraordinary store stocks every kind of soda under the sun. And we mean *every* kind: colas and cherry limeades, sarsaparillas and root beers, more than 450 varieties in total. And that's not all: you'll also find a similarly wild variety of candies, plus one of the best beer selections in LA and even a deli counter serving knockout sandwiches. Awesome. *Photo p155*.

Silverlake Wine

2395 Glendale Boulevard, at Brier Avenue, Silver Lake (1-323 662 9024, www.silverlakewine.com). Bus 92/US 101, exit Glendale Boulevard north. **Open** 10am-9pm Mon, Sun; 10am-10pm Thur-Sat. **Credit** AmEx, DC, Disc, MC, V. **Map** p314 D2.
The owners of this store take pleasure in making their favourite artisanal wines known to customers. Tastings are held three times a week, and boutique beers and sakés round out the careful selection.

General

Supermarket chains include **Ralphs** (www.ralphs.com), **Vons** (www.vons.com) and **Albertsons** (www.albertsons.com). **Trader Joe's** (www.traderjoes.com) is good for gourmet and organic foods, as are the various branches of **Whole Foods** (www.wholefoods market.com), dubbed 'Whole Paycheck' by many people for obvious

reasons. Just as **Fresh & Easy** (http://fresh andeasy.com), the US version of UK stalwart Tesco, is starting to improve, selling good-quality ready meals and British treats for homesick expats, there are indications it may pull out of the US market altogether. If it's still here by the time you read this, the branch at 7021 Hollywood Boulevard (1-323 466 0097) is a handy location if you're staying in Hollywood.

Markets

From Leimert Park to Little Tokyo, Los Angeles is dotted with farmers' markets, at which local producers sell fresh fare (some of it organic) directly to shoppers. But the goods on offer are not limited to just fruit and vegetables; alongside the farmers you'll find other retailers selling hot food, flowers, juices, coffee and knick-knacks.

There are farmers' markets in **West Hollywood** (9am-2pm Mon at Plummer Park, N Vista Street & Fountain Avenue, 1-951 544 8399, www.sfma.net), **Beverly Hills** (9am-1pm Sun at 9300 block of Civic Center Drive, www.beverlyhills.org), **Hollywood** (8am-1pm Sun at 1500 block of Ivar Avenue, between Hollywood & Sunset Boulevards) and **Downtown** (11am-3pm Thur at 735 South Figueroa Street, between W 7th and 8th Streets). **Santa Monica** has four: on Wednesday at the Third Street Promenade, Arizona Avenue & 3rd Street (8.30am-1.30pm); an organic version on Saturday at the same location (8.30am-1pm) and at Virginia Park (corner of Pico & Cloverfield Boulevards, 8am-1pm); and on Sunday at Main Street & Ocean Park Boulevard (9.30am-1pm). For others, see www.farmernet.com.

The numerous stalls at the **Grand Central Market** in Downtown LA (317 S Broadway, between W 3rd & W 4th Streets, 1-213 624 2378, www.grandcentralsquare.com) offer fruit, vegetables, meat, fish, herbs, spices and flowers. In this location since 1917, the market is still open daily, and a visit is a lively way to pass a couple of hours.

Specialist

★ Cheese Store of Silverlake

3926-28 W Sunset Boulevard, between Hyperion & Sanborn Avenues, Silver Lake (1-323 644 7511, www.cheesestoresl.com). Bus 2, 4, 302, 704/US 101, exit Silver Lake Boulevard north. **Open** 10am-6pm Mon-Sat; 11am-5am Sun.
Credit AmEx, DC, Disc, MC, V. **Map** p314 B3.
To go with the fromage from cows, sheep and goats, there's an impressive array of epicurean treats: chocolates, cured meats, olives and teas, for example. A delightful shop.

CONSUME

Home-made Heroes

Get to know some of the best LA food artisans.

CONSUME

HANDSOME COFFEE ROASTER
Who: Tyler Wells.
What: Coffee.
Where it's made: Downtown.
Taste it at: Handsome Coffee Roasters, Bäco Mercat (*see p110*), Ink (*see p104*).
Downtowners get their caffeine fix from Handsome's roasting plant/coffee bar (582 Mateo Street, 1-213 621 4194, www.handsomecoffee.com), where 1,000 bags of coffee beans are roasted and shipped to 80 wholesale accounts a week. It's also found on the menus of a select few of the city's best restaurants. 'I love what's happening with coffee', says Wells. 'It parallels what happened with food a few years ago – it's become something culinary'. Wells opened and managed Intelligentsia's Pasadena outpost in 2010. There, he met Michael Phillips and Chris Owens. The trio bonded over all things coffee and decided to work together. Offerings are limited to single-origin espresso – either served straight up or with whole Clover milk – no additions, no sugar. Whether or not coffee drinkers accept the no-sugar rule, they're intent on doing things their way and with a

Handsome Coffee Roaster.

of small-batch jams, she also fills requests like dill pickles for clients like Nancy Silverton's Short Order. In October 2012, Koslow opened Sqirl with G&B with Intelligentsia alums Kyle Glanville and Charles Babinski, a 'sort-of café' (720 N Virgil Avenue, 1-213 394 6526, http://sqirlla.com), which serves coffee and menu items that showcase Koslow's penchant for preserving. You can also find the goods at local stores like Proof Bakery (3156 Glendale Boulevard, Atwater Village, 1-323 664 8633, www.proofbakeryla.com).

SQIRL
Who: Jessica Koslow.
What: Artisanal preserves from jams to pickles and preserved lemons.
Where it's made: Silver Lake (technically Virgil Village).
Taste them at: Sqirl with G&B, Proof Bakery, and more.
'Jammer' Jessica Koslow hunts down 'the dodo birds of produce' – uncommon heirloom varieties, only briefly available during growing season. She captures them at their peak, preserves them into jars, then hand labels them. In addition to creating six different seasonal flavours

BRASSICA & BRINE
Who: Jordan 'Uri' Laio.
What: Fermented goods like sauerkraut, kimchi and kombucha.
Where it's made: Van Nuys
Taste it at: Farmshop (*see p98*).
Jordan was a year into law school when he asked himself, 'Why am I in law school when my passion is fermentation?' Enter: Brassica & Brine. Launched in November 2012 at Westwood and West LA's farmers markets, Uri's sauerkraut and spicy Korean cousin, kimchi, are made using a centuries-old technique of fermentation, namely wild lacto fermentation. Salt – as opposed to vinegar and canning – is the only ingredient used to preserve vegetables. The result? Delicious pickled cabbage that's savoury to tangy to downright funky. Good to know: Laio also moonlights as an urban beekeeper – he's working with Farmshop to create their own rooftop beehives.

MOTHER MOO
Who: Karen Klemens.
What: Handmade ice-cream.

Sqirl.

Where it's made: Sierra Madre.
Taste it at: Mother Moo Creamery.
Karen Klemens is one of LA's master preservers and a self-described urban homesteader. She founded Mother Cluck preserves and continues the preserving tradition with Mother Moo's ice cream. 'Icecream,' she says, 'is one of the most social foods.' At her Mother Moo ice cream parlour in Sierre Madre (17 Kersting Court, 1-626 355 9650, www.mothermoo.com), locals and families stop in for a root beer float, milkshake and ice-cream in signature flavours like chocolate (three types of chocolate, flecked with salt) and triple milk (a combination of buttermilk, cream and non-fat Strauss milk).

ANGELO & FRANCO
Who: Angelo Tartaglia and Franco Russo, cheese makers.
What: Fresh cheeses like mozzarella, burrata and ricotta made by real Italians.
Where it's made: Hawthorne.
Taste it at: Fox Pizza Bus.
Two Italian friends Angelo Tartaglia and Franco Russo met in Bagnoli, Italy, where Russo's family has been making mozzarella cheese for three generations. They brought the same cheese-making tradition (and machinery) to LA's South Bay with fresh cheeses made with California dairy. While the company distributes to Whole Foods, Russo oversees the five-hour production every morning, and hand makes its burrata. Fox Pizza Bus – yes, it's a double-decker bus (red, natch) – uses their mozzarella and ricotta exclusively on its wood-fired pizzas.

Brassica & Brine.

Erewhon Natural Foods Market
7660 Beverly Boulevard, at The Grove Drive, Fairfax District (1-323 937 0777, www. erewhonmarket.com). Bus 14/I-10, exit Fairfax Avenue north. **Open** 8am-11pm Mon-Sat; 9am-11pm Sun. **Credit** AmEx, DC, Disc, MC, V. **Map** p310 C3.
The best organic supermarket in town sells a range of produce, natural remedies, cosmetics and toiletries. The excellent food counters feature salads, soups, sushi, deli items, fresh juices and coffee.

Petrossian
321 N Robertson Boulevard, at Beverly Boulevard, West Hollywood (1-310 271 6300, www.petrossian.com). Bus 14, 16/I-10, exit Robertson Boulevard north. **Open** 11am-10pm Mon-Fri; 10am-10pm Sat; 10am-4pm Sun. **Credit** AmEx, DC, Disc, MC, V. **Map** p310 A3.
A French-owned and -run resource for delights beloved by Francophiles: caviar, truffles, smoked salmon and so on. A recent expansion has resulted in a larger restaurant space, a bigger patio out front and a longer menu. Thankfully, the laid-back atmosphere remains.

Surfas
8777 W Washington Boulevard, at National Boulevard, Culver City (1-310 559 4770, www.surfasonline.com). Bus 33, 733, C1/I-10, exit Robertson Boulevard south. **Open** 9am-6pm Mon-Sat; 11am-5pm Sun. **Credit** AmEx, DC, MC, V.
This family-run business, a huge gourmet food and restaurant supply emporium, was founded in 1937, which makes it virtually prehistoric by LA standards. The food is as fresh and tasty as ever, and there's an upmarket café attached.

GALLERIES

Following the recessions of the 1990s and late noughties, the LA art scene has bounced back, with exciting venues all over town joining those that survived the slump. Below is a rundown of our favourites, by area. In addition, art events dot the calendar: highlights include the Venice Art Walk in May (www.veniceartwalk.org); the Culver City Art Walk (www.ccgalleryguide.com) in late May/early June; the Miracle Mile Artwalk (www.miraclemileartwalk.com), held four times a year; and the Downtown Art Walk on the second Thursday of the month (www.downtownartwalk.com). January is officially 'arts month' in Los Angeles (www.losangelesartsmonth.com), with events including the LA Art Show at the LA Convention Center (www.laart show.com), photo l.a. (www.photola.com) and Art Los Angeles Contemporary (www.artlosangelesfair.com).

CONSUME

Santa Monica & the beach towns

The centre of Santa Monica's art scene is **Bergamot Station** (2525 Michigan Avenue, www.bergamotstation.com), a former trolley stop that's now home to 30-plus galleries. The galleries are generally open 10am-6pm Tuesday to Friday and 11am-5.30pm on Saturdays; check the website for details for all tenants. Venice, meanwhile, boasts a healthy and prominent community of artists. Head to venerable **LA Louver** (45 N Venice Boulevard, 1-310 822 4955, www.lalouver. com), which deals in LA's contemporary masters and younger artists from New York, South America and the UK. Over on Abbot Kinney Boulevard, **G2** (No.1503, 1-310 452 2842, www.theg2gallery.com) exhibits a range of environmentally conscious art.

Brentwood to Beverly Hills

The heart of Culver City's burgeoning gallery district is W Washington Boulevard at La Cienega Boulevard. **Koplin del Rio** (No.6031, 1-310 836 9055, www.koplindelrio.com) makes good use of its large space by hosting figurative painting from an impressively diverse collection. **Susanne Vielmetter** (No.6006, 1-310 837 2117, www.vielmetter.com) shows intense figurative work side by side with first-rate minimalist abstractions. East on Washington from La Cienega sit several galleries with very different aesthetics. **Carmichael** (No.4619, 1-323 939 0600, www.carmichaelgallery.com) deals in graffiti-based figurative painting, while high-profile **Roberts & Tilton** (No.5801, 1-323 549 0223, www.robertsandtilton.com) offers an acclaimed roster of local and European artists. Century City is home to the small but interesting **Annenberg Space for Photography** (2000 Avenue of the Stars, 1-213 403 3000, www.annenbergspacefor photography.org), which hosts thought-provoking photo exhibitions on topics such as endangered wildlife. Prestigious galleries in Beverly Hills include **Gagosian** (456 N Camden Drive, 1-310 271 9400, www.gagosian.com), which remains the place to head for notable post-war painting, sculpture and star-studded openings, while the Beverly Hills outpost of **ACE** (9430 Wilshire Boulevard, 1-310 858 9090, www.acegallery.net) is often replete with work by A-listers such as Robert Wilson. At the nearby **Taschen Store** (354 N Beverly Drive, 1-310 274 4300, www.taschen.com), a mix of art and pop culture glamour-pusses are canonised in the pages of high-end tomes and on the walls of the store's gallery.

West Hollywood, Hollywood & Midtown

WeHo's arts scene is focused on the streets around the intersection of Melrose Avenue and N Robertson Boulevard, where a group of businesses together promote themselves under the umbrella of **Avenues of Art & Design** (www.avenuesartdesign.com). On N Almont Drive sit **Manny Silverman** (No.619, 1-310 659 8256, www.manny silvermangallery.com), which deals in American abstract expressionism.

On San Vicente Boulevard, the hard-to-miss **Pacific Design Center** (*see p49*) houses 130-plus showrooms containing architects, dealers and designers, plus a design-oriented annexe of **MoCA**. Nearby, the north end of N La Cienega Boulevard is home to Los Angeles Art Association-run **Gallery 825** (No.825, 1-310 652 8272, www.laaa.org). There's more action further east, courtesy of the incomparable **MAK Centre** and the underground star-makers at **New Image Art** (7920 Santa Monica Boulevard, 1-323 654 2192, www.newimageartgallery.com). In the Fairfax District, Beverly Boulevard is home to **Michael Kohn** (No.8071, 1-323 658 8088, www.kohngallery.com), a major dealer in representational and abstract art, while further east along Beverly, **Stephen Cohen** (No.7354, 1-323 937 5525, www.stephencohen gallery.com) shows photography. The stretch of La Brea Avenue between Melrose Avenue and W 3rd Street is also dotted with galleries. The Miracle Mile has **LACMA** (*see p55*) and a pair of interesting non-profit galleries (the **Craft & Folk Art Museum** and the **A+D Museum**; for both, *see p55*). Elsewhere, most of the notable galleries are on Wilshire Boulevard, close to Fairfax Avenue. The building at **6150 Wilshire Boulevard** houses a number of enterprises, among them **ACME** (1-323 857 5942, www. acmelosangeles.com) and the inscrutably avant-garde **Marc Foxx** (1-323 857 5571, www.marcfoxx.com). Reticent classicist **Daniel Weinberg** (1-323 782 0957, www.danielweinberggallery.com) is at No.6363.

Silver Lake, Los Feliz & Echo Park

Galleries are a mainstay on the funky East Side, none more so than Los Feliz's **La Luz de Jesus** (4633 Hollywood Boulevard, 1-323 666 7667, www.laluzdejesus.com). With Wacko and Soap Plant (*see p156*), it provides a one-stop shopping experience with paintings, books and toys that nod to high art, low art and everything in between.

Galco's Soda Pop Stop. *See p151.*

CONSUME

Over in Silver Lake is the all-outdoors **Materials & Applications** (1619 Silver Lake Boulevard, 1-323 739 4668, www.emanate.org), which aims to combine art (architecture) and nature (landscape), and the **Los Angeles Municipal Art Gallery** (4800 Hollywood Boulevard, 1-323 644 6269, www.culturela.org/lamag), a 10,000-square-foot venue operated by the LA Department of Cultural Affairs that features art from all mediums.

In Echo Park, Shepard Fairey's Obey Giant spin-off **Subliminal Projects** (1331 Sunset Boulevard, 1-213 213 0078, www.subliminal projects.com) shows gritty, fantastical painting with a flair for the dramatic, while **Tropico de Nopal** (1665 Beverly Boulevard, 1-213 481 8112, www.tropicodenopal.com) describes itself, more or less accurately, as a 'swap-meet-church-machine-shop-chemistry-lab installation'.

Downtown

While Chinatown continues to thrive, the real story is the explosive success of **Gallery Row**, the semi-official nickname for the stretches of Main and Spring Streets between 2nd and 9th Streets, where you'll find first-rate outfits such as installation engineers **Morono Kiang** (in the historic Bradbury Building, 218 W 3rd Street, 1-213 628 8208, www.moronokiang.com). For a full guide to the scene, see www.galleryrow.org. The art community has also taken hold just north of the 101 freeway in Chinatown, where

a tenacious and still-expanding concentration of galleries has set up on pedestrianised Chung King Road. **Drkrm** (933 Chung King Road, 1-213 928 0973, www.drkrm.com) focuses on photographs that illuminate once-subversive subcultures. Also here is **Telic** (No.951, 1-213 344 6137, www.telic.info), which runs hypnotic multimedia installations.

GIFTS & SOUVENIRS

Museum shops are good for presents. Try the **Craft & Folk Art Museum** (*see p55*), the **Getty Center** (*see p41*), the **Getty Villa** (*see p31*), the **Japanese American National Museum** (*see p67*), **LACMA** (*see p55*) and **MoCA** (*see p71*).

A+R

1121 Abbot Kinney Boulevard, at San Juan Avenue, Venice (1-800 913 0071, www.aplusr store.com). Bus 33, 733, SM1, SM2/I-10, exit 4th/5th Street south. **Open** 11am-7pm daily. **Credit** AmEx, DC, Disc, MC, V. **Map** p310 A5. Run by and named after British expat Andy Griffith and Los Angeles style journalist Rose Apodaca, A+R offers a super-fresh selection of desirable designer goodies: mostly homewares, alongside a few other gift ideas (books, artworks and other chic novelties). Goods are sourced from around the world, making it a good place to find something unusual. **Other locations** 171 South La Brea Avenue, Fairfax District (1-800 913 0071).

THE BEST UNIQUE SOUVENIRS

For people lacking scents
Strange Invisible Perfumes. *See p159.*

For gifts everybody will love
Skeletons in the Closet. *See p156.*

For your AC/DC lunchbox
Soap Plant/Wacko. *See p156.*

For the Hawaii Five-O fan in your life
Surfing Cowboys. *See p161.*

Clover

2756 Rowena Avenue, at Glendale Boulevard, Silver Lake (1-323 661 4142, www.cloversilver lake.com). Bus 92/I-5, exit Glendale Boulevard south. **Open** 10am-7pm Mon-Sat; noon-6pm Sun. **Credit** AmEx, DC, MC, V. **Map** p314 D2.

This local favourite is packed with a lovely selection of goodies: clothes and bags, lotions and candles, green teas and household trinkets. There's a little something for everyone here.

Firefly

1409 Abbot Kinney Boulevard, at California Avenue, Venice (1-310 450 6288, www.shopfirefly. com). Bus 33, 733, SM1, SM2/I-10, exit 4th/5th Street south. **Open** 11am-7pm Mon-Sat; 11am-5pm Sun. **Credit** AmEx, DC, MC, V. **Map** p310 A6.

One of the most charming shops on Abbot Kinney, Firefly offers a catch-all selection of gifts suitable for more or less every occasion (assuming, that is, that you're not buying for a guy): a few clothes, some books, plenty for the bathroom and a nice selection of cards. Also visit the kids'-only store at No.1405 (1-310 450 6283).

Mohawk General Store

4011 W Sunset Boulevard, at Sanborn Avenue, Silver Lake (1-323 669 1601, www.mohawk generalstore.net). Bus 2, 175, 302/US 101, exit Silver Lake Boulevard north. **Open** 11am-7pm Mon-Sat; noon-6pm Sun. **Credit** AmEx, MC, V. **Map** p314 B3.

The cardinal rule of gifting states that you should give that which you would want to receive yourself. If that's the case, this serene space is the ideal place for present-shopping. Standouts include the delicate jewellery by LA brands Hortense and Gabriela Artigas, candles by venerable brand Cire Trudon, polygonal terrariums by Score + Solder, and printed stationery by Postalco. Also worth noting: the shop's impressive collection of modernist furniture and lighting.

Skeletons in the Closet

LA County Coroner, 1104 N Mission Road, at Marengo Street, Downtown (1-323 343 0760,

www.lacoroner.com). Bus 70, 71/I-5, exit E César E Chávez Avenue west. **Open** 8.30am-4.30pm Mon-Fri. **Credit** Disc, MC, V.

Gallows humour meets capitalism at this bizarre coroner's department shop. Gifts 'to die or kill for' include beach towels, doormats and T-shirts emblazoned with corpse outlines.

Soap Plant/Wacko

4633 Hollywood Boulevard, at N Vermont Avenue, Los Feliz (1-323 663 0122, www.soap plant.com). Metro Vermont-Sunset/bus 4, 156, 204, 754/US 101, exit Vermont Avenue north. **Open** 11am-7pm Mon-Wed; 11am-9pm Thur-Sat; noon-6pm Sun. **Credit** AmEx, DC, MC, V. **Map** p314 A2.

This Los Feliz building houses a trio of zany enterprises: there are two stores, Soap Plant and Wacko, along with a gallery, La Luz de Jesus (*see p154*). The stock – tchotchkes, artworks and stocking-stuffers – is a mix of the kitsch, the silly and the just plain bizarre.

HEALTH & BEAUTY

Hairdressers and spas are everywhere in LA; as are nail salons, which don't always require clients to have made an appointment.

Hairdressers & barbers

Argyle Salon & Spa

Sunset Tower, 8358 Sunset Boulevard, between N Kings Road & N Sweetzer Avenue, West Hollywood (1-310 623 9000, www.argylela.com). Bus 2, 302/I-10, exit La Cienega Boulevard north. **Open** 9am-7pm Tue; 9am-9pm Wed-Sat; noon-6pm Sun. **Credit** AmEx, DC, Disc, MC, V. **Map** p312 B1.

The spa at the Sunset Tower Hotel (*see p178*) offers a full menu of facials, massages and more, but the real reason to visit is the hairdressing. Among the talent on offer is Mauricio: he's famed for his Brazilian blowouts, designed to leave the frizziest of hair smooth for weeks.

Baxter Finley Barber & Shop

515 N La Cienega Boulevard, at Rosewood Avenue, West Hollywood (1-310 657 4726, www.baxterfinley.com). Bus 4, 105, 550, 704/ I-10, exit La Cienega Boulevard north. **Open** 11am-9pm Tue-Sat; 11am-7pm Sun. **Credit** AmEx, Disc, MC, V. **Map** p312 B3.

Dudes looking to graduate from drugstore blades need look no further than this old-timey barber shop. Along with shave brushes, razors and after-shave balms, the Baxter of California brand also encompasses skincare, hair products, body washes, candles and soaps. Be sure to also spring for a signature cut-and-shave when you visit, administered the retro way with hot towels and straight razors.

★ Drybar

*8595 W Sunset Boulevard, at Sunset Plaza
Drive, West Hollywood (1-323 843 4777,
www.thedrybar.com). Bus 2, 105, 302, 705/
I-10, exit La Cienega Boulevard north.* **Open**
8am-8pm Mon-Wed; 8am-9pm Thur-Sat;
9am-7pm Sun. **Credit** AmEx, Disc, MC, V.
Map p312 B1.

Drybar's tagline pretty much says it all: 'No cuts. No
color. Just blowouts. Only $35.' But this is no back-
to-basics chain – leather seats and flat-screen TVs
set the tone for the decor, and you also get a wash
thrown in, plus, at certain times, a free cocktail or
glass of champagne. Great for special occasions or
girlie get-togethers.

Other locations throughout LA.

▶ *Need a look to go with your fancy new up-do?
Stop in next door for a pro make-up application
at Blushington (No.8591, 1-310 652-5874,
www.blushington.com), which also runs classes
and does essential maintenance such as eyebrow
waxing and tweezing.*

Kinara Skin Care Clinic & Spa

*656 N Robertson Boulevard, between Melrose
Avenue & Santa Monica Boulevard, West
Hollywood (1-310 657 9188, www.kinara
spa.com). Bus 4, 105, 550, 704/I-10, exit La
Cienega Boulevard north.* **Open** *Skincare Clinic
& Spa* noon-5pm Mon; 9am-6pm Tue-Thur;
9am-7pm Fri, Sat; 10am-6pm Sun. *Hair studio*
9am-6pm Tue-Sat; 10am-5pm Sun. **Credit**
AmEx, DC, MC, V. **Map** p312 A2.

Despite being favoured by celebs, there's not a hint
of snobbery at this day spa. Treatments on offer
include massages, wraps, face treatments (including the must-have Red Carpet Facial), manicures
and pedicures. Can't decide? Book a package. The
retail area stocks Kinara's excellent own-brand
products, and there's also a hair salon attached
to the premises.

Rudy's Barber Shop

*4451 W Sunset Boulevard, at Hollywood
Boulevard, Los Feliz (1-323 661 6535,*

CONSUME

Strange Invisible Perfumes. *See p159.*

www.rudysbarbershop.com). Metro Vermont-Sunset/bus 2, 4, 302, 704/I-10, exit Vermont Avenue north. **Open** 9am-9pm Mon-Sat; 9am-7pm Sun. **Credit** AmEx, DC, Disc, MC, V. **Map** p314 B3.

Formerly a garage, this salon is now one of the hippest places in LA to get coiffed. Check out the art on the walls while you're being shorn.
Other locations throughout LA.

Sol Salon

10115 Washington Boulevard, between Clarington & Jasmine Avenues, Culver City (1-310 836 9166). Bus 33, 733, C1/I-10, exit Robertson Boulevard south. **Open** 10am-7pm Tue-Fri; 9am-5pm Sat. **Credit** DC, MC, V.

At this excellent salon, staff can handle anything from a simple trim to a total overhaul. Prices are low ($50 for a women's cut); as a result, it's popular.

Opticians

There are several branches of **Sunglass Hut** in LA, including three at the Beverly Center (*see p138*; 1-310 855 1220, www.sunglasshut.com).

LA Eyeworks

7407 Melrose Avenue, at N Martel Avenue, Fairfax District (1-323 653 8255, www.laeyeworks.com). Bus 10/I-10, exit Fairfax Avenue north. **Open** 10am-7pm Mon-Fri; 10am-6pm Sat; noon-5pm Sun. **Credit** AmEx, DC, Disc, MC, V. **Map** p312 D2..

The frames at LA Eyeworks are so hip that people with 20/20 vision have been known to wear them.
Other locations 7386 Beverly Boulevard, Fairfax District (1-323 931 7795).

Oliver Peoples

8642 W Sunset Boulevard, between Sunset Plaza & N Sherbourne Drives, West Hollywood (1-310 657 2553, www.oliverpeoples.com). Bus 2, 105, 302, 705/I-10, exit La Cienega Boulevard north. **Open** 10am-7pm Mon-Fri; 10am-6pm Sat; noon-5pm Sun. **Credit** AmEx, DC, MC, V. **Map** p312 A1.

Oliver Peoples' fab retro-style sunglasses have been spotted on everyone from Angelina Jolie to Kate Moss. The friendly staff can also help you select prescription glasses.
Other locations Malibu Country Mart, 3835 Cross Creek Road, Malibu (1-310 456 1333); South Coast Plaza (*see p141*; 1-714 557 7000).

Pharmacies

There are branches of **Rite Aid** (1130 N La Brea Avenue, West Hollywood, 1-323 463 8539, www.riteaid.com) and **CVS** (8491 W Santa Monica Boulevard, West Hollywood, 1-310 360 7303, www.cvs.com) across LA.

Shops

Excellent national chain **Sephora** has several branches in LA, including one at the Beverly Center (*see p138*; 1-310 657 9670).

Surfing Cowboys. *See p161.*

CONSUME

INSIDE TRACK BLACK FRIDAY

Unless you're a masochist, shopping on the day after Thanksgiving is to be avoided like the plague. 'Black Friday' does promise some real steals – hence people camping out overnight to snag a giant-screen TV for $100 – but it also promises stress levels through the roof and a paucity of parking.

Larchmont Beauty Center

208 N Larchmont Boulevard, between Beverly Boulevard & W 1st Street, Hancock Park (1-323 461 0162, www.larchmontbeauty.com). Bus 14, 210, 710/I-10, exit La Brea Avenue north. **Open** 8.30am-8pm Mon-Sat; 10.30am-6pm Sun. **Credit** AmEx, DC, Disc, MC, V. **Map** p313 B3.
This small local operation sells all manner of prettifying products (skincare, haircare, make-up) from high-end brands such as Dr Hauschka, REN, Diptyque and Molton Brown.

Lather

17 E Colorado Boulevard, at N Fair Oaks Avenue, Pasadena (1-626 396 9636, www.lather.com). Metro Memorial Park/bus 180, 181, 260, 762/Hwy 110 to Pasadena (hwy ends at Glenarm Street). **Open** 11am-9pm Mon-Thur; 11am-10pm Fri, Sat; 11am-7pm Sun. **Credit** AmEx, DC, MC, V.
A clinical-looking place (we mean that in a good way), Lather sells face, body and hair products that eschew synthetic fragrances and colours in favour of natural ingredients such as cranberry, lemongrass and eucalyptus.

★ Strange Invisible Perfumes

1138 Abbot Kinney Boulevard, at San Juan Avenue, Venice (1-310 314 1505, www.siperfumes.com). Bus 33, 733, SM1, SM2/I-10, exit 4th/5th Street south. **Open** 11am-7pm Mon-Sat; noon-6pm Sun. **Credit** AmEx, DC, Disc, MC, V. **Map** p310 A5.
Alexandra Balahoutis weaves arcane stories into her unique line of handmade organic perfumes, with essences gathered from around the world. Her serene store now also stocks her own line of body washes and lotions, in gorgeous combinations like frankincense and coriander and sage and rose. *Photos p157.*

Spas & salons

For a round-up of the best hotel spas, *see p171* **Spa for a Day**.

Burke Williams

8000 W Sunset Boulevard, at N Crescent Heights Boulevard, West Hollywood (1-323 822 9007,

www.burkewilliamsspa.com). Bus 2, 218, 302/I-10, exit Fairfax Avenue north. **Open** 9am-10pm daily. **Credit** AmEx, DC, Disc, MC, V. **Map** p312 C1.
Treatments to uplift your body and spirit, from manicures to seaweed wraps, are the speciality here. Create your own simple rejuvenation package: warm up in the jacuzzi, cool down in the plunge pool, detox in the sauna.
Other locations throughout LA.

★ Kate Somerville

8428 Melrose Place, at N Croft Avenue, West Hollywood (1-323 655 7546, www.katesomerville.com). Bus 10, 105/I-10, exit La Cienega Boulevard north. **Open** 10am-7pm Mon-Sat; 10am-4pm Sun. **Credit** AmEx, DC, Disc, MC, V. **Map** p312 B2.
Somerville's facials are consistently voted one of the best in LA. At her swanky salon, luxurious potions and modern equipment combine to ensure great results. The aestheticians are as skilled as they are charming; clients include Christina Aguilera, Katherine Heigl and… Simon Cowell.

Ole Henriksen

8622A W Sunset Boulevard, at Sunset Plaza Drive, West Hollywood (1-310 854 7700, www.olehenriksen.com). Bus 2, 105, 302, 705/I-10, exit La Cienega Boulevard north. **Open** 8am-5pm Mon, Sun; 8am-8pm Tue-Sat. **Credit** AmEx, DC, MC, V. **Map** p312 B1.
Danish-born Henriksen has been making faces glow and bodies gleam for nearly four decades. The spa is a Zen-style retreat for both Hollywood stars and ordinary hipsters, where clients sip green tea as they soak in a candlelit hydrotherapy tub. There's also a nail boutique onsite.

Paint Shop Beverly Hills

7938 W 3rd Street, between S Edinburgh & S Hayworth Avenues (1-323 658 1930, www.paintshopbeverlyhills.com). Bus 14, 16/I-10, exit Fairfax Avenue north. **Open** 10am-6pm Tue, Wed; 10am-8pm Thur; 10am-7pm Fri; 9am-6pm Sat; 11am-5pm Sun. **Credit** AmEx, DC, MC, V. **Map** p312 C3.
Misnomer aside – it's actually near the Grove – this is a funky, friendly, down-to-earth nail shop. The menu of services includes the must-have, tequila-themed 'Ritas & Rocks' pedicure (cocktail not included, sadly).

Tattoos & piercings

Zulu Tattoo

165 S Crescent Heights Boulevard, at W 3rd Street, Fairfax District (1-323 782 9977, www.zulutattoo.com). Bus 14, 16/I-10, exit Fairfax Avenue north. **Open** by appointment only. **Credit** AmEx, DC, Disc, MC, V. **Map** p312 C3.

CONSUME

Zulu offers high-quality tattoo work using organic inks, with professional, friendly service to boot.

HOUSE & HOME
Antiques

While some of the city's long-time antiques stores have recently closed, there's still worthwhile browsing to be had in West Hollywood, along Robertson and Beverly Boulevards and La Brea Avenue. Also check out the **Pasadena Antique Center & Annex** (444 & 480 S Fair Oaks Avenue, Pasadena, 1-626 449 7706, www.pasadena antiquecenter.com), which hosts around 100 dealers, who set up shop daily.

Several markets merit mention. The biggest, with over 800 sellers, is the **Long Beach Outdoor Antique & Collectible Market** (Long Beach Veterans Memorial Stadium, Clark Avenue & E Conant Street, 1-323 655-5703, www.longbeachantiquemarket.com), on the third Sunday of the month from 5.30am to 2pm. The **Santa Monica Outdoor Antique & Collectible Market** is held at Santa Monica Airport on the first and fourth Sunday of the month (1-323 933 2511, www.santamonica airportantiquemarket.com; check the website for hours). And both the **Pasadena Flea Market** (at the Rose Bowl, 8am-4.30pm on the second Sunday of the month, http://rgcshows.com) and the **Melrose Trading Post** in the Fairfax Senior High School car park (7850 Melrose Avenue, Fairfax District; 9am-5pm every Sunday; http://melrosetradingpost.org), also offer bargains.

Blackman Cruz
836 N Highland Avenue, between Waring & Willoughby Avenues, Hollywood (1-323 466 8600, www.blackmancruz.com). Bus 14, 714/US 101, exit Melrose Avenue west. **Open** 10am-6pm Mon-Fri; noon-5pm Sat. **Credit** AmEx, DC, Disc, MC, V. **Map** p313 A3.
The speciality here is rare and peculiar antiques: expect to find all manner of odd furniture, lights and other trinkets.

Liz's Antique Hardware
453 S La Brea Avenue, between W 4th & W 6th Streets, Miracle Mile (1-323 939 4403, www.lahardware.com). Bus 20, 212/I-10, exit La Brea Avenue north. **Open** 10am-6pm Mon-Sat. **Credit** AmEx, DC, MC, V. **Map** p312 D4.
With more than a million pieces of vintage and contemporary hardware for doors, windows and furniture in stock, you're sure to find what you need.

General
*See also p155 **A+R**.*

Crate & Barrel
438 N Beverly Drive, between Brighton Way & Little Santa Monica Boulevard, Beverly Hills (1-310 247 1700, www.crateandbarrel.com). Bus 4, 16, 20, 720/I-10, exit Robertson Boulevard north. **Open** 10am-8pm Mon-Fri; 10am-7pm Sat; 11am-6pm Sun. **Credit** AmEx, DC, Disc, MC, V. **Map** p311 C3.
This nationwide chain is a reliable choice for homewares. The kitchen department is particularly noteworthy, stocking interesting gadgets, bakeware, books and cookery kits. There are other locations at major malls in the greater LA area, including the Grove (*see p140*). Also worth a look is edgier spin-off CB2 (www.cb2.com), with branches at 8000 W Sunset Boulevard, West Hollywood (1-323 848 7111), and at Santa Monica Place (*see p140*).

HD Buttercup
3225 Helms Avenue, at Venice Boulevard, Culver City (1-310 558 8900, www.hdbuttercup.com). Bus 33, 733, C1/I-10, exit Robertson Boulevard south. **Open** 10am-7pm Mon-Sat; 11am-6pm Sun. **Credit** AmEx, DC, Disc, MC, V.
The old Helms Bakery in Culver City is now filled with around 15 homewares and design stores, which sell everything from rugs to ceiling fans. Selling goods from more than 50 different manufacturers, HD Buttercup is perhaps the most interesting of the lot; for others, see www.helmsbakerydistrict.com.

Jonathan Adler
8125 Melrose Avenue, at N Kilkea Drive, West Hollywood (1-323 658 8390, www.jonathanadler.com). Bus 10/I-10, exit Fairfax Avenue north. **Open** 10am-7pm Mon-Fri; 10am-6pm Sat; noon-5pm Sun. **Credit** AmEx, DC, MC, V. **Map** p312 C2.
Coolly creative pottery, pillows, rugs, chairs, bedding, light and table-top items from the legendary ceramicist turned all-round design guru.
Other locations Fashion Island (1-949 759 0017, *see p140*); 1318 Montana Avenue, Santa Monica (1-310 458 4545).

★ Yolk
1626 Silver Lake Boulevard, between Effie Street & Berkeley Avenue, Silver Lake (1-323 660 4315, www.shopyolk.com). Bus 2, 4, 302, 704/US 101, exit Silver Lake Boulevard north. **Open** noon-6pm Mon, Sun; 11am-7pm Tue-Fri; 10am-7pm Sat. **Credit** AmEx, DC, MC, V. **Map** p314 C3.
'Free Range Design' is the tagline at this colourful shop in Silver Lake, at which the products are sourced from around the world. Find fresh, modern ideas for the home, along with children's furniture and accessories.

Specialist

★ Surfing Cowboys
1624 Abbot Kinney Boulevard, at Venice Boulevard, Venice (1-310 450 4891, www.surfingcowboys.com). Bus 33, 733, SM1, SM2/ I-10, exit 4th/5th Street south. **Open** 11am-6pm Mon, Sun; 11am-7pm Tue-Sat. **Credit** AmEx, MC, V. **Map** p310 A6.

Donna and Wayne Gunthers' California lifestyle store showcases their inspired collection of mid-century modern furniture and home pieces, surf and skate collectibles, jewellery (vintage, modernist and Native American), books and own-brand clothing, which is made locally. *Photo p158.*

Tortoise General Store
1208 Abbot Kinney Boulevard, between San Juan & California Avenues, Venice (1-310 314 8448, www.tortoiselife.com). Bus 33, 733, SM1, SM2/I-10, exit 4th/5th Street south. **Open** 11.30am-6.30pm Tue-Sat; noon-6pm Sun. **Credit** MC, V. **Map** p310 A5.

A symbol of longevity in Japan, the tortoise is the theme for this shop, which showcases traditional Japanese crafts and items designed to last, such as cast-iron ornaments. Nearby sister store, Tortoise (No.1342, 1-310 396 7335), focuses on artist-related pieces including jewellery and furniture.

MUSIC & ENTERTAINMENT
CDs & records

★ Amoeba Music
6400 Sunset Boulevard, at N Cahuenga Boulevard, Hollywood (1-323 245 6400, www.amoeba.com). Metro Hollywood-Vine/ bus 2, 302/US 101, exit Sunset Boulevard west. **Open** 10.30am-11pm Mon-Sat; 11am-9pm Sun. **Credit** DC, Disc, MC, V. **Map** p313 B2.

While the longstanding likes of Rhino in Westwood and House of Records in Venice have fallen by the wayside, the LA branch of SF's Amoeba has gone from strength to strength; indeed, this is the largest independent record store in the US. The variety of stock (CDs and DVDs, new and used) is awesome, the prices are fair and the staff know their onions.

Fingerprints
420 E 4th Street, at N Frontenac Court, Long Beach (1-562 433 4996, www.indierecord shop.com). Metro Transit Mall/I-710, exit Broadway. **Open** 10am-10pm Mon-Thur, Sun; 10am-11pm Fri, Sat. **Credit** AmEx, DC, Disc, MC, V.

This fine independent store is bigger than it looks from the outside: the premises are unexpectedly capacious, and every shelf is crammed with CDs both new and used.

CONSUME

Amoeba Music.

Rockaway Records

2395 Glendale Boulevard, at Silver Lake Boulevard, Silver Lake (1-323 664 3232, www.rockaway.com). Bus 92/US 101, exit Silver Lake Boulevard north. **Open** 11am-7pm daily. **Credit** AmEx, DC, MC, V. **Map** p314 D2.

Used CDs, rare vinyl, new alternative and LA-based bands, 1960s memorabilia and videos are the specialties of this unassuming shop. Prices are keen.

DVDs

For **Amoeba Music**, *see p161*. For **CineFile Video**, *see p197*.

Vidiots

302 Pico Boulevard, at 3rd Street, Santa Monica (1-310 392 8508, www.vidiotsvideo.com). Bus 33, 733, SM7, SM8/I-10, exit Lincoln Boulevard north. **Open** 10am-11pm Mon-Thur; 10am-midnight Fri; noon-midnight Sat; noon-11pm Sun. **Credit** AmEx, DC, MC, V. **Map** p310 A3.

This wonderfully named store has all the usual commercial fare and plenty more besides: foreign flicks, art house videos and rare films, on video, DVD and Blu-ray, for sale or rental.

Musical instruments

If you want to make rather than listen to music, visit the Hollywood branch of the **Guitar Center** (7425 W Sunset Boulevard, 1-323 874 1060, www.guitarcenter.com), which stocks most kinds of musical instruments alongside the axes. Two guitar shops merit mention: the wonderful **McCabe's Guitar Shop** in Santa Monica (3101 Pico Boulevard, 1-310 828 4497, www.mccabesguitar.com) is a favourite of folkies, while the instruments at East LA's **Candelas Guitars** (2724 E César E Chávez Avenue, 1-323 261 2011, www.candelas.com) have been favoured by everyone from Andres Segovia to Ozomatli.

SPORTS & FITNESS

Several chains dot LA, all offering a wide range of products. The biggest is **Big 5 Sporting Goods**; one of its many stores is at 3121 Wilshire Boulevard, Santa Monica, 1-310 453 1747, www.big5sportinggoods.com). The most central **Sport Chalet** is at 11801 W Olympic Boulevard (1-310 235 2847, www.sportchalet.com); the most central **Sports Authority** is in West Los Angeles (1919 S Sepulveda Boulevard, 1-310 312 9600, www.sportsauthority.com). Outdoor specialist **REI** has several stores in the metropolis, including one in Santa Monica (402 Santa Monica Boulevard, 1-310 458 4370, www.rei.com).

Adventure 16

11161 W Pico Boulevard, between S Sepulveda Boulevard & I-405, West LA (1-310 473 4574, www.adventure16.com). Bus C3, SM7, SM8, SM12, SM13/I-10, exit Overland Boulevard north. **Open** 10am-9pm Mon-Fri; 10am-7pm Sat; 10.30am-6pm Sun. **Credit** AmEx, DC, MC, V. **Map** p311 A6.

Whether you're off on an extended desert expedition or a little hillside hike, the city's best outward-bound shop will be able to kit you out.

ZJ Boarding House

2619 Main Street, at Ocean Park Boulevard, Santa Monica (1-310 392 5646, www.zjboarding house.com). Bus 33, 733, SM1, SM2, SM8, SM10/I-10, exit 4th/5th Street south. **Open** 10am-7pm Mon-Sat; 10am-6pm Sun. **Credit** AmEx, DC, Disc, MC, V. **Map** p310 A4.

There are several surf shops in this part of the city, and many others further down the coast in surfer-friendly towns such as Huntington Beach. With its friendly service and adjoining Hurley and Billabong stores (the latter offersing wetsuit and board rentals), ZJ is a good bet.

TICKETS

If you want tickets for a performance or a sporting event in Los Angeles, you'll probably have to go through **Ticketmaster**. The large global chain sells tickets on behalf of countless institutions, adding often-high booking fees to the face-value ticket price. Buy online at www.ticketmaster.com, by phone on 1-213 480 3232 or at one of several ticket windows (the most central is at the Beverly Center; *see p138*). However, it's always worth trying the venue first. You can also book tickets to some events and make restaurant reservations via the Time Out Los Angeles website (www.timeout.com/los-angeles).

TRAVELLERS' NEEDS

For **Traveler's Bookcase**, *see p142*. For computer repairs and cellphone rentals, *see p143*.

Distant Lands

20 S Raymond Avenue, at Colorado Boulevard, Pasadena (1-800 310 3220, www.distant ands.com). Metro Memorial Park/bus 180, 181, 260, 762/Hwy 110 to Pasadena (hwy ends at Glenarm Street). **Open** 10.30am-8pm Mon-Thur; 10.30am-9pm Fri, Sat; 11am-6pm Sun. **Credit** AmEx, DC, Disc, MC, V.

Maps, guidebooks, luggage, binoculars, electrical adaptors, passport holders... This fine retailer stocks pretty much everything that you need.

CONSUME

Hotels

Sleek sleeps and luscious lodgings.

In July 2012, according to a survey by the LA Tourism & Convention Board, the city's hotel occupancy rate had bounced back from an all-time low in 2009 to 83.9 per cent, the highest rate in 25 years. The boom was credited to a rise in domestic and foreign tourists, comprised of Americans who'd put their travel plans on hold during the depths of the recession, plus visitors from countries with relatively healthy economies, such as China, Japan and Australia. That's the good news. The bad news is that LA is still a very expensive place to stay. Although many hotels had been forced to slash their rates in order to survive the economic crisis, it's all relative. If money's no object and $500-a-night rooms are within your budget, you're in luck. But for visitors travelling without an unlimited expense account it can be tricky to find something affordable and decent. On the plus side, at least we're starting to see new/revamped and, in some cases (comparatively) cheap properties in previously under-represented areas, such as the Miracle Mile, Burbank, Culver City and – when the renovated historic Hotel Normandie (www.hotelnormandiela.com) is unveiled in late 2013 – Koreatown.

CONSUME

HOTEL HOTSPOTS

Where you choose to stay will greatly affect your time here, and will also affect how much you pay. Even basic hotels can charge a premium if they're near the beach; conversely, a room in a business-friendly Downtown property can be had for a song on weekends.

INFORMATION AND PRICES

Room rates vary wildly, both from hotel to hotel and within a single property: public holidays, big conventions and awards shows are just three events that affect rates. Obtained from the hotels, the prices listed here reflect that disparity. The rates listed are for double rooms.

Rates can be high, but the hidden extras are the real killer. Quoted room rates will exclude the room tax, which varies from 12 per cent to 17 per cent, depending on the area. And while parking is free in a few hotels, most charge heavily for the privilege: we've included nightly parking rates (before tax) in our listings, but you can expect to pay $25-$30 in many properties, and even up to $40. So, in other words, a double room with a quoted rate of $300 will probably set you back $375

cent mark-up. And that's before you open the minibar or tried to access the internet.

When making a reservation, first call the hotel or, better still, go to the hotel's website: many properties offer internet-only specials. It's also worth visiting sites such as www.priceline.com, www.lastminute.com and www.expedia.com: they may have better deals, though be sure to check the small print as add-ons vary. And always check cancellation policies: many hotels won't charge you if you cancel more than 24 hours ahead, but you might not be eligible for a refund if you book through an outside website.

We've listed a selection of services for each hotel at the end of its review, from entertainment (all hotels have in-room TVs unless stated) to pools (perhaps surprisingly, not all properties have one; all are outdoors unless stated). For internet access, 'wireless'

> ❶ Red numbers given in this chapter correspond to the location of each bar as marked on the street maps. *See pp310-315.*

denotes Wi-Fi, while 'high-speed' is used where high-speed access is available only via a cable. California law requires all hotels to provide non-smoking rooms (some properties are entirely non-smoking) and facilities for disabled visitors (although that doesn't apply to some older buildings, so always check in advance).

For more accommodation reviews and features, go to www.timeout.com/los-angeles.

Santa Monica & the Beach Towns

MALIBU
Expensive

Malibu Beach Inn
22878 Pacific Coast Highway, between Malibu Pier & Carbon Canyon, Malibu, CA 90265 (1-800 462 5428, 1-310 456 6444, www.malibu beachinn.com). Bus 534/I-10, exit PCH north. **Rates** $385-$1,200. **Rooms** 47. **Credit** AmEx, DC, MC, V.

Chain of Thought

Reliable options when inspiration fails.

All the following have branches in and/or around LA.

MODERATE
Hilton 1-800 445 8667, www.hilton.com.
Hyatt 1-888 591 1234, www.hyatt.com.
Marriott 1-888 236 2427, www.marriott.com.
Radisson 1-800 967 9033, www.radisson.com.
Sheraton 1-800 325 3535, www.sheraton.com.

BUDGET
Best Western 1-800 780 7234, www.bestwestern.com.
Comfort Inn 1-877 424 6423, www.comfortinn.com.
Days Inn 1-800 225 3297, www.daysinn.com.
Hampton Inn 1-800 426 7866, http://hamptoninn.hilton.com.
Holiday Inn 1-800 465 4329, www.holiday-inn.com.
Motel 6 1-800 466 8356, www.motel6.com.
Ramada 1-888 854 9517, www.ramada.com.

A $10 million renovation a few years ago added a number of deluxe amenities to this contemporary-style beachfront hotel: custom-stocked bars, private balconies and even in-room wine cellars; some also have fireplaces. Bathrooms feature large, multi-head showers and Molton Brown products. The friendly staff are determined to help guests feel at home on Carbon Beach, making a stay here a pleasant all-round experience.
Bar. Business centre. Concierge. Internet (free wireless). Parking ($27). Restaurant. Room service. Spa. TV: DVD & pay movies.

Moderate

Casa Malibu Inn on the Beach
22752 Pacific Coast Highway, between Malibu Pier & Carbon Canyon, Malibu, CA 90265 (1-800 831 0858, 1-310 456 2219). Bus 534/I-10, exit PCH north. **Rates** $169-$499. **Rooms** 21. **Credit** AmEx, DC, MC, V.
Located on the sand, Casa Malibu is the only hotel on this stretch that has a beach for exclusive use of guests. Malibu Colony is within walking distance; so is Malibu Pier, where fabulous breaks provide some of the best longboard surfing in Southern California. The inn offers four types of room, including two mini-suites with king-size beds, fireplaces and kitchens. The beachfront and ocean-view rooms are coveted, but all have private decks and some include adjacent rooms for families. Considering the location and amenities, rates are very reasonable.
Internet (free wireless). Parking (free). Room service. TV: DVD.

SANTA MONICA
Expensive

Casa del Mar
1910 Ocean Way, at Pico Boulevard, Santa Monica, CA 90405 (1-800 898 6999, 1-310 581 5533, www.hotelcasadelmar.com). Bus 33, 733, SM1, SM7, SM10/I-10, exit 4th-5th Street south. **Rates** $340-$499. **Rooms** 129. **Credit** AmEx, DC, Disc, MC, V. **Map** p310 A3 ❶
Located on the sand, close to Santa Monica's shops and restaurants, this elegant and architecturally significant hotel, sister to Shutters on the Beach (*see p167*), is a local landmark. Most of the plush rooms and suites offer ocean views; for a really opulent stay, reserve one of the two-storey penthouse suites or the super-deluxe presidential suite. An afternoon at the Sea Wellness Spa is a vacation in itself, while the in-house restaurant, Catch, helmed by chef Sven Mede, serves inspired comfort food and fish dishes. The hotel also offers a Live Music Series in the Lobby Lounge from Monday to Saturday evenings.
Bar. Business centre. Concierge. Gym. Internet ($12 wireless). Parking ($33). Pool. Restaurant. Room service. Spa. TV: DVD & pay movies.

CONSUME

Huntley Hotel.

Fairmont Miramar Hotel & Bungalows

101 Wilshire Boulevard, at Ocean Avenue, Santa Monica, CA 90401 (1-866 540 4470, 1-310 576 7777, www.fairmont.com/santa-monica). Bus 20, 534, 720, SM1, SM7/I-10, exit 4th-5th Street north. **Rates** *$309-$1,429.* **Rooms** *302.* **Credit** AmEx, DC, Disc, MC, V. **Map** p310 A2 ❷

The Miramar has been pampering the glamorous and the powerful in California for nearly 90 years: past guests have included everyone from Greta Garbo to Bill Clinton. Families clamour for the 32 bungalows with private patios surrounded by lush tropical landscaping; the other guest rooms boast the ocean and city views. FIG bistro gets rave reviews for its seasonal cuisine, while Exhale Spa focuses on mind-body treatments.
Bars (2). Business centre. Concierge. Gym. Internet ($5.99 wireless & high-speed). Parking ($33). Pool. Restaurants (2). Room service. Spa. TV: pay movies.

Hotel Oceana

849 Ocean Avenue, at Montana Avenue, Santa Monica, CA 90403 (1-800 777 0758, 1-310 393 0486, www.hoteloceanasantamonica.com). Bus 534, SM4/I-10, exit 4th-5th Street north. **Rates** *$350-$750.* **Rooms** *70.* **Credit** AmEx, DC, Disc, MC, V. **Map** p310 A2 ❸

A multi-million-dollar renovation several years ago catapulted this boutique hotel into chic status. Designer Chris Barrett fine-tuned the interior spaces, but managed to retain the warm ambience that has long characterised the property. While the Oceana is a destination spot for holidaymakers, business travellers and aspiring screenwriters will find nice touches throughout: rooms have exec-size desks and there's Wi-Fi even by the pool. Tower 8, the hotel's revamped restaurant, debuted in January 2013 with a menu overseen by Mélisse's Josiah Citrin (*see p97*).

Business centre. Concierge. Gym. Internet (free wireless). Parking ($36). Pool. Restaurant. Room service. TV: DVD.

Huntley Hotel

1111 2nd Street, at California Avenue, Santa Monica, CA 90403 (1-888 532 5155, 1-310 394 5454, www.thehuntleyhotel.com). Bus 4, 20, 534, 704, 720, SM1, SM7, SM8, SM10/I-10, exit 4th-5th Street north. **Rates** *$369-$469.* **Rooms** *209.* **Credit** AmEx, DC, Disc, MC, V. **Map** p310 A2 ❹

There's something of the W chain about this operation, located in the building that previously housed a Radisson. The design of the public areas makes the most of the sunlight that so often illuminates Santa Monica: the occasional shiny surface and lots of light colours, including a daring amount of white that must have the cleaners working overtime. The most memorable space is the Penthouse, a handsome, airy and altogether quite impressive bar-restaurant that affords dramatic views over the Pacific. Many of the rooms also look out towards the ocean. There's no pool, but the beach is a mere pebble's throw away.
Bar. Business centre. Concierge. Gym. Internet ($9.95 wireless). Parking ($33). Restaurants (2). Room service. Smoking rooms. TV: DVD & pay movies.

Loews Santa Monica Beach Hotel

1700 Ocean Avenue, between Colorado Avenue & Pico Boulevard, Santa Monica, CA 90401 (1-800 235 6397, 1-310 458 6700, www.loews hotels.com). Bus 33, 534, 733, SM1, SM7, SM10/I-10, exit 4th-5th Street south. **Rates** *$300-$489.* **Rooms** *342.* **Credit** AmEx, DC, Disc, MC, V. **Map** p310 A3 ❺

This is pretty much a quintessential corporate-Californian property: light and airy, warm and beachy, casual but elegant in an almost entirely

CONSUME

nondescript way. Although the pool area is pretty nice, the most eye-catching part of the building is the four-storey glass atrium. Except, that is, for the inevitable ocean views: the location is its main selling point. The spa and fitness centre includes a Blow hair salon, and there's food at Ocean & Vine and drinks in the Blue Streak bar.

Bar. Business centre. Concierge. Gym. Internet ($11.95 wireless in room; free wireless in lobby). Parking ($36). Pool. Restaurants (3). Room service. Smoking rooms. Spa. TV: pay movies.

Le Merigot

1740 Ocean Avenue, between Colorado Avenue & Pico Boulevard, Santa Monica, CA 90401 (1-888 539 7899, 1-310 395 9700, www.lemerigothotel. com). Bus 33, 534, 733, SM1, SM7, SM10/I-10, exit 4th-5th Street south. **Rates** $249-$1,200. **Rooms** 175. **Credit** AmEx, DC, Disc, MC, V. **Map** p310 A3 ❻

Sure, there are trendier and swankier properties in the area, but Le Merigot has a lot going for it, not least its low-key vibe. It's now part of the JW Marriott group, and while it continues to attract the business brigade, it also comes with plenty of comforts for vacationers, including 37in LCD TVs and Cloud Nine beds, which live up to their name. Other draws include an outdoor pool, a high-tech gym and a serene spa. Check the website for interesting packages that include sports-car rentals and surfing lessons.

Bar. Business centre. Concierge. Gym. Internet ($14.95 wireless, high-speed & shared terminal). Parking ($35). Pool. Restaurant. Room service. Spa. TV: DVD & pay movies.

★ Shutters on the Beach

1 Pico Boulevard, at Ocean Avenue, Santa Monica, CA 90405 (1-800 334 9000, 1-310 458 0030, www.shuttersonthebeach.com). Bus 33, 733, SM1, SM7, SM10/I-10, exit 4th-5th Street south. **Rates** $445-$820. **Rooms** 198. **Credit** AmEx, DC, Disc, MC, V. **Map** p310 A3 ❼

Still a cool retreat for hot Hollywood stars, Shutters has a relaxed but decidedly upscale style. Filled with comfortable sofas, club chairs and prints by modern masters such as David Hockney, the lobby mirrors the beach-cottage ambience of the rooms and suites, which in turn feature lovely, dark hardwood floors and the hotel's signature white shutters. Guests who prefer gentle pampering to the myriad outdoor beach activities can spend a day at the spa or sit poolside sipping wine and taking in the ocean views. The luxury is low-key, but it's luxury all the same.

Bars (2). Business centre. Concierge. Gym. Internet ($12 wireless). Parking ($34). Pool. Restaurants (2). Room service. Spa. TV: DVD & pay movies.

★ Viceroy

1819 Ocean Avenue, at Pico Boulevard, Santa Monica, CA 90401 (1-800 622 8711, 1-310 260
7500, www.viceroysantamonica.com). Bus 33, 534, 733, SM1, SM7, SM10/I-10, exit 4th-5th Street north. **Rates** $399-$599. **Rooms** 163. **Credit** AmEx, DC, Disc, MC, V. **Map** p310 A3 ❽

After more than a decade, the Viceroy remains the hippest hotel on the West Side. More crucially, though, it's also its most stylish and impressive operation. Interiors diva Kelly Wearstler is behind the design: sleek and chic yet quietly playful, with modern amenities set amid an overall look that nods both to a camped-up British country-house aesthetic and the hotel's history (it was built in 1969). The bar hums with activity, though many drinkers take their cocktails to the bijou pool area out back; Whist restaurant provides sustenance. Light sleepers should note that the oceanside rooms are a tad louder than those on the other side of the building.

Bar. Business centre. Concierge. Gym. Internet ($15 wireless). Parking ($35). Pool. Restaurant. Room service. TV: DVD & pay movies.

Moderate

Ambrose

1225 20th Street, between Wilshire Boulevard & Arizona Avenue, Santa Monica, CA 90404 (1-877 262 7673, 1-310 315 1555, www. ambrosehotel.com). Bus 20, 720, SM2/I-10, exit 4th-5th Street north. **Rates** $229-$279. **Rooms** 77. **Credit** AmEx, DC, Disc, MC, V. **Map** p310 C2 ❾

This sustainably minded boutique avoids the stereotypical super-sunny decor prevalent in so many Santa Monica hotels, preferring a cultured mixture of sturdy Craftsman tradition and Asian chic. The latter influence extends to the faintly Asian-inspired garden; however, the stately rooms, some of which come with terraces and fireplaces, are more tangibly American in style. The hotel's environmental friendliness covers everything from energy-efficient LED signs to low-flow toilets. There's also complimentary local transport within a three-mile radius.

Concierge. Gym. Internet (free wireless & high-speed). Parking (free). Room service. TV: DVD & pay movies.

Georgian Hotel

1415 Ocean Avenue, at Santa Monica Boulevard, Santa Monica, CA 90401 (1-800 538 8147, 1-310 395 9945, www.georgianhotel.com). Bus 4, 534, 704, SM1, SM7, SM8, SM10/I-10, exit 4th-5th Street north. **Rates** $250-$479. **Rooms** 84. **Credit** AmEx, DC, Disc, MC, V. **Map** p310 A3 ❿

Built in 1933 during the peak period of California coastal expansion, the Georgian Hotel is a finely conceived amalgamation of Romanesque revival and art deco styles, and a renovation several years ago succeeded in bringing out the building's most flattering assets. The rooms are elegantly modern yet maintain some original features, such as exposed water pipes and solid wood doors; the old-

CONSUME

Custom Hotel. *See p170.*

school elevator won't get you there in a hurry but it will get you there in style. One of the hotel's best attributes is the lovely veranda on which guests can take their morning coffee or evening cocktail. *Bar. Business centre. Concierge. Gym. Internet (free wireless). Parking ($26). Restaurant. Room service. TV: DVD & pay movies.*

Hotel California

1670 Ocean Avenue, between Pico Boulevard & Colorado Avenue, Santa Monica, CA 90401 (1-866 571 0000, 1-310 393 2363, www.hotel ca.com). Bus 33, 733, SM1, SM7, SM10/I-10, exit 4th-5th Street south. **Rates** *$129-$189.* **Rooms** 36. **Credit** AmEx, DC, Disc, MC, V. **Map** p310 A3 ⑪

It might be just next to the Loews (*see p165*), but this jaunty motel offers its guests a different type of Californian experience. Surfboards hanging from the façade underline the location; surfers even get a 10% discount if they turn up with board (call ahead first to check). The decor is homey rather than stylish, old-fashioned rather than old-school. But prices are good.

Concierge. Internet (free wireless). Parking ($36). Room service. TV.

Hotel Shangri-La

1301 Ocean Avenue, at Arizona Avenue, Santa Monica, CA 90401 (1-310 394 2791, www. shangrila-hotel.com). Bus 20, 534, 720, SM1, SM7, SM8, SM10/I-10, exit 4th-5th Street north. **Rates** $305-$935. **Rooms** 71. **Credit** AmEx, DC, Disc, MC, V. **Map** p310 A2 ⑫

Following a $30 million renovation, this art deco beauty reopened in 2009, just as it turned 70. Thankfully the streamline moderne exterior has been preserved; inside, the rooms have been upgraded with hardwood floors, windows that open (yes, it's a rarity), flat-screen TVs and iPod docking stations. All offer ocean views and many have balconies and kitchenettes. There's also a pool and a restaurant serving dishes using produce from the local farmers' market, and, on the rooftop, guests can enjoy a drink at the Suite 700 lounge or a spa treatment at the Sybaris Rejuvenation Lounge.

Bars (3). Business centre. Concierge. Gym. Internet (free wireless). Parking ($34). Pool. Restaurants (2). Room service. TV: DVD & pay movies.

Sheraton Delfina

530 W Pico Boulevard, between 4th & 7th Streets, Santa Monica, CA 90405 (1-888 627 8532, 1-310 399 9344, www.sheratonsantamonica. com). Bus 33, 733, SM1, SM7, SM10/I-10, exit 4th-5th Street south. **Rates** $199-$500. **Rooms** 310. **Credit** AmEx, DC, Disc, MC, V. **Map** p310 B3 ⑬

Down the road from the beach, the Delfina was designed by the über-stylish Kor (now Viceroy) Hotel Group for the über-corporate Sheraton chain. A little of both approaches is evident throughout the property: the design is handsome and modern but also overfamiliar. Still, the amenities are excellent (stop by the new Link Café and Poolside Grille), the rooms are in good nick (some have balconies and ocean views) and the service is as reliable as you'd expect. A nice alternative for those who want a bit of the

Viceroy's style without worrying about whether they're wearing the right label jeans in the bar. *Bar. Business centre. Concierge. Gym. Internet (free wireless in lobby, $15 high-speed in rooms). Parking (free-$25). Pool. Restaurants (2). TV: pay movies.*

Budget

Bayside Hotel

2001 Ocean Avenue, at Bay Street, Santa Monica, CA 90405 (1-800 525 4447, 1-310 396 6000, www.baysidehotel.com). Bus 33, 733, SM1, SM7, SM10/I-10, exit 4th-5th Street south. **Rates** $109-$287. **Rooms** 45. **Credit** AmEx, DC, Disc, MC, V. **Map** p310 A3 ⓮

At this unpretentious hotel, parking is cheap, rates are reasonable and advance reservations will secure a clean, comfortable room with an ocean view. One appealing feature is the retro blade sign on the corner, which harks back to the days when Santa Monica truly was a laid-back beach town at the end of Route 66. *Internet (free wireless). Parking ($17). TV.*

HI-Santa Monica

1436 2nd Street, between Santa Monica Boulevard & Broadway, Santa Monica, CA 90401 (1-888 464 4872 ext 137, 1-310 393 9913, www.hilosangeles.org). Bus 4, 20, 534, 704, 720, SM1, SM7, SM8, SM10/I-10, exit 4th-5th Street north. **Rates** $33-$38 dorm bed. **Beds** 260. **Credit** AmEx, DC, MC, V. **Map** p310 A3 ⓯

You'll need to book far in advance for this four-floor, 260-bed Santa Monica hostel: the location ensures that demand is always high. The rooms more than cover the basics: the dorms sleep between six and ten. There's a café for breakfast, video games, TV and movie rooms, a kitchen, a courtyard and all the other budget-travel basics you could possibly want. *Internet (free wireless).*

VENICE
Budget

Cadillac Hotel

8 Dudley Avenue, at Speedway & Ocean Front Walk, Venice, CA 90291 (1-310 399 8876, www.thecadillachotel.com). Bus 33, 733, C1, SM1, SM2/I-10, exit 4th-5th Street south. **Rates** $95-$139. **Rooms** 47. **Credit** AmEx, DC, MC, V. **Map** p310 A5 ⓰

After a long run as a budget beach hostel, the pink Cadillac was transformed into a boutique hotel by a new team a while back. The lobby and all the rooms have been renovated and the exterior has been given a fresh coat of paint, and, thankfully, the management has kept the Venice vibe alive. *Business centre. Concierge. Internet ($3 wireless & shared terminal). Parking ($15). TV.*

Venice Beach House

15 30th Avenue, at Speedway, Venice, CA 90291 (1-310 823 1966, www.venicebeachhouse.com). Bus 108, 358, C1/I-10, exit 4th-5th Street south. **Rates** $145-$235. **Rooms** 9. **Credit** AmEx, DC, MC, V. **Map** p310 A6 ⓱

This Craftsman-style inn was built in 1911 by Warren Wilson, the owner of the now-defunct *Los Angeles Daily Journal*. Now on the National Register of Historic Places, it's been faithfully restored and furnished with exceptional antique pieces; many of the rooms are named after characters with ties to the area (Venice founder Abbot Kinney, sometime local Charlie Chaplin). Each of the nine rooms has its own character and amenities, though four share a bath. The more extravagant suites offer an ocean view, a fireplace, a patio or a private entrance. Further freebies: a hot breakfast and teatime snacks. *Internet (free wireless). Parking ($14). TV.*

★ Venice Beach Suites

1305 Ocean Front Walk, at Westminster Avenue, Venice, CA 90291 (1-888 877 7602, 1-310 396 4559, www.venicebeachsuites.com). Bus C1, SM1/I-10, exit 4th-5th Street south. **Rates** $129-$350. **Rooms** 25. **Credit** AmEx, Disc, MC, V. **Map** p310 A5 ⓭

Many hotels exaggerate with the term 'beachfront', but this place couldn't be closer to the sand – walk out the front door and you're right on the boardwalk. Rooms feature exposed brick walls, hardwood floors

---

Carry on Camping

Sleep under the stars, not with them.

Perhaps the most scenic camping in LA is found at **Malibu Creek State Park** (four miles south of US 101 on Las Virgenes/Malibu Canyon Road). The park offers 4,000 acres for hiking, fishing and horse riding, as well as 15 miles of stream-side trails. (*M*A*S*H* fans may recognise it as the backdrop to the TV show). Not far away in Malibu is **Leo Carrillo State Beach** (35000 PCH, Malibu), which has 1.5 miles of beach for swimming, surfing and fishing. Reservations for both parks – staff recommend booking six months ahead for summer – can be made at 1-800 444 7275; see www.parks.ca.gov for more. Private campsites tend to be less scenic than their state counterparts, but offer more amenities. **Malibu Beach RV Park** (25801 PCH, 1-800 622 6052, 1-310 456 6052, www.maliburv.com) has 50 tent sites, priced from $42 to $60 depending on the view and the time of year.

CONSUME

and well-stocked kitchenettes (complete with toaster, fridge, microwave and even pots and pans) and bathrooms are spotless. Further bonuses: bars and restaurants are nearby, and staff are helpful. A bargain on the beach.
Internet (free wireless). TV.

MARINA DEL REY TO LAX
Moderate

Custom Hotel
8639 Lincoln Boulevard, between W Manchester Avenue & Loyola Boulevard, Playa del Rey, CA 90045 (1-877 287 8601, 1-310 645 0400, www.jdvhotels.com). Bus 115/I-405, exit Jefferson Boulevard west. **Rates** $170-$250. **Rooms** 250. **Credit** AmEx, DC, Disc, MC, V.
You can't miss this Joie de Vivre-owned property as you drive up from LAX or Marina del Rey: topped with a glowing neon sign announcing its name, it's the only all-black building on the horizon. Things are more colourful inside, but no less stylish: the lobby opens out into a sleek but playful bar area (say hello to the sheep), and there's also a new restaurant and lounge, Deck 33, by the beautifully designed pool. The rooms are lovely, with comfortable beds and supplemented by quirky design touches and all mod cons. There's not much in the vicinity, but you'd be forgiven if you didn't want to leave the hotel. *Photo p168.*
Bars (2). Business centre. Concierge. Gym. Internet (free wireless). Parking ($20). Pool. Restaurants (2). Room service. TV: DVD & pay movies.

Inn at Playa del Rey
435 Culver Boulevard, Playa del Rey, CA 90293 (1-310 574 1920, www.innatplayadelrey.com). Bus 115/I-405, exit Culver Boulevard west. **Rates** $195-$450. **Rooms** 21. **Credit** AmEx, DC, MC, V.
The Inn at Playa del Rey has the rare distinction of being minutes from LAX and yet also within easy walking distance of the beach. Rooms are decorated individually; all are comfortable and have a homey ambience. Some come with fireplaces and jacuzzis, as well as balconies overlooking the nature reserve and Marina del Rey. Parents with children in tow will be relieved to find that there are also family suites available. The hotel offers complimentary bike rentals to guests, and there's free wine and hors d'oeuvres every evening.
Concierge. Internet (free wireless & shared terminal). Parking (free). TV: free movies.

Jamaica Bay Inn
4175 Admiralty Way, at Palawan Way, Marina del Rey, CA 90292 (1-888 823 5333, 1-310 823 5333, www.jamaicabayinn.com). Bus C1, 108, 358/I-405, exit hwy 90 west. **Rates** $195-$399. **Rooms** 111. **Credit** AmEx, DC, Disc, MC, V.
A welcome addition to Marina del Rey, Jamaica Bay Inn opened in 2010. Part of the property was

formerly a Best Western, but you'd never know it: rooms are stylishly done out in shades of brown, gold and orange, with extras such as robes and small fridges, while bathrooms feature biodegradable toiletries. Many rooms have balconies, some facing the marina, where activities include volleyball and kayaking; there's also an extensive running trail. Onsite bar-restaurant Beachside includes a DIY bloody mary bar at weekends. The location – on a calm inlet and in close proximity to Venice, Santa Monica and LAX – is a major boon, but this is a nice place to stay in its own right.
Bar. Business centre. Concierge. Gym. Internet (free wireless). Parking ($16-$24). Pool. Restaurant. Room service. TV: free movies.

Sheraton Gateway
6101 W Century Boulevard, between Airport & S Sepulveda Boulevards, Los Angeles, CA 90045 (1-800 325 3535, 1-310 642 1111, www.sheraton lax.com). Bus 117, 439/I-405, exit Century Boulevard west. **Rates** $99-$209. **Rooms** 802. **Credit** AmEx, DC, Disc, MC.
Presumably in an attempt to differentiate the property from the cluster of over-familiar hotels that ring LAX, Sheraton engaged the services of the fashion-friendly Kor (Viceroy) Hotel Group to sprinkle its magic dust on this place a few years ago. The result is the most handsome hotel in the airport's immediate shadow, albeit one that doesn't match the likes of the Viceroy itself in the style stakes. On the other hand, it doesn't try to: the Gateway offers instead a likeable interpretation on modern boutique decor, and, unusually for an airport hotel, amenities include an outdoor pool.
Bar. Business centre. Concierge. Gym. Internet ($12.95 high-speed & wireless). Parking ($17-$33). Pool. Restaurant. Room service. TV: pay movies.

Brentwood to Beverly Hills
CULVER CITY
Moderate

Culver Hotel
9400 Culver Boulevard, at Main Street, Culver City, CA 90232 (1-888 328 5837, 1-310 558 9400, www.culverhotel.com). Metro Culver City/ bus CM1/I-10, exit Robertson Boulevard south. **Rates** $245-$405. **Rooms** 46. **Credit** AmEx, DC, Disc, MC, V.
Culver City's historic, neo-Renaissance Culver Hotel, which celebrates 90 years in 2014, was once the part-time residence of Old Hollywood stars – from Clark Gable to Greta Garbo. Charlie Chaplin supposedly sold it to John Wayne for a buck, while tales of apparitions and antics by the Munchkins – who slept three

Spa for a Day

Spas are everywhere in LA, but the best are found at hotels.

OK, so the rooms at the five-stars may break the bank, but surely you can splurge on a treatment? Most hotel spas cater to visitors as well as guests, and many have become destinations in their own right. Two tips: it's always worth checking the hotel's websites for deals and packages, and it's a little-known fact that some hotel spas let you use their pool for the day if you book a treatment.

Though the clinical-feeling Bliss spa at Hollywood's **W** hotel (*see p172*) emphasises results rather than full-on pampering, guests are treated to a glass of champers and mini-brownie bites as part of the deal. If blind masseur Moeul can't get those knots out during the Blissage massage ($155/75 minutes), no one can.

Boasting a similarly white palette but a more luxurious vibe is Ciel, at the **SLS at Beverly Hills** (*see p175*). Its signature treatments include the absurdly indulgent Sweet Loving Souls ($495/120 minutes), where you and your significant other get to soak in deep tubs and are then massaged (champagne and candle included).

Indeed, Beverly Hills is home to many raved-about spas, not least the two gorgeous ones at the **Four Seasons** hotels. The menu at the **Wilshire** property (*see p174*) includes Natura Bissé facials and themed treatments aimed at kids and teenagers, while the **Doheny** location focuses on incredible mind-and-body experiences such as Manipura ($260/90 minutes), which, as billed, leaves your 'mind, body and spirit sparkling'.

Another top spa in the area is the **Beverly Hills Hotel & Bungalows** (*see p173*), where the La Prairie spa showcases the luxe Swiss skincare brand (during awards season, demand soars for the legendary Caviar Firming facial, $300/90 minutes).

City workers, meanwhile, can escape the stress of Downtown at the **Ritz-Carlton** (*see p181*), whose spa includes a divine, all-white 'sanctuary' for post-treatment chilling. Some services are inspired by – and use ingredients from – the hotel's garden; for ultra-smooth skin, book the Cranberry Pomegranate Holiday treatment ($150/50 minutes).

Orange County, the byword for extravagance, also has some stunners. Superbly set on a bluff overlooking the ocean, Spa Montage at the **Montage Laguna Beach** (*see p184*) is known for its Surrender treatments (from $455/120 minutes) and ocean-inspired therapies, but it also provides more straightforward fare. Its city sister, the **Montage Beverly Hills** (*see p175*), has won a number of awards for the beautiful design of its spa, which features a huge heated whirlpool and luxurious treatments such as the scary-sounding but sublime Anointing ($270/90 minutes).

CONSUME

Four Seasons Beverly Wilshire.

to a bed while filming the *Wizard of Oz* at the nearby MGM lot – surround the property. Following a renovation in 2007, the light-filled guest rooms now have a classic-meets-modern feel, with chandeliers, antiques and marble bathrooms. Locals and tourists enjoy the lobby bar and restaurant, which serves a complimentary continental breakfast to overnighters. *Bar. Business centre. Gym. Internet (free wireless). Parking ($10-$20). Restaurant. Room service. TV.*

WESTWOOD
Expensive

W
930 Hilgard Avenue, at Le Conte Avenue, Westwood, CA 90024 (1-310 208 8765, www.wlosangeles.com). Bus 2, 302, 720, SM1, SM2, SM3, SM8/I-405, exit Wilshire Boulevard east. **Rates** $269-$649. **Rooms** 258. **Credit** AmEx, DC, Disc, MC, V.
Westwood is a wonderful place to walk, eat and attend university, but it's not really a thrill-a-minute urban hub. As such, the W has become essential to the area: located on a sidestreet lined with apartment complexes, the hotel offers a sleek environment in which locals and outsiders can indulge their inner hipster. The recently revamped rooms include all the comforts you'd expect; the public areas include the Backyard poolside restaurant and WET, the gorgeous heated pool; further pampering comes in the form of a Bliss spa. Intriguingly, pets under 40lbs are welcome for an additional fee, and are given their own bed and dishes. Woof! *Bar. Business centre. Concierge. Gym. Internet ($14.95 high-speed; free wireless in lobby). Parking ($36). Pool. Restaurants (3). Room service. Spa. TV: DVD & pay movies.*

Moderate

Hotel Palomar
10740 Wilshire Boulevard, at Selby Avenue, Los Angeles, CA 90024 (1-800 472 8556, 1-310 475 8711, www.hotelpalomar-lawestwood.com). Bus 20, 720/I-405, exit Wilshire Boulevard east. **Rates** $199-$369. **Rooms** 268. **Credit** AmEx, DC, Disc, MC, V. **Map** p311 A4 ⑲
Kimpton bought this former Doubletree property a while back, sprucing it up so that it's more or less unrecognisable. The style throughout is handsome and pleasingly muted, and Kimpton's long-held reputation for excellent service is another selling point. The restaurants on the UCLA campus are within walking distance, but the hotel itself is home to BLVD 16, serving California cuisine. Panoramic views and a pet-friendly attitude are further boons. *Bar. Business centre. Concierge. Gym. Internet ($11.99 wireless). Parking ($35). Pool. Restaurant. Room service. TV: pay movies.*

BEL AIR
Expensive

★ Hotel Bel-Air
701 Stone Canyon Road, at Bellagio Road, Bel Air, CA 90077 (1-800 648 4097, 1-310 472 1211, www.hotelbelair.com). I-405, exit Sunset Boulevard east. **Rates** $565-$10,000. **Rooms** 103. **Credit** AmEx, DC, Disc, MC, V.
This elite and quietly decadent Mission-style 1920s hotel, a dreamy getaway on 12 fairytale acres of lush landscaping, reopened in October 2011 after a two-year overhaul. The additions – which include new lofts and hillside suites, a La Prairie spa (for guests and residents of Bel Air only) and fitness centre –

W.

are suitably impressive, but thankfully other draws have stayed the same, including the gardens, the resident swans and the pool, where Marilyn Monroe famously posed for *Vogue* six weeks before she died. One welcome change: Wolfgang Puck now oversees the menu at the posh restaurant, where diners subtly try to spot which Hollywood player is sitting at the next table. If that's beyond your budget, stop by for a drink at the swanky bar.

Bars (2). Business centre. Concierge. Gym. Internet ($10 wireless). Parking ($35). Pool. Restaurant. Room service. TV: pay movies.

CENTURY CITY
Moderate

★ Hyatt Regency Century Plaza
2025 Avenue of the Stars, between Constellation & W Olympic Boulevards, Century City, CA 90067 (1-877 787 3452, 1-310 277 2000, www.centuryplaza.hyatt.com). Bus 4, 28, 316, SM5/I-405, exit Santa Monica Boulevard east. **Rates** $275-$500. **Rooms** 726. **Credit** AmEx, DC, Disc, MC, V. **Map** p311 B4 ⑳

No surprises: this is simply a comfortable and efficient hotel that offers plenty of services designed to please the Hyatt's legions of business travellers. That said, it's nice for families, too, especially in summer, when the pool area comes into its own. The architecture is rather corporate (the views from the building are more appealing than the views of it) and the interior is predictable. Still, there's something to be said for the convenience, the reliability and the sheer size of the place. An Equinox gym and the huge Westfield mall (*see p141*) are just steps away.

Bars (2). Business centre. Concierge. Internet ($9.95 wireless & high-speed; free wireless in lobby). Parking ($36). Pool. Restaurants (2). Room service. Smoking rooms. Spa. TV: pay movies.

BEVERLY HILLS
Expensive

Avalon
9400 W Olympic Boulevard, at S Canon Drive, Beverly Hills, CA 90212 (1-310 277 5221, www.avalonbeverlyhills.com). Bus 28/I-10, exit Overland Avenue. **Rates** $270-$389. **Rooms** 83. **Credit** AmEx, DC, MC, V. **Map** p311 D4 ㉑

Opened as the Beverly Carlton back in the 1940s, this street-side property was renovated and regenerated by the Kor (Viceroy) Hotel Group in 1999, setting the tone for the boutique-hotels-in-old-buildings schtick that was later brought to something approaching perfection by the company at the Viceroy in Santa Monica (*see p167*). Revamped a few years ago by Kelly Wearstler, the retro-handsome rooms feature mid 20th-century decor and toiletries by celeb hairdresser Neil George. Through the lobby,

Beverly Hills Hotel & Bungalows.

hidden behind a fabulous boomerang façade and a cluster of trees, is a kidney-shaped pool that provides a focal point for a buzzy bar scene and the gorgeous al fresco Italian restaurant, Oliverio.

Bar. Business centre. Concierge. Gym. Internet ($10.95 wireless). Parking ($31-$35). Pool. Restaurant. Room service. TV: DVD.

★ Beverly Hills Hotel & Bungalows
9641 Sunset Boulevard, at N Crescent Drive, Beverly Hills, CA 90210 (1-800 283 8885, 1-310 276 2251, www.thebeverlyhillshotel.com). Bus 2, 302/I-405, exit Sunset Boulevard east. **Rates** $510-$13,650. **Rooms** 208. **Credit** AmEx, DC, Disc, MC, V. **Map** p311 B2 ㉒

The famous pink stucco façade, the manicured grounds and the sumptuous rooms of the Beverly Hills Hotel look as fresh as they did on opening day in 1912. It oozes exclusivity: every screen legend from Valentino to Arnie has slept in this fabled hideaway or held court in its still-popular Polo Lounge. The biggest draw are the bungalows, where Liz Taylor spent six of her honeymoons, although these paled into insignificance when the hotel unveiled its two new 5,000sq ft Presidential Bungalows in 2011 – the epitome of lavishness, and yours for a cool $13,650. If your budget won't stretch that far, at least stop by for a treatment at the lovely La Prairie spa.

Bars (2). Concierge. Gym. Internet ($10 wireless & high-speed, free shared terminal). Parking ($36). Pool. Restaurants (3). Room service. Smoking rooms. Spa. TV: DVD & pay movies.

Beverly Hilton
9876 Wilshire Boulevard, between Santa Monica Boulevard & Whittier Drive, Beverly Hills, CA

CONSUME

90210 (1-310 274 7777, www.beverlyhilton. com). Bus 16, 20, 316, 720/I-405, exit Wilshire Boulevard east. **Rates** *$295-$475.* **Rooms** *569.* **Credit** AmEx, DC, Disc, MC, V. **Map** p311 C3
For a long time, this hotel was a dowdy property famous only as the home of the Golden Globes. These days, it's known as the hotel where Whitney Houston died in February 2012. A refit several years ago spruced the place up no end, when the rather tired decor was replaced by a look that's both comfortable and handsome, classic but not wedged in the past. The Aqua Star Spa offers a string of upscale treatments; unusually for a hotel in this part of town, the heated pool – the largest in Beverly Hills – is big enough to swim in. Dining and drinking options are provided by Circa 55 and tiki lounge Trader Vic's; up in the rooms, all mod cons are present and correct.
Bars (2). Business centre. Concierge. Gym. Internet ($14.95 wireless). Parking ($38). Pool. Restaurant. Room service. Spa. TV: pay movies.

SLS Hotel at Beverly Hills.

★ Beverly Wilshire, A Four Seasons Hotel

9500 Wilshire Boulevard, at S Rodeo Drive, Beverly Hills, CA 90212 (1-800 427 4354, 1-310 275 5200, www.fourseasons.com/beverlywilshire). Bus 4, 14, 16, 20, 316, 704, 720/I-405, exit Wilshire Boulevard east. **Rates** *$495-$895.* **Rooms** *395.* **Credit** AmEx, DC, Disc, MC, V. **Map** p311 D3 ᠒
The ornate detailing on this Four Seasons-operated gem, famous for its role in *Pretty Woman*, recalls 19th-century French splendour, but more recent additions such as a Richard Meier-designed, Wolfgang Puck-operated bar, Sidebar, and restaurant, CUT (*see p101*), lend 21st-century sophistication. The beautiful spa, with its Aromatherapy Crystal Steam Room, is well worth a splurge. The proximity to Rodeo Drive ensures a wealthy and occasionally sniffy crowd, but there's still something warm about the place. If the rooms are out of your price range, stop by and relax with a coffee or a cocktail at the Blvd, the lovely sidewalk café.
Bar (2). Business centre. Concierge. Gym. Internet (free wireless & high-speed). Parking ($40). Pool. Restaurants (3). Room service. Spa. TV: DVD.

★ Four Seasons Los Angeles at Beverly Hills

300 S Doheny Drive, at Burton Way, Beverly Hills, CA 90048 (1-800 332 3442, 1-310 273 2222, www.fourseasons.com/losangeles). Bus 20, 28/I-10, exit Robertson Boulevard north. **Rates** *$455-$785.* **Rooms** *285.* **Credit** AmEx, DC, Disc, MC, V. **Map** p311 D2 ᠒
Following a $38 million renovation, completed in 2012, the Four Seasons continues to pamper its guests something silly. From the fragrant, flower-filled lobby to the immaculate rooms, which come with chinoiserie headboards and Frette linens, every detail is calculated to spoil visitors. Limos to Rodeo Drive or anywhere within two miles are available; the revamped pool area features a state-of-the-art alfresco fitness centre and the lovely shaded Cabana café. Other major draws include the superb spa and Culina, the ground-floor modern Italian restaurant and crudo bar.
Bars (2). Business centre. Concierge. Gym. Internet (free wireless & high-speed). Parking ($38). Pool. Restaurants (2). Room service. Spa. TV: DVD & pay movies.

Luxe Rodeo Drive

360 N Rodeo Drive, between Brighton & Dayton Ways, Beverly Hills, CA 90210 (1-866 589 3411, 1-310 273 0300, www.luxerodeo.com). Bus 14, 16, 20, 316, 720/I-405, exit Wilshire Boulevard east. **Rates** *$309-$359.* **Rooms** *86.* **Credit** AmEx, DC, Disc, MC, V. **Map** p311 C3 ᠒
The design of this hotel is an exercise in restraint. Located on Rodeo Drive (it's the only hotel on Beverly Hills' most famous street), the Luxe has an intimate lobby defined by its monochromatic palette and sleek decor, and 86 rooms and suites that share an equally polished aesthetic. The high-priced luxury is tangible in the quality of the linens, the generous amenities and the professional service. The hotel is alluring for Hollywood movers and shakers, but it's also a good option for families. The new onsite On Rodeo Bistro & Lounge is a handy option if you'd rather stay in than explore the myriad options nearby. For total seclusion, the Sunset location, at the intersection of Bel-Air and Brentwood, is a hidden gem.
Bar. Business centre. Concierge. Gym. Internet (free wireless & high-speed). Parking ($28). Restaurant. Room service. TV: DVD & pay movies.
Other locations Luxe Sunset Boulevard, 11461 Sunset Boulevard, Los Angeles, CA 90049 (1-800 468 3541); Luxe City Center, 1020 S Figueroa Street, Los Angeles, CA 90015 (1-866 589 3411).

CONSUME

Montage Beverly Hills

225 N Canon Drive, at Clifton Way, Beverly Hills, CA 90210 (1-888 860 0788, 1-310 860 7800, www.montagebeverlyhills.com). Bus 4, 14, 16, 20, 316, 704, 720/I-405, exit Wilshire Boulevard east. **Rates** $595-$9,000. **Rooms** 201. **Credit** AmEx, DC, Disc, MC, V. **Map** p311 D3 ⑤

It may have been daring for the Montage to unveil a temple to extravagance during the depths of the recession, in 2008, but the Montage already feels as if it's been here forever. The rooms don't quite have the wow factor of the public areas, but they're luxurious, with plush furnishings and marble and mosaic-tiled bathrooms. Further reasons to stay here include the lovely heated rooftop pool, with sweeping views, upscale Italian restaurant Scarpetta (*see p103*) and the award-winning spa, a destination in itself. If you can't afford to spend the night, consider stopping by for afternoon tea or a craft cocktail against a backdrop of live music in Parq Bar.

Bars (2). Business centre. Concierge. Gym. Internet (free wireless). Parking ($35). Pool. Restaurants (2). Room service. Spa. TV: DVD & pay movies.

Mosaic

125 S Spalding Drive, between Wilshire & Charleville Boulevards, Beverly Hills, CA 90212 (1-800 463 4466, 1-310 278 0303, www.mosaic hotel.com). Bus 4, 16, 20, 316, 704, 720/I-405, exit Wilshire Boulevard east. **Rates** $300-$400. **Rooms** 49. **Credit** AmEx, DC, Disc, MC, V. **Map** p311 C3 ㉘

The old Beverly Hills Inn was brought into the 21st century with some style just over a decade ago, and it remains an impressive operation. The luxury here is all in the best possible taste: the earth-toned rooms come complete with Bose stereo systems, 450-thread-count linens, immense shower-heads and free Wi-Fi, with the one- and two-bedroom suites simply continuing the theme on a larger scale. With only 49 rooms, the Mosaic has the feel of a boutique hotel, a welcome change from some of its more impersonal neighbours. Rodeo Drive is a short stroll from the door.

Bar. Business centre. Concierge. Gym. Internet (free wireless & high-speed). Parking ($30). Pool. Restaurant. Room service. TV: DVD & pay movies.

Peninsula Beverly Hills

9882 Santa Monica Boulevard, between Wilshire & Charleville Boulevards, Beverly Hills, CA 90212 (1-800 462 7899, 1-310 551 2888, http:// peninsula.com/beverlyhills). Bus 4, 16, 20, 316, 704, 720/I-405, exit Santa Monica Boulevard east. **Rates** $520-$8,500. **Rooms** 193. **Credit** AmEx, DC, Disc, MC, V. **Map** p311 C3 ㉙

Designed to look and feel like a private estate, the Peninsula exudes opulence. There are 193 recently renovated rooms, suites and private villas situated on the lushly landscaped grounds, along with a fitness centre, a spa, a rooftop outdoor bar and restaurant and a pool complete with private cabanas. Elsewhere,

the gorgeous Club Bar is a popular meeting place for movers and shakers, the Belvedere restaurant provides a classy dining experience and afternoon tea in the Living Room is justifiably renowned.

Bar. Business centre. Concierge. Gym. Internet (free wireless & high-speed). Parking ($36). Pool. Restaurants (4). Room service. Spa. TV: DVD & pay movies.

SLS Hotel at Beverly Hills

465 S La Cienega Boulevard, at Clifton Way, Beverly Hills, CA 90048 (1-310 247 0400, www.slshotels.com). Bus 28, 105, 328/I-10, exit La Cienega Boulevard north. **Rates** $279-$489. **Rooms** 297. **Credit** AmEx, DC, Disc, MC, V. **Map** p312 B3 ㉚

On the very edge of Beverly Hills, this property was part of the Méridien chain until 2008, when it was given a dramatic $230 million makeover by SBE Group (headed by restaurateur and nightlife promoter Sam Nazarian), in collaboration with Philippe Starck. The result was sensational, from the beautiful lobby to the rooms themselves, which feature D Porthault linens, faux mink throws, Cassina chaises longues and floor-to-ceiling mirrors that cleverly conceal plasma-screen TVs. Other highlights include the gorgeous pool deck, with two pools and panoramic views, and the spa, Ciel, a white vision of loveliness (a Robert Vetica hair salon was recently added). The SLS also gets a lot of attention for its celeb-cheffed restaurant, the Bazaar by José Andrés (*see p101*).

Bar. Business centre. Concierge. Gym. Internet (free wireless & high-speed). Parking ($36). Pool. Restaurants (2). Room service. Spa. TV: DVD & pay movies.

Moderate

Maison 140

140 S Lasky Drive, at Charleville Boulevard, Beverly Hills, CA 90212 (1-866 891 0945, 1-310 281 4000, www.maison140beverlyhills.com). Bus 4, 14, 16, 20, 316, 704, 720/I-405, exit Santa Monica Boulevard east. **Rates** $229-$319. **Rooms** 43. **Credit** AmEx, DC, Disc, MC, V. **Map** p311 C3 ㉛

The intimate rooms at this Gemstone Hotel and Resorts property seem designed to prove that form is more important than function. The Kelly Wearstler decor in the individually decorated rooms, a chic return to 18th-century Paris with a few contemporary Asian twists, is every bit as glamorous a look as you'd hope to find in a building that was once owned by Lillian Gish. Bar Noir provides guests with somewhere to unwind in a neighbourhood that's strangely short on nightlife. There's no pool, but guests are welcome to use the facilities at nearby sister hotel, the Mosaic (*see above*).

Bar. Business centre. Concierge. Gym. Internet (free wireless). Parking ($28). Room service. TV.

CONSUME

Budget

Hotel Beverly Terrace

469 N Doheny Drive, at Santa Monica Boulevard, Beverly Hills, CA 90210 (1-800 842 6401, 1-310 274 8141, www.hotelbeverlyterrace.com). Bus 4, 14, 16, 20, 316, 704, 720/I-405, exit Wilshire Boulevard east. **Rates** $169-$199. **Rooms** 39. **Credit** AmEx, DC, Disc, MC, V. **Map** p311 D2 **32**
The rooms are smaller and less luxurious than other Beverly Hills hotels, but this mid-century spot does offer one of the best deals in the area. Teak furniture and planted palms hint playfully towards a tropical getaway, though the decor in the rooms themselves (which aren't huge) is retro and minimal. Continental breakfast is included in the rates; Trattoria Amici, the hotel's restaurant, offers Cal-Italian cooking. There's a small garden and a nice little pool.
Business centre. Internet (free wireless). Parking ($10). Pool. Restaurant. TV.

West Hollywood, Hollywood & Midtown

WEST HOLLYWOOD

Expensive

★ Andaz West Hollywood

8401 Sunset Boulevard, at N Kings Road, West Hollywood, CA 90069 (1-323 656 1234, www. westhollywood.andaz.hyatt.com). Bus 2, 302/I-10, exit La Cienega Boulevard north. **Rates** $229-$1,200. **Rooms** 239. **Credit** AmEx, DC, Disc, MC, V. **Map** p312 B1 **33**
You wouldn't know it today, but this snazzy hotel from the Hyatt chain was once the hardest partying spot on the Sunset Strip. Known then as the Hyatt House, it was the place where rock royalty boozed all night long and, as legend has it, where Keith Richards and Keith Moon once threw a TV set off the balcony. In 2009, the hotel underwent a $48 million makeover to emerge as a sleek boutique property. The hotel pays homage to its history with decorative touches (contemporary art and vintage images of its famous guests) throughout the modern-designed rooms and lobby. There's also a show-stopper of a rooftop sun-deck, with sweeping views of the city.
Bar. Concierge. Gym. Internet (free wireless). Parking ($32). Pool. Restaurant. Room service. Smoking rooms. TV: pay movies.

Chamberlain

1000 Westmount Drive, at W Knoll Drive, West Hollywood, CA 90069 (1-800 201 9652, 1-310 657 7400, www.chamberlainwesthollywood.com). Bus 2, 302/I-10, exit La Cienega Boulevard north. **Rates** $309-$399. **Rooms** 113. **Credit** AmEx, DC, Disc, MC, V. **Map** p312 B2 **34**

**THE BEST
HOTELS FOR MOVIE FANS**

Featured in *American Gigolo*
Beverly Hills Hotel & Bungalows.
See p173

Appeared in *Catch Me If You Can*
Hollywood Roosevelt. *See p179.*

Starred in *Ghostbusters* and
Pretty in Pink
Millennium Biltmore. *See p181.*

Open less than a decade, the most discreet of all the Kor (Viceroy) Hotel Group's properties is also one of its most appealing. Tucked away in a quiet West Hollywood sidestreet, the Chamberlain is less buzzy than the Viceroy (*see p167*) and subtler than the Avalon (*see p173*), but the understated look is perfect for the location and part of the property's appeal. The rooms, in an attractive palette of periwinkle, cream, gold and bronze, feature 42in-screen TVs and Sferra linens, and some boast vaulted ceilings. But don't be surprised if you spend a lot of your time with cocktail in hand up in the atmospheric pool area.
Bar. Concierge. Gym. Internet ($10.95 wireless & high-speed). Parking ($36). Pool. Restaurant. Room service. TV: DVD & pay movies.

★ Chateau Marmont

8221 Sunset Boulevard, between Crescent Heights Boulevard & Roxbury Road, West Hollywood, CA 90046 (1-800 242 8328, 1-323 656 1010, www. chateaumarmont.com). Bus 2, 302/I-10, exit La Cienega Boulevard north. **Rates** from $535. **Rooms** 63. **Credit** AmEx, DC, Disc, MC, V. **Map** p312 B1 **35**
One of the many beautiful things about this Hollywood Hills fixture is that it's barely changed over the decades. The hotel still attracts the brazen and the beautiful (everyone from Led Zeppelin to Lindsay Lohan has stayed here; John Belushi OD-ed in bungalow 3); it still offers a quintessentially glamorous LA experience; and it still promises its guests absolute discretion. No two rooms are the same, but most come with kitchenettes or full kitchens, and some have balconies or terraces. Can't afford to stay? Treat yourself to lunch or dinner – executive chef Carolynn Spence oversees a menu of New American dishes – or linger over a drink at the adjacent Bar Marmont (*see p121*).
Bar. Business centre. Concierge. Gym. Internet (free wireless). Parking ($32). Pool. Restaurant. Room service. Smoking rooms. TV: DVD & pay movies.

★ London West Hollywood

1020 N San Vicente Boulevard, at Sunset Boulevard, West Hollywood, CA 90069 (1-866

282 4560, 1-310 854 1111, www.thelondon westhollywood.com). Bus 4, 105, 550, 704/I-10, exit La Cienega Boulevard north. **Rates** $279-$629. **Rooms** 200. **Credit** AmEx, DC, Disc, MC, V. **Map** p312 A2 ❸❻

Thanks to a total makeover by design guru David Collins several years back, the London now boasts some of the nicest guest quarters in LA. All 200 rooms are generous suites, featuring subtle sage and tan palettes, Italian linens and luxurious white bathrooms. Each has a private deck or a balcony with decent views; for truly extraordinary panoramic vistas, especially at dusk, head to the rooftop pool deck. The off-Sunset location makes it a popular location with leisure-seekers, while businessfolk enjoy free phone calls to London. Other draws include a Gordon Ramsay restaurant and the Alex Roldan hair salon.
Bars (2). Business centre. Concierge. Gym. Internet (free wireless & high-speed). Parking ($32). Pool. Restaurants (3). Room service. TV: DVD & pay movies.

Mondrian

8440 W Sunset Boulevard, at N Olive Drive, West Hollywood, CA 90069 (1-800 525 8029, 1-323 650 8999, www.mondrianhotel.com). Bus 2, 302/I-10, exit La Cienega Boulevard north. **Rates** $335-$475. **Rooms** 237. **Credit** AmEx, DC, Disc, MC, V. **Map** p312 B1 ❸❼

Built as an apartment block in the 1950s, this tower was converted into a hotel by businessman Ian Schrager and designer Philippe Starck in the mid

'90s, and immediately became the hottest spot in the city. It still carries a certain amount of star quality, despite several recent changes, not least a redesign by Benjamin Noriega Ortiz (who sensitively enhanced Starck's original design rather than do away with it entirely). Funky additions to the rooms include combined mirror/TV showpieces and sustainable bamboo flooring. Elsewhere in the hotel, Skybar still draws a starry crowd.
Bars (3). Business centre. Concierge. Gym. Internet ($10 wireless & high-speed). Parking ($32). Pool. Restaurant. Spa. Room service. TV: DVD & pay movies.

Sofitel Los Angeles

8555 Beverly Boulevard, at N La Cienega Boulevard, West Hollywood, CA 90069 (1-800 763 4835, 1-310 278 5444, www.sofitel.com). Bus 14, 16, 105, 316, LDF/I-10, exit La Cienega Boulevard north. **Rates** $300-$385. **Rooms** 295. **Credit** AmEx, DC, Disc, MC, V. **Map** p312 B3 ❸❽

A shopper's paradise but a driver's nightmare – that's the best way to describe the location of this hotel, close to the Beverly Center in the heart of one of the most congested areas in LA. The good news, though, is that there are countless shops, restaurants and bars just a short walk from here. And once you've made it through the traffic, you'll find a very impressive hotel operation: smart, reliable and also, thanks to the presence of the chic LeSpa, the French restaurant, Estérel, and the Riviera 31 bar, surprisingly fashionable.
Bar. Business centre. Concierge. Gym. Internet ($14.95 wireless; free high-speed). Parking ($33). Pool. Restaurant. Room service. Spa. TV: pay movies.

Sunset Marquis Hotel & Villas

1200 N Alta Loma Road, between W Sunset Boulevard & Holloway Drive, West Hollywood, CA 90069 (1-800 858 9758, 1-310 657 1333, www.sunsetmarquishotel.com). Bus 2, 302/I-10, exit La Cienega Boulevard north. **Rates** $295-$645. **Rooms** 150. **Credit** AmEx, DC, Disc, MC, V. **Map** p312 B1 ❸❾

Celebrating its half-century in 2013, the Sunset Marquis has attracted a steady stream of A-listers to its discreet, secluded surroundings since it first opened. Some of the amenities are aimed at a niche audience: such as the on-site, state-of-the-art recording studio. However, the pair of outdoor pools and the divine Bar 1200, which offers classes in its Cocktail Lab, have wider appeal. A major renovation a few years ago added 40 new villas to the existing 12, and updated the hotel's suites into a casually cosy style. Guests get free passes to nearby celeb-favoured gym, Equinox.
Bar. Business centre. Concierge. Internet ($11.95 wireless & high-speed). Parking ($30). Pools (2). Restaurant. Room service. Smoking rooms. Spa. TV: DVD & pay movies.

Chamberlain.

CONSUME

INSIDE TRACK
TURN IN, TUNE OUT, DROP OFF

If you're a light sleeper and are staying in a nightlife-heavy part of town (such as Hollywood, West Hollywood and certain parts of Downtown and Santa Monica) or near LAX, be sure to request a quiet room.

Sunset Tower

8358 Sunset Boulevard, between N Sweetzer Avenue & Olive Drive, West Hollywood, CA 90069 (1-323 654 7100, www.sunsettower hotel.com). Bus 2, 302/I-10, exit La Cienega Boulevard north. **Rates** *$295-$395.* **Rooms** *73.* **Credit** *AmEx, DC, Disc, MC, V.* **Map** *p312 B1* ⓺

One of the most memorable buildings on the Sunset Strip (it's on the National Register of Historic Places), this beautiful tower opened in 1931 as an apartment block, but it's been a hotel for years. These days, the decor is a fine-tuned balance of Old Hollywood charm and contemporary chic, and service is excellent. The elevated pool and lounge afford wonderful views of the city below, although equally breathtaking vistas can be enjoyed through floor-to-ceiling windows in the nicely sized rooms and suites.

Bar. Business centre. Concierge. Gym. Internet (free wireless). Parking ($32). Pool. Restaurants (2). Room service. Spa. TV: DVD & pay movies.

Moderate

Élan

8435 Beverly Boulevard, at N Croft Avenue, Los Angeles, CA 90048 (1-866 203 2212, 1-323 658 6663, www.elanhotel.com). Bus 14, 16, 105, 316, LDF/I-10, exit La Cienega Boulevard north. **Rates** *$179-$249.* **Rooms** *49.* **Credit** *AmEx, DC, Disc, MC, V.* **Map** *p312 B3* ⓻

The simplicity of the Élan's modernist architecture, especially its concrete and plate glass façade, continues inside the property: the lobby area is crisp and welcoming, and renovation several years ago updated the formerly slightly drab rooms with a sharper look. Unusually, there's no pool, restaurant or bar, but the reasonable rates do include continental breakfast and an evening wine and cheese reception.

Business centre. Concierge. Internet (free wireless & high-speed). Parking ($24). Room service. TV.

Orlando

8384 W 3rd Street, at Orlando Avenue, West Hollywood, CA 90048 (1-800 624 6835, 1-323 658 6600, www.theorlando.com). Bus 16/I-10, exit La Cienega Boulevard north. **Rates** *$179-$329.* **Rooms** *95.* **Credit** *AmEx, DC, Disc, MC, V.* **Map** *p312 B3* ⓼

A $6 million renovation in 2011 brought a breath of fresh air to the family-owned Orlando. Done out in

crisp white linens, the rooms include comfy beds, larger marble bathrooms and 42in plasma-screen TVs. The property also boasts a sparkling saltwater rooftop pool and sundeck and the Churchill, serving American grub and draft beers (the outdoor patio, complete with fireplace, is a lovely spot to sit – and sip – in the evening). The location is excellent, too, slap on pedestrian-friendly West 3rd Street, lined with shops and restaurants, and within walking distance of the Beverly Center, and, slightly further away, the Farmers Market and the Grove.

Bar. Concierge. Internet (free wireless & shared terminal). Parking ($29). Pool. Restaurant. Room service. Spa. TV: DVD & pay movies.

HOLLYWOOD
Expensive

★ Redbury

1717 Vine Street, at Hollywood Boulevard, Hollywood, CA 90048 (1-877 962 1717, 1-323 962 1717, www.theredbury.com). Metro Hollywood-Vine/bus 163, 180, 181, 210, 212, 217, 312, 363, 780, LDH/US 101, exit Vine Street south. **Rates** *$295-$1,000.* **Rooms** *57.* **Credit** *AmEx, DC, MC, V.* **Map** *p313 B1* ⓽

A collaboration between SBE Group and esteemed photographer Matthew Rolston, this bachelor pad-cum-boutique hotel opened in 2010. Three years on, it's still receiving rave reviews. 'Home-from-home feel' may sound like a cliché but here it's appropriate: the 57 generously sized 'flats' feature paisley prints, old-fashioned English sofas and vintage record players (vinyl supplied), plus modern amenities such as LCD TVs, Wi-Fi and kitchenettes with microwaves and washer-dryers. Each has a balcony – some overlooking the iconic Capitol Records building. Guests are given preferential access to other SBE properties, although with the fabulous Library Bar, Glade courtyard lounge and Cleo restaurant (*see p105*), why would you ever want to leave? *Photo p180.*

Bar. Business centre. Concierge. Internet ($10 wireless). Parking ($38). Restaurant. Room service. TV: DVD.

W Hollywood

6250 Hollywood Boulevard, between Vine Street & Argyle Avenue, Hollywood, CA 90028 (1-888 625 4955, 1-323 798 1300, www.whollywood hotel.com). Metro Hollywood-Vine/bus 163, 180, 181, 210, 212, 217, 312, 780, LDH/US 101, exit Hollywood Boulevard west. **Rates** *$239-$659.* **Rooms** *305.* **Credit** *AmEx, DC, Disc, MC, V.* **Map** *p313 B2* ⓾

Occupying a huge space at the corner of the iconic Hollywood & Vine intersection, this 12-storey development, which includes a 305-room hotel, 143 W-branded residences and 20,000sq ft of retail space, opened in 2010 to huge fanfare. Despite its size, it manages to pull off an Old Hollywood-glamour-

Sunset Tower.

the hotel also counts theatre in its repertoire. Look out for the occasional subtly placed photographic nod to the starry location.
Bars (4). Concierge. Gym. Internet ($15 wireless). Parking ($32). Pool. Restaurants (3). Room service. TV: DVD & pay movies.

Loews Hollywood Hotel

1755 N Highland Avenue, at Yucca Street, Hollywood, CA 90028 (1-855 563 9749, 1-323 856 1200, www.loewshotels.com). Metro Hollywood-Highland/bus 163, 180, 181, 210, 212, 217, 312, 780, LDH/US 101, exit Hollywood Boulevard west. **Rates** $289-$349. **Rooms** 632. **Credit** AmEx, DC, MC, V. **Map** p313 A1 **46**
This property, in the heart of tourist land, has changed hands many times during its 40-year lifespan. Most recently it was the Renaissance Hollywood, before the Loews group took it over in 2012 with a view to treating it to a $26 million makeover (ongoing as this guide went to press). The rooms – some of which offer views of the Hollywood sign – will no doubt remain stylish and comfy. A grand staircase leads to the Hollywood & Highland mall (*see p140*). And if all the hustle and hassle outside gets too much, repair to the Exhale spa.
Bar. Business centre. Concierge. Gym. Internet ($12.95 wireless & high-speed). Parking ($10-$38). Pool. Restaurant. Room service. Spa. TV: pay movies.

Magic Castle Hotel

7025 Franklin Avenue, between N Sycamore Avenue & N Orange Drive, Hollywood, CA 90028 (1-800 741 4915, 1-323 851 0800, www.magic castlehotel.com). Metro Hollywood-Highland/bus 163, 180, 181, 210, 212, 217, 312, 780, LDH/ US 101, exit Hollywood Boulevard west. **Rates** $194-$214. **Rooms** 43. **Credit** AmEx, Disc, DC, MC, V. **Map** p313 A1 **47**
This unusual property is connected to the Academy of Magical Arts, an exclusive organisation made up of roughly 2,500 American magicians; guests have access to the otherwise private Magic Castle, where AMA members perform nightly for clued-up crowds. However, the hotel itself is no illusion. Of the 43 units, three-quarters are apartment-style suites with kitchenettes and living areas; some have balconies overlooking the pool. Amenities include continental breakfasts with baked goods from Susina, one of LA's best bakeries (*see p135*).
Concierge. Internet (free wireless). Parking ($11). Pool. TV: DVD.

Budget

Highland Gardens Hotel

7047 Franklin Avenue, at N Sycamore Avenue, Hollywood, CA 90028 (1-800 404 5472, 1-323 850 0536, www.highlandgardenshotel.com). Metro Hollywood-Highland/bus 163, 180, 181, 210, 212, 217, 312, 780, LDH/US 101, exit Hollywood

meets-cutting-edge vibe. The rooms, which all feature Egyptian cotton sheets, plasma-screen TVs and marble bathrooms, are luxurious. Thanks to the W's crafty marketing department, even the most basic accommodations are dubbed 'Wonderful', but it's worth splurging on a suite. R&R can be had via the well-appointed gym, Bliss spa, rooftop pool, Drai's bar/club (*see p122*) and Delphine Eatery & Bar.
Bars (4). Business centre. Concierge. Gym. Internet ($10.95-$14.45 wireless; free wireless in lobby). Parking ($36). Pool. Restaurants (2). Room service. Spa. TV: DVD & pay movies.

Moderate

★ Hollywood Roosevelt

7000 Hollywood Boulevard, at N Orange Drive, Hollywood, CA 90028 (1-800 950 7667, 1-323 466 7000, www.thompsonhotels.com). Metro Hollywood-Highland/bus 163, 180, 181, 210, 212, 217, 312, 780, LDH/US 101, exit Hollywood Boulevard west. **Rates** from $299. **Rooms** 300. **Credit** AmEx, DC, Disc, MC, V. **Map** p313 A1 **45**
After a restoration by designer Dodd Mitchell in 2005, this 1927 landmark, a beautiful example of Spanish colonial design, once more welcomes the A-listers who frequented it during Hollywood's heyday (the Roosevelt was the location of the first-ever Academy Awards). The hotel is at its most dramatic in the historic lobby, which leads to the Public Kitchen & Bar, 25 Degrees, Spare Room, Teddy's nightclub and the hidden-gem Library Bar. The rooms are sleek and dark; the cabana rooms have direct access to the pool (which boasts an underwater mural by David Hockney), where you'll also find the buzzing Tropicana Bar. And thanks to Beacher's Madhouse,

CONSUME

Boulevard west. **Rates** $109-$129. **Rooms** 72. **Credit** AmEx, DC, MC, V. **Map** p313 A1 ⑱

This hotel opened as the Hollywood Landmark hotel in the 1950s; while it's been renovated since, it still feels pretty old-fashioned both inside and out. The mid-century post-and-beam architecture and court-yard pool with tropical landscaping are memorable assets, but the rooms are forgettable. Still, if you plan on spending most of your time at the many sights within a short distance of the hotel, you'll get from it what you need: a place to sleep, a place to shower and a safe place to store your bags. The free parking is a big plus too. Janis Joplin fans note: this is where the singer died of a heroin overdose in 1970.

Internet ($8.99 wireless). Parking (free). Pool. TV.

FAIRFAX DISTRICT
Moderate

Farmer's Daughter
115 S Fairfax Avenue, at W 1st Street, Los Angeles, CA 90036 (1-800 334 1658, 1-323 937 3930, www.farmersdaughterhotel.com). Bus 217, 218, LDF/I-10, exit Fairfax Avenue north. **Rates** $199-$279. **Rooms** 66. **Credit** AmEx, DC, MC, V. **Map** p312 C3 ⑲

This was once a basic motel, so it's a credit to the owners of the gingham-giddy Farmer's Daughter that these days it feels pretty fresh. The rooms have been duded up in blue and yellow checks and denim bed-spreads; farm and barnyard humour abounds. Other amenities include a DVD library, a small pool and Tart, which serves good ol' country cooking. The rates are high given the amenities. However, you could say the same about countless other LA hotels,

including many with far worse locations: this one is right by the Farmers Market and the Grove.

Bar. Concierge. Internet (free wireless). Parking ($18). Pool. Restaurant. Room service. TV: DVD.

Budget

Beverly Laurel
8018 Beverly Boulevard, between S Laurel & S Edinburgh Avenues, Los Angeles, CA 90048 (1-323 651 2441). Bus 14, 217, 218, LDF/I-10, exit La Cienega Boulevard north. **Rates** $109-$150. **Rooms** 52. **Credit** AmEx, DC, MC, V. **Map** p312 C3 ⑳

This '50s motel is one of the best buys on Beverly, its location and attitude making it popular with younger movers and shakers who would rather save than splurge. Luxury is conspicuous by its absence: the rooms are unashamedly basic, and the pool area is about as plain as you'll ever find. Still, the funkiness is all part of the appeal, the hotel's diner (Swingers) is a real winner, and the price is most definitely right.

Internet ($5.95 wireless). Parking ($5). Pool. Restaurant. TV.

MIRACLE MILE & MIDTOWN
Expensive

Hotel Wilshire
6317 Wilshire Boulevard, at S Crescent Heights Boulevard, Los Angeles, CA 90048 (1-323 852 6000, www.hotelwilshire.com). Bus 20, 217, 218, 720, 761/I-10, exit Fairfax Avenue north. **Rates** $279-$499. **Rooms** 74. **Credit** AmEx, DC, MC, V. **Map** p312 C4 ㉑

Redbury. *See p178.*

CONSUME

THE BEST LUXURY GETAWAYS

Still going strong, over
100 years on
Beverly Hills Hotel & Bungalows.
See p173.

Renovated and rejuvenated
Hotel Bel-Air. See p172.

Heaven on the edge of the Pacific
Shutters on the Beach. See p167.

R&R, OC-style
St Regis Monarch Beach. See p184.

This boutique property, owned and operated by Kimpton, sits right on Wilshire Boulevard, but nonetheless provides an escape from the daily grind. Rooms are primed for comfort, with Frette linens and, in the bathrooms, rainforest showers and toiletries by Lather, but a bigger draw is the rooftop pool and restaurant, which boast sweeping views. During weekend brunch, tuck into chef Eric Greenspan's pancake lasagna as you sip bottomless mimosas, or come during the week for sunset drinks and bites. Guests can bring their pooch to stay bedside, while enjoying free access to the nearby LA Fitness gym. *Photo p182. Bar. Business centre. Concierge. Internet (free wireless). Parking ($32). Pool. Restaurant. Room service. TV.*

DOWNTOWN
Expensive

★ Ritz-Carlton, Los Angeles
900 W Olympic Boulevard, at Georgia Street, Los Angeles, CA 90015 (1-213 743 8800, www. ritzcarlton.com). Metro Pico/bus 81, 381, 442, 460/I-110, exit Adams Boulevard. **Rates** $269-$429. **Rooms** 123. **Credit** AmEx, DC, MC, V. **Map** p315 A4 ⓮

Since it opened in 2010 within the mammoth L.A. LIVE complex, the Ritz-Carlton has brought a touch of glamour to the otherwise dowdy Downtown hotel scene. In the rooms, which come with espresso machines, huge walk-in closets and Bulgari toiletries, no detail has been overlooked – there are six types of clothes hanger alone. Still, it's worth considering paying a little extra to upgrade to the Club Lounge Level, where there's free Wi-Fi and snacks and drinks all day. Among the hotel's major draws are the rooftop pool and bar, Wolfgang Puck's WP24 restaurant (*see p115*) and the white, futuristic-feel spa, where all treatments kick off with a glass of champagne. *Photo p183. Bar. Business centre. Concierge. Gym. Internet (wireless $12.95). Parking ($38). Pool. Restaurant. Room service. Spa. TV (DVDs & pay movies).*

Other locations 4375 Admiralty Way, Marina del Rey, CA 90292 (1-310 823 1700).
▶ *Within the same massive building is the 878-room JW Marriott (1-888 832 9136, www. marriott.com), a slightly cheaper alternative with its own pool, plus eating and drinking options that include a coffee bar, cocktail lounge, wine bar, restaurant and pool bar.*

Moderate

Millennium Biltmore
506 S Grand Avenue, at W 5th Street, Los Angeles, CA 90071 (1-800 245 8673, 1-213 624 1011, www.thebiltmore.com). Metro Pershing Square/bus 14, 37, 70, 71, 76, 78, 79, 96/I-110, exit 6th Street east. **Rates** $159-$375. **Rooms** 683. **Credit** AmEx, DC, Disc, MC, V. **Map** p315 B3 ⓬

Built in 1923, the Biltmore retains the Italian-Spanish renaissance elegance that once enticed such dignitaries as Winston Churchill and JFK. The ground level is striking, one gorgeous room after another peeling off the exquisite lobby (where afternoon tea is served Wednesday through Sunday); a number of them, such as the Crystal Ballroom and the Gold Room, are available only for private hire, but if there's no event being staged and you ask nicely at reception, someone will show you around. Next to such extravagance, the rooms can hardly compete, but they're comfortable in an old-fashioned way. *Bars (3). Business centre. Concierge. Gym. Internet ($9.95 high-speed & wireless). Parking ($40). Pool (indoor). Restaurants (3). Room service. TV: pay movies.*

Omni Los Angeles
California Plaza, 251 S Olive Street, between W 2nd & W 3rd Streets, Los Angeles, CA 90012 (1-800 843 6664, 1-213 617 3300, www.omni hotels.com). Metro Civic Centre/bus 16, 18, 55, 62/I-110, exit 4th Street east. **Rates** $159-$329. **Rooms** 453. **Credit** AmEx, DC, Disc, MC, V. **Map** p315 C2 ⓮

Located close to Downtown's growing cultural district, the Omni offers theatre and concert packages for those wanting to come here and catch a show or attend a party. However, this is chiefly a business hotel, and an efficient one. Rooms are comfy, and some have views over Bunker Hill; 'club level' guests get free breakfasts and cocktails. Other amenities include a smallish pool and a largeish exercise room. *Bar. Business centre. Concierge. Gym. Internet ($9.95 wireless & high-speed). Parking ($40). Pool. Restaurants (2). Room service. Spa. TV: pay movies.*

Standard Downtown
550 S Flower Street, between W 5th & W 6th Street, Los Angeles, CA 90071 (1-213 892 8080, www.standardhotels.com). Metro 7th Street-Metro Center/bus 16, 18, 55, 62/I-110, exit 6th Street

CONSUME

Hotel Wilshire. *See p180.*

east. **Rates** $155-$368. **Rooms** 207. **Credit** AmEx, DC, Disc, MC, V. **Map** p315 B3 ⑮

The Downtown version of the Sunset Strip shag pad pokes fun at jet-setting '60s bachelors, with the lobby setting the tone. Swinger-style rooms come equipped with platform beds, tubs for two and peek-a-boo showers. Complete with DJs, vibrating waterbeds and views, the rooftop pool bar (*see p128*) can be a tough ticket on weekends for non-guests; you'd do as well to hang out in the ground-level bar. In case you're wondering about the artefacts in the lobby, the hotel was once the HQ of Superior Oil.

Bars (3). Business centre. Concierge. Gym. Internet (free wireless). Parking ($33). Pool. Restaurant. Room service. Smoking rooms. TV: DVD & pay movies.

Other locations Standard Hollywood, 8300 W Sunset Boulevard, West Hollywood, CA 90069 (1-323 650 9090).

Budget

Hotel Figueroa

939 S Figueroa Street, between W 9th Street & W Olympic Boulevard, Los Angeles, CA 90015 (1-800 421 9092, 1-213 627 8971, www.figueroa hotel.com). Metro 7th Street-Metro Center/bus 16, 18, 55, 62/I-110, exit 9th Street east. **Rates** $148-$184. **Rooms** 285. **Credit** AmEx, DC, MC, V. **Map** p315 B4 ⑯

This striking hotel near L.A. LIVE is a dramatic mix of Morocco and Mexico, and oozes the kind of charisma after which boutique hotel designers flail but so often fail to achieve. Built in 1925 as a YWCA, the Figueroa is now more exotic, but it's still an absolute bargain. The hotel's airy lobby is a pot-pourri of Moroccan chandeliers, huge cacti and woven rugs; towards the back, there's a popular bar and a lovely pool area that's at its atmospheric best after dark. The rooms, which vary in size, are done out in funky casbah chic with Mexican-tiled bathrooms. Mod cons are few and far between, but they're not really the point. *Bar. Internet ($5 wireless). Parking ($12). Pool. Restaurant. TV.*

The Valleys

SAN FERNANDO VALLEY
Budget

★ Tangerine Hotel

3901 W Riverside Drive, at N Kenwood Street, Burbank, CA 91505 (1-877 843 1121, 1-818 843 1121, www.tangerinehotel.com). Bus 155, 222/Hwy 134, exit Buena Vista Street. **Rates** $129-$169. **Rooms** 31. **Credit** AmEx, Disc, MC.

Burbank may not be the most obvious choice of hotel location, but if visiting Warner Bros, NBC Studios or Universal Studios are on your agenda, this revamped former nondescript motel is hard to beat. You won't find a spa on site – or restaurant or bar, for that matter – but you will find comfortable beds, free Wi-Fi, 32in LCD TVs, iPod docking stations, fridges and nice touches such as Crabtree & Evelyn toiletries. There's also a pool and complimentary breakfast in the form of hot drinks and pastries from the excellent Porto's bakery. As the tagline says, 'Tangerine is the independent alternative you've been looking for' – and we couldn't agree more. *Photo p184.*
Internet (free wireless). Parking (free). Pool. TV.

SAN GABRIEL VALLEY
Expensive

★ Langham Huntington

1401 S Oak Knoll Avenue, at Wentworth Avenue, Pasadena, CA 91106 (1-877 499 7161, 1-626 568 3900, http://pasadena.langhamhotels.com). I-110, exit Glenarm Street east. **Rates** $249-$4,700. **Rooms** 380. **Credit** AmEx, DC, Disc, MC, V.

Formerly a Ritz-Carlton, this landmark hotel changed hands in 2008. The Langham group has thankfully preserved the heritage of the elegant 100-plus-year-old property, and invested millions of dollars in the renovation of the cottages, dining room, bar and spa. The dining room is now the Royce, serving New American cuisine; the bar has been rechris-

tened the Tap Room (*see p130*), pouring well-crafted cocktails; and the spa now offers treatments based on traditional Chinese medicine, as well as more standard fare. Swanky and historic.
Bar. Business centre. Concierge. Gym. Internet (free wireless & high-speed). Parking ($25). Pools (2). Restaurants (2). Room service. Spa. TV: DVD & pay movies.

Heading South

MANHATTAN BEACH
Moderate

★ Shade
1221 N Valley Drive, at Manhattan Beach Boulevard, Manhattan Beach, CA 90266 (1-310 546 4995, www.shadehotel.com). Bus 126/I-405, exit Manhattan Beach Boulevard. **Rates** $225-$425. **Rooms** 38. **Credit** AmEx, DC, Disc, MC, V.
This sparkling property hasn't been solely responsible for the regeneration of Manhattan Beach, but its influence has been huge. It's a small place but pretty perfectly formed: slick yet approachable, stylish yet not without a sense of humour. The 38 guest rooms make great use of the space: multi-purpose tables can be rolled back and forth over the beds for breakfast or for use as a desk, while all rooms have vast spa-baths, DVD players and colour-adjustable lighting. Downstairs is a big central courtyard and the slick Zinc lounge; upstairs is the handsome Skydeck, complete with a bijou pool. There's no gym, but guests get complimentary passes to the nearby branch of Equinox and free use of the hotel's beach cruiser bikes. Rates include continental breakfast too. An impressive spot.

Bar. Business centre. Concierge. Internet (free wireless). Parking ($20). Pool. Restaurant. Room service. TV: DVD.
▶ *Further south of Manhattan Beach, on the Palos Verdes peninsula, the luxurious Terranea Resort (100 Terranea Way, CA 90275, 1-310 265 2800, www.terranea.com) overlooks the Pacific and has a top-notch golf course and spa.*

LONG BEACH
Moderate

★ Queen Mary
1126 Queens Highway, Long Beach, CA 90802 (1-877 342 0742, 1-562 435 3511, www.queen mary.com). Metro Transit Mall then bus or taxi/ I-405, then I-710 south. **Rates** $119-$400. **Rooms** 314. **Credit** AmEx, DC, Disc, MC, V.
This grand ocean liner hasn't sailed since the 1960s; these days, it multitasks as a tourist attraction (*see p88*), an eating and drinking spot (the bar is an art deco glory) and, of course, a hotel. Unsurprisingly, given the boat's age (it was built in 1936), guest cabins are modest in size, but as of a sensitive ship-wide update a few years ago, they were given a makeover and now feature mod cons such as iPod docking stations and flat-screen TVs. Above all, they're handsome and well maintained. An intriguing novelty.
Bar. Business centre. Concierge. Gym. Internet ($9.95 wireless & high-speed). Parking ($15). Restaurants (4). Room service. Spa. TV: pay movies.

ORANGE COUNTY

Other good OC options include the funky **Shorebreak Hotel** in Huntington Beach (500 Pacific Coast Highway, CA 92648, 1-714 861 4470, www.shorebreakhotel.com) and, for

CONSUME

Ritz-Carlton, Los Angeles. *See p181.*

Tangerine Hotel. *See p182.*

those with limitless budgets, the über-luxurious **Resort at Pelican Hill** (22701 Pelican Hill Road South, Newport Coast, CA 92657, 1-949 467 6800, www.pelicanhill.com).

Expensive

Disney's Grand Californian Hotel & Spa

1600 S Disneyland Drive, between Ball Road & Katella Avenue, Anaheim, CA 92802 (1-714 635 2300, http://disneyland.disney.go.com/hotels). I-5, exit Disneyland Drive south. **Rooms** 745. **Credit** AmEx, DC, Disc, MC, V.

This Disney hotel aims to blur the lines between luxury and fantasy: the large property is effectively an extension to Disney's California Adventure, so much so that guests even have their own entrance to the park. Grown-ups may take to the Mandara Spa, a suitably peaceful escape from the theme-park chaos mere yards away; kids, on the other hand, will probably prefer the slides in the Redwood Pool or the activities in Pinocchio's Workshop. A getaway for children and their parents, albeit a pricey one.

Bar. Business centre. Concierge. Gym. Internet (free high-speed). Parking ($17). Pools (3). Restaurants (3). Room service. TV: DVD.

★ Montage Laguna Beach

30801 South Coast Highway, Laguna Beach, CA 92651 (1-888 715 6700, 1-949 715 6000, www.montagelagunabeach.com). I-405, exit PCH south. **Rates** $595-$995. **Rooms** 250. **Credit** AmEx, DC, Disc, MC, V.

Consuming 30 acres of land at the top of a bluff overlooking the Pacific, the Montage was designed to be a self-contained village of luxury. There are four dining and drinking venues, a massive indoor/outdoor spa and two outdoor pools, all set in immaculately landscaped grounds that overlook a beautiful stretch of beach. Accommodation ranges from spacious doubles to a vast suite; all include floor-to-ceiling windows

with views of the Pacific. Among the other draws are the delightful Spa Montage and Studio, the elegant bluff-top restaurant serving California-French cuisine.

Bars (4). Business centre. Concierge. Gym. Internet ($19.95 wireless & high-speed). Parking ($30). Pools (2). Restaurants (3). Room service. Spa. TV: DVD & pay movies.

★ St Regis Monarch Beach

1 Monarch Beach Resort, at Niguel Road, Dana Point, CA 92629 (1-877 787 3447, 1-949 234 3200, www.stregismb.com). I-5, exit Crown Valley Parkway west. **Rates** $345-$1,075. **Rooms** 400. **Credit** AmEx, DC, Disc, MC, V.

Part of the swanky St Regis chain, this Tuscan-inspired resort is an Orange County icon. Although it's not a beachfront property, it has lovely views of the coastline, and even runs a shuttle to carry sunbathers to the sand. Still, you might not actually want to leave the property, what with the superb Spa Gaucin, the 18-hole golf course, the three outdoor pools and the upscale Stonehill Tavern restaurant (*see p117*). The daily $25 resort fee includes internet, gym and 1-800-number phone calls.

Bars (2). Business centre. Concierge. Gym. Internet (wireless & high-speed included with resort fee). Parking ($30). Pools (3). Restaurants (5). Room service. Spa. TV: DVD & pay movies.

▶ *Completing the triumvirate of luxury hotels in the area is the Ritz-Carlton, Laguna Niguel (1 Ritz-Carlton Drive, Dana Point, CA 92629, 1-949 240 2000, www.ritzcarlton.com).*

Moderate

Disneyland hotels

Disneyland Hotel *1150 W Magic Way, between Ball Road & Katella Avenue, Anaheim, CA 92802 (1-714 778 6600).* **Rates** $310-$410.
Disney's Paradise Pier Hotel *1717 Disneyland Drive, at Katella Avenue, Anaheim, CA 92802 (1-714 999 0990).* **Rates** $290-$315.
Both *1-714 956 6425, http://disneyland.disney. go.com/hotels. I-5, exit Disneyland Drive.* **Credit** AmEx, DC, Disc, MC, V.

The **Disneyland Hotel** is the original, classic property next to the Disney Downtown entrance. It's very big and very Disney. The huge pool with a water slide is great for kids. **Paradise Pier**, meanwhile, has different amenities – a rooftop pool, fitness centre – and is considerably smaller than its counterpart. However, service is as slick as you'd expect and rooms were recently remodelled with a boardwalk theme.

If you'd rather not stay so close to Disneyland, it's worth looking into Disney's 32 'Good Neighbour' hotels, dotted throughout the Anaheim area. Prices and quality vary, but there are many reputable chains among the options. If you'd prefer a hotel with its own identity, consider the **Candy Cane Inn** (1747 S Harbor Boulevard, Anaheim, 1-714 774 5284, www.candycaneinn.net), handily close to the parks.

Praising the Bar

Our favourite hotel bars, from beachside Santa Monica to gritty Downtown.

The **Hollywood Roosevelt** (*see p179*) draws its share of tourists, located as it is across from Grauman's (TCL) Chinese Theatre, right in the middle of the madness. But it has been gorgeously refurbished to its original Golden Age grandeur with soaring beamed ceilings and Mediterranean tiles around a central indoor fountain. Order a cocktail from the Library Bar – we love the whisky, basil, tomato mix that's Seriously Dangerous – and settle on a black leather couch or take it for a wander through the hotel's many nooks and crannies to stalk out a hidden corner.

Hollywood gets all the credit for creating movies, but Culver City is where most of the 'lights, camera, action' actually happened. As movie posters and memorabilia dotting the lobby of the **Culver Hotel** (*see p170*) will remind you, the historic hotel has housed countless silver screen legends since opening in 1924. Despite the dramatic outfitting – massive stone fireplace, heavy draping over arched windows– the lobby bar has a low-key, neighbourhood feel.

While the airy, bright lobby lounge at the renovated **Hotel Bel-Air** (*see p172*) is for hotel guests, plebeian visitors can head for the darker, sexier bar. Settle on the front patio or fireside (and piano side, in the evenings) in a stylish, art deco-inspired space. With Wolfgang Puck behind the drink and food menus, bar treats include caviar and schmancy, egg-topped club sandwiches, and seasonal cocktails served in crystal stemware, lest you forget where you are.

The **Figueroa** (*see p182*) is in no way fancy. And, just a block away from the overly lit drone that is the Staples Center, the Downtown hotel's bar is, in keeping with its Moroccan theme, an oasis. You wouldn't know by the wrought-iron lanterns and coloured tiles that you're standing in an old, brick-façaded YMCA. Sip a staycation cocktail as you gaze across the pool deck among flowering bougainvillea.

At **Shutters on the Beach** (*see p167*), the Living Room is all upholstered couches and antiques, the better for year-round fulfilment of a luxe, Capeside fantasy. The cocktails tend towards the light and summery – try the coconut rum Starfish Mojito or Cucumber Splash – and the small plates menu is a surf 'n' turf celebration. Call ahead to request the round table in front of the main french doors, if it's a see-and-be-seen kind of night, or drop in for sunset cocktails on the heated patio.

The main draw for civilians at the **Chateau Marmont** in West Hollywood (*see p176*) is the celeb-spotting, but whatever you do, play it cool. Act like you belong among the pretty young things who sprawl on oversized seats and couches in the lobby. Partying is encouraged here, and a what-happens-in-the-Chateau-stays-in-the-Chateau ethos prevails – though no jumping (or late-night swimming) in the pool for non-guests. The shabby chic-meets-Spanish-Gothic-revival decor pairs with nothing better than a bottle of champagne. Oh, if these walls could talk.

CONSUME

Figueroa.

Arts & Entertainment

Children

Big fun for the little people.

Although a city designed around the car might not seem an ideal place for a family holiday, LA is actually great for children. The climate and the topography help: you can spend hours on one of the many beaches or up in the mountains – or combine them in the same day. But LA's family-friendliness is also due in part to the nature of the locals, who insist on the best for their offspring.

The area's attractions are many and varied, with different neighbourhoods offering all sorts of cultural experiences. Want Johnny to hear a mariachi band? Take him to a park in East LA on a Saturday. Want him to ride horses? Head to Griffith Park. Want the true, quintessential American entertainment experience? Welcome to Disneyland.

SIGHTSEEING

Attractions & museums

Budget permitting – none is exactly a cheap day out – the various LA-area theme parks are all child-pleasers. There's **Disneyland** (*see p90*) and **Knott's Berry Farm** (*see p91*) in Orange County, and **Universal Studios** (*see p80*) and **Six Flags California** (*see p79*) in the San Fernando Valley. And if you're planning on driving to San Diego, there's **Legoland** (*see p260*), off the I-5 in Carlsbad.

Without doubt one of the best attractions for kids in LA is Noah's Ark at the **Skirball Cultural Center** (*see p43*), a brilliant display of pure imagination: three rooms transformed into a wooden ark and filled with full-sized animals made of found objects, as well as steampunk-style interactive gizmos that create the sensations of a flood.

Los Angeles had two large children's museums: Pasadena's **Kidspace Children's Museum** (*see p83*), an inside–outside learn-while-you-play environment with climbing towers and a mock bug food kitchen, and the currently closed **Children's Museum of Los Angeles** at the Hansen Dam Recreation Area in the San Fernando Valley. The museum went bankrupt in 2009 but in December 2012 the city approved an agreement to allow the **Discovery Science Center** in Santa Ana to operate the facility in its existing location; the new space is tentatively titled **Discovery Science Center**

– Los Angeles and is due to open in late 2014/early 2015. To see real bugs, as well as other educational exhibits, visit Exposition Park, home to a pair of kid-friendly museums in the shape of the **Natural History Museum of Los Angeles County** (*see p77*) and the **California Science Center** (*see p200*), which now has the added attraction in the form of the Space Shuttle Endeavour.

Animal attractions are a favourite with youngsters, and LA's no exception. The **Los Angeles Zoo** (*see p61*) and the **Star Eco Station** (*see p44*) are supplemented by a string of marine-oriented draws: the **Santa Monica Pier Aquarium** (*see p36*), the **Cabrillo Marine Aquarium** (*see p86*) in San Pedro and the **Aquarium of the Pacific** (*see p87*) in Long Beach.

Other kid-friendly diversions include the low-key but delightful **Travel Town Museum** (*see p61*) in Griffith Park and, at the other end of the scale, the touristy but fun trappings of Hollywood, including **TCL** (formerly Grauman's) **Chinese Theatre** (*see p52*), the **Hollywood Walk of Fame** (*see p50*), **Madame Tussauds** and **Ripley's Believe it or Not!** (for both, *see p52*). Also popular with youngsters are the **La Brea Tar Pits** and **Page Museum**, and the **Petersen Automotive Museum** (for both, *see p56*).

On Santa Monica Pier is **Pacific Park** (1-310 260 8744, www.pacpark.com), which boasts a rollercoaster, a big wheel, some smaller rides for little kids, amusement arcades and a carousel. There's a free concert series in summer: bring a picnic.

And for kids drawn to the stars, the **Griffith Observatory** (*see p60*), one of the premier public observatories in the world, is a must-visit.

Zimmer Children's Museum

6505 Wilshire Boulevard, at San Vicente Boulevard, Miracle Mile (1-323 761 8984, www.zimmermuseum.org). Bus 20, 217, 218, 720, 761/I-10, exit Fairfax Avenue north. **Open** 10am-5pm Tue-Fri; 12.30-5pm Sun. **Admission** $8; $5 under-18s; under-1s free. **Credit** AmEx, MC, V. **Map** p312 B4.

This socially minded Jewish institution, set within the Goldsmith Jewish Federation building, is the only Los Angeles museum dedicated to kids and families. Interactive exhibits, classes and field trips are all designed to help youngsters 'play their way to a better world'. The museum is for VIBs only (that's 'Very Important Babies' under two years old) every Wednesday from 9am until 10am. Kids must have an adult with them at all times. Also note: the museum closes at 4pm on Fridays in winter, and there's free parking in the (shared) visitor lot, but it fills up quickly.

OUTDOORS & NATURE
Beaches & swimming pools

On **Santa Monica Beach** (*see p35*) and **Venice Beach** (*see p39*), between Santa Monica Pier to the north and Venice Pier to the south, there's sand, sea, bike and skate paths, with cycles and in-line skates available for hire and, in Venice, a skate park (*see p242*). Near the bike path are a number of small play-parks; the largest is at the Venice Recreation Center. And there are even regular surf camps for over-sevens at Santa Monica Beach and, further south, at **El Segundo Beach**. For more, call 1-310 663 2479 or check www.learntosurfla.com.

If your kids want to swim but are nervous of the ocean's strong currents, big waves and cold temperatures, they might prefer to use one of LA's public swimming pools. Two of the most family-friendly are listed below; there's also the lovely pool at the **Annenberg Community Beach House** in Santa Monica, open seasonally (*see p37*).

Rose Bowl Aquatic Center

360 N Arroyo Boulevard, in Brookside Park, Pasadena (1-626 564 0330, www.rosebowl aquatics.org). Metro Memorial Park/bus 51, 52, 264, 267/Hwy 134, exit Orange Grove Boulevard/Colorado Boulevard. **Open** *Recreational/family swim* 2.30-5pm, 7.30-8.30pm Mon-Fri; 2-4.30pm Sat, Sun. **Admission** $2; $1 under-17s. **Credit** DC, MC, V.

This open-air swimming centre has two Olympic-sized pools, but also provides plenty of access for families and lessons for beginners. One adult is required to supervise each child under eight.

Santa Monica Swim Center

Santa Monica College, 2225 16th Street, at Pico Boulevard, Santa Monica (1-310 458 8700, www.smgov.net/aquatics). Bus 534, SM6, SM7/ I-10, exit Lincoln Boulevard south. **Open** 3-6.30pm Mon-Fri; 10.30am-5pm Sat, Sun. **Admission** $6.50; $2.50 under-18s; $12.50 families with 2 children & 2 adults at weekends. **Credit** DC, Disc, MC, V. **Map** p310 C4.

A clean, cheerful, brightly tiled and not overly chlorinated pair of open-air pools. One is competition size; the other is large enough for laps but shallow enough for children to enjoy. Private and group swimming lessons are available.

Parks

With its picnic areas, miles of hiking and horse-riding trails, 1920s merry-go-round and zoo, the rolling hills of **Griffith Park** (*see p59*) make a great outdoor experience for kids. That said, most of LA's parks are good for families. The best are the **Kenneth Hahn State Recreation Area** and the **Will Rogers State Historic Park** (*see p33*).

The botanical gardens at the **Huntington Library** (*see p82*) feature a lovely children's garden, containing kinetic sculptures that explore the natural elements of earth, light, air and water. Children aged two and older can walk under a rainbow in a circle of mist, vanish into a sea of billowing fog and feel sound waves moving through water in a sonic pool.

TreePeople

12601 Mulholland Drive, at Coldwater Canyon Drive, Beverly Hills (1-818 753 4600, www. treepeople.org). No bus/US 101, exit Coldwater Canyon Boulevard south. **Open** *Park* sunrise-sunset daily. **Admission** free.

This non-profit group plants and cares for native and exotic trees and the environment. The centre is located in the idyllic 45-acre Coldwater Canyon Park, a welcome break from the urban sprawl.

Playgrounds

How times have changed. LA's children no longer spend hours playing in parks that consist only of a slide, a few bars and some battered old swings. Tots today get to develop their muscles in clean and safe neighbourhood play-parks, many of which come with hanging bridges, towers, tubes, slides in multiple wave forms and, on the ground, sand or padded rubber to protect from bumps. Most of these

ARTS & ENTERTAINMENT

kids' parks are in bigger parks with football and basketball fields, and many of the better ones are in more affluent parts of town.

The best play-parks on the Westside include **Venice Beach** (at Windward Avenue), **Santa Monica Beach** (at Ocean Park Boulevard), **Roxbury Park** in Beverly Hills and the park in the **Playa Vista** development at the south end of Playa Vista Drive. However, there are plenty of others. There are good online resources for details For details on all the parks in Los Angeles County, see http://parks.la county.gov; for Santa Monica, visit www.sm gov.net/parks; and for Beverly Hills, go to www.beverlyhills.org/living/recreationparks.

RESTAURANTS & CAFÉS

While many LA restaurants accommodate children, some actively welcome them. Chinese and Mexican restaurants are often a good bet: the service is fast and there's finger food for tiny hands.

Café 50s
11623 Santa Monica Boulevard, between Barry & Federal Avenues, West LA (1-310 479 1955, www.cafe50s.com). Bus 1, 4, 11, 704, SM1, SM10/I-10, exit Bundy Drive north. **Open** 7am-midnight Mon-Thur, Sun; 7am-1am Fri, Sat. **Credit** DC, MC, V.
Kitschy dining for those weary of the Johnny Rockets chain but still craving the fun of an occasional old-fashioned burger and milkshake. Brunch is served on Saturdays and Sundays. Mini-jukeboxes sit at each table; children (and adults) eat for free if they dress in pyjamas on the last Wednesday of the month. The restaurant also holds private parties for children.
Other locations 850 N Vermont Avenue, Silver Lake (1-323 906 1955).

California Pizza Kitchen
Throughout LA (www.cpk.com).
The numerous kid-friendly branches of the California Pizza Kitchen are a favourite fallback among LA families.

Cheesecake Factory
Throughout LA (www.cheesecakefactory.com).
The eclectic and lengthy menu offers something for every tastebud. You'll find branches all over the city.

★ Farmers Market
See p107.
No restaurant in the city surpasses the energy and variety of edibles on offer at the food court at the Farmers Market at 3rd and Fairfax. While the children munch on pizza or burgers, adults can try more interesting fare – Brazilian food at the Pampas Grill (1-323 931 1928), say, or cajun cooking at the Gumbo Pot (1-323 933 0358) – before all the generations reunite for dessert at Gill's Old Fashioned Ice Cream, still there after more than 75 years (1-323 936 7986). Also here is Du-Pars, a longtime family favourite that serves hearty comfort food and ice-cream. Aside from its Farmers Market location (1-323 933 8446), it has branches in Studio City and Thousand Oaks.
▶ *For more on the Farmers Market and the neighbouring open-air, kid-friendly Grove shopping centre, see p140.*

Pitfire Pizza Company
Throughout LA (www.pitfirepizza.com).
Pitfire professes to loving kids, but it makes itself clear to parents, threatening that 'unattended children will be given multiple shots of espresso and a puppy'. It offers great pizzas, pastas and salads, and the North Hollywood branch (5211 Lankershim Boulevard) also has plenty of outside tables.

Wolfgang Puck Express
1315 Third Street Promenade, at Arizona Avenue, Santa Monica (1-310 576 4770, www.wolfgangpuck.com). Bus 20, 720, SM2, SM3, SM4, SM5, SM9/I-10, exit 4th/5th Street north. **Open** 11am-9.30pm Mon-Thur, Sun; 11am-10.30pm Fri, Sat. **Credit** AmEx, DC, Disc, MC, V. **Map** p310 A2.
Puck's top-end eateries, such as Spago (*see p103*), are by no means ideal for families. However, this rather cheaper chain is very child-friendly.

ARTS & ENTERTAINMENT

For details of what's on, check the 'Calendar' section of the Sunday *Los Angeles Times*, the *LA Weekly* and the free monthly *LA Parent*, which can be found in any location that caters for children and is also available online (http://losangeles.parenthood.com). Also useful is http://gocitykids.parentsconnect.com.

Activities

Color Me Mine
1335 4th Street, between Santa Monica Boulevard & Arizona Avenue, Santa Monica (1-310 393 0069, www.colormemine.com). Bus 20, 720, R3/

Griffith Park. *See p189.*

I-10, exit Lincoln Boulevard north. **Open** 11am-9pm Mon-Thur; 11am-10pm Fri, Sat; noon-7pm Sun. **Rates** $10/session for adults; $6/session under-10s. **Credit** AmEx, DC, Disc, MC, V. **Map** p310 A2.

For a few hours of creative fun, visit one of Color Me Mine's locations. Choose from a selection of ceramic plates, bowls, teapots or animals, which you then paint and have fired.

Other locations throughout LA.

Duff's Cakemix

8302 Melrose Avenue, at N Sweetzer Avenue, West Hollywood (1-323 650 5555, www.duffs cakemix.com). Bus 10, 48, 217, 218/I-405 exit La Cienega Boulevard south. **Open** 11am-6.30pm Mon-Thur; 11am-10pm Fri; 10am-10pm Sat; 10am-6.30pm Sun. **Credit** AmEx, MC, V. **Map** p312 B2.

If your kids are crazy for cake, head for this bakery/cake-decorating studio, the brainchild of celeb baker Duff Goldman (the star of reality show *Ace of Cakes*). Select your baked cake or cupcake, then your fillings and toppings, then get creative. There's a maximum of two people per kit; reservations are taken for parties of six kits; otherwise it's first come, first served.

Storyopolis

16740 Ventura Boulevard, between Balboa & Petit Avenues, Encino (1-818 990 7600, www.storyopolis. com). Bus 150, 236, 237, 240/US 101, exit

Hayvenhurst Avenue south. **Open** 11am-5pm Mon-Fri; 10am-5pm Sat; 11am-4pm Sun. **Credit** AmEx, DC, MC, V.

This book and toy store hosts family-friendly events including storytime sessions for babies and toddlers on Tuesday and Thursday mornings.

Bookstores & libraries

Much to the surprise of many visitors, LA is full of bibliophiles. The children's section of the **Richard J Riordan Central Library** (*see p71*) has plenty of kids' books and a strong programme of children's events. The LA region also has a number of children's booksellers that offer author and illustrator meet-and-greets, dress-up parties, crafts workshops, singalongs and story times. Listed below are some of the best-loved bookstores; check their websites for events. For **Children's Book World**, another kids' specialist, *see p142*; for **Storyopolis**, *see left*; and for **Vroman's**, which has children's events, *see p142*. For kids' fashion and toy stores, *see pp142-143*.

★ Chevalier's Books

126 N Larchmont Boulevard, between W 1st Street & Beverly Boulevard, Hancock Park (1-323 465 1334, http://chevaliersbooks.blogspot.com). Bus 14, 37/US 101, exit Melrose Avenue west. **Open** 10am-6pm Mon-Fri; 9am-6pm Sat, Sun. **Credit** AmEx, DC, MC, V. **Map** p313 B4.

San Marino Toy & Book Shoppe

2424 Huntington Drive, between San Marino & Del Mar Avenues, San Marino (1-626 309 0222, www.toysandbooks.com). Bus 79/I-110, exit Sierra Madre Boulevard. **Open** 10am-6pm Mon-Sat; 11am-4pm Sun. **Credit** DC, Disc, MC, V.

Music & theatre

On weekdays during July and August, the LA Philharmonic lays on performances and workshops for under-tens in a series called **Summer Sounds at the Hollywood Bowl** (*see p228*). During autumn, winter and spring, take the young 'uns to a youth concert by the LA Philharmonic at the marvellous **Walt Disney Concert Hall** (*see p229*).

During long car journeys, tune in to **KDIS** (1110 AM), Disney's 24-hour radio station.

★ Bob Baker Marionette Theater

1345 W 1st Street, at Glendale Boulevard, Echo Park (1-213 250 9995, www.bobbaker marionettes.com). Bus 37/I-110, exit 3rd Street west. **Open** *Box office* 9am-2pm Tue-Fri. *Shows* 10.30am Tue-Fri; 2.30pm Sat, Sun. **Tickets** $20; free under-2s. **Credit** AmEx, Disc, MC, V. **Map** p314 D6.

The entertainment that most kids enjoy today is of the spoon-fed variety, passed through a sieve to remove any taint of weirdness. LA's tykes, then, are lucky to have the merry band of puppeteers led by Bob Baker, who's been staging original shows in his own theatre since 1961. During a typical performance, as many as 100 characters might caper under the able hands of black-clad young artists trained

Bob Baker Marionette Theater.

INSIDE TRACK GET MOVING

For more child-friendly sporting activities, from bowling to tennis to whale-watching, *see pp237-245.*

by the master. There's no stage: grown-ups get folding chairs while kids sit in a big U-shape on a rug. The entertainment ends with a complimentary cup of ice-cream in the attached Party Room. Sadly, mounting financial debts are an ongoing problem, so catch a show while you can (booking is essential).

Geffen Playhouse

10886 Le Conte Avenue, between Tiverton Avenue & Westwood Boulevard, Westwood (1-310 208 5454, www.geffenplayhouse.com). »Bus 1, 2, 8, 11, 233, 702, 761, C6/I-405, exit Wilshire Boulevard east. **Box office** 10am-6pm Mon-Fri; noon-6pm Sat, Sun. **Tickets** $20. **Credit** AmEx, DC, Disc, MC, V.

On certain Saturday mornings, the Geffen hosts Story Pirates, a programme for children offering performances by a troupe that reads and acts out the stories written by elementary students.

Hollywood Bowl

See p228.

One of the most gorgeous attractions in LA, the Bowl runs a programme of children's concerts, plus an outdoor arts studio that's held each weekday morning over a six-week span in July and August. For tickets and information, call 1-323 850 2000.

★ Pasadena Symphony Musical Circus

Americana at Brand, 889 Americana Way, between Central Avenue & Grand Boulevard, Glendale (Pasadena Symphony 1-626 793 7172, www.pasadenasymphony-pops.org). Bus 92, 180, 181, 183, 201/I-5, exit Colorado Street east. **Open** some Sun; call or check online. **Tickets** free.

Musicians and teachers help kids aged three to eight discover the joy of music-making at these periodic Sunday afternoon sessions. After a musical petting zoo (2pm), where children get a close-up look at various instruments, there's a family concert (3pm).

BABYSITTERS

Babysitters Guild

1-310 837 1800. **Open** *Office* 10am-4.30pm Mon-Fri. **No credit cards.**

LA's largest and oldest babysitting service serves hotels all over the city for $13-$19/hr plus $7 flat travel fee. There's a four-hour daily minimum except on Saturdays, when it's five hours. Staff suggest at least 24 hours' notice, but they'll provide same-day service if they can

ARTS & ENTERTAINMENT

Film & TV

And… Action!

Below the gleaming typographic splendour of the Hollywood sign stretches the picture-postcard landscape of greater Los Angeles, all palm tree s, white beaches and scattered skylines. The world's most photographed megalopolis, LA thrives on the snap-snap fuss that it's attracted ever since it took the movie industry under its wing a century ago. Unfortunately, recent mainstream cinema has been loaded with sequels, remakes and lacklustre rip-offs, while television programming seems to consist almost entirely of unwatchable reality drivel and cutesy sitcoms such as the derivative *New Girl* (starring Zooey Deschanel), a modern version of *Three's Company*, itself based on the UK's *Man About the House*, which aired four decades ago. Maybe, just maybe, someone will think up a new plot one day.

Film

MOVIE THEATRES

Cinemas are everywhere in Los Angeles, their varied architecture, artistic slants and client bases approximating *la ciudad*'s multilingual diversity. From Bruckheimer blockbusters to fancies of yesteryear, Bauhaus abstracts to Iranian comedies, all cinematic life is here, assuming you know where to look.

For weekly listings and reviews, check the film section of the Time Out LA website (www.timeout.com/los-angeles/film); it also has links to buy tickets via Fandango (www.fandango.com). For more reviews, go to the Film Radar website (www.filmradar.com), which provides a special focus on the arthouse and repertory movie scenes.

PREMIERES & PREVIEWS

Woody Allen once wisecracked that the only cultural advantage to Los Angeles is that you're able to make a right turn on a red light. Still, moviegoers have at least one other perk: the chance to see new films before anybody else. In areas that attract heavy foot traffic (the Hollywood Walk of Fame, Santa Monica's Third Street Promenade, Universal CityWalk), studio recruiters tempt non-industry passers-by into attending test-the-market preview screenings, at which the latest studio movies are screened well in advance of their release.

Tickets are free; payback comes with the expectation that attendees pass comment on what they've just seen by filling out a lengthy form afterwards.

Multiplexes

Most of Los Angeles' ultra-modern cineplexes are located in consumer paradises: malls, shopping centres and the like. Five of the most popular are detailed below.

INSIDE TRACK PIC YOUR SEAT

Bum-numbing seats and rustling bags of popcorn just not doing it for you any more? **iPic Theaters**, a national mini-chain with a location at the One Colorado outdoor mall in Pasadena (42 Miller Alley, www.ipictheaters.com) and a new one opening in Westwood in summer 2013, offers the latest movies but with a backdrop of plush reclining seats and a menu that includes chicken satay and house-made doughnuts. You pay more, of course, but for your $29 (less if you join the membership programme) you get to book your seat in advance and turn up a few minutes before the start of the show. Extra pillows and blankets? They're on their way.

Pacific's the Grove Stadium 14

AMC Century 15

Westfield Century City, 10250 Santa Monica Boulevard, between Century Park W & Avenue of the Stars, Century City (1-310 277 2262, www. amctheatres.com/CenturyCity). Bus 4, 16, 28, 316, 704, 728/I-405, exit Santa Monica Boulevard east. **Screens** 15. **Tickets** $13.75; $7-$11.75 discounts. $4 extra for 3D, $5-$6 extra for IMAX. **Credit** AmEx, DC, Disc, MC, V. **Map** p311 B4.

AMC CityWalk Stadium 19 with IMAX

Universal CityWalk, 100 Universal City Plaza, Universal City (1-818 508 0711, www.amc theatres.com/Citywalk). Metro Universal City/Studio City/bus 150, 156, 224, 240, 750/US 101, exit Universal Center Drive. **Screens** 19. **Tickets** $12.50; $6-$10.50 discounts. **Credit** AmEx, DC, Disc, MC, V.

Landmark

10850 W Pico Boulevard, at Westwood Boulevard, Westwood (1-310 470 0492, www.landmark theatres.com). Bus C3, SM4, SM7, SM8, SM12, SM13/I-10, exit Overland Avenue north. **Screens** 12. **Tickets** $13; $10 discounts; $16 3D. **Credit** AmEx, DC, MC, V. **Map** p311 A5.

Pacific's the Grove Stadium 14

The Grove, 6301 W 3rd Street, between N Fairfax Avenue & N Gardner Street, Fairfax District (1-323 692 0829, www.pacifictheatres.com). Bus 16, 217, 218, 318, 780, LDHWI/I-10, exit Fairfax Avenue north. **Screens** 14. **Tickets** $10.50-$13.75; $10.50-$11.75 discounts. **Credit** AmEx, DC, MC, V. **Map** p312 C3.

Regal Cinemas

L.A. LIVE, 1000 W Olympic Boulevard, at Georgia Street, Downtown (1-213 763 6070, *www.regmovies.com). Metro Pico/bus 28, 30, 81, 330, 442, 460/I-110, exit Olympic Boulevard east.* **Screens** 14. **Tickets** Mon-Thur $13.75; $11.75 discounts; Fri-Sun $14; $11.75 discounts; $4 extra for 3D. **Credit** AmEx, DC, Disc, MC, V. **Map** p315 A4.

Classic picturehouses

★ ArcLight Hollywood

6360 W Sunset Boulevard, between Ivar Avenue & Vine Street, Hollywood (1-323 464 1478, www. arclightcinemas.com). Bus 2, 180, 181, 210, 212, 217, 222, 310, 780, LDH, LDHWI/US 101, exit Vine Street south. **Screens** 15. **Tickets** $14-$16; $17-$19.50 3D. **Credit** AmEx, DC, MC, V. **Map** p313 B2.

A local favourite, the ArcLight offers comfortable seats, state-of-the-art sight and sound, fantastic snack bars and, for some extra Dionysian indulgence, an in-house café-bar. The programming is an astute mix of first-run flicks, indies, foreign fare and premières; and, unusually for Los Angeles, alcohol is allowed in some screenings. It's the most appealing modern multiplex in the city, but it nevertheless falls under the 'Classic' section for the Cinerama Dome, a fabulous and unique domed movie theatre that opened in 1963. Note that parking is usually a nightmare in this area: allow plenty of time to find a space. *Photo p198.*

Regency Bruin

948 Broxton Avenue, at Weyburn Avenue, Westwood (1-310 208 8998, www.regency movies.com). Bus 20, 233, 302, 761, SM1, SM2, SM3, SM6, SM8, SM11, SM12/ I-405, exit Wilshire Boulevard east. **Screens** 1. **Tickets** $11.50; $8-$9.50 discounts; $2.50 extra for 3D. **Credit** AmEx, DC, Disc, MC, V.

Built in 1937, this streamline moderne cinema draws sometimes-rowdy college crowds from nearby UCLA, who gather in front of its single screen to take in the latest mainstream favourites. Westwood is also home to the Regency Village Theater (961 Broxton Avenue, 1-310 208 5576), another single-screen, 1930s-vintage operation that seats 1,400.

TCL Chinese Theatre

6925 Hollywood Boulevard, between N Orange Drive & N McCadden Place, Hollywood (1-323 461 3331, www.tclchinesetheatres.com). Metro Hollywood-Highland/bus 212, 217, 222, 312, 780/US 101, exit Highland Avenue south. **Screens** 1. **Tickets** $13.75-$16. **Credit** AmEx, Disc, DC, MC, V. **Map** p313 A1.
In terms of both variety and technology, there are better options in Hollywood. However, the famous hand- and footprints outside this iconic theatre

(see p52) – formerly known as Grauman's Chinese Theatre – only enhance the experience, and the innumerable galas that pass beneath its renowned pagoda add to its star quality. A more modern six-screen multiplex (same website and phone number) adjoins it in the Hollywood & Highland mall.

Arthouse & independent

You should also find arthouse and independent movies at some of the cinemas mentioned above, among them the **Landmark** and the **ArcLight Hollywood**.

Laemmle's Monica 4-plex

1332 2nd Street, at Santa Monica Boulevard, Santa Monica (1-310 394 9744, www.laemmle. com). Bus 4, 33, 704/I-10 exit 4th Street. **Screens** 4. **Tickets** $11; $8 discounts. **Credit** AmEx, DC, MC, V. **Map** p310 A3.

Festivals Film

A round-up of LA movie marathons.

Pan African Film & Arts Festival
1-310 337 4737, www.paff.org. **Date** Feb.
A slate of African and African American films, many addressing issues of cultural and racial tolerance. The ten-day festival also features live music, poetry and performance art and Artfest, a show that exhibits the work of more than 100 established and emerging artists and craftspeople.

Los Angeles Asian Pacific Film Festival
1-213 680 4462, www.vconline.org/festival. **Date** May.
A variety of Asian and Asian American films, screened in several venues in West Hollywood and Little Tokyo.

Last Remaining Seats
1-213 623 2489, www.laconservancy.org. **Date** May/June.
The LA Conservancy offers a wonderful time-machine trip by reopening Downtown's grand old movie palaces for one-night-only screenings of classic films.

Film Independent's Los Angeles Film Festival
1-866 345 6337, www.lafilmfest.com. **Date** June.
With 200-plus features, shorts and music videos, this prestigious ten-day festival at various Downtown venues is cardio cinema.

Downtown Film Festival
www.dffla.com. **Date** July.
Celebrates the resurgence of Downtown LA across a wide variety of venues.

Outfest
1-213 480 7088, www.outfest.org. **Date** July/Aug.
A ten-day festival of gay and lesbian shorts and features, spread across ten venues dotted around LA.

Los Angeles Latino International Film Festival
1-323 446 2770, www.latinofilm.org. **Date** Aug.
Mexican and Latin American filmmakers come to Hollywood to promote their work.

Los Angeles International Short Film Festival
1-818 508 0800, www.lashortsfest.com. **Date** Sept.
The world's largest shorts festival crams 400 entries into a typically dense programme.

AFI Los Angeles International Film Festival
1-866 234 3378, www.afi.com/afifest. **Date** Nov.
This ten-day festival shows some 130 films from 40 countries, along with special events.

While the Sunset location is now a Sundance cinema (*see p197*), the Laemmle group still operates this Santa Monica outpost of the family-run arthouse chain, which has premières and screenings, as well as the Royal (11523 Santa Monica Boulevard, West LA, 1-310 478 0401) and the Music Hall 3 (9036 Wilshire Boulevard, Beverly Hills, 1-310 274 6860).

★ **Nuart Theatre**
11272 Santa Monica Boulevard, at Sawtelle Boulevard, West LA (1-310 473 8530, www. landmarktheatres.com). Bus SM1, SM4/I-405, exit Santa Monica Boulevard west. **Screens** 1. **Tickets** $10.50; $8.50 discounts. **Credit** AmEx, DC, MC, V. Exclusive engagements of independent movies, foreign flicks, arthouse curios and restored classics

Caught on Camera

Hollywood, the biggest movie star of all.

On 24 October 1907, a Chicago judge ruled that 'Colonel' William N Selig's movie equipment, acquired on the black market, infringed Edison Motion Picture patents. Banned from filming in Illinois, Selig read an LA Chamber of Commerce brochure promising '350 days a year of sunshine!', and duly sent Francis Boggs to film a scene for his **The Count of Monte Cristo**.

Boggs liked LA so much that he never left. His film **In the Sultan's Power** (1909), shot on a vacant Downtown lot (at 751 S Olive Street, now a parking garage), was the first dramatic film shot wholly in the city, and kicked off LA's 100-year reign as the most filmed town on earth. Since his arrival, the city has been captured in countless movies, playing itself with various degrees of enthusiasm and commitment in everything from surf flicks (John Milius's 1978 flick **Big Wednesday**) to movies about car theft (the original 1974 version of **Gone in 60 Seconds**). Here are some of the best.

CRIME AND PUNISHMENT
Just as LA gave birth to noir literature, so Hollywood took up the mantle of filming it. **Double Indemnity** (1944), **Mildred Pierce** (1945) and **The Postman Always Rings Twice** (1946, remade 1981) are steamy tales of hapless schlubs done in by femme fatales. Stephen Frears' rough-and-tumble **The Grifters** (1990) ploughs a similar furrow. And then there are the escapades of Chandler's Philip Marlowe: played by Hollywood smoothie Dick Powell in **Farewell, My Lovely** (1944), urbane tough guy Humphrey Bogart in **The Big Sleep** (1946), restrained grump James Garner in **Marlowe** (1969), crumpled mumbler Elliot Gould in **The Long Goodbye** (1973) and ageing battler Robert Mitchum in another version of **Farewell, My Lovely** (1975).

Other crime films have used LA in opaque ways. Take **DOA** (1949, dismally remade in 1988), whose LA is edgy and artless, or **Heat** (1995) and **Collateral** (2004), Michael Mann's sumptuous travelogues; contrast them with **Memento** (2000), a dizzying puzzle of revenge, and **Training Day** (2001), which offers a vivid tour that hits East LA, Downtown, Echo Park and South Central in a single day. David Lynch demonstrated that LA noir needn't be confined to the detective genre in **Mulholland Dr.** (2001), arguably the best film about LA's incestuous relationship to the Hollywood fantasy machine. And then, of course, there are the crooks and ninnies in the movies of Quentin Tarantino, with the malls, diners and warehouses of Inglewood, Toluca Lake and Torrance taking centre stage in **Reservoir Dogs** (1992) and **Pulp Fiction** (1994).

However, two crime films really stand from the pack. Roman Polanski's creepy **Chinatown** (1974) follows the tough, well-meaning but ultimately ineffectual PI Jake Gittes (Jack Nicholson) through seedy, sun-kissed pre-war LA as he tries to unravel the mystery of a phoney drought, a doomed mystery woman and her monstrous tycoon father. **L.A. Confidential** (1997), based on the James Ellroy novel, is a more stylised but no less fascinating re-creation of the seedy city in the 1950s. Its release imbued the city itself with a new iconography

WEALTH AND POVERTY
Filmmakers have had plenty of fun detailing the lifestyles of LA's rich and famous. Paul Bartel essays the perversions of the idle rich in **Scenes from the Class Struggle in Beverly Hills** (1989); Hal Ashby's **Shampoo** (1975) follows the romantic travails of a bed-hopping Hollywood hair stylist played by (who else?) Warren Beatty; and **Clueless** (1995) paints a satirical yet winning portrait of LA rich kids and their pampered lives. *Clueless*, indeed, could hardly provide a greater contrast to **Rebel**

ARTS & ENTERTAINMENT

fill the calendar at this long-standing operation. There are midnight screenings on Fridays and Saturdays, with the latter always dedicated to the *Rocky Horror Picture Show*. Just nearby stands CineFile Video (11280 Santa Monica Boulevard, 1-310 312 8836, www.cinefilevideo.com), a cult rental store that specialises in rare, unusual and hard-to-find films.

Sundance Sunset Cinemas

8000 W Sunset Boulevard, at N Crescent Heights Boulevard, West Hollywood (1-323 654 2217, www. sundancecinemas.com). Bus 2, 217, 302/I-10, exit Fairfax Avenue north. **Screens** 5. **Admission** $11-$12; $10 discounts. **Credit** DC, MC, V. **Map** p312 C1.
After a $2 million renovation, the former Laemmle Sunset 5 space reopened in late 2012 as a glitzy new

Without a Cause (1955), shot in part at the Griffith Observatory.

However, filmmakers have also revelled in the city's seedy and deprived subcultures, amplifying the voices of characters whose cries are largely unheard in day-to-day LA. **Barfly** (1987) finds Mickey Rourke mumbling through a part-autobiographical Charles Bukowski script set in LA's fleabag hotels and odiferous dive bars. In John Cassavetes' **The Killing of a Chinese Bookie** (1976), a strip club provides a home for an extended family of lonely dancers. And **Permanent Midnight** (1998) chronicles the heroin addiction of former TV writer Jerry Stahl (Ben Stiller).

Although Charles Burnett's **Killer of Sheep** (1977) was set in Watts, it was another 15 years before South Central LA's poverty-wrecked black communities found a cinematic focus. John Singleton's **Boyz N the Hood** (1991) launched a trend of movies that indicted, glorified and poked fun at black LA culture. The Hughes Brothers' quite terrifying **Menace II Society** (1993) and Carl Franklin's adaptation of Walter Mosley's **Devil in a Blue Dress** (1995) provide alternative perspectives on LA's black communities.

FILM AND FAME

Dreams of stardom have been tackled ad nauseam, from **Sullivan's Travels** (1941) via **A Star Is Born** (1937, remade in 1954 and 1976) through to the more modern likes of **Postcards from the Edge** (1990), **Guilty by Suspicion** (1991), **Barton Fink** (1991), **The Player** (1992), **Swimming with Sharks** (1994) and **Get Shorty** (1995). Other movies, though, have imbued the subject with a little more pathos. Tim Burton's **Ed Wood** (1994) links the laughable films of 'the worst director of all time' with the underbelly of Hollywood's has-beens, wannabes and never-weres. Paul Thomas Anderson's **Boogie Nights**

(1997) journeys into the heart of the San Fernando Valley's fabled porn industry, while Paul Schrader's **Auto Focus** (2002) tackles the sex addiction that led to the downfall of *Hogan's Heroes* star Bob Crane. The gothic vivisection of Hollywood's self-loathing detailed by Billy Wilder in **Sunset Boulevard** (1950) is still horrifying; Edgar G Ulmer's **Detour** (1945) plays like its cancerous brother. And then, of course, there's **Singin' in the Rain** (1952), about stumbling into the Sound Era.

SPRAWL AND DECAY

LA has had plenty of affection smothered on to it by its native chroniclers. **LA Story** (1991) is Steve Martin's Left Coast equivalent of Woody Allen's *Manhattan*; **Swingers** (1996) captures the rise of cocktail culture; and in the sleek, silky form of **Pretty Woman** (1990), LA found its *Pygmalion*. Others have appeared ambivalent but ultimately affectionate: witness Robert Altman's **Short Cuts** (1993), Alan Rudolph's earlier **Welcome to LA** (1976) and even, perhaps, Paul Thomas Anderson's **Magnolia** (1999).

However, a few directors have provided a fearsome counterpoint to their affections, depicting the city as smog-choked, monstrous and alienating. As LA entered the 1990s with floods, fires, earthquakes and riots, in film it became almost synonymous with urban fear and paranoia. The New Agey **Grand Canyon** (1991) essays pre-Rodney King white malaise at the turn of the decade; Todd Haynes' **Safe** (1995) focuses on a rich LA wife who believes she's being poisoned by the modern world; and **Crash** (2004) updates the city's multi-ethnic tensions post-9/11. Still, the last word on LA's sprawl belongs to **Falling Down** (1993), which tracks an Angry White Man (Michael Douglas) as he cuts a violent swathe from East LA to Venice Beach after getting stuck in rush-hour gridlock. Don't follow his lead.

ARTS & ENTERTAINMENT

ArcLight Hollywood. *See p194.*

682-seat theatre, complete with refurbed lobby, lounge, art gallery and patio. Check the website for its schedule of independent screenings, lectures and special series. The open-air 8000 Sunset mall is also home to a Burke Williams spa, CB2 home furnishings store and several restaurants, including Veggie Grill.

Repertory & experimental

Raging against wholesale homogenous modernity, Los Angeles' stand-alone repertory cinemas are eureka-evoking resources. In addition to the movie houses detailed below, LA's museums also contribute to the scene: the **Museum of Contemporary Art** (*see p71*) concentrates on avant-garde and experimental offerings; while **LACMA** (*see p55*) programmes enlightened retrospectives and, on Tuesday lunchtimes, Hollywood classics for $4 a ticket.

★ American Cinematheque

Egyptian Theatre *6712 Hollywood Boulevard, between N Highland & N Las Palmas Avenues, Hollywood. Metro Hollywood-Highland/bus 156, 212, 217, 222, 312, 780/US 101, exit Highland Avenue south.* **Map** p313 A1.
Aero Theatre *1328 Montana Avenue, at 14th Street, Santa Monica. Bus SM3, 41/I-10, exit Lincoln Boulevard north.* **Map** p310 B2.
Both *1-323 466 3456, www.american cinematheque.com.* **Screens** 1. **Tickets** $11; $9 discounts. **Credit** AmEx, DC, MC, V.
Its design inspired by King Tutankhamun's sepulchre, the Egyptian Theatre edges its Santa Monica counterpart for sheer dramatic majesty. However, the main attraction at both venues is still the programme: the not-for-profit American Cinematheque delivers a wide range of excellent themed mini-festivals and one-off Q&As with legendary figures. On Sunday nights at the Egyptian Theatre, the LA Filmforum screens experimental films and video art.

Billy Wilder Theatre

Hammer Museum, 10899 Wilshire Boulevard, at Westwood Boulevard, Westwood (1-310 206 8013, www.cinema.ucla.edu). Bus 11, 12, 20, 720, 761, SM1, SM2, SM3, SM6, SM8/I-405, exit Wilshire Boulevard east. **Screens** 1. **Tickets** $9-$10; free-$8 discounts. **Credit** AmEx, DC, MC, V. **Map** p311 A4.
The Hammer Museum's intimate, state-of-the-art spot boasts 1970s game-show decor and 295 pink stadium-style seats. Programming consists of screenings tied to the museum's exhibition schedule and the excellent UCLA Film & Television Archive.

Cinefamily at the Silent Movie Theatre

611 N Fairfax Avenue, at Clinton Street, Fairfax District (1-323 655 2520, www.cinefamily.org). Bus 10, 48, 217, 218, 780, LDHWI/I-10, exit

Essential LA Films

The City of Angels in six celluloid gems.

CHINATOWN
dir Roman Polanski, 1974
This is as ingenious as screenwriting gets: Robert Towne's 1930s detective tale seamlessly blends glamour and action with then-current paranoia, when 'follow the money' was the phrase on everyone's lips. Here, it's 'follow the water' – diverted from orange groves in the Valley to future suburban tracts. Based on true events, the crime is colossal; private eye Jack Nicholson is in over his head.

FALLING DOWN
dir Joel Schumacher, 1992
Stuck in a traffic jam while trying to reach his ex-wife's house for his daughter's birthday party, unemployed defence engineer William Foster (Michael Douglas) abandons his car on the baking freeway, becoming increasingly frustrated and violent as he makes his way across town, pursued by retiring cop Martin Prendergast (Robert Duvall). So relevant it could've been made yesterday.

JACKIE BROWN
dir Quentin Tarantino, 1997
Tarantino's adaptation of Elmore Leonard's *Rum Punch* adds the perfect sense of lived-in verisimilitude by grounding it in the less-than-glamorous South Bay region. Shooting in the area's actual dive bars and bail-bond offices, the film offers a kind of pulp-perfect LA, where career criminals hold court and desperate stiffs concoct escape plans. Pam Grier excels in the title role.

SUNSET BOULEVARD
dir Billy Wilder, 1950
Desperate to keep his car from repossession, deadbeat screenwriter Joe Gillis (William Holden) takes shelter at the Sunset Boulevard mansion-turned-mausoleum of silent-screen star Norma Desmond (Gloria Swanson). He becomes a kept man, swathed in bespoke suits and smothered by self-loathing. The film epitomises the film industry's pathological nostalgia for past glories.

L.A. CONFIDENTIAL
dir Curtis Hanson, 1997
Both a gorgeous throwback to 1950s Hollywood tough guys and a piercing comment on the post-Rodney King '90s, Hanson's tightly wound cop drama runs on the tension between LA's dream-factory mechanics and the sordid reality. It's a place where one could run into a hooker at the Formosa Café who looks like Lana Turner – or into the real Turner herself.

MULHOLLAND DR.
dir David Lynch, 2001
Lynch's hallucinatory tale of blonde ingénue Naomi Watts caught up in a mystery involving an amnesiac brunette begins with a car accident on the eponymous road and basks in LA's boozy, nightmarish atmosphere. One of the director's most devastatingly emotional works – a mournful love poem to those who have been chewed up and spat out by the Hollywood machine.

ARTS & ENTERTAINMENT

Chinatown.

Fairfax Avenue north. **Screens** 1. **Tickets** $8-$12. **Credit** AmEx, DC, Disc, MC, V. **Map** p312 C2.
LA's equivalent of the Cinémathèque Française responds to Truffaut's inquiry – 'Is the cinema more important than life?' – with a wholehearted 'Yes'. Curated by the Cinefamily organisation of enthusiasts, Fairfax's historic Silent Movie Theatre still screens early films – and talkies too, from classics to more modern picks. It also hosts Q&As, live music and potlucks.

New Beverly Cinema

7165 Beverly Boulevard, at N Detroit Street, Fairfax District (1-323 938 4038, www.newbev cinema.com). Bus 14, 37, 212, 312/I-10, exit La Brea Avenue north. **Screens** 1. **Tickets** $8-$9; $6-$7 discounts. **No credit cards**. **Map** p312 D3.
Cinephiles study their ABCs at this beloved grindhouse, defined by its bargain prices, shabby charm and film-for-film's-sake attitude. All the regular repertory presentations are double features; midnight screenings help get movie buffs through the night.

Other cinemas

California Science Center IMAX

California Science Center, 700 State Drive, between S Figueroa Street & S Vermont Avenue, Exposition Park (1-213 744 2019, www.casciencectr.org). Metro Expo Park/USC/bus 102, 550/I-110, exit Exposition Boulevard west. **Screens** 1. **Tickets** $8.25; $5-$6 discounts. **Credit** AmEx, DC, Disc, MC, V.
The Science Center's gargantuan screen engenders wonder with its flora and fauna explorations and way-of-the-world programming.

Cinespia at the Hollywood Forever Cemetery

6000 Santa Monica Boulevard, at Gordon Street, Hollywood (no phone, www.cinespia.org). Bus 4, 10, 48/US 101, exit Santa Monica Boulevard west. **Screens** 1. **Tickets** $10-$15. **No credit cards**. **Map** p311 C2.
A slide show of vintage film posters and a mood-setting DJ combine to relax the picnicking crowd at this famous cemetery before the main event: a classic film projected on to a wall of one of the larger mausoleums. The *carpe diem* ambience enchants, though the fact that alcohol is permitted also helps. Check the website for details of screenings at other venues, such as Downtown's Los Angeles Theatre.

Echo Park Film Center

1200 N Alvarado Street, at W Sunset Boulevard, Echo Park (1-213 484 8846, www.echoparkfilm center.org). Bus 2, 4, 200, 302, 603, 704/US 101, exit Glendale Boulevard north. **Screens** 1. **Tickets** $5. **No credit cards**. **Map** p314 D5.
Aimed at locals and aspiring filmmakers, this community media arts organisation holds a film school, and also has a rental shop and a 50-seat microcinema.

TV

Tickets to TV shows are easy to obtain – you can apply online ahead of time through a specialist agency or, in some cases, through the relevant TV network. However, if you haven't booked in advance, clipboard-touting agents can be found at tourist hangouts such as TCL (formerly Grauman's) Chinese Theatre, Universal CityWalk, Santa Monica's Third Street Promenade and Venice Beach, dispensing tickets for that week's shows.

Tickets for shows are free, but be warned that the experience may involve three to four hours and a lot of sitting around. And check the fine print: tickets may not guarantee admission (early arrival is usually required), and shows have age restrictions. For tours of studios, *see p29*.

INDIVIDUAL SHOWS

Ellen

Tickets *1-818 954 5929, www.ellentv.com/ tickets.* **Shows** 1pm, Mon-Thur.
This popular talk show, hosted by comedian Ellen DeGeneres, is filmed at the Warner Bros. studio in Burbank. Tickets book up weeks in advance; it's worth persevering, as guests tend to be high profile.

Tonight Show with Jay Leno

Tickets *3000 W Alameda Avenue, Burbank, CA 91523 (1-818 840 3537, www.nbc.com/the-tonight-show/tickets).* **Shows** 4pm Mon-Fri.
Tickets for this longtime favourite, filmed at NBC in Burbank, are available around four to six weeks in advance by the website or mail. A limited number are handed out for the same day's show, with distribution from 8am. Even with tickets, you'll need to arrive by 1.45pm at the latest to stand a chance of entry. The excellent house band, led by Rickey Minor, is entertainment in itself.

TICKET AGENCIES

Audiences Unlimited

1-818 260 0041, www.tvtickets.com.
Audiences Unlimited deals largely with sitcoms, providing tickets to favourites such as *Two and a Half Men* and *The Big Bang Theory*.

On Camera Audiences

1-818 295 2700, www.ocatv.com.
American Idol, Dancing with the Stars, The Price is Right and *Chelsea Lately* are among the shows served by OCA.

TV Tix

1-818 985 8811, www.tvtix.com.
Deal or No Deal, Wheel of Fortune, Jeopardy and others are just a few mouse-clicks away. The company also enlists movie extras.

ARTS & ENTERTAINMENT

Gay & Lesbian

Where to stay and play.

In 2013, Los Angeles continues to live up to its reputation as a place where fantasy becomes reality against the backdrop of what might best be described as a perfectly appointed set. Everything may be a bit too tightly pulled, too meticulously manicured and too over the top, but the City of Angels is a town that revels in its quirkiness. Likewise, Hollywood is a très gay land of dreams, glamour and re-invention, and if you don't honour that truth at the door, then you're not 'getting' the unique charm of California's largest urban jungle (and America's second most populous city).

Whether you want to be a star, see a star or make a star, you can be as much a part of the landscape as a Kardashian, a Los Angeles Laker or the palm trees that line Sunset Boulevard.

Beckoning beneath the famous Hollywood sign is the epicentre of the world's gayest candy store: West Hollywood. Venture just a little east and you'll hit Hollywood, cleaning up its once-lost glory as a glamour nightlife hub. Further east sits one of gay LA's brightest stars, Silver Lake, where the grittier gay scene offers respite from the twinkie turns of WeHo.

INFORMATION & RESOURCES

For gay and lesbian resources, including the LA Gay & Lesbian Center and health clinics, *see p293*. Admission to venues is free unless stated.

THE SCENE

If you want to mingle with the movers and shakers of gay LA, you have to know where to find them. A good start is the annual gay power parties, which are teeming with out insiders. Whether it's a celebration of the arts, equality or each other, these soirées know how to fête what's important – and always include who's important. A few of the not-to-be missed annual events each year include the **GLAAD Media Awards** (www.glaad.org/mediaawards/losangeles) every April, which brings out the who's who of gay Hollywood and those who love them, the **LA Gay & Lesbian Center Anniversary Gala & Auction** (http://laglc.convio.net), and **Macy's Glamorama** (www.macys.com/glamorama), one of the biggest fashion happenings in Los Angeles every September. **LA Pride** (www.lapride.org), held in June in – where else? – West Hollywood, doesn't compare to other Prides held around the

world, but is nonetheless hugely popular; the official City of West Hollywood website (www.weho.org) has details of all the events, from film screenings to a comedy festival, leading up to and following the Pride weekend.

THEATRE & FILM

LA's gay theatre scene remains intimate and accessible. The **Celebration Theatre** (7051 Santa Monica Boulevard, West Hollywood, 1-323 957 1884, www.celebrationtheatre.com) is the most renowned LGBT theatre in SoCal, and offers both irreverent and socially conscious works. The two theatres at the **Los Angeles Gay & Lesbian Center** (*see p293*) have staged everything from musicals about Dusty Springfield to plays by Tennessee Williams and one-woman shows by the likes of Jenifer Lewis and Miss Coco Peru. Conversely, the shows at **Highways** (1651 18th Street, Santa Monica, 1-310 315 1459, www.highwaysperformance.org) are edgy for LA, while the **Cavern Club Theater** nights at Silver Lake's Casita del Campo (1920 Hyperion Avenue, 1-323 969 2530, www.cavernclubtheater.com) are campier and more raw.

Outfest, LA's gay film festival (*see p195*), retains a presence all year. Outfest Wednesdays, held roughly twice a month at the American Cinematheque's Egyptian Theatre (*see p198*), were on hold as this guide went to press, but it's worth checking to see if they're back on.

Gay

Gay LA is coloured dramatically by the city's entertainment industry: a number of gay clubs feel like studio soundstages, and big-name designers art-direct venues as if they were film sets. The climate plays its part, too; come sun, Santa Ana winds or heatwave, LA's glorious gay scene belongs to the great outdoors. Gorgeous, sun-filtered patios are where the gays play: sunbathing, after all, is a Californian art form. And when temperatures drop below 60°F (15°C) and local TV anchors deliver stern 'Storm Watch' warnings, the restaurants and bars just bring out their gas lamps.

INFORMATION

To find out what's on, pick up one of the free magazines found in bars, cafés and shops in West Hollywood. Titles include Frontiers (www.frontiersla.com). Also check out www.visitwesthollywood.com for the most up-to-date WeHo happenings.

WEST HOLLYWOOD

Despite an influx of straight immigration – blame it on the reality shows immortalising the area – West Hollywood belongs to the gays. A modern experiment in habitation (there's a curious subculture of conservative Russian immigrants who co-exist peacefully with the homos), WeHo has risen from ghetto to upscale gay suburb, but the area retains its edge. Today, it succeeds beautifully as both an elegant residential enclave and an exuberant party town. It's safe, serene and, thankfully, never subtle.

Main Street WeHo is **Santa Monica Boulevard** between N Doheny Drive and N Fairfax Avenue, a notorious stretch of bars, clubs and über-gay coffeehouses. The area's epicentre, though, is **Robertson Boulevard**, where gorgeous gays and lesbians with lipo-sculptured bodies leave little to the imagination.

Where to stay

As a general rule, West Hollywood hotels (*see p176*) are gay- and lesbian-friendly, but the **Le Montrose Suite Hotel** is particularly popular given its proximity to the best of gay WeHo. Other good choices in the neighbourhood are the **Chamberlain** (*see p176*) and the **London West Hollywood** (*see p177*).

Le Montrose Suite Hotel

900 Hammond Street, at Cynthia Street (1-310 855 1115, www.lemontrose.com). Bus 2, 30, 105, 302, 330/I-10, exit La Cienega Boulevard north. **Rates** $250-$400. **Credit** AmEx, DC, Disc, MC, V. **Map** p312 A2.

All suite, all fabulous, all the time. Some rooms have fireplaces and patios with views. Quiet and residential, Le Montrose is an excellent respite from the hustle and bustle of Sunset Boulevard to the north and Santa Monica Boulevard to the south, while simultaneously being within a five-minute walk of each.

Palihouse Hotel

8465 Holloway Drive, at Hacienda Place (1-323 656 4100, www.palihouse.com). Bus 4, 30, 105, 330/I-10, exit La Cienega Boulevard north. **Rates** $250-$400. **Credit** AmEx, DC, Disc, MC, V. **Map** p312 B2.

Ideal for longer stays (nightly rates go down the longer you book), the Palihouse offers everything from beautifully appointed classic guest suites to two-bedroom loft residences (1,800-2,000sq ft). The neighbourhood is a bit more mixed but star-studded restaurants and bars await on nearby La Cienega Boulevard.

Ramada

8585 Santa Monica Boulevard, at W Knoll Drive (1-310 652 6400, www.ramadaweho.com). Bus 4, 105, 550, 704/I-10, exit La Cienega Boulevard north. **Rates** $139-$199. **Credit** AmEx, DC, Disc, MC, V. **Map** p312 B2.

The Ramada may be West Hollywood's gayest accommodation because of its location, in the heart

---

INSIDE TRACK
TAKING THE MICKEY?

It may sound unlikely, but Gay Days at Disney is a weekend-long event that is celebrated once a year at the Disneyland and Disney California Adventure theme parks. Events include a kick-off party, musical performances, Saturday's Gay Day and Magic Mountain's one-night-only private party (*see p90*). While Disney does not officially endorse the event, PRIDE, its LGBT group, works closely with Gay Days organisers. The event attracts 30,000 enthusiastic fans. Those not dressed as Disney characters in drag don red shirts to stand out among the crowds. Additional dough can purchase tickets to VIP parties, events and lounges. Hotel discounts of up to 40 per cent are offered at Disney hotels.

Abbey.

of Boys Town, but there's more here than just convenience: friendly staff, clean quarters in art deco style and modern accoutrements (including 42 in flat-screen TVs). It's also right next door to popular gay hangouts including Kitchen 24 and what is arguably the gayest (and cruisiest) Starbucks in the whole of LA (so much so that it's known among locals as 'Gaybucks').

Bars & nightclubs

Abbey
692 N Robertson Boulevard, at Santa Monica Boulevard (1-310 289 8410, www.abbeyfood andbar.com). Bus 4, 105, 550, 704/I-10, exit La Cienega Boulevard north. **Open** 8am-2am daily. **Main courses** $17. **Credit** AmEx, DC, Disc, MC, V. **Map** p312 A2.
The grande dame of WeHo, the Abbey is still very popular, and increasingly so with celebrities and hets. On any given night of the week you'll find a busy scene. The large outdoor patio, with statues and fairy lights, is a pleasant spot; the food is decent and won't break the bank; and the martinis are beyond reproach. As an added bonus, a troupe of male dancers is on tap almost every night of the week to whip the crowd into a frenzy.

Eleven
8811 Santa Monica Boulevard, at Palm Avenue (1-310 855 0800, www.eleven.la). Bus 4, 105, 550, 704/I-10, exit La Cienega Boulevard north. **Open** 5pm-2am Mon-Fri; 10am-2am Sat, Sun. **Credit** AmEx, DC, Disc, MC, V. **Map** p312 A2.
This two-floor megaclub has become one of WeHo's most popular watering holes. The $5 daily happy hour (5-8pm Mon-Fri, 2-8pm Sat, Sun) makes the bar an excellent early option any night of the week. Fans of musicals go mad for Musical Mondays, where local talent takes to the boards and Broadway show tunes are on blast, while Tuesday's Tiger Heat is a twink fest and Saturday's Private Society delivers a sea of go-go boys on every surface imaginable.

Factory/Ultra Suede
Factory: 652 N La Peer Drive, between Santa Monica Boulevard & Melrose Avenue (1-310 659 4551, www.factorynightclub.com). Ultra Suede: 661 North Robertson Boulevard, between Santa Monica Boulevard & Melrose Avenue. Both: Bus 4, 105, 550, 704/I-10, exit La Cienega Boulevard north. **Open** Factory 10pm-2am Wed, Fri, Sat. Ultra Suede 9pm-2am Thur-Sat. noon-2am daily. **Admission** free-$10. **Credit** (bar only) AmEx, DC, MC, V. **Map** p312 A2.
Two great venues run by the same team and connected by adjoining doors that are on occasion thrown open for major events and holiday weekends. The Factory's line-up is highlighted by a glossy young crowd and Friday's Hype party, which has attracted performers ranging from Nikki Minaj and Kelly Rowland to Jordin Sparks and Robyn. Word to the wise, always check ahead before turning up at this hotspot because not every night is a gay night and, because the space is often used for big events, it isn't always open to the public.

Fiesta Cantina
8865 Santa Monica Boulevard, at Larrabee Street (1-310 652 8865, www.fiestacantina.net). Bus 4, 105, 550, 704/I-10, exit La Cienega Boulevard north. **Open** noon-2am daily. **Credit** AmEx, DC, Disc, MC, V. **Map** p312 A2.
Cheap drinks and a daily two-for-one happy hour from 4pm to 8pm make this bar one of the loudest and busiest stops on Santa Monica Boulevard any day of the week.

★ Fubar
7994 Santa Monica Boulevard, between N Laurel & N Edinburgh Avenues (1-323 654 0396, www.fubarla.com). Bus 4, 217, 218, 704/I-10, exit Fairfax Avenue north. **Open** 4pm-2am daily. **Admission** usually free but varies. **Credit** AmEx, DC, Disc, MC, V. **Map** p312 C2.
The easternmost WeHo gay bar on Santa Monica Boulevard, Fubar is the most alternative of the Boys Town cabal of bars and clubs. Ripped, tattooed and pierced bartenders pour strong drinks in the steamy dark space. Hooking up is always in the air, thanks to the underground vibe, so make no mistake: this is not the bar you go to for a casual drink, this is the bar you go to looking for casual sex. The most popular nights are the Mario Diaz-hosted BFD (Big Fat Dick), which features a contest where patrons agree to have their private parts photographed and be voted on by the crowd at the end of the night (the winning title is obvious).

Gold Coast
8228 Santa Monica Boulevard, at N La Jolla Avenue (1-323 656 4879, www.goldcoast weho.com). Bus 4, 217/I-10, exit La Cienega Boulevard north. **Open** 11am-2am Mon-Fri; 10am-2am Sat, Sun. **No credit cards. Map** p312 B2.

Saint Felix.

Leather daddies and cocktailin' senior gays swing east to this WeHo rough diamond. It's dark and dive bar-ish, but there's a classic locals feel – and drinks cost less than at most other nearby joints. Late night happy hour from 11pm to midnight is one of the best bargains in town.

★ Gym Sportsbar

8737 Santa Monica Boulevard, at Hancock Avenue (1-310 659 2004, www.gymsports bar.com). Bus 4, 105, 550, 704/I-10, exit La Cienega Boulevard north. **Open** 4pm-2am Mon-Fri; 10am-2am Sat, Sun. **Credit** MC, V. **Map** p312 A2.

As West Hollywood's only sports bar, Gym Bar is the go-to bar for sports-loving jocks on the Boulevard. Saturday and Sunday Beer Bust are particularly busy, as are sports-themed nights like Dodgeball Tuesdays and It's a Slam Dunk Thursdays. Otherwise, any night on which a major sporting event is taking place, from the NBA play-offs to the Superbowl, is likely to be a winner.

Here Lounge

696 N Robertson Boulevard, at Santa Monica Boulevard (1-310 360 8455, www.herelounge.com). Bus 4, 105, 550, 704/I-10, exit La Cienega Boulevard north. **Open** 8pm-2am Mon-Sat; 4pm-2am Sun. **Admission** free-$10. **Credit** DC, MC, V. **Map** p312 A2.

Located off the Santa Monica Boulevard drag, the minimalist, upscale Here Lounge accommodates a large crowd comprised of the scene's prettiest and cruisiest guys. The Sunday afternoon/early evening Size event is when the locals come out in force, while Wednesday's Stripper Circus attracts LA's hottest porn stars and DJ Chi Chi LaRue to the turntables.

Micky's

8857 Santa Monica Boulevard, between Larrabee Street & N San Vicente Boulevard (1-310 657 1176, www.mickys.com). Bus 2, 4, 2, 30, 105, 302, 330, 704/I-10, exit La Cienega Boulevard north. **Open** 4pm-2am Mon-Fri; noon-4am Sat; noon-2am Sun. **Admission** $7-$10. **Credit** AmEx, DC, Disc, MC, V. **Map** p312 A2.

At this historic bar, go-go boys entertain a mix of the young and the broke nursing nightly drink specials – all under the watchful eye of seasoned sugar daddies. Saturday nights after hours here are the hottest on the Boulevard, if only because it's the only bar still open (though not serving cocktails) after 2am for those who need a little more time to make a connection.

★ Motherlode

8944 Santa Monica Boulevard, at N Robertson Boulevard (1-310 659 9700, www.motherlode-westhollywood.com). Bus 4, 105, 550, 704/I-10, exit La Cienega Boulevard north. **Open** 3pm-2am daily. **No credit cards**. **Map** p312 A2.

Everyone's favourite beer bust is held on Sunday afternoons at LA's friendliest gay bar. An unexpectedly straightforward hangout, especially for this part of town, Motherlode is experiencing a renaissance among the younger crowd, who have adopted it as their favourite unpretentious spot in the 'hood.

★ Revolver

8851 Santa Monica Boulevard, at Larrabee Street (1-310 694 0430, www.revolverweho.com). Bus 4, 105, 550, 704/I-10, exit La Cienega Boulevard north. **Open** 4pm-2am Mon-Fri; noon-2am Sat, Sun. **Credit** AmEx, DC, MC, V. **Map** p312 A2.

The former East West Lounge is now the Boulevard's hottest hipster bar. But don't call it a comeback – because it's as if the original Revolver only took a hiatus and has now returned to its former digs with a slick new look. Strong drinks, a bevy of hunky (often shirtless bartenders) and a stable of LA's A-list promoters taking turns ruling the roost combine to attract a glossy, video-loving crowd nearly every night of the week.

★ Saint Felix

8945 Santa Monica Boulevard, at N Robertson Boulevard (1-310 275 4428, www.saintfelix. net). Bus 2, 4, 302, 550/I-10, exit La Cienega Boulevard north. **Open** 4pm-2am daily. **Credit** AmEx, DC, Disc, MC, V. **Map** p312 A2.

WeHo's newest star has become the most popular neighbourhood bar in the game, with a mood that is conducive to conversation, a simple menu of upscale bar food offered at down-to-earth prices, an exceptional cocktail menu and friendly devoted staff who make each visit a pleasant one.

Restaurants & coffeehouses

In addition to the venues listed below, **Urth Caffé** on Melrose Avenue (*see p134*) is a see and be seen kind of spot that attracts a clubby, celebrity crowd. **Hugo's** (8401 Santa Monica Boulevard, 1-323 654 3993, www.hugos restaurant.com) is also reliable and popular, while **Tender Greens** (8759 Santa Monica Boulevard; *see p100*) draws in protein-craving gym bods.

★ Bossa Nova

685 N Robertson Boulevard, at Santa Monica Boulevard (1-310 657 5070, www.bossanova food.com). Bus 4, 105, 550, 704/I-10, exit La Cienega Boulevard north. **Open** 11am-11.30pm Mon-Thur; 11am-3.30am Fri, Sat; 11am-3.30am Sun. **Main courses** $11-$19. **Credit** AmEx, DC, Disc, MC, V. **Map** p312 A2.

Pasta, pizza, burgers and grilled meats, all prepared with a uniquely Brazilian flair, are the speciality of this always-packed West Hollywood institution located steps away from all the local hotspots. It's the ideal place to grab a bite before a big night out, if not for the sake of fortification, for the ample eye candy that keeps it humming until the wee hours of the morning at weekends. It also has branches in Hollywood and West LA.

Café D'Etoile

8941½ Santa Monica Boulevard, between Hilldale Avenue & Robertson Boulevard (1-310 278 1011, www.cafedetoile.net). Bus 2, 4, 302, 550/I-10, exit La Cienega Boulevard north. **Open** 11am-late Mon-Fri; 10am-late Sat, Sun. **Main courses** $12-$25. **Credit** AmEx, DC, Disc, MC, V. **Map** p312 A2.

With over 30 years in the game, Café D'Etoile is the granddaddy of eateries along the Santa Monica strip. Like its clientele, its menu tends towards more traditional fare – but that is precisely its charm. While its neighbours have come and gone, Café D'Etoile continues to thrive with an old-school flair that defies WeHo's sometimes ageist attitudes.

Café La Bohème

8400 Santa Monica Boulevard, at N Orlando Avenue (1-323 848 2360, www.cafelaboheme.us). Bus 4, 105, 704/I-10, exit La Cienega Boulevard north. **Open** 5-10pm Mon-Thur, Sun; 5-11pm Fri, Sat. **Main courses** $19-$26. **Credit** AmEx, DC, Disc, MC, V. **Map** p312 B2.

Fine dining goes gay and goth at this sophisticated but unstuffy restaurant. You get the feeling that this is what Cher's dining room looks like: glamorous, OTT and a bit tacky. Gays, celebs and industry folk bask under chandeliers and down martinis.

Five Guys

8731 Santa Monica Boulevard, at Hancock Avenue (1-310 289 1175, www.fiveguys.com). Bus 4, 105, 550, 704/I-10, exit La Cienega Boulevard north. **Open** 11am-10pm Mon-Thur, Sun; 11am-2am Fri, Sat. **Main courses** $3-$7. **Credit** AmEx, Disc, MC, V. **Map** p312 A2.

It's one of the few mainstream chains to infiltrate Santa Monica Boulevard's health-conscious core and as such it's also among the guiltiest pleasures in which locals allow themselves to indulge. With a menu of hamburgers, hot dogs and fries, Five Guys is one of the few places where being seen is a deficit. **Other locations** throughout LA.

Hamburger Mary's

8288 Santa Monica Boulevard, at N Sweetzer Avenue (1-323 654 3800, www.hamburgermarys. com/weho). Bus 4, 704/I-10, exit Fairfax Avenue north. **Open** 11am-1am Mon-Thur, Sun; 11am-2am Fri, Sat. **Main courses** $11-$18. **Credit** AmEx, DC, Disc, MC, V. **Map** p312 B2.

Burger hounds have a tricky choice. Do they go to this gay-oriented mini-chain, which hosts a celeb-infested drag queen bingo on Wednesday night? Or head across the street to try Irv's Burgers (8289 Santa Monica Boulevard, 1-323 650 2456), a tiny mainstay for decades? The answer is simple: do both. ▶ *Just a couple of doors along from Irv's, at No.8279, a WeHo branch of New York restaurant/ piano bar/cabaret venue Don't Tell Mama opened in February 2013.*

★ Marix

1108 Flores Street, at Santa Monica Boulevard (1-323 656 8800, www.marixtexmex.com). Bus 4, 105, 217/I-10, exit La Cienega Boulevard north. **Open** 11.30am-11pm Mon-Fri; 11am-11pm Sat, Sun. **Main courses** $14. **Credit** AmEx, DC, Disc, MC, V. **Map** p312 B2.

Tour of Booty

A fascinating guide to gay LA.

Forget the cheesy 'stars' homes' tours and instead try the Out & About Tour, a lively and insightful look at LGBTQ Los Angeles that, of course, includes cocktails. The three-hour tours take in monumental locations in WeHo, Echo Park and Silver Lake, including notorious gay homes and hotbeds of famous gay activity. It's all delivered with saucy, comedic monologues from a guest lesbian or gay actor/tour guide. Tours are held on Saturday and Sunday afternoons; the SunGay Brunch Tour, held occasionally, includes a stop-off for brunch at a popular gay restaurant (venues vary). Tours take place in everything from a vintage double-decker bus to a luxury minibus or 'VIP SUV', and private tours are available. For reservations and more information, go to www.outandabout-tours.com.

ARTS & ENTERTAINMENT

This local institution has been a hotspot for nearly three decades, which practically qualifies it for senior citizen status by West Hollywood standards. Owned by two local lesbians, it serves up decent Tex-Mex cuisine and what some swear are the best margaritas in town. Come down on Sunday afternoons when patrons party, or on all-you-can-eat Taco Tuesdays. *Photo p208.*
Other locations 118 Entrada Drive, Santa Monica (1-310 459 8596).
▶ *Around the corner from Marix is Basix (8333 Santa Monica Boulevard, 1-323 848 2460, www.basixcafe.com), a comfort food fave.*

★ Sur

606 N Robertson Boulevard, at Melrose Avenue (1-310 289 2824, www.surrestaurantandbar.com). Bus 4, 105, 550, 704/I-10, exit La Cienega Boulevard north. **Open** noon-3pm, 5-10.30pm Mon-Thur; noon-3pm, 5-11pm Fri, Sat; 5-10.30pm Sun. **Main courses** *Lunch* $16. *Dinner* $26. **Credit** AmEx, DC, Disc, MC, V. **Map** p312 A2.
Romance and dining go hand in hand at this southern European-inspired eatery, co-owned by one of the Real Housewives of Beverly Hills. Delicious Cal/Med dishes are enjoyed by an upscale mixed crowd, which turns especially lesbian on Thursday nights.

Gyms

Gay-friendly gyms include **24-Hour Fitness** (www.24hourfitness.com), distinguished by its pool and cruisey atmosphere (the West Hollywood branch, at 8612 Santa Monica Boulevard, 1-323 652 7440, has a particularly lively gay scene), and **Equinox** (8590 W Sunset Boulevard, 1-310 289 1900, www.equinox.com), a high-end but friendly facility with a top-notch spa and classes from abs to yoga.

Crunch

8000 W Sunset Boulevard, at N Laurel Avenue (1-323 654 4550, www.crunch.com). Bus 2, 217, 302/I-10, exit Fairfax Avenue north. **Open** 5am-11pm Mon-Thur; 5am-10pm Fri; 7am-8pm Sat; 8am-8pm Sun. **Rates** $25/day. **Credit** AmEx, DC, Disc, MC, V. **Map** p312 C1.
It's hard to know which is more breathtaking: the views of the Hollywood Hills, or the Adonises who choose the hills as the backdrop for their exercise. Flirtation can be part of the workout: wash up in the oft-discussed 'peek-a-boo' see-through showers.

Bathhouses & sex clubs

Midtowne Melrose Spa

7269 Melrose Avenue, at N La Brea Boulevard, Fairfax District (1-323 937 2122, www.midtowne.com). Bus 10, 212, 312/I-10, exit La Brea Avenue north. **Open** 24hrs daily. **Admission** *Per 8hrs* $29 room; $17 locker;

$4 processing fee. **Credit** AmEx, DC, MC, V. **Map** p312 D2.
This two-storey spa close to WeHo attracts a varied clientele. Amenities of note include a rooftop patio, a huge adult movie room, a darkened maze for anonymous action, and a resident sex therapist.

Shops & services

If you're looking to soak up the LA sunshine and snap the stars, head to the **Grove** (*see*

Bear Necessities

The bears are back in town.

Bears in Space

Blame it on a reaction to LA's obsession with babyfaces, but a 'bear' revolution is taking root in Silver Lake – in what appears to be a direct assault on the culture of WeHo twink bars where the music of Rihanna and Taylor Swift is always on blast. **Bears in Space**, a self-described 'sexy cosmic bear beats disco', held on the third Thursday of the month at Akbar (*see right*), is the most popular of the recent influx, and it's a wildly successful antidote to the usual scene. Crowds consist of all ages, colours, shapes and sizes, and there's a rowdier, retro-fuelled air to the proceedings. You'll find all sorts here: Radical Faeries, leather worshippers, S&M guys and anyone headed East for a respite from WeHo.

Other favourites are **Cub Scout**, on the first Friday of the month at Eagle LA, and **Brutus**, a collaborative effort between promoter Chris Bowen and Mario Diaz (Big Fat Dick) held on the second Saturday of the month at Faultline (for both, *see p208*). Other clubs that attract bears (and their admirers) include **A Club Called Rhonda at Los Globos**, held around once a month (3040 West Sunset Boulevard, Silver Lake, 1-323 666 6669, www.clublosglobos.com).

p140). Whether you're navigating the Studio 54-like circuit scene of Abercrombie & Fitch, peeping at the filming of an episode of *Extra*, or cruising the eateries at the neighbouring Farmers Market, this open-air mall is the local homos' favourite shopping haunt.

Brick & Mortar

8713 Santa Monica Boulevard, at W Knoll Drive (1-310 652 6605, www.bricknmortar.com). Bus 4, 105, 550, 704/I-10, exit La Cienega Boulevard north. **Open** noon-8pm Mon-Thur; noon-10pm Fri; 11am-10pm Sat; 11am-7pm Sun. **Credit** AmEx, DC, Disc, MC, V. **Map** p312 B2.

Expect to find clothes, housewares and coffee-table books at this gay-owned store, one of the most fashion-forward shops on this stretch.

Chi Chi LaRue's

8932 Santa Monica Boulevard, between N Robertson & N San Vicente Boulevards (1-323 337 9555, www.chichilarue.com). Bus 2, 4, 302, 550/I-10, exit La Cienega Boulevard north. **Open** 10am-midnight Mon-Wed; 10am-2am Thur-Sun. **Credit** AmEx, DC, Disc, MC, V. **Map** p312 A2.

Famous drag queen and porn producer extraordinaire Chi Chi LaRue presides over this gay-themed adult megastore. The retail clerks are porn stars, and there's a playful vibe that's sexy, not seedy.

LA Jock

8915 Santa Monica Boulevard, at Robertson Boulevard (1-323 848 8088, www.lajock.com). Bus 4, 105, 550, 704/I-10, exit La Cienega Boulevard north. **Open** noon-6pm daily. **Credit** AmEx, DC, Disc, MC, V. **Map** p312 A2.

One of the most extensive selections of men's underwear and swimwear in the whole of LA. It's like Victoria's Secret for men and it's the first place all the boys in WeHo hit when they want to find sexy and cute undergarments for a big date or a swimsuit for the hottest pool party in town.

LASC

8592 Santa Monica Boulevard, at W Knoll Drive (1-310 657 2858, www.shoplasc.com). Bus 4, 105, 550, 704/I-10, exit La Cienega Boulevard north. **Open** 10am-8pm daily. **Credit** AmEx, Disc, MC, V. **Map** p312 B2.

Not only is LASC a popular West Hollywood landmark, it's also ground zero for local events and parties. Ask any of the attractive, friendly staff for nightlife advice, while trying on the latest threads.

HOLLYWOOD

Cleaner and safer than it's been for years, Hollywood has undergone an urban facelift of late, with the addition of a mall and a number of paparazzi-infested clubs. Gay nightlife revolves around designated nights in the gymnasium-sized danceplexes.

Bars & nightclubs

Circus Disco (6655 Santa Monica Boulevard; *see p213*) is also popular, both the gay Boys Night Out on Tuesdays and Club Macho Man on Fridays. On Thursdays, a trendy crowd heads to **Avalon** (1735 N Vine Street; *see p212*) for TigerHeat.

Spotlight Bar

1601 N Cahuenga Boulevard, at Selma Avenue (1-323 467 2425). Metro Hollywood-Vine/bus 162, 163, 180, 181, 210, 212, 217, 312, 780, LDH/ US 101, exit Hollywood Boulevard west. **Open** 6am-2am daily. **No credit cards**. **Map** p313 B2.

Trannies abound midweek, but there's a diverse clientele most nights and days (including a few straights and the occasional celeb) at Spotlight, LA's oldest gay bar.

Bathhouses & sex clubs

Hollywood Spa

1650 N Ivar Avenue, between Hollywood Boulevard & Selma Avenue (1-323 464 0445, www.hollywoodspa.com). Metro Hollywood-Vine/bus 162, 163, 180, 181, 210, 212, 217, 312, 780, LDH/US 101, exit Vine Street south. **Open** 24hrs daily. **Admission** *Per 8hrs* $35-$50 room; $25-$28 locker. **Credit** AmEx, DC, Disc, MC, V. **Map** p313 B2.

A Hollywood mainstay most LA locals have visited (though few will admit it). An after-hours mix swarms under soft lights through the palatial Hollywood digs, plus there's a steam room, sauna and cabins. **Other locations** 5636 Vineland Avenue, North Hollywood (1-818 760 6969).

SILVER LAKE

If the West Hollywood scene seems too vanilla and whitewashed, head over to Silver Lake. Its rougher queer scene may be fancier than it used to be, but it is still the destination where all the other kids with their pumped-up kicks like to work and play. Best of all, when you describe Silver Lake as a mixed neighbourhood it doesn't just refer to the straight-gay ratio but also to the fact that you'll find S&M, bears, Spanish, leather, cubs, daddies and older homos and lesbians who lived here when the neighbourhood was an edgy barrio.

Bars & nightclubs

★ Akbar

4356 W Sunset Boulevard, at Fountain Avenue (1-323 665 6810, www.akbarsilverlake.com).

ARTS & ENTERTAINMENT

Metro Vermont-Sunset/bus 2, 175, 302/US 101, exit Echo Park Avenue north. **Open** 4pm-2am daily. **Admission** free-$5. **Credit** (bar only) AmEx, DC, Disc, MC, V. **Map** p314 B3.
Silver Lake's most famous gay bar is where the alterna-boys and cool straights hang equally loose. Come for the rock-themed Friday and Saturday night dance parties.

★ Eagle LA

4219 Santa Monica Boulevard, at W Sunset Boulevard (1-323 669 9472, www.eaglela.com). Metro Vermont-Santa Monica/bus 2, 4, 302, 704/ US 101, exit Vermont Avenue. **Open** 4pm-2am Mon-Fri; 2pm-2am Sat, Sun. **Admission** free-$5. **No credit cards**. **Map** p314 B3.
Porn plays alluringly on the monitors as leather daddies get their boots polished at LA's premier leather and fetish bar. Throbbing Thursdays are the busiest; other events come with self-explanatory names such as Boot Camp and Meat Rack.

Faultline

4216 Melrose Avenue, at N Vermont Avenue (1-323 660 0889, www.faultlinebar.com). Metro Vermont-Beverly/bus 10, 204, 754/US 101, exit Vermont Avenue north. **Open** 5pm-2am Wed-Fri; 2pm-2am Sat, Sun. **Admission** free-$10. **Credit** AmEx, MC, V. **Map** p314 A4.
Leather men hold Faultline in the highest regard, but other fetishes are catered for, too: bikers, bodybuilders and body piercers are all regulars. The DJs have a strict 'no divas' music policy, spinning an edgy mix of electronica and rock. The weekly beer bust is Silver Lake's most popular Sunday soirée.

Marix. See p205.

MJs

2810 Hyperion Avenue, at Rowena Avenue (1-323 660 1503, www.mjsbar.com). Bus 175/US 101, exit Silver Lake Boulevard east. **Open** 4pm-2am Mon-Sat; 3pm-2am Sun. **Admission** free-$10. **Credit** AmEx, DC, Disc, MC, V. **Map** p314 C2.
This bar is more West Hollywood than Slakers care for, but outlandish theme nights keep everyone happy. Tuesday belongs to Rim Job, a homage to homo sleaze that unites WeHo queers and Silver Lake boys; Fresh Meat Fridays spin glossy pop and a troupe of scantily clad boys dancing on every available surface. Arrive before 10pm to beat the long line.

★ Other Side

2538 Hyperion Avenue, between Evans & Tracy Streets (1-323 661 0618, www.flyingleapcafe.com). Bus 175/US 101, exit Silver Lake Boulevard east. **Open** 4pm-2am Mon-Thur; noon-2am Fri-Sun. **Admission** varies. **Credit** AmEx, DC, Disc, MC, V. **Map** p314 C2.
The average age may be 60-plus, but the talent performing at this classy piano bar is phenomenal and the atmosphere is always welcoming. LA kitsch at its finest, increasingly sought out by straights.

Bathhouses & sex clubs

Flex Los Angeles

4424 Melrose Avenue, at US 101 (1-323 663 7786, www.flexspas.com). Bus 10, 48. **Open** 24/7. **Admission** Lockers $11-$18. Rooms $23-$38. **Credit** MC, V.
This popular sex club near Downtown attracts its biggest crowds once the bars close around 2am on the weekends and after or before work hours during the week.

Slammer

3688 Beverly Boulevard, between N Virgil & N Vermont Avenues (1-213 388 8040, www.slammerclub.com). Metro Vermont-Beverly/bus 14/US 101, exit Beverly Boulevard west. **Open** 8pm-late Mon-Fri; 2pm-late Sat, Sun. **Admission** $23. **No credit cards**. **Map** p314 B5.
A sex club mostly for the leather crowd. Tuesdays are for gym buffs and Wet Wednesdays attract those into watersports. Don't expect many of Hollywood Spa's pretty guys. Free HIV testing is available.

DOWNTOWN

Bars & nightclubs

Mustache Mondays

Every Monday at La Cita (see p213). **Open** 4pm-2am. **Admission** free 4-10pm; $5 10-11pm; $8 11pm-2am. **Credit** AmEx, MC, V. **Map** p315 C3.
Mustache Mondays hosts world-class DJs, performance artists, drag queen luminaries and a polysexual crowd. Come mustachioed and get in free.

Lesbian

From bi-curious Lindsay Lohan smooching for the cameras at Sunday's girl night at the Abbey or a Melissa sighting at Marix, LA's lesbian scene is nothing if not glamorous. But it's more intimate than you might expect. That's not to say there isn't a prolific community: there is, but you'll need to look a little harder for it.

INFORMATION

For information, see free monthly mag *Lesbian News* (www.lesbiannews.com) or *Frontiers* (www.frontiersla.com), which covers women's issues as well.

BARS & NIGHTCLUBS

Few LA venues devote themselves to lesbians seven days a week, so pick events carefully. Thursdays are big lesbian nights all over WeHo but on Fridays the **Here Lounge** (*see p204*) hosts the super-sexy, super-grungy Truckstop. Meanwhile, Sundays at the **Abbey** (*see p203*) have been known to bring out a slew of local lesbian celebrities (particularly early afternoon).

Jewel's Catch One

4067 W Pico Boulevard, at S Norton Avenue, Midtown (1-323 734 8849, www.jewelscatch one.com). Bus 30, 210/I-10, exit Crenshaw Boulevard north. **Open** 9pm-2am Mon; 10pm-3am Fri; 10pm-4am Sat. **Admission** $2-$5. **Credit** AmEx, DC, Disc, MC, V. **Map** p313 B6.
Opened in 1972 as the first nightclub aimed at the African American gay communities, Jewel's Catch One continues to draw a mixed clientele with a variety of nights that stretch from hip hop to industrial rock. It's not located in the greatest neighbourhood, so take extra precautions, especially when parking.

Oil Can Harry's

11502 Ventura Boulevard, between Colfax Avenue & Tujunga Avenue, Studio City (1-818 760 9749, www.oilcanharrysla.com). Bus 150/US 101, exit Tujunga Boulevard south. **Open** 7.30pm-12.30am Tue, Thur; 9pm-2am Fri; 8pm-2am Sat; 11.30am-midnight Sun. **Admission** varies. **Credit** AmEx, DC, MC, V.
Bring your cowboy boots and affect your best country twang at this femme-dominated line-dancing joint. There's always someone to dance with. Lessons are held on Tuesdays and Thursdays (7.45-9.15pm). The crowd isn't always particularly heavy on lesbians, but it's a welcoming environment for ladies who like to get their two-step on.

Palms

8572 Santa Monica Boulevard, between Westbourne Drive & W Knoll Drive, West Hollywood (1-310 652 1595, www.thepalms bar.com). Bus 4, 105, 550, 704/I-10, exit La Cienega Boulevard north. **Open** 8pm-2am Mon-Sat; 6pm-2am Sun. **Admission** free-$10. **Credit** AmEx, DC, MC, V. **Map** p312 B2.
The oldest lesbian bar in LA is still going strong, supplementing its mellower evenings with regular dance nights inside its cosy confines. The Sunday afternoon beer bust remains popular.

RESTAURANTS & CAFÉS

Popular gay venues include the **Abbey** (*see p203*), **Marix** (*see p205*), froyo **Yogurt Stop** (*see p134* **Cold Comfort**) and **Coffee Bean & Tea Leaf** (8595 Santa Monica Boulevard, 1-310 659 8956) in West Hollywood. In Silver Lake, try **Intelligentsia** (*see p136*).

Gay Beaches

Sand, sea and sexy bodies.

Many of Southern California's beaches are gay-friendly, but those listed below are three of the best. Gay men and lesbians both head here, but the scenes are male-dominated.

Laguna Beach

Laguna Beach: off PCH, 30 miles south of Long Beach. Gay beach: just past the pier; look for the rainbow flag.
It's a long drive from LA and it's not as gay as it once was, but Laguna Beach is still busy on the weekends (and even when it's not, the water is clean and the beach is hot).

Venice Beach

Venice: see p38. Gay beach: where Windward Avenue meets the beach, next to the wall, just down from Muscle Beach.
It figures that LA's most bohemian district should also welcome the gay community. The quasi-legendary Roosterfish (1302 Abbot Kinney Boulevard, 1-310 392 2123, www.roosterfishbar.com) is a must-see for the guys.

Will Rogers State Beach

Will Rogers State Beach: on PCH, two miles north of Santa Monica Pier, in front of the Beach Club.
This cruisey beach is packed on sunny weekends, and it's easy to see why: it's free, it's got tons of guys playing volleyball and it lasts until sunset.

Nightlife

Nocturnal manoeuvres in the dark.

The worldwide recession has done wonders for Southern California nightlife. While bottle service still reigns, some now consider it over the top. People ask what's on the menu and who's DJing, but not who's in the club. Likewise, where five years ago every kid who got turntables for Christmas was doing a club night in LA, the economic slump has weeded out the demand – and thus the supply has become sharper. Hollywood club life has become more than a destination for top global DJs.

When it comes to the city's music scene, most Angelenos can say about at least one big-name act: 'I knew them when…' It's inevitable in a city that serves as the epicentre of the music industry, the kind of place where festival headliners hold weekly residencies. Even less-than-cutting edge listeners have a good chance of stumbling into a surprise set from the far-flung likes of Thom Yorke, Erykah Badu or Skrillex. Serving simultaneously as the birthplace of new sounds and the guardian of a rich history, LA's immense landscape of live music venues serves up everything from back room jazz to main stage hip hop, top 40 pop stars to obscure indie rock acts, every night of the week.

The comedy scene in Los Angeles is arguably one of the strongest in the US, and certainly one of the most varied. From nationally known stand-ups warming up for a *Tonight Show* turn via Chicago-style improv to experimental sketch comedy, you'll find a little of everything.

ARTS & ENTERTAINMENT

NIGHTCLUBS

If Las Vegas is a capital of bad taste, just keep in mind that, spiritually, it really comprises LA's own backyard party. And so if Jersey Shore, South Beach at midnight or, yes, a white-limo entourage on the Vegas Strip make you cringe, you should be prepared for more of the same in the City of Angels. Spikey hair, girls who go 'woo-woo', moneyed, irreverent young people, bottle service – Los Angeles has all of these in spades. If we didn't have Vegas and, at one time, Tijuana, as escape valves, LA would be a global capital of cheese.

THE LOCAL SCENE

A new generation of kids has created a pop phenomenon in LA – a mix of electronic dance music's love of all-night bacchanalia and punk rock's irreverence – and it's going off at spots like the Echoplex and Arena. We call these ravers dressed in pink Ray-Bans and American Apparel tights neon punks. And, yeah, they could care less about valet service.

And all of this is happening in a tighter, more appreciative scene where, it seems, the platinum cards of yesteryear have been weeded out in favour of nightlife aficionados. The amateurs have given way to the professionals once more.

Of course, the economy has been taking a turn for the better, and the velvet ropes will always be in full effect in LA. Just follow your own tastes, and say 'woo-woo' just for tradition's sake.

The scene is also varied, if you know where to look. Care to witness the electro resurgence at first hand, complete with original artists such as Egyptian Lover or Arabian Prince on the turntables? Word up! How about hipsters dancing to rootsy, Colombian *vallenato* music? *Aquí, en LA.* If you want to join some of the sexiest Asian American partiers in the world, you've come to the right place. This is perhaps the most diverse city in the United States, and clubland reflects the ethnic variety.

Since the 1980s, when East Side Latinos turned backyard parties into DJ-driven massives and British expats introduced the city to a rave-like underworld, LA has had a thriving dance scene below the surface. Today's standout one-offs come in the form of Doc Martin's house music hoedowns (www.sublevelcalifornia.com), DJ Harvey's dub-disco affairs (www.harvey sarcasticdisco.com) and Droid Behavior's techno throwdowns (www.droidbehavior.com). Some of these underground events are held in legit locales, but many others skirt the line of legality: LA boasts various warehouse districts with few neighbours to complain and even fewer police to respond. However, don't expect anarchy: most of these gigs are offered with pre-sale tickets, 21-and-up bars (from licensed caterers) and plenty of security guards. It's the music, not the punters, that provides the edginess.

Contrast these underground scenes with the city's starstruck mini-clubs, where you might not be made to feel welcome unless you're rocking gold or platinum plastic and are willing to rack up a fat bar tab that might top your air fare. That's all well and good if you're in the market for once-in-a-lifetime actor-spotting (in which case, get in line behind the 'paps'). However, the experience will fill your ears with top 40 fluff and then expose your eyes to the ugliest pretty people you've ever seen. And after you've added valet parking ($10 and up) and either bottle-service fees or cocktails (as much as $30 each) to your cover charge, your wallet will be lighter

than Nicole Richie. Many of the stars are there for open-bar charity events or organised parties; in some cases, they're even being paid by the management simply to add a little kudos to their nightclub. These ventures are counting on you to subsidise their clientele's *Entourage* lifestyle – and their own profits. Invest wisely.

PRACTICAL INFORMATION
While men are generally dressing fancier these days, some still look like slobs at a car show. Women, meanwhile, suffer in heels, dresses and $300 jeans. Whatever your gender, travel light: many larger venues ban gum, pens, cameras and even cigarettes. And if you stash anything resembling a weapon, a pill or a powder in your

ARTS & ENTERTAINMENT

Avalon. *See p212.*

Zanzibar. *See p216.*

pockets, you can expect delays and loss of property. If you come face to face with the LAPD, do as they say: officers have a low tolerance for clubland high jinks. If you can bear the extra expense, always try and tip your bartender or server well: if you look after them, they'll look after you.

Venues crank different sounds and attract different crowds from night to night, thanks to out-of-house promoters who slice up the city's musical demographics like a chef at Benihana. The currents of clubland are constantly changing, so stay up-to-date by going to the Time Out Los Angeles website (www.timeout. com/los-angeles), which has reviews and features; you can also buy tickets to some events on the site, via Ticketmaster. Tickets for most of the larger events can also be bought in advance at www.wanttickets.com and www.grooteickets.com, both of which are also good resources for information on what's coming soon in the City of Angels.

Arena

6655 Santa Monica Boulevard, between N Las Palmas & Seward Streets, Hollywood (1-323 462 1291, www.arenanightclub.com). Metro Hollywood-Vine/bus 163, 180, 181, 210, 212, 217, 312, 363, 780, LDH/US 101, exit Vine Street south. **Open** 9pm-2am Wed, Sun; 9pm-3am Sat. **Admission** $10-$20. **Credit** AmEx, DC, Disc, MC, V. **Map** p313 A2.

This former ice factory has become a newfound playground for cool kids who dance to Daft Punk mashups. Its wall of video screens and neon trim can make it feel like a relic of the '80s, but its minimal expanse is timeless and utilitarian. Arena has youthful energy thanks, in part, to an 18-and-older door policy. It's on the same property as Circus Disco (*see p213*).

★ Avalon

1735 N Vine Street, at Hollywood Boulevard, Hollywood (1-323 462 8900, www.avalon hollywood.com). Metro Hollywood-Vine/bus 163, 180, 181, 210, 212, 217, 312, 780, LDH/US 101, exit Vine Street south. **Open** 10pm-6am Sat. **Admission** $15-$60. **Credit** AmEx, DC, MC, V. **Map** p313 B1.

Completed in 1927, this huge theatre remains LA's pre-eminent superclub more than 85 years on. Avalon's Saturday-night bookings have embraced Europe's techno renaissance and aim for a Fabric-like critical edge with nary any trance, so leave the glowsticks at home. And bring earplugs: the venue has the best sound system in the city, a floor-shaking EAW Avalon Series set-up that cost a cool $1 million. Thursday plays host to the hugely popular TigerHeat gay night (www.clubtigerheat.com). *Photo p211.*

Bardot

1737 Vine Street, at Yucca Street, Hollywood (1-323 462 1307, www.bardothollywood.com). Metro Hollywood-Vine/bus 163, 180, 181, 210, 212, 217, 312, 780, LDH/US 101, exit Vine Street south. **Open** times vary; usually until 2am Mon-Wed, Fri, Sat. **Credit** AmEx, DC, Disc, MC, V. **Admission** free-$10. **Map** p313 B1.

This is the exclusive, upstairs sister venue that's attached to superclub Avalon (*see above*). Its tighter quarters, Moroccan-themed decor and EAW sound system make for some serious clubbing, even if its clientele is more focused on star-spotting than music. Cosy, dark and intimate, Bardot is one of the city's most adventurous propositions for Friday after-hours.

Bootsy Bellows

9229 W Sunset Boulevard, between N Sierra Drive & Doheny Road, West Hollywood (1-310 274 7500, www.bootsybellows.com). Metro

Hollywood-Vine/bus 2, 302, 305 4, 48, 105, 220, 550, 704, 780/US 101, exit Santa Monica Boulevard west. **Open** 10pm-2am Thur-Sat. **Admission** varies. **Credit** AmEx, DC, MC, V.
Formerly Trousdale, this is one of LA's more exclusive dance clubs. It's got promoters, velvet ropes and a sizable VIP section for the Hollywood B-listers. And it's impossible to get in. Clearly, however, it's worth a try. Bring your camera and a bribe for the door if you want to skip the wait.

Boulevard3

6523 Sunset Boulevard, at Wilcox Avenue, Hollywood (1-323 466 2144, www.boulevard3. com). Metro Hollywood-Vine/bus 163, 180, 181, 210, 212, 217, 312, 780, LDH/US 101, exit Sunset Boulevard west. **Open** 9.30pm-2am Fri, Sat. **Admission** $20. **Credit** AmEx, DC, Disc, MC, V. **Map** p313 B2.
This indoor-outdoor expanse, owned by the folks behind Skybar at the Mondrian (*see p177*), nobly attempts to bring a little dignity to a tipsy and often crass community of celebutantes and actors. Dress up, bring your wallet and try to behave yourself. Hip hop is the weekend soundtrack, but DJs sometimes venture into house on off-nights.

★ Circus Disco

6655 Santa Monica Boulevard, at N Las Palmas Avenue, Hollywood (1-323 462 1291, www.circus andarena.com). Bus 4, 210, 704/US 101, exit Vine Street south. **Open** 9pm-2am Tue; 9pm-3am Fri. **Admission** $3-$15. **Credit** MC, V. **Map** p313 A2.
One of the city's oldest clubs, the 3,300-capacity Circus is a gay mecca on most evenings, but Saturdays are home to DJ-centric electronic music nights aimed chiefly at straight audiences.

La Cita

336 S Hill Street, between 3rd & 4th Streets, Downtown (1-213 687 7111, www.lacitabar.com). Metro Pershing Square/bus 2, 4, 30, 40, 42, 45, 48/I-110, exit 3rd Street east. **Open** 10am-2am daily. **Admission** free-$8. **Credit** AmEx, DC, MC, V. **Map** p315 C3.
One of a handful of old-school Mexican watering holes in the inner city that have been taken over by new-school hipsters, La Cita serves as a bar, a restaurant and a club, complete with a dancefloor and an outdoor patio. Edgy dance-punks and big-name artist-DJs (Shepard Fairey, to name one) have called the red-velvet-adorned venue home in recent times, but you can still find Downtown throwbacks, including many Latinos, sipping modelos at happy hour.
▶ *For the Mustache Mondays gay night, see p208.*

Conga Room

L.A. LIVE, 800 W Olympic Boulevard, at S Figueroa Street, Downtown (1-213 745 0162, www.congaroom.com). Metro 7th Street-Metro Center/bus 28, 66, 81/I-110, exit Olympic
Boulevard east. **Open** 9pm-2am Mon, Wed-Sun. **Admission** $20, $10 before 10pm. **Credit** AmEx, DC, MC, V. **Map** p315 B4.
Co-owned by Latino stars Jimmy Smits, Jennifer Lopez and Sheila E, among others, this fabled and fabulous showcase of Latin music and musicians features hip hop on Fridays and salsa on Saturdays. The 1,100-capacity venue also offers dining alongside the music and is sometimes open on Thursdays for concerts, when ticket prices are higher.
▶ *For more on the L.A. LIVE complex, see p72.*

Exchange LA

618 S Spring Street, at E 6th Street, Downtown (1-213 627 8070, www.exchangela.com). Metro Pershing Square/bus 2, 4, 30, 40, 42, 45, 48/ I-110, exit 3rd Street east. **Open** 9pm-3am Fri, Sat. **Admission** free-$20. **Credit** AmEx, DC, MC, V. **Map** p315 C3.
This 25,000sq ft, multi-level mega-club wonderland is in the heart of Downtown's revived nightlife district, yet locals barely hear a peep about it. But you can still find the occasional superstar DJ, along with regular, Asian American-themed nights here. It's worth a peep just to check out its gorgeous, moderne architecture. Oh, and the magnificent 1929 building really was once the Los Angeles Stock Exchange – and part of LA's 'Wall Street of the west' district.

Mayan

1038 S Hill Street, at W Olympic Boulevard, Downtown (1-213 746 4674, www.clubmayan. com). Metro Pershing Square/bus 2, 4, 30, 40, 42, 45, 48/I-110, exit 9th Street east. **Open** varies. **Admission** $10-$50. **Credit** AmEx, DC, MC, V. **Map** p315 B4.
In recent decades, this Downtown landmark has been the backdrop for many televised music performances, hosted some of the region's biggest salsa parties, and provided good vibes for spin sessions from the likes of John Digweed and Paul Van Dyk. Unfortunately, while its architecture is amazing, it could use a little nip-tuck. Security is hands-on and about as friendly as a New York City sanitation worker.

★ Playhouse

6506 Hollywood Boulevard, at Wilcox Avenue, Hollywood (1-323 656 4600, www.playhousenight club.com). Metro Hollywood-Vine/bus 163, 180, 181, 210, 212, 217, 312, 780, LDH/US 101, exit Hollywood Boulevard west. **Open** 10pm-4am Mon; 10pm-4am Thur-Sat. **Admission** free-$20. **Credit** AmEx, DC, Disc, MC, V. **Map** p313 B1.
This 13,000sq ft, three-level venue is one of the boulevard's hottest dance clubs. While it can get a little *Jersey Shore* on its tightly packed floor (we once witnessed a young, shirtless clubber down a bottle of vodka as he stood atop a platform), it's a revelation to see celebutantes dancing to serious dance music at its must-see Monday Social nights, which feature top spinners from around the globe. *Photo p216.*

ARTS & ENTERTAINMENT

Sound of the Underground

Get down and party.

Rihanna and fun have their place, but if you want to escape the mainstream and lose yourself on the dancefloor, an underground venue is the solution. You'll find soulful house, techno, hip hop, disco on the decks at these top LA dance parties, where the freaks come out at night (and sometimes during the day). Here are our top five; for more, visit the Time Out Los Angeles website (www.timeout.com/los-angeles).

MAKING SHAPES

Thrown By: Jeniluv, Alexandre Mouracade, DJ Hoff

Why it Kills: Making Shapes (www. facebook.com/making.shapes.events) started with a clear mission: to fill a void in LA nightlife by throwing an authentic party for the creative types who like their nights out a little dirty. By hosting local Hollywood talent and attracting international headliners in a renegade warehouse venue, it has become a badge of honour for visiting DJs to play. As the party starts to host other events, look for Making Shapes to pop up poolside at hotels and other creative venues.

The Music: An international hit list of the biggest DJs in the game – Kim Ann Foxmann, Mark E (Fabric UK), Benoit & Sergio (DC), Mark E Quark and Matais Aguayo (Chile).

The Scene: About 700 of greater LA's fashion-philes, drag queens, artists, musicians, designers and actors all party pretty along with those who make the pilgrimage from San Diego and the Inland area.

A CLUB CALLED RHONDA

Thrown By: Gregory Alexander and Goddollars; hosted by POPtART gallery owner and photographer Phyliss Navidad

Why it Kills: What started as an adverse reaction to LA's celebutante-heavy and TMZ-soaked club scene has flourished into one of the artsy-est, most inclusive parties in the city. The promoters of A Club Called Rhonda (http://rhondasays.net) steer clear of top 40 by wrangling talent from Europe and American underground scenes. Eccentric dressers are rewarded with line privileges and free entry, and for an extra dash of irreverence, free

Jell-O shots are passed out to partygoers to help keep the energy up.

The Music: Rhonda takes the best DJs and acts – Monty Luke, Jacques Renault, Metro Area and Peanut Butter Wolf – off their superclub tour stops and places them in a homespun atmosphere.

The Scene: This polysexual crowd of extreme dressers know they'll score instant entry for donning daring looks. Still, the be-whoever-you-want-to-be message prevails, so everyone from streetwear-soaked artists to familiar faces such as Leona Lewis and Dita Von Teese rock everything from wedding dresses to wife beaters.

HARVEY SARCASTIC DISCO

Thrown By: DJ Harvey and Paul T & Junior

Why it Kills: The incomparable DJ Harvey, who has graced everything from Ministry of Sound to House of Burberry parties, is the only DJ billed to throw down six-plus hours of body-rocking beats. Harvey Sarcastic Disco (www.harveysarcasticdisco.com) is the quintessential party for purists – there are no international mystery DJs flown in to bloat cover charges and no gimmicks. If you're here, you're dancing.

The Music: Expect a mix of soul, house, hip hop, funk, breaks, you name it. Harvey's speciality is uncovering long-lost tracks and exposing them to the masses.

A Club Called Rhonda.

ARTS & ENTERTAINMENT

Harvey Sarcastic Disco.

The Scene: This party's elusive 'if you don't know, ask somebody' motto keeps the crowd control to a legit 800-1,000 joyful souls (multi-generational disciples of disco, soul and house) who treasure the underground vibe of this under-the-radar event. This crowd is there for one reason only – to dance.

LIGHTS DOWN LOW
Thrown By: Sleazemore and Richie Panic (of Frisco Disco and Blow Up)
Why it Kills: Corey Sleazemore brought banger electro with him when he decamped from Florida to San Francisco more than seven years ago. As the scene evolved, so did Lights Down Low (www.lightsdownlow.net); he and partner Richie Panic later brought their signature dark, gritty aesthetic to the southland, pouring heart, soul and major coin into their first LA party. With more than 700 people showing up to LA's first LDL, the event has paved the way for more epic parties to come; going forward, look for quarterly throwdowns at both club and warehouse venues.
The Music: Everything from a Yeah Yeah Yeahs' Nick Zinner DJ set to a Blaqstarr performance.
The Scene: Panic's DIY punk background and Sleazemore's baby-raver upbringing mix to create a deliberately understyled atmosphere where music is the thing. The gritty atmosphere attracts a wide span of house-lovers in the know, but it's the plain-clothed house heads that keep the dancefloor throbbing.

DEEP
Thrown By: Marques Wyatt
Why it Kills: While 'deep' refers to the dark, gut-reaching, heart-shaking brand of house that's often played at this party (http://prelaunch.deep-la.com), the event could just as easily be called 'soul'. Month after month, Wyatt works to provide a transformative experience for its revellers by way of spirit-lifting beats, low lighting and artistic images. And it's a conscientious approach that's been working for an unheard-of decade and a half, since it launched in the Viper Room (of all places). Since, Deep has hosted everything from an air-guitar wailing Prince to Classic Nights, where longtime fans bust out their throwback Deep-issue tees and DJs dig in the crates for timeless cuts.
The Music: Marques Wyatt, a house music legend in his own right, uses his contact list to keep Deep one of the most true-school parties in town. Look for heavy hitters such as Miguel Migs, Louie Vegas, Mark Farina and Doc Martin. Meanwhile, Deep's Innovator Series features up-and-coming talent.
The Scene: Its organic vibe makes for a bare-bones atmosphere. Veteran house-lovers co-mingle with fresh, young things to comprise a crowd of 400 people who are there to bliss out and just dance.

Sevilla

140 Pine Avenue, at N Tribune Court, Long Beach (1-562 495 1111, www.sevillanightclub. com). Metro Transit Mall/I-110, exit 9th Street east. **Open** 10pm-2am Wed-Sat. **Admission** $5-$20. **Credit** AmEx, DC, Disc, MC, V.

Well-heeled patrons entering Long Beach's tapas haven for a bite often have to trip over a line of teenage hopefuls waiting to get into its second-floor sister club of the same name. Its young clientele often draws stern looks from Los Angeles' cops posted across the street but Sevilla, the club, is mostly mild-mannered, even as its hip hop beats breathe subwoofer fire for what seem to be blocks. With the demise of superclub V20 nearby, this is one of the LBC's few dance club choices these days.

Vanguard

6021 Hollywood Boulevard, at N Bronson Avenue, Hollywood (1-323 463 3331, www.vanguard la.com). Metro Hollywood-Vine/bus 163, 180, 181, 210, 212, 217, 312, 780, LDH/US 101, exit Hollywood Boulevard west. **Open** 9pm-2am Mon-Fri; 9pm-4am Sat. **Admission** $10-$40. **Credit** AmEx, DC, MC, V. **Map** p313 C1.

This former rave warehouse is now one of the city's finest superclubs, complete with an enchanting, Buddha-lined patio and a Funktion One sound system that can and should be heard for miles. On Friday nights, quality progressive and techno spinners make this one of Hollywood's best dance venues.

Villains Tavern

1356 Palmetto Street, at S Santa Fe Avenue, Downtown (1-213 613 0766, www.villainstavern. com). Bus 18/I-10, exit Mateo Street. **Open** 5pm-12.30am Mon-Wed; 5pm-2am Thur; 3pm-2am Fri, Sat; 3pm-1am Sun. **Admission** free. **Credit** AmEx, DC, Disc, MC, V.

Walls of dust-covered bottles (for decoration only) and artfully prepared cocktails served up in mason jars lend an apothecary atmosphere to this Downtown arts district mainstay. Candlelit outdoor tables and live bluegrass bands round off the charm, and though it's a geographical outlier – you'll have to drive to hit the next spot – it's well worth a visit.

Zanzibar

1301 5th Street, at Arizona Avenue, Santa Monica (1-310 451 2221, www.zanzibarlive.com). Bus 4, 20, 33, 733, SM1, SM5, SM7, SM8, SM10/I-10, exit 4th/5th Street north. **Open** usually 9pm-2am daily. **Admission** free-$15. **Credit** AmEx, DC, MC, V. **Map** p310 B2.

This African-themed hangout is a West Side institution, and offers some of the region's most eclectic and forward-thinking DJs – soul, indie-hip hop and world-beat spinners who cater for a well-heeled, international crowd. Groove on the small dancefloor, order a Chimay at the bar or grab a pillow and relax on the benches at the back. *Photo p212.*

Music

ROCK & POP

From the dizzy heights of the Sunset Strip during the 1960s to the stagnant waters of the '90s, LA's music scene has had its highs and lows. However, since the turn of the millennium, local groups have begun to make an impression

Playhouse. *See p213.*

once again. Among the highlights: the underground hip hop of Stones Throw Records acts such as Madlib, breakout indie-rock bands including Rilo Kiley, and such unique products of the city's musical melting pot as Dengue Fever. Social networking and online downloads have also changed the shape of the scene as many unsigned artists can now draw crowds through their internet presence creating a much richer and more diverse array of musical offerings to the smaller venues. The melding of cultures ensures a rich variety of sounds that bubbles with ideas. At the same time, LA attracts a steady flow of hot-ticket touring acts, from slick pop stars to gritty hip hoppers via a constant turnover of indie buzz bands. And even if the recession has led to the demise of a few venues, the city is still home to a huge number of venues to suit anyone's taste, from vast arenas to hole-in-the-wall neighbourhood bars.

Bring photo ID to every venue: some shows are open only to over-18s or over-21s, and you'll need to be 21 or older to get served at the bar. For free events, *see p232* **Notes for Nothing**.

Arenas, theatres & large clubs

Two traditionally classical venues have seen a recent uptick in the number of rock and pop shows they stage: **Disney Hall** (*see p229*) has welcomed everyone from Grizzly Bear to the Chieftains, while the **Hollywood Bowl** (*see p228*) has featured everyone from Florence + The Machine to Animal Collective.

Gibson Amphitheatre

Universal CityWalk, 100 Universal City Plaza, Universal City (1-818 622 4440, www.gibson-amphitheatre.net). Metro Universal City/Studio City/bus 96, 156, 166/US 101, exit Universal Center Drive. **Box office** *In person* 1-8.30pm Mon-Fri. *By phone/online* Ticketmaster (*p162*). **Tickets** $25-$150. *Parking* $10-$20. **Credit** AmEx, DC, Disc, MC, V.

Located at the far end of Universal CityWalk, this slick, semi-circular mid-sized room serves a wide array of major pop, R&B and Latin artists – plus the odd soprano and comedy act – with everyone from Sarah Brightman to No Doubt on the calendar. The sterile setting and sometimes frigid air-conditioning are downsides, but clean sightlines and good sonics make this a popular spot.

Greek Theatre

2700 N Vermont Avenue, in Griffith Park (1-323 665 5857, www.greektheatrela.com). Bus 180, 181/US 101, exit Vermont Avenue north. **Box office** *In person* noon-6pm Mon-Fri; 10am-4pm Sat, Sun. *By phone/online* Ticketmaster (*p162*). **Tickets** $25-$150. *Parking* $15. **Credit** AmEx, DC, MC, V. **Map** p314 A1.

This pleasant, open-air, 6,000-seat theatre has the visual advantage of being nestled neatly into the flora of Griffith Park. Excellent acoustics and show bills featuring everyone from Al Green to Gotye guarantee a sell-out season from April to October. Pro tip: pack a picnic and take advantage of 'non-stacked parking' ($20).

Hollywood Palladium

6215 W Sunset Boulevard, between Argyle & N El Centro Avenues, Hollywood (1-323 962 7600, www.livenation.com). Metro Hollywood-Vine/bus 2, 212, 217, 302, LDHWI/US 101, exit Vine Street south. **Box office** 10am-2pm Sat & 2hrs before shows. *By phone/online* Ticketmaster (*p162*). **Tickets** $40-$75. **Credit** *Ticketmaster* AmEx, DC, Disc, MC, V. **Map** p313 B2.

Once ruled by the big band sounds of Glenn Miller and Tommy Dorsey, this vintage ballroom is part of Live Nation these days. Over the years it has hosted awards ceremonies, celebrity parties and an impressive array of music shows, from hip hop to punk bands to classic rock and indie faves and it continues to present big-name artists.

House of Blues

8430 W Sunset Boulevard, at N Olive Drive, West Hollywood (1-323 848 5100, www.house ofblues.com). Bus 2, 302/I-10, exit La Cienega Boulevard north. **Box office** *In person* show days only. *By phone/online* Ticketmaster (*p162*). **Admission** $20-$50. **Credit** AmEx, DC, Disc, MC, V. **Map** p312 B1.

This club's faux blues-shack exterior stands in odd contrast to the major-to-rising rock, punk and rap acts that fill its calendar. The cramped conditions are annoying, but the food is good (come for Gospel Brunch on Sundays) and the sound is above average, except under the balcony. There's also a (less revered) branch in Anaheim.

ARTS & ENTERTAINMENT

ARTS & ENTERTAINMENT

Music Box

6126 Hollywood Boulevard, between N El Centro Avenue & N Gower Street, Hollywood (1-323 930 7100). Metro Hollywood-Highland/bus 212, 217/ US 101, exit Hollywood Boulevard west. **Box office** *In person* 10am-6pm Mon-Fri. *By phone/ online* Ticketmaster (*p162*). **Admission** $15-$40. **Credit** AmEx, DC, Disc, MC, V. **Map** p313 B1.

Built in the 1920s, this Hollywood institution has had more facelifts than most of its performers. After a stint as the Henry Ford Theater, staging Broadway shows and theatre productions, in 2002 the Music Box revived its original name and began presenting music, attracting the likes of Stevie Wonder and Green Day. Yet another renovation in 2010 restored much of its Golden Age splendour. Parking nearby can be trying but there are two private lots.

Nokia Theatre at L.A. LIVE

777 Chick Hearn Court, 11th & Figueroa Streets, Downtown (1-213 763 6030, http://nokia theatrelalive.com). Metro Pico/bus 81, 246, 381, 442, 460/I-110, exit Olympic Boulevard east. **Box office** *In person* from Staples Center (*see right*); or show days only. *By phone/online* Ticketmaster (*p162*). **Tickets** $30-$150. *Parking* $10-$25. **Credit** AmEx, DC, Disc, MC, V. **Map** p315 A5.

This slick, 7,100-capacity hall is part of the $2.5 billion L.A. LIVE entertainment complex. The sound system is fantastic and the seating is plush, but the offerings are less than interesting, falling back on variety and kids' shows. Parking can be tough if there's an event at the Staples Center (*see right*) next door: it's quicker to park further away and walk, or to take public transport.

Orpheum

842 S Broadway, between 8th & 9th Streets (1- 877 677 4386, www.laorpheum.com). Metro Pershing Square/bus 2, 4, 30, 40, 42, 45, 48/I-110, exit 9th Street east. **Box office** *In person* show days and cash only. *By phone/ online* Ticketmaster (*p162*). **Tickets** $30-$100. **Credit** AmEx, DC, Disc, MC, V. **Map** p315 C4.

Judy Garland once graced the stage of this landmark, which opened in 1926. Nowadays, it prefers rock and pop acts such as Ben Harper, Joe Jackson and Ani DiFranco, alongside the occasional comic. The sound, especially from under the balcony on the main floor, is fine, and the space grand. Unfortunately, the seats have to be the most knee-crunchingly close-set in town, and parking can be a chore if you don't want to opt for one of the nearby lots.

▶ *For more about the Orpheum, see p70* **Broadway Booming.**

★ El Rey Theatre

5515 Wilshire Boulevard, between Burnside & Dunsmuir Avenues, Miracle Mile (information 1-323 936 6400, www.theelrey.com). Bus 20, 21, 720, LDF/I-10, exit La Brea Avenue north. **Box office** *In person* Music Box box office (*see left*). *By phone/online* See website for details. **Tickets** $15-$40. **Credit** AmEx, DC, Disc, MC, V. **Map** p312 D4.

This original art deco movie house was converted into a 900-capacity music venue in 1994. Sound and sightlines are excellent (it's general admission). With a roster that continues to be inspired and interesting, El Rey has become a classic on the LA music scene.

Staples Center

1111 S Figueroa Street, at 11th Street, Downtown (1-213 742 7340, www.staplescenter.com). Metro Pico/bus 81, 246, 381, 442, 460/I-110, exit Olympic Boulevard east. **Box office** *In person* 10am-6pm Mon-Sat; from 10am event days. *By phone/online* Ticketmaster (*p162*). **Tickets** $50-$250. **Credit** AmEx, DC, MC, V. **Map** p315 A5.

Downtown's sports shrine also hosts big musical acts, from Madonna to Morrissey. Though it's plush and modern, the sound quality in the 20,000-capacity arena is surprisingly variable. At the concession stand, don't miss the *nachos camachos*, an LA favourite.

★ Wiltern

3790 Wilshire Boulevard, at S Western Avenue, Koreatown (1-213 388 1400, www.livenation. com). Metro Wilshire-Western/bus 20, 21, 207, 209, 720, LDHWI/I-10, exit Western Avenue north. **Box office** *In person* show days only, or at Hollywood Palladium box office (*see p217*), 10am-2pm Sat. *By phone/online* Ticketmaster (*p162*). **Tickets** $30-$70. **Credit** MC, V. **Map** p313 D5.

This classy art deco gem packs 'em in for shows from the alt-rock likes of My Morning Jacket and Ellie Goulding, as well as the odd comic act. For general admission shows you can stand downstairs or sit in the balcony. The sightlines are a plus, but elbow room in the best spots can be at a premium.

Bar & club venues

In addition to the clubs below, other venues in the city stage live music. The **Key Club** (9039 W Sunset Boulevard, West Hollywood, 1-310 274 5800, www.keyclub.com) offers occasional shows alongside its club programming, while **Los Globos** (3040 W Sunset Boulevard, Silver Lake, 1-323 666 6669, www.clublosglobos.com) is a two-storeyed hotspot for everything from local house DJs to vaudeville variety acts. Club shows in LA generally start between 8pm and 9pm and finish between 11pm and midnight, though there are exceptions. Tickets for club shows are usually available on the door for cash (credit card information given below is usually for the bar), though some venues do sell tickets in advance; check websites for details. As always, be sure to have some form of ID.

Essential Los Angeles Albums

Sounds of the city.

AJA
STEELY DAN (1977)

'Black Cow', 'Peg', 'Deacon Blues', ... Becker and Fagen's finest, and an LA archetype for the New York-founded group, which became its best-selling album. Its follow-up, *Gaucho* (1980), epitomised the souring of the Hollywood dream, with addiction, legal woes and perfectionist standards dogging the interminable recording.

L.A. WOMAN
THE DOORS (1971)

The sixth studio album by the quintessential LA quartet, it was also the last recorded with Jim Morrison, who laid down his vocals in the studio's bathroom to get the right echo. It's tough to choose between the sublime title track and the haunting 'Riders on the Storm'. A testament to Mr Mojo Risin', who died three months after the record's release.

GRAND PRIX
TEENAGE FANCLUB (1995)

In which four pasty Scottish lads journey to LA and leave with the sunniest rock record of the last two decades. The lyrics are at their most heartfelt on the melancholic 'Mellow Doubt', and while it's not the most obvious soundtrack choice for driving through the City of Angels on a bright day, somehow it works. Essential.

TODAY!/SUMMER DAYS AND SUMMER NIGHTS
THE BEACH BOYS (2001)

Splendid two-for-one reissue of a pair of early albums – both first released in 1965 – by this most quintessentially Californian band. Stellar hits collection *Endless Summer* (1974) also does the trick, although, frustratingly, the seminal 'Good Vibrations' wasn't added until the album's CD reissue in 1987.

FOREVER CHANGES
LOVE (1967)

One of the few records from the LA rock scene of the late 1960s that's held up. And how: *Forever Changes* is a blissed-out folk-rock diamond, despite the Hendrix-esque 'Bummer in the Summer'. Seriously under-appreciated at the time, the album is now a critics' favourite and was inducted into the Grammy Hall of Fame in 2008.

THE WORLD IS A GHETTO
WAR (1972)

Fearsome, funky and fantastic, this is the sound of black LA in the early '70s, courtesy of the multi-sound, multi-ethnic SoCal band. The title track could've come from a Tarantino movie, while 'the Cisco Kid' is both iconic and interminable. Hard to believe it but Eric 'The Animals' Burdon was a founding member.

Airliner

2419 N Broadway, between Daly Street & S Avenue 24, Lincoln Heights (1-323 221 0771, http://theairlinerla.com). Bus 45, 83, 251/I-5, exit Broadway/Daly Street. **Admission** free-$10. **Credit** AmEx, DC, MC, V.

Although off the beaten path, the Airliner is well worth the extra mileage. Recently renovated, the bar and live music venue features two floors, large outdoor and upstairs patios, and an unrivalled sound system. Every Wednesday night it hosts the LA-based Low End Theory, a haven for hip hop heads and beat junkies. Be warned: the crowd is young, and the decibels are off the chart.

Bootleg Theater

2220 Beverly Boulevard, at Roselake Avenue, Silver Lake (1-213 389 3856, www.bootleg theater.org). Bus 14, 37, 200/US 101, exit N Alvarado Street. **Admission** free-$25. **Credit** AmEx, Disc, MC, V. **Map** p314 C6.

This 1930s warehouse space now plays home to local artists working in theatre, music, dance and film. With shows presented by the Fold, which takes pride in discovering and showcasing burgeoning acts, it pretty much guarantees high-quality, hand-picked, indie bands and singer-songwriters any night of the week.

Café Fais Do-Do

5253 W Adams Boulevard, between S Cloverdale Avenue & S Redondo Boulevard, West LA (1-323 931 4636, www.faisdodo.com). Bus 37/I-10, exit La Brea Avenue south. **Admission** $5-$20. **Credit** AmEx, DC, MC, V.

Once mostly the province of blues and zydeco acts, Fais Do-Do (Cajun dialect for 'dance party') now stages a 'gumbo of eclectic music', anything from rockabilly and Brazilian bands to hip hop turntablists. The faded opulent interior and desolate West Side location add to the exotic vibe.

Cinema Bar

3967 Sepulveda Boulevard, between Washington Place & Venice Boulevard, Culver City (1-310 390 1328, www.thecinemabar.com). Bus C1, C6/I-405, exit Washington Boulevard east. **Admission** free. **Credit** AmEx, DC, Disc, MC, V.

This tiny, rustic spot, the oldest bar in Culver City, draws a bohemian crowd to its nightly shows. You'll find a high percentage of fine local acts, such as singer-songwriters Randy Weeks and Duane Jarvis and retro-rocker Ben Vaughan. Added bonus: drinks are cheap.

Echo

1822 W Sunset Boulevard, at Glendale Boulevard, Echo Park (1-213 413 8200, www.attheecho.com). Bus 2, 4, 96, 302, 304/US 101, exit Glendale Boulevard north. **Admission** free-$25. **Credit** AmEx, DC, MC, V. **Map** p314 D4.

Hotel Café.

Hipsters flock to this often-jammed club for all flavours of indie, dub reggae and electronica. Saturday nights feature Funky Sole fare, and the bar serves up drinks alongside slices of Two Boots pizza from the restaurant next door. A back patio offers a quaint retreat from the crowds, and its poster-lined walls pay homage to the venue's rich (though fairly recent) history.

Echoplex

1154 Glendale Boulevard, at W Sunset Boulevard, Echo Park (1-213 413 8200, www.attheecho.com). Bus 2, 4, 96, 302, 304/US 101, exit Glendale Boulevard north. **Admission** $5-$25. **Credit** AmEx, DC, MC, V. **Map** p314 D5.

This big, low-slung space is situated under the Echo (*see above*), but it's a separate venue with a different entrance. The roster is similar to that offered at the Echo: local indie acts, the occasional residency by LA luminaries, and touring artists who draw bigger crowds (Ed Harcourt, Built to Spill, Dizzie Rascal). Like the Echo, it can be sweltering when crowded.

★ Hotel Café

16232 N Cahuenga Boulevard, between Hollywood Boulevard & Selma Avenue, Hollywood (1-323 461 2040, www.hotelcafe.com). Metro Hollywood-Vine/bus 156, 210, 212, 217, 710, LDH/US 101, exit Hollywood Boulevard west. **Admission** $8-$15. **Credit** MC, V. **Map** p313 B1.

After more than a decade, this intimate haven continues to be a staple on the singer-songwriter circuit, hosting local favourites such as the Cary Brothers and Jim Bianco as well as national and international touring acts such as Rachael Yamagata and Imogen

Heap. You can't go wrong with the line-up: that is, if you can hear over the bar chat, which can overwhelm the music when it's busy. Get there early if you want to nab one of the few tables and settle in for the night.

Joint

8771 W Pico Boulevard, at S Robertson Boulevard, Beverly Hills (1-310 275 2619, www.thejointlive.com). Bus 28/I-10, exit Robertson Avenue north. **Admission** $5-$15. **Credit** AmEx, MC, V. **Map** p312 A5.

Joint has a chaotic booking policy, encompassing everything from hip hop DJs to folk singers and local wannabe bands. Check out the club's jam sessions, where you might see some major stars let rip.

King King

6555 Hollywood Boulevard, between Whitney Avenue & Schrader Boulevard, Hollywood (1-323 960 5765, www.kingkinghollywood.com). Metro Hollywood-Highland/bus 156, 212, 217, 222, 312, LDH/US 101, exit Highland Avenue north. **Admission** free-$30. **Credit** AmEx, MC, V. **Map** p313 B1.

A club with many hats, King King's event calendar may seem haphazard – live Latin and Tropical music shares weeknight slots with hip hop dance troupes and local DJs – but the venue's vibe is consistently fresh. Expect to see partygoers of all ages and orientations, and despite being set in the middle of Hollywood, the experience is anything but.

Largo

Coronet Theatre, 366 N La Cienega Boulevard, at Oakwood Avenue, West Hollywood (1-310 855 0350, www.largo-la.com). Bus 4, 105, 550, 704/I-10, exit La Cienega Boulevard north. **Admission** $20-$40. **Credit** AmEx, DC, MC, V. **Map** p312 C3.

This 280-seat theatre is LA's home for cultured, bankable singer-songwriters, with the likes of Aimee Mann, John Doe, Jill Sobule and perennial hot-ticket artist-in-residence Jon Brion plying their trade here. The strictly enforced no-talking policy can feel a bit excessive and, combined with no drinks in the performance space, makes it feel more like a church than a music venue. Ideal for folk purists.

▶ *Next door, the speakeasy-style Roger Room (370 N La Cienega Boulevard, 1-310 854 1300) is a great venue for a pre- or post-performance cocktail.*

Mint

6010 W Pico Boulevard, at Stearns Drive, Midtown (1-323 954 9400, www.themintla.com). Bus 217/I-10, exit Fairfax Avenue north. **Admission** $8-$20. **Credit** AmEx, DC, MC, V. **Map** p312 C5.

Once hosting the likes of Stevie Wonder and Ray Charles, this classy venue is more than 75 years old. Today's schedule of primarily roots- and blues-oriented acts includes notable touring acts (Rebirth Brass Band, the Dirty Dozen Brass Band) and fine local stalwarts (Café R&B, Leo Nocentelli, Diane Birch) along with more unremarkable fare. Excellent food and, following an expansion a few years ago, a comfortable room to spend an evening.

Mr T's Bowl

5621 N Figueroa Avenue, between Avenue 56 & Avenue 57, Highland Park (1-323 256 7561, http://mrtsbowl.tripod.com). Metro Highland

ARTS & ENTERTAINMENT

Smell. *See p222.*

Park/bus 83, 256/Highway 110, exit Avenue 52.
Admission free-$10. **Credit** AmEx, DC, MC, V.
Mr T passed away in 2005 and with him some of the magic that made this old bowling alley-cum-music venue such a legendary venue. But ageing locals and young hipsters still rub shoulders to a line-up of rock/punk/grunge and the sound is pretty decent.

Roxy

9009 W Sunset Boulevard, between San Vicente Boulevard & Doheny Drive, West Hollywood (1-310 276 2222, www.theroxyonsunset.com). Bus 2, 105, 302/I-10, exit La Cienega Boulevard north. **Admission** $12-$35. **Credit** AmEx, DC, Disc, MC, V. **Map** p312 A2.
In its 40 years as a Sunset Strip stalwart, the Roxy has been both a major player (hosting Neil Young, early Springsteen and Guns N' Roses shows) and a disappointing has-been (insert name of horrible '80s hair band here). Now that the Roxy has settled comfortably into middle age, the club offers a more mellow fare of singer-songwriters, bluegrass and country and the occasional local up-and-comer, plus comedy and club nights. The tables offer the best views, but the sightlines from the standing risers are fine – and closer to the bar.

Satellite

1717 Silver Lake Boulevard, at Effie Street, Silver Lake (1-323 661 4380, www.thesatellitela.com). Bus 201/US 101, exit Silver Lake Boulevard north. **Admission** $7-$20. **Credit** AmEx, DC, MC, V. **Map** p314 C3.
Previously Spaceland, the sprawling dive now known as the Satellite opened in 1995, and it remains the leading LA shrine to all things indie. The sound isn't great and parking is a combat sport, but it's still popular. The Monday-night programme, which features free monthly residencies for local buzz bands on their way up, is always worth a look.

Silverlake Lounge

2906 W Sunset Boulevard, at Parkman Avenue, Silver Lake (1-323 663 9636, www.thesilverlake lounge.com). Bus 2, 4, 302, 304/US 101, exit Silver Lake Boulevard north. **Admission** free-$12. **No credit cards. Map** p314 C4.
Depending on the night, this hangout is either a grungy watering hole favoured by transvestites or a grungy rock club favoured by indie bands. The sound is dire, the sightlines terrible and the smell of beer fierce, but ascendant out-of-towners (Scanners, Tame Impala) and local acts (Family of the Year, White Arrows) usually deliver.

Smell

247 S Main Street, between 2nd & 3rd Streets, Downtown (www.thesmell.org). Metro Pershing Square/bus 16, 316/I-110, exit 4th Street east. **Admission** $5. **Credit** AmEx, DC, MC, V. **Map** p315 C3.

The closest thing to a European squat-style venue in Los Angeles, this stark, hard-to-find warehouse-like space near Skid Row hosts the latest in indie-noise, political art-punk and the like. The Smell doesn't serve booze, and thus attracts an all-ages crowd skewed towards the younger end of the range. Veggie-friendly snacks are available. *Photo p221.*

★ Troubadour

9081 Santa Monica Boulevard, at N Doheny Drive, West Hollywood (1-310 276 1158, www.troubadour.com). Bus 4, 304/I-405, exit Santa Monica Boulevard east. **Admission** free-$30. **Credit** AmEx, DC, MC, V. **Map** p312 A2.
Still one of LA's best clubs, the Troubadour has a rich musical history: Randy Newman got his start here, and Elton John made his US debut on its stage in 1970. It continues to present old favourites, new international names and local talent, from the Cure's first US club show in 20 years to Lily Allen's US debut. The sound is great and the views are decent – just stay out from under the balcony.

Viper Room

8852 W Sunset Boulevard, at Larrabee Street, West Hollywood (1-310 358 1880, www.viper room.com). Bus 2, 105, 302/I-10, exit La Cienega Boulevard east. **Admission** free-$20. **Credit** AmEx, MC, V. **Map** p312 A2.
Clumsy punk acts, actors' bands, Hollywood detritus and the occasional singer-songwriter of varying vintages play this faux-deco hole on the Sunset Strip. It's also famous for being the place where River Phoenix died in 1993.

Whisky A Go-Go

8901 W Sunset Boulevard, at N San Vicente Boulevard, West Hollywood (1-310 652 4202, www.whiskyagogo.com). Bus 2, 105, 302/I-10, exit La Cienega Boulevard north. **Admission** $10-$15. **Credit** AmEx, DC, MC, V. **Map** p312 A2.
The Doors were once the house band at the Whisky, until the owner objected to the lyrics of 'The End' and banned the group. Its place in Sunset Strip lore can't be denied, but these days the music comes mostly from rock tribute acts and young bands of the punk/metal variety, few of whom you'll ever hear of again.

ROOTS & BLUES

Country, folk and Irish music join imported beers on the menu at **Molly Malone's** (575 S Fairfax Avenue, Miracle Mile, 1-323 935 1577, www. mollymalonesla.com). The nostalgic **Dresden** (*see p125*) in Los Feliz comes complete with old-Hollywood decor and lounge singers performing Sinatra-era classics five nights a week.

Harvelle's

1432 4th Street, between Broadway & Santa Monica Boulevard, Santa Monica (1-310 395

Baked Potato.

Admission $5-$30. **Credit** AmEx, DC, Disc, MC, V. **Map** p310 D4.

By day a revered guitar shop (*see p162*, McCabe's doubles as an intimate performance space. The roster of acts has included rootsy singers such as Odetta and Chris Hillman, but also indie perennials such as Kristin Hersh and Peter Case, and more unexpected acts such as Nels Cline and Eugene Chadbourne. Gigs are usually held on Fridays, Saturdays and Sundays.

JAZZ

The city's jazz venues are scattered from pillar to post, although the economic downturn has seen the closure of old institutions such as **La Ve Lee**. But all is not lost: there is a quietly blossoming alternative scene thanks to organisations and promoters like **Los Angeles Jazz Collective** (www.lajazzcollective.com) and **Rocco Somazzi** (www.roccoinla.com), both of whom present various events around town. In 2007, Rocco founded **Angel City Jazz Festival** (www.angelcityjazz.com), held in October at a handful of major venues.

Aside from the venues listed below, you'll find all manner of bars, hotels and restaurants hosting jazz acts, many of them top-notch sessioneers playing as much for pleasure as for pay. Downtown, jazz is also presented most weekends at **Café Metropol** (923 E 3rd Street, 1-213 613 1537, www.cafemetropol.com).

Baked Potato
3787 Cahuenga Boulevard W, at Lankershim Boulevard, Studio City (1-818 980 1615, www. thebakedpotato.com). Bus 96, 150, 156, 240, 750/US 101, exit Lankershim Boulevard south. **Admission** $10-$30; 2-drink min. **Credit** AmEx, DC, Disc, MC, V.

Don Randi's pint-sized room spawned the LA jazz fusion sound in the 1970s. It's still the site of synth-driven romps, though nowadays Latin jazz acts appear too. Famous session sidemen show up frequently and, the menu is full of – yes! – potatoes.

★ Blue Whale
123 Astronaut Ellison S Onizuka Street, Suite 301, between E 1st & S San Pedro Streets, Little Tokyo (1-213 620 0908, www.bluewhalemusic. com). Metro Little Tokyo/Arts District or Union Station/bus 1, 2, 30, 40, 42, 442/US 101, exit Los Angeles Street south. **Admission** $10-$20. **Credit** AmEx, DC, Disc, MC, V. **Map** p315 D2.

On the third floor of Weller Court, in the heart of Little Tokyo, this gem is a fave on the local scene Thursday to Sunday nights; Monday is a jam session. Good-quality musicians, attentive staff, tasty Korean fusion fare and a mature crowd that's there to listen to, rather than talk over, the music. Free parking in the lot downstairs (with validation) is another boon.

1676, www.harvelles.com). Bus 4, 304, SM1, SM2, SM3, SM4, SM10/I-10, exit 4th/5th Street north. **Admission** $5-$15; 2-drink min. **No credit cards**. **Map** p310 A3.

Established in 1931, this sleek and sultry spot is Santa Monica's self-styled home of the blues, a little jazz and some serious burlesque. Check out Harlow Gold, a burlesque show with a modern twist (book seats at the bar and hold on to your glass!), held on the last two Thursdays of the month. The comfortable bar/lounge setting is often packed at weekends, and it pays to show up early.

Other locations 201 E Broadway, Long Beach (1-562 293 3700).

★ McCabe's
3101 Pico Boulevard, at 31st Street, Santa Monica (1-310 828 4497, www.mccabes.com). Bus SM7/I-10, exit Centinela Avenue south.

Vibrato.

Catalina Bar & Grill

6725 W Sunset Boulevard, between N Highland
& N Las Palmas Avenues, Hollywood (1-323 466
2210, www.catalinajazzclub.com). Bus 2, 302/
US 101, exit Sunset Boulevard west. **Admission**
$15-$35; 2-drink min except for diners. **Credit**
AmEx, DC, Disc, MC, V. **Map** p313 A2.

Catalina Popescu pulls some of jazz's heaviest hitters
to her civilised Hollywood establishment: old-timers
such as McCoy Tyner and Pharoah Sanders, plus
younger stars of the calibre of Joshua Redman and
a good proportion of dinner jazz-friendly vocalists.
The food isn't as good as the music, however.

★ Jazz Bakery

1-310 275 8961, http://jazzbakery.org.
Admission $10-$35. **Credit** DC, MC, V.

In 2009, after 16 years in the old Helms Bakery, this
not-for-profit enterprise lost its lease. In 2011, fans
were delighted to learn that it had been given a $2
million grant by the Annenberg Foundation to
develop a new home, next to the Kirk Douglas
Theatre on Washington Boulevard in Culver City
(*see p233*). When it opens (likely in 2015) the new
space, designed by Frank Gehry no less, will
include a performance area, a jazz museum and a
bakery-café, and will host around 250 shows each
year. In the meantime, check out the website for
itinerant shows.

Vibrato

2930 Beverly Glen Circle, at Beverly Glen
Boulevard, Bel Air (1-310 474 9400,
www.vibratogrilljazz.com). I-405, exit Sunset
Boulevard east. **Admission** free. **Credit** AmEx,
DC, MC, V.

Co-owned by Herb Alpert, this high-end steakhouse
books better talent; and, while the food and drinks
can be quite pricey, there's rarely a cover charge or
a drinks minimum. The food is very good, and you
might catch Will Smith or former LAPD police chief
William Bratton nodding their heads to the likes of
Bobby Hutcherson, Kenny Barron and local bass legend John Heard. Reservations are recommended.

COMEDY

Long-established laughatoriums such as the
Comedy Store and the Improv keep packing 'em
in, but there are alternatives (so to speak). And
keep your eyes peeled for oddball shows staged
in coffeehouses and other unexpected locations.
Reservation policies vary by club, but you
should try and book ahead if possible.

COMEDY CLUBS

Acme Comedy Theatre

135 N La Brea Avenue, between Beverly
Boulevard & W 1st Street, Hollywood (1-323
525 0202, www.acmecomedy.com). Bus 14, 37,
212, 312/I-10, exit La Brea Avenue north. **Shows**
8pm, 9pm, 10pm Fri; 7pm, 10pm Sat; other nights
vary. **Admission** *Regular shows* $10 & 1-drink
min. *Special shows* $10-$20. *All-evening pass* $15.
Credit AmEx, DC, MC, V. **Map** p313 A4.

This small and well-kept Hollywood theatre hosts *Saturday Night Live*-quality nights, and you can take that analogy however you please. Sketch comedy is the Acme's speciality; however, there's also improv. Russell Brand has been known to play here when he's in town.

Comedy & Magic Club

1018 Hermosa Avenue, between 10th Street & Pier Avenue, Hermosa Beach (1-310 372 1193, www.comedyandmagicclub.com). Bus 130/I-405, exit Rosecrans Boulevard west. **Shows** 8pm Tue-Fri; 8pm Sat; 7pm Sun; special events vary. **Admission** $15-$35; 2-item min. **Credit** AmEx, DC, MC, V.

The biggest names in stand-up come to this hallowed yet funky beach club miles from the Sunset Strip. Jay Leno tries out new material for his talk show every Sunday, and Jerry Seinfeld sometimes plays when he's in LA. Up-and-coming comics sometimes play the smaller-scale Live at the Lounge series.

Comedy Central Stage

6539 Santa Monica Boulevard, between Seward Street & Wilcox Avenue, Hollywood (1-323 960 5519, www.comedycentral.com). Bus 4/US 101, exit Vine Street south. **Shows** 8pm, nights vary. **Admission** free. **Map** p313 B2.

Developing comedians get a chance to hone their skills in front of a live audience at this low-key, always-free theatre run by the Comedy Central TV network. The result is intelligent comedy of all varieties. Unsurprisingly, the place is popular and booking ahead is a must. If you're lucky, you may see the next Flight of the Conchords. If you're unlucky, don't blame us.

ComedySportz

733 Seward Street, at Melrose Avenue, Hollywood (1-323 871 1193, www.comedysportzla.com). Bus 10, 48/US 101, exit Vine Street south. **Shows** 8pm Thur; 8pm, 10.30pm Fri, Sat; 7pm Sun; other nights vary. Admission $10-$19. **Credit** AmEx, DC, Disc, MC, V. **Map** p313 B3.

At ComedySportz's eponymous flagship show (8pm Fri, 8pm & 10.30pm Sat), teams of improvisers go head-to-head in a challenge, complete with a referee. Other shows take a similar improv bent: in the sporadically staged U-Sical, an entire musical is improvised around a single audience member.

Comedy Store

8433 W Sunset Boulevard, at N Olive Drive, West Hollywood (1-323 650 6268, www.the comedystore.com). Bus 2, 302/I-10, exit La Cienega Boulevard north. **Shows** nightly, times vary. **Admission** free-$20; 2-drink min. **Credit** AmEx, DC, MC, V. **Map** p312 B1.

The site that once held notorious Sunset Strip club Ciro's morphed into the Comedy Store in 1972.

Three separate stages host a monstrous array of stand-ups more or less every night of the week: check the website for precise times. If Chris Rock doesn't show up, you're bound to see someone who's almost as funny. Probably.

Comedy Union

5040 W Pico Boulevard, between S Sycamore & S La Brea Avenues, Midtown (1-323 934 9300, www.thecomedyunion.com). Bus 7, 13, 33, 212, 312, 733/I-10, exit La Brea Avenue north. **Shows** 9pm Mon-Thur; 10pm Fri; 8pm, 10.30pm Sat. **Admission** free-$12; 2-drink min. **Credit** AmEx, DC, Disc, MC, V. **Map** p312 D5.

Damon Wayans and DL Hughley are among the comics who've starred at this mid-city club, which specialises in talented African American stand-ups famous from their appearances on the likes of HBO's *Def Comedy Jam.*

Garrett Morris Downtown Blues & Comedy Club

501 S Spring Street, at W 5th Street & W 6th Street, Downtown (information 1-213 841 3940, http://bluesandcomedy.com). Metro Pershing Square/bus 16, 18, 30, 40, 45, 53, 68, 84, 316, 330/I-110, exit 6th Street east. **Shows** 8pm, 9pm Fri, Sat. **Admission** $10. **Credit** AmEx, DC, Disc, MC, V. **Map** p315 B3.

Garrett Morris, an original *Saturday Night Live* Not Ready for Prime-Time Player, runs one of the only regular comedy clubs in Downtown LA, located in the Alexandria Hotel, specialising in savvy stand-up. Morris himself often joins the headliners on stage, and even offers a money-back guarantee.

★ Groundlings Theatre

7307 Melrose Avenue, at N Poinsettia Place, West Hollywood (1-323 934 4747, www.groundlings.com). Bus 10, 48/I-10, exit Fairfax Avenue north. **Shows** 8pm Wed, Thur; 8pm, 10pm Fri, Sat; 7.30pm Sun. **Admission** $10-$20. **Credit** AmEx, DC, Disc, MC, V. **Map** p312 D2.

The holy hall of improvisational and character-based sketch comedy operates a popular theatre alongside an extensive programme of improv classes. Kathy Griffin, Will Ferrell, Phil Hartman and innumerable *Saturday Night Live* cast members have all shot to stardom from here.

Ice House

24 N Mentor Avenue, at E Colorado Boulevard, Pasadena (1-626 577 1894, www.icehousecomedy. com). Metro Lake/bus 20, 180, 181, 187, 256, 485, 686, 687, 720/I-210, exit Lake Avenue south. **Shows** 8pm Wed; 8pm, 10pm Thur; 8.30pm, 10.30pm Fri; 8pm, 10pm Sat; 7pm, 9pm Sun; other nights vary. **Admission** $10-$30; 2-drink min. **Credit** AmEx, DC, Disc, MC, V.

Nationally known touring comics such as Craig 'the Lovemaster' Shoemaker and Gabriel Iglesias are

ARTS & ENTERTAINMENT

regulars at this stand-up specialist up in Pasadena. The Ice House is also home to Rudy Moreno's popular Latino Comedy Showcase, held every Wednesday night.

Improv

8162 Melrose Avenue, between N Kilkea Drive & N La Jolla Avenue, West Hollywood (1-323 651 2583, www.improv.com). Bus 10, 48, LDF/I-10, exit La Cienega Boulevard north. **Shows** 8pm Mon; 8pm, 10pm Tue-Fri; 8pm, 10pm, midnight Sat; 7.30pm, 9.30pm Sun. **Admission** free-$30. **Credit** AmEx, DC, Disc, MC, V. **Map** p312 C2.

The oldest brick wall in town hosts two stand-up shows each night, with an early-evening open-mic on Tuesdays and Fridays at 6pm and popular black comedy night Mo' Betta Monday. Big-name drop-ins are frequent. Check the website, as special performances sometimes crop up at different times.

IO West

6366 Hollywood Boulevard, at Ivar Avenue, Hollywood (1-323 962 7560, http://west.ioimprov.com). Metro Hollywood-Vine/bus 210, 212, 217, 222, 312, 780 LDH/US 101, exit Vine Street south. **Shows** various shows nightly; check website for details. **Admission** free-$10. **Credit** DC, MC, V. **Map** p313 B1.

The LA outpost of the Chicago-based comedy set-up (formerly ImprovOlympic) offers several shows a night, many featuring the house improv speciality known as 'the Harold'. Weekly staples include Opening Night: the Improvised Musical (Fridays at 9pm); the cover charges and drinks prices are among the lowest on Hollywood Boulevard. If you're here in June, look out for the improv festival and the LA Scripted Comedy Festival, which launched in 2013.

LA Connection

13442 Ventura Boulevard, Sherman Oaks (1-818 710 1320 ext 2, www.laconnectioncomedy.com). Bus 150, 240/US 101, exit Coldwater Canyon Avenue south. **Shows** 8pm, 9pm, 10.30pm Fri; noon, 5.30pm, 8pm, 9pm, 10.30pm Sat; 3.30pm, 8pm Sun; other nights vary. **Admission** $7-$12. **Credit** AmEx, DC, Disc, MC, V. **Map** p312 B1.

Dedicated to nurturing comic talent, LA Connection is your best – OK, only – choice for improv, sketch and stand-up comedy in the Valley. If there's available seating, a single cover charge admits you to all three shows on any given night. Kids perform for kids on weekend afternoons.

Largo

Coronet Theater, 366 N La Cienega Boulevard, at Oakwood Avenue, West Hollywood (1-310 855 0350, www.largo-la.com). Bus 14, 37, 105, 705/US 101, exit Santa Monica Boulevard west. **Shows** call or see website for details. **Admission** $20-$25. **No credit cards**. Map p312 C3.

Largo is chiefly a music venue (*see p221*), but there's also plenty of smart, inventive comedy on the schedule. Major names such as Zach Galifianakis, Sarah Silverman and Patton Oswalt play the 280-seat main space; a cosy 60-seat club hosts the famed Largo Comedy Night on Monday, where drop-ins by the likes of Janeane Garofalo, Eddie Izzard and Flight of the Conchords keep audiences excited.

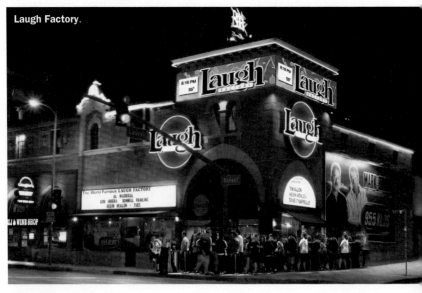

Laugh Factory.

Laugh Factory

8001 W Sunset Boulevard, at Laurel Canyon Boulevard, West Hollywood (1-323 656 1336 Ext. 1, www.laughfactory.com). Bus 2, 217, 218, 302, 780/I-10, exit La Cienega Boulevard north. **Shows** 8pm, 10pm Mon-Thur; Sun; 8pm, 10pm, midnight Fri, Sat. **Admission** $20-$30 Mon-Thur; $25-$35 Fri-Sun; $30-$35 VIP seating; 2-drink min. **Credit** DC, MC, V. **Map** p312 B1.

Comedian Kevin Nealon performs here regularly on Tuesdays, schedule permitting. On other nights, this Sunset Strip staple showcases touring stand-ups alongside themed evenings (Latino Night on Mondays, the outrageous urban comedy of Sunday's Chocolate Sundae). You'll need a VIP ticket to guarantee a seat. Dane Cook made it big here, but don't hold that against what is generally a dependable joint.

M Bar

1253 N Vine Street, at Fountain Avenue, Hollywood (1-323 856 0036, www.mbaronline.com). Bus 210/US 101, exit Vine Street south. **Shows** 8pm, 10pm nightly. **Admission** $5-$20; $10 food min. **Credit** AmEx, DC, Disc, MC, V. **Map** p313 B2.

This 100-seat venue, which is an Italian restaurant – visitors are expected to dine – features local comics and occasional special guests. The schedule varies: call for details of what's on when you're in town.

Second City Studio Theatre

6560 Hollywood Boulevard, at Schrader Boulevard, Hollywood (1-323 464 8542, www.secondcity.com). Metro Hollywood-Vine/bus 210,

212, 217, 222, 312, LDH/US 101, exit Vine Street south. **Shows** Mon-Sat, times vary. **Admission** free-$10. **Credit** AmEx, DC, Disc, MC, V. **Map** p313 B1.

Tucked away in an upstairs room on Hollywood Boulevard, this tiny theatre hosts regular improv shows that continue the kind of comedy experimentation made famous by Chicago legends such as John Belushi. There's a Friday night Showcase every week, featuring original material created by grads and alumni of Second City; check the website for details of other regular events.

Steve Allen Theater

Center for Inquiry, 4773 Hollywood Boulevard, at N Berendo Street, Los Feliz (1-323 666 4268, www.steveallentheater.com). Metro Vermont-Sunset/bus 180, 181, 204, 206, 217, 780/US 101, exit Vermont Avenue north. **Shows** midnight Sat; other nights vary. **Admission** $8-$20. **No credit cards. Map** p314 A2.

The Tomorrow Show, a bizarre variety performance with music and comedy, runs every Saturday at midnight, hosted by hotshots Craig Anton, Brendon Small and Ron Lynch. The programme also often includes fantastic, oddball shows by former Kids in the Hall, Emo Phillips and Mary Lynn Rajskub, among others. A true gem.

★ Upright Citizens Brigade Theatre

5919 Franklin Avenue, at N Bronson Avenue, Hollywood (1-323 908 8702, http://losangeles.ucbtheatre.com). Bus 180, 181, 217, LDH/US 101, exit Gower Street north. **Show** times vary, daily; see website. **Admission** free-$10. **No credit cards. Map** p313 C1.

The Upright Citizens Brigade Theatre puts on three or four shows per night across a variety of disciplines. Highlights include the flagship Asssscat improv show, $10 on Saturdays but free on Sundays, and the consistently star-studded Comedy Put Your Hands Together (8pm on Tuesdays), where you might find big names such as Bobcat Goldthwait or Aziz Ansari.

Westside Comedy Theater

1323A Third Street Promenade, at Arizona Avenue, Santa Monica (1-310 451 0850, www.westsidecomedy.com). Bus 20, 704, SM1, SM2, SM3, SM4, SM5, SM6, SM7, SM8, SM9, SM10/ I-10, exit 4th/5th Street north. **Shows** nightly; times vary. **Admission** free-$10. **Credit** AmEx, DC, Disc, MC, V. **Map** p310 A2.

Upstart improv comedy comes to the beach at the Westside Comedy Theater (formerly Westside Eclectic), where you'll find fine performers perfecting their craft in solid troupes such as the Ed Galvez Punk House, Mission IMPROVable, The Grind and Neal Brennan (co-creator of Chappelle's Show) and Friends. There is no drinks minimum, and the venue features a beer and wine bar.

ARTS & ENTERTAINMENT

Performing Arts

Starry, starry nights.

Los Angeles is too big to have a single coherent performing arts scene – and that's what brings a perpetual sense of adventure and surprise to its concert halls and venues. For every big-bucks musical extravaganza at Disney Hall there's a group of enthusiastic young actors eager to entertain you in a 50-seat space in the suburbs. As a result, your experience could be as immense as the city itself or as intimate as a quiet night at home. LA's dance scene, meanwhile, is small but includes some notable companies, with performances held most weekends.

ARTS & ENTERTAINMENT

CLASSICAL MUSIC & OPERA

LA's classical scene is one of the strongest in the US. The **LA Philharmonic** has had an excellent reputation for years, but the city's other, smaller ensembles also deliver the goods.

TICKETS & INFORMATION

Big-name concerts often sell out, so buy tickets in advance if possible. For listings and information, check the Time Out LA website (www.timeout.com/los-angeles, *LA Weekly* (www.laweekly.com) and the *LA Times* (www.latimes.com). For tickets, www.ticketmaster.com is incomparable.

CLASSICAL VENUES

In addition to the following, concerts are held at a number of venues around the LA region: the grand **Pasadena Convention Center** (300 E Green Street, Pasadena, 1-626 793 2122, www.pasadenacenter.com); a handful of churches; museums such as **LACMA** (*see p55*) and the **Skirball Center** (*see p43*); and college venues such as **Schoenberg Hall** and the beautiful **Royce Hall** at UCLA (1-310 825 2101, http://cap.ucla.edu) and the **Harriet & Charles Luckman Fine Arts Complex** at Cal State University in East LA (1-323 343 6600, www.luckmanarts.org).

For the weekly concerts at LACMA's **Leo S Bing Theatre**, *see p232* **Notes for Nothing**. And it's worth considering a trip out of town to the **Ojai Festival** in June

(www.ojaifestival. org), which offers a strong programme that ranges from familiar classics to modern works.

Dorothy Chandler Pavilion

Music Center, 135 N Grand Avenue, between W 1st & W Temple Streets, Downtown (1-213 972 7211, www.musiccenter.org). Metro Civic Center/Grand Park/Tom Bradley/bus 10, 14, 37, 48, 55, 60, 355, 701/I-110, exit 4th Street east. **Box office** *In person* 10am-6pm Tue-Sat. *By phone/online* Via individual companies (eg LA Opera) or Ticketmaster (*see p162*). **Tickets** $19-$310. *Parking* $9-$23. **Credit** AmEx, DC, MC, V. **Map** p315 B2.

The arrival of Disney Hall left this 1960s-era concert hall in the shade, almost taunting its rather dated exterior architecture (the interior is nicer) and, more pertinently, exposing its acoustics as substandard. The music at the 3,200-capacity theatre is now mostly limited to performances by the LA Opera (*see p230*) and dance companies; the sound is best from the upper floors, although the views from the top can be vertiginous.

★ Hollywood Bowl

2301 N Highland Avenue, at US 101 (1-323 850 2000, www.hollywoodbowl.com). Bus 156, 222/US 101, exit Highland Avenue north. **Box office** *In person* May-Sept noon-6pm Tue-Sun. *By phone/online* Via individual companies (eg LA Philharmonic) or Ticketmaster (*see p162*). **Tickets** $1-$150. *Parking* $17-$19. **Credit** AmEx, DC, Disc, MC, V.

This gorgeous outdoor amphitheatre has been hosting concerts since the LA Philharmonic first played here in 1922. Nestled in an aesthetically blessed fold in the Hollywood Hills, the 18,000-seat venue can bring out the romantic in the terminally cynical, and the glorious setting almost makes up for the somewhat dodgy acoustics. It's the summer home of the LA Philharmonic, but it's hosted everyone from the Beatles to Big Bird via Kylie and Coldplay, and today mixes classical concerts with rock and pop. Parking is limited, so patrons are encouraged to use the Park and Ride service – check the website for details.

★ Walt Disney Concert Hall

111 S Grand Avenue, between W 2nd & W 3rd Streets, Downtown (1-323 850 2000, www.laphil.com). Metro Civic Center/Grand Park/Tom Bradley/bus 10, 14, 37, 48, 55, 60, 355, 701/I-110, exit 4th Street east. **Box office** *In person* noon-6pm Tue-Sun; 2hrs before show. *By phone/online* Via individual companies (eg LA Philharmonic) or Ticketmaster *(see p162)*. **Tickets** $18-$185. *Parking* $9-$23. **Credit** AmEx, DC, Disc, MC, V. **Map** p315 B2.

The $274 million crown jewel of the LA Music Center, Disney Hall opened in 2003 to rave reviews. Even after a decade, the novelty hasn't yet worn off: both inside and out, this is a terrific venue. Designed by Frank Gehry, the hall features a 2,265-capacity auditorium with an open platform stage. Chief acoustician Yasuhisa Toyota combined the best aspects of orchestral halls in Tokyo, Berlin, Amsterdam and Boston in a bid to provide aural warmth and clarity; the result of his endeavours is a virtually perfect acoustic that works almost as well for amplified events as for orchestral performances. The hall is home to the LA Philharmonic and the LA Master Chorale, but the programme is surprisingly varied throughout the year. The complex also includes the 250-seat Roy and Edna Disney/CalArts

Theatre (aka the REDCAT; *see p231*), a gallery and a roof garden. For tours of the building, call 1-213 972 7483, or see online for a schedule.

▶ *Disney Hall is also home to one of Downtown's best upscale restaurants, Patina (see p113).*

Ensembles

In addition to the ensembles below, check out the **Da Camera Society**'s Chamber Music in Historic Sites programme (1-213 477 2929, www.dacamera.org), which presents concerts by first-rate ensembles and soloists in some of the city's more interesting buildings.

Elsewhere, the **Pasadena Symphony** (1-626 793 7172, tickets 1-626 584 8833, www.pasadenasymphony-pops.org) gives five concerts a year at the Pasadena Civic auditorium, five at the LA County Arboretum & Botanic Garden in Arcadia (*see p84*), a holiday concert at all Saints Church in Pasadena and a free annual concert at Pasadena City Hall. The **Long Beach Symphony** (1-562 436 3203, www.lbso.org) and **Long Beach Opera** (1-562 432 5934, www.longbeachopera.org) both perform semi-regularly in the region, while the **Pacific Symphony** (information 1-714 755 5788, tickets 1-714 755 5799, www.pacificsymphony. org) keeps Orange County entertained.

Los Angeles Chamber Orchestra

1-213 622 7001, www.laco.org.
Founded in 1968, the LA Chamber Orchestra is 40-strong and offers a broad range of programming from baroque classics to new works. It performs at the Alex Theatre in Glendale, UCLA's Royce Hall (*see p44*), Zipper Hall in Los Angeles and the Broad Stage in Santa Monica (*see p231*).

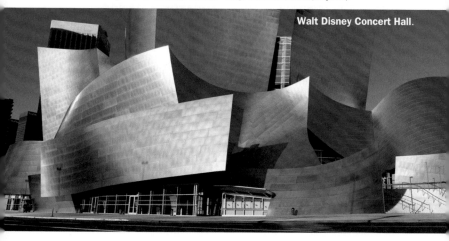

Walt Disney Concert Hall.

Pantages Theatre.

Los Angeles Master Chorale

*Information 1-213 972 7282, tickets 1-213 972
7282, www.lamc.org.*
The 120-voice LA Master Chorale is the largest choir
of its kind in the US. Presenting a crowd-pleasing
repertoire for almost 50 years, it performs roughly
a dozen concerts each year at Disney Hall (*see p229*),
some a cappella and others with accompanying
musicians (often the LA Chamber Orchestra).

Los Angeles Opera

1-213 972 8001, www.laopera.com.
The LA Opera made its debut in 1986 with an
acclaimed production of Verdi's *Otello*. Now led by
Plácido Domingo and James Conlon, the company
specialises in high-concept stagings of popular
favourites, interspersed with the occasional new
work. The 2013-14 season includes *Carmen* and *The
Magic Flute*. Performances are held at the Dorothy
Chandler Pavilion (*see p228*).

★ Los Angeles Philharmonic

1-323 850 2000, www.laphil.org.
Established in 1919 by tycoon William Andrews
Clarke, the LA Philharmonic has long served as
proof that the city isn't a cultural wasteland. After
the orchestra's 1964 move to the Dorothy Chandler
Pavilion, and the concurrent tenure of Zubin Mehta
as musical director, the Phil began to attract international attention. But its reputation has really
soared since its 2003 move to Disney Hall, giving the
orchestra the acoustic that its talents deserved.

Under acclaimed Finnish conductor Esa-Pekka
Salonen, the Phil introduced a forward-thinking sensibility to its programme, with modern works and
rarely performed pieces supplementing more widely

heard selections. UpBeat Live, a series of lectures that
precede some concerts, adds insight; there are also
events aimed at children. Most concerts are staged at
Disney Hall (Oct-May; *see p229*); in summer, the Phil
moves outside to the Hollywood Bowl (June-Sept; *see
p228*) and concentrates on crowd-pleasers.

At the end of the 2008-09 season Venezuelan
Gustavo Dudamel took over from Salonen as music
director; he continues to thrill audiences and critics
with his passion and energy. He is now spearhead-
ing the development of LA Phil's Youth Orchestra
of Los Angeles (YOLA), modelled after the
Venezuelan music system that moulded his career.

THEATRE & DANCE

In a city with so many actors, writers and
directors, it shouldn't be surprising that LA has
a varied and vibrant theatre community. In the
past decade, the standard of productions has
risen dramatically, particularly in the smaller
houses. And while the Big Apple might have all
the bells-and-whistles shows, LA excels with its
intimate venues and daring productions. Going
to the theatre here is a worthwhile experience:
tickets are generally cheaper than in London
or New York, and most seats in small and
mid-sized theatres offer excellent sightlines
and a remarkable sense of intimacy.

TICKETS & INFORMATION

Visit the Time Out Los Angeles website
(www.timeout.com/los-angeles), the *LA
Times* (www.latimes.com) and *LA Weekly*
(www.laweekly.com). For half-price tickets,
try www.goldstar.com.

THEATRE

Large theatres

Keep an eye out for updates on the new **Wallis Annenberg Center for the Performing Arts**, located between North and South Santa Monica Boulevards and Crescent and Canon Drives in Beverly Hills (1-310 246 3800, www.bhculturalcenter.com). Staging theatre, music and dance performances, the venue will incorporate a 500-seat theatre, a 150-seat studio space (on the site of the old Beverly Hills Post Office), a theatre school, gift shop and café. Completion is scheduled for autumn 2013.

Eli & Edythe Broad Stage

Santa Monica College Performing Arts Center, 1310 11th Street, at Santa Monica Boulevard, Santa Monica (1-310 434 3200, http://the broadstage.com). Bus 1,4,7/I-10, exit Lincoln Boulevard. **Box office** noon-6pm Mon-Fri. **Tickets** $15-$110. **Credit** AmEx, DC, Disc, MC, V. **Map** p310 B2.

The stage named for and by LA's top Downtown arts philanthropists might seem a bit out of place, miles away from their Grand Avenue Corridor, but the Broad Stage is an elegant venue for theatre, dance and music performances throughout the year. It's not Disney Hall West, but the 499-seat auditorium, inspired by Italian horseshoe-shaped theatres, boasts impeccable acoustics and seats so comfortable you'll be hoping for an encore or two. The jazz series is sparse but important: Rickie Lee Jones and Madeleine Peyroux both played here in 2012.

Ford Amphitheater

2580 Cahuenga Boulevard, north of Cahuenga Terrace, Hollywood (1-323 461 3673, www.ford amphitheater.org). Bus 156, 222/US 101, exit Cahuenga Boulevard north. **Box office** *Apr-Oct* noon-5pm Tue-Sun; 2hrs before show. **Tickets** $20-$55. **Credit** AmEx, DC, Disc, MC, V.

Owned by Los Angeles County, the 1,145-seat Ford Amphitheater has performances from May to October. The programme includes live music, dance and children-oriented events that are often written and performed by local artists. Some exceptions in the 2013 programme include actor Mandy Patinkin singing Broadway showtunes with the Pasadena Pops backing him and a contemporary ballet performance by the Lula Washington dance company.

★ Music Center Theaters

135 N Grand Avenue, between W 1st & W Temple Streets, Downtown (1-213 628 2772, www.musiccenter.org). Metro Civic Center/Grand Park/Tom Bradley/bus 10, 14, 37, 48, 55, 60, 355, 701/I-110, exit 4th Street east. **Box office** *In person* noon-8pm Tue-Sat; 11am-7pm Sun. *By phone* 10am-6pm Mon; 10am-8pm Tue-Fri; noon-

8pm Sat; 11am-7pm Sun. **Tickets** $20-$200. **Credit** AmEx, DC, Disc, MC, V. **Map** p315 B2.

The Center Theatre Group programmes two of the halls that make up LA's primary cultural complex. At the north end, the Ahmanson Theatre presents pre- or post-Broadway fare, with seating capacities ranging from 1,600 to 2,100. And in the Center's centre, the 745-seat Mark Taper Forum stages new plays.

Also part of the Music Center, the Dorothy Chandler Pavilion (*see p228*) stages occasional dance events. And on the south side of the Music Center's Walt Disney Concert Hall, the forward-thinking RED-CAT (aka the Roy & Edna Disney/CalArts Theater, 1-213 237 2800, www.redcat.org) includes some theatre performances in its cutting-edge programming.

Pantages Theatre

6233 Hollywood Boulevard, between Argyle Avenue & Vine Street, Hollywood (information 1-323 468 1770, tickets 1-800 982 2787, www.broadway la.org). Metro Hollywood-Vine/bus 180, 181, 210, 212, 217, 222, 312, 780, LDH/US 101, exit Hollywood Boulevard west. **Box office** 10am-6pm Mon-Sat; 10am-4pm Sun. **Tickets** $25-$270. **Credit** AmEx, DC, Disc, MC, V. **Map** p313 B1.

This vintage entertainment palace is the HQ of Broadway/LA, which specialises in big-budget musicals such as *West Side Story* and *Hair*.

INSIDE TRACK
WANDERING STARS

While many theatre groups dream of one day owning their own space, others are content to roam from venue to venue around LA. Among such groups are the **Playwrights' Arena** (1-231 489 0994, www.playwrightsarena.org), which produces only new plays by LA writers, as well as regular 'flash' theatre performances on the city's streets (check www.facebook. com/flashtheaterLA for updates).

However, one company has turned its itinerant status into a major selling point, specialising in site-specific works that explore the city's cultural and sociological diversity. Most productions from the **Cornerstone Theater Company** (1-213 613 1700, www.cornerstonetheater.org) begin with the team interviewing members of an identified community: sometimes people linked by geography, sometimes people linked by a common interest. When this process is complete, the group's actors work with a playwright, a director and volunteers to create a play addressing that group's particular issues, before staging the finished piece in an unexpected venue.

ARTS & ENTERTAINMENT

Notes for Nothing

It's a free-for-all at the following venues.

Ticket prices remain high for major shows in Los Angeles, and the booking fees added to them by ticket agencies continue to horrify. However, it's not all bad news: from the clutch of outdoor festivals in summer to the year-round in-store PAs at **Amoeba Music** (*see p161*), there are still plenty of places to catch music for free in LA.

LACMA (www.lacma.org; *see p55*) supplements its massive art collections and oft-changing special exhibitions with long-standing live music performances, from the Sundays Live series featuring chamber music in the Leo S Bing Theatre every Sunday at 6pm to the Latin Sounds series held every Saturday at 5pm in Hancock Park.

Summer programming is rampant and widespread. **Active Arts at the Music Center** (www.musiccenter.org) offers various programmes designed to inspire and encourage audience participation, such as the live-accompanied Friday Night Sing-Alongs (June-Aug) and the free beginner dance lessons of Dance Downtown. For those on the West Side, the **Culver City Boulevard Music Summer Series** (7pm Thur, July-Aug, www.boulevardmusic.com) – four free concerts under the stars in the courtyard of the Culver City City Hall – is a steal, with free parking and plenty of dining and bar options within walking distance. After the popular Sunset Junction music festival was shut down by city officials in 2011, **Echo Park Rising** (http://echo parkrising.com) rose to take its place. A micro-local celebration of art, music and business, it's free, and features stages spread throughout venues among the bars, restaurants and galleries of Sunset and Glendale Boulevards.

Other museums that stage regular free or almost-free concerts include the **Skirball Center** (folk and roots music; *see p228*) and the **Getty Center** (mostly jazz and classical; *see p41*). Some of the Skirball's concerts, much like the excellent, hipster-friendly First Friday shows at the **Natural History Museum of Los Angeles County** (*see p77*), come free with regular museum admission.

Out by the ocean, the **Twilight Concert Series** (7-10pm Thur, July-Sept, www.twilightseries.org) offers a broad range of acts on a stage at Santa Monica Pier, with everyone from Bettye LaVette to Ben Lee. If you don't want to stand with the crowds on the pier itself, bring a blanket and settle down on the beach. Also by the coast are the rather more low-key summer concerts at Marina del Rey (www.visitmarina.com).

★ Pasadena Playhouse

39 S El Molino Avenue, at E Green Street, Pasadena (information 1-626 792 8672, tickets 1-626 356 7529, www.pasadenaplayhouse.org). Metro Memorial Park/bus 10, 187, 256, 686, 687/I-210, exit Lake Avenue south. **Box office** noon-6pm Tue-Sun. **Tickets** $32-$100. **Credit** AmEx, DC, Disc, MC, V.

Built in the 1920s and revived in the '80s, this gracious 672-seat venue made an impressive comeback in 2010 when it reopened after an eight-month 'intermission' following bankruptcy. The main space offers mostly new plays and musicals. Upstairs, in the Carrie Hamilton Theatre, is the brash young Furious Theatre Company (1-626 792 7116, www.furioustheatre.org).

Valley Performing Arts Center (VPAC)

18111 Nordhoff Street, at Lindsey Avenue, Northridge (1-818 677 3000, www.valley performingartscenter.org). Bus 166, 167, 239, 364/I-405, exit Nordhoff Street west. **Box office** 10am-4pm Tue-Sat. **Tickets** $20-$115. **Credit** AmEx, DC, Disc, MC, V.

The San Fernando Valley's $125 million glass-panelled theatre, located on the Cal State Northridge campus, opened in 2011 with a high-profile performance by the Moscow Symphony. The 1,700-seat hall functions as the area's main arts hub with year-round dance, theatre, classical and world music programming that covers everything and everyone from flamenco guitarist Paco Peña to the Mark Morris Dance Group to chef Jacques Pépin.

Other large theatres

A quartet of theatres south of LA stages regular large-scale productions. **La Mirada Theatre** presents staid but polished fare under husband-and-wife team Tom McCoy and Cathy Rigby. The **Segerstrom Center for the Arts** offers professional-quality musicals, mostly familiar titles; it's a similar story at the **Redondo Beach Performing Arts Center**, where musicals are staged by Civic Light Opera of South Bay Cities (1-310 221 0254, www.civiclightopera.com), and the **Richard & Karen Carpenter**

Performing Arts Center, courtesy of Musical Theatre West (1-562 856 1999, www.musical.org).

La Mirada Theatre *14900 La Mirada Boulevard, between Excelsior Drive & Rosecrans Avenue, La Mirada (1-562 944 9801, www.lamirada theatre.com). I-5, exit Rosecrans Boulevard east.* **Box office** 11am-5.30pm Mon-Fri; noon-4pm Sat. **Tickets** $20-$70. **Credit** AmEx, DC, MC, V.

Redondo Beach Performing Arts Center
1935 Manhattan Beach Boulevard, at Aviation Boulevard, Redondo Beach (1-310 937 6607, www.rbpac.com). Bus 126/I-405, exit Inglewood Avenue south. **Box office** 1hr before show. **Tickets** $45-$60. **Credit** AmEx, DC, MC, V.

Richard & Karen Carpenter Performing Arts Center *California State University, 6200 Atherton Street, at Palo Verde Avenue, Long Beach (1-562 985 7000, www.carpenterarts.org). I-405, exit Palo Verde Avenue south.* **Box office** 11am-6pm Mon-Fri; noon-4pm some Sats. **Tickets** $20-$68. **Credit** AmEx, DC, MC, V.

Segerstrom Center for the Arts *600 Town Center Drive, Costa Mesa (1-714 556 2787, www.scfta.org). I-405, exit Bristol Street.* **Box office** 10am-6pm daily. **Tickets** $20-$100. **Credit** AmEx, DC, MC, V.

Mid-sized theatres

Look out also for the ancient Greek or Roman play staged each September at the **Getty Villa**'s outdoor amphitheatre (*see p31*).

A Noise Within

3352 East Foothill Boulevard, at Sierra Madre Villa Avenue, Pasadena (1-626 356 3100, www. anoisewithin.org). Metro Sierra Madre Villa/bus 32, 40, 60, 180, 181, 264, 266, 267, 487, 489/ I-210, exit Sierra Madre Villa Avenue north. **Box office** 2-6pm Tue-Sat & 2hrs before show. **Tickets** $36-$52. **Credit** AmEx, DC, MC, V. The LA region's leading classical theatre company, formerly in Glendale, presents two annual seasons, each containing three productions in repertory.

Colony Theatre

555 N 3rd Street, between E San Jose Drive & E Cypress Avenue, Burbank (1-818 558 7000, www.colonytheatre.org). Bus 94, 154, 164, 165, 292, 794/I-5, exit Burbank Boulevard east. **Box office** 2-6pm Tue-Sat. **Tickets** $20-$42. **Credit** AmEx, DC, Disc, MC, V.
A mix of reliably satisfying new plays and recent revivals is presented to a loyal audience in this warm Burbank theatre.

East West Players

120 N Judge John Aiso Street, between E 1st & Temple Streets, Downtown (1-213 625 7000, www.eastwestplayers.org). Metro Little Tokyo/Arts District/bus 10, 442, 481, 487, 489, 493, 497, 498, 499, 707/US 101, exit Alameda Street south.* **Box office** 2hrs before show. **Tickets** $30-$56; $25-$51 discounts. **Credit** AmEx, DC, MC, V. **Map** p315 D2.
EWP specialises in Asian American plays and musicals, and Asian-flavoured revivals of non-Asian shows. A former church, the company's 240-seat David Henry Hwang Theatre lacks the wraparound intimacy you might expect from a space of this size.

Falcon Theatre

4252 Riverside Drive, at N Rose Street, Burbank (1-818 955 8101, www.falcontheatre.com). Hwy 134, exit Buena Vista Street. **Box office** noon-6pm Tue-Fri; 10am-4pm Sat, Sun; 1hr before show. **Tickets** $27-$46. **Credit** DC, MC, V.
Hollywood director Garry Marshall (*Pretty Woman, Beaches*) built this small, inviting venue in the mid 1990s. Its most successful shows are by the deliciously rowdy Troubadour Theater (www.troubie. com), whose mastermind Matt Walker incorporates pop music into seemingly incongruous contexts (such as *Fleetwood Macbeth* and *A Midsummer Saturday Night's Fever Dream*).

★ Geffen Playhouse

10886 Le Conte Avenue, between Tiverton Avenue & Westwood Boulevard, Westwood (1-310 208 5454, www.geffenplayhouse.com). Bus 1, 2, 3, 8, 11, 12, 233, 302, 761/I-405, exit Wilshire Boulevard east. **Box office** 10am-6pm Mon-Fri; noon-6pm Sat, Sun. **Tickets** $37-$150. **Credit** AmEx, DC, MC, V.
The West Side's most glittery theatrical venue is home to a good-sized main stage and the cosier Audrey Skirball Kenis Theatre. The company offers a mix of new work and local premières, frequently with big-name (OK, second-tier) Hollywood talent.

International City Theatre

300 E Ocean Boulevard, at Long Beach Boulevard, Long Beach (1-562 436 4610, www. ictlongbeach.org). Metro 1st Street/bus 21, 22, 23, 61, 71, 72, 121, 151/I-710, exit Shoreline Drive east. **Box office** 9am-5pm Mon-Fri. **Tickets** $29-$50. **Credit** AmEx, DC, MC, V.
Long Beach's ICT offers a well-executed mix of plays and musicals, including some local premières. It's an 825-seat facility, but for the sake of economy and intimacy, only 289 of the seats are used. Perched between a massive convention centre and a 3,000-seat hall, it's hard to find. The box office is a couple of blocks away at the administrative office (110 Pine Avenue, Suite 820).

★ Kirk Douglas Theatre

9820 W Washington Boulevard, at Culver Boulevard, Culver City (1-213 628 2772, www.centertheatregroup.org). Metro Culver

ARTS & ENTERTAINMENT

*City/bus C1, C5, C7, 33/I-10, exit Robertson
Boulevard south.* **Box office** *By phone* 10am-
6pm Mon-Fri; noon-6pm Sat, Sun. *In person* 2hrs
before show. **Tickets** $20-$65. **Credit** AmEx,
DC, MC, V.
The West Side branch of the Center Theatre Group
(*see p231*) offers the company's most adventurous
fare, along with intermittent collaborations with
some of LA's smaller troupes. The theatre itself was
originally built as a cinema and retains its iconic old
neon sign out front.

Laguna Playhouse

*Moulton Theater, 606 Laguna Canyon Road,
Laguna Beach (1-949 497 2787, www.laguna
playhouse.com). I-405, exit Hwy 133 south.* **Box
office** 10am-5pm Tue-Sun; open until 8pm on
show nights. **Tickets** $35-$85. **Credit** AmEx,
DC, Disc, MC, V.
Located a few blocks from an enticing beach, the
enterprising Laguna Playhouse produces many
American or West Coast premières in its appealing
420-seat theatre. Ireland's Bernard Farrell is a
favourite writer here.

★ Los Angeles Theatre Center

*514 S Spring Street, between W 5th & W 6th
Streets, Downtown (1-213 489 0994, tickets
1-866 811 4111, http://thelatc.org). Metro
Pershing Square/bus 16, 18, 30. 40, 45, 53, 55,
62, 68, 84, 316, 330, 355, 460, 745/US 101,
exit Main Street south.* **Box office** *By phone*
6am-6pm Mon-Fri; 7am-3pm Sat, Sun. *In person*
9am-5pm Mon-Fri; 1hr before show. **Tickets**
$10-$30. **Credit** AmEx, DC, MC, V. **Map** p315 C3.
This city-owned, four-theatre complex is housed in
a former bank close to Skid Row in Downtown, and

INSIDE TRACK WILL I AM

Shakespeare plays crop up from time to
time around LA theatres, but two troupes
specialise in al fresco productions of the
Bard's finest works. Every summer, the
Shakespeare Center (1-213 481 2273,
www.shakespearecenter.org) performs
an often LA-spiced production in two
contrasting settings: one urban (1238
West 1st Street, Downtown), the other
sylvan (usually on the Westside).
Meanwhile, the **Independent Shakespeare
Company** (1-818 710 6306, www.
independentshakespeare.com) stages
a rep season of three more traditional
interpretations between June and August.
Originally in Barnsdall Park, 2010 saw
the location change and the Griffith Park
Shakespeare Festival make its debut
in the old zoo in the park (*see p59*).

can be one of the city's most exciting venues. The
Latino Theater Company also operates from here.

El Portal Theatre

*11206 Weddington Street, at Lankershim
Boulevard, North Hollywood (1-818 508 4200,
www.elportaltheatre.com). Metro North Hollywood/
bus 152, 154, 162, 163, 224, 353/Hwy 170,
exit Magnolia Boulevard east.* **Box office** 3pm-
showtime. **Tickets** $20-$75. **Credit** AmEx, DC,
Disc, MC, V.
The 360-seat main theatre at this former cinema is
used by a variety of tenants, but the building also
houses two sub-100-seat theatres. One of them is
home of Theatre Tribe (1-818 763 3232, www.the-
atretribe.com).

South Coast Repertory

*655 Town Center Drive, at Park Center Drive,
Costa Mesa (1-714 708 5555, www.scr.org). I-405,
exit Bristol Street north.* **Box office** 10am-6pm
Mon; 10am-showtime Tue-Sat; noon-showtime Sun.
Tickets $24-$70. **Credit** AmEx, DC, Disc, MC, V.
One of America's outstanding resident theatre companies, the South Coast Repertory has long been
acclaimed for its development of new work.
However, it also stages glossy classics, sometimes
with an innovative streak. The theatre's modernist
façade is warmed up by the cosy interiors.

Will Geer Theatricum Botanicum

*1419 N Topanga Canyon Boulevard, at
Cheney Drive, Topanga (1-310 455 3723,
www.theatricum.com). I-10, exit PCH north.*
Box office noon-6pm Tue-Fri; 11am-7.30pm Sat,
Sun. **Tickets** $25-$34. **Credit** AmEx, DC, MC, V.
Located in a seductive, rustic setting in Topanga in
the heart of the Santa Monica Mountains, this under-
the-stars theatre offers Shakespeare works, other
classics and occasional new plays, performed in an
annual repertory season that runs from June until
October. The site was founded in the 1950s by Will
Geer ('Grandpa' in *The Waltons*), who was black-
listed during the McCarthy era. He and his wife
made their home and living here, growing and selling fruit and vegetables and staging plays by similarly unemployed actors. The theatre opened in its
current guise in 1973.

Small theatres

In addition to the enterprises listed below, two
sections of town hold an unusually large number
of theatres. In **Hollywood**, more than a dozen
small venues are clustered around a seven-block
stretch of Santa Monica Boulevard in what's
become known as **Theater Row**. Several
of LA's more accomplished and audacious
groups are based here, among them **Unknown
Theatre**, the **Blank Theatre Company,
Elephant Stageworks** and **Open Fist**.

On the other side of the Hollywood Hills, more than 20 small theatres sit within a half-mile of the intersection of Magnolia and Lankershim Boulevards in **North Hollywood**. The list includes the **Road Theatre Company**, the classically minded **Antaeus Company** and **Deaf West Theatre**, where the productions are also in sign language. For more, see www.nohoartsdistrict.com.

Actors' Gang

9070 Venice Boulevard, between Culver & Robertson Boulevards, Culver City (1-310 838 4264, www.theactorsgang.com). Metro Culver City/bus 6, 12, 33, 733, C1/I-10, exit Robertson Boulevard south. **Box office** 9am-6pm Mon-Wed; 9am-10pm Thur-Sat. **Tickets** free-$35. **Credit** AmEx, DC, MC, V.

Tim Robbins remains in charge of the Actors' Gang, the company that he co-founded back in the 1980s. Productions remain hard-edged and presentational, and often rely on politically charged material. Performances take place in a century-old electricity substation.

Atwater Village Theatre Complex

3269 Casitas Avenue, at Silver Lake Boulevard, Atwater Village (1-323 644 1929, www.atwater villagetheatre.com). Bus 90, 91, 94, 603/US 101, exit Alvarado south. **Box office** noon-4pm Tue-Fri; 1hr before show. **Tickets** $25. **Credit** AmEx, DC, Disc, MC, V.

This two-staged space is under the joint stewardship of two of LA's veteran theatre companies, Ensemble Studio Theatre LA (www.ensemble studiotheatrela.org) and Circle X Theatre Co

(www.circlextheatre.org), which both develop and produce thought-provoking, original work.

Bootleg Theater

2220 Beverly Boulevard, at Roselake Avenue, Westlake (1-213 389 3856, www.bootlegtheater. org). Bus 14, 37, 200/US 101, exit Alvarado south. **Box office** 30mins before show. **Tickets** free-$25. **Credit** AmEx, DC, Disc, MC, V. **Map** p314 C5.

This interesting space takes the unusual stance of presenting live bands and theatre. Throughout the week and after theatrical performances, the front reception area is a music venue. The founder and artistic director is LA theatre veteran Alicia Adams, and programming is original and explorative.

★ Boston Court

70 N Mentor Avenue, at Boston Court, Pasadena (1-626 683 6883, www.bostoncourt.com). Metro Lake/bus 20, 180, 181, 187, 256, 485, 686, 687, 780/I-210, exit Lake Avenue south. **Box office** 11am-5pm Tue-Sat. **Tickets** $34; $29 discounts. **Credit** AmEx, DC, MC, V.

Exciting new plays and revivals are staged by this well-regarded group in a lavishly appointed sub-100-seat venue.

Fountain Theatre

5060 Fountain Avenue, between N Normandie & N Mariposa Avenues, Hollywood (1-323 663 1525, www.fountaintheatre.com). Metro Vermont-Sunset/bus 175, 206/US 101, exit Santa Monica Boulevard east. **Box office** 2-6pm Tue-Sat; noon-5pm Sun. **Tickets** $25-$30; $18-$23 discounts. **Credit** AmEx, DC, MC, V. **Map** p313 D2.

ARTS & ENTERTAINMENT

Bootleg Theater.

This widely acclaimed group generally concentrates on masters of 20th-century realism, but sometimes adds more recent works into the mix. And, for something completely different, it also produces a flamenco series in Barnsdall Park (see p59).

Odyssey Theatre Ensemble

2055 S Sepulveda Boulevard, between La Grange & Mississippi Avenues, West LA (1-310 477 2055, www.odysseytheatre.com). Bus 4, 5, C6/ I-405, exit Santa Monica Boulevard east. **Box office** 1-6pm Tue, Sun; 1-8pm Wed-Sat. **Tickets** $25-$30. **Credit** AmEx, DC, MC, V.

For more than four decades, Ron Sossi's three stages have stimulated and entertained West Siders and others, often with politically minded or metaphysically themed work. The OTE is the main attraction, but other companies also appear here, such as the often-notable New American Theatre (www.circus theatricals.com).

Pacific Resident Theatre

703-707 Venice Boulevard, at Oakwood Avenue, Venice (1-310 822 8392, www.pacificresident theatre.com). Bus 33, 733/I-10, exit 4th/5th Street south. **Box office** 3-7pm Tue-Sat; noon-2pm Sun. **Tickets** $20-$30. **Credit** DC, MC, V. **Map** p315 A6.

The productions turned out by this theatrical co-op, which frequently include lesser-known works from 20th-century European and American writers, often become critical favourites. There are three stages.

★ Sacred Fools

660 N Heliotrope Drive, between Melrose Avenue & Clinton Street, Hollywood (1-310 281 8337, www.sacredfools.org). Bus 10, 48/US 101, exit Melrose Avenue east. **Box office** show nights only. **Tickets** $7-$25. **Credit** AmEx, DC, Disc, MC, V. **Map** p314 A4.

One of LA's most prolific companies, having produced around 120 plays since its establishment in 1997, the award-winning Sacred Fools presents often-playful and humorous theatre.

▶ *Ever fancied treading the boards but were too afraid to try? Just across the street, the Lifebook Playhouse (665 N Heliotrope Drive, 1-323 244 4620, www.lifebookacting.com) has acting classes for all levels, run by the excellent Lifebook Acting Academy, which also operates from theatres in Studio City and Santa Monica.*

Theatre Banshee

3435 W Magnolia Boulevard, between N Avon & N Lima Streets, Burbank (1-818 846 5323, www.theatrebanshee.org). Bus 183, 222/Hwy 134, exit Buena Vista Street north. **Box office** show nights only. **Tickets** $20; $16 discounts. **No credit cards.**

This Burbank theatre is the LA area's most frequent producer of Irish plays, though it also offers a sprinkling of British and American work. The 2012-13 season included *The Importance of Being Earnest* and *The Merchant of Venice*.

Theatre of Note

1517 N Cahuenga Boulevard, between Sunset Boulevard & Selma Avenue, Hollywood (1-323 856 8611, www.theatreofnote.com). Metro Hollywood-Vine/bus 2, 302/US 101, exit Sunset Boulevard west. **Box office** 30mins before show. **Tickets** $25. **Credit** DC, MC, V. **Map** p313 B2.

Founded in 1981, Theatre of Note is one of LA's most solid theatre companies, producing innovative and original work as well as occasionally providing space for guest companies.

Victory Theatre

3324-3326 W Victory Boulevard, between N Avon & N Lima Streets, Burbank (1-818 841 5422, www.thevictorytheatrecenter.org). Bus 164, 222/Hwy 134, exit Buena Vista Street north. **Box office** 1-6pm Mon-Fri. **Tickets** $22-$34. **Credit** DC, MC, V.

For several decades now, the Victory has been one of the most consistently active smaller theatres in LA. It frequently produces new plays in its two side-by-side venues, the Big Vic and Little Vic.

DANCE & PERFORMANCE ART

Major national and international ballet companies appear at the **Music Center's Dorothy Chandler Pavilion** (see p228), including, recently, the Joffrey Ballet and Alvin Ailey American Dance Theater. The region's most daring dance programmes are staged by **UCLA** in Royce Hall (see p44) and at **REDCAT** in the Music Center (see p231). Fans of modern dance should also investigate **Diavolo** (1-323 225 4290, www.diavolo.org), in the Brewery Arts Complex north of Downtown. Aside from hosting the resident Diavolo company, it also welcomes modern groups such as the **Los Angeles Contemporary Dance Company** (www.la contemporarydance.org), **Brockus Project** (www.brockusproject.org) and **Ledges & Bones** (1-310 998 6698, www.ledgesandbones.org).

During summer, there's dance at the open-air **Ford Amphitheatre** (see p231) and at the **Grand Performances** in Downtown LA (see p232 **Notes for Nothing**). Smaller theatres with worthwhile dance programmes include **Unknown Theater** on Theater Row in Hollywood; gay-oriented **Highways Performance Space** in Santa Monica (see p201); and the lively, solar-powered **Electric Lodge** (1416 Electric Avenue, Venice, 1-310 306 1854, www.electriclodge.org). The list of local companies is led by the **Los Angeles Ballet** (www.losangelesballet.org), which performs at several venues around the region.

Sports & Fitness

No pain, no gain.

Blessed with a climate that simply demands outdoor activities, Southern Californians are legendary for indulging in everything under the glorious sun when it comes to getting physical. Sure, people spend hours each week in their cars, the air quality challenges even the hardiest lungs and there's not much of a pedestrian culture. But don't be fooled: this is still one of the healthiest cities in America. And forget the perception that you have to be a gorgeous Adonis before you even think about setting foot in a gym or hiking up Runyon Canyon: no one actually cares what you look like – they're all too busy ogling themselves in the mirror.

ARTS & ENTERTAINMENT

SPECTATOR SPORTS

The second-largest sports market in the US (after New York), LA features an abundance of athletic franchises, most of which have devoted fans. Several of them – including a hockey team, an arena football outfit and all three of LA's basketball teams – are based at the Staples Center in Downtown LA, which hosts everything from concerts (*see p218*) to political conventions.

INFORMATION AND TICKETS

The sports section of the *LA Times* lists the games and broadcast schedules each day. If you want to look further ahead, check teams' individual websites, or the comprehensive and easy-to-navigate site run by sports TV network ESPN at www.espn.com.

It's best to approach teams' box offices for tickets, but prepare to be disappointed. LA Lakers games routinely sell out, while the very best seats at Dodgers games are sold as part of season-ticket packages. If you get no luck at the team's own box office, try Ticketmaster (*see p162*) or StubHub (www.stubhub.com), where fans resell tickets, with StubHub aking a cut.

A riskier approach is to buy tickets from touts – aka scalpers – who wait outside the venues before the game. If you do decide to buy from them, be sure to double-check the date before you hand over your money: selling tickets for games that have already happened is the oldest trick in the scalper's book.

Baseball

The Major League Baseball (MLB) season runs from April until late September/early October, whereupon the top four teams from each of the two leagues (the American and the National) begin four weeks of playoff games that end with the World Series.

Los Angeles Angels of Anaheim

Angel Stadium of Anaheim, 2000 Gene Autry Way, between Katella & Orangewood Avenues, Anaheim (information 1-888 796 4256, tickets 1-714 663 9000, http://losangeles.angels.mlb.com). Anaheim Amtrak stop/I-5, exit Katella Avenue east. **Tickets** $5-$200. *Parking* $8. **Credit** AmEx, DC, MC, V.

Having muddled through the 1990s, the Angels have spent much of the 21st century as a team to beat in the American League West division. The turnaround began in 2002, when manager Mike Scioscia led the team to their first World Series. The Angels haven't fared as well as of late, but hopes are high with the more recent signing of sure-to-be hall of famer Albert Pujols and other major players such as slugger Josh Hamilton. The Angels' ballpark lacks character compared to Dodger Stadium, but it's still a pleasant place to take in a game, and the fans are known for their enthusiasm.

Los Angeles Dodgers

Dodger Stadium, 1000 Elysian Park, at Stadium Way, Echo Park (1-323 224 1507, tickets 1-866 363 4377, http://losangeles.dodgers.mlb.com). Bus 2, 3, 4, Express from Union Station/I-110, exit

ARTS & ENTERTAINMENT

Dodger Stadium north. **Tickets** $11-$1,650. *Parking* $10, $35 for preferred parking. **Credit** AmEx, DC, Disc, MC, V.

The Dodgers were perennial underachievers in the National League West division for a long time. They managed to start making their way into the playoffs in the mid 2000s, but have disappointed again in more recent years. The future could be bright, with a $500 million stadium renovation under way, as well as a talented roster that includes Matt Kemp and Hanley Ramirez. Though the team has their ups and downs, the loyal fan base keeps coming.

Basketball

The National Basketball Association (NBA) season starts in late October/early November and runs until mid April. At this point, the league's best teams enter the playoffs, which end in mid June.

When the regular season is finished, the WNBA hoves into view, beginning in May and wrapping up in September. The women's team the **Los Angeles Sparks** draw pretty good crowds to their games at the Staples Center. Star player Candace Parker leads the team, but she has had to deal with several injuries. However, the Sparks could get new life now that they're coached by Joe 'Jellybean' Bryant, a former NBA player and father of Los Angeles Lakers superstar Kobe. For tickets, call 1-877 447 7275 or see www.wnba.com/sparks.

Los Angeles Clippers

Staples Center, 1111 S Figueroa Street, at 11th Street, Downtown (1-888 895 8662, www.nba. com/clippers). Metro Pico/bus 30, 81, 442, 460/ I-110, exit Olympic Boulevard east. **Tickets** $10-$1,100. *Parking* $15-$25. **Credit** AmEx, DC, Disc, MC, V. **Map** p315 A5.

The Los Angeles Clippers were the laughing stock of the NBA for years; now they are one of the teams to beat. With the signing of point guard Chris Paul and forward Blake Griffin, they are one of the most dynamic teams in the league, sometimes even out-classing their more famous local NBA draw, the Lakers. Though not as popular as the latter, the Clippers could nonetheless score a championship win if they manage to keep their current roster.

Los Angeles Lakers

Staples Center, 1111 S Figueroa Street, at 11th Street, Downtown (information 1-310 426 6000, tickets 1-800 745 3000, www.nba.com/lakers). Metro Pico/bus 30, 81, 442, 460/I-110, exit Olympic Boulevard east. **Tickets** $30-$1,000. *Parking* $15-$25. **Credit** AmEx, DC, Disc, MC, V. **Map** p315 A5.

While baseball has the New York Yankees and soccer Manchester United, the Los Angeles Lakers are the NBA team everybody loves to hate. For 'hate',

read 'beat': there's not a player in the league who doesn't enjoy putting one over on the most glamorous team in American sports. At the turn of the millennium, they won the NBA Finals three years in succession. There followed a slump of a few years, but led by coach Phil Jackson and superstar guard Kobe Bryant, they returned to form in the 2007-08 season and then went on to win back-to-back championships. Since then, Jackson has left and the Lakers have been in a slump, meaning early exits from the playoffs, but with the signings of superstars Dwight Howard and Steve Nash, championships could again be seen in the near future.

Like the Clippers, the team play at the Staples Center. Unlike the Clippers, they draw a crowd packed with Hollywood royalty – including, courtside, a permanently sunglassed Jack Nicholson. That said, the Clippers' recent success has begun to add to their celebrity appeal as well.

Football

Los Angeles has been without an NFL team since the Raiders returned to Oakland in 1995. Since then a variety of plans have been put forward for discussion, with the Coliseum, the Rose Bowl, Anaheim and even the Dodger Stadium parking lot all suggested as possible locations for a new NFL team in the city. However, AEG and Farmers Insurance are planning to build Farmers Field, a $1.5 billion stadium, to be located near the Staples Center and L.A. LIVE, once a group signs on to bring a team to the area.

In the absence of the NFL, LA football fans turn their heads to the college game, which runs from September to November, before the bevy of bowl games played across the country around New Year's Day. The most famous of these, and the most prestigious, is the Rose Bowl game, held at the stadium of the same name in Pasadena (www.rosebowl stadium.com).

The storied **USC Trojans** (1-213 740 4672, www.usctrojans.com) have won more Rose Bowls than any other college team. However, a three-season winning streak came to an end in 2010 and since then, off the field, they have been plagued with public reprimands and sanctions after a four-year NCAA investigation into violations of ineligible players participating in championship games. They were banned from post-season play for two years but were eligible to play in bowl games again as of 2012. The Trojans play their regular-season games at the Los Angeles Coliseum (3911 S Figueroa Street). The **UCLA Bruins** (1-310 825 2101, www.uclabruins.com), who play their homes games at the Rose Bowl, struggle by comparison, but still draw passionate crowds.

Horse racing

There are three racetracks in the LA area, all of which feature flat racing.

Hollywood Park Race Track & Casino

1050 S Prairie Avenue, between 90th Street & Century Boulevard, Inglewood (1-310 419 1500, www.betfairhollywoodpark.com). Bus 117, 211, 212/I-405, exit Manchester Boulevard east. **Admission** $10; $5 seniors on Thur; free under-17s. *Parking* $3, $5, $10.

Los Alamitos Race Course

4961 Katella Avenue, between Walker Street & Lexington Drive, Los Alamitos (1-714 820 2800, www.losalamitos.com). I-5, exit Katella Avenue west, or I-605, exit Katella Avenue east. **Admission** $3-$10. *Parking* free-$5 preferred.

Santa Anita Park

285 W Huntington Drive, between Santa Anita & Holly Avenues, Arcadia (1-626 574 7223, www.santaanita.com). Bus 78, 79, 378/I-210, exit Baldwin Avenue south. **Admission** $5-$20. *Parking* $4-$6.

Wheel-life Adventures

The car may be king in Los Angeles, but there's room on the roads for everyone.

Believe it or not, Los Angeles does have a contingent of cyclists who navigate the city on two wheels. Despite the overwhelming freeway configurations and miles of congested boulevards, groups such as the **Los Angeles County Bicycle Coalition** (LACBC, www.la-bike.org) are determined to convince Angelenos that cyclists deserve to move as freely and safely through the city as their motorised counterparts.

Formed in 1994, the LACBC is the largest and most vocal bicycle advocacy group in Southern California. Working in tandem (sorry) with the LA County Metropolitan Transportation Authority, the coalition has been the driving force behind improved bike paths along several bus lines and thoroughfares, an increase in the number of bike racks on buses, and improved bike access on public transport.

Although it's less politically and more socially active, **CICLE** (Cyclists Inciting Change thru Live Exchange; www.cicle.org) has a broadly similar mission. The highlight of its website is the 'Back Roads' section: hardcore cyclists detail their favoured routes, listing the streets, landmarks, specific turns and hazards that will take a cyclist from one side of the city to the other.

LA cyclists will tell you that despite aggressive drivers, wormhole storm-drains and a dearth of proper bike lanes, traversing the city can be quite simple and fairly enjoyable. The attitude of these optimistic souls is reinforced at places such as the **Bicycle Kitchen** (4449 Fountain Avenue, 1-323 662 2776, www.bicyclekitchen.com), a volunteer-run organisation that offers neophytes courses on bike repair. Along with **Orange 20 Bikes** (4351 Melrose Avenue, 1-323 662 4537, www.orange20bikes.com), it's at the heart of LA bike culture and is

a great place to meet like-minded riders.

Between the LACBC, the Bicycle Kitchen and a number of other bike clubs and shops, there's a range of happenings held throughout the year. Bicycle Kitchen events tend to attract an assortment of hipster bike messengers and adrenaline junkies, while LACBC affairs bring out the full gamut of cyclists. The festive **Los Angeles River Ride** is the LACBC's premier fundraiser, held each year in June, and offering six different bike rides. And then there are the **Midnight Ridazz** (www.midnightridazz.com), a very loose collective of cyclists that organises highly informal night rides around LA.

Visiting cyclists should do their homework in advance, sourcing routes and perhaps contacting the LACBC. LA is a drivers' city, but the cycling community is very happy to welcome visitors to its side of the road.

ARTS & ENTERTAINMENT

Hockey

The National Hockey League (NHL) regular season runs from October to early April, and is followed by two months of playoffs.

Anaheim Ducks

Honda Center, 2695 Katella Avenue, at Douglass Road, Anaheim (information 1-877 945 3946, tickets 1-714 703 2545, http://ducks.nhl.com). Anaheim Amtrak stop/I-5, exit Disney Way. **Tickets** $25-$290. *Parking* $15-$25. **Credit** AmEx, DC, MC, V.

The Mighty Ducks of Anaheim changed their name to the more restrained Anaheim Ducks before the 2006-07 season, but their might remained intact: the team won the Stanley Cup for the first time. They made it to the conference quarter-finals in 2007-08 and semi-finals in 2008-09, but following seasons have proved less successful. Nonetheless, they remain competitive and the fans as enthusiastic as ever.

Los Angeles Kings

Staples Center, 1111 S Figueroa Street, at 11th Street, Downtown (1-888 546 4752, www.lakings.com). Metro Pico/bus 30, 81, 442, 460/I-110, exit Olympic Boulevard east. **Tickets** $30-$388. *Parking* $15-$25. **Credit** AmEx, DC, Disc, MC, V. **Map** p315 A5.

Ice hockey in SoCal may seem ridiculous, but all of that changed when the Kings won the Stanley Cup in 2012. Even before that major victory, the crowds they drew were surprisingly enthusiastic.

Motor racing

The annual glamour event is the **Toyota Grand Prix of Long Beach**, held on a street circuit in April (www.gplb.com). The **Auto Club Speedway** in Fontana (1-909 429 5000, www.californiaspeedway.com), 90 minutes east of LA just off the I-10, hosts events between March and October.

Irwindale Speedway

13300 E Live Oak Avenue, at I-605, Irwindale (1-626 358 1100, www.irwindalespeedway.com). I-605 north, exit E Live Oak Avenue west. **Tickets** $15; free under-12s. **Credit** AmEx, DC, Disc, MC, V.

This half-mile paved oval has 6,500 seats and hosts a range of racing events from April to November.

Soccer

Numerous bars and cafés show overseas matches on satellite TV – if you want to catch up on the English Premier League, try British pubs such as the **Cock & Bull** in Santa Monica (2947 Lincoln Boulevard, 1-310 399 9696, www.cocknbullbritishpub.com) or the **Village Idiot** in the Fairfax District (*see p130*).

While **LA Galaxy** have the higher profile in the local game, they face fierce competition from rivals **Chivas USA** (1-877 244 8271, www.cdchivasusa.com), with which they share a stadium. The season runs from March to November.

LA Galaxy

Home Depot Center, 18400 Avalon Boulevard, Carson (1-877 342 5299, www.lagalaxy.com). I-110, exit 190th Street east. **Tickets** $12.50-$172.50. *Parking* $15-$30. **Credit** AmEx, DC, Disc, MC, V.

The initial fanfare surrounding David Beckham in 2007 at the start of his five-year deal with the Galaxy catapulted the team's popularity into near-mainstream support. While his first couple of seasons proved disappointing his acquisition paid off when the team won the MLS Cup in 2011 and 2012. With Beckham now gone and high-profile player Landon Donovan's future with the team uncertain, it remains to be seen whether the Galaxy can sustain their form.

PARTICIPATION SPORTS

Also check the Time Out Los Angeles website (www.timeout.com/los-angeles) for round-ups of everything from Christmas ice rinks to free yoga.

Bowling

In addition to the following, the **Spare Room** at the Hollywood Roosevelt hotel (*see p179*) has two bowling lanes.

AMF Bay Shore Lanes

234 Pico Boulevard, between Main & 3rd Streets, Santa Monica (1-310 399 7731, www.amf.com).

*Bus 33, 333, SM1, SM2, SM8, SM10/I-10, exit
4th/5th Street south.* **Open** 9am-midnight Mon-
Thur, Sun; 9am-1.30am Fri, Sat. **Rates** $20/person
incl shoe rental. **Credit** AmEx, DC, Disc, MC, V.
Map p310 A3.
Santa Monica's main bowling alley can get pretty
busy at weekends.

Lucky Strike Lanes

*Hollywood & Highland mall, 6801 Hollywood
Boulevard, at N Highland Avenue, Hollywood
(1-323 467 7776, www.bowlluckystrike.com).
Metro Hollywood-Highland/bus 156, 212, 217,
222, 312, 780, LDH/US 101, exit Hollywood
Boulevard west.* **Open** noon-2am Mon-Fri;
11am-2am Sat, Sun. **Rates** $5.95-$7.95/person;
$4 shoe rental. **Credit** AmEx, DC, Disc, MC, V.
Map p313 A1.
This slick, party-friendly 12-lane alley within the
Hollywood & Highland mall is a retro homage to
bowling alleys of the 1960s, though it's unlikely that
alleys back then operated such strict dress codes (no
baggy clothes, no plain white T-shirts, no hats). It's
also over-21s only after 7pm.
Other locations L.A. LIVE, 800 W Olympic
Boulevard, Downtown (1-213 542 4880).

Cycling

If you don't feel quite brave enough to cycle
around the LA streets (*see p239* **Wheel-life
Adventures**), there are plenty of alternatives.
The most appealing bike trails in the city run
along the beaches: the **South Bay Bicycle
Trail**, also known as the Strand, covers 22
miles from Will Rogers State Beach to
Torrance, while the **Huntington Beach
Bicycle Trail** extends eight miles south
from Sunset Beach. Many oceanfront stalls

in Santa Monica and Venice rent beach bikes,
usually with one gear and pedal brakes.
Riding off-road isn't legal, but not much effort
has been made to stop the cyclists who weave
through the Santa Monica Mountains, home to
the most popular and accessible mountain biking
areas: numerous fire trails jut off Mulholland
Boulevard from Beverly Hills to Topanga and
Malibu. You may have to squeeze under a gate
or two, but keep pedalling until you reach the
peaks. Further inland, Griffith Park has more
than 14 miles of bike trails, but some are MTB-
accessible only and many are hilly.

Fishing

Public fishing is popular at the piers of many
local beaches, in part because you don't need
a permit when fishing from public piers into
ocean waters. In particular, try Santa Monica
Pier, Redondo Beach and Manhattan Beach. But
if you're lucky enough to catch a fish, current
pollution levels suggest you might be better off
throwing it back than preparing it for dinner.
If you're fishing anywhere else, you'll need
a licence. Available from Big 5 Sporting Goods,
K Mart and a variety of other locations, licences
cost $14.61 for a single day, $22.94 for two days
and $45.93 for ten days. For full details on
licensing, including details on other locations
that sell them, see the California Department
of Fish and Wildlife's website at www.dfg.
ca.gov or call 1-916 928 5805.
For freshwater fishing in LA, try **Echo
Park Lake** in Echo Park (*see p62*; 1-213 250
3578) and **Lincoln Park Lake** in Lincoln
Heights (1-323 906 7953); information on both
is available at www.laparks.org.
Alternatively, several companies in the region
ferry fishers out into the Pacific on fishing boats.
Contact **Marina del Rey Sportfishing** (1-310
822 3625, www.marinadelreysportfishing.com)
or **Redondo Beach Sportfishing** (1-310 372
2111, www.redondosportfishing.com); expect to
pay around $35 for a half-day trip or $50-$55 for
a full day's fishing.

Golf

The Department of Recreation & Parks runs
13 municipal courses around the city: seven
18-hole courses, three nine-hole circuits and a
trio of par-three set-ups (one 18-holer, two nine-
holers). In order to book a tee time, you'll need
a registration card, available at any course,
from 1-818 291 9980 and at www.golf.lacity.org
(where you can also find a full list of municipal
courses). Among them are a nine-hole, par-three
course in **Los Feliz** (reservations not required;
3207 Los Feliz Boulevard, 1-323 663 7758); a
popular complex containing an 18-hole course

Runyon Canyon.

and a nine-hole, par-three course in **Rancho Park** (10460 W Pico Boulevard, 18-hole: 1-310 838 7373, nine-hole: 1-310 838 7561); an 18-hole set-up in **Encino** (16821 Burbank Boulevard, 1-818 995 1170); and the Harding and Wilson courses in **Griffith Park** (4730 Crystal Springs Drive, 1-323 663 2555). Rates for non-residents run from $16 to $42, depending on the size of the course, day and time. Always call ahead to find out your chances before setting out, although you can sometimes get lucky if you just turn up. Orange County has some lavish courses, including the nine-hole **Links at Terranea** (www.terranea.com, rates start at $40) overlooking the Pacific.

Hiking

There's lots of great hiking around Los Angeles: **Griffith Park** (*see p59*), the **Santa Monica Mountains** (including the Hollywood Hills) and the **San Gabriel Mountains** all offer plenty of variety, and are easily accessible by car. Other popular locations include **Runyon Canyon** (*see p53*), **Temescal Gateway Park** and **Topanga Canyon**, where you'll find the TreePeople environmental group (*see p189*). *See also p243* **View from the Top**.

The local chapter of the **Sierra Club** (1-213 387 4287, www.angeles.sierraclub.org) runs an impressive 4,000 outings each year in the area. Particularly noteworthy are the evening hikes in Griffith Park, which depart from the upper carousel car park at 7pm every Tuesday, Wednesday and Thursday – they're suitable for all levels of fitness. Booking isn't required: just turn up on the night (get there early to complete a waiver form before your first hike).

Horse riding

Horse riding is popular here. In Griffith Park, you can hire horses at the **Los Angeles Equestrian Center** (480 W Riverside Drive, Burbank, 1-818 840 9063, www.la-equestrian center.com); for riding in the Hollywood Hills,

try **Sunset Ranch** (3400 N Beachwood Drive, 1-323 469 5450, www.sunsetranchhollywood. com). Expect to pay around $25-$40 an hour at both. Both offer lessons.

Rock climbing

Some of the best rock climbing in the LA region can be found at **Malibu Creek State Park** (1-818 880 0367, www.parks.ca.gov). Further out, there's also good climbing in **Joshua Tree National Park** (*see p256*), where the **Joshua Tree Rock Climbing School** (1-760 366 4745, www.joshuatreerockclimbing.com) offers a variety of lessons. A useful resource for other climbing sites throughout LA County is www.rockclimbing.com.

Rockreation
11866 La Grange Avenue, at S Westgate Avenue, West LA (1-310 207 7199, www.rockreation.com). Bus SM10, SM14/I-10, exit Bundy Drive north. **Open** noon-11pm Mon, Wed; 6am-11pm Tue, Thur; noon-10pm Fri; 10am-6pm Sat, Sun. **Credit** AmEx, DC, MC, V.
Use of the facilities here, at one of LA's better indoor climbing walls, costs $17 a day, or $12 for children. There are classes available for everyone from beginners to experts.

Rollerskating & in-line skating

For in-line skaters, there's no place like the **Strand**, an immaculate paved path that stretches along the coast from Will Rogers State Beach in the north to Torrance County Beach in the south and is open to cyclists and skaters. Public parks along the beach also serve as gathering points for quality skaters who like to rehearse their tricks before an audience. In Venice, **Venice Beach Park**, which has a dedicated skate park, is popular, as is the adjoining Ocean Front Walk. Other tranquil spots include **Griffith Park** and the **Sepulveda Dam Recreation Center** just west of Encino in the San Fernando Valley.

View from the Top

Vital vistas: five of the most glorious hikes in LA.

RUNYON CANYON, HOLLYWOOD

Runyon's the spot for views of the toned bodies and even tonier homes endemic to this part of LA. The busy dirt path leads hikers and runners on a loop around the canyon, with countless moments to pause and utter, 'This is so LA'. You can catch the loop from the east (Fuller Avenue) or West (North Vista Street) side of the canyon. Either way, it's a mostly gradual ascent, except for a steep and narrow section near the top of the eastern canyon wall. At the top, the trail follows a ridge, giving views of the architectural hodgepodge of the Hollywood Hills, Hollywood, WeHo's tidy grid and the high-rises of Miracle Mile.
Address 2001 N Fuller Avenue.
Hours Dawn to dusk.
Length 1.5 miles with possibilities to extend.
Time 30-60mins.

CHARLIE TURNER TRAIL TO MOUNT HOLLYWOOD, GRIFFITH PARK

At the top of Mount Hollywood, 360-degree views make this an ideal vantage point for checking out the Los Angeles basin, the edge of the San Fernando Valley, the skyline of Downtown Los Angeles with the observatory in the foreground, and the money shot: a close-up of the Hollywood sign at eye level. To get to the summit, Griffith's highest peak, pick up the trail at the north side of the Observatory parking lot. Starting off amid scrubby evergreens, the path quickly emerges into the hills, with the Hollywood sign appearing to the left. After about 40 minutes, you'll reach the top: a big, dusty clearing with picnic tables.
Address 2800 E Observatory Avenue.
Hours 5am-10.30pm. Trails close at sunset.
Length: 3 miles.
Time: 90mins.

SARA WAN TRAILHEAD AT CORRAL CANYON

Malibu's Corral Canyon is the only coastal canyon in Los Angeles County that was never developed. That means raw nature – coastal sage scrub and willows clinging to parched hills, plus the occasional bunny or lizard – experienced over a fairly gentle hike. As the trail begins, the noise of PCH and the sea breeze follow you up. But things quieten down – and heat up – quickly

on this shadeless trail. Hang a left at the first fork – this way you can face the ocean during your descent. The path leads you on switchbacks along the east side and top of the canyon. There's no crowning 'inspiration point', but the descent towards the ocean has sweeping views of Santa Monica beaches all the way to Point Dume.
Address 5623 Pacific Coast Highway.
Hours Dawn to dusk.
Length 2.5 miles.
Time 60-90mins.

BALDWIN HILLS SCENIC OVERLOOK, CULVER CITY

An oil rig-studded hill on the edge of Culver City's industrial zone is an odd place for a state park. But that's all part of this urban overlook's understated charm. The park's main draw is the steps: more than 260 stone slabs that deliver hikers – breathless, aching – to the top in under 20 minutes. Your reward is a north-gazing view of LA's east-to-west spine. Peer east towards Downtown's skyline and the sprawl of South LA. To the north and west, Century City high-rises and Westwood's Mormon temple cut imposing figures; the Santa Monica Mountains are a smoky backdrop.
Address 6300 Hetzler Road.
Hours 8am to dusk. Visitor centre is usually open Thursday to Saturday mornings.
Length Less than 1 mile, but very steep.
Time 30mins.

ECHO MOUNTAIN, ALTADENA

Hikers begin by scaling the wall of a canyon and emerging on to the face of the mountain about 15 minutes later. The views of Downtown, Pasadena and the San Gabriel Valley are stellar even at low levels. But once you get to the top, there's the added bonus of a piece of LA history: old train tracks and the remains of White City, an alpine resort built in the late 19th century. Two fires burned everything to the ground within a decade of its opening. All that's left now are ruined foundations and the tracks for hikers to explore and picnic on.
Address E Loma Alta Drive at Lake Avenue.
Hours Part of the Angeles National Forest, the trail doesn't officially close and is popular with night hikers.
Length 5 miles.
Time 2.5-3.5hrs.

ARTS & ENTERTAINMENT

Catch a Break

Surfing USA.

Although the beach breaks in LA are often given low marks by well-travelled surfers, the below-average reputation isn't always deserved, and the water is surprisingly clean outside the hit-or-miss rainy season that runs from November to April. However, the northern currents of the Pacific here are cold (58-66°F from October to June), so bring or hire a full wetsuit, and onshore winds are relentless most afternoons. Working north to south, here are some of LA's best breaks.

Four decades after the throngs first descended on **Malibu's Surfrider Beach** (23200 Pacific Coast Highway; roadside and pay-lot parking; *see also p34*). It's still a world-class, right-breaking wave shaped by an alluvial stone bottom. And it's still over-populated. 'First Point', closest to the pier, is where newcomers, longboarders and beginners go to fight for surf. Water quality is an issue at Surfrider, so think twice if you have health conditions. Attempt to avoid the crowds (and the murk) by heading to **County Line Beach**, across from Neptune's Net restaurant (42505 Pacific Coast Highway; roadside parking).

In Santa Monica, **Bay Street** (at the foot of Bay; pay-lot parking) can have a strong west swell. There are several great surf stores here. If you need to rent a stick or rubber, ZJ Boarding House (*see p162*) has the hard and soft goods.

A few miles south, Venice's surf-meets-the-streets allure has been buried under million-dollar condos. When the cold-weather swells are tasty, surly locals rule the **Breakwater** (at the foot of Windward Avenue; pay-lot parking) and **Venice Pier** (at the foot of Washington Boulevard; pay-lot parking); the rest of the time, it's usually a free-for-all. You can rent gear at Ocean Echo Surf Shop (23 Washington Boulevard, Venice; 1-310 823 5850). Be sure to lock your car tight and keep valuables out of sight: Venice is the home of the smash-and-grab.

Further south, **Dockweiler State Beach** (Vista Del Mar and Imperial Highway; pay-lot parking) is a three-mile strip of uncrowded waves beneath the flight path of LAX. Cross into Manhattan Beach and you're at the beloved **El Porto** (on the Strand, at the foot of 45th Street, Manhattan Beach; pay-lot parking). Underwater contours give the waves focus and organisation, even when other spots are shutting down. It gets mobbed, so remember the golden rule: respect the locals.

Scuba diving

The best places to dive are off **Leo Carrillo State Beach**, **Laguna Beach**, **Redondo Beach** and **Palos Verdes**, but if you're really serious, head to **Santa Catalina Island** (*see p258*) or the **Channel Islands** (*see p249*). The LA coastline consists of miles of sloping sand, but the coastal islands have rocky shores with plenty of kelp beds and shipwrecks to explore.

Surfing

If you really want to hook into the California lifestyle, you need to get on a surfboard. But don't expect to ride a wave quickly: it can take weeks just to learn to sit on the board properly. Most novice surfers opt for the easier-to-learn alternatives: boogie-boards (aka bodyboards), body surfing and skim-boarding.

If you're learning to surf, choose a wide-open beach break such as **Zuma Beach** (*see p34*) or **Will Rogers State Beach** (*see p209*). Alternatively, sign up for lessons with a surf school: **Surf Academy** (1-424 903 9500, www.surfacademy.org) has group classes in Santa Monica and private classes in a number of locations down the coast; and the **Santa Monica Surf School** (1-310 526 3346, www.santamonicasurfschool.com) runs a summer day camp for children and private lessons for adults. Experienced surfers should check the rundown of the best breaks along the coast; *see above* **Catch a Break**.

For information on conditions, plus a full listing of surf shops and surf schools, check the

ARTS & ENTERTAINMENT

excellent website www.surfline.com. And for a round-up of the best beaches in Los Angeles, *see p34* **Beachy Keen**.

Swimming

For the best beaches for swimming, *see p34* **Beachy Keen**. The majority of the city's **YMCAs** (see www.ymcala.org) also contain swimming pools, as do many hotels. For child-friendly swimming, *see p189*.

Tennis

There are tennis courts in many LA parks; for a full list, see www.laparks.org. **Griffith Park** has courts ($5-$8/hr) at two sites: 12 lit courts at Griffith/Riverside ($8/hr; 1-323 661 5318) and 12 courts at Griffith/Vermont Canyon ($5/hr 8am-noon; $8/hr 3-7pm; 1-323 664 3521). On weekdays before 4pm, the courts are available on a walk-up basis; after 4pm, you can also do walk-ups, but to secure a private court, you must book with a registration card, which costs $30 for non-residents.

Alternatively, try one of several tennis centres around LA. The most central is the 16-court **La Cienega Tennis Center** (325 S La Cienega Boulevard, Midtown, 1-310 652 7555).

Whale-watching

Whale-watching provides California's most extraordinary wildlife experience. The annual season, off the Southern California coastline, is in winter (December to March), following the migratory habits of the gray and blue whales, the two most common species. In Santa Barbara, whale-watching reaches its peak in summer, ending in mid-September. Most marinas have numerous boats offering whale-watching trips.

FITNESS

Gyms

There are gyms all over LA; the following are open to non-members. Many YMCAs and hotels have gyms. For gay-friendly gyms, *see p206*.

Gold's Gym
360 Hampton Drive, at Rose Avenue, Venice (1-310 392 6004, www.goldsgym.com). Bus 33, SM1/I-10, exit 4th/5th Street south. **Open** 4am-midnight Mon-Fri; 5am-11pm Sat, Sun. **Rates** *Non-members* $20/day; $70/wk. **Credit** AmEx, DC, Disc, MC, V. **Map** p310 A5.
Gold's bills itself as 'the mecca of bodybuilding', and perhaps with some justification: this is where one ex-Governor of California honed his body.
Other locations throughout LA.

Santa Monica Family YMCA
1332 6th Street, between Santa Monica Boulevard & Arizona Avenue, Santa Monica (1-310 393 2721, www.ymcasm.org). Bus 4, 20, 33, 333, 704, 720, SM1, SM3, SM4, SM5, SM7, SM8, SM10/ I-10, exit 4th/5th Street north. **Open** 6am-10pm Mon-Fri; 7am-8pm Sat; 8am-8pm Sun. **Rates** *Non-members* $15/day. **Credit** AmEx, DC, Disc, MC, V. **Map** p310 B3.
This centre offers racquetball and handball, weights, a lap pool, a spa, aerobics, yoga, rock climbing and volleyball, as well as a wide variety of classes .
Other locations throughout LA (www.ymcala.org).

Yoga

YAS
1101 Abbot Kinney Boulevard, at Westminster Avenue, Venice (1-310 396 6993, www.go2 yas.com). Bus 33, 733, SM1/I-10, exit 4th/5th Street south. **Open** 5.15am-2pm, 3.30-9pm Mon-Fri; 6.30am-1pm, 3.30-8pm Sat, Sun. **Classes** $17. **Credit** AmEx, DC, MC, V. **Map** p310 A5.
Kimberly Fowler's Venice operation offers the unexpected combination of yoga and spinning. It clearly works for the locals: three more branches have sprung up in the LA area, and more are planned.
Other locations throughout LA.

YogaWorks
230 N Larchmont Boulevard, between Beverly Boulevard & 1st Street, Larchmont Village (1-323 464 1276, www.yogaworks.com). Bus 14, 37, 210/I-10, exit La Brea Avenue north. **Open** daily, class times vary. **Classes** $22. **Credit** AmEx, DC, MC, V. **Map** p311 B4.
With more than a dozen locations throughout LA and Orange County, YogaWorks is a local favourite.
Other locations throughout LA.

ARTS & ENTERTAINMENT

Escapes & Excursions

Escapes & Excursions

Hit the highway.

The Los Angeles urban area may have many and varied attractions, but it's also the gateway to some stunning sights and scenery. Travelling north up the coast will lead you to the well-dressed but easy-going town of Santa Barbara. Taking the coast road south will bring you to sunbleached San Diego and, across the border, the infamous Mexican town of Tijuana. And if you head east, you'll soon be in the desert, whether isolated in Joshua Tree or Death Valley National Parks, or crammed into Palm Springs and the Coachella Valley. The easiest – and sometimes the only – way to get to the places listed in this chapter is by car. Reaching all the destinations involves a drive of at least an hour and a half and usually more. For car hire and driving tips, *see pp288-289*.

More gems sit further afield. To the north are the natural glories of Big Sur and the buzzing town of San Francisco, LA's polar opposite in so many ways. To the north-east lie the photogenic wonders of Sequoia National Park and Yosemite National Park, not to mention the delightful B&Bs of the Gold Country. And north-east – nearly 300 miles away, makeable in under four hours if you're lucky with both traffic and police – is the incomparable Nevadan city of Las Vegas.

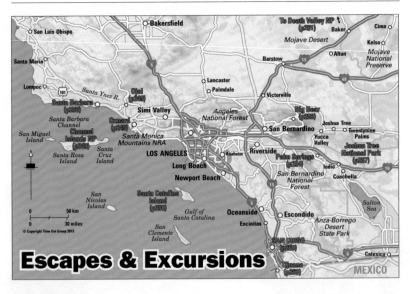

Escapes & Excursions

The Coast Road to Riches

Conspicuous wealth and natural beauty make for some great sights north of the metropolis, the former in the shape of man-made architectural splendours (and enjoyably OTT monstrosities) and the latter in some of the most stunning scenery imaginable.

LOS ANGELES TO OJAI

The drive north from LA is lovely, however you choose to begin it. If you take US 101 from Hollywood, cut through the untamed Santa Monica Mountains. Taking route N1 (aka Las Virgenes Road) will bring you down via the start of the **Las Virgenes View Trail**, a two-and-a-half-mile uphill hike that begins at the intersection of N1 and the Mulholland Highway. But it's the coastal road that really appeals. The

stretch of Highway 1 north from Malibu to the small town of **Oxnard** is dotted with surfer-friendly beaches: **Leo Carrillo State Park** is popular, as are the beaches that form rugged **Point Mugu State Park** (for both: 1-310 457 8143, www.parks.ca.gov).

Close by sits **Ventura**, a largely unspoiled piece of Middle America by the sea and the jumping-off point for the **Channel Islands National Park** (1-805 658 5730, www.nps.gov/chis). Diving, hiking, fishing, kayaking and simple wildlife observation are on offer at this sanctuary, set across a five-island archipelago. Boat transport from Ventura to the islands is organised by Island Packers Cruises (1-805 642 1393, www.islandpackers.com): for details on how to reach the islands, see the park's website.

Located a dozen miles north of Ventura, **Ojai** is a sweet village in a gorgeous setting with a disarming preponderance of wide-eyed hippie residents. The town has long been a magnet for those of a spiritual bent, a fact borne witness by

---

Hollywood and Vines

California's other wine country.

Napa and Sonoma may grab the headlines, but there's a long tradition of winemaking around LA. And, indeed, in LA: the **San Antonio Winery** (737 Lamar Street, 1-323 223 1401, www.sanantoniowinery.com) has been making wine less than a mile from the centre of Downtown since 1917. It's not the only working winery in the city, but it's the only one that's open to the public. For others, you'll have to head out.

North of LA, it's 90 minutes to the **Ojai Valley** (*see above*), where there are more than 15 small wineries. The most interesting is **Casa Barranca** (208 East Ojai Drive, Ojai, 1-805 640 1255, www.organic-wine.com), where you can taste organic and biodynamic wines in a spectacular Craftsman-style mansion. Santa Barbara, too, is making a name for itself among wine buffs: the Urban Wine Trail (www.urbanwinetrailsb.com) covers some terrific new boutique wineries.

Another easy day trip from LA is the 45-minute ride north to the **Antelope Valley**, where the prettiest winery is **Agua Dulce** (9640 Sierra Highway, Agua Dulce, 1-661 268 7402, www.aguadulcevineyards.com). Stop in for a meal at **Le Chêne** (12625 Sierra Highway, 1-661 251 4315, www.lechene.com, mains $30), where winemaker Juan Alonso has transformed an old cottage into a fine-dining destination.

Continue a few miles down the Antelope Valley Highway and you'll be in Lancaster, where you'll find the **Antelope Valley Winery** (42041 20th Street W, 1-661 722 0145, www.avwinery.com). The owners are friendly, and the winemaker is happy to chat when time allows.

Just under an hour east of Downtown, Rancho Cucamonga has two noteworthy wineries. **Galleano Winery** (4231 Wineville Road, Mira Loma, 1-951 685 5376, www.galleanowinery.com) and **Joseph Filippi** (12467 Base Line Road, Rancho Cucamonga, 1-909 899 5755, www.josephfilippiwinery.com) both produce from old vines. Both also make Angelica, the fortified wine of the Spanish missions that's the only wine style native to Southern California.

Those with time for a weekend getaway should consider a trip to Temecula, about two hours south-west from LA. While there are dozens of hotels, wineries and restaurants in the area, only one place combines all three – the **South Coast Winery Resort & Spa** (34843 Rancho California Road, Temecula, 1-951 587 9463, www.wineresort.com). This luxurious complex of rambling villas is a perfect base for exploring the area, taking a hot-air balloon ride (call in advance) or tasting around the Valley.

---

the art galleries of Ojai Avenue and the esoteric businesses on the fringes of the town. If you've already found yourself, content yourself with a search for bargains at fabulously chaotic **Bart's Books** (302 W Matilija Street, 1-805 646 3755, www.bartsbooksojai.com). If you're here in June, check out the **Ojai Music Festival** (*see p228*).

Eating & drinking

In Ventura, **71 Palm** (71 N Palm Street, 1-805 653 7222, www.71palm.com, closed Sun, mains $23) offers fine French cuisine; the **Anacapa Brewing Company** (472 E Main Street, 1-805 643 2337, www.anacapabrewing.com, mains $16) serves smart bar food to go with its own brews. And in Ojai, try the French-American fare at **Suzanne's Cuisine** (502 West Ojai Avenue, 1-805 640 1961, www.suzannescuisine. com, closed Tue, mains $26) or the high-class Californian cooking at the **Ranch House** (102 Besant Road, 1-805 646 2360, www.theranch house.com, closed Mon, mains $30).

Tourist information

Oxnard California Welcome Center *1000 Town Center Drive (1-800 269 6273, 1-805 385 7545, www.visitoxnard.com).* **Open** 9am-5pm Mon-Sat; 10am-5pm Sun.
Ventura Visitors & Convention Bureau *101 S California Street (1-800 333 2989, 1-805 648 2075, www.ventura-usa.com).* **Open** 8.30am-5pm Mon-Fri; 9am-5pm Sat; 10am-4pm Sun.

SANTA BARBARA

The wealthy resort town of Santa Barbara is almost too perfect to be true. And, boy, does it know it. A well-heeled, conservation-minded coterie works hard to keep Santa Barbara handsome, almost immaculate. You don't come here for urban thrills, but for history, culture, top-end eating and an old-world aesthetic.

Sheltered between towering green mountains and deep blue ocean, this has long been sought-after land. The local Chumash Indians lived here for 5,000 years, before the Spanish arrived in 1786 and set about building the **Santa Barbara Mission** (2201 Laguna Street, 1-805 682 4713, www.sbmission.org, $5), one of the loveliest in the state. The current building dates from 1870 and is still an active Catholic church, although parts of it are run as a museum.

For a different historical perspective on the region, try the **Museum of Natural History** (2559 Puesta del Sol Road, 1-805 682 4711, www.sbnature.org, $7-$12), or go Downtown to the **Santa Barbara Historical Society Museum** (136 E De la Guerra Street, 1-805 966 1601, www.santabarbaramuseum.com, closed

Mon). Just down De la Guerra Street from here is historic De la Guerra Plaza, flanked by City Hall and the site of the raucous **Old Spanish Days Fiesta** (first weekend in August; 1-805 962 8101; www.oldspanishdays-fiesta.org). Nearby is what's left of the **Presidio** (123 E Canon Perdido Street, 1-805 965 0093, www.sb thp.org): now a state park, it's currently being restored, though it remains open to the public.

Perhaps the finest example of the town's Spanish-Moorish colonial architectural heritage is the **Santa Barbara County Courthouse** (1100 Anacapa Street), with lofty towers, an interior covered with murals and sprawling grounds. It's worth taking the elevator up to the top to breathe in the billion-dollar views, from the 4,000-foot tips of the Santa Ynez Mountains to the beach: not for nothing has Santa Barbara been nicknamed the American Riviera.

Two blocks away is the main drag of State Street, a strip of uppity boutiques, decent restaurants and upscale bars. Near the top of the Downtown core is the **Santa Barbara Museum of Art** (1130 State Street, 1-805 963 4364, www.sbmuseart.org), a worthwhile display of ancient creativity and modern-day pretenders. In the other direction, State Street ends at Pacific-side **Stearns Wharf** (www. stearnswharf.org). Up the coast, soft waves make **Leadbetter Beach** the perfect littoral playground; down the coast is the sweet, sandy **East Beach**. Alternatively, head back inland and take in the altogether mellower **Santa Barbara Botanic Garden** (1212 Mission Canyon Road, 1-805 682 4726, www.sbbg.org).

Eating & drinking

There's plenty of variety – and quality – here. **Bouchon** (9 W Victoria Street, 1-805 730 1160, www.bouchonsantabarbara.com, mains $30) and **Downey's** (1305 State Street, 1-805 966 5006, www.downeyssb.com, mains $32) serve upscale Californian cuisine with local wines; **Ca'Dario** (37 E Victoria Street, 1-805 884 9419, www.cadario.net, mains $28) offers traditional Italian cooking. At the harbour, **Brophy Bros** (119 Harbor Way, 1-805 966 4418, www. brophybros. com, mains $22) turns out fresh fish and justly celebrated clam chowder. More affordable fare can be found at the **Sojourner** (134 E Canon Perdido Street, 1-805 965 7922, www.sojournercafe.com, mains $11), the organic old-timers' favourite, and renowned low-budget Mexican spot **La Super-Rica** (No.622, 1-805 963 4940, mains $5).

Tourist information

Santa Barbara Visitor Center *1 Garden Street (1-805 965 3021, www.sbchamber.org).*

Santa Barbara

Sun, Sand & Snow

Nature played a cruel trick on the early Western pioneers. Just where the barrier of the Sierra Mountains peters out in the south, a great desert swathe cuts across to the coast. Technically, much of Southern California is desert, receiving less than ten inches of rain a year. Were it not for irrigation, air-conditioning and the automobile, large areas would be nigh-on uninhabitable for modern man.

Inhospitable, perhaps, but also spectacular. **Death Valley** and **Joshua Tree National Parks** are both breathtaking; the drive to the former is one of the state's most undervalued road trips. In the middle of this alien landscape, in what's known as the Coachella Valley, sit a cluster of sunbleached resort towns, of which **Palm Springs** is easily the most notable. Despite the heat, however, there's skiing close by at **Big Bear Lake** and **Lake Arrowhead**.

The drive to **Death Valley** from LA via **Mojave** and **Red Rock Canyon State Park**, having picked up Highway 14 at Santa Clarita, is desert driving at its most beguiling. However, engaging with the environment more closely, preferably on foot, pays large dividends. Go on an interpreted or ranger-led trail to familiarise yourself with some of the basics of geology, flora and fauna. For more, see www.desertusa.com.

DEATH VALLEY NATIONAL PARK

Enlarged and redesignated a national park under the 1994 Desert Protection Act, Death Valley is now the largest national park outside Alaska, covering roughly 5,200 square miles. It's also, famously, one of the hottest places on the planet. The park's website calmly offers that 'Death Valley is generally sunny, dry and clear throughout the year'. True, but the word 'generally' masks a multitude of curiosities. Air temperatures regularly top 120°F (49°C) in July and August, and are 50 per cent higher on the ground; fearsome by anyone's standards.

Although you'll pass several points of interest on your way into the park, regardless of whether you enter from the west (via Mojave) or the east (via Death Valley Junction), it's a good idea to head directly to the **Furnace Creek Visitor Center** (*see p252*) to get your bearings. Here, you'll find an excellent bookshop, decent exhibits, a useful orientation film and helpful staff. Stop in for advice on current weather and road conditions (some tracks are only accessible to 4X4s), pay your fee of $20 per car and take the opportunity to fill up at one of the park's three expensive gas stations.

From the visitor centre, take the 190 heading east. Just three miles south of Furnace Creek lies ragged, rumpled **Zabriskie Point**. Further south, roughly 13 miles off the 190 and standing 5,475 feet above sea level, **Dante's View** is a wonderful place from which to first survey the park's otherworldly landscape.

At **Golden Canyon**, south of Furnace Creek, there's a simple two-mile round-trip hike that's best walked in the late afternoon sunlight, when you'll see how the canyon got its name. Continuing south, the landscape gets plainer. Nine miles down the road is the **Devil's Golf Course**, a striking, scrappy landscape formed by salt crystallising and expanding; a few miles further is bleak, eerie **Badwater**, just two miles as the crow flies from Dante's View but more than 5,000 feet lower. Indeed, this is the second lowest point in the Western Hemisphere, 282 feet below sea level. Unexpectedly, it's only 85 miles from the highest point in the US, the

ESCAPES & EXCURSIONS

14,494-foot Mount Whitney in the Sierra Nevada. An annual 'ultramarathon' race is held between the two (www.badwater.com), although it no longer extends all the way to Whitney's summit.

Driving north from Furnace Creek offers a greater variety of sights. The remains of the **Harmony Borax Works** have been casually converted into a short trail; there's a similarly simple walk, less historic but more aesthetically pleasing, at nearby **Salt Creek** (look for desert pupfish in the stream in spring). Following the road around to the left will lead you past the eerie **Devil's Cornfield** and the frolic-friendly **Sand Dunes**, which rise and dip in 100-foot increments, and on to the small settlement at **Stovepipe Wells**. Taking a right and driving 36 miles will lead you to the luxurious **Scotty's Castle** (1-877 444 6777, www.recreation.gov); built in the 1920s for Chicago millionaire Albert Johnson, it was named after Walter Scott, his eccentric chancer of a friend. Rangers tell the story on 50-minute tours (usually hourly, 9am-4pm, $15).

It's often too hot to hike, but there are plenty of trails in Death Valley, short and long. The options include the 14-mile round trip to the 11,000-foot (3,300-metre) summit of **Telescope Peak**, a good summer hike (the higher you climb, the cooler it gets). Starting at Mahogany Flat campground, you climb 3,000 feet (900 metres) for some spectacular views of Mount Whitney. In winter, only experienced climbers with ice axes and crampons should attempt it.

Where to stay and eat

Set into the hillside above Furnace Creek Wash, the **Furnace Creek Inn** (reservations 1-800 236 7916, hotel/same-day reservations 1-760 786 2345, www.furnacecreekresort.com, closed mid May-mid Oct, double $345-$460) was built in the 1930s, and retains a cultured dignity reminiscent of the era from which it emerged. The rooms are charming and well equipped, the landscaped gardens are a refined delight, and the inn's upscale Californian food is far better than you might expect.

Elsewhere, the **Ranch at Furnace Creek** (same phone & URL, double $169-$199) has 200 motel-style rooms and cabins, as well as a pool, tennis courts and the world's lowest golf course, plus a pretty basic bar and restaurant. The 83-room **Stovepipe Wells Village** (1-760 786 2387, www.escapetodeathvalley.com, double $95-$160) also has food on offer, but few other amenities. Four of Death Valley National Park's campgrounds are free, with others costing between $12 and $18 a night. The most central, and the only one for which reservations are taken, is at Furnace Creek (1-877 444 6777, www.recreation.gov).

Tourist information

Furnace Creek Visitor Center *Furnace Creek (1-760 786 3200, www.nps.gov/deva).* **Open** 8am-5pm daily.

Death Valley National Park.
See p251.

Getting there

By car To reach Death Valley, take I-10 west to Ontario, follow I-15 north-east to Baker, drive on Highway 127 to Death Valley Junction and then take Highway 190 west into the park. Alternatively, leave LA to the north-west and, at Sylmar, pick up Highway 14. This eventually turns into Highway 395; from here, take Highway 190 west into the park. Both journeys are around 300 miles; allow 5-6hrs.

Lake Arrowhead & Big Bear Lake

LAKE ARROWHEAD

Nestled on top of one of Southern California's few mountain ranges, two small towns and a handful of scattered neighbourhoods make up the community of Lake Arrowhead. **Blue Jay**, at the west side of the region, consists of a number of small, forgettable shops, while **Lake Arrowhead Village** offers gift and outlet shops on a water-ringed peninsula.

Although the boat tours on the **Arrowhead Queen** (1-909 336 6992, http://lakearrowhead queen.com) provide a little history, sightseeing is largely usurped by the sports and activities: **McKenzie's Water Ski School** in Arrowhead Village (1-909 337 3814, http:// mckenziewaterskischool.com), the oldest water-ski school in the United States. The main disappointment, apart from the plethora of speedboats, is the lack of swimming: the lake is privately owned.

Winter sees skiers from the LA conurbation descend on the area. The Discovery Center (1-909 382 2790, www.bigbeardiscoverycenter. com) can offer guidance on current conditions for cross-country skiing and snow-shoeing. About ten miles up from Lake Arrowhead on US 18 sits the Snow Valley Resort (information 1-909 867 2751, snow report 1-800 680 7669, www.snow-valley.com), where you can buy a range of ski and snowboarding passes. The resort is located at a low altitude, but makes its own snow to ensure that the slopes are always in service.

Eating & drinking

The range of eating and lodging options in the area is underwhelming; your best bets are the large, handsome, Marriott-owned **Lake Arrowhead Resort** (27984 Hwy 189, 1-909 336 1511, www.laresort.com, double $229-$329) and its smart eatery **Bin 189** (1-909 337 4189). European-influenced B&Bs in the area include

the **Fleur de Lac** (285 Hwy 173, 1-909 337 8178, www.fleurdelac.com, double $89-$199).

Tourist information

Lake Arrowhead Chamber of Commerce
*28200 Hwy 189 (1-909 337 3715, http://
lakearrowhead. net).* **Open** 10am-4pm daily.

BIG BEAR LAKE

Big Bear Lake offers a less charming and more rugged experience than its near-neighbour. But there's also a greater variety of activities available here all year round, with no need to rely on the fake snow that's often required at Lake Arrowhead. Visitors can even swim in the lake here, which is also a first-rate fishery. And many hiking trailheads are easily accessible, with most providing fine views.

During the winter, **Snow Summit** (1-800 232 7686, www.snowsummit.com) is one of the most popular ski/snowboard resorts in Southern California. In summer, its East Mountain Express high-speed chairlift is converted into the **Scenic Sky Chair** (1-800 232 7686): running to an 8,200-foot summit, it offers magnificent views of the San Gorgonio Mountains. There are also golfing, hiking and biking opportunities, while families may enjoy careening down the bobsleigh-esque **Alpine Slide** or the summer-only **Alpine Water Slide** (800 Wildrose Lane, 1-909 866 4626, www.alpineslidebigbear.com).

Eating & drinking

The restaurants along Big Bear Boulevard include the **Old Country Inn** (41126 Big Bear Boulevard, 1-909 866 5600, www.oldcountry innrestaurant.com), which specialises in Mexican seafood. B&Bs around the lake include the **Windy Point Inn** (39015 North Shore Drive, 1-909 866 2746, www.windypointinn. com, double $145-$265).

Tourist information

Big Bear Lake Visitor Center *630 Bartlett Road (1-800 424 4232, www.bigbear.com).* **Open** 9am-5pm daily.

Getting there

By car Take I-10 and then I-215 to San Bernardino. Pick up Highway 30 eastbound for a mile and then head north on Highway 18; the Lake Arrowhead turn-off is around 30-40mins before Big Bear Lake. The journey from LA should take around 2hrs.

Coachella Valley

PALM SPRINGS

Tucked into an abutment of the San Jacinto and Santa Rosa mountain ranges, Palm Springs first found fame as a destination for the infirm and the tubercular, who were able to soothe their aches and pains at the town's eponymous natural springs. However, after Hollywood began filming silent Westerns and Arabian-themed romances in the deserts during the 1920s, the town transformed itself into a winter playground for the Hollywood elite. By the 1950s and '60s, nearly every major American entertainer owned a home in Palm Springs.

When the same stars moved on to more lavish spreads elsewhere in the Valley, the town itself metamorphosed into a tawdry tourist trap. However, it's turned itself around once more. Though late mayor Sonny Bono is given most of the credit, the town's resurgence is really down to the combination of a solid economy and an active, town-proud gay community. Renewed interest in mid 20th-century modernist architecture and the opulent trappings of the leisure-obsessed Rat Pack era have also proved welcome shots in the arm. In addition, the non-profit Palm Springs Modern Committee (www.psmodcom.com) seems determined to preserve Palm Springs' architectural aesthetic and keep the city from mutating into another ugly Riverside County exurb.

The city consists simply of a commercial spine: **N Palm Canyon Drive**, home to most of the town's eating, drinking and shopping options. Mid 20th-century antiques shops abound on Palm Canyon and the parallel **N Indian Canyon Drive**; bargains are no longer easy to find, but you can score a lucite table for less than on LA's Beverly Boulevard. On Thursday nights, a mile-long stretch of Palm Canyon is closed to traffic for **Villagefest** (www.palmspringsvillagefest.com), when shops open late and stalls line the road.

Though it takes less than an hour to traverse the lengths of Palm Canyon and Indian Canyon by car, don't keep driving in a straight line. Nearly every turn opens up yet another eye-popping mountain view, as well as striking examples of mid 20th-century modern architecture, from simple tract homes to Jetsonian structures. The Palm Springs Modern Committee publishes a map, available for $5 online or from the visitor centre (*see p256*), that details the most notable buildings in the city; for more, *see p255* **Back to the Future**.

The town is dotted with small attractions. In the heart of Palm Springs sits the impressive **Palm Springs Art Museum** (101 Museum Drive, 1-760 322 4800, www.psmuseum.org, $12.50), which supplements selections from its permanent collection with temporary shows. Across from the airport, the excellent **Palm Springs Air Museum** (1-760 778 6262, www.palmspringsairmuseum.org, $15) has a collection of propeller-driven World War II aircraft, many still in flying condition. South of town sits the wilfully eccentric **Moorten Botanical Garden & Cactarium** (1701 S Palm Canyon Drive, 1-760 327 6555, www.moortengarden.com, $4), a living museum with nature trails, sculpture, rusted-out cars, dinosaur footprints and 3,000 varieties of cacti, succulents and flowers.

Outdoor types are well served. There are hundreds of hiking trails throughout the San Jacintos and Santa Rosas, but the **Indian Canyons** (1-760 323 6018, www.indian-canyons.com, $9), located five miles south of Downtown on S Palm Canyon Drive, are a must-see. Owned and preserved by the Agua Caliente Indians, the Canyons contain miles of hiking trails that wind through an unspoiled wilderness of palm groves, barrel cacti, waterfalls and dramatic rock formations.

For a change of ecosystem, take the **Palm Springs Aerial Tramway** (1-888 515 8726, www.pstramway.com, $23.95) to the crest of San Jacinto. The rotating tram cars lift you 5,873 feet (1,791 metres) through four different 'life zones' into a lush pine forest that's typically 30°F to 40°F (18°C to 24°C) cooler than on the desert floor. It's worth the journey just to enjoy a drink or a meal at E Stewart William's Tramway Mountain Station.

Eating & drinking

While Palm Springs offers plenty of culinary variety, top-quality cooking is harder to find. Too many restaurants coast by comfortably on location alone, and plenty of mediocre eateries attach eye-catchingly high prices to dishes that should be retailing for considerably less. Beware, in particular, of a lot of ordinary Mexican and Italian food.

By and large, you're on safest ground at the lower end of the market. **Tyler's Burgers** (149 S Indian Canyon Drive, 1-760 325 2990, http://tylersburgers.com, mains $7) is a genuine local favourite, a cute little patio on which residents and weekenders chomp on uncomplicated burgers. There's excellent sushi at **Wasabi** (333 S Indian Canyon Drive, 1-760 416 7788, mains $17, sushi $8), unexpectedly good Belgian cuisine at **Pomme Frite** (256 S Palm Canyon Drive, 1-760 778 3727, www.pomme-frite.com, mains $24) and reasonable Mexican food at **El Mirasol Cocina Mexicana** (140 E Palm Canyon Drive, 1-760 323 0721, www.elmirasolrestaurants.com,

mains $13). **Manhattan in the Desert** (2665 E Palm Canyon Drive, 1-760 322 3354, mains $12) is the closest thing to a New York-esque Jewish deli that you're likely to find out here; and dropped into the middle of the Coachella Valley is **John Henry's Cafe** (1785 E Tahquitz Canyon Way, 1-760 327 7667, www.johnhenrysps.com, mains $17), good for solid American comfort cooking far from the madding crowd. If you want to push the boat out, consider **Melvyn's**

Back to the Future

Thrill to a 1950s architectural aesthetic.

What art deco did for Miami Beach in the 1980s, modernism has done for Palm Springs in recent years. Although many of the city's great structures have been razed or changed (invariably in pseudo-Spanish style) beyond recognition, you can still find gems by modernist architects such as William Cody, Richard Neutra, John Lautner, Donald Wexler, E Stuart Williams and Albert Frey. Indeed, Frey's classic 1963 **Tramway Gas Station**, a dramatically angled structure that came perilously close to demolition, now serves as a tourist information centre.

It's not the only must-see modernist site. The upside-down arches of E Stewart Williams' **Washington Mutual Bank** (499 S Palm Canyon Drive) were built in 1961 across the street from Rudy Baumfeld's blue-tiled 1959 **Bank of America Building** (588 S Palm Canyon Drive, *below*). William Cody's sensually curved **St Theresa's Church** (2800 E Ramon Road), built in

1968, is a quick drive from the equally fantastic **Palm Springs City Hall** at 3200 E Taquitz Canyon Way (Albert Frey, 1952) and the nearby **Palm Springs International Airport** (Donald Wexler, 1965).

A map to more than 50 significant structures is available at the visitor centre (*see p256*). It's also fun to get lost in the winding streets of the Las Palmas and Little Tuscany locales west of Palm Canyon Drive at the foot of Mount San Jacinto, where hundreds of ranch-style modern mansions have been preserved in all of their space-age glory. Famous homes include Frank Sinatra's **Twin Palms** (1148 E Alejo Road), where Ol' Blue Eyes lived with Ava Gardner; Liberace's **Casa de Liberace** (501 N Belardo Road), still adorned with the pianist's trademark 'L' logo; and two John Lautner buildings on Southridge Drive, the **Elrod House** and Bob Hope's **Flying Saucer House**.

(200 W Ramon Road, 1-760 325 2323, www. inglesideinn.com, mains $29), a high-priced relic where the food takes second billing to the old-school Palm Springs ambience. The lounge is a real beauty.

Where to stay

Most of the impressive hotels in Palm Springs are housed in classic mid 20th-century buildings. Some have even been decorated in space-age fashion: take the mid 20th-century **Orbit In** (562 W Arenas Road, 1-760 323 3585, www.orbitin.com, double $129-$259), funkily appointed with furniture by Eames et al, or the tiki-on-a-budget theme at the **Caliente Tropics** (411 E Palm Canyon Drive, 1-888 277 0999, www.calientetropics.com, double $41-$127). Another fun option is the cute **Palm Springs Rendezvous** (1420 N Indian Canyon Drive, 1-760 320 5308, www.palmsprings rendezvous.com, double $139-$259), whose themed rooms include Route 66, Stagecoach and Pretty In Pink, where Marilyn Monroe stayed during the 1950s.

Other local hotels, meanwhile, have been ushered gently into the 21st century. The best of them is the beautiful **Movie Colony** (726 N Indian Canyon Drive, 1-760 320 6340, www.moviecolonyhotel.com, double $99-$299), an Albert Frey-designed construction with a lovely pool area. Alternatives include the understated **Horizon** (1050 E Palm Canyon Drive, 1-760 323 1858, www.thehorizon hotel.com, double $229-$309) and the sublime **Parker** (4200 E Palm Canyon Drive, 1-760 770 5000, www.theparkerpalmsprings.com, double $179-$695). Gay lodgings include the smart **East Canyon Hotel** (288 E Camino Monte Vista, 1-760 320 1928, www.eastcanyon hotel.com, double $109-$219), which boasts a full-service spa. A trendier option is the **Ace Hotel** (701 E Palm Canyon Drive, 1-760 325 9900, www.acehotel.com, double $99-$599), where some of the stylish rooms are equipped with turntables and retro vinyl. Chances are you'll have a private patio or fireplace at your disposal too.

The waters that lend their name to the neighbouring town of **Desert Hot Springs** have been exploited by several hotels in the town, each with their own natural mineral pools. The **Desert Hot Springs Spa Hotel** (10805 Palm Drive, 1-760 329 6000, www.dhs spa.com, double $89-$139) offers good value, but **Hope Springs** (68075 Club Circle Drive, 1-760 329 4003, www.hopespringsresort.com, double $150-$195) is more stylish. For a full list, see the Desert Hot Springs Chamber of Commerce site at 1-760 329 6403, www.desert hotsprings.com.

Tourist information

Palm Springs Visitors Center *2901 N Palm Canyon Drive (1-800 347 7746, 1-760 778 8418, www.visitpalmsprings.com).* **Open** 9am-5pm daily.

OTHER COACHELLA TOWNS

The climate remains just as delicious around the Coachella Valley. However, outside the recuperative waters of **Desert Hot Springs** (*see left*), there's not much of interest. **Cathedral City** is notable only as the last resting place of Frank Sinatra (at the Desert Memorial Park cemetery); **Rancho Mirage**'s sole claim to fame is the Betty Ford Clinic.

Palm Desert's appeal rests on the **Living Desert Zoo & Gardens** (47-900 Portola Avenue, 1-760 346 5694, www.livingdesert.org, $8.75-$17.25), a 1,200-acre wildlife and botanical park with animals from local and African deserts. Nearby **Indio** is home to the annual Coachella (www.coachella.com) and Stagecoach (www.stagecoachfestival.com) music festivals each spring, and a date industry that thrives all year. The **Shields Date Garden** (80-225 Highway 111, 1-760 347 7768, www.shieldsdate garden.com, free) is one of the area's oldest tourist traditions: stop by for a date shake.

To the west of Palm Springs is **Cabazon**, chiefly known for its **Desert Hills Premium Outlets** (48400 Seminole Drive, 1-951 849 6641, www.premiumoutlets.com), where tenacious bargain-hunters can find big markdowns on Burberry, Dior and the like.

Getting there

By bus Greyhound (1-800 231 2222, www. greyhound.com) runs up to 4 buses a day. The 3hr trip from LA costs around $58 (round-trip). **By car** To reach Palm Springs from LA, take I-10 eastbound for just over 100 miles. The journey can take anywhere between 2hrs and 3hrs.

Joshua Tree

Whether you're approaching from LA or Palm Springs, Joshua Tree National Park is best entered from the north via Highway 62: many of the park's highlights are in this northern section.

North of Yucca Valley, **Pipes Canyon Preserve** (1-909 797 8507, www.wildlands conservancy.org) is owned by a private conservation group but is every bit as wild as a national park. Ask at the visitor centre (*see p258*) for information about cougars, bears and bobcats, petroglyphs and active springs. Admission is free.

Joshua Tree National Park.

East of Yucca Valley are two smaller settlements, both of which offer entrances into Joshua Tree National Park. The towns of **Joshua Tree** itself and, around 16 miles further along Highway 62, **Twentynine Palms** are both small and rather plain, with a few hotels and restaurants but not much else.

JOSHUA TREE NATIONAL PARK

North of Palm Springs, the desert valley gives way to massive granite monoliths and strange, jagged trees with spiky blooms. These are Joshua trees, a form of cactus named by early Mormon settlers after the prophet Joshua, which they believed pointed the way to the Promised Land. The trees lend their name to the 794,000-acre **Joshua Tree National Park** (1-760 367 5500, www.nps.gov/jotr), a mecca for modern-day explorers that's home to 17 different types of cactus, palm-studded oases, ancient petroglyphs, spectacular rock formations and all manner of wildlife. The park straddles two desert ecosystems, the Mojave and Colorado. The remote eastern half is dominated by cholla cactus, small creosote bushes and some adrenaline-pumping 4WD routes. The cooler and wetter western section is what the Joshua Tree tourists come to see.

Entering via the West Entrance at the town of Joshua Tree (the $15 per car fee is valid for seven days), you'll soon come to Hidden Valley, a collection of climbs, hikes and picnic spots stretching as far as the eye can see. There's walking, too, with more than a dozen trails revisiting remnants of the gold mining era. The **Hidden Valley** mile-long loop winds around a dramatic, rock-enclosed valley, while the nearby **Barker Dam Trail** leads to a lake built by early ranchers; at dusk, it's possible to spot bighorn sheep

taking a sip. Try to take at least one of the trails during your visit.

Keys View, due south of Hidden Valley, is worth a side trip; on a clear day, you can see all the way to Mexico. You can also pick up 18-mile **Geology Tour Road** (high clearance vehicles are a must) showing off some of Joshua Tree's most dramatic landscapes. Off-road adventures continue on **Berdoo Canyon Road**, which intersects Geology Tour Road and passes the ruins of a camp constructed in the 1930s by builders of the California Aqueduct.

Where to stay and eat

Once a cantina set for numerous Westerns, **Pappy & Harriet's Pioneertown Palace** (53688 Pioneertown Road, Yucca Valley, 1-760 365 5956, www.pappyandharriets.com, mains $10) is now a popular local hangout serving heaped portions of mesquite BBQ and all manner of live music. In Joshua Tree, locals swear by the home cooking at the **Crossroads Café** (61715 Twentynine Palms Highway, 1-760 366 5414, www.crossroadscafejtree.com, mains $7), a hippie-ish eaterie that serves sandwiches, salads and the like; nearby **Royal Siam** (61599 Twentynine Palms Highway, 1-760 366 2923, mains $9) serves decent Thai fare. The best of a so-so bunch of restaurants in Twentynine Palms is the **Twentynine Palms Inn** (73950 Inn Avenue, 1-760 367 3505, www.29palms inn.com, mains $21), which serves steaks, chops and veggies from its own garden (yes, in the desert).

Lodgings are cheap and characterful. Yucca Valley's **Pioneertown Motel** (5040 Curtis Road, 1-760 365 7001, www.pioneertown-motel.com, double $70-$120) hosted actors such as Barbara Stanwyck when they filmed in the area. In Joshua Tree, try the hacienda-style **Joshua Tree Inn** (61259 Twentynine Palms Highway, Joshua Tree, 1-760 366 1188, www.joshuatreeinn.com, double $89-$159). Built in the 1950s as a getaway for movie stars, it then drew rock star guests such as the Rolling Stones and the Eagles during the 1960s; Gram Parsons spent his final hours in room 8. Over in Twentynine Palms, skip the vanilla motels on Highway 62 in favour of funky, old-school **Twentynine Palms Inn** (*see p257*, double $85-$155) or the 1950s-style **Harmony Motel** (71161 Twentynine Palms Highway, 1-760 367 3351, www.harmonymotel.com, double $65-$77), where U2 stayed while recording *The Joshua Tree*. In the park, there are nine campsites (see www.nps.gov/jotr), but only two have water. Remember to drink two litres a day.

Tourist information

Joshua Tree National Park *Oasis of Mara, 74485 National Park Drive, Twentynine Palms (1-760 367 5500, www.nps.gov/jotr).* **Open** 8am-5pm daily.
Joshua Tree National Park Cottonwood Spring *Joshua Tree National Park, 8 miles N of I-10, Joshua Tree (1-760 367 5500, www.nps.gov/jotr).* **Open** 9am-4pm daily.
Joshua Tree National Park *6554 Park Boulevard, Joshua Tree ((1-760 367 5500, www.nps.gov/jotr).* **Open** 8am-5pm daily.

Getting there

By car Joshua Tree National Park can be reached from the south via I-10, or from the north via Highway 62 in the towns of Joshua Tree and Twentynine Palms.

Southern Charms

SANTA CATALINA ISLAND

The most Mediterranean island in North America, Santa Catalina Island juts more than 2,000 feet (600 metres) above the Pacific Ocean at its highest point, 22 miles off Long Beach. Privately owned for two centuries and now 86 per cent owned and run by the **Santa Catalina Island Conservancy** (125 Claressa Avenue, 1-310 510 2595, www.catalinaconservancy.org), it's protected from overdevelopment.

The first street you walk will be Crescent Avenue, in the tiny town of **Avalon**. Lined with shops and restaurants, the street curves along a postcard-perfect harbour towards the art deco Casino building, home to a theatre and the **Catalina Island Museum** (1 Casino Way, Avalon, 1-310 510 2414, www.catalina museum. org, $4-$5, 10am-5pm daily). Busy, wave-free **Crescent Beach** is a big draw, though the **Descanso Beach Club** (closed Oct-Apr), a ten-minute walk along Via Casino from Avalon, is a quieter alternative and is open to the public for a small fee. From the north end of Crescent Avenue, it's a half-hour stroll on Avalon Canyon to the **Wrigley Memorial & Botanical Gardens** (1400 Avalon Canyon Road, 1-310 510 2897, $3-$7, 8am-5pm daily). The 1934 memorial recognises gum magnate William Wrigley Jr, who bought the island in 1915. The harbour views are beautiful. Perched along the harbour, the theatre at the breathtaking **Catalina Casino** (1 Casino Way, 1-800 626 1496, $10) shows

Santa Catalina Island.

first-run movies. The art deco landmark, which was recently treated to a facelift, also host October's annual **JazzTrax Festival** (www.jazztrax.com).

You'll need a permit from the Conservancy to either hike (free) or bike ($35/year pass) outside Avalon or Two Harbors, the rustic settlement at the island's northern isthmus. There's good scuba diving; try **Catalina Divers Supply** (1-310 510 0330, www.catalina diverssupply.com) or, for something a bit different, consider the **Catalina Zipline Eco Tour** (1-800 626 1496, $109-$120). It starts at Hog's Back gate and, two hours later, exits at Descanso Beach, after making several stops along the way. The less adventurous can enjoy one of a variety of boat trips; call the **Santa Catalina Island Company** (1-310 510 8687) or visit www.visitcatalinaisland.com, which also has information about other attractions and amenities on the island.

Where to stay and eat

Most eateries are in Avalon. For surf and turf, try **Steve's Steakhouse** (417 Crescent Avenue, 1-310 510 0333, www.stevessteakhouse.com, mains $25) on the harbour. Want to know where everyone is scoring those saliva-inducing, ice-cream-packed waffle cones? It's **Big Olaf's** (220 Crescent Avenue, 1-310 510 0798).

It's no wonder most visitors are day-trippers: lodging is scarce and pricey. You'll pay to be in the thick of things, but the casual elegance of **Hotel Vista del Mar** (1-800 601 3836, www.hotel-vistadelmar.com, double $145-$495), steps from the beach, and the plainer but still handsome **Metropole** (1-800 541 8528, www.hotel-metropole.com, double $159-$359) are worth it. **Hermit Gulch** is one of five campsites near Avalon (reservations required; 1-310 510 8368, $21); for others, such as the stunning seaside hike-in at Little Harbor, see www.visitcatalinaisland.com.

Tourist information

Catalina Island Chamber of Commerce & Visitors Bureau *1 Green Pleasure Pier, Avalon (1-310 510 1520, www.catalinachamber.com).* **Open** 8am-5pm Mon-Sat; 9am-3pm Sun.

Getting there

By boat Long Beach (1hr), San Pedro (75mins) and Dana Point (90mins) are served by Catalina Express (1-800 481 3470, www.catalinaexpress. com, $72.50-$74.50 round-trip). For the 75-min trip from Newport Beach, use the less regular Catalina Flyer (1-800 830 7744, www.catalina info.com, $70 round-trip).

San Diego

To the casual visitor, San Diego might come across as a little bland. It lacks the bohemian earthiness that defines San Francisco (despite an active gay community). It lacks the cascade of competing cultures that makes up LA's urban sprawl. It lacks a little charisma.

Of course, one man's charisma is another man's freak show, which explains how San Diego has grown into America's sixth largest city. Once known for its naval base and its climate, it's blossomed into a cheery centre of business and tourism. It's unashamedly nice: as sunny as the day is long, Californian conservatism at its most approachable. The Mexican and gay communities have shaken the town out of its woozy stasis, but you don't really come here for an edgy urban experience. Indeed, you don't really come here for an urban experience at all: you come here to find Middle America under Southern Californian skies.

DOWNTOWN SAN DIEGO

The heart of San Diego is its well-scrubbed, thriving **Downtown**, which combines a high-rise business district with a popular commercial core. The area, like Downtowns in many major US cities, had become moribund, but has been revived by a mix of commercial development and high-quality in-fill urban housing. Start at **Horton Plaza** (324 Horton Plaza, 1-619 239 8180, www.westfield.com), a complex of shops and restaurants on six open-air levels now run by the national Westfield chain.

Surrounding Horton Plaza is the historic, 16-block **Gaslamp Quarter**. Built in the 19th century, the area has been polished into a busy entertainment district, home to a number of neat, tidy and rather predictable restaurants and bars. Much of the street furniture is modern, including the mock-Victorian street lamps (powered not by gas but electricity) and brick sidewalks; conversely, many of the buildings are original. A walking tour of the area departs every Saturday at 11am from the **William Davis Heath House** (410 Island Avenue, 1-619 233 4692, www.gaslampquarter. org), which was built in 1850 and is the city's oldest building. Tour tickets cost $15.

West on Broadway, just a stone's throw from the waterfront stands one of San Diego's most recognisable landmarks, the **Santa Fe Depot** (1050 Kettner Boulevard). Constructed in 1915, the Spanish Mission-Colonial revival building is still an important travel hub under its modern name of **Union Station**. Across the street is the futuristic, two-storey **Museum of Contemporary Art** (1001 Kettner Boulevard,

ESCAPES & EXCURSIONS

San Diego.

1-858 454 3541, www.mcasd.org, $10), the sister to the original venue in La Jolla (*see p261*).

Continue west, and you'll reach the tree-lined **Embarcadero**, which affords panoramic views of the city and numerous reminders of San Diego's naval history: the excellent **Maritime Museum** (1492 N Harbor Drive, 1-619 234 9153, www.sdmaritime.org, $8-$16) sits close to the **USS Midway Museum** (910 N Harbor Drive, 1-619 544 9600, www.midway.org, $9-$19), the longest-serving aircraft carrier in US naval history. Some visitors choose to experience San Diego's water at closer quarters: **San Diego Harbor Excursions** (990 N Harbor Drive, 1-619 234 4111, www.sdhe.com) offers a variety of tours from Broadway Pier.

BALBOA PARK

Like Central Park in New York, 1,200-acre Balboa Park occupies a prominent piece of real estate. But, unlike its Manhattan equivalent, San Diego's city park is dotted with around two dozen fine cultural institutions. Stop by the **Visitor Center** (1549 El Prado, 1-619 239 0512, www.balboapark.org) for a map and other orientation aids. If you're planning on visiting a number of attractions, ask about the Balboa Park Passport, which entitles the bearer to entry to many of the park's attractions. If $49 is too dear, come on Tuesday, when some of the museums are free on a rotating basis.

The park itself is a lovely place, handsomely landscaped and smartly kept. Though most tourists just swing by and whistle-stop through a handful of the museums, it's worth taking time out to wander away from the crowds.

Culture vultures will want to take in the temporary exhibitions and permanent displays in the decent **San Diego Museum of Art** (1450 El Prado, 1-619 232 7931, www.sdmart. org, $4.50-$12); the regularly changing exhibits in the modern **Museum of Photographic Arts** (1649 El Prado, 1-619 238 7559, www.mopa. org, $4-$6); and the Dutch paintings and ancient Italian religious works in the **Timken Museum of Art** (1500 El Prado, 1-619 239 5548, www. timkenmuseum.org, free), a modernist building compared to its neighbours; all three are closed on Mondays. Families are better served by the interactive, kid-friendly exhibits in the **Reuben H Fleet Science Center** (1875 El Prado, 1-619 238 1233, www.rhfleet.org, $9.75-$15.75), the **Natural History Museum** (1788 El Prado, 1-619 232 3821, www.sdnhm.org, $11-$17) and the **San Diego Air & Space Museum** (2001 Pan American Plaza, 1-619 234 8291, www.sandiegoairandspace.org, $7-$18).

However, the park's real highlight is the 100-acre **San Diego Zoo** (2920 Zoo Drive, 1-619 234 3153, www.sandiegozoo.org, $34-$44 or with CityPass; *see p28*). Start by taking a 35-minute bus tour of the highlights, or riding the aerial Skyfari air tram across the park. The pandas (including the young Xiao Liwu, born in summer 2012 at the zoo), elephants and tigers are very popular, as are the polar bears; the hummingbird exhibit is the best place to avoid the crowds. And do notice the fabulous plant life: the site is a botanical garden of no little repute. A new Australian Outback exhibit was due to debut as this guide went to press. The zoo also runs the Safari Park in Escondido, 30 miles north of San Diego. Check the zoo's website for more details. And further north of Escondido, in Carlsbad, is another well-known family attraction, **Legoland** – see http://california.legoland.com.

HILLCREST AND OLD TOWN

San Diego's two most famous neighbourhoods have little in common save their interest for the casual visitor. A short drive north of Downtown sits **Hillcrest**, a few handsome streets lined with vintage shops, old-fashioned cafés and gay bars. The main drag is University Avenue; if you continue east along it for ten minutes, you'll reach **North Park**, a fast-rising district dotted with interesting bars and restaurants.

A little to the west of Hillcrest is **Old Town**, the first Spanish settlement in California and the original centre of San Diego. The two dozen original buildings now comprise a State Historic Park, albeit one dotted with a number of rather ordinary restaurants. The visitor centre in the Robinson-Rose building offers further information (4002 Wallace Street, 1-619 220 5422, www.parks.ca.gov); tours leave from here at 11am and 2pm every day of the year.

CORONADO

You can get a sense of the might of the US Navy driving across the two-mile **Coronado Bay Bridge**, which swoops over the harbour from Downtown to the 'island' (actually a peninsula) of Coronado: it yields a dramatic view of the cruisers and other vessels anchored in the bay. Most of Coronado is military, but it's also home to a comfortable downtown area and the 1888 **Hotel del Coronado** (*see p262*), one of the US's largest all-wood structures. The hotel overlooks a lovely beach, tying together the sum total of Coronado's other attractions.

HEADING NORTH

The Pacific Ocean sits a ten-minute drive from Old Town, and facing it are a number of beaches and resorts. The stretch of coastline covering shambling **Ocean Beach**, tidier **Mission Beach** and happy-go-lucky **Pacific Beach** is one long blur of mellowed-out beach bummery. The summer never ends around here – weatherbeaten men, old and young, ease through the mellow days with nothing more than a beer, a fish taco, a surfboard and the sun.

Aside from the weather and the waves, this stretch holds two notable attractions. In Mission Beach, **Belmont Park** (3146 Mission Boulevard, 1-858 488 1549, www.belmont park.com, $15.95-$26.95) offers old-fashioned beachside entertainments, including a rollercoaster built in 1925. It's harmless fun, but it's rather overshadowed by the wildly popular aquatic-themed family attractions at **SeaWorld** (1720 South Shores Drive, 1-619 226 3901, www.seaworld.com, $70-$78), which opened a new rollercoaster, Manta, in late 2012.

A ten-minute drive north of here, **La Jolla** ('La Hoy-a') is a very different town. You'll see the occasional bum and surf dog loitering around on its street corners, but this is an altogether wealthier and grander part of the world, prim and precious to the last. The shops along Girard Avenue are a mix of familiar chains and unique boutiques; few of the latter are anything other than upscale.

The **Museum of Contemporary Art, San Diego** (700 Prospect Street, 1-858 454 3541, www.mcasd.org, $5-$10) features more than 4,000 post-1950 works, including impressive collections of pop art and Latin American art, and there are some elegant modern buildings scattered amid plenty of architectural mediocrity: in particular, seek out Louis Kahn's **Salk Institute for Biological Studies** (10010 N Torrey Pines Road, 1-858 455 4100, www.salk.edu) and the **Scripps Institute of Oceanography** (2300 Expedition Way, 1-858 534 3474, www.aquarium.ucsd.edu, $9.50-$14), parts of which were designed by early California modernist Irving Gill. The Birch Aquarium at the Scripps is an excellent place at which to get acquainted with the local marine life. However, the main attraction of La Jolla is its location. Perched above the Pacific and fronted by a swooping coastline, the town could hardly have been blessed with a more impressive aspect. It's little wonder that the real estate here is the most expensive in San Diego.

Eating & drinking

Downtown San Diego is packed with bars and restaurants, although the quality, especially in the Gaslamp Quarter, is spotty. For comfort cooking, try the excellent burgers and beers at airy **Neighborhood** (777 G Street, 1-619 446 0002, www.neighborhoodsd.com, mains $10); down the street, **Zanzibar** (707 G Street, 1-619 230 0125, www.zanzibarcafe.com, mains $15) has sandwiches, salads and coffees. The French cooking at cosy **Café Chloe** (721 9th Avenue, 1-619 232 3242, www.cafechloe.com, mains $24) is solid but pricey. There are expensive steaks at **Donovan's** (570 K Street, 1-619 237 9700, www.donovanssteakhouse.com, mains $50) and cheap, agreeably jolly breakfasts at **Café 222** (222 Island Avenue, 1-619 236 9902, www.cafe222.com, mains $9).

Heading north, there are several worthwhile options in Bankers Hill en route to Hillcrest. There's bright, European-influenced Californian cooking at **Bertrand at Mister A's** (2550 5th Avenue, 1-619 239 1377, www.bertrandatmisteras.com, mains $33), which affords great views of the city, and some extraordinary desserts at, er, **Extraordinary Desserts** (2929 5th Avenue, 1-619 294 2132,

ESCAPES & EXCURSIONS

ESCAPES & EXCURSIONS

Ocean Beach. *See p261.*

www.extraordinarydesserts.com, desserts $9). And in Balboa Park, the Latin-inflected American cuisine served at the **Prado** (1549 El Prado, 1-619 557 9441, www.pradobalboa.com, mains $28) is far better than it needs to be given the touristy location. If your tastes run towards the carnivorous, a can't-miss local joint in the Midway is **Phil's BBQ** (3750 Sports Arena Boulevard, 1-619 226 6333, www.philsbbq.net, mains $13); there's another location in San Marcos (579 Grand Avenue, 1-760 759 1400).

Up in Hillcrest, try the diner staples at the **Crest Café** (425 Robinson Avenue, 1-619 295 2510, www.crestcafe.net, mains $11). Further east in fast-gentrifying North Park, your best bet is the cheap Mexican basic cuisine served at **Super Cocina** (3627 University Avenue, 1-619 584 6244, http://supercocinasd.com, mains $8.99). On Prospect Street in La Jolla, **Georges at the Cove** (No.1250, 1-858 454 4244, www.georgesatthecove.com, mains $34) sets the standards for California cuisine. And out in Pacific Beach, try the lively and likeable comfort cooking at relaxed, affordable **Café 976** (976 Felpar Street, 1-858 272 0976, www.cafe976.com, mains $8).

Hotels

The handsome and ultra-hip **W** (421 W B Street, 1-619 398 3100, www.whotels.com, double $129-$529) has been joined by the gracious **Sofia**, 150 W Broadway, 1-800 826 0009, www.thesofiahotel.com, $88-$319) and the **Hotel Solamar** (435 6th Avenue, 1-877 230 0300, www.hotelsolamar.com, double $136-$319), a sunny Kimpton property. The **Hotel Indigo** (509 9th Avenue, www.ichotels group.com, 1-619 727 4000, double $171-$225) is popular for amenities such as free Wi-Fi; it also has a rooftop bar that overlooks the city. For

old-school luxury, try the **US Grant** (326 Broadway, 1-619 232 3121, www.usgrant.net, double $189-$439). On Bankers Hill you'll find the **Britt Scripps Inn** (406 Maple Street, 1-619 230 1991, www.brittscripps.com, double $240-$299), a Victorian-style boutique hotel with nine guestrooms. Budget travellers should head, instead, for **HI-San Diego** (521 Market Street, 1-619 223 4778, www.sandiegohostels. org, $19-$34 per person, $85 family room).

Outside Downtown, the landmark property is the immaculate **Hotel del Coronado** (1500 Orange Avenue, Coronado, 1-619 435 6611, www.hoteldel.com, double $289-$1,500), which famously featured in *Some Like It Hot*, among other films. Amenities at the 125-year-old grande dame include a superior spa and several restaurants. In Point Loma, not far from Downtown, you'll find the stylish **Pearl** (1410 Rosecrans Street, 1-619 226 6100, www.thepearl sd.com, double $164-$204). Pacific Beach offers the glamorous **Tower 23** (723 Felspar Street, 1-866 869 3723, www.tower23hotel.com, double $199-$350). And north in La Jolla, the boutiquey **Hotel Parisi** (1111 Prospect Street, 1-858 454 1511, www.hotelparisi.com, double $239-$589) offers a little modish East Coast style.

Tourist information

Balboa Park Visitors Center *House of Hospitality, 1549 El Prado (1-619 239 0512, www.balboapark.org).* **Open** 9.30am-4.30pm daily.
San Diego Convention & Visitors Bureau *1140 North Harbor Drive (1-619 236 1212, www.sandiego.org).* **Open** *June-Sept* 9am-5pm daily. *Oct-May* 9am-4pm daily.

Getting there

By car From Downtown LA, take the I-5 south. From West LA, take the I-405 south and then join the I-5. From LA, it takes about 2hrs with no traffic.
By bus Greyhound (1-800 231 2222, www. greyhound.com) runs up to 20 buses a day. The fare is $30-$37 and the journey takes 2-3hrs.
By train Amtrak (1-800 872 7245, www.amtrak. com) runs about ten trains per day between Union Station and San Diego. A round trip costs about $64; journey time 2hrs 40mins.

Getting around

San Diego Transit Corporation buses cover much of the city, or use the San Diego Trolley between Downtown and Old Town (to the north) or Tijuana (to the south). For details on public transport, visit the **San Diego Transit Store** (102 Broadway, 1-619 234 1060, www.sdmts.com). For route information, call 511 (within San Diego) and select 'public transportation' or call 1-619 233 3004.

Borderline Madness

Take a walk on the wilder side of the West Coast.

On the northern side of the westernmost US–Mexico border crossing, you'll see a massive parking lot, usually filled with newish cars owned by American day-trippers who've crossed over in search of a little fun and games. On the southern side, meanwhile, is a massive breaker's yard filled with the remains of now-useless Mexican cars. Between them, these two lots provide a useful metaphor for the vast differences in attitudes, aspirations and wealth between nice, middle-class Southern California and earthy, dirty **Tijuana**, the most famous border town on earth.

After squeaky-clean San Diego, Tijuana smacks you upside the head like the third margarita of the night. A classic untamed border town, it's messy, edgy and loud, a vibrant reminder of the ongoing tensions between the mutually dependent gringo north and the impoverished south. Prostitutes ply their trade as sharks offer discount drinks; mariachi musicians roam the streets in search of work and tips, hunting in packs like wolves. Mexicans do the selling; Americans are doing the buying.

It's all about commerce: get your picture taken with a donkey, buy three tacos for a buck, stock up on discount drugs (mostly for depression and erectile dysfunction, two conditions in which the US seems to be a world leader). On Avenida Revolución, shops and street vendors hawk religious kitsch and cheap cigarettes; several big US chains (Burger King et al) cater to astonishingly unadventurous tourists. Nightfall brings boozy exuberance (the legal drinking age is 18, which is why the town is popular with San Diego students) and an increase in crime, with locals preying on drunk visitors.

Some visitors grumble that Tijuana isn't authentically Mexican. Certainly, the country is different the further south you travel. But in truth this Americanised border town is no less authentic than Downtown San Diego, with its airbrushed industrial buildings and electricity-powered ersatz gaslamps. The rip-offs are different on either side of the border – fake Zoloft in Tijuana, $30 parking in San Diego – but they're all cut from the same fiercely capitalist cloth.

To reach Tijuana, drive south on I-5 or I-805 from San Diego for 25 miles to the San Ysidro International Border. You're best off parking here, then walking across the border into Tijuana. Alternatively, from Downtown San Diego, take the San Ysidro trolley ($5 return; 1-619 233 3004, www.sdcommute.com), which runs until 1am daily and until 2am on Saturdays; it connects with various stations in Downtown, including 5th Avenue (at C Street), Civic Center (C Street between 2nd & 3rd Avenues) and Santa Fe Depot. There's a tourist information office just over the border, but the maps it distributes are pretty useless. Travellers can stay without a visa for up to 72 hours, but need a passport as ID. Children also require a passport.

Note: While millions of people travel safely to and from Tijuana every year, due to ongoing violence on the border, safety remains an issue. Always check the US Department of State's website (www.travel. state.gov/travel, then select Mexico) for updates and warnings before travelling.

History

From cow town to boom town to Tinseltown.

TEXT: WILL FULFORD-JONES AND LESLEY MCCAVE

Now the second most populous city in the United States (after New York), Los Angeles has achieved that status against all odds. The fact that it is built on arid land prone to tremors, fires and floods has proved no boundary to the nearly four million people who call the area home. That's not to say that life here has ever been easy: in its 230-plus years LA has seen oil shortages, water shortages, earthquakes, riots, police brutality, gruesome murders, suburban sprawl and deflating house prices, and even during the city's various boom decades, riots and racial tension were commonplace. Maybe that's par for the course in a place where nearly half the citizens are 'outsiders' looking for a community to settle down in (more than 40 per cent of LA's population is foreign-born). The reality is that Los Angeles may have attracted its fair share of chancers and hustlers, but those who manage to make it here, regardless of their ethnic background, are here for the long haul.

EARLY SETTLEMENT

Given the city's recent developmental history, perhaps it's appropriate that settlement in Los Angeles began with a series of single-family suburbs scattered haphazardly across its landscape. Prior to the arrival of Spanish colonists in the latter part of the 18th century, what is now metropolitan Los Angeles was populated by 30,000 Native Americans. But they weren't farmers: they relied on hunting and native plants for food. And, unlike the Iroquois and other tribes in North America, they hadn't yet organised themselves into strong political confederations. Instead, they lived in small settlements surrounding the area's few rivers, each group adopting a separate identity.

Backed by military muscle, the Spanish arrived and began to establish a string of Franciscan missions along the coast. The first was established in San Diego during 1769; two years later, the San Gabriel Mission marked the initial Spanish foray into what would latter become Los Angeles County. The missionaries' supposed ambition was to spread the Christian faith, but life on their new missions proved feudal and even brutal. The reluctant Native American converts were rounded up from their small settlements and virtually enslaved by the Franciscans. Thousands died, leading the missionaries to head deep into the surrounding countryside in search of more 'converts'.

A PLANNED PUEBLO

The history of Los Angeles as a city begins in 1781, the year the British surrendered to George Washington in Virginia and effectively ended the War of Independence, when the Spaniards decided that they needed a settlement (or pueblo) in Southern California to serve as a way-station for the military. At a site nine miles east of the San Gabriel Mission, where the Los Angeles River widened, Governor Felipe de Neve laid out a plaza measuring 275 feet by 180 feet (84 metres by 55 metres). Around it were marked a series of lots, each with a 55-foot (17-metre) frontage on the plaza.

De Neve commissioned his aides to recruit 24 settlers and their families from

'The 1880s transformed LA from a cow town into a fast-growing hustlers' paradise.'

Sonora, more than 350 miles north. On 18 August 1781, after a forced march of 100 days through desert heat, the 12 men, 11 women and 21 children who survived the trip arrived at the plaza. Thus did El Pueblo de Nuestra Señora la Reina de Los Angeles de Porciúncula begin as it has always since grown: not with a hardy band of motivated settlers, but with a real estate agent looking for customers. (The remains of this early settlement stand just north of modern-day Downtown LA, on now-touristy Olvera Street. They were designated a California State Historic Landmark in 1953.)

Although other missions were established in and near the region, among them San Buenaventura, San Fernando and San Juan Capistrano, de Neve's new settlement remained, literally, a dusty cow town for decades: the population in 1800 was made up of 315 people and 12,500 cows. However, after Mexico declared itself independent from Spain in 1821 and annexed California during the following year, the Spanish-born priests were ordered out of the area. The mission system soon broke down, and powerful local families, eager to exploit mission land, received dozens of large land grants from the Mexican government. Most of these *ranchos*, which were typically several thousand acres in size, were recognised as valid claims of title when California entered the United States in 1850. Many remained intact into the 20th century, one of numerous factors that allowed large-scale, mass-production land development to occur in the region.

Americans had been informally colonising Los Angeles throughout the era of Mexican rule, as wandering opportunists arrived in the town, married into prominent

IN CONTEXT

'Spanish' families and renamed themselves 'Don Otto' or 'Don Bill'. The transfer of the cow town into US hands occurred during the forcible annexation of California that triggered the Mexican-American war of 1846-48. On 13 August 1846, Commodore RF Stockton landed at San Pedro with 500 marines and started his march to the pueblo. With political support from the 'Dons', he captured the settlement without firing a shot. The US-Mexican treaty of 1848 confirmed US dominion over California; on 9 September 1850, it officially became the 31st state of the Union.

BOOMS AND BUSTS

Los Angeles grew steadily but somewhat unspectacularly over the next 20 years, becoming a centre of California's 'hide and tallow' trade: farmers would raise cattle, then sell the hides for coats and the fat for candle-tallow to trading companies from the East Coast and Europe. Richard Henry Dana's *Two Years Before the Mast* (1840), California's first literary masterpiece, includes descriptions of the author trudging through the shallow waters of San Pedro harbour with cowhides on his back. But when the gold rush hit Northern California, the cattle barons of Los Angeles discovered they could sell the cows for beef at $30 a head to the gold fields, rather than at $3 a head to the traders.

In 1883, the transcontinental railroad from New Orleans to Los Angeles was finally completed, bringing with it the long-expected boom. A price war broke out among the railroads, and the cost of a one-way ticket to LA dropped from $125 to a mere dollar. Naturally enough, more and more people took the westbound railroad: in 1887, the Southern Pacific Railroad transported 120,000 people to LA, at the time a city of just 10,000 residents. The instability of the local economy meant that the real estate boom didn't last: one of the reasons that LA's population had grown so dramatically was that many immigrants simply couldn't afford to leave. But despite the crash, the 1880s transformed Los Angeles from a cow town into a fast-growing hustlers' paradise.

After the short-lived prosperity of the 1880s, the land barons and real estate operators who came to dominate LA became determined to lay more solid foundations for the city's expansion. Forming the Los Angeles Chamber of Commerce in 1888, they took the unprecedented step of embarking on a nationwide campaign to attract new immigrants to the region, sending advertisements, brochures and even quasi-evangelical speakers to spread the word of the Golden State in the Midwest. It was this commercial offensive that led journalist Morrow Mayo to conclude that LA was not a city but 'a commodity; something to be advertised and sold to the people of the United States like automobiles, cigarettes and mouthwashes.'

Still, the charm offensive had a tangible effect. As commodity prices rose in the first decade of the 20th century, thousands of Midwestern farmers sold up, moved west and set in motion the wheels of a new boom. Encouraged by the influx of new residents, the city's land barons soon pulled off one of the most audacious and duplicitous schemes ever devised to ensure a city's greatness.

WATER, WATER EVERYWHERE

In 1904, former Los Angeles mayor Fred Eaton travelled to the Owens Valley, a high-desert region 230 miles north of Los Angeles. Claiming that he was working on a dam project for the federal government, Eaton began purchasing land along the Owens River. But after he'd bought huge swathes of the area, Eaton revealed his true purpose: to divert the Owens River through an aqueduct to LA.

Whipped into a frenzy by trumped-up fears of a drought in 1905, Los Angeles voters approved a bond issue that called for the construction of an aqueduct from the Owens Valley to the city. LA had enough water to serve the population at the time, but not enough to enable its growth. As William Mulholland, the city's water engineer, put it: 'If we don't get it, we won't need it.' Mulholland, a self-taught Irish immigrant, went on to direct one of the great engineering feats in US

Times of the Sign

How nine letters stole the city's heart.

It seems wholly appropriate that the most famous landmark in Los Angeles was built as a wildly ostentatious piece of advertising. Stuck for ideas as to how best to promote their new real estate development in the Hollywood Hills, *Los Angeles Times* publisher Harry Chandler and Keystone Cops creator Mack Sennett hit upon a solution. Some 50 feet tall, 450 feet wide and lit by 4,000 light bulbs, their unmissable HOLLYWOODLAND sign was unveiled on 13 July 1923.

The sign was meant to stand for just 18 months, but it remained long after Chandler and Sennett had sold their properties. It briefly returned to the news in 1932, when 24-year-old British-born actress Peg Entwistle threw herself off the top of the 'H'. But the sign was otherwise left to rot: vandals laid waste to its lights in the 1930s; and in the mid 1940s, ownership of the land slipped into the hands of the local government.

Only when the 'H' collapsed in 1949 did the authorities decide to take action. Some lobbied to get rid of it, while others campaigned to keep it. In the end, a compromise was reached: the last four letters were removed, but the first nine were given a refurbishment (albeit without their lights). HOLLYWOODLAND was dead; hooray, instead, for HOLLYWOOD. Despite being granted landmark status in 1973, no effort was made to protect the sign.

Graffiti was scratched on it, some parts of it were stolen, and, in 1977, an arsonist tried to torch the second 'L'.

It took an unlikely figure to restore a little star power to the landmark. When it was estimated that a new sign would cost $250,000, Hugh Hefner hosted a fundraising gala at which individual letters were sponsored, to the tune of $27,700, by the likes of Andy Williams (the 'W') and Alice Cooper (the middle 'O'). The old sign came down in 1978 andthe new version, its letters 45 feet tall and between 31 and 39 feet wide, was unveiled to much fanfare. It's this incarnation that still looks down over LA.

In 2005 Dan Bliss put the original sign up for sale on eBay, having bought it from Berger two years earlier. It netted $450,400, roughly 20 times what the sign had cost to build 82 years earlier. Bliss's reason for selling? He needed to raise funds to invest in a movie.

Less than five years later, however, a proposed development of the land around the sign put it in danger once again. In February 2010 a campaign to raise the $12.5 million necessary to buy and protect the land was launched. For a few months people were on tenterhooks, fearing that the city could really lose its best-known landmark. But gradually donations began to trickle in and by April there was relief when the last of the money was raised. Who had stepped in at the last minute with the final $900,000? LA's favourite playboy, Hugh Hefner. The sign received another makeover – its biggest in 35 years – in December 2012, in time for its 90th birthday. No Botox required.

For a local's perspective, check out Hope Anderson's *Under the Hollywood Sign* 2009 documentary (www.under thehollywoodsign.com), an homage to – and a history of – the sign, featuring interviews with famous fans and nearby residents.

IN CONTEXT

history. A century after its completion, his 233-mile aqueduct still operates without electrical power, entirely on a gravity system. The aqueduct didn't actually come to the heart of Los Angeles: it went only as far as the San Fernando Valley, an adjacent farming region. But in the last and perhaps most masterful part of the scam, it turned out that LA's land barons had secretly bought the valley on the cheap, annexed it to the city and then splashed irrigating Owens Valley water on it, all in a successful attempt to increase its value. (Roman Polanski's masterpiece *Chinatown* is based in part on the so-called water wars). Today, the San Fernando Valley, population 1.8 million, is the prototypical US suburb, and its people chafe under the Los Angeles city controls that brought water to their valley in the first place.

MOTORS AND MOVIES

With its water supply in place, Los Angeles boomed in the 1910s and 1920s like no other American city. The expansion was partly dependent on real estate speculation, but it was also due to the rise of three new industries: petroleum, aircraft and movies. With little natural wood and almost no coal, the city suffered regular fuel crises that, in some cases, were as severe as its water problem. However, the discovery of oil in metropolitan LA between 1900 and 1925, particularly around the La Brea Tar Pits, in Huntington Beach and at Santa Fe Springs, put an end to the troubles. The result was a plentiful supply of oil that enriched the region and helped to fuel the city's growing love affair with the automobile.

Its residents scattered far and wide, Los Angeles took to the car more readily than any city except Detroit. Car sales were high: the city soon developed its own thriving oil, automobile and tyre industries, each with its own monuments. In 1928, Adolph Schleicher, president of the Samson Tire & Rubber Co, constructed an $8 million tyre plant modelled after a royal palace once built by the king of Assyria. The plant (5675 Telegraph Road, City of Commerce) has since been reborn as a shopping mecca.

Movies and aircraft came to Los Angeles during the 1910s for the same reasons as its incoming residents: temperate weather, low rainfall and cheap land, the last of these providing the wide open spaces that both industries needed in order to operate. In 1921, Donald Douglas founded his aircraft company, a predecessor to McDonnell-Douglas, at Clover Field in Santa Monica (now Santa Monica Municipal Airport); the Lockheed brothers moved their business from Santa Barbara to LA in 1926; and Jack Northrop, who had worked with both Douglas and the Lockheeds, started his own company in Burbank in 1928. Together, the three firms later formed the foundation of the US's 'military-industrial' complex.

Filming began in Los Angeles around 1910, moving to Hollywood in 1911 when the Blondeau Tavern at Gower Street and Sunset Boulevard was turned into a movie studio. At the time, Hollywood was being

'LA now attracted poor white refugees from the Dust Bowl of Oklahoma and Texas.'

marketed as a pious and sedate suburb, and the intrusion of the film industry was resented. The business was never really centred on the neighbourhood: Culver City and Burbank, both home to a number of studios, have stronger claims on the title of the industry's capital. Nevertheless, Hollywood became the financial and social centre of the film world, as the area's population grew from 4,000 in 1910 to 30,000 in 1920 and 235,000 in 1930. The wealth that defined the period is still visible in the magnificent commercial architecture along Hollywood Boulevard between Cahuenga and Highland Avenues. However, the town's earliest movie palaces were built not in Hollywood but on Broadway in Downtown LA.

IN CONTEXT

PROGRESS OF SORTS

During the 1920s, a decade that saw the population of Los Angeles double, the city became a kind of national suburb, where the middle classes sought refuge from the teeming immigrant groups so prevalent in other large metropolises. Civic leaders worked hard to build the type of edifices and institutions that they thought a big city deserved: the Biltmore Hotel and the adjacent Los Angeles Central Library, Los Angeles City Hall, the Los Angeles Coliseum, the University of Southern California and Exposition Park. And with the creation of the Los Angeles Stock Exchange (now the Pacific Stock Exchange), LA became the financial capital of the West Coast.

However, this process of making Los Angeles the great 'white' city served to marginalise the minority groups that had long been a part of local life. The Mexican and Mexican American population, which had grown rapidly and had provided the city with a much-needed labour force, was pushed out of Downtown into what is now the East LA barrio. And the African Americans, who had previously lived all over the city, found themselves confined to an area south of Downtown straddling Central Avenue, which became known as South Central. Both of these mini-migrations laid the foundation for serious social unrest in later decades.

Despite these problems, Los Angeles in the 1920s had an irrepressible energy. The arrival of so many newcomers created a rootlessness that manifested itself in many ways. Those in need of companionship were drawn to the city's many cafeterias (invented in LA), which served as incubators of social activity. Those in need of a restored faith had, and still have, their choice of any number of faith healers. And those searching for a quick profit were drawn to the tantalising claims of local oil companies in search of investors. Indeed, nothing captures a sense of LA's primal energy during the 1920s like the rampant oil business.

With a steady supply of gushers, often in residential areas, oil promoters had a ready-made set of samples with which to promote their products. And with an endless stream of equity-rich farm refugees from the Midwest, they also had a ready-made pool of gullible investors. The most skilled promoter was a Canadian named CC Julian, who attracted millions of dollars to his oil company with a string of newspaper ads that had the narrative drive of a soap opera. When it became clear that he couldn't deliver on his promises, he was elbowed out of his own firm by other swindlers who continued the scam, issuing millions of bogus shares and bribing the district attorney in a bid to stay out of trouble. The end came in 1931, when a defrauded investor opened fire in an LA courtroom on a banker who had been involved in the scam. The failed investor had ten cents to his name when he was arrested. The crooked banker's pockets held $63,000.

GROWING UP

As was the case elsewhere in the US, the 1930s proved rather more sober than the roaring '20s in Los Angeles. With the boom over and the Depression in full swing, the city's growth slowed, and the city's new arrivals were very different from their predecessors. Instead of greeting wealthy Midwestern farmers, LA now attracted poor white refugees from the Dust Bowl of Oklahoma and Texas, the 'Okies' made famous in John Steinbeck's novel *The Grapes of Wrath*. These unskilled workers wound up as farm labourers and hangers-on in the margins of society.

Dealing with these newcomers proved difficult for Los Angeles, but the problem was intertwined with another conundrum: how to handle the equally poor and unskilled Mexican and Mexican American population. After farm owners chose to hire Okies over Mexicans, LA County became overwhelmed by the cost of public relief. The authorities resorted to repatriating even those Mexicans who were born and raised in Los Angeles.

The arrival of the Okies and other hobos caused a nasty public backlash. But it also built a liberal political mood among the have-nots, which culminated in the near-election of reformer and novelist Upton Sinclair as California's governor. In the early '30s, Sinclair wrote a diatribe

IN CONTEXT

'Okies' head for California, 1937.

called *I, Governor of California, and How I Ended Poverty*, before going on to found the End Poverty in California (EPIC) movement and eventually winning the Democratic gubernatorial nomination for the 1934 elections. Only a concerted effort by reactionary political forces, aided by movie-house propaganda from the film industry, defeated his bid. After his failure, Sinclair followed his original pamphlet with a book entitled *I, Governor of California, and How I Got Licked*.

The region also had other problems with which to contend: the 1933 Long Beach earthquake, for example. But optimism gradually returned, with a handful of developments lending the locals some new-found pride. Held at the Coliseum, the 1932 Olympics saw the expansion and aesthetic redevelopment of 10th Street: the street was renamed Olympic Boulevard and lined with palm trees, thus setting the fashion for palms in LA. Seven years later, the first local freeway was built: the Arroyo Seco Parkway, now the Pasadena Freeway. And in 1941, a new aqueduct brought water from the Hoover Dam along the Colorado River, helping to cater for the city's continued growth.

World War II caused the single biggest upheaval Los Angeles had seen to that point, laying the foundations for the modern metropolis it went on to become. Already at the forefront of aviation, the city rapidly grew industrialised during the war, becoming both a major military manufacturing centre and a staging ground for the American fight against Japan in the Pacific. More than 5,000 new manufacturing plants were built in LA during the war, mostly in outlying locations. Dormitory communities sprang up to accommodate the workers, many of them 'model' towns sponsored by industrialists or the military. These new settlements helped to establish the sprawling pattern of urban development that came to characterise LA in the postwar years.

COLOUR CLASH

The population of Los Angeles diversified still further during the '40s. During the war, more than 200,000 African Americans moved to the city, mostly from Louisiana and Texas, to take advantage of the job opportunities. But the restrictive property laws meant that the South Central ghetto didn't expand geographically in order to accommodate these new arrivals, and the area became seriously overcrowded. It wasn't until 1948, when the Supreme Court threw out restrictive covenants and paved the way for an exodus of middle-class blacks west into the Crenshaw district, that the South Central's burden began to ease.

In desperate need of labourers, Los Angeles welcomed the return of the Mexicans and Mexican Americans who had been pushed out a decade earlier. However, tensions between white Angelenos and Mexicans were widespread and constantly threatened to boil over. In 1942, roughly 600 Mexican Americans were arrested in connection with the murder of José Gallardo Díaz, found dying near a reservoir in the area today known as Bell. No fewer than 22 were charged, and, in January 1943, 17 were eventually convicted following a trial thick with racial epithets. There was more to come.

When a white sailor on shore leave was injured during a group brawl with a number of Mexican Americans in May 1943, more than 100 sailors left their ships and stampeded into East LA in search of Latinos. A number of Mexicans were injured in the ensuing skirmishes, which became known as the Zoot Suit Riots after the baggy suits favoured by Mexican American men at the time. A national civil rights outcry ensued and a committee was set up to investigate the trouble. However, no punishment was ever meted out to the sailors, and some sections of the local press even praised their actions. On 2 October 1944, the 17 Mexican Americans found guilty at the 1943 murder trial each had their convictions quietly quashed at appeal, but the tensions nonetheless remained.

Discrimination against LA's growing Japanese community was even more pronounced. Most Japanese Americans on the West Coast were interned in camps by the federal government during World War II, no matter how patriotic their attitude to their new home. (Indeed, in a supreme irony, some young men were permitted to leave the internment camps to join the US armed forces, which many did enthusiastically.) Most Japanese lost their property during these years, much of it concentrated in the Little Tokyo area of LA just east of City Hall. It took decades for the neighbourhood to return to prosperity.

When the African Americans, Latinos and Japanese who fought for the US during the war returned to continued housing discrimination, police brutality and the general Angeleno attitude that they were not 'real Americans', their sense of alienation grew further. But because Los Angeles was a highly segregated city, most whites were able to ignore the race problem – especially after the war, when the city reaped the benefits of industrialisation and a new suburban boom began.

AFTER THE WAR

The postwar era in Los Angeles is often recalled as an idyllic spell of prosperity and harmony. In fact, it was an unsettled period during which the city struggled to keep up with the demands of massive growth. Taxes rose in order to fund new facilities and heavily oversubscribed schools went on 'double-sessions', teaching two classes in the same classroom.

In the decade after the war, the entire LA region devoted itself to building anything and everything. Freeway construction, which had been stymied by the war, exploded in 1947 after California imposed an additional petrol tax to pay for a new road network. Over the next two decades, virtually the entire freeway system was constructed, a marvel of modern engineering and the driving force behind the city's unstoppable expansion. The new road network opened up vast tracts of land for urban development in outlying areas: chief among them were the San Fernando Valley and Orange County, linked to Los Angeles by the I-5 (aka the Golden State Freeway). A crucial event in the success of this suburbanisation was the opening, in 1955, of Disneyland, the world's first theme park.

IN CONTEXT

Other leisure attractions helped to establish Los Angeles as a major city during the same period. In 1958, the city achieved 'major league' status by luring New York's Brooklyn Dodgers baseball team to the West Coast. But, as so often in LA's history, even this event was marred by racial tensions. In order to attract the Dodgers, the city gave them a spectacular site in Chavez Ravine, overlooking Downtown LA. Located in a low-income Latino neighbourhood, the site had been earmarked for use as a public housing project. The project, though, was never built; Dodger Stadium still stands today.

As suburbanisation continued in the 1950s and '60s, some areas prospered but others were left behind. On a hot summer night in 1965, the pent-up frustrations of the black ghetto exploded into one of the first and most destructive of the US's urban disturbances. The Watts Riots began after an African American man was pulled over on a drink-driving charge. By the time they were over, dozens of locals had been killed and hundreds of buildings had been destroyed; some estimates pinned the cost at around $40 million, a huge figure at the time. For many Angelenos living in their comfortable suburbs, the riots were the first indication that all was not well in their metropolis.

ONWARDS AND OUTWARDS

After the Watts Riots, Los Angeles began to struggle with its image problem, as national newspapers and magazines began to proclaim the end of the California Dream. Under a series of hard-line chiefs, the Los Angeles

Eau Yes We Can!

An amazing feat of engineering.

'There it is... take it,' William Mulholland famously told the crowds who had gathered for the opening of the Los Angeles aqueduct on 5 November 1913. The brainchild of Mulholland, a former ditch digger from Belfast, and engineer (and later mayor) Fred Eaton, the aqueduct was an incredible undertaking – as reflected in the figures below – involving massive manpower in the form of itinerant workers who camped out in the desert, and using gravity alone to push the water along. The fact that it came in on time and under budget only added to its awe.

5,000: labourers on the project
164: number of tunnels
233 miles: length
$25 million: budget
6 years: duration of the project
40,000: people who turned up for the opening ceremony
600 million: gallons of drinking water supplied by the aqueduct to modern-day LA

To mark the project's centennial, 2013 has been declared the 'Year of the LA Aqueduct' by the LA city council, with various activities and events, culminating in a celebration on 5 November 2013, 100 years to the day since the aqueduct opened.

To download a free, 90-minute self-guided car audio tour of the Owens Valley along US Route 395, complete with commentaries and opinions about the aqueduct's controversial background from a selection of residents, environmentalists and historians, go to http://thereitistakeit.org.

Police Department continued to treat minority neighbourhoods as if they were occupied territories. As they did so, a violent gang culture gradually began to develop in pockets of South Central LA.

Although he had no previous political experience, former actor Ronald Reagan was elected as the state governor on a law-and-order platform in 1966. But despite his efforts, the city continued to grab the national headlines in a number of undesirable ways. Three years after Reagan's election, the Charles Manson cult killed actress Sharon Tate and others at a home in Benedict Canyon, disturbing the sense of tranquillity that permeated the high-end Beverly Hills suburb. And in 1971, the city suffered its worst earthquake in 38 years, escaping a high death toll only because the quake struck at the early hour of 6am. Out of this troubled period, however, emerged a towering political figure: Tom Bradley, an African American police captain who had grown up in the segregated world of Central Avenue and who later held his own in such white-dominated enclaves as UCLA and the LAPD.

While at the LAPD in the 1950s, Bradley was assigned to improve relations with beleaguered Jewish shopkeepers in black neighbourhoods, an opportunity he used to help forge a cross-racial political alliance that sustained him for years. After retiring from the police, Bradley was elected to the City Council and, with strong support in South Central and the largely Jewish West Side, ran for mayor. He lost in 1969 but won four years later, becoming the first African American mayor of a predominantly white city (according to a 2010-11 census, the black population of the City of Los Angeles is only 9.6 per cent, and that of Los Angeles County a mere 9.3 per cent). By moving into the mayor's mansion, Bradley helped desegregate the Hancock Park neighbourhood, which had violently resisted the arrival of Nat 'King' Cole some years before.

A low-key man with a calming personality, Bradley successfully ruled the city for 20 years through the power of persuasion. During the 1970s, he sought to heal the city's long-open racial wounds. And in the early 1980s, he turned his attention to development, reviving Downtown and courting international business: the 1984 Olympics were to prove his greatest triumph. Bradley's efforts also benefited from a huge flow of Japanese capital into Los Angeles real estate in the 1980s. However, his popularity levels fell in the early 1990s, due in part to his handling of the Rodney King affair, and he was replaced as mayor by Richard Riordan in 1993 after deciding not to seek a sixth term in office. He died five years later.

TROUBLED TIMES

For all the optimism engendered by Bradley's work, the period during which he led the city offered only a partial respite from LA's chronic social and racial tensions. Public opinion in the region became more polarised in the 1970s, as affluent whites grew more conservative and found little in common with the immigrants who were turning LA into a melting pot. The decline of agriculture in Latin America made the city a magnet for legal and illegal immigrants from Mexico and elsewhere, while political strife in Central America led to the arrival of thousands more new arrivals. The city's position on the edge of the burgeoning Pacific Rim also attracted people (and capital) from Korea, the Philippines, Taiwan and Hong Kong.

The vast central areas of Los Angeles were re-energised by these newcomers. Tourism, trade and the garment industry boomed, as did the rapidly expanding Koreatown. But as the neighbourhoods changed, so friction grew. Latin American immigrants began crowding into historically black South Central, creating a culture clash with middle- and working-class home-owners. African Americans, in particular, felt more alienated than ever.

These tensions turned Los Angeles into a social tinderbox at the beginning of the 1990s. The arrest and beating of black motorist Rodney King by four LAPD officers in 1991, captured on tape by a home video enthusiast, proved to be the turning point. When a jury acquitted the officers of assault in 1992, it touched off a three-day

IN CONTEXT

riot during which 50 people died and 1,000 buildings were destroyed by fire and looting. The events were more widespread and destructive than the Watts disturbances of 1965: indeed, it was the worst urban riot in US history. A natural event, the 1994 earthquake, caused further damage to the city's infrastructure. Then, in 1995, the trial of OJ Simpson, an African American football star accused of killing his white ex-wife and another man, gripped the city. Simpson's acquittal stunned white residents, but reassured doubting black locals that the legal system could be on their side.

INVENTING THE FUTURE

Yet despite racial tensions, an economic renaissance that began in the mid 1990s brought new life to LA. As the aerospace industry declined, so the entertainment industry rapidly expanded. In 1997, house prices started to rocket once more, just as they had in the 1970s and '80s. Meanwhile, the Latino community grew into the dominant racial group in Los Angeles County, a dramatic demographic change that affected everything from shopping malls to city government. Latinos are now the pivotal voting group in the city: for evidence, look no further than the triumph of Antonio Villaraigosa in the

mayoral elections of 2005. By defeating incumbent candidate James Hahn in a run-off election, Villaraigosa became the city's first Latino mayor in more than a century, and went on to win a second (and final) term in 2009, running to June 2013.

But Los Angeles has moved into the second decade of the 21st century with uncertainty. The good news is that serious crime is at a near-historic low, with the overall crime rate falling in 2012 for the tenth year in a row. The bad news is that LA, like the rest of California, hasn't escaped the recent worldwide economic meltdown. Far from it: budget cuts have affected everything from schools to museums to the fire and police departments and animal shelters. However, heading into 2013 there were some flutters of improvement: house prices are showing initial signs of bouncing back, the state's previously disastrous unemployment rate hit single digits for the first time in four years in October 2012, and in January 2013 Governor Jerry Brown went so far as to declare that California's budget – previously billions of dollars in the hole – was 'fixed', thanks to deep spending cuts and tax hikes. Wobbly steps they may be, but there's a sense of guarded optimism in the air that's been lacking in LA for half a decade.

OJ Simpson trial, 1995.

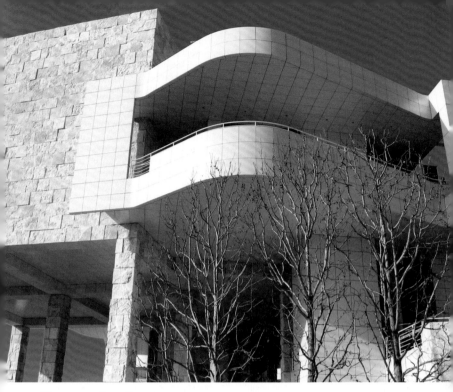

Architecture

Dig deep to discover LA's surviving gems.

TEXT: FRANCES ANDERTON

Los Angeles was founded and repeatedly reinvented by adventurers and fortune-seekers. Some showed up with 'nothing to declare but my genius', as Oscar Wilde once famously told a US customs officer. However, many others came laden with cultural baggage and the desire to carve a piece of their past into their future. The presence of these outsiders helps explain why much of LA's architectural landscape is a chaotic mishmash of borrowed styles, often executed with little finesse or imagination. For the most part, LA appears bewilderingly vast: featureless and horizontal, at least from the freeways. And although there's been a spurt of noteworthy civic building in the last decade or so, the city boasts relatively few major public buildings or landmark corporate structures. To discover its architectural diversity, you really need to visit its residential districts.

A CITY IS BORN

Little remains of the original 18th-century settlement of El Pueblo de Nuestra Señora la Reina de los Ángeles de Porciúncula, and the newer buildings that have attempted to follow in its tradition are largely unmemorable. Misty-eyed preservationists often blather on about the city's roots and the adobe tradition, but the evidence is unconvincing: dull, provincial buildings, rebuilt or prettified.

Just north of today's Downtown, the **Olvera Street** district was the city's original hub, and today serves as a low-key, Mexican-themed tourist attraction. A handful of 19th-century buildings remain in place, many standing on or around an appealing square that hosts regular markets and sporadic festivities. Among the more notable structures is the Italianate **Pico House**: built in 1870, it was the city's first hotel with indoor plumbing.

Other neighbourhoods hold a rich legacy of residential buildings that went up during the land boom of the late 1880s. In Echo Park, north of Downtown, stand a number of handsome houses built in the Queen Anne and Eastlake styles: the most impressive are located on the 1300 block of **Carroll Avenue**, between Douglas Street and Edgeware Road. And to the north-east, at the foot of the San Gabriel Mountains, **Pasadena** is home to many handsome bungalows built during the same period in the Craftsman style, an offshoot of the Victorian Arts and Crafts movement. The standout is Charles and Henry Greene's 1908 Gamble House (4 Westmoreland Place; *see p82*), a marvel of polished mahogany and Tiffany glass.

The most remarkable Victorian structure in LA, though, is south of Olvera Street in Downtown and explicitly not designed for residential use. The brick façade of the **Bradbury Building** (304 S Broadway; *see p72*), constructed as a garment factory by George Wyman in 1893 and now used as offices, is perfectly handsome, but it offers no hint of the astonishing interior: pass through the main doors (the building is open to the public) and you'll be greeted by a stunning sky-lit atrium, ringed by tiled galleries and ornamented with polished wood balustrades and open-cage lifts. The design was reputedly inspired by Edward Bellamy's science-fiction novel *Looking Backward*; appropriate, then, that it featured prominently in *Blade Runner*.

BETWEEN THE WARS

During the 1920s, Southern California embraced Mediterranean and Spanish-style traditions (*see p284* **Y Viva España**). Local architects erected a panoply of pocket haciendas, Churrigueresque car showrooms and abstracted Andalucían farmhouses, and LA developed an insatiable and indiscriminate appetite for all things foreign and exotic. George Washington Smith and Wallace Neff set the pace: the town of **San Marino**, south-east of Pasadena, contains several examples of their Spanish revivalist tendencies. However, all Beaux Arts-trained architects were masters of period style, and every builder could run up a mosque, a medieval castle or an Egyptian tomb.

The city's favourite fantasy house sits, perhaps appropriately, in Beverly Hills. The **Spadena House** (Walden Drive, at Carmelita Avenue, Beverly Hills; *see p46*), commonly known as the Witch's House and the Hansel & Gretel House, was built as a movie set by Henry Oliver in 1921; five years later, it was moved to its present location and converted into a private residence. LA's greatest personal fantasy, though, is not a cinematic creation or a rich man's folly. Built between 1921 and 1954 with dogged, irrational but ultimately heroic persistence by an Italian tilesetter named Simon Rodia, the **Watts Towers** (1727 & 1765 E 107th Street, Watts; *see p74* **Towers of Strength**) have assumed landmark status in the last half-century.

The city's yen for fantasy found a grander and more public outlet in a parade of exotic movie palaces built during the 1920s. Hollywood Boulevard boasts a trio of classics, all still open: Grauman's Chinese Theatre, recently renamed the **TCL Chinese Theatre** (No.6925; *see p52*), built in 1927; the **El Capitan Theatre** (No.6838), completed a year earlier and returned to its former glory by a 1991 renovation; and the **Egyptian Theatre** (No.6712; *see p198*), part of Sid Grauman's empire when it opened in 1922 and now home to the American Cinematheque. Other cinemas from the '20s and '30s have found new life in later life: the **Pantages Theatre** (6233 Hollywood Boulevard, Hollywood; *see p132*) stages theatrical blockbusters, while the **Wiltern Theatre** (3790 Wilshire Boulevard, Koreatown) is now a rock venue.

Architecture in '20s LA wasn't only about such flights of fantasy: many Downtown buildings of the period were driven by a more cultured Beaux Arts sensibility. **Bertram Goodhue's Central Library** (630 W 5th Street, Downtown; *see p71*) includes spirited murals and lofty inscriptions; likewise, the vast, pyramid-capped 1928 City Hall (200 N Spring Street, Downtown; *see p68*) was intended to impress to the point of pomposity. Its commercial counterpart was **Bullocks Wilshire** (3050 Wilshire Boulevard, near Koreatown), the grandest of the old department stores, a 1929 art deco gem now owned by a law school.

During the same period, LA's architectural eclecticism extended to residential construction. Frank Lloyd Wright designed several buildings here, among them the **Hollyhock House** (4800 Hollywood Boulevard, Los Feliz; *see p59*;

public tours suspended during renovations, until mid 2013) and the **Ennis-Brown House** (2655 Glendower Avenue, Los Feliz; check with the Los Angeles Conservancy, *see p58*, for details of tours). Later, two Austrian-born protégés of Wright made their first marks on the city. Rudolph Schindler's notable buildings include his own live-work space, now the **MAK Center for Art & Architecture** (835 N Kings Road, West Hollywood; *see p50*), and, in Orange County, the concrete-frame **Lovell Beach House** (13th Street, at Beach Walk, Balboa Island). Among Richard Neutra's finest residences, meanwhile, are the 1929 Lovell House (4616 Dundee Drive, Griffith Park; *see p58*), designed for the same clients as Schindler's abovementioned house, and the **Strathmore Apartments** (11005 Strathmore Drive), stacked up a Westwood hillside and completed in 1937.

The Los Angeles area fared better than most American cities during the Depression. However, the old extravagance vanished, and a New World streamline moderne style replaced the European models. One classic example of the idiom is Robert Derrah's **Coca-Cola Bottling Plant** (1334 S Central Avenue, Downtown), an ocean liner moored amid warehouses since 1937. **Union Station** (800 N

Lovell Beach House.

Alameda Street; *see p66*), completed two years later as the last of the great US passenger terminals, successfully fuses streamline moderne styling with old-fashioned Spanish revivalism. But as so often in LA, the sublime was accompanied by the ridiculous.

IN THE VERNACULAR

As automotive travel became a central part of Angeleno existence in the '20s and '30s, local entrepreneurs quickly grew to understand the value of eye-catching roadside advertising. Untroubled by zoning laws or good taste, they built an array of cartoonish roadside buildings that effectively served both to advertise and describe themselves. You could buy ice-cream from a towering ice-cream cone, grab a ham sandwich from the mouth of a whale-sized pig, or even buy silk stockings inside a colossal leg.

These structures weren't built to last. And those whose plaster-and-chicken-wire façades didn't crumble with age typically fell victim to the march of progress. However, a few remain. The most striking is **Randy's Donuts** (805 W Manchester Boulevard, Inglewood), built in the 1950s and one of three donut-shaped donut shops in the city. But there's also the tamale-shaped former tamale stand (most recently a beauty parlour) at 6421 Whittier Boulevard in East LA; Hollywood's Capitol Records Building (1750 N Vine Street), reputedly built to resemble a stack of 45s on a spindle; and the Crossroads of the World mall (6671 Sunset Boulevard), with an 'international' flavour reflected by an ocean liner-like centrepiece and its European-themed bungalows. Built in 1936, it pre-dates LA's strip mall explosion by 50 years; now it's home to offices.

POST-WAR GROWTH

The population of Southern California exploded in the 1950s. New suburbs obliterated fields and citrus orchards, extending, with the freeways, into the desert. Business interests spurred the renewal of Downtown, razing the decaying Victorian mansions atop Bunker Hill and creating, from the early '60s, a corridor of office towers. But thanks to clogged

freeways and abysmal public transport, Downtown LA never took off. Instead, Century City and other new commercial hubs began to serve the increasingly fragmented metropolis. Between 1945 and 1962, influential magazine *Arts + Architecture* sponsored the Case Study House programme, a visionary project with a mission to create prototypical low-cost houses using new prefabricated materials and building methods. Although they never achieved mass popularity, the houses stand as icons of Southern Californian design, characterised by the use of glass walls and doors, and open-plan glass-and-steel volumes. One of the best is the steel-framed **Eames House** (203 Chautauqua Boulevard, Pacific Palisades; *see p31*), a fusion of poetry and technology by famed husband-and-wife design team Charles and Ray Eames.

Several post-war LA architects were heavily influenced by Frank Lloyd Wright's organic modern tradition. When John Lautner first came to LA in 1939 in order to supervise construction of **Wright's Sturges House** (441-449 Skyeway Road, Brentwood), he was sickened by the ugliness of the city. But it occurred to him, as it had to Wright in the 1920s, that he could realise his vision here as he never could in the tradition-bound East or Midwest. Among his more daring properties were the 1960 **Chemosphere** (7776 Torreyson Drive, north of Mount Olympus), now home to publisher Benedikt Taschen and, in Palm Springs, the **Elrod House** (2175 Southridge Drive, Palm Springs), later famous as a location in *Diamonds Are Forever*.

GOOGIE WONDERLAND

On the whole, the decades after the war produced little architecture of note in LA. One notable exception was the short-lived trend for Googie in the 1950s and '60s. After the Depression and World War II, a mood of optimism and faith in technology swept the country. Cars were designed to resemble jet fighters, while coffeehouses and car washes strove to look as though they were moving at warp speed. Lloyd Wright (Frank's son) and John Lautner led the charge; in 1949, Lautner designed

Talking Frank

How the Canadian architect stamped his mark on LA.

Just as Frank Lloyd Wright inspired the first generation of modernists in Southern California, so Frank Gehry – born in Toronto in 1929 but resident in LA since childhood – has the free-spirited architects of today. Although it took until 1997, and the opening of the Guggenheim Museum in Bilbao, Spain, for him to attain worldwide fame, Gehry has been known to Angelenos for years.

One of his early works in LA is the 1964 **Danziger Studio/Residence** (7001 Melrose Avenue, Hollywood), two bold, simple cubic structures, remodelled in 2008 by the studio of Glenn Williams Architect). Soon, Gehry began to grow more experimental, drawing inspiration from artists rather than architects. Witness his 1978 remodelling of his own home (1002 22nd Street, Santa Monica), a collage of chainlink fencing, plywood and exposed structure. Must-see examples from the 1980s and early 1990s include the **Loyola Law School** (1441 W Olympic Boulevard, Downtown); the *Edgemar Center for the Arts* (2437 Main Street, Santa Monica); and the former **TBWA Chiat/Day office** (340 Main Street,

Venice), with its eye-catching binoculars portico designed by Claes Oldenburg and Coosje van Bruggen. His Santa Monica Place mall (Broadway & 4th Street, Santa Monica), was torn down in 2008 and rebuilt as a new, less claustrophobic shopping centre.

In the 1990s, Gehry's work moved from raw, makeshift construction to complex, sensuous structures clad in rich materials and designed with the aid of sophisticated computer programs. Two buildings in Anaheim – the **Team Disney administration building** (800 W Ball Road), with its undulating façade, and the muscular **Disney Ice Arena** (300 W Lincoln Avenue) – inspired and amazed. But even these structures pale in comparison with the LA building, completed in 2003, for which Gehry will surely be best remembered.

The **Walt Disney Concert Hall** (111 S Grand Avenue, Downtown; *see p22*) was actually commissioned and designed a decade before the Guggenheim Museum in Bilbao, but years of financial problems and construction delays nearly killed it. Its undulating aluminium exterior is similar to that of the Guggenheim (where the exterior is titanium), but the interior of the Disney Hall is arguably superior. The highlight is the auditorium, with warm wooden surfaces, a curved ceiling and marvellous acoustics. Gehry has also been involved in the ambitious Grand Avenue Project, also Downtown, although, given the economy, it remains to be seen whether his contribution – a residential/hotel/retail tower costing $3 billion – will ever come to fruition.

Nonetheless, Gehry's influence runs far and wide across LA, and there are several must-see buildings by architects working under his influence. The finest are in Culver City, where Eric Owen Moss has remodelled a succession of warehouses into workspaces on land known as the **Hayden Tract** (*see p43*).

an angular wood-and-glass coffeehouse called Googie's on the Sunset Strip. It has long since vanished, replaced by a pastel shopping-and-cinema complex, but the name lives on as shorthand for the single-storey, neon-topped coffeehouses epitomised by the futuristic drive-by design of the 1950s and '60s: slick and angular, their decor a mix of cosy and gee-whizz (Naugahyde booths and space-age lamps). The best of the survivors may be **Pann's** (still open at 6710 La Tijera Boulevard, Inglewood), used in the diner scene in *Pulp Fiction*, and **Ship's Culver City** (now a Starbucks; 10705 W Washington Boulevard, Culver City); the earliest surviving **McDonald's** (10207 Lakewood Boulevard, Downey), built in 1953, also shares the aesthetic. But although Googie itself didn't last long, it briefly influenced a handful of LA architects in the 1990s: check out Stephen Ehrlich's **Robertson Library** (1719 S Robertson Boulevard, Beverly Hills), for example, or the vibrant primary colours of Kanner Architects' **In-n-Out Burger** (922 Gayley Avenue, Westwood).

MODERN LOVE

The 1980s saw Morphosis and Eric Owen Moss develop a recognisable local aesthetic, their whimsical designs characterised by skewed planes, contorted structures and elaborate details. You can get a taste of this style at the **Hayden Tract** (*see p281*), a collection of converted warehouses designed by Moss for development company Samitaur Constructs in Culver City. More recently, Moss added the **Cactus Tower**, a collection of 28 oversized steel pots, each containing a live cactus, suspended within a steel frame; his current ambitious projects for the surrounding area include the dramatic nine-'wing' **Pterodactyl**, an office space and parking garage, and the Waffle, a bendy steel-framed multi-use space; as well as a hotel at the intersection of Sunset and Doheny in West Hollywood.

Around this time, Los Angeles began to change dramatically, as a bewildering succession of recessions, riots, earthquakes and floods jolted the city into a sense of civic responsibility. Local architects organised seminars and community workshops, out of which came numerous well-intentioned plans for LA. Most never left the drawing board, and many areas were eventually rebuilt by developers and politicians in the most expedient way possible. However, this brief period of reflection did produce some notable legacies: designed by Frank Gehry alumnus Michael Maltzan, **Inner-City Arts** (720 S Kohler Street, Downtown) quickly came to life in a converted car repair shop after a post-riot rush of donations. Later, it bore fruit in new schools and libraries.

As LA started to emerge from recession in the early 1990s, all the major movie studios embarked on expansion plans, developing restaurants, leisure centres and themed entertainment/retail destinations. There's no greater example of the trend than Universal CityWalk, an artificial street of noise and colour at **Universal City** built by the Jerde Partnership International in 1992.

As it did in buzzing cities the world over, the hotel sector soon became a driving force behind forward-thinking design in LA. Many of the more interesting developments came not through new construction but within the frameworks of existing buildings: old hotels or apartment blocks that were renovated, remodelled and, in some cases, partly rebuilt. The most notable conversions have been the **Mondrian** (8440 W Sunset Boulevard, West Hollywood; *see p177*), a 1959 apartment building redesigned by Philippe Starck; and the cheap, chic interiors created by Shawn Hausman for the **Standard Hotel** properties in West Hollywood (8300 W Sunset Boulevard) and Downtown (550 S Flower Street; for both, *see p181*). And then there are the hotels restored by designer Kelly Wearstler: the mid-century modern **Avalon** (9400 W Olympic Boulevard, Beverly Hills; *see p173*); the Chinoiserie-inspired **Maison 140** (140 S Lasky Drive, Beverly Hills; *see p175*); and the **Viceroy** (1819 Ocean Avenue, Santa Monica; *see p167*), where English country house meets the future.

A very different colour of money paid for perhaps the most exciting architectural commission in LA's recent history. Although its lengthy genesis meant that it eventually opened a year after his crisp **Paley Center for Media** (465 N Beverly Drive, Beverly Hills; *see p48*) opened in 1996, it was the long-awaited completion of the **Getty Center** (1200 Getty Center Drive, Brentwood; *see p41*) that really introduced Richard Meier's brand of cool international modernism to LA. Some found the buildings a little too cool, but the outdoor areas, including a main garden designed by artist Robert Irwin, are a real catch. It didn't come cheap: total construction costs topped $1 billion.

The Getty Center has been supplemented by several other notable museum projects in recent years. The original Getty Museum, a replica Roman villa in Pacific Palisades now known as the **Getty Villa** (17985 Pacific Coast Highway; *see p31*), was beautifully restored and remodelled in 2006 by Machado & Silvetti Associates as a centre for classical antiquities and comparative archaeology. And 2008 saw the opening of the **Broad Contemporary Art Museum** (aka BCAM) at the Los Angeles County Museum of Art (5905 Wilshire Boulevard; *see p55*). A simple travertine box designed by Renzo Piano after Rem Koolhaas's plans for a more substantial renovation of LACMA were rejected, its bright red exterior escalator affords stunning views to the Hollywood Hills.

GOING DOWNTOWN

After the spread of the freeway network helped decentralise the city in the '50s, Downtown LA went into steep decline. Many of the area's gracious early 20th-century office buildings fell into disrepair, and the only people seen at night were the growing army of homeless people centred on the city's infamous Skid Row.

By the mid 1990s, Downtown had begun to stir. Some commentators have pinned Frank Gehry's **Disney Hall** (*see p281* **Talking Frank**), completed in 2003, as the spur for this re-emergence. However, its roots lie with a slew of other public buildings built in the 1980s and '90s. Four years after Gehry had completed his 1983 remodelling of an old hardware

store into the **Geffen Contemporary** (152 N Central Avenue; *see p71*), Japanese architect Arata Isozaki built the **Museum of Contemporary Art** (250 S Grand Avenue; *see p71*), a complex of geometric solids and sky-lit galleries. And the revival was later helped by the arrival of Rafael Moneo's austere **Catholic Cathedral of Our Lady of the Angels** (555 W Temple Street; *see p68*), completed in 2002, which sits at the opposite end of Downtown to Pei Cobb Freed's soaring extension for the **Los Angeles Convention Center** (1201 S Figueroa Street).

Construction work on other major public projects continues today. Near Disney Hall, the **Grand Avenue Project** will apparently include cinemas, shops, offices and a new park. While the current economic climate has seen off some of the more ambitious parts of the project, including, according to the rumours, a Frank Gehry-designed hotel, the **Grand Park** opened in autumn 2012 at S Grand Avenue and W 1st Street, and construction has begun on a 19-storey apartment complex by Arquitectonica. Also well under way as this guide went to press was the **Broad** (*see p69*), a contemporary art museum designed by Diller Scofidio + Renfro. Dubbed 'the veil and the vault' for the honeycomb-like exoskeleton that wraps the building and the 'vault' for its archive and storage space, the space is slated to open in 2014. (Like the Broad Contemporary Art Museum, the new space will house works from the collection of philanthropists Eli and Edythe Broad.)

Downtown's continuing revival would have been impossible without the explosion of residential development in the neighbourhood's old commercial buildings. For the first time in years, the district has a moneyed local community that doesn't desert the area at 6pm. Things began to change during the 1990s, when the city's growing population began to find property prices too high in much of the Los Angeles basin. Around the same time, the LA Conservancy helped bring about a change in the law that allowed commercial buildings to be converted for residential use. As a result, more than 100 commercial buildings dating from the turn of the century to the 1970s have been

IN CONTEXT

transformed, among them the century-old structures around 4th and Spring Streets; the **General Petroleum Building** (612 S Flower Street), designed by Welton Becket, now the Pegasus Apartments; and Claude Beelman's **Eastern Columbia Building** (849 S Broadway), an eye-catching zig-zag moderne building from 1930. The trend has even reached the streets east of Little Tokyo, in the burgeoning Arts District, with the conversions of a 1924 warehouse into the **Toy Factory** apartment complex (1855 Industrial Street) and, across the road, a former Nabisco factory into the **Biscuit Company Lofts** (corner of Mateo and Industrial Streets).

ONWARDS AND UPWARDS

With historic, convertible buildings now in shorter supply than they were a decade

Y Viva España

The reign of Spain.

IN CONTEXT

Among architects in LA, belief in modernism is so strong that you'd be forgiven for thinking everybody wants to live in industrial-looking buildings with large windows, tons of light and no applied decoration. But the reality is that by far the favoured residential style among Angelenos is Spanish revival. From Santa Barbara to San Diego, Southern California is covered with properties boasting red-tiled roofs, arched doorways and fake adobe walls.

Most of these houses, especially newer ones, are kitschy descendants of the Spanish revival style that flourished from the 1920s to the 1940s, which grew out of the Mission revival style popular in the late 19th century. Architects of the time drew their inspiration from the early Spanish missions in California and from Helen Hunt Jackson's Ramona, a hugely popular 1884 novel that romanticised Spanish Californian society.

Some marvellous civic structures emerged from the early fashion for Spanish revival architecture. **Scripps College** in Claremont remains very handsome more than 85 years after its construction, and **Union Station** (*see p66*) is still in good shape. But the Spanish revival aesthetic became most prevalent in residential neighbourhoods, as architects such as Richard Requa, George Washington Smith, Wallace Neff, Lillian Rice and Paul Williams built detached houses for well-to-do

clients. A typical Spanish revival house of the time features a picturesque combination of white-stuccoed arches, towers, balconies and terraces, with colourful tiling, wrought-iron window grilles and heavy wooden doors.

The style was and is seen by many as nostalgic and romantic. But according to LA writer DJ Waldie, co-author with Diane Keaton of House, a coffee-table book about classic Spanish-style houses in Los Angeles, it was also forward-thinking. The houses contained the most modern conveniences of the era; and, unlike the Victorian architecture imported from the east, they were tailored to the climate and light of Southern California. They had, wrote Waldie, such 'astonishing sympathy and presence that they continue to be the common memory of what many Californians call home'.

Many classic Spanish-style houses have been torn down, and those that survive tend to be in private hands. However, a few are open to the public. Designed by Mark Daniels and completed in 1928, **Villa Aurora** (www.villa-aurora.org) in Pacific Palisades is an artists' residence and sometimes opens for lectures. The Carl Lindbom-designed **Casa Romantica** (www.casaromantica.org) in San Clemente is now a cultural centre. Further south, in Carlsbad, near San Diego, stands **Rancho de los Quiotes** (www.carrillo-ranch.org), designed by actor Leo Carrillo.

ago, developers have begun to erect new residential high-rises in Downtown. The most concentrated developments have been in South Park, near the Staples Center and adjacent new L.A. LIVE complex. The Johnson Fain-designed **Met Lofts** (1050 S Flower Street) come complete with an exterior digital light display activated by people walking into the building. Nearby, at 11th Street and Grand Avenue, stand the **Elleven**, **Luma** and **Evo** condo buildings. This trio are the work of the South Group, whose commitment to sustainable design extended to widening the sidewalks and adding bike racks.

Whether in converted commercial buildings or new structures, this fresh wave of residential buildings shares a common influence: the boutique hotels mentioned above. Most of the new condo developments include high-design lobbies, shared lounges and computer rooms. A number also feature high-rise roof gardens with open-air pools and cabanas, providing residents with even greater exclusivity than even the Standard Downtown can offer at its rooftop pool parties.

HOMES AT LAST

Los Angeles is gradually being transformed from a suburban city to a semi-urban one, as politicians, planners and architects struggle to provide for the rising population while facing the twin challenges of growing traffic and no comprehensive public transport system. 'Smart growth' is the buzz phrase of the moment. The mayor and city planners have designated certain parts of town, typically located near major transit connections, as ripe for denser residential redevelopment through the addition of multi-family apartment or condo buildings. Several residential high-rises have been proposed for Century City; in other areas, residential streets have been re-zoned to allow the construction of multi-family properties in place of single-family residences.

The formerly shambling beach town of Venice has seen an explosion of such structures: check out Abbot Kinney Boulevard between Main Street and W Washington Boulevard, and, running parallel to it, Electric Avenue. Both West Hollywood and Hollywood also have their share of stylish multi-family apartment and condo buildings: Lorcan O'Herlihy, designer of the Lexton-MacCarthy House in Silver Lake (3228 Fernwood Avenue) and his own Vertical House (116 Pacific Avenue, Venice), designed both the very striking **Habitat 825** (825 N Kings Road, next door to the MAK Center) and **Gardner 1050** (1050 N Gardner Street).

Another recent phenomenon has been the emergence of a sustainable design sensibility, as designers try to integrate solar power and energy-efficient technologies into clean, modern buildings. One of the more worthwhile examples is **Colorado Court** (502 Colorado Avenue, Santa Monica), a complex of affordable apartments with a wall of solar panels. Pugh Scarpa architects, who designed it, were also responsible for Larry Scarpa's own home in Venice: the **Solar Umbrella House** (615 Woodlawn Avenue), at which solar panels form a canopy over the house and wrap the southern side. Another proponent of green building is David Hertz, designer of his own **McKinley Residence** (2420 McKinley Avenue, Venice). Such ethics extend to public buildings, too, not least the new Gold LEED-certified **Shore Hotel** in Santa Monica (1515 Ocean Avenue), whose commitment to low energy and water use is laudable.

LA's most interesting architecture continues to be residential, then, but the innovation that characterised the city's best housing in the 20th century has come up against some hurdles of late. Most visible are the ghastly, oversized McMansions that dominate parts of the region, but architectural invention is also being challenged by the emergence of militant design review boards that are becoming increasingly protectionist and dictatorial. This preservationism is testament to the maturation of LA, but it's also made the city less of a design frontier. The Angeleno creative architecture spirit lives on, but within tighter parameters than of yore.

IN CONTEXT

Essential Information

Hollywo

ion Station

Getting Around

ARRIVING & LEAVING

Airports

Los Angeles International Airport (LAX)
1-310 646 5252, www.lawa.org/lax.
LAX is situated in Westchester on the west side of LA, between Marina del Rey and Manhattan Beach. It has nine terminals; most flights from Europe arrive at the Tom Bradley International Terminal, which was most of the way through a $4.1 billion upgrade at press time; Virgin Atlantic, based at Terminal 2, is the main exception. The renovation has so far included, among other things, 45,000 square feet (4,180 square meters) of space for baggage screening and handling to ease the notorious congestion at the ticket counters and check-in. The food scene, too, has improved, with a slew of new eateries and shops being lured here.

The cheapest, yet most time-consuming, way to reach your hotel from LAX is by public transport. From the airport, take either the C or G shuttle buses, both free. The C will ferry you to the bus centre at Vicksburg Avenue and 96th Street, from where you can take a bus; the G heads to the Aviation station on the Metro's Green Line (*see p291*). But this route isn't recommended. Alternatively, there's the FlyAway bus service (1-866 435 9529, www.lawa.org/flyaway), which operates several routes between the airport and Union Station, Westwood, Van Nuys and Irvine (Orange County); fares are $7 each way; under-5s free.

A fleet of **shuttles** flits between LAX and every neighbourhood in LA. Most services are able to drop you at your hotel; fares start at around $15. You can pick up a shuttle outside the arrival terminals from **Prime Time** (1-800 733 8267, www.primetimeshuttle.com) and **SuperShuttle** (1-800 258 3826, www.supershuttle.com). Both firms can also pick you up from your hotel and take you back to LAX, given 24 hours' notice.

Taxis can be found outside arrivals. Fares from LAX come with a $4.50 surcharge; each additional mile is $2.70, and the minimum fare is $15. If you're staying on the West Side, a taxi

from LAX will cost $20-$25 plus tip; it'll be twice that to Hollywood or beyond. There's a flat rate of $40 (including surcharge) from West Hollywood (or $38 from Beverly Hills). For details of local taxi firms, *see p291*.

Burbank–Glendale–Pasadena Airport (Bob Hope Airport)
1-818 840 8840, www.burbank airport.com.
If you're flying from a US airport, you may land at Burbank. There are many ways to travel from Burbank to your hotel: by **public transport** (a free shuttle will take you to the Metro bus stop at Hollywood Way and Thornton Avenue; the airport is also served by Metrolink rail), by **shuttle** (firms are numerous) and by **taxi**.

Major airlines

Air Canada *1-888 247 2262, www.aircanada.com.*
Air New Zealand *1-800 262 1234, www.airnewzealand.com.*
Alaska Air *1-800 252 7522, www.alaskaair.com.*
America West *1-800 428 4322, www.americawest.com.*
American Airlines *1-800 433 7300, www.aa.com.*
British Airways *1-800 247 9297, www.britishairways.com.*
Delta *1-800 221 1212, www.delta.com.*
Lufthansa *1-800 645 3880, www.lufthansa.com.*
Southwest Airlines *1-800 435 9792, www.iflyswa.com.*
United Airlines *1-800 864 8331, www.united.com.*
Virgin Atlantic *1-800 862 8261, www.virgin-atlantic.com.*

By bus

LA's main **Greyhound** station is Downtown, at 1716 E 7th Street. However, Greyhound buses arriving in LA stop at several smaller stations around town. For more on Greyhound, call 1-800 231 2222 or check www.greyhound.com.

By rail

Trains to LA terminate at **Union Station**, at 800 N Alameda Street

in Downtown. From here, you can take the Purple, Red or Gold Metro lines to your destination, or connect with any number of buses. For more on **Amtrak**, which runs services from LA to all corners of the US, call 1-800 872 7245 or see www.amtrak.com.

DRIVING

Although public transport in LA is improving, it's a brave soul who chooses to tackle the town without a car. It is possible to get around without one, but you'll need to plan your movements in advance and be prepared to spend ages on seemingly interminable bus journeys. The subway system is less time consuming but currently doesn't extend to some major tourist destinations such as Santa Monica. (This is due to change in a few years; *see p291*). Of course, driving in LA presents its own challenges. Those used to driving in towns or smaller cities may blanche at the five-lane freeways. However, LA is less terrifying for drivers than, say, New York, in part because the traffic often moves at a snail's pace. Traffic can be atrocious during the morning and evening rush hours, which can run from 6am to 10am and as early as 2pm to 7pm. For traffic information, call the **CalTrans Highway Information Service** on 1-800 427 7623, or see www.dot.ca.gov/roadsandtraffic.html. Radio station KNX (1070 AM) has traffic reports every six minutes during the day; KFWB (980 AM) gives traffic reports every ten minutes, 24-7.

Freeways in LA are referred to by their relevant numbers (the 10, the 110, the 405, and so on) but also by nicknames: west of Downtown, the I-10 ('I' for Interstate), for example, is the Santa Monica Freeway. There's a limit of 65mph on the freeways, or 70mph where posted, but you'll see cars going much faster (outside of rush hour). Don't expect people to signal when they change lanes. The outside lanes are the fast lanes, though it's normal to overtake on the inside. It's best to stay in the middle lanes until you need to exit.

Many freeways have a carpool lane, which only cars carrying at

ESSENTIAL INFORMATION

least two or three people (depending on the signs) can use. This is not a members-only scheme – if you fit the criteria, you can use the lane, but make sure you get out of it well before your exit. On your own? Keep out of carpool lanes fines are steep.

All non-freeways are known as surface streets. When you merge onto a freeway from a surface street, accelerate to freeway speed; similarly, be prepared to slow right down when exiting. Freeway exits are marked by the name of the surface street with which they link; for all businesses in this guide, we've included a convenient freeway route and exit. However, always plan your route before you leave. If you don't know your entrance and exit and the direction you need to go when you find it (north, south, east or west), you may find yourself being forced off at the wrong intersection. Most rental-car agencies will include GPS systems at an additional charge; if you're going to be doing a lot of driving, fork over the extra cash. Of course, if your cell phone service provides GPS in the US, you're good to go.

On surface streets, you can turn right on a red light if your way is clear, unless signs say otherwise. Speed limits vary, and may be as low as 15mph around schools, so pay attention to the signs. At four-way stop signs, 'courtesy driving' is expected: cars cross in the order they arrive at the junction, with drivers going forward or turning right having the right-of-way over those turning left. Seatbelts are compulsory. If you break down, look for yellow call boxes on the sides of major freeways and some roads in LA County, but a cell phone provides more security. However, note that using a non-hands-free cell phone while driving is illegal, as is texting while driving. Also note that the drink-driving laws across LA are strict and not to be tested.

The **American Automobile Association** (or 'Triple A') offers maps and guides, which are free if you're a member or belong to an affiliated club (such as the British AA). Many hotels offer discounts to AAA members. There are offices all over LA; check online for more.

American Automobile Association (AAA) *2601 S Figueroa Street, at W Adams Boulevard, Downtown (1-213 741 3686, www.aaa-calif.com).* I-110, exit Adams Boulevard west. **Open** 9am-5pm Mon-Fri.

Car hire

To rent a car, you'll need a credit card and a driver's license (British licenses are valid). Most firms won't rent to anyone under 25 – those that do often add a surcharge – and if you're under 21, you might not be able to rent a car at all. The national rental firms, which tend to offer the best deals, have 1-800 numbers and offer online booking.

Rates seesaw wildly. It can pay to book weeks ahead: you can put a hold on a car without committing yourself to pay for it. You may qualify for a discount: members of the AAA and affiliated foreign clubs are eligible, and corporate deals are often available. As a rule, you won't be allowed to take a rental car into Mexico, nor can you smoke in rental cars.

All quotes from US websites will exclude insurance. US travellers may be covered by your car rental insurance at home; always check before setting out. If not, you'll need to take out liability insurance (SLI) and collision damage waiver (CDW) with the rental firm, which together usually total around $25-$30 a day.

Travellers from outside the US have several choices. The simplest is to book via the firm's US website and pay the pricey insurance premiums. UK residents should try the car hire firms' dedicated UK sites, where quotes include insurance. UK travellers who regularly travel in the US should consider www.insurance4carhire. com, where the comprehensive annual policies can save drivers a fortune over the rates levied by the rental firms themselves.

Car rental companies

Alamo *US: 1-877 222 9075, www.alamo.com. UK: 0871 384 1086, www.alamo.co.uk.*
Avis *US: 1-800 230 4898, www.avis.com. UK: 0844 581 0147, www.avis.co.uk.*
Budget *US: 1-800 527 0700, www.budget.com. UK: 0844 544 3470, www.budget.co.uk.*
Dollar *US: 1-800 800 3665, www.dollar.com. UK: 020 3468 7685, www.dollar.co.uk.*
Enterprise *US: 1-800 261 7331, www.enterprise.com. UK: 0800 800 227, www.enterprise.com/uk.*
Hertz *US: 1-800 654 3131, www.hertz.com. UK: 0870 844 8844, www.hertz.co.uk.*
National *US: 1-877 222 9058, www.nationalcar.com. UK: 0871 384 1140, www.nationalcar.co.uk.*

Rent-a-Wreck *1-877 877 0700, www.rentawreck.com.*
Thrifty *US: 1-800 847 4389, www.thrifty.com. UK: 01494 751500, www.thrifty.co.uk.*

Parking

Parking restrictions vary by street, and the signs detailing them are far from clear. Don't b lock driveways or fire hydrants, and pay attention to curb markings: if they're red, you're risking a big fine or, worse, getting towed. Check signs on your side of the block, which should detail parking laws; many seem incomprehensible at first glance, so read the sign twice. Most streets have street-cleaning days/times when parking is illegal; others allow permit parking only after 6pm and at weekends. All parking tickets accrued while in a rented vehicle are your responsibility.

Most parking meters take quarters (25¢), and meters that accept credit and debit cards are increasingly common. Most bars, restaurants and malls and some shops offer valet parking; you'll need to tip the valet ($2-$5) on top of the parking fee, but it's cheaper than paying a fine and it saves time. If you do get nabbed, call t he number listed on the ticket; you can usually pay with a credit card.

Otherwise, there are public parking lots all over town (including several in Beverly Hills' Golden Triangle), as well as privately run lots that charge between $5 and $10 for a full day. Some establishments – in particular restaurants and shops – offer free parking for a certain amount of time; remember to ask them to validate the ticket.

The LAPD suggests you keep your rental agreement with you at all times in case your car gets towed or stolen (most people stick it in the glove compartment – bad idea). If you do get towed, call the nearest police precinct to find out where the car has been taken. To reclaim it, you'll need your rental papers, the car's license number, your passport or driving license and cash to pay the parking ticket, anywhere from $100 and up.

PUBLIC TRANSPORT

LA's public transport system is run by the **Metropolitan Transportation Authority** (or just Metro). For information on the network, see **www.metro.net**, where you'll find timetables, maps,

ESSENTIAL INFORMATION

fare information and a handy trip planner; for the latter you can also call 1-323 466 3876. Its Twitter account (http://twitter.com/metro losangeles) is also worth following for frequent updates on delays, temporary station closures etc.

We've listed a variety of bus routes for almost every venue featured in this book. Note, though, that Downtown is served by innumerable buses. We've included buses for these venues, but if you catch any bus that passes through central Downtown, you'll be no more than a 15-minute walk from your destination when you get off the bus.

Buses in LA run every 5-10 minutes on the main routes, less often at night. On main crosstown routes, the service is 24-hour, but there's only one bus an hour after 1am. For lost property, see p294.

Note that routes can change or be dropped, sometimes at short notice, so it's worth checking details before setting off.

Metro Customer Centres

See also www.metro.net/about/contact/customer-centers.

Miracle Mile 5301 Wilshire Boulevard, at S La Brea Avenue, Miracle Mile. Bus 20, 212, 312/I-10, exit La Brea Avenue. **Open** 9am-5pm Mon-Fri. **Map** p312 D4.
Union Station 800 N Alameda Street, at Los Angeles Street. Metro Union Station/bus 33, 40, 42, 68, 70, 71, 78, 79/US 101, exit Alameda Street north. **Open** 6am-6.30pm Mon-Fri. **Map** p315 D1.
East LA 4501B Whittier Boulevard, at S Ford Boulevard. Bus 18, 256, 720/I-5, exit Olympic Boulevard east. **Open** 10am-6pm Tue-Sat.
Baldwin Hills 3650 Martin Luther King Boulevard, at Crenshaw Boulevard. Bus 40, 42, 210, 710, 740/I-10, exit Crenshaw Boulevard south. **Open** 10am-6pm Tue-Sat.

Metro buses

Metro's 2,500-plus local orange buses cover more than 180 routes across LA. Red 'Rapid' buses cover many of the major routes but make fewer stops.

The fare on all Metro bus routes is $1.50; a further 35¢ is required for a transfer to a bus run by a separate agency (for example, Culver City buses; see p291). Paper tickets have now been replaced by plastic TAP (Transit Access Pass) cards

– available for a one-off $1 (at bus stations) and $2 (at vending machines in stations) fee – which can be topped up at stations, certain retail locations, by phone (1-866 827 8646) or online (http://taptogo.net). If you're planning on doing a lot of travelling, consider an all-day pass ($5, though this may rise to $6), a weekly pass ($20) or a monthly pass ($75).

The recently approved Wilshire Bus Rapid Transit Project, which will see the installation of a nearly eight-mile bus lane along Wilshire Boulevard between South Park View Street near MacArthur Park and Centinela Avenue in West LA, should be completed by 2015.

All Metro bus routes in LA are given a number according to the areas they cover:

1-99	Local services to and from Downtown
100-199	Local east–west services that don't pass through Downtown
200-299, 902	Local north–south services that don't pass through Downtown
300-399	Limited-stop services, usually on routes also served by local services; for example, the 302, which takes the same route along Sunset Boulevard as the 2 but makes fewer stops
400-499	Express services to and from Downtown
500-599	Express services in other areas
600-699	Special services (such as the 605, a shuttle bus to the LA County/USC Medical Center)
700-799	Rapid bus services (similar to limited-stop services detailed above)

The following are among LA's more useful crosstown services. Maps and timetables are available at www.metro.net/around/maps and at Metro Customer Centers.

2 Runs along Sunset Boulevard from its junction with the PCH to Westwood. From here, it runs along the southern border of the UCLA and then follows Sunset through Hollywood, Silver Lake and Echo Park to Downtown, where it follows

Hill Street south to Venice Boulevard. The return route is identical save for the fact that it heads north through Downtown on Broadway rather than Hill. The 302 takes an identical route as far as the northern edge of Downtown, but makes fewer stops.
4 Runs along Santa Monica Boulevard from Santa Monica to the junction with Sunset Boulevard in Silver Lake, whereupon it follows the same route as the 2. The 704 is its limited-stop version.
16 Runs between Century City and Downtown LA, following 3rd Street for almost its entire length. The main exception is between Beverly Hills and Century City, where it runs along Santa Monica Boulevard, and within Downtown, where it runs along either 5th Street (westbound) or 6th Street (eastbound). The 316 is its limited-stop alternative.
20 Runs the length of Wilshire Boulevard from Santa Monica to Downtown, whereupon it takes 7th Street. The 720 offers a limited-stop alternative.
212 Runs between the Hollywood-Vine Metro station and Hawthorne, along Hollywood Boulevard and La Brea Avenue.
217 Runs between the Vermont-Sunset Metro station and the West LA Transit Center, along Hollywood Boulevard, Fairfax Avenue and La Cienega Boulevard.

LA DASH buses

DASH stands for Downtown Area Short Hop; its five express shuttles (A, B, D, E and F) run every 5-20 minutes and serve many of Downtown's important sites, including the Convention Center, City Hall and Union Station.

Despite its name, there are a number of DASH shuttles in other areas of LA. Fares on all DASH routes are 50¢. For more, see http://ladottransit.com/dash, or call 1-213 808 2273, 1-310 808 2273 or 1-323 808 2273. The following are among the most useful routes:
Fairfax (abbreviated in our listings to LDF) Links the Beverly Center with the Melrose District, the Fairfax District and the Miracle Mile.
Hollywood (LDH) Loops around Hollywood, chiefly (but not

exclusively) on Highland, Franklin, Fountain and Vermont Avenues.
Hollywood-Wilshire (LDHWI) Runs between the Hollywood-Vine and Wilshire-Western Metro stations, via Vine Street, Sunset Boulevard, Gower Street, Melrose Avenue and Western Avenue.

Municipal buses

Some areas have their own municipal bus services that complement Metro's services. Among them are the following:

Santa Monica (denoted with prefix 'SM' in this book; SM1, SM2, etc) The Big Blue Bus company serves Santa Monica, Venice and parts of West LA. The fare on all routes is $1 on local and $2 on express routes, with a 50¢ inter-agency transfer; day ($4), month ($60-$80) and 13-ride ($12) passes are also available. For more, call 1-310 451 5444 or see http://big bluebus.com.
Culver City (denoted with prefix 'C') Fares on all bus routes are $1 (25¢-75¢ discounts), with inter-agency transfers costing 40¢ (80¢ discounts). Call 1-310 253 6510 or see www.culvercity.org/bus.
West Hollywood Cityline is a free shuttle service in West Hollywood. The service runs 9am-6pm Mon-Sat. For more, call 1-800 447 2189 or see www.ci.west-hollywood.ca.us.
San Gabriel Valley The Foothill Transit service mostly serves the San Gabriel and Pomona Valleys. Fares are $1.25-$4.90; monthly passes are $18-$22. For details, call 1-800 743 3463 or see www.foothilltransit.org.
Orange County (denoted with prefix 'OC'). For details, call 1-714 636 7433 or see www.octa.net. Most fares are $1.50; see website.

Trains

LA's **Metro Rail** system currently only covers a limited area of the city at present, but a major expansion is under way. It can be a very convenient way to get around, especially to and from Downtown. The fare structure is identical to that on the Metro buses; daily, weekly and monthly passes can be used on both trains and buses. Trains run approximately 5am to 12.30am daily. For a map of the network, *see p319*; below is a summary of its six lines. Note that some minor name changes were being proposed at press time.

Blue Line Starting at the Red Line station of 7th Street/Metro Center, the Blue Line heads south through South Central all the way to Long Beach.
Expo Line The Expo Line run south from the 7th Street/Metro Center to Exposition Park, before heading west to Culver City. Phase 2 – scheduled for completion in 2015 or 2016 – will see it extend all the way to Santa Monica.
Gold Line The Gold Line's hub is Union Station, where it connects with the Red Line, and heads north-east through Chinatown, Highland Park and Pasadena to Sierra Madre; it also runs south of Union Station through Little Tokyo and out through Boyle Heights and into East LA. Further work will see the line extend to Azusa (due for completion in 2015) and, ultimately, Montclair.
Green Line This overground route links the area around LAX (there's currently no station at LAX itself, but shuttle buses take passengers from Aviation station to the airport) with Redondo Beach to the west and South Central and Norwalk to the east.
Purple Line The Purple Line follows the Red Line route from Union Station to Wilshire-Vermont, then continues along Wilshire for two further stops before terminating at Wilshire-Western. Construction on the controversial Westside Subway Extension, which will extend the line all the way to Westwood via Century City, began in autumn 2012.
Red Line The most useful line for visitors, the Red Line links Downtown, Westlake, Hollywood, Universal Studios and North Hollywood. At North Hollywood, travellers can connect to the Metro Orange Line: it's a bus service that looks and acts like a train line, running Metroliner articulated buses along its own dedicated busway between North Hollywood and Chatsworth. At the other end of the line, the Red Line connects with Union Station and the Gold Line.

The route map also includes the Silver Line, an express bus service that runs from El Monte in the east down through South Central, finishing in Artesia.

TAXIS & LIMOS

Because of the city's size, taxis aren't a cheap way of getting around LA. Nor are they convenient – there are some taxi ranks, including one outside the Beverly Center across from the Sofitel hotel, but in most

areas you can't hail a passing cab on the street – or especially straightforward (you may even have to give the driver directions). The basic fare is $2.85; each additional one-ninth of a mile (or 37 seconds of waiting time) will cost you a further 30¢; the minimum fare for local trips is $10 if you're paying by credit card. There's a $4.50 surcharge on all fares leaving LAX,. Large, licensed firms include **Bell Cab** (1-888 481 2345, www.bellcab.com), **Checker Cab** (1-800 300 5007, www.ineedtaxi.com), **Independent Taxi** (1-800 521 8294, www.taxi4u.com), **United Independent** (1-800 822 8294, www.unitedtaxi.com), **Beverly Hills Cab Company** (1-800 273 6611, www.beverlyhillscab co.com) and **Yellow Cab Co** (1-877 733 3305, www.layellowcab.com). For more details, see www.taxicabs la.org. Don't forget to tip the driver!

If you're really flush, you might want to consider hiring a limousine. The cost of hiring one starts at around $60-$75 an hour, usually with a three- to four-hour minimum; on top of this, the driver will expect a decent tip. Companies include **Alliance** (1-800 954 5466, www.alliancelimo.net) and Crown Limo LA(1-800 933 5466, www.crown limola.com).

CYCLING

There are bike paths down the coast through Santa Monica and Venice, and there are bike lanes in other parts of LA; you can also mountain-bike in Griffith Park and Topanga Canyon. Otherwise, though, the volume of traffic and distances involved make cycling tough. For more on bikes and cycling, *see p239* **Wheel-life Adventures**.

WALKING

Certain sections of Los Angeles – Santa Monica and Venice, Beverly Hills, parts of West Hollywood, central Hollywood, the centres of Los Feliz and Silver Lake, pretty much all of Downtown – are easily covered on foot. Jaywalking – crossing the street anywhere except at a designated pedestrian crossing – can get you a fine of up to $191; police don't generally enforce the penalty on tourists, but it's best to be on the safe side. Be sure to take extra caution when walking in LA, even at a crossing, and particularly at night: drivers are notorious for ignoring anything on the road but cars, especially when they're making a left turn across traffic.

ESSENTIAL INFORMATION

Resources A-Z

ESSENTIAL INFORMATION

ADDRESSES

Written addresses follow the standard US format. Where applicable, the apartment or suite number usually appears after the street address, followed on the next line by the city name and zip code.

AGE RESTRICTIONS

Buying alcohol 21
Drinking alcohol 21
Driving 16
Sex 18
Smoking 18

ATTITUDE & ETIQUETTE

LA is casual, but there are distinct codes within that standard. If you're here on business, make it expensive, stylish casual; if you're here to go out, dress up – even in a casual way – rather than down. Few restaurants operate a specific dress code, but nor do the posher places approve of torn jeans and scruffy sneakers.

BUSINESS

Angelenos work hard, with early starts and late finishes. Long commutes mean little drinking; business is usually done over still or sparkling, not red or white.

The LA affliction of 'flaking' (making and then rescheduling appointments) occurs both in business and socially – it's nothing personal. That said, if you're here with cap in hand, don't do the flaking yourself: know your route and leave time to find parking.

Conventions & conferences

The **LA Convention Center** (1201 S Figueroa Street, at W Pico Boulevard, Downtown,1-213 741 1151, www.lacclink.com) is located at the intersection of I-10 and I-110. Next door is the huge **L.A. LIVE** complex (*see p72*).

Couriers & shippers

DHL *1-800 225 5345, www.dhl.com.* **Credit** AmEx, DC, Disc, MC, V.
FedEx *1-800 463 3339, www.fedex.com.* **Credit** AmEx, DC, Disc, MC, V.
UPS *1-800 742 5877, www.ups.com.* **Credit** AmEx, DC, MC, V.

Office services

FedEx *5500 Wilshire Boulevard, at S Dunsmuir Avenue, Miracle Mile (1-323 937 0126, www.office depot.com).* *Bus 20, 212/I-10, exit La Brea Avenue north.* **Open** 24hrs daily. **Credit** AmEx, DC, Disc, MC, V. **Map** p312 D4.
Other locations throughout LA.
Mail Boxes Etc *1-800 789 4623, www.mbe.com.* **Open** hrs vary. **Credit** AmEx, DC, Disc, MC, V. Mail forwarding services.
Office Depot *2020 Figueroa Street, at 20th Street, Downtown (1-213 741 0576, www.office depot.com).* *Metro Grand/bus 81, 381/I-110, exit Adams Boulevard west.* **Open** 8am-8pm Mon-Fri; 9am-7pm Sat; 10am-7pm Sun. **Credit** AmEx, DC, Disc, MC, V. Other locations throughout LA.

Useful organisations

Los Angeles Area Chamber of Commerce *350 S Bixel Street, at W 3rd Street, Downtown, CA 90017 (1-213 580 7500, www.lachamber.org).* *Bus 14, 16/I-110, exit 3rd Street west.* **Open** 8am-5pm Mon-Fri.

CONSUMER

Department of Consumer Affairs *1-800 952 5210, deaf callers 1-800 326 2297, www.dca.ca.gov.* Investigates complaints.
Better Business Bureau of the Southland *315 North La Cadena Drive, Colton (1-909 825 7280, www.bbbsouthland.org.* Useful if you need to file a complaint.

CUSTOMS

International travellers go through US Customs after Immigration. Hand over to the official the white form you were given, and should have completed, on the plane. Some common items that may require licences or permits are food products ordered from a commercial vendor, plant, animal and dairy products, prescription medications, trademarked articles such as name-brand shoes, handbags, luggage, golf clubs, toys, and copyrighted material such as CDs, DVDs and tapes.

Foreign visitors can import the following items duty-free: 200 cigarettes or 50 cigars (not Cuban; over-18s only) or 2kg of smoking tobacco; one litre of wine or spirits (over-21s); and up to $100 in gifts ($800 for returning Americans). You must declare and maybe forfeit plants or foodstuffs. See the US Customs site (www.cbp.gov/xp/cgov/travel) for more information.

DISABLED

California's strict building codes ensure equal access to all city facilities, businesses, parking lots, restaurants, hotels and other public places. Only older buildings are likely to present problems, and many of those have been retrofitted. All Metro buses have wheelchair lifts, and large-type and Braille-encoded 'Metro Flash Cards' are available for signalling the correct bus. For more information, call the Disabled Riders line on 1-800 621 7828 or check www.metro.net.

Access Services *1-800 827 0829, www.asila.org.* Refers mobility-impaired people to door-to-door transportation services.

Department on Disability *1-213 202 2764, www.ci.la.ca.us/dod.* Information and resources.

Society for the Advancement of Travel for the Handicapped *1-212 447 7284, www.sath.org.* Gives referrals for disabled travellers planning trips to the US.

DRUGS

Drugs are not uncommon in LA's nightlife, but the local authorities take a zero-tolerance approach to drug use and trafficking. Be careful.

ELECTRICITY

The US uses a 110-120V, 60-cycle AC voltage. Except for dual-voltage flat-pin shavers, most foreign visitors will need to run appliances through an adaptor. Note that DVDs purchased here will only work in DVD players equipped with multi-region capabilities.

EMBASSIES & CONSULATES

Australia *2029 Century Park East, Suite 3150, at W Olympic Boulevard, Century City, CA 90067 (1-310 229 2300, www.losangeles. consulate.gov.au). I-405, exit Olympic Boulevard.*

Canada *550 S Hope Street, between W 5th & W 6th Streets, Los Angeles, CA 90071 (1-213 346 2700, www.losangeles.gc.ca). I-110, exit 6th Street east.*

New Zealand *2425 Olympic Boulevard, Suite 600E, Santa Monica, CA 90404 (1-310 566 6555, www.nzcgla.com). I-10, exit Cloverfield Boulevard north.*

Republic of Ireland *1631 Beverly Boulevard, Los Angeles, CA 92648 (1-714 658 9832). I-101, exit Glendale Boulevard/Union Avenue.*

United Kingdom *11766 Wilshire Boulevard, Suite 1200, at Granville Avenue, Los Angeles, CA 90025 (1-310 481 0031, www.britainusa. com/la). I-405, exit Wilshire Boulevard west.*

EMERGENCIES

For **hospitals** and **helplines**, *see below.*
Police, fire, ambulance 911.
Coast Guard 1-310 215 2112.
Poison Information Center 1-800 222 1222, www.calpoison.org.

GAY & LESBIAN

LA Gay & Lesbian Center *1625 N Schrader Boulevard, between Hollywood Boulevard & Selma Avenue, Hollywood (1-323 993 7400, www.lagaycenter.org). Metro Hollywood-Vine/bus 163, 180, 181, 210, 212, 217, 312, 780, LDH/US 101, exit Vine Street south.* **Open** 9am-9pm Mon-Fri; 9am-1pm Sat (pharmacy only). **Map** p313 B2.
Myriad resources for LGBT locals.

HEALTH

Ensure you have full medical insurance, preferably the kind that pays upfront. Emergency rooms are obliged by law to treat emergencies, though they will try to make you pay.

If it's not an emergency and you don't have insurance, try the Saban Free Clinic, which offers free medical, dental and mental health care. However, don't abuse the service and don't expect an immediate appointment.

Saban Free Clinic *8405 Beverly Boulevard, at N Orlando Avenue, West Hollywood (appointments 1-323 653 1990, www.thesabanfree clinic.org). Bus 14/I-10, exit La Cienega Boulevard north.* **Open** *Medical & Behavioural health* 7.30am-8pm Mon-Thur; 7.30am-4.30pm 1st, 3rd & 5th Fri of mth; noon-4.30pm 2nd & 4th Fri of mth. *Dental* 7.30am-8.30pm Mon-Thur; 7.30am-5pm Fri. **Map** p312 B3.
Other Saban-run locations, with the same phone number, are **S Mark Taper Foundation Health Center** (6043 Hollywood Boulevard, Hollywood) and **Hollywood Wilshire Health Center** (5205 Melrose Avenue, Fairfax District).

Accident & emergency

The hospitals below have 24-hour emergency rooms.
Cedars-Sinai Medical Center *8700 Beverly Boulevard, at George Burns Road, West Hollywood (1-310 423 3277, www.csmc.edu). Bus 14, 105/I-10, exit La Cienega Boulevard north.* **Map** p312 A3.
Children's Hospital of Los Angeles *4650 W Sunset Boulevard, at N Vermont Avenue,*

Los Feliz (1-323 660 2450, www.chla.org). Metro Vermont-Sunset/bus 2, 204, 702, 754/US 101, exit Vermont Avenue north. **Map** p314 A3.
St John's Health Center *2121 Santa Monica Boulevard, between 20th & 23rd Streets, Santa Monica (310 829 5511, www.stjohns.org). Bus 4, SM1, SM10/I-10, exit 26th Street north.* **Map** p310 C3.

Contraception & abortion

Family Planning Associates Medical Group *12304 Santa Monica Boulevard, at Wellesley Avenue, West LA (1-877 833 7264/ 1-310 820 8084, www.fpamg.net). Bus 4, SM1, SM10/I-405, exit Santa Monica Boulevard west.* **Open** 8am-5pm Mon-Fri; 8am-4pm Sat.

Dentists

The LADS offers referrals to approved practices. For the **Saban Free Clinic**, *see left.*
LA Dental Society *1-213 380 7669, www.ladentalsociety.com.* **Open** 8.30am-4.30pm Mon-Thur; 8.30am-4pm Fri.

Hospitals

See left **Accident & emergency**.

Opticians

See p158.

Pharmacies

See p158.

STDs, HIV & AIDS

There is also an HIV/AIDS clinic at the LA Gay & Lesbian Center (*see above*).
AIDS Healthcare Foundation *99 N La Cienega Boulevard, Suite 200, at S San Vicente Boulevard, West Hollywood (24hr hotline 1-800 797 1717, 1-310 657 9353, www.aids health.org). Bus 16, 105/I-10, exit La Cienega Boulevard north.* **Open** 8.30am-5.30pm Mon-Fri. *Night clinic* 5.30-8pm Tue. **Map** p312 B3.
Quality care, regardless of the patient's ability to pay. For other locations, check the website.

HELPLINES

Alcoholics Anonymous *1-323 936 4343, www.lacoaa.org.*
CDC STD & AIDS Hotline *1-800 232 4636, www.cdc.gov/hiv.*

ESSENTIAL INFORMATION

Child Abuse Hotline
1-800 540 4000.
Gamblers Anonymous
*1-877 423 6752, www.gamblers
anonymous.org.*
LA Suicide Prevention Hotline
*1-877 727 4747, www.suicide
preventioncenter.org.*
Narcotics Anonymous
1-800 863 2962, www.todayna.org.
**Peace over Violence: Rape
& Battering Hotline** *1-310
392 8381, 1-213 626 3393,
www.peaceoverviolence.org.*

ID

Even if you look 40, you will still
need a photo ID – preferably a
driver's licence with a photograph
included – in order to buy alcohol
or get served in most of the city's
liquor stores and bars.

INSURANCE

Non-nationals should organise
comprehensive insurance, including
medical insurance, before they
leave home. Medical centres will
ask for details of your insurance
company and your policy number
if you require treatment; keep the
information with you at all times.

INTERNET

Almost all hotels in LA offer some
form of in-room, high-speed access
for travellers, usually wireless;
many also have a communal
computer on which guests can get
online. Many cafés (see pp131-136)
also offer wireless access, often for
free, though a few make a point of
not having it. And free Wi-Fi zones
have been set up in parts of Culver
City, Hermosa Beach and Long
Beach, as well as Pershing Square
in Downtown.

If you don't have your own
laptop, you can get online at
branches of the LA Public
Library system (see right).

LEFT LUGGAGE

The LAX International Baggage
Service, while unrelated to LAX
itself, offers storage of baggage
outside the airport. For details, call
1-310 863 4109. There are no lockers
at Union Station.

LEGAL HELP

If you get sued, or if you think you
have a claim against someone, there
are hundreds of attorneys listed in
the Yellow Pages, but you're best off

getting a recommendation. If you're
arrested and held in custody, call
your insurer's emergency number or
contact your consulate (see p293).

LIBRARIES

The main branch of the LA Public
Library network is the **Richard
J Riordan Central Library** in
Downtown LA, where facilities
include free internet access. For
details of other libraries, see
www.lapl.org. For county
libraries, including the swanky
new West Hollywood one, see
www.colapublib.org.

LOST PROPERTY

If you've lost something at LAX, try
your airline, then the general lost
property number (1-310 417 0440).
For goods lost on Metro buses or
trains, call 1-323 937 8920. For items
left in taxis, call the cab firm.

MEDIA

Newspapers

The *Los Angeles Times*
(www.latimes.com) has been the
only big newspaper in town for
years. Strengths include arts and
entertainment; weaknesses include
spotty business coverage and a
below-par sports section.

Magazines

The monthly *Los Angeles Magazine*
(www.lamag.com) is an enjoyable
blend of fawning celebrity profiles,
insider enthusiasms and long-form
reporting. The *Hollywood Reporter*
(www.hollywoodreporter.com),
which is weekly, and *Variety*
(www.variety.com), which has
both a daily and weekly edition,
have the scoop on industry deals.
The biggest of the city's free
weeklies, *LA Weekly* (www.la
weekly.com) is a mix of solid but
sometimes over-long reportage,
and criticism that ranges from the
excellent to the abysmal.

Commercial music radio

LA's major hip hop station is
Power 106 (KPWR, 105.9 FM,
www.power106.fm). **Hot 92.3**
(KHHT, 92.3 FM, www.hot923.com)
serves up old-school R&B; alt-rock
comes courtesy of **KROQ** (106.7
FM, www.kroq.com). **KLOS** (95.5
FM, www.955klos.com) mixes soft
and classic rock. **Jack** (93.1FM,
http://931jackfm.cbslocal.com)

plays hits from the 1960s, '70s
and '80s, as does **Sound** (100.3,
www.thesoundla.com), which
also plays 'album rock'.

Public & college radio

The best station in LA, and one of
the most influential stations in the
US, is the NPR-affiliated **KCRW**
(89.9 FM, www.kcrw.com), which
mixes intelligent news and talk
with approachable but slightly off-
radar music. Elsewhere on the dial,
Loyola Marymount's **KXLU** (88.9
FM, www.kxlu.com) provides noisy
and nice indie sounds, while USC's
KUSC (91.5 FM, www.kusc.org)
mixes classical music and talk.
Classical fans should also try
Cal State's **KCSN** (88.5 FM,
www.kcsn.org); jazz radio is limited
to Long Beach State's **KKJZ** (88.1
FM, www.jazzandblues.org).

Talk radio

KFI (640 AM, www.kfiam640.com)
hosts Rush Limbaugh (9am-noon
Mon-Fri). **KABC** (790 AM, www.
kabc.com) offers the outspoken
likes of Sean Hannity (noon-3pm
Mon-Fri); liberals have **KCRW**'s
Warren Olney, whose *Which Way,
LA?* (7-8pm Mon-Thur) and national
To the Point (1-2pm Mon-Fri) are
the best issues-forum radio shows
in California.

For news, **KNX** (1070 AM,
www.knx1070.com), **KFWB**
(980 AM, http://kfwbam.com) and
KNNZ (540 AM) offer 24-hour,
up-to-the-minute coverage.

Television

LA has affiliates of the four major
networks: **CBS** (KCBS, channel 2),
NBC (KNBC, channel 4), **ABC**
(KABC, channel 7) and **Fox**
(KTTV, channel 11). Competition
comes from the **CW** (KTLA,
channel 5) and **MyNetworkTV**
(KCOP, channel 13). **KWHY**
(channel 22), **KMEX** (channel
34) and **KVEA** (channel 52) serve
the city's Latino population, while
KSCI (channel 18) and **KDOC**
(channel 56) offer a mix of
Japanese, Korean, Chinese and
Armenian programming.

Websites

In 2012 Time Out launched a
dedicated Los Angeles website
(www.timeout.com/los-angeles),
with listings and features on
everything from museums to
clubs to restaurants.

MONEY

The US dollar ($) is divided into 100 cents (¢). Coins run from the copper penny (1¢) to the silver nickel (5¢), dime (10¢), quarter (25¢), the less common half-dollar (50¢) and the rarely seen dollar (silver and gold). Notes or 'bills' are all the same green colour and size; they come in denominations of $1, $5, $10, $20, $50 and $100. There's also an occasionally seen $2 bill.

Credit cards are accepted almost everywhere in LA. MasterCard (abbreviated as MC throughout this book) and Visa (V) are the most popular, with American Express (AmEx) and Discover (Disc) common. Phone the numbers listed below if your card is lost or stolen..

Travellers' checks are still accepted in some shops and restaurants, albeit with proof of identity (such as a passport). Draw the checks in US dollars before your trip.

Banks & ATMs

Banks in LA are usually open from 9am or 10am to 5pm Monday to Thursday; until 6pm on Friday; and from 9am or 10am until any time up to 3pm on Saturday. Some have bureaux de change. Call the numbers below or go to their websites to locate your nearest bank branch.

There are ATMs all over LA: in banks, and in some stores and bars. ATMs accept AmEx, MC and V, as well as some debit cards. However, you may be charged a small fee each time you make a withdrawal, not only from your bank, but also by the machine itself.

Bank of America *1-800 432 1000, www.bankofamerica.com.*
Citibank *1-800 374 9700, www.citibank.com.*
Wells Fargo *1-800 869 3557, www.wellsfargo.com.*

Bureaux de change

There are a number of bureaux de change at LA airport. However, you may get a better rate at bureaux away from the airport.

If you need money wired to you, **Western Union** (1-800 325 6000, www.westernunion.com) can receive funds from anywhere in the world.

American Express Travel Services *327 N Beverly Drive, between Brighton & Dayton Ways, Beverly Hills (1-310 274 8277, http://travel.americanexpress.com). Bus 20, 720/I-10, exit Robertson Boulevard north.* **Open** 10am-6pm Mon-Fri; 10am-3pm Sat. **Map** p311 C3.
Other locations 8493 W 3rd Street, West Hollywood (1-310 659 1682); 269 S Lake Avenue, Pasadena (1-626 449 2281).

Lost/stolen credit cards

American Express *1-800 992 3404, www.americanexpress.com.*

Diners Club *1-800 234 6377, www.dinersclub.com.*
Discover *1-800 347 2683, www.discovercard.com.*
MasterCard *1-800 627 8372, www.mastercard.com.*
Visa *1-800 847 2911, www.visa.com.*

Tax

Sales tax in Los Angeles County is 9% (8% in Orange County); food bought as groceries is exempt. Hotel tax varies from 12% to 17%.

OPENING HOURS

Though many establishments open at 8am or 9am, the magic hour for shoppers is 10am. Shops are usually open until 6pm, with malls open until 9pm or later. Many museums are open until 6pm, although if you're making a special trip, be sure to arrive well before half an hour before the official closing time. Many have late-night openings one or two days during the week. Bars must stop serving alcohol by 2am.

POLICE

In an emergency, dial **911**. For non-emergencies, use the police stations below; www.lapdonline.org has details of others.
Beverly Hills *464 N Rexford Drive, at Santa Monica Boulevard (1-310 550 4951, www.beverlyhills.org). Bus 4, 14, 16, 20, 316, 704, 720/I-405, exit Wilshire Boulevard east.*
Downtown *251 E 6th Street, at Maple Avenue (1-213 485 3294, www.lapdonline.org). Metro Pershing Square/bus 16, 18, 28, 53, 62/I-110, exit 6th Street east.*
Hollywood *1358 N Wilcox Avenue, between De Longpre & Fountain Avenues (1-213 972 2971, www.lapdonline.org). Metro Hollywood-Vine/bus 1180, 181, 210, 212, 217/US 101, exit Hollywood Boulevard west.*
Santa Monica *333 Olympic Drive, between Main & 4th Streets (1-310 395 9931, www.santamonicapd.org). Bus 33, 733, SM1, SM2, SM3, SM10/I-10, exit 4th-5th Street south.*
West Hollywood *780 N San Vicente Boulevard, at Santa Monica Boulevard (1-310 855 8850, www.wehosheriff.com). Bus 4, 105/I-10, exit La Cienega Boulevard north.*

POSTAL SERVICES

Post offices are usually open from 9am to 5pm Mon-Fri, but often have last collections at 6pm. Many are

SIZE CHARTS

WOMEN'S CLOTHES

British	French	US
4	32	2
6	34	4
8	36	6
10	38	8
12	40	10
14	42	12
16	44	14
18	46	16
20	48	18

WOMEN'S SHOES

British	French	US
3	36	5
4	37	6
5	38	7
6	39	8
7	40	9
8	41	10
9	42	11

MEN'S CLOTHES

British	French	US
34	44	34
36	46	36
38	48	38
40	50	40
42	52	42
44	54	44
46	56	46
48	58	48

MEN'S SHOES

British	French	US
6	39	7
7.5	40	7.5
8	41	8
8	42	8.5
9	43	9.5
10	44	10.5
11	45	11
12	46	11.5

ESSENTIAL INFORMATION

open on Saturdays from 9am to 1pm or 2pm. Stamps for postcards within the US cost 33¢ or, for large postcards, 46¢; for Europe, it's $1.10. Postage rates for letters vary by size and destination. Below are listed several post offices around the city; for others, dial 1-800 275 8777 or check www.usps.com.

Beverly Hills *325 N Maple Drive, between Burton Way & W 3rd Street. Bus 16/I-10, exit Robertson Boulevard north.* **Open** 9am-5pm Mon-Fri; 9.30am-1pm Sat. **Map** p311 D2.

Downtown *505 S Flower Street, at W 5th Street. Metro 7th Street-Metro Center/bus 16, 18, 55, 62/I-110, exit 6th Street east.* **Open** 8.30am-5.30pm Mon-Fri. **Map** p315 B3.

Santa Monica *1248 5th Street, at Arizona Avenue. Bus 4, 304, SM2, SM3, SM4/I-10, exit 4th-5th Street north.* **Open** 9am-6pm Mon-Fri; 9am-3pm Sat. **Map** p310 B2.

West Hollywood *1125 N Fairfax Avenue, at Santa Monica Boulevard. Bus 4, 217, 218, 704/I-10, exit Fairfax Avenue north.* **Open** 8.30am-5.30pm Mon-Fri; 8.30am-3.30pm Sat. **Map** p312 C2.

Poste restante

If you need to receive mail but don't know what your address will be, have it sent to: [your name], General Delivery, 1055 N Vignes Street, Los Angeles, CA 90012, USA. You can collect it from this Downtown address (8am-4.30pm Mon-Fri).

RELIGION

All Saints Episcopal Church *504 N Camden Drive, at Santa Monica Boulevard, Beverly Hills (1-310 275 0123, www.allsaintsbh.org). Bus 4, 16, 20,720/I-10, exit Robertson Boulevard north.* **Map** p311 C3.

Beth Israel Synagogue *8056 Beverly Boulevard, at S Crescent Heights Boulevard, West Hollywood (1-323 651 4022). Bus 14, 217, 218/I-10, exit La Cienega Boulevard north.* **Map** p312 C3.

Beverly Hills Presbyterian Church *505 N Rodeo Drive, at Santa Monica Boulevard, Beverly Hills (1-310 271 5194, www.bhpc.org). Bus 4, 16, 20, 316/I-10, exit Robertson Boulevard north.* **Map** p311 C3.

First Baptist Church of Hollywood *6682 Selma Avenue, at Las Palmas Avenue, Hollywood (1-323 464 7343, http://fbc hollywood.org). Metro Hollywood-Highland/bus 156, 163, 212, 217, 656/US 101, exit Hollywood Boulevard west.* **Map** p313 A2.

Islamic Cultural Centre *434 S Vermont Avenue, between W 4th & W 5th Streets, Koreatown (1-213 382 9200). Metro Wilshire-Vermont/ bus 204, 754/I-10, exit Vermont Avenue north.* **Map** p314 A6.

St Monica Roman Catholic Church *725 California Avenue, at Lincoln Boulevard, Santa Monica (1-310 566 1500, www.stmonica.net). Bus 20, 720, SM2/I-10, exit Lincoln Boulevard north.* **Map** p310 B2.

Wat Thai Buddhist Temple *8225 Coldwater Canyon Avenue, at Roscoe Boulevard, North Hollywood (1-818 785 9552, http://www.watthai.com). Bus 167/I-405, exit Roscoe Boulevard east.*

SAFETY & SECURITY

LA is pretty safe on the whole, but it pays to be cautious: don't fumble with your wallet or a map in public; avoid walking alone at night; keep your doors locked while driving; avoid parking in questionable areas. On foot, walk with confidence. As a motorist, avoid coming off the freeway in unfamiliar areas, never drive too slowly or too fast, and always carry a map and a phone with you. Areas in which to take particular care include parts of Venice, Koreatown, Silver Lake, Echo Park, Highland Park, Downtown, Watts and Compton. Hollywood is much improved compared with even just a few years ago, but the presence of so many tourists is tempting to petty thieves, so use caution.

SMOKING

Smoking is banned in all enclosed public areas: shops, restaurants, cinemas, hotels (except some private rooms) and bars, as well as parks, beaches, playgrounds, outdoor cafés and food courts. In addition, most restaurants, bars and shops request you stand at the curb or at least 15 feet from the entrance. Be prepared for dirty looks from passers-by.

STUDY

Aside from the universities detailed below, there are numerous colleges devoted to film and TV. USC's **School of Cinematic Arts** (1-213 740 2235, www-cntv.usc.edu) has a great reputation, as does UCLA's **School of Theater, Film & Television** (1-310 825 5761, www.tft.ucla.edu).

California Institute of Technology *1200 E California University, Pasadena, CA 91125 (1-626 395 6811, www.caltech.edu).*

California State University *LA-area campuses in Alhambra, Fullerton, Long Beach & Northridge (www.calstate.edu).*

Loyola Marymount University *1 LMU Drive, Los Angeles, CA 90045 (1-310 338 2700, www.lmu.edu).*

Pepperdine University *24255 Pacific Coast Highway, Malibu, CA 90263 (1-310 506 4000, www.pepperdine.edu).*

UCLA *Los Angeles, CA 90095 (1-310 825 4321, www.ucla.edu).*

USC *Los Angeles, CA 90089 (1-213 740 2311, www.usc.edu).*

TELEPHONES

Dialling & codes

LA is covered by a number of different area codes. Calling outside your area code from your hotel can be very costly – you're generally better off using a payphone or your cellphone. Calls to numbers prefixed 1-800, 1-866, 1-877 or 1-888 are free. Unless you are dialling from a US-based mobile phone, you must always dial 1 + area code + seven-digit number, even if you're calling from a phone in the same code as the number you're dialling. All numbers in this book have been listed in this 11-digit format. For international calls, dial 011 (the international access code), followed by the country code, followed by the number.

Local area codes

213 Downtown
310 Malibu, Santa Monica, Venice, Culver City, West LA, Westwood, Beverly Hills, parts of West Hollywood, Inglewood
323 parts of West Hollywood, Hollywood, East LA, South Central, Silver Lake
562 Long Beach
626 San Gabriel Valley, Pasadena
714 North Orange County
818 San Fernando Valley, Glendale
949 Laguna & Newport Beaches

International country codes

61 Australia
81 Japan
64 New Zealand
44 UK

Mobile phones

LA operates on the 1900mHz GSM frequency. Travellers with tri-band (or greater) handsets should be able to connect to one of the networks, assuming their service provider has an arrangement with a local network; the majority do, but it's worth checking before you depart. European visitors with only dual-band phones will need to rent a handset on arrival from a company such as TripTel (*see p143*).

Check the price of calls with your home service provider before you arrive. Rates are generally hefty and you'll be charged for receiving as well as making calls – if you need to make a lot of calls rental may be a better option.

Operator services

Collect/reverse-charge calls 0. **Local directory enquiries** 411. **National directory enquiries** 1 + [area code] + 555 1212 (if you don't know the area code, dial 0 for the operator). **International operator** 00.

Public phones

Payphones are no longer common in LA, and many seem permanently broken. If you find one that works, pick up the receiver, listen for a dialling tone and feed it change (50¢ for a local call). To make long-distance or international calls, buy a phonecard (sold at some supermarkets, convenience stores, such as 7-Eleven, and pharmacies. The card will give you a fixed amount of talk-time.

TIME

California is on Pacific Standard Time, eight hours behind GMT (London) and three hours behind Eastern Standard Time (New York). Clocks go forward by an hour on the second Sunday in March, and back on the first Sunday in November.

TIPPING

Tipping is a way of life in the US, and workers in service industries rely on gratuities. Tip bellhops and baggage handlers $1-$3 a bag; cab drivers, wait staff and food delivery agents 15-20 per cent; parking valets $3-$5; bartenders $1 a drink; and housekeepers $2-$5 a night.

TOILETS

There are virtually no public restrooms in LA. Duck into a mall, a department store, a hotel or a chain coffeehouse to use their facilities.

TOURIST INFORMATION

LA Inc has a wealth of information online (www.discoverlosangeles.com) and at its information centres. For local tourist offices in the likes of Santa Monica, see the relevant Sightseeing chapter (*pp30-91*).
LA Inc Downtown *685 S Figueroa Street, at Wilshire Boulevard (1-213 689 8822). Metro 7th Street-Metro Center/bus 16, 18, 55, 62/I-110, exit 6th Street east.* **Open** 9am-5pm Mon-Fri. **Map** p315 B3.
LA Inc Hollywood *6801 Hollywood Boulevard, at N Highland Avenue (1-323 467 6412). Metro Hollywood-Highland/bus 156, 163, 212, 217, 363, 656, 780/US 101, exit Hollywood Boulevard west.* **Open** 10am-10pm Mon-Sat; 10am-7pm Sun.* **Map** p313 A1.

VISAS & IMMIGRATION

Under the Visa Waiver Program, citizens of 35 countries – including the UK, Ireland, Australia and New Zealand – do not need a visa for stays in the US of less than 90 days (business or pleasure) as long as they

have a machine-readable passport valid for the full 90-day period, a return ticket and authorisation to travel through the Electronic System for Travel Authorization (ESTA) system (see www.cbp.gov/esta). Visitors must fill in the online ESTA form (and pay $14) at least 24 hours before travelling (72 hours is recommended) and pay a $14 fee. The form can be found on US embassy websites and, once completed, is valid for two years or until the visitor's passport expires.

Other visitors need visas. Allow plenty of time for your application to be processed. For details, see http://travelstate.gov. UK citizens can consult www.usembassy.org.uk, or call the embassy's Visa Information Hotline on 09042 450100.

WHEN TO GO

Climate

With an annual average of 300 clear days, LA offers generally idyllic weather. However, the smog can be awful, especially when combined with the dry summer heat and the Santa Ana winds.

The best times to visit are between March and May, and from September to November, when temperatures are cooler and the air is nicer. June and July are best avoided: the coastal cities are swathed in sea mist, referred to as 'June gloom', and temperatures inland soar. In comparison to the averages in the chart below, summer temperatures are 5-8°F (3-5°C) warmer in the Valleys, and around 3-5°F (2-3°C) cooler on the coast.

For 24-hour smog and air-quality checks, contact the South Coast Air Quality Management District (1-800 288 7664, www.aqmd.gov).

PUBLIC HOLIDAYS

New Year's Day 1 Jan.
Martin Luther King, Jr Day 3rd Mon in Jan.
Presidents Day 3rd Mon in Feb.
Memorial Day last Mon in May.
Independence Day 4 July.
Labor Day 1st Mon in Sept.
Columbus Day 2nd Mon in Oct.
Veterans Day 11 Nov.
Thanksgiving 4th Thur in Nov.
Christmas Day 25 Dec.

WORKING IN LA

Contact the US embassy in your home country for details on work visas; working in Los Angeles without one is a bad idea.

THE LOCAL CLIMATE

Average temperatures and monthly rainfall in Los Angeles.

	High (°C/°F)	Low (°C/°F)	Rainfall (mm/in)
Jan	20/68	9/48	85/3.3
Feb	21/70	10/50	94/3.7
Mar	21/70	11/52	80/3.1
Apr	23/73	12/54	21/0.8
May	24/75	14/58	8/0.3
June	27/80	16/61	2/0.1
July	29/84	18/65	1/0
Aug	29/85	19/66	3/0.1
Sept	28/83	18/65	8/0.3
Oct	26/79	16/60	9/0.4
Nov	23/73	12/53	27/1.1
Dec	21/69	9/48	49/1.9

ESSENTIAL INFORMATION

Further Reference

BOOKS

Non-fiction

Kenneth Anger *Hollywood Babylon*
The dark side of Tinseltown.
Leon Bing *Do or Die*
LA gang culture uncovered.
Carolyn Cole & Kathy Kobayashi *Shades of LA: Pictures from Ethnic Family Albums*
A beautifully rendered scrapbook of the ethnic family in LA.
Douglas Flamming *Bound for Freedom*
The history of African-Americans in LA from its birth to Jim Crow.
Otto Friedrich *City of Nets*
A portrait of Hollywood in the '40s.
Barney Hoskyns *Waiting for the Sun; Hotel California*
Hoskyns surveys Californian music in the 1960s.
Steven L Isoardi *The Dark Tree: Jazz and the Community Arts in LA*
A history of the South Central arts movement of the 1960s and '70s.
Norman Klein *The History of Forgetting: Los Angeles and the Erasure of Memory*
A part-factual, part-fictional analysis of LA's myth creation by an always-readable cultural critic.
Chris Kraus, Jan Tumlir & Jane McFadden *LA Artland*
The city's contemporary art scenes.
Mötley Crüe with Neil Strauss *The Dirt: Confessions of the World's Most Notorious Rock Band*
Sunset Strip's 'hair metal' days, from those who survived.
Carey McWilliams *Southern California: An Island on the Land; North From Mexico: The Spanish-Speaking People of Los Angeles*
A history of LA's sinfulness and scandals; a pioneering celebration of the Mexican heritage in the Southwest (written in 1948).
Leonard Pitt & Dale Pitt *Los Angeles A-Z*
An interesting and occasionally invaluable encyclopaedia of LA's people, places and institutions.
Domenic Priore *Riot on Sunset Strip*
The Southern California music scene in the '60s.
Kevin Roderick *Wilshire Boulevard: Grand Concourse of Los Angeles*
The Miracle Mile and beyond.

Josh Sides *LA City Limits*
A history of African-Americans in LA from the Depression to today.
Kevin Starr *California*
Starr has chronicled the state's history in a number of books down the years; this abbreviated history is a good place to start.
Paul Theroux *Translating LA*
Around the neighbourhoods.
David Thomson *The Whole Equation*
An engaging history of Hollywood.
DJ Waldie *Holy Land*
'A suburban memoir' set in Waldie's home town of Lakewood.

Fiction

Charles Bukowski *Hollywood*
The drunk poet's incisive musings on making a movie in Tinseltown.
James M Cain *Double Indemnity, Mildred Pierce*
Classic 1930s/'40s noir.
Raymond Chandler *The Big Sleep; Farewell, My Lovely; The Long Goodbye*
Philip Marlowe in the classic hard-boiled detective novels.
Joan Didion *Play It as It Lays*
Despair and breakdown in LA. A big influence on…
Bret Easton Ellis *Less Than Zero*
The classic 1980s coke-spoon-chic novel about being young and fast on both coasts.
James Ellroy *The Black Dahlia, The Big Nowhere, LA Confidential, White Jazz*
Ellroy's LA Quartet is a masterpiece of contemporary noir; the black and compelling *My Dark Places* recounts his search for his mother's killer.
John Fante *Ask the Dust*
Depression-era Los Angeles as seen by an Italian émigré.
David Fine (ed) *Los Angeles in Fiction*
This fine anthology includes work by, among others, Walter Mosely, Norman Mailer and James M Cain.
F Scott Fitzgerald *The Pat Hobby Stories*
Short stories about Hollywood from a writer who died there.
Elmore Leonard *Get Shorty*
A Miami loan shark turns movie producer in this gutsy thriller.
John Miller (ed) *Los Angeles Stories*
Fiction and essays by Henry Miller, Fitzgerald, Chandler et al.

Walter Mosely *The Easy Rawlins Mystery Series*
Mosely's Easy Rawlins is an African American PI in LA. See also *Always Outnumbered, Always Outgunned.*
Budd Schulberg *What Makes Sammy Run?*
A furious attack on the studio system by one of its employees.
Bruce Wagner *I'm Losing You; I'll Let You Go; Still Holding*
Biting Hollywood satire.
Evelyn Waugh *The Loved One*
Waugh's hilarious and accurate satire on the American way of death.
Nathaniel West *The Day of the Locust*
A classic, apocalyptic raspberry blown at the movie industry.

FILM

See also p199 **Essential LA**.
The Aviator (2004)
The glory days of Old Hollywood and Howard Hughes.
The Big Lebowski (1998)
John Goodman. Jeff Bridges. Dude.
Boogie Nights (1997)
The 1970s and '80s San Fernando Valley porn industry uncovered.
Boyz N the Hood (1991)
Can a right-thinking father stop his son falling prey to the culture of gang violence in South Central LA?
Bulworth (1998)
This political satire starred and was co-written by Warren Beatty, who plays a rapping Democrat senator.
City of Angels (1998)
LA has never looked more dreamily beautiful than in this remake of Wim Wenders' *Wings of Desire.*
Clueless (1995)
A satirical portrait of LA rich kids and their lives at Beverly Hills High.
Colors (1988)
Gritty locations, plausible dialogue and a laudable lack of sensationalism define Dennis Hopper's take on cops versus LA's murderous gangs.
Crash (2005)
An Altmanian, Oscar-winning run around 48 hours in LA.
Double Indemnity (1944)
Billy Wilder's sexy, sweaty, classic film noir, with dialogue by Raymond Chandler.
The End of Violence (1997)
The Griffith Observatory has a starring role in Wim Wenders' love-hate letter to Hollywood.

Heat (1995)
Michael Mann's intense crime drama, starring Pacino and De Niro.

In Search of a Midnight Kiss (2008)
Hipsters struggle to find love in Los Feliz and Downtown.

LA Story (1991)
Steve Martin's love letter to LA is a sentimental but sweet look at a group of affluent Angelenos.

The Limey (1999)
Terence Stamp heads to LA in a vengeful state of mind.

The Long Goodbye (1973)
Robert Altman's superb homage to Chandler is held together by Elliott Gould playing Marlowe as a shambling slob.

Los Angeles Plays Itself (2003)
This epic bootleg history of the world's most filmed city is well worth seeking out.

Million Dollar Baby (2004)
A nice pastiche of the city's gritty Downtown boxing world.

The People vs Larry Flynt (1996)
An engaging portrayal of LA's very own porn king.

The Player (1992)
Robert Altman's semi-affectionate evisceration of the Hollywood world he worked to hard to avoid.

Pretty Woman (1990)
Richard Gere and Julia Roberts in an unlikely Hollywood love story.

Point Break (1991)
Keanu Reeves never looked – or acted – better in this surfing flick.

Pulp Fiction (1994)
Tarantino's witty, vivid, violent interweaving of three LA stories.

Shampoo (1975)
In which Warren Beatty single-handedly takes on womankind and almost wins.

Short Cuts (1993)
More than Altman, this time a epic series of interconnected lives, adapted from stories by Raymond Carver.

Singin' in the Rain (1952)
The greatest movie about Hollywood.

Strange Days (1995)
Kathryn Bigelow's dystopian view of Los Angeles on the eve of 2000.

Swingers (1996)
An out-of-work actor and his pals trawl the town looking for honeys.

The Take (2008)
Armoured-truck driver John Leguizamo goes in search of the thugs who hijacked him in East LA.

Timecode (2000)
Mike Figgis's inventive, four-screen piece of LA realism.

Training Day (2001)
Denzel Washington plays bad cop to Ethan Hawke's rookie.

MUSIC

See also p219 **Essential LA**.

Bad Religion *Suffer*
SoCal punks. More than 20 years later, they're still plugging away.

Dengue Fever *Escape from Dragon House*
Cambodian pop meets indie-rock in an instantly classic piece of Angeleno fusion.

Dr Dre *The Chronic*
Released in 1992, The Chronic flipped hip hop on its head.

The Eagles *Hotel California*
The defining album of the 1970s, for better or worse.

Elliott Smith *From a Basement on a Hill*
Echo Park hermit Elliott Smith's haunting ode to himself.

Hole *Celebrity Skin*
'This album is dedicated to all the stolen water of Los Angeles.'

Mötley Crüe *Girls, Girls, Girls*
The girls! The guitars! The spandex! The haircuts!

Nels Cline with Devin Sarno *Buried on Bunker Hill*
Avant-garde paean to a vanished Downtown neighbourhood.

Randy Newman *Trouble in Paradise*
The closest LA's finest songwriter has come to making an LA album.

NWA *Straight Outta Compton*
The moment at which gangsta rap went mainstream. Hard to overestimate its influence.

Ozomatli *Ozomatli*
Best experienced live, but this isn't a bad representation of East LA's genre-busting Latino-rock outfit.

Tom Waits *Small Change*
Streetcorner balladry from the longtime resident of the Tropicana.

X *Los Angeles*
A punk classic, still fresh.

WEBSITES

Blog Downtown
http://blogdowntown.com
The most useful of the many blogs chronicling Downtown's resurgence.

City of Los Angeles
www.ci.la.ca.us
The LA government's home page.

Curbed LA
http://la.curbed.com
Architecture, construction and real estate in LA.

Discover LA
www.discoverlosangeles.com
The LA Tourism & Convention Board's official tourist-industry resource.

Eater LA *http://la.eater.com*
Restaurants, bars and clubs in the city, brought to you by the folks

behind Curbed. The shopping equivalent is at http://la.racked.com.

LA Cowboy
http://lacowboy.blogspot.com
The blog of influential Downtown booster Brady Westwater.

LA Observed
www.laobserved.com
Politics and the politics of media in Los Angeles.

LA Times *www.latimes.com*
Not the most easily navigable of sites, but it's all up here somewhere. For listings, go straight to http://findlocal.latimes.com.

LA Weekly *www.laweekly.com*
Listings information for bars, clubs, music venues and so on.

LA.com *www.la.com*
Bars, shops, restaurants and after-hours culture.

MTA *www.metro.net*
Public transportation information, including maps and timetables.

People *www.people.com*
The 'best' of the celebrity magazine sites – though that's a relative term – with gossip, news and interviews.

Public Art in LA
www.publicartinla.com
An excellent guide to public works in all corners of the city.

Seeing Stars *www.seeing-stars.com*
Not the best-looking site on the net, by any means, but there's some good celeb-related stuff buried here.

Time Out Los Angeles
www.timeout.com/los-angeles
Reviews of all the latest restaurants, bars, clubs and more… plus features and interviews.

Traffic News *http://cad.chp.ca.gov*
The latest incidents on the road.

APPS

Go Metro
Metro's app features fares, maps and other trip-planning info. Plus service alerts, closures and a petrol price comparison, should you decide to drive instead.

Perez Hilton
Celeb gossip a-go-go, courtesy of love-him-or-hate-him Hilton. Plenty of LOLz moments!

Time Out Los Angeles
Arts and ents coverage, from cinemas to nightclubs, plus food and drink. Also has a handy 'Restaurants & bars nearby' search facility.

TMZ
Exclusives, clips and videos on the stars du jour (or, more usually, du minute).

Tripeze (Travel + Leisure)
Tours, trips and tips from the publishers of the venerable travel mag.

ESSENTIAL INFORMATION

Index

INDEX

INDEX

INDEX

INDEX

INDEX

Maps

LA Overview

Santa Monica & Venice

Will Rogers State Beach

PACIFIC OCEAN

Santa Monica State Beach

PALISADES BEACH ROAD

Annenberg Community Beach House

Santa Monica Municipal Pier

Santa Monica Pier Aquarium

Visitor Center

California Heritage Museum

THE PROMENADE

Venice City Beach

OCEAN PARK

VENICE

SANTA MONICA

Brentwood Country Club

St John's Hospital

Bergamot Station/Santa Monica Museum of Art

Memorial Park

Woodlawn Cemetery

Penmar Golf Course

Clover Park

Donald Douglas Loop N

Santa Monica Airport

Donald Douglas Loop S

Museum of Flying

W CHANNEL RD ENTRADA DR

SAN VICENTE BLVD

MONTANA AVE

CALIFORNIA AVE

WILSHIRE BLVD

SANTA MONICA BLVD

BROADWAY

COLORADO AVE

OLYMPIC BLVD

PICO BLVD

OCEAN PARK BLVD

ROSE AVE

PALMS BLVD

AIRPORT AVE

DEWEY AVE

SANTA MONICA FREEWAY

LINCOLN BLVD

OCEAN AVE

MAIN ST

ABBOT KINNEY BLVD

BEETHOVEN ST

S CENTINELA AVE

CLOVERFIELD BLVD

26TH ST

20TH ST

14TH ST

7TH ST

VENICE BLVD

WASHINGTON BLVD

0   2600
0   900 m
0   900 yds

© Copyright Time Out Group 2013

●	Restaurants pp94-117
●	Bars pp118-130
●	Coffeehouses pp131-136
●	Hotels pp163-185

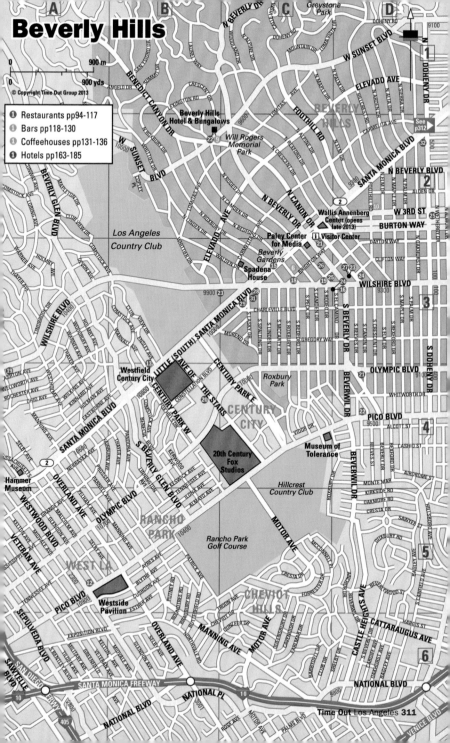

Beverly Hills

© Copyright Time Out Group 2013

0   900 m
0   900 yds

❶ Restaurants pp94-117
❶ Bars pp118-130
❶ Coffeehouses pp131-136
❶ Hotels pp163-185

Beverly Hills
Hotel & Bungalows

Will Rogers
Memorial
Park

BEVERLY
HILLS

Wallis Annenberg
Center (opens
late 2013)

Los Angeles
Country Club

Paley Center
for Media

Visitor Center

Beverly
Gardens

Spadena House

Westfield
Century City

CENTURY
CITY

Roxbury
Park

20th Century
Fox
Studios

Museum of
Tolerance

Hillcrest
Country Club

Hammer
Museum

RANCHO
PARK

Rancho Park
Golf Course

WEST LA

CHEVIOT
HILLS

Westside
Pavilion

SANTA MONICA FREEWAY

NATIONAL PL

West Hollywood

© Copyright Time Out Group 2013

0 — 900 m
0 — 900 yds

A | **B** | **C** | **D**

HOLLYWOOD BLVD

SUNSET BLVD

Chateau Marmont 35

SUNSET BLVD (SUNSET STRIP)

WEST HOLLYWOOD

Post Office

SANTA MONICA BLVD

Warner Studios

Schindler House/MAK Center

Pacific Design Center

West Hollywood Park

MELROSE AVE

MELROSE AVE

CRESCENT HEIGHTS BLVD

CBS Television City

BEVERLY BLVD

LA Museum of the Holocaust

BEVERLY BLVD

Beverly Center

Pan Pacific Park

FAIRFAX DISTRICT

BURTON WAY

W 3RD ST

W 3RD ST

BEVERLY HILLS

Farmers Market

The Grove

MIRACLE MILE

WILSHIRE BLVD

Zimmer Children's Museum

La Cienega Park

LA County Museum of Art

Page Museum at the La Brea Tar Pits

W 6TH ST

Petersen Automotive Museum

WILSHIRE BLVD (MIRACLE MILE)

Craft & Folk Art Museum

OLYMPIC BLVD

OLYMPIC BLVD

SAN VICENTE BLVD

W PICO BLVD

W PICO BLVD

VENICE BLVD

W 18TH ST

VENICE BLVD

CADILLAC AVE

W WASHINGTON BLVD

SANTA MONICA FREEWAY

❶ Restaurants pp94-117
❶ Bars pp118-130
❶ Coffeehouses pp131-136
❶ Hotels pp163-185

See p313 ▶

◀ See p311

Hollywood & Midtown

A **B** **C** **D**

HOLLYWOOD HILLS

Hollywood Bowl

101

HOLLYWOOD FRWY

BEACH DR

5800

FRANKLIN AVE

Los Feliz

FRANKLIN AVE

39

48 47
TCL Chinese Theater
Madame Tussauds

Hollywood & Highland
Hollywood Wax Museum

YUCCA ST

YUCCA ST

Pantages Theatre

46

45

Ripley's

Hollywood Museum

N CAHUENGA BLVD

HOLLYWOOD BLVD

Hollywood-Vine

Hollywood-Western

HOLLYWOOD BLVD

CARLOS AVE

CARLTON WAY

SELMA AVE

HAROLD WAY

N Serrano AVE

SUNSET BLVD

SUNSET BLVD

Hollywood-Highland

LELAND WAY

6500

DE LONGPRE AVE

DE LONGPRE AVE

FOUNTAIN AVE

HOLLYWOOD

N HIGHLAND AVE

FOUNTAIN AVE

LA MIRADA AVE

N BRONSON AVE

N VAN NESS AVE

LA MIRADA AVE

N NORMANDIE AVE

N LA BREA AVE

LA MIRADA AVE

LEXINGTON AVE

LEXINGTON AVE

VIRGINIA AVE

101

SANTA MONICA BLVD

SANTA MONICA BLVD

6800

N VINE ST

N GOWER ST

Hollywood Forever Cemetery

N WILTON PL

N WESTERN AVE

ROMAINE ST

ROMAINE ST

WILLOUGHBY AVE

ELEANOR AVE

BARTON AVE

LEMON GROVE AVE

WARING AVE

N CAHUENGA BLVD

GREGORY AVE

Paramount Studios

MARATHON ST

700

MELROSE AVE

6600

36

CAMERFORD AVE

MELROSE AVE

34

5700

20

MELROSE AVE

4700

3

CLINTON ST

ROSEWOOD AVE

N GOWER DR

N BRONSON AVE

N VAN NESS AVE

N GRAMERCY PL

N OXFORD AVE

N SERRANO AVE

N HARVARD BLVD

N KINGSLEY DR

OAKWOOD AVE

Wilshire Country Club

BEVERLY BLVD

4600

BEVERLY BLVD

See p312

BEVERLY BLVD

5300

N RIDGEWOOD PL

W 1ST ST

S MANHATTAN PL

W 1ST ST

LARCHMONT VILLAGE

S ROSSMORE AVE

W 2ND ST

W 3RD ST

W 3RD ST

HANCOCK PARK

5000

W 4TH ST

S NORMANDIE AVE

S ALEXANDRIA AVE

5700

W 3RD ST

S HIGHLAND AVE

S PLYMOUTH BLVD

S LUCERNE BLVD

S WINDSOR BLVD

S IRVING BLVD

S LORRAINE BLVD

WESTMINSTER AVE

S ST ANDREWS PL

W 5TH ST

S KINGSLEY DR

W 6TH ST

W 6TH ST

WILSHIRE BLVD

Wilshire-Western

WILSHIRE BLVD

Wilshire-Normandie

28

S LA BREA AVE

5300

WILSHIRE BLVD

4300

INGRAHAM ST

Wiltern Theater

5

IROLO ST

W 8TH ST

W 9TH ST

OLYMPIC BLVD

LEEWARD AVE

S WILTON PL

S WESTERN AVE

W 8TH ST

KOREATOWN

EDGEWOOD PL

FRANCIS AVE

W 9TH ST

64

OLYMPIC BLVD

51

3200

50

49

6

52

CRENSHAW BLVD

S COUNTRY CLUB DR

PICO BLVD

W 12TH ST

W 15TH ST

0   900 m
0   900 yds

① Restaurants pp94-117
① Bars pp118-130
① Coffeehouses pp131-136
① Hotels pp163-185

© Copyright Time Out Group 2013

Time Out Los Angeles **313**

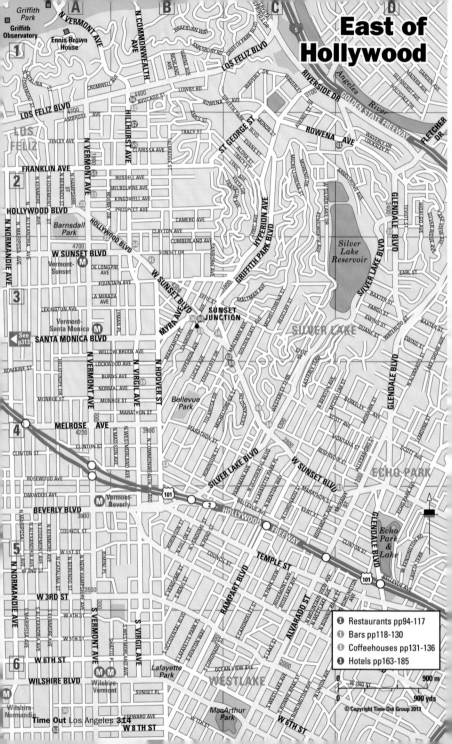

East of Hollywood

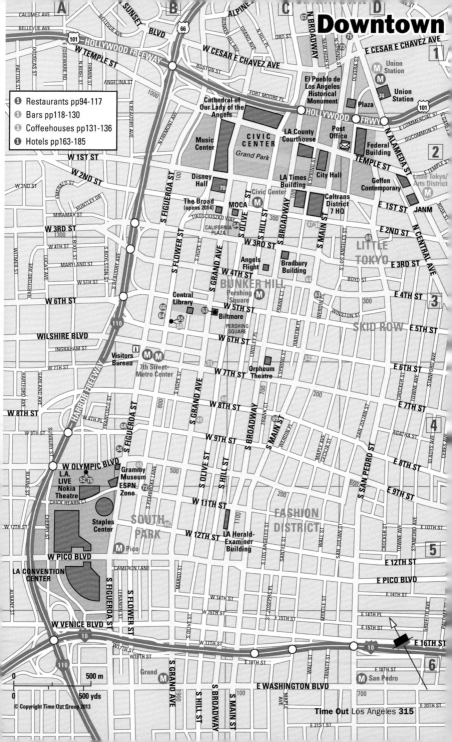

Downtown

① Restaurants pp94-117
① Bars pp118-130
① Coffeehouses pp131-136
① Hotels pp163-185

© Copyright Time Out Group 2013

Street Index

STREET INDEX

Metro Rail Network

Go Metro

metro.net

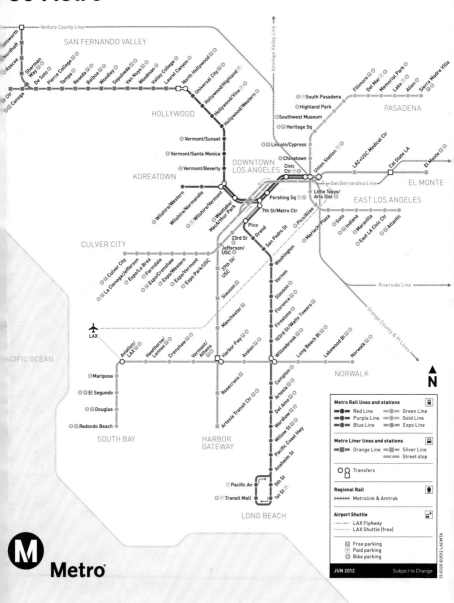

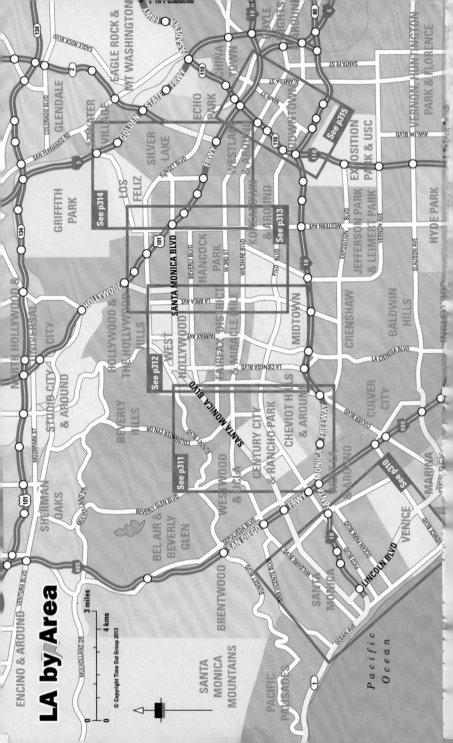